What Is the Mishnah? The State of the Question

What Is the Mishnah? The State of the Question:
Proceedings of a Conference at Harvard University

What Is the Mishnah?
The State of the Question

The Proceedings of a Conference at Harvard University

edited by Shaye J. D. Cohen

THE JEWISH LAW AND CULTURE PUBLICATION SERIES

JULIS-RABINOWITZ PROGRAM ON JEWISH AND ISRAELI LAW/
CENTER FOR JEWISH STUDIES/HARVARD UNIVERSITY

Harvard University Press | Cambridge, Massachusetts & London, England

© Copyright 2022 Harvard Law School,
Julis-Rabinowitz Program on Jewish and Israeli Law/
Center for Jewish Studies/Harvard University

Distributed by Harvard University Press on behalf of the
Julis-Rabinowitz Program on Jewish and Israeli Law and the
Harvard Center for Jewish Studies

First printing.

ISBN 978-0-674-27877-6 (cloth)
ISBN 978-0-674-29370-0 (epub)
ISBN 978-0-674-29371-7 (web-ready PDF)

Library of Congress Control Number: 2022919130

Jacket image: *Mishnah Codex* (Kaufmann A50, folio number 1v).
By courtesy of the Oriental Collection of the Library of the
Hungarian Academy of Sciences

Contributors

Elitzur A. Bar-Asher Siegal	Associate Professor, Department of Hebrew Language, Hebrew University
Beth A. Berkowitz	Ingeborg Rennert Chair of Jewish Studies and Professor, Department of Religion, Barnard College
Shaye J.D. Cohen	Nathan Littauer Professor of Hebrew Literature and Philosophy, Department of Near Eastern Languages and Civilizations, Harvard University
Naftali S. Cohn	Professor, Department of Religions and Cultures, Concordia University, Montreal
Shamma Friedman	Distinguished Service Professor Emeritus of Talmud and Rabbinics, Jewish Theological Seminary
Uziel Fuchs	Head of the Department of Oral Torah, Herzog College and Department of Talmud, Bar-Ilan University
Yair Furstenberg	Assistant Professor and Chair, Talmud Department, Hebrew University
Chanan Gafni	Rothberg International School at the Hebrew University and Ben-Gurion University of the Negev
Martin Goodman	Professor of Jewish Studies, Fellow of Wolfson College, and Fellow of the Oxford Centre for Hebrew and Jewish Studies, University of Oxford
Sarit Kattan Gribetz	Associate Professor of Classical Judaism, Department of Theology, Fordham University

Moshe Halbertal	Gruss Professor of Law, Hebrew University
Catherine Hezser	Professor of Jewish Studies, School of Oriental and African Studies, University of London
Jonathan S. Klawans	Professor of Religion, Department of Religion, Boston University
Gail Labovitz	Professor of Rabbinic Studies, Ziegler School of Rabbinic Studies, American Jewish University
Hayim Lapin	Robert H Smith Professor of Jewish Studies and History and Director of the Joseph and Rebecca Meyerhoff Program and Center for Jewish Studies, University of Maryland
Jonathan Milgram	Associate Professor of Talmud and Rabbinics, Department of Talmud and Rabbinics, The Jewish Theological Seminary
Vered Noam	Professor of Talmud, Department of Jewish Philosophy and Talmud, Tel Aviv University
Tzvi Novick	Abrams Jewish Thought and Culture Professor of Theology at the University of Notre Dame.
Ishay Rosen-Zvi	Professor of Rabbinic Literature, Department of Jewish Philosophy and Talmud, Tel-Aviv University
Adiel Schremer	Professor of Jewish History, The Israel & Golda Koschitzky Department of Jewish History and Contemporary Jewry, Bar Ilan University
Moshe Simon-Shoshan	Senior Lecturer, The Joseph and Norman Berman Department of Literature of the Jewish People, Bar-Ilan University
David Stern	Harry Starr Professor of Classical and Modern Jewish and Hebrew Literature, Professor of Comparative Literature, and Director of the Center for Jewish Studies, Harvard University
Azzan Yadin-Israel	Professor of Jewish Studies, Department of Jewish Studies, Rutgers University

Contents

Preface   ix
Introduction   xi
List of Abbreviations   xv

PART I. THE MISHNAH AND ITS PREDECESSORS   1

  1. Tzvi Novick: The Mishnah and the Bible   3
  2. Jonathan S. Milgram: The Mishnah and Ancient
     Near Eastern Law   23
  3. Vered Noam: The Mishnah and the Dead Sea Scrolls   47
  4. Shamma Friedman: Mishnah and Tosefta   73
  5. Yair Furstenberg: The Literary Evolution of the Mishnah   98

PART II. ROMAN CONTEXT AND HISTORY   127

  6. Martin Goodman: The Presentation of the Past
     in the Mishnah   129
  7. Catherine Hezser: The Mishnah and Roman Law   141
  8. Hayim Lapin: Mishnah and History   167

PART III. READING THE MISHNAH   185

  9. Beth A. Berkowitz: The Rhetoric of the Mishnah   187
  10. Naftali S. Cohn: Mishnah as Utopia   204
  11. Moshe Halbertal: Mishnah and *Halakhah*   232
  12. Moshe Simon-Shoshan: Nomos and Mishnah   253
  13. Sarit Kattan Gribetz: Holiness in the Mishnah   275
  14. Elitzur A. Bar-Asher Siegal: The Language of the Mishnah   305

PART IV. THE PRESENTATION OF PERSONS
         AND GROUPS IN THE MISHNAH   327

15. Jonathan Klawans: Priests and Pietists in the Mishnah   329
16. Gail Labovitz: Mishnah, Women, Gender   354
17. Ishay Rosen-Zvi: *Goyim* in the Mishnah   379
18. Adiel Schremer: Heretics and Heresy in the Mishnah   401

PART V. RECEPTION AND TRANSMISSION
        OF THE MISHNAH   423

19. Azzan Yadin-Israel: The Halakhic Midrashim
    and the Canonicity of the Mishnah   425
20. David Stern: The Publication and Early Transmission
    of the Mishnah   444
21. Uziel Fuchs: The Reception of the Mishnah from
    the Geonic Period to the Age of Print   471
22. Chanan Gafni: The Reception of the Mishnah
    in the Modern Era   489

Notes on the Contributors   511
Index   517

Preface

In January 2021 the Julis-Rabinowitz Program on Jewish and Israeli Law at Harvard Law School, chaired by Professor Noah Feldman, and the Center for Jewish Studies at Harvard University, chaired by Professor David Stern, co-sponsored a conference on the theme "What is the Mishnah." Our original plan was to hold a traditional conference, but the realities of the COVID pandemic forced us to reprogram the conference as a series of remote workshops featuring pre-circulated papers and open discussion among the participants. My colleagues have tasked me with editing the proceedings of the conference. In order to produce a reasonably coherent volume, I have reorganized the papers under new headings and have solicited some additional papers that had not been presented at the conference itself. We asked the contributors to focus on the state of the question in Mishnah studies. I am grateful to all the contributors for sharing their erudition with us. In the organization of the conference and the volume Dr. Susan Kahn provided essential support, as did Ms. Dalia Wolfson in editing the proceedings; warm thanks to them both.

I would like to dedicate this volume to my grandson Caleb. I look forward to the time when he and I will be able to study Mishnah together.

—Shaye J. D. Cohen

Introduction

The Mishnah ("repetition" or "teaching"), the first rabbinic book, composed in Hebrew in the land of Israel around 200 CE, is a large anthology devoted primarily to matters of practice, ritual, and law. In addition to statements, whether anonymous or attributed to named individuals, the Mishnah contains other literary forms as well, notably lists, disputes, anecdotes, maxims, Scriptural exegesis, and ritual narratives (descriptions of the rituals of the Jerusalem Temple and of the High Court).

THE MISHNAH AND ITS PREDECESSORS

What was there before the Mishnah? What sources were available to its creators? In what form? The Mishnah drew on the Torah, of course, directly and indirectly; in particular the influence of halakhic midrash, especially midrashim of the school of R. Akiva, is apparent (see chapters 18 and 19). The Mishnah's creators also incorporated a fair amount of Near Eastern law, in particular laws of marriage and divorce (chapter 2). The *Temple Scroll*, the Damascus Document, and 4QMMT of the Dead Scrolls show that there were written halakhic compositions before the time of the Mishnah (chapter 3) but the question of the Mishnah's sources remains open. The Mishnah itself gives evidence of development: some tractates seem to be earlier than others (chapter 5) and some passages seem to be revisions of earlier material now to be found in our Tosefta (chapter 4). But scholarship on the question of what the Mishnah looked like before it became our Mishnah has not yet achieved consensus.

ROMAN CONTEXT AND HISTORY

Another remarkable feature of the Mishnah is its obliviousness to its time and place (chapter 6). The Mishnah seldom mentions the destruction of the Temple. It treats at great length the rituals of the Temple (chapters 10 and

12), although the Temple is no longer standing; priests and their prerogatives figure prominently, rabbis and their prerogatives hardly at all; the Mishnah sets out in great detail the rules of ritual purity, even though most of the purity system was falling into disuse after the destruction of the Temple, and even though purification from the most severe forms of impurity was impossible without the Temple system being in place. The replacements that Jewish society was developing for the Temple, its rituals, and its personnel (e.g. synagogues, prayer, rabbis), are of little interest to the Mishnah; there is almost no rabbinic "biography" in the Mishnah (chapter 6). The Mishnah is not living in historical time and does not seem interested in the affairs of its own period (chapter 8).

The Mishnah's denial of contemporary history is all the more remarkable if the Mishnah had a Roman context and a Roman function. Catherine Hezser suggests that the Mishnah was composed in order to serve the Romans as the law book of the civic body of the Jews of Judaea (chapter 7). In this conception the context and purpose of the Mishnah were as much Roman as Judaean (chapter 8).

READING THE MISHNAH

The Mishnah is a text; whether oral or written is still an open question (see chapter 19). It is a text meant to be read, recited, studied, and memorized. Recent scholarship emphasizes that there are different ways to read the Mishnah, depending on the goal and manner of our reading (see chapter 15). As Beth Berkowitz explains, the Mishnah is not just law; it is also a representation of its own conceptions of reality (chapter 9). These conceptions may or may not be consonant with historical facts. When the Mishnah describes the rituals of the Jerusalem Temple, it emphasizes the unity of the people and the authority of the rabbinic elite. In other words, from the perspective of the rabbinic sages the Jerusalem Temple is a utopia, an ideal community in which everything and everyone upholds the ideal social order. The mishnaic account also contains some decidedly non-utopianic elements, but for the most part in the Mishnah's Temple everything works in timeless perfection (chapter 10).

The Mishnah is a compendium of legal materials, but it is more than just legal materials. Through its narrative and narratives the Mishnah expresses its values, what might be called "rabbinic Judaism" (see chapter 12). At the heart of this system is *halakhah,* usually translated "law." The Torah, of course, is full of laws, commandments, and prohibitions. Among the things that make the Torah different from the Mishnah is the scale of the Mishnah, the overwhelming obsession with details. There is nothing in the Torah's legislation about the Sabbath, for example, that can compare with the Mishnah's twenty-four chapters of detailed legislation about the Sabbath. We are in a different world (see chapter 11). Among the things that make the Torah similar to the Mishnah is that both have a conception of holiness: even in a world without a temple there are holy times, holy objects, holy people (chapter 13).

THE PRESENTATION OF PERSONS
AND GROUPS IN THE MISHNAH

As already indicated, rabbis and members of the rabbinic estate speak in the Mishnah, usually in discussion of points of law. The people they speak about are usually adult Jewish men, householders, landowners, people who are bound by rabbinic law but are not necessarily sages themselves. The sages regularly talk about women and slaves, who are bound by rabbinic law to a lesser degree than adult males (chapter 15), and about gentiles, who are not bound by rabbinic law at all (chapter 16). Passages about the Temple, purity law, and marriage law inevitably also speak about priests (chapter 14), who enjoy special privileges and are bound by special laws. From time to time the Mishnah also speaks about sinners and heretics, but exactly who they are and what place they have in society is not clear. Adiel Schremer argues that rabbinic society did not have "heretics," strictly speaking, at all (chapter 17).

RECEPTION AND TRANSMISSION OF THE MISHNAH

How and when the Mishnah became the canonical text of rabbinic Judaism is a complicated story, not fully documented. How and when the Mishnah became the canonical *written* text of rabbinic Judaism is another complex process. The halakhic midrashim aim to connect rabbinic law with Scripture; the Mishnah, in contrast, seems uninterested in doing so (with a few exceptions; see chapter 18). The Hebrew of the Mishnah is not the Hebrew of the Torah (chapter 19), another sign that the creators of the Mishnah were not even attempting to make the Mishnah sound like the Torah or share in the Torah's authority. The Mishnah emerges from the shadows, as it were, in the early Islamic period, known in Jewish historiography as the Geonic period (7th/8th century–ca.1100), by which time the Mishnah is a written book and, as such is studied in the rabbinic academies. The ongoing question for students of the Mishnah now becomes: May the Mishnah be studied as an independent work, or does the Mishnah's authority derive solely from the fact that it is the basis of the Talmud? This question will be pursued vigorously in the centuries that follow (chapters 20–22).

Abbreviations for the Citation of Mishnah and Talmud

b (followed by the name of the tractate)   Bavli, Babylonian Talmud
m (followed by the name of the tractate)   Mishnah
t (followed by the name of the tractate)   Tosefta
y (followed by the name of the tractate)   Yerushalmi, Talmud of the land
                                            of Israel

The tractates:

Zera'im

Ber	Berakhot
Pe'ah	Pe'ah
Dem	Demai
Kil	Kila'im
Shevi	Shevi'it
Ter	Terumot
Ma'as	Ma'aserot
MS	Ma'aser Sheni
Ḥal	Ḥalah
'Orl	'Orlah
Bik	Bikurim

Mo'ed

Shab	Shabat
'Eruv	'Eruvin
Pes	Pesaḥim
Shek	Shekalim
Yom	Yoma'
Suk	Sukkah
Bets	Betsah
RH	Rosh Ha-Shanah
Ta'an	Ta'anit
Meg	Megilah
MK	Mo'ed Katan
Ḥag	Ḥagigah

Nashim

Yev	Yevamot
Ket	Ketubot
Ned	Nedarim
Naz	Nazir
Sot	Sotah
Git	Gitin
Kid	Kidushin

Nezikin

BK	Bava Kama
BM	Bava Metsi'a
BB	Bava Batra
San	Sanhedrin
Mak	Makot
Shevu	Shevu'ot
'Eduy	'Eduyot
'AZ	'Avodah Zarah
Avot	Avot
Hor	Horayot

Kodashim

Zev	Zevaḥim
Men	Menaḥot
Ḥul	Ḥulin
Bekh	Bekhorot
'Arakh	'Arakhin
Tem	Temurah
Ker	Keritot
Me'il	Me'ilah
Tam	Tamid
Mid	Midot
Kin	Kinim

Tohorot (or *Teharot*)

Kel	Kelim
Ohal	Ohalot
Neg	Nega'im
Parah	Parah
Toh	Tohorot (or Teharot)
Mik	Mikva'ot
Nid	Nidah
Makh	Makhshirin
Zavim	Zavim
TY	Tevul Yom
Yad	Yadayim
'Ukts	'Uktsin

Part I

The Mishnah and Its Predecessors

1. The Mishnah and the Bible

Tzvi Novick

INTRODUCTION

The opening sentence of tractate *Berakhot*, which represents the beginning of the Mishnah according to the prevailing arrangement, offers a good illustration of the complex relationship between the Mishnah and the Bible.[1] It reads as follows: "From when does one read (קורין) the *Shema* in the evening (ערבים)?"[2] The word *Shema* is a quotation from Deut 6:4, and in context it denotes a collection of biblical texts that begins with that verse. The notion that this collection ought to be recited, and in the evening in particular, comes from a later verse in this collection, Deut 6:7, although this verse does not employ the verb קרא or the word ערב. Thus, for its content this sentence depends heavily on the Bible, in direct but also mediated ways.

In its form or language, by contrast, the sentence differs markedly from antecedents in biblical law. Legal units in the Pentateuch very rarely include questions, and never employ a question in the way that mBer 1.1 does, to set the stage for a rule.[3] The verb קורין is a masculine plural participle with no

---

1. I thank Ishay Rosen-Zvi for his comments on an earlier draft of this chapter. On the arrangement of the six orders of the Mishnah, and of the tractates therein, see Menahem Kahana, "The Arrangement of the Orders of the Mishnah" (Hebrew), *Tarbiz* 76.1–2 (2006): 29–40.

2. For this and other quotations from the Mishnah, the underlying Hebrew text is from MS Kaufmann. Translations from rabbinic literature and the Dead Sea Scrolls are my own. For the Bible I make use of but often diverge from the NRSV.

3. A rare case of a question in biblical law occurs in Ex 22:26: "On what will he lie down?" See Assnat Bartor, "The Representation of Speech in the Casuistic Laws of the Pentateuch," *JBL* 126.2 (2007): 236–38, noting that this question, though attributed to the lawgiver, "voices" the perspective of the pauper.

explicit subject, and its usage, too, represents a sharp departure from biblical law. The Bible always names legal subjects—in the most general case, figures like the "man" (איש) or "person" (אדם)—and uses imperfect verbs to specify actions.

These observations can serve as starting points for this chapter, which offers an overview of the Mishnah's relationship to the Bible (or in almost all cases, the Pentateuch in particular).[4] The first part of the chapter concerns the presence of the Bible in the substance of mishnaic law. It will inquire not only into the Mishnah's substantive debt to the Bible, but also into the degree to which the Mishnah makes this debt visible, either explicitly or implicitly, through citation of Scripture and through adherence to the order of biblical passages. The second part concerns the legal language of the Mishnah, and its similarities to and differences from the legal language of the Bible.

1. SCRIPTURE IN MISHNAIC LAW

a. Topics

A pericope from the Mishnah, mḤag 1:8, famously reflects on the relationship between biblical law and some of the legal topics addressed in the Mishnah.

> The dissolution of vows flies in the air, and has nothing on which to lean. The *halakhot* of the Sabbath, festival offerings, and trespasses, these are like *harar* bushes hanging by a hair: little Scripture and many *halakhot*. The civil laws and the temple services and the pure foods and the impurities, they have something on which to lean. They are the very bodies of Torah.[5]

Even if the dissolution of vows, the subject of mNed 9, "flies in the air," without a scriptural basis on which to rest, the Bible (in Numbers 30) is the

4. This chapter does not address tractate *Avot*, which, as a work of rabbinic wisdom on the model of Proverbs and Sirach, manifests a very different relationship to the Bible from the rest of the Mishnah. On *Avot* and the Bible see, e.g., Isaac B. Gottlieb, "Pirqe Abot and Biblical Wisdom," *VT* 40.2 (1990): 152–64; Shimon Sharvit, *Language and Style of Tractate Avoth through the Ages* (Hebrew; Beer-Sheva, 2006), 18–59.

5. The *harar* bush is a plant with a shallow root system; on this, see Michal Bar-Asher Siegal, "Mountains Hanging by a Strand? Rereading *Mishnah Ḥagigah* 1:8," *JAJ* 4.2 (2013): 233–56. For the translation "pure foods," and for discussion of parallels to and other scholarship on this pericope, see Yair Furstenberg, "Eating in the State of Purity during the Tannaitic Period" (Hebrew) (PhD diss., Hebrew University, 2010), 74–76.

source for the institution of vows itself. Likewise, going beyond the laws named in the above pericope, although the Bible does not recognize an impurity specific to the hands, the subject of tractate *Yadayim*, it has much to say on the broader topic of impurity. The marriage contract that gives its name to tractate *Ketubot* is a post-biblical innovation, but the rabbis' interest in it follows directly from the Bible's investment in the laws governing the marital relationship.[6] In this way, all of the major topics of the Mishnah trace ultimately to the Bible, though some of them only at a considerable remove.

Another way to think about the relationship between the Bible and the Mishnah is through the prism of the commandments. When the medieval jurist-philosopher Maimonides set to work composing a revision of the Mishnah, his *Mishneh Torah*, he thought it important, first, to enumerate the commandments, positive and negative, so that they might organize the revision and ensure its comprehensiveness. Maimonides' enumeration, *The Book of the Commandments*, thus represents a prefatory foundation for the *Mishneh Torah*. The header to each book of the *Mishneh Torah* identifies the commandments covered therein, and the commandments serve as lodestars in the structuring of these books.[7]

The tractates of the Mishnah do not, of course, include headers listing relevant commandments, and yet it is possible to discern what we may call a commandment-based orientation underlying the organization of the Mishnah. Most tractates center on an action or set of actions connected with obligations, prohibitions, or ritual procedures. Perhaps the most significant exception is the sixth order, "Purities," and even its tractates systematize the laws of purity that as a whole rest on a body of prohibitions and ritual procedures. Notably, there are no tractates organized by status, no tractate devoted to "priests" or "gentiles" or "slaves."[8] Nor, likewise, with the exception of tractate *Midot*, which concerns the layout and measurements of the temple, does any tractate orient itself around spaces.[9] The structure of the

---

6. On the biblical foundations (or lack thereof) for the topics covered by the Mishnah see Ishay Rosen-Zvi, *Between Mishna and Midrash: The Birth of Rabbinic Literature* (Hebrew; Ra'ananah, 2020), 61–62.

7. See Moshe Halbertal, *Maimonides: Life and Thought* (Princeton, 2013), 107–11.

8. This lacuna becomes visible through the supplementary contributions of some of the later "minor tractates," in particular *Gerim* (on converts), *Kuttim* (on Samaritans), and *'Avadim* (on slaves). On these and the other minor tractates see M. B. Lerner, "The External Tractates," in *The Literature of the Sages: First Part: Oral Torah, Halakha, Mishna, Tosefta, Talmud, External Tractates*, ed. S. Safrai and P. J. Tomson (Philadelphia, 1987), 367–409.

9. On tractate *Midot* see Avraham Walfish, "Conceptual Ramifications of Tractates *Tamid* and *Middot*" (Hebrew), *Judea and Samaria Research Studies* 7 (1997): 79–92. Tractate *Ohalot* concerns a space—the tent—but only insofar as the tent is relevant for the laws of corpse impurity, and this space itself becomes a legal abstraction.

Mishnah foregrounds actions, and in doing so implicitly constructs the law as an expression of an underlying set of biblical commandments.

The prominence of the commandments in the thought world of the Mishnah also emerges from the extended reflection on the commandments in the second half of mKid 1, and from other passages that develop the distinction between positive and negative commandments, especially the beginning of tractate *Keritot*.[10] It is notable in this regard that while the Mishnah is strongly affiliated with the exegetical works attributable to the school of R. Akiba, it does not uniformly adopt the definition of positive and negative commandments assumed in these works. As Aharon Shemesh has shown, the school of R. Ishmael adheres to an action-based distinction: Positive commandments are commandments fulfilled through action, while negative commandments are commandments that one fulfills by refraining from action. The school of R. Akiba, by contrast, treats the distinction as a linguistic phenomenon: Commandments in the Torah that employ negations are negative commandments, and those phrased positively are positive commandments.[11] Yet in the beginning of Mishnah *Keritot* and elsewhere, the Mishnah adheres to the school of R. Ishmael's understanding of the nature of the distinction between positive and negative commandments.[12]

b. Explicit Citation of Scripture

Four book-length studies or dissertations have been devoted to the topic of biblical interpretation in the Mishnah: Aicher, *Das alte Testament in der Mischna* (1906); Rosenblatt, *The Interpretation of the Bible in the Mishnah* (1935); Pettit, "*Shene'emar*: The Place of Scripture Citation in the Mishnah" (1993); and Samely, *Rabbinic Interpretation of Scripture in the Mish-*

10. On the commandments in the Mishnah and other tannaitic texts see Marc Hirshman, "On the Nature of Mitzva and Its Rewards in the Mishnah and Tosefta" (Hebrew), *WCJS* 10.C.1 (1990): 54–60; Tzvi Novick, *What Is Good, and What God Demands: Normative Structures in Tannaitic Literature* (Leiden, 2010), 89–107.

11. See Aharon Shemesh, "The Development of the Terms 'Positive' and 'Negative' Commandments" (Hebrew), *Tarbiz* 72.1–2 (2003): 133–50.

12. See Shemesh, "Development," 134–37, on the passage in mKer 1, and likewise mHor 2:4. For another case in which the Mishnah incorporates—and indeed gives pride of place to—an Ishmaelian perspective (one that also finds its way into later strata of Akiban midrash itself), see Amit Gvaryahu, "The Tannaitic Laws of Battery" (Hebrew) (MA thesis, Hebrew University, 2013), 44–51. My thanks to Ishay Rosen-Zvi for drawing my attention to this case.

nah (2002).[13] All of them attempt to develop taxonomies of the Mishnah's exegetical methods. Jason Kalman's review of these works highlights one limitation of this scholarship, and especially of the first three works: They do not account sufficiently for the dubious manuscript attestation of some biblical citations in the Mishnah.[14]

Samely's book manifests considerably greater awareness of the importance of textual criticism, and as the only work among the four to appear in the current millennium, it is naturally more attentive to contemporary methods in rabbinics across the board. However, the value of his book, and the other three works, for rabbinics scholarship is limited by the fact that their taxonomic categories for systematizing the various interpretive approaches to the Bible in the Mishnah are etic, and thus do not necessarily find resonance in the thought world of the rabbis themselves. In Samely's self-conscious formulation: "My language of description is independent of specifically rabbinic terminology."[15] Samely's taxonomy is by far the most conceptually sophisticated and comprehensive of the four, but for the same reason, it is also cumbersome. He offers such coinages as Opposition 1.4 ("Explication of the number of a biblical expression in the light of its opposition to another grammatical number") and Cotext 7 ("Explication of the meaning of an expression in the light of an extension of the grammatical period to co-text beyond the Masoretic verse boundary").[16] As Samely observes, his taxonomy enables comparison with works far beyond the rabbinic corpus. But rabbinics scholars who look to Samely's rich work for help answering questions specific to the field must penetrate and forage in a dense forest of technical neologisms.

Approaching the Mishnah from within a rabbinics framework, rather than with a taxonomic eye, one might compare explicit citation of Scripture in the Mishnah to the interpretation of Scripture in the tannaitic midrashim, which reached their final form after the Mishnah and sometimes make use of it. A recent article by Menahem Kahana takes up this comparison with a specific interest in the ways in which the Mishnah was received

13. See Georg Aicher, *Das alte Testament in der Mischna* (Freiburg im Breisgau, 1906); Samuel Rosenblatt, *The Interpretation of the Bible in the Mishnah* (Baltimore, 1935); Peter A. Pettit, *"Shene'emar*: The Place of Scripture Citation in the Mishnah" (PhD diss., Claremont Graduate School, 1993); and Alexander Samely, *Rabbinic Interpretation of Scripture in the Mishnah* (Oxford, 2002).

14. See Jason Kalman, "Building Houses on the Sand: Scripture Citation in the Mishnah," *Journal for Semitics* 13.2 (2004): 186–244.

15. Samely, *Rabbinic Interpretation*, 2.

16. See Samely, *Rabbinic Interpretation*, 403, 407.

differently by the schools of Rabbi Akiba and Rabbi Ishmael.[17] Below we will draw on some of the data that Kahana collects to reflect on what the reformulation of mishnaic interpretation of Scripture by midrashic works from the school of R. Akiba can tell us about the Mishnah.[18]

An example of explicit scriptural citation in the Mishnah occurs in mSan 2:5, in the laws concerning the king:

> One does not ride on his horse, nor sit on his throne, nor use his scepter, nor see him when he is naked, nor in his coiffure, nor in the bathhouse, as it says, "You shall place upon yourself a king" (Deut 17:15), that his fear should be upon you.

The exegesis is brief, consisting of nothing more than an explanatory paraphrase: "that his fear should be upon you." The Mishnah offers no argument to justify the paraphrase. When Sifre Deut 157 (Finkelstein ed., 209) references this pericope, it supplies the missing justification.

> "You shall place upon yourself a king." But does it not already say "placing, you shall place a king"? What is taught by "upon yourself a king"? That his fear should be upon you. From here they said: A king, "one does not ride on his horse," etc.[19]

The exegesis in this passage turns on the apparent superfluity of the prepositional phrase "upon yourself" (עָלֶיךָ); it should go without saying that it is over Israel whom the king will rule. According to the midrash, the phrase

---

17. See Menahem Kahana, "The Relations between Exegeses in the Mishnah and *Halakhot* in the Midrash" (Hebrew), *Tarbiz* 84.1–2 (2015): 17–76. The first appendix provides a comprehensive list of cases in which the Mishnah cites a verse from the Pentateuch in support of a conclusion, with notes on parallels or lack of parallels in the tannaitic midrashim. See Kahana, "Relations between Exegeses," 49–58 and 28–29 n. 62 for detailed considerations governing the formulation of the list. Note that a citation to Lev 19:16 in mSan 3:7 occurs in Kahana's list ("Relations between Exegeses," 52), even though, as Kalman shows (Kalman, "Scripture Citation," 224–26), it is missing in all early witnesses.

18. To judge from Kahana's notes to the list of exegeted verses in the Mishnah ("Relations between Exegeses," 49–58), such reformulation occurs specifically in Akiban works. Ishmaelian works quote from the Mishnah but do not reformulate it.

19. Citations from Sifre Deuteronomy otherwise depend on Vatican 32, but in this case I use the Berlin manuscript, which seems to preserve the more original text. On the use of "from here they said" in the tannaitic midrashim see Kahana, "Relations between Exegeses," and the brilliant reconstruction of the literary context of tPes 3:12 in Shamma Friedman, *Tosefta Atiqta: Pesaḥ Rishon: Synoptic Parallels of Mishna and Tosefta Analyzed with a Methodological Introduction* (Hebrew; Ramat-Gan, 2002), 333–47.

instead conveys an imperative to maintain the king's superior status. The key difference between the Mishnah and Sifre Deuteronomy concerns the relationship between the legal teaching and the verse. The Mishnah adduces the verse in order to justify the legal teaching, while Sifre Deuteronomy arrives at the legal teaching in order to justify the verse. In service of the latter end, the midrash introduces explicit exegetical reasoning, and technical exegetical terminology: "but does it not already say" (והלא כבר נאמר); "what is taught" (מה תלמוד לומר). These are absent from the Mishnah. The same set of differences recurs in many cases; we will consider two others.

In mBK 8:1, the Mishnah confines the penalty for shaming to cases involving the intention to shame.

> If he fell from the roof and caused damage and shamed, he is liable
> for the damage and exempt for the shame, as it says, "and she sends
> forth her hand and holds fast to his shameful things," (Deut 25:11): He
> is not liable for the shame until he acts with intention.

This rule also appears in Sifre Deut 292 (Finkelstein ed., 311):

> Rabbi says: For we find that there are damagers in the Torah who
> even when they act unintentionally are treated as if they acted inten-
> tionally. Perhaps also here? Hence it says, "and she sends forth her
> hand and holds fast to his shameful things" (Deut 25:11); it tells that
> he is not liable for the shame until he acts with intention.

We may suppose that the attribution to "Rabbi," or Rabbi Judah the Patriarch, represents an allusion to the Mishnah passage. Sifre Deuteronomy reiterates the Mishnah's teaching, but its aim is to justify the verse, and to this end, it introduces explicit exegetical reasoning: The fact that lack of intention does not matter in other areas of damages might lead one to think that it does not matter in the case of shame as well, hence the verse comes to "tell" (מגיד) that this is not in fact so.

As a final illustration of this phenomenon we may consider the rule concerning the offering of marginal body parts in mZev 9:5.

> The wool on the sheep's heads and the hair in the goats' beard, the
> bones and the sinews and the horns and the hooves, when they are
> attached, they ascend (on the altar), as it says, "and the priest shall
> render all of it into smoke on the altar" (Lev 1:9). If they separate,
> they do not ascend, as it says, "and you shall make your whole offer-
> ings (with) the flesh and the blood" (Deut 12:27).

This passage is paralleled in Sifra Nedava 5:3 (Weiss ed., 7c).

"All of it" (Lev 1:9). To include the bones and the sinews and the horns and the hooves and the wool on the sheep's heads and the hair in the goats' beards. Perhaps even though they separate? Hence it says, "and you shall make your whole offerings (with) the flesh and the blood" (Deut 12:27). Or, "and you shall make your whole offerings (with) the flesh and the blood": Perhaps one must pull away sinews and bones, and offer the meat on the altar? Hence it says, "all of it"; it has included. How, thus? When they are attached, they ascend. If they separate, even if they are atop the altar, they must descend.[20]

Both passages revolve around the tension between, on the one hand, Lev 1:9, which has the priest offer up "all" of the animal, and, on the other, Deut 12:27, which specifies the flesh and the blood. And both passages resolve the tension by adverting to parts of the animal that are not flesh and blood, and by assigning Lev 19 to the case where these parts remain attached to the flesh, and Deut 12:27 to the case where they have become detached. But in mZev 9:5, the reasoning is implicit, because the verses are introduced only as sources for the law. The Sifra, aiming instead to justify the verses, recasts the legal teaching within an exegetical apparatus awash in technical terminology: "to include" (לרבות); "perhaps" (יכול); "hence it says" (תלמוד לומר); "how, thus" (הא כיצד, i.e., how, thus, are the two verses to be reconciled).[21]

The Mishnah does not altogether eschew explicit exegetical reasoning, or technical exegetical terminology. In mSot 3:5, for example, R. Akiba, as in the above passage from the Sifra, introduces two verses, notes that one cannot affirm either of them (אי אפשר לומר "one cannot say") because the one contradicts the other, and then resolves the contradiction by applying the verses to two different scenarios.[22] The term "one cannot say" occurs in the same usage once elsewhere in the Mishnah, at m'Arakh 8:7, in the name of R. Ishmael, and in passages from tannaitic midrash.[23]

But the dearth of technical exegetical terminology in connection with citation of Scripture in the Mishnah is nevertheless notable. Thus, for example, a standard and extremely prevalent exegetical term in Akiban midrash

---

20. The text is from MS Vatican 66.

21. On הא כיצד as a characteristically Akiban reflex see J. N. Epstein, *Introduction to Tannaitic Literature*, ed. E. Z. Melamed (Hebrew; Jerusalem, 1957), 568–69.

22. In tSot 5:13 this exegesis is attributed by R. Joshua to a certain Judah b. Peṭiri.

23. See, e.g., Mek. R. Ish. ba-ḥodesh 7 (Horovitz-Rabin ed.), 227.

is לרבות "to include"; it occurs in the above passage from the Sifra, both in the infinitive and in the perfect. But this terminology is not only absent in the Mishnah parallel, mZev 9:5; it never occurs at all in the Mishnah.[24] The term מלמד "it teaches" occurs pervasively in Akiban midrash as a bridge between the lemma and its interpretation, but it is found in only four pericopes in the Mishnah.[25] Strikingly, in one of them, mSuk 4:8, it bridges not from a biblical lemma but from a halakhah.[26]

Abraham Goldberg suggests that as a matter of form, the way the above passages from the Mishnah introduce scripture, with the accompaniment of minimal or no reasoning or technical terminology, is a sign of "early exegesis," from the Pharisees and other sectarians of the Second Temple period, in contrast with the forms of "late exegesis" on view in the tannaitic midrashim.[27] It is certainly not the case that all pericopes formally like the above ones are early. In mPes 1:12, for example, the Mishnah rules as follows concerning leaven after Passover.

> Leaven that passed Passover in the possession of a non-Jew is permitted with respect to benefit; but of an Israelite, it is forbidden, as it says, "[leaven] shall not be seen for you" (Ex 13:7).

Shamma Friedman has shown that this pericope represents a revision of tPes 1:12 and 1:8.[28] In tPes 1:8, R. Judah takes the view that one who eats leaven that passed Passover (evidently in the possession of an Israelite) transgresses a negative commandment. The Mishnah, in adapting this passage, identifies what it assumes to be the negative commandment to which R. Judah refers: Ex 13:7. Thus, in this pericope the appearance of the exegetical form of interest—a concluding prooftext, with minimal or no accom-

---

24. See Liora Elias Bar-Levav, *The Mekhilta de-Rabbi Shimeon Ben Yohai on the Nezikin Portion* (Hebrew; Jerusalem, 2013), 112. My thanks to Ishay Rosen-Zvi for drawing my attention to Bar-Levav's discussion.

25. See Bar-Levav, *The Mekhilta de-Rabbi Shimeon Ben Yohai*, 126. The four cases are mBik 1:9; mSuk 4:1; mKer 6:9; mMid 3:1. In m'Eduy 5:6, MS Kaufmann has ללמד; here, as in, e.g., mSan 4:5, ללמד evidently represents a distinct usage, signaling the interpretation of an event rather than a text. In mSot 5:5, MS Kaufmann has לימד.

26. The pericope interprets the halakhic tradition in mSuk 4:1.

27. See Abraham Goldberg, המדרש הקדום והמדרש המאוחר, *Tarbiz* 50 (1981), 94–106, reprinted in Goldberg, *Literary Form and Composition in Classical Rabbinic Literature: Selected Literary Studies in Mishna, Tosefta, Halakhic and Aggadic Midrash and Talmud* (Jerusalem, 2011), 119–31.

28. See Friedman, *Tosefta Aitqta*, 156–67.

panying exegetical apparatus—is a result of late editing, and not a sign of antiquity.

More important than the chronological factor that Goldberg adduces are the interrelated considerations of purpose and form to which we alluded above. Even when the Mishnah cites and interprets verses, its goal is distinct from the project of Akiban midrash. In such cases, the Mishnah in general aims not, in the first instance, to explain the biblical text, but to provide support for a legal teaching. It is for this reason that the exegetical apparatus of the Mishnah is minimalist. The midrashic works of the school of R. Akiba, insofar as they make use of such minimalist pericopes from the Mishnah, "reformat" them to incorporate the legal teaching, with its associated proof-text, into a systematic exegetical framework. The difference in substantive aim corresponds to the basic formal difference between these works: In the Mishnah, in the default case, the legal teaching comes first, and then comes the prooftext (when it comes at all), whereas in tannaitic midrash, the biblical lemma comes first, then the legal teaching.

In the above cases from the Mishnah (mSan 2:5; mBK 8:1; mZev 9:5; mPes 1:12), the Mishnah supports each assertion with a concluding prooftext. The usage in these pericopes should be distinguished from another category of concluding citation, where the prooftext is introduced with the words על זה נאמר "concerning this was it said" and similar formulations.[29] In mSuk 2:6, for example, the Mishnah cites the view of R. Eliezer that if a person did not eat in the sukkah on the evening of the first day of the festival, he may make up the omission by eating in the sukkah on the supplementary eighth evening of the festival. The sages disagree:

> There is no making up for the matter. Concerning this it was said: "What is crooked cannot be made straight, and what is lacking cannot be counted." (Eccl 1:15)

The exegesis is familiar from the *petiḥta* form, most prevalent in amoraic literature from Roman Palaestina but with earlier precedents: The rabbi identifies a concrete fact pattern as an instance of a general principle articulated by Scripture.[30] In this and other cases, the form has a "merely" homiletical rather than exegetical force; we are obviously not meant to suppose

29. On this use of Scripture see Samely, *Rabbinic Interpretation*, 104–9, and the secondary literature cited in 106 n. 93.

30. On the *petiḥta* form see, e.g., Tzvi Novick, *Midrash and Piyyut: Form, Genre, and History* (Göttingen, 2019), 12–17.

that the author of Ecclesiastes had in mind specifically the missed Sukkot meal.

But the form can also be deployed in a genuinely exegetical way, as in the following example, from mḤag 1:5.[31] The pericope concerns offerings associated with the pilgrimage festivals: well-being offerings, which are consumed in part by the sacrificiant and his party, and whole offerings, which are entirely consumed on the altar.

> One who has many eaters and little property brings many well-being offerings and few whole offerings. [One who has] much property and few eaters, he brings many whole offerings and few well-being offerings. If this and this are few, concerning this did they say, "one *ma'ah* of silver and two [*ma'ah* of] silver." If this and this are many, concerning this it was said, "Each man according to what he can give, according to the blessing that the Lord your God has given you" (Deut 16:17).

As Samely suggests, the Mishnah seems to locate two criteria in Deut 16:17: a person's wealth ("what he can give"), and the size of his family ("the blessing that the Lord your God has given you").[32] The Mishnah supposes that the verse itself speaks to a case when both wealth and family are present in abundance: In this case, one brings many well-being offerings (to feed the family) and many whole-offerings. This exegesis has a homiletical ring, but makes something closer to a legal claim than the exegesis in mSuk 2:6.

More notable for our purposes than the blurring of the homiletical and the legal is the implicit equivalence in this passage between biblical verse and mishnaic halakhah. Just as the phrase "concerning this was it said" introduces Deut 16:17 as referring to the case of abundance of resources and eaters, so the Mishnah uses the phrase "concerning this did they say" to identify a passage from the Mishnah itself—the house of Hillel's ruling in mḤag 1:2, legislating the expenditure of one *ma'ah* on a whole offering, and two on a well-being offering—as a minimum, for the case of little wealth and few consumers.

Ishay Rosen-Zvi has suggested that the effect of the Mishnah's haphazard, non-systematic engagement with the Bible is to establish a sort of

31. On "standard" and "substandard" usages of the form see N. A. van Uchelen, "The Formula על זה נאמר in the Mishnah: A Form-Analytical Study," in *History and Form: Dutch Studies in the Mishnah*, ed. A. Kuyt and N. A. van Uchelen (Amsterdam, 1988), 83–92.

32. See Samely, *Rabbinic Interpretation*, 105 and n. 91.

equivalence between the biblical and the non-biblical, and thus to situate the ultimate authority of the laws in the fact of their appearance within the framework of the Mishnah.[33] Whatever the macroscopic effect of the Mishnah's citation practices, cases like mḤag 1:2, which directly pair a verse with a legal teaching from the Mishnah itself, effect such equivalence on a smaller scale. We will examine below another instance of pairing of this sort.[34]

c. Implicit Presence of Scripture

Scholars have observed that besides drawing on the Bible for its topics, and explicitly citing biblical verses, the Mishnah often includes interpretive paraphrases of a verse or sequence of verses. In other cases still, a series of pericopes or even chapters reflects the order of the relevant biblical verses. In both of these circumstances, the Mishnah can be said to manifest implicit interpretation of or dependence on Scripture. Here as an example of an interpretive paraphrase is mBK 5:5, which introduces the law of damages from a pit; I juxtapose to it the biblical verses on pit damage, Ex 21:33–34.[35]

> mBK 5:5: One who digs a pit in the public domain and an ox or ass fell into it and died, he is liable. It is all the same for a pit and a ditch and a cave, a groove or a trench. If so, why is a "pit" said? Just as a pit is sufficient to kill, to ten handbreadths, so anything that is sufficient to kill, to ten handbreadths. If they were less than ten handbreadths, and an ox or ass fell into it and died, he is exempt. But if it was damaged in it, he is liable. One who digs a pit in a private domain and opens it up into the public domain; in the public domain and opens it up into another public domain, he is liable.
> Ex 21:33–34: If a man opens a pit, or if a man excavates a pit, and he does not cover it, and an ox or ass fell into it, the owner of the pit shall make restitution.

This case is especially interesting because it features both an interpretive paraphrase and explicit biblical interpretation. Let us begin with the latter. The Mishnah insists that liability extends to the digging of any depression in the ground. Why, then, it asks, does the biblical verse specify a pit? The answer: A pit is typically ten handbreadths deep, and is therefore of sufficient

33. See Rosen-Zvi, *Between Mishna*, 69.
34. See also mSuk 4:8, noted above.
35. For discussion of some aspects of this paraphrase see Rosen-Zvi, *Between Mishna*, 67 n. 116.

depth to kill a normal ox or ass. If, by contrast, the depression is less than ten handbreadths deep, the person who dug it is liable only for damages. If the ox or ass died, we suppose that the death reflects an unusual weakness in the animal.

The expansion from a named biblical instance to a category, expressed through the term "so anything" (אף כל), is a phenomenon in tannaitic midrash, but it is typically bound up, in the latter context, with a complex, technically defined apparatus of exegesis, such as "rule and specification and rule" (כלל ופרט וכלל) or "the common denominator" (הצד השווה), that justifies the expansion.[36] But such apparatuses rarely occur in the Mishnah, and in mBK 5:5 the expansion is in fact stated as a law ("It is all the same for a pit and a ditch and a cave, a groove or a trench") prior to the turn to the verse. Likewise, in Akiban midrash, the expansion through "so anything" is typically followed by an explicit term of exclusion: Something "exits" (יצא) the category, or there is an exception (פרט ל-) to it. In mBK 5:5, too, there is an exclusion statement—exemption from liability for a depression shallower than ten handbreadths—but the statement is articulated separately, without the technical term to glue it to the exegesis, even though the exclusion is precisely the point of the exegesis.[37] Unlike the cases in the previous section, the Mishnah's explicit exegesis in mBK 5:5 seeks to justify the verse ("If so, why is 'pit' said?"), and in this respect the Mishnah uses "midrashic" reasoning. And yet even here, its exegetical apparatus is characteristically minimalist, and the pericope as a whole, insofar as it takes the law rather than a verse as its starting point, is mishnaic. The oddly unmoored character of the exegesis in mBK 5:5 is the result of this tension.

Alongside the explicit exegesis of the word "pit," the Mishnah engages in extensive exegetical paraphrase of the biblical verse. It lifts the phrase "an ox or an ass fell" (ונפל . . . שור או חמור) from the verse. It also replaces the rare root כר"י ("to excavate") with the more common root חפ"ר ("to dig"). Per our observation in connection with the opening analysis of mBer 1:1, the Mishnah characteristically conceals the biblical subject ("a man") behind the impersonal participle החופר "one who digs." The Mishnah also adds limitations to the Bible's case: The pit is situated in the public domain, and the animal dies from the fall. After the explicitly exegetical aside on excavations other than pits, the Mishnah returns to implicit exegetical paraphrase, this time by taking up the reference to "opening" a pit in Ex 21:33. The Mish-

---

36. See, e.g., Mek. R. Ish. ba-ḥodesh 8 (Horovitz-Rabin ed., 234); Sifra Nedava 2:1 (Weiss ed., 3c).

37. Contrast Samely, *Rabbinic Interpretation*, 232, 278, who locates the exegesis in the expansion rather than in the exclusion.

nah evidently assumes that the verse cannot refer to someone who simply exposes a pit in the public domain, for to do so is the same as (or at least not materially different from) excavating it. Again attentive (unlike the biblical text) to the question of the location of the pit, the Mishnah interprets the case of "opening" as one involving a tunnel, where the excavation point (i.e., the point where one breaks ground) is different from the "opening" point. The Mishnah reverses the order in the verse, beginning with "excavating" and ending with "opening," presumably because in the Mishnah's construal of the biblical cases, digging is the paradigmatic case of pit damage, whereas opening is an altogether rarer alternative.

There is a blurry line between paraphrases of this sort on the one hand, which are addressed to the substance of the biblical text that they reformulate, and on the other hand, more playful or literary allusions.[38] A case closer to the latter occurs in mBB 1:5, where the anonymous voice of the Mishnah says that one who dwells in a city can be compelled by the other city dwellers to contribute "to build for a city a wall, and a double gate, and a bar." The Mishnah borrows Moses' words in his account of the conquest of the cities of Bashan in Deut 3:5: "All these were fortress cities, with a high wall, a double gate, and a bar." It is not clear whether the Mishnah means implicitly to rely on Deut 3:5 as a source for the essential features of a city, or whether it is merely introducing a literary flourish.

J. N. Epstein observes that "the older the Mishnah pericopes, the more they are influenced by the language of Scripture."[39] Exegetical paraphrases like the one in mBK 5:5 are, as Ishay Rosen-Zvi notes, formally continuous with the halakhic cases of "rewritten Bible" that one finds in Second Temple literature like Josephus's summary of the law in his *Biblical Antiquities*, and some legal texts from Qumran.[40] Paraphrases are rarer in later strata of the Mishnah. The same chronological factor may also figure in cases where the Mishnah, without necessarily paraphrasing, tracks the order of biblical verses or passages. Thus, for example, Yair Furstenberg traces a relatively early stratum of tractate *Nezikin* (i.e., the three "gates") that follows the sequence of relevant biblical topics from Exodus to Leviticus to Deuteronomy. I refer the reader to Furstenberg's own contribution to this volume,

38. See Nathan Braverman, לשונות מקרא במשנה, *Netuim* 10 (2003): 9–17, and the literature cited there.

39. See J. N. Epstein, *Introduction to the Mishnaic Text* (Hebrew; Jerusalem, 2001 [1948]), 1129.

40. See Rosen-Zvi, *Between Mishna*, 69 and n. 119. See also Menahem I. Kahana, *Sifre Zuta Deuteronomy: Citations from a New Tannaitic Midrash* (Hebrew; Jerusalem, 2005), 242–44, identifying a probable implicit interpretation of Deut 13:15 and 17:4 in an early layer underlying mSan 5:1.

where he takes up this case, along with references to other scholarship on this phenomenon.

2. SCRIPTURE AND MISHNAIC LEGAL LANGUAGE

We turn now from the presence of the Bible in the substance of the Mishnah—as the source for the Mishnah's topics and through explicit and implicit reference—to the relationship between the legal language of the Bible and that of the Mishnah. It will be helpful to start at a point chronologically in between these works: the Damascus Document, from a time near the end of the Second Temple period. The Sabbath laws of the Damascus Document (CD x 14–xi 17) have a consistent form, exemplified in the two excerpts below.[41]

Let not a man do (אל יעש איש) work on the sixth day from the time that the sun's disk is distant from the gate by its fullness, for this is what it said, "keep watch over the day of the Sabbath to sanctify it" (Deut 5:12). (x 14–17)[42]

Let not a man go (אל ילך איש) after an animal to graze it outside his city, save two thousand cubits. (xi 5)

Each law begins with the negation אל, followed by the imperfect or jussive, and the subject איש.[43] This construction resembles biblical law, which employs imperfects and named subjects, but diverges from it in that the Bible predominantly employs the negation לא rather than אל for law, and

41. For the Hebrew text I rely on the online Historical Dictionary Project of the Academy of the Hebrew Language (Ma'agarim).

42. This sentence opens the section on the Sabbath laws (after a titular prepositional phrase). Strikingly, the section includes no other prooftexts from the Bible until the very end: "Let not a man raise up on the altar on the Sabbath anything save the whole offering for the Sabbath, for thus is written, 'except for your Sabbath [offerings]'" (xi 17–18). This envelope structure—with prooftexts only at the beginning and end—may be designed implicitly to convey that the entire unit of Sabbath laws has its roots in Scripture.

43. See also the related bodies of Sabbath laws in 4Q264a and 4Q421, on which see Vered Noam and Elisha Qimron, "A Qumran Composition of Sabbath Laws and Its Contributions to the Study of Early Halakah," *DSD* 16.1 (2009): 55–96, esp. 80–81 and n. 69. On the use of the negation אל in the Dead Sea Scrolls in general see Elisha Qimron, "The Negative Word אל in our Early Sources" (Hebrew), in *Studies Presented to Professor Zeev Ben-Ḥayyim*, ed. M. Bar-Asher et al. (Jerusalem, 1983), 473–82. The use of the jussive is visible in the first excerpt and again in xi 6, 17, but contrast, e.g., the imperfect יוציא in xi 7.

reserves אל for "wisdom" purposes, to convey advice or counsel.[44] In contrast to the Damascus Document, when the Mishnah negates the imperfect in legal contexts, it retains, as a rule, the biblical negation לֹא, and very rarely employs אל outside of certain limited and well-defined rhetorical contexts.[45] But as noted at the outset of this chapter, the Mishnah diverges from the legal language of the Bible by making regular use of the subjectless participle where the Bible uses only the named subject with the imperfect verb.[46]

In the absence of the Damascus Document, one might suppose that the Mishnah's preference for לֹא represents nothing other than inertia, a default adoption of biblical style. But the fact that the Damascus Document employs אל enables us to appreciate the Mishnah's use of לֹא as a considered choice. This conclusion is reinforced by the fact that Mishnah-like articulations of law in the "Zuta" works of tannaitic midrash (Sifre Zuta Numbers and Sifre Zuta Deuteronomy) also often use אל, like the Damascus Document.[47] It appears that the preference for אל in both the Damascus Document and

44. See Qimron, "Negative Word," 475; Jacobus A. Naudé and Gary A. Rendsburg, "Negation: Pre-Modern Hebrew," in *Encyclopedia of Hebrew Language and Linguistics*, ed. G. Kahn (Leiden, 2013), 804.

45. See Qimron, "Negative Word"; Hallel Baitner, "Studies in the Mishnah of Sifre Zuta and Its Integration into the Midrash" (Hebrew) (PhD diss., Hebrew University, 2017), 80–83. Among the important rhetorical contexts for אל is the expression of a preference for a non-ideal course of action over a still less ideal course of action. See, e.g., mTer 8:10–12, and especially mHal 2:3; the latter pericope gives explicit expression to the impossibility of the ideal course of action. Baitner ("Studies in the Mishnah of Sifre Zuta," 81 n. 188) lists five cases of אל in apparently ordinary halakhic contexts in the Mishnah, but this list must be nuanced. First, analysis of the usage of אל should distinguish between the anonymous voice of the Mishnah and named rabbis. Of these five cases, only three (mBM 2:8, 10, 3:11) occur in the anonymous voice of the Mishnah, all of them within a span of two chapters in a single tractate. The other two instances (mTer 8:8 and mPes 3:3) both occur in the speech of a named rabbi from the Yavneh generation (Rabban Gamaliel and R. Eliezer). Second, these two cases, unlike the three from mBM, concern the same question: what to do with defiled priestly food (*terumah, ḥallah*) in specific circumstances that constrain disposal possibilities. Thus, in the end, these cases instantiate, if in abbreviated form, the standard usage of אל, to advocate for a particular course of action in non-ideal circumstances; in fact, mTer 8:8 is continuous with mTer 8:10–12, where this usage occurs in its standard form, and mPes 3:3 concerns a different dimension of the case of impure *ḥallah* that is the topic of mHal 2:3, which likewise exemplifies the standard usage. On mPes 3:3 see Friedman, *Tosefta Atiqta*, 275–88.

46. On the participle for the expression of law in mishnaic Hebrew see Mordechay Mishor, "The Tense System in Tannaitic Hebrew" (Hebrew) (PhD diss., Hebrew University, 1983), 264–65.

47. See Kahana, *Sifre Zuta Deuteronomy*, 79–80; Baitner, "Studies," 80–83.

the Zuta midrashim stems from a perception of אל as belonging to a high or literary register.[48] Paradoxically, their use of אל may represent an attempt to invoke the Bible by departing from it: To produce a patina of Bible-like authority, these texts use the more poetic, vaguely archaic negation אל, even though the Bible itself deploys לא in law. By the same token, the Mishnah's preference for לא with imperfects may indicate not primarily a debt to biblical style, but a view that the law should be presented prosaically or impersonally, in a way that does not draw attention to its own literariness. The intended effect of the subjectless participle is arguably the same.[49]

The beginning of this chapter highlighted an important distinction between the legal language of the Bible and that of the Mishnah: Even within its anonymous voice, the Mishnah is often dialogical, presenting the law through questions and answers.[50] We may consider, as an example, the question כיצד "How so?"[51] One common usage of this question in the Mishnah is to clarify a rule, as in mNed 2:3.

> There is a vow within a vow, but there is no oath within an oath. How so? If he said: Behold I am a nazirite if I eat; behold I am a nazirite if I eat; behold I am a nazirite if I eat, and he ate, he is liable for each [vow]. [If he said:] An oath that I will not eat; an oath that I will not eat; an oath that I will not eat, and he ate, he is only liable for one [oath violation].

The Mishnah states a rule, then follows with a "how so?" question, which prompts the description of a case that illustrates and thus clarifies the rule: Multiple vows bound to the same act have effect, whereas if one has bound oneself by oath to refrain from an act, further identical oaths have no effect.[52] The illustration is casuistic ("If he said," etc.), and thus mirrors much bib-

---

48. Thus Kahana, *Sifre Zuta Deuteronomy*, 80 and n. 17. Baitner, "Studies," 81, separates the Qumran evidence from that of the Zuta midrashim, and suggests that the latter is merely one instance of a later, post-mishnaic trend of more prevalent use of אל, attested also in the Tosefta and the Yerushalmi.

49. For this construal of the participle see Mishor, "The Tense System," 277–80.

50. On this phenomenon see, in brief, Rosen-Zvi, *Between Mishna*, 11 and n. 46.

51. Other examples: איזהו "what is" (and variants); אימתי "when" (and variants); מהיכן "whence"; מה בין "what is the difference between."

52. On the use of "how so" not to explain but to qualify a rule see Abraham Goldberg, "כיצד": כמילת ניב לשון המשנה, לטיב :הגבלה *Leshonenu* 41.1 (1977): 6–20, reprinted in Goldberg, *Literary Form and Composition*, 102–16. Oddly, Goldberg does not compare "how so" in this usage to the question במי דברים אמורים "In what are these matters said?," which occurs commonly with just this qualifying sense in the Mishnah.

lical law. But the dialogical structure of the pericope allows the Mishnah to articulate at the outset a generalization, and thus to subsume the casuistry under an abstract rule. The dynamic of question and answer, perhaps a reflection of the scholastic context from which the Mishnah emerged, introduces a didactic or performative element into the work that modulates the impersonal posture constructed by the Mishnah's preference for the subjectless participle and the negation לא.

A different and especially interesting usage of "how so" occurs later in the same tractate, at mNed 11:9.

> The vow of a widow or divorcee shall be binding on her. How so? If she said: Behold I am a nazirite after thirty days, even if she married within thirty days, he cannot annul.
>
> If she vowed, and she is under the authority of the husband, and he annulled for her—if she said: Behold I am a nazirite after thirty days, even if she became widowed or divorced within thirty days— behold, it is annulled.

The pericope divides into two parallel units. The first begins with words drawn directly (with an ellipsis) from Num 30:10: "The vow of a widow or divorcee . . . shall be binding on her." The law itself is straightforward enough: If a woman is no longer under her husband's authority, her vow is not subject to annulment, and hence binds her. Unlike the case in mNed 2:3, the "how so" question does not seek illustration of an abstract principle, but rather does exegetical work: It calls for a case where one might have thought that the vow of a woman not under a husband's authority would *not* bind her, such that it was necessary for scripture to say that she is in fact bound.[53] The Mishnah's answer: The case is one in which a woman makes a vow that will take effect in thirty days, and in the interim, she marries. One might have thought that since thirty days on, when the vow is set to take effect, she is now married, the husband may annul the vow; hence the biblical rule comes to teach that he may not annul it, because he was not her husband when she made the vow.

The second half of the pericope introduces the mirror case: A married woman makes a vow that will take effect in thirty days, and her husband annuls it, but she becomes widowed or divorced before the vow is set to take

---

53. The exegetical conundrum becomes more acute in light of the apparently expansive כל "everything" in the elided portion of the verse. The verse as a whole runs thus: "The vow of a widow or divorcee, everything that she bound on herself, shall be binding on her."

effect. In printed editions, the form of the second half of the pericope precisely matches the first, with a statement of the principle followed by a "how so" question. In MS Kaufmann, the basis for the above translation, and in other manuscripts, the "how so" question is missing, but even in them, there is a basic formal parallel to the first half, with a division between an apparently obvious assertion ("If she vowed, and she is under the authority of the husband, and he annulled for her . . . behold it is annulled."), and the identification of the case that would make this assertion non-obvious.

Epstein cites the observation of the medieval commentator, R. Yom Tov b. Avraham of Seville, on this pericope: "This is like a midrash and not a midrash."[54] There is indeed a remarkable synthesis here of the language and methods of Mishnah and midrash. In the first half of the pericope, an apparently superfluous verse and its justification are clothed in a characteristically mishnaic dialogical form, the "how so" question. Moreover, the Mishnah does not mark the biblical text as a quotation; the text is rather voiced by the Mishnah. Even more strikingly, in the second half of the pericope, the Mishnah makes an utterly obvious assertion (that a husband may annul his wife's vow) simply in order to mirror the biblical assertion in the first half of the pericope (that there is no annulment for the vow of an independent woman), and thus reproduce the pattern of "lemma" and exegesis from that first half. The parallelism of biblical and mishnaic teachings in mNed 11:9 recollects the similar pairing of verse and halakhah in mḤag 1:5, discussed above.

CONCLUSION

We have surveyed some key contributions in the history of scholarship on the relationship between the Mishnah and the Bible, from the work of J. N. Epstein and Abraham Goldberg of an earlier generation to that of contemporary scholars like Alexander Samely and Menahem Kahana. The results do not allow for easy summary, precisely because the defining feature of the Mishnah's relationship to the Bible is its independence therefrom, especially in structure and form. The Bible's presence in the Mishnah is haphazard, orthogonal, interstitial, often silent. It is also on the move: One consistent finding in the scholarship on this topic is that the Mishnah's relationship to the Bible shifts over time, and in particular that implicit dependence on the Bible, in the forms of paraphrase and adherence to the order of the relevant verses, declines from earlier strata to later.

---

54. See Epstein, *Introduction to the Mishnaic Text*, 1132.

One area that calls for further research is the context for the emergence of the distinctive legal language of the Mishnah. As we have observed, the Mishnah in this respect departs sharply from the Bible, and the one way noted above in which it returns to biblical language—its choice of לא for the negation of imperfects—may not derive from a desire to biblicize but from other considerations. A comprehensive, positive account of the legal language of the Mishnah, as distinct from mishnaic Hebrew more generally—an account that is attentive to, among other things, Second Temple antecedents at Qumran and beyond, as well as contemporaneous legal language elsewhere in the Semitic world, especially Aramaic—falls outside the scope of this chapter, and remains a desideratum.

2. The Mishnah and Ancient Near Eastern Law

Jonathan S. Milgram

I. INTRODUCTION[1]

Possible parallels between ancient Near Eastern[2] law and mishnaic law have intrigued scholars since the great discoveries of the cuneiform law collec-

1. My thanks to Shamma Friedman for encouraging me to write this article; Shalom Holtz for reading parts of it; Aaron Koller for reading an earlier draft of the entire essay and offering his typically insightful comments; David Danzig and Bernard Jackson for fruitful discussion and bibliography. Finally, I especially wish to thank Shaye J. D. Cohen, honored at the conference resulting in this publication, for the invitation to participate and for his continued support of my work. Note that transliterations of Akkadian and Aramaic follow the conventions of Ancient Near Eastern Studies; of Hebrew, the style sheet of *JQR*. I only discuss overlap in the area of "private law" (laws dealing with the property and relationships of private persons) such as marriage, divorce, and inheritance, for which scholars have found significant parallels in Babylonian legal literature. Ancient Near Eastern cultic laws that correspond to tannaitic traditions tend to be rooted in sources from Phoenicia, Syria, and Anatolia. For examples and bibliography, see Noga Ayali-Darshan, "The Origin and Meaning of the Crimson Thread in the Mishnaic Scapegoat Ritual in Light of an Ancient Syro-Anatolian Custom" *JSJ* 44 (2013): 1–23, and Noga Ayali-Darshan, "The Seventy Bulls Sacrificed at Sukkot (Num 29:12–34) in Light of a Ritual Text from Emar (6, 373)," *VT* 65:1 (2015): 9–19.

2. I use the terms "ancient Near Eastern law," "Akkadian law," and "cuneiform law" interchangeably to refer to laws evidenced in ancient Near Eastern codes and transactional records (all the product of Mesopotamia in the last three millennia BCE). Assyriologists distinguish between transactional records—such as marriage, divorce, adoption, and testamentary documents—and the codes of ancient Mesopotamian law (among the most famous, Hammurabi, ca. 1750 BCE, and Lipit Ishtar, ca. 1930 BCE, for example). The transactional records are documentary evidence for practices. The codes, never cited in court cases or transactional records, are likely theoretical laws that are the

tions in the nineteenth and early twentieth centuries.[3] A number of studies in the last few decades have broadly addressed these parallels.[4] As regards mishnaic law specifically, a source book listing a great number of laws in the Mishnah (and related literatures) that are comparable to ancient Near Eastern traditions was recently published.[5] Yet while robust comparative studies have discussed linkages between tannaitic laws and Greek and Roman sources,[6] scholars of rabbinics have only recently attempted more comprehensive treatments of parallels between ancient Near Eastern and tannaitic

---

product of scribal schools. On the codes' normativity see the essays in, Edmond Lévy, *La codification des lois dans l'antiquité: Actes du colloque de Strasbourg: 27–29 Novembre 1997* (Paris, 2000).

3. For a partial listing, see Yochanan Muffs, *Love and Joy: Law, Language, and Religion in Ancient Israel* (New York, 1992), 139. In his important survey, Shaye Cohen lists ancient Near Eastern law as one of the sources from which mishnaic law draws; see Shaye J. D. Cohen, "The Judaean Legal Tradition and the *Halakhah* of the Mishnah," in *The Cambridge Companion to The Talmud and Rabbinic Literature*, ed. C. E. Fonrobert and M. S. Jaffee (Cambridge, 2007), 121–43.

4. See M. J. Geller, "The Influence of Ancient Mesopotamia on Hellenistic Judaism," in *Civilizations of the Ancient Near East*, ed. J. Sasson (New York, 2002), 43–54. A list of works on the overlap between ancient Near Eastern law and rabbinic law appears in Muffs, *Love and Joy*, 139–41. For a more recent list, see Shamma Friedman, "The Plotting Witness and Beyond—A Continuum in Ancient Near Eastern, Biblical, and Talmudic Law," in *Birkat Shalom: Studies in the Bible, Ancient Near Eastern Literature and Post-biblical Judaism Presented to Shalom M. Paul on the Occasion of His Seventieth Birthday*, ed. C. Cohen (Winona Lake, Ind., 2008), 827 n. 81. On potential parallels in the Babylonian Talmud, see M. J. Geller, "The Survival of Babylonian Wissenschaft in Later Tradition," in *The Melammu Symposia I: The History of Assyria. Proceedings of the Opening Symposium of the Assyrian and Babylonian Intellectual Heritage Project*, ed. S. Aro and R. M. Whiting (Helsinki, 2000), 1–6. For a parallel between the Code of Hammurabi and Genesis Rabbah (a document from the land of Israel of the third or fourth century), see Yaakov Elman, "Babylonian Echoes in a Late Rabbinic Legend" *JANES* 4 (1972): 12–19.

5. Samuel Greengus, *Laws in the Bible and in Early Rabbinic Collections: The Legal Legacy of the Ancient Near East* (Eugene, Ore., 2011). The book builds on the author's important earlier work; see, for example, Samuel Greengus, "Filling Gaps: Laws Found in Babylonia and in the Mishna but Absent in the Hebrew Bible" *Maarav* 7 (1991): 149–71 (among other studies).

6. See, for example, the following classic studies: Saul Lieberman, *Greek in Jewish Palestine* (New York, 1942) and *Hellenism in Jewish Palestine* (New York, 1950); republished in one volume, Saul Lieberman, *Greek in Jewish Palestine / Hellenism in Jewish Palestine*, with a new introduction by Dov Zlotnick (New York and Jerusalem, 1994), and Boaz Cohen, *Jewish and Roman Law* (New York, 1966); republished as Boaz Cohen, *Jewish and Roman Law*, introduction by Natalie B. Dohrmann (Piscataway, N.J., 2018).

laws.[7] This may be in part because scholars have struggled to formulate what "channels of transmission"[8] could have brought about legal overlap with cuneiform law. It is highly unlikely, for example, that the rabbis had any direct exposure to ancient Near Eastern codes or documents. In contrast, possible direct contact with Greek and Roman sources is more easily substantiated.[9]

In this article, I treat two separate, but interrelated, topics: legal parallels between ancient Near Eastern and mishnaic laws, and the mechanisms that may have brought them about. The legal parallels draw on three types of "interconnections."[10] Significantly, the parallels are attested in both ancient Near Eastern codes and transactional documents,[11] demonstrating that the rabbinic tradition drew on scribal and scholastic traditions, as well as lived practices. In my discussion of the channels of transmission I argue that each channel was likely to result in a certain type of parallel.

II. FORMS OF LEGAL PARALLELS AND CHANNELS OF TRANSMISSION

Among the greatest challenges for scholars of comparative ancient law is to determine when a parallel is evidence of intercultural contact. The laws of peoples in neighboring civilizations may be based on similar values, outlooks, and methods of problem solving, and may, therefore, result in similar laws.[12] As I have written elsewhere, at times a great degree of similarity in legal materials across ancient cultures actually prevents us from concluding anything substantive about the interdependence of said laws.[13] While determining antecedents and interdependence based on conceptual con-

---

7. See, for example, Jonathan S. Milgram, *From Mesopotamia to the Mishnah: Tannaitic Inheritance Law in its Legal and Social Contexts* (Tübingen, 2016); paperback with new preface and postscript (Boston, 2019) and the literature cited below.

8. I thank Bernard Jackson for suggesting this phrase.

9. See n. 6 and Milgram, *From Mesopotamia to the Mishnah*, 14–16.

10. Here I borrow the fluid, yet useful, term in Muffs, *Love and Joy*, 139.

11. See n. 2.

12. Compare Saul Lieberman, *"Mashehu 'al sifro shel yulianus me'ashkelon 'ḥukei palestina uminhageha'" Tarbiz* 40 (1971): 409.

13. Regarding some similarities between tannaitic inheritance laws and those in other ancient law collections, I have written, for example, "the parallels from the distinct collections supply essential data for determining to what degree the inheritance laws formulated by the tannaim are representative of concepts, customs, and laws generally known in the ancient Mediterranean" (Milgram, *From Mesopotamia to the Mishnah*, 16). In relation to this, see my discussion of what to consider "internal" vs. "external" when comparing the laws in tannaitic works to the laws in other ancient collections in Milgram, *From Mesopotamia to the Mishnah*, 16 (and especially n. 86).

sistency alone poses methodological challenges, criteria can be developed for determining possible historical connections.[14] The examples below are not based on thematic overlap alone. Each example includes "anchors" that demonstrate the presence of a historical connection between specific laws of the ancient Near East and the laws of the Mishnah. These anchors may be terminological, formulaic, or parallel in concept and formal literary presentation (see below).

By "terminological overlap" I mean the occurrence of a Hebrew term in the Mishnah that is the equivalent of an Akkadian legal term. Accordingly, in example (1) I deal with terms referring to the assets that make up the rabbinic dowry: Hebrew *melug* and its antecedent Akkadian *mulūgu*, and *tson barzel* and its possible correspondence to *šá AN.BAR šú-nu*. By "formulaic parallel" I refer to a set series of words found in both ancient Near Eastern sources and the Mishnah that constitutes a declaration that effects legal change. In example (2) I examine the possible ancient Near Eastern antecedents to the mishnaic divorce formula "You are permitted to go and marry any man that you please." Lastly, I treat laws that are "parallel in concept and formal literary presentation," specifically laws regarding payment for inflicting "disgrace" on another.

The presentation of the scholarship in each example is accompanied by some methodological observations and a discussion of one of three channels of transmission suggested by scholars: (a) the presence of local traditions; that is, customs transmitted by communities of practice, (b) the diffusion of Aramaic law and the accompanying persistence of scribal traditions, and (c) the oral transmission of scholastic traditions. I argue that each particular channel of transmission is more conducive for the preservation of a specific form of parallel. The terms for assets in the dowry *melug* and *tson barzel*, for example, are likely evidence of local traditions adopted by the tannaim. The overlap in divorce formula between ancient Near Eastern and tannaitic traditions—also present in the Aramaic papyri at Elephantine—represents

---

14. In my own work, when terminological or formulaic overlap is not present, I have only argued for a possible relationship when the data shows that rabbinic thinking is not grounded in biblical precedent or tannaitic interpretation of Scripture and when the presumed parallel only occurs in one body of law (in addition to tannaitic law) and not in others from the ancient Mediterranean. Two examples from my book on inheritance include: (1) in both the Mishnah and at Nuzi property gifted in contemplation of death that had a lien attached to it remained claimable by creditors (see Milgram, *From Mesopotamia to the Mishnah*, 58–59) and (2) according to the Mishnah, the Code of Hammurabi, and possibly some Sumerian transactional documents the widow retained a right of residence in her deceased husband's home (Milgram, *From Mesopotamia to the Mishnah*, 135–36 and 139–43).

the effects of ancient Near Eastern scribal traditions preserved and promulgated by the Aramaic legal tradition. Scholastic traditions about damages for "disgrace," originating in cuneiform law and transmitted orally, in all likelihood informed the rabbinic interpretations of specific biblical verses.

1. Terminology and the Transmission of Local Traditions: The Dowry

a. *Mulūgu/Melûg*

In his important study "'*Mulūgu/Melûg*': The Origins of a Talmudic Legal Institution,"[15] Baruch Levine advanced the question by using etymological methods to study the word *melug* in tannaitic sources, ultimately pointing to Akkadian origins (see below).[16] Levine correctly noted that the Hebrew root *mlg/mlk* (in sources from the land of Israel) means "to pluck, break off" and its usage in tannaitic sources is indicative of a major feature of the *melug* assets (*nikhsei melug*) brought into the marriage by the wife (and given to her by her father as part of her dowry, in tannaitic literature called the *parnasah*).[17] According to the Mishnah (mYev 7.1–2), the wife retains ownership of these assets;[18] the husband only manages them and has the right to (pluck from) the usufruct (see mKet 8.3 and 8.5). At the time of the dissolution of the marriage or the husband's death, the *melug* assets revert to the wife's sole ownership and usage at their current value (i.e., after profit or loss since the inception of marriage).

Within the legal orbit of Akkadian law, *mulūgu* property (primarily in documents from Nuzi and in Neo-Babylonian texts) was also property given

---

15. Baruch Levine, "'*Mulūgu/Melûg*': The Origins of a Talmudic Legal Institution" *JAOS* 88 (1968): 271–85.

16. Levine, "'*Mulūgu/Melûg*,'" 272. Importantly, however, Levine tells us that a clear etymology is not available: "[I]t has not been possible to relate *mulūgu* to any Semitic root extant in the second or first millennium B.C.E." (272). Accordingly, we do not translate the term here.

17. See, for example, tKet 4.17 and the comments in Saul Lieberman, *Tosefta: Nashim* (New York, 1973), 70 n. 56. On the Aramaic term used for dowry in later talmudic sources, *nedunya*, see Boaz Cohen, *Jewish and Roman Law*, 350–51, and the bibliography in Schremer, *Male and Female He Created Them* (Hebrew; Jerusalem, 2003), 292 n. 115. Here too the word is originally Akkadian (*nudunnû*). On the use of *nudunnû* as property from the bride's parents (as opposed to being from the groom) in the Neo-Babylonian period, see M. J. Geller, "New Sources for the Origins of the Rabbinic Ketubah" *HUCA* 49 (1978): 237 n. 29.

18. The nature of these assets, whether landed property or movables, is not clearly delineated in the sources; see Schremer, *Male and Female*, 272.

to the wife by her father in the context of marriage (or dowry given to the wife for the inheritance of her sons),[19] as we see from the following Neo-Babylonian document:

1. As for the 1 2/3 minas, 2 shekels of silver, which Ṭabia
2. son of Nabu-apal-iddin, to the creditors
3. who (held a debt) against Nabu-eṭir . . .
4. out of his own resources has paid, in place of the two
5. servants, the remainder of the *mulūgu* personnel of Nabu-eṭir
6. and Amat-Ninlil, which Ṭabia had given them . . .

This text, cited by Levine,[20] concerns Ṭabia, who had given his daughter and son-in-law a *mulūgu* of two slaves. The son-in-law gave the *mulūgu* slaves to creditors as collateral for debt. Subsequently, Ṭabia restored the two slaves by making a payment to the creditors. Later in the document we see that the son-in-law agreed to give two of his own slaves as collateral, thereby getting Ṭabia his money back. *Mulūgu* here, as elsewhere in the documents surveyed by Levine, is used in the context of a dowry.

Admittedly, significant differences remain between the mishnaic model and the Neo-Babylonian; the overlap is only partial.[21] Note that the text here implies the *mulūgu* belonged both to the woman and to her husband (line 6 reads: "which Ṭabia had given *them*"). Another important general difference—although the context in this text does not require mention of it—is that the husband's right to usufruct is not explicit.[22] In spite of these

---

19. Levine, "'*Mulūgu/Melûg*,'" 280; *cf.* Geller, "Ketubah," 237–38.

20. Levine, "'*Mulūgu/Melûg*,'" 278–79; originally in *Vorderasiatische Schriftdenkmäler der (Königlichen) Museen zu Berlin* IV (Berlin, 1907), 46.

21. Indeed, comparatists continue to demonstrate that the parallels between tannaitic laws and those in other bodies of ancient law are typically partial. That is, the rabbis did not absorb legal institutions in toto. For a methodological debate on the partial overlap between tannaitic traditions and those in other ancient legal systems see the review of *From Mesopotamia to the Mishnah*, Yair Furstenberg, "Inheritance Laws in their Greco-Roman Context: Review Essay on *From Mesopotamia to the Mishnah*, by Jonathan S. Milgram," (Hebrew) *Shenaton Ha-mishpat Ha-'ivri* 29 (2016–18): 250–54; my rebuttal, Jonathan S. Milgram, "*Min ha-mizraḥ ha-kadum ve-'ad la-mishnah: hilkhot ha-yerushah shel ha-tannaim be-heksheran ha-mishpati ve-ha-ḥevrati*," ('*im teguvah le-vikoret sefarim me'et Dr. Yair Furstenberg)*," *Shenaton Ha-mishpat Ha-'ivri* 30 (2019–20) 175–78 (esp. 176 n. 180); and Milgram, *From Mesopotamia to the Mishnah*, paperback edition, 203–11.

22. On the fact that usufruct is not detailed in Babylonian or Assyrian law, see Geller, "Ketubah," 238 and especially n. 33. Despite the absence, Geller writes that in Mesopotamia, "the husband probably had the usufruct of his wife's property" (238). He relies

differences, the linguistic connection (Akkadian *mulūgu* and Hebrew *melug)* coupled with the parallel contexts of dowered property definitively demonstrates a historical relationship between the terms.[23]

b. *Tson barzel* and *šá AN.BAR šú-nu*

Other assets that made up the mishnaic dowry included *tson barzel* ("iron sheep") property, over which the husband assumed ownership and administration during the marriage (mYev 7.1–2). At the husband's death or in the event of divorce, the wife received these assets at their original value. A. L. Oppenheim argued for the possible correspondence between *tson barzel* and *šá AN.BAR šú-nu* (meaning "they are made of iron"), found in two Neo-Babylonian contracts and referring to capital, such as cattle, that must be returned in the same amount as it was borrowed (i.e., their value will be maintained).[24] The contracts were of field leases in which the oxen were leased as well. Despite the possible conceptual overlap (assets retaining value) and the linguistic evidence (the meaning of "iron"), M. J. Geller objected to Oppenheim's argument for correspondence, since Akkadian contracts do not record this type of asset in the context of marriage (unlike *mulūgu/melûg* above).[25] However, as pointed out by Ranon Katzoff, the term *tson barzel* also appears in the Mishnah in the context of leasing animals (see, for example, mBekh 2.4).[26] The term, therefore, may have initially moved into mishnaic discourse regarding the leasing of animals, as in the original Akkadian, and only then have also been applied in the context of dowries.

---

on the fact that it seems usufruct is the background for the case of divorce of a wife who has no sons and whose husband is required to restore (and not just return) the dowry (Hammurabi ¶138). Due to the absence of the explicit mention of usufruct in the context of dowries, we should ask ourselves if usufruct of *mulūgu* was not native to the original Akkadian and only in rabbinic literature, due to the Hebrew root *mlg*'s meaning, was the principle of plucking usufruct imposed on the meaning of the word? Or, alternatively, does the rabbinic tradition preserve an element of the ancient Near Eastern institution unrecorded in the documents that have surfaced to date? The matter requires further investigation.

23. However, see the critical comments in Steven Kaufman, *The Akkadian Influences on Aramaic* (Chicago and London, 1974), 73.

24. A. L. Oppenheim, "A Note on *ṣôn barzel*" *IEJ* 5 (1955): 87–92.

25. Geller, "Ketubah," 239.

26. See Asher Gulak, *Legal Documents in the Talmud: In Light of Greek Papyri and Greek and Roman Law*, edited and supplemented by Ranon Katzoff (Hebrew; Jerusalem, 1994), 99 n. 76.

c. Terms and Local Traditions

In my study of tannaitic inheritance law,[27] I claimed that (a) due to the absence of biblical verses dealing with many of the specifics of inheritance procedure and (b) the lack of creative tannaitic interpretation of Scripture for the few biblical verses that do deal with inheritance, it is difficult to argue that tannaitic inheritance laws are the result of internal developments.[28] Rather, legal traditions external to the rabbinic corpus—including ancient Near Eastern, Greek, and Roman—at times provided terms that were eventually absorbed into tannaitic law.[29] Regarding our examples as well, as one scholar concisely put it, "in biblical law, no laws regarding a dowry were formulated."[30] Therefore, neither *melug* nor *tson barzel* should be viewed as having biblical antecedents, nor are they the product of rabbinic creative biblical interpretation.[31] Note also that the original usage of the Akkadian terms appeared in ancient Near Eastern transactional documents. This datum would indicate that—at least in these cases—the rabbinic movement drew from traditions that were part of a broad web of customs, presumably preserved and transmitted by communities of practice.

2. Formulae: Divorce and the Diffusion of Aramaic Law

a. Aramaic Law as Agent for the Circulation of Akkadian Law

In *Studies in the Aramaic Legal Papyri from Elephantine*, treating the papyri as a result of a long development in the history of ancient Near Eastern law, Yochanan Muffs posited that the Aramaic sale formula known from Elephantine *ṭyb lbby* (= "my heart is satisfied"), used in the context of compensation and expressing satisfaction with the price, could be traced back

---

27. Milgram, *From Mesopotamia to the Mishnah*.

28. For a concise statement, see Milgram, *From Mesopotamia to the Mishnah*, 33.

29. On the Roman legal terms *donatio* and *hereditas* as translated into tannaitic discourse as *mattanah* and *yerushah*, for example, see Milgram, *From Mesopotamia to the Mishnah*, 60–64. My thesis spawned a fruitful methodological discussion. See the review of my book, Furstenberg, "Inheritance Laws in their Greco-Roman Context," 254, and my response, Milgram, "Min ha-mizraḥ ha-kadum ve-'ad la-mishnah," 175–78. See also the abbreviated response to Furstenberg (in English) in Milgram, *From Mesopotamia to the Mishnah*, paperback, 207–8.

30. Joseph Fleishman, "A Daughter's Demand and a Father's Compliance: The Legal Background of Achsah's Claim and Caleb's Agreement: Joshua 15, 16–19; Judges 1, 12–15," *ZAW* 118:3 (September 2006): 355. On the scholarly dispute regarding the evidence for dowry in the Bible, see Milgram, *From Mesopotamia to the Mishnah*, 107 n. 8.

31. Indeed, the terms seem not to be addressed in *midrash halakhah*.

to the Old Babylonian Akkadian *libbašu ṭāb* (= "his heart is satisfied").[32] Such a progression from Akkadian to Aramaic formulation, argued Muffs, would affirm the degree to which Akkadian law lent elements of its character to Aramaic law. As a corollary to studying the terms for satisfaction in sale, Muffs also analyzed the function of *ina ḫūd libbišu* (= "in the joy of his heart"), the most common phrase of volition—that is, the willingness to part freely with property—in Neo-Babylonian cuneiform deeds of sale (for more on this, see below).[33] In the conclusion to his book, Muffs emphasized that further study of such formulaic trajectories could have potential for understanding the role of the Aramaic legal tradition—and its Akkadian antecedent—in the production of subsequent legal documents, including those authored by the rabbis.[34] Indeed, in a later work, *Love and Joy: Law, Language and Religion in Ancient Israel*, Muffs returned to the idea. He identified the trope of giving "of one's own free will" (akin to *ina ḫūd libbišu* addressed in his first study) in the use of the words *be-simha* (= "in joy") and *be-ratzon* ("willingly") in a tannaitic midrashic interpretation of Num 18:8. The verse, dealing with the giving of tithes, states:

> The Lord spoke further to Aaron: I [*va-'ani*] hereby [*hinne*] give [*na-tatti*] you charge of My gifts, all the sacred donations of the Israelites; I grant them to you and your sons as a perquisite, a due for all time.

On this verse, *Sifre Bemidbar* records in the name of R. Yishmael, "'*va-'ani*'—*beratzon*, '*hinne*' *be-simha*"; that is, "'I'—with full volition, "hereby"—with joy."[35] For the tanna, the verse's words assume a legal connotation analogous to the Akkadian formulation: giving in joy means giving freely.

Muffs's thesis for the trajectory of legal formulae and conceptualization from cuneiform law to Aramaic or tannaitic sources is attractive because it grounds the developments in identifiable linguistic and thematic processes. In Muffs's model, the data speaks for itself. Overlap in terms and formu-

32. Muffs, *Studies*, 30–62. See also Raymond Westbrook, "The Phrase 'His Heart is Satisfied' in Ancient Near Eastern Legal Sources," *JAOS* 111 (1991): 219–24. Muffs, *Studies*, 128–41.

33. Muffs, *Studies*, 128–41.

34. Muffs, *Studies*, 192–94. Compare the comments of M. J. Geller on Jewish texts of the Hellenistic period and beyond, "[t]hrough Aramaic much of the technical vocabulary of the Near East found its way into Jewish texts" ("Influence," 43).

35. Muffs, *Love and Joy*, 127. *Sifre to Numbers*, 117 (*Sifre bemidbar mahadurah mevo'eret*, ed. M. Kahana (Jerusalem, 2015), vol. 2, 342). See also the expansive commentary to this section in Part 4, 885–86, of the same edition.

lae (even if there is only semantic equivalence and not etymological, *per se*)[36] can teach about interconnections. Legal language, its function, and its meaning are retained, even as the formulations are expressed in new legal milieus. In this case, Aramaic law is the channel of transmission for the diffusion of cuneiform terms and formulae into tannaitic legal discourse. The spread of the Aramaic legal tradition caused the continued use of originally Akkadian terms and formulae, albeit in their new Aramaic form.[37]

Importantly, in his own research Muffs only documented the path from Akkadian to Aramaic law and, separately, from Akkadian to tannaitic traditions. He only suggested that the trajectory could be from Akkadian to Aramaic to tannaitic. As the work of Shalom E. Holtz on divorce formula shows (see below), the movement from Akkadian to Aramaic to tannaitic law can be more concretely theorized in specific cases.[38]

b. Divorce Formula from Hammurabi to the Mishnah

Expanding on the model proposed by Yochanan Muffs for the transformation of Akkadian legal terms and formulae into Aramaic and their eventual incorporation into tannaitic texts, Shalom E. Holtz examined the possible Mesopotamian antecedents to a formula found in the tannaitic *get* (writ of divorce).[39] In mGit 9.3, we find the following dispute regarding the formula of the *get*:

> The essential formula in the bill of divorce is, "You are hereby permitted to [marry] anyone." Rabbi Judah says: "Let this be to you from me a writ of divorce and letter of dismissal and deed of liberation, that you may go and marry any man you please."[40]

36. As per the Landsberger-Held method. For a discussion of the method, see Chaim Cohen, "The 'Held Method' for Comparative Semitic Philology" *JANES* 19:1 (1989): 9–23.

37. For more on this see below, "Conclusions and Further Research." See also, most recently, Shamma Friedman, *"Hotsi'u li ketubbat imotekhem,"* in *Semitic, Biblical, and Jewish Studies in Honor of Richard C. Steiner*, ed. A. J. Koller et al. (Jerusalem and New York, 2021), 176–255.

38. This channel of transmission could not have been theorized regarding *mulūgu* and *tson barzel* (see above in the body of the article), since evidence from the Aramaic tradition has not surfaced.

39. Shalom E. Holtz, "'To Go and Marry Any Man That You Please': A Study of the Formulaic Antecedents of the Rabbinic Writ of Divorce" *JNES* 60:4 (2001): 241–58.

40. Translation as cited in Holtz, "To Go and Marry," 253.

The formula suggested in the first opinion is in Hebrew, while the tradition attributed to R. Judah promotes an Aramaic formula for releasing the wife from the marriage: "*limhakh lehitnaseba lekhol gevar detitzbayin,*" "go and marry any man you please,"[41] and is the subject of Holtz's study. Significantly, this Aramaic formula is attested in a *get* found in the Judaean Desert[42] (and was used even into medieval times),[43] a matter I will address again below.

Holtz's search for antecedents to R. Judah's Aramaic formula begins with a discussion of both the linguistic and thematic overlap in divorce formulae in a number of ancient Near Eastern codes. These include the Code of Hammurabi (see below), the Middle Assyrian Laws,[44] and the Neo-Babylonian Laws[45]—all of which explicitly state that upon divorce the wife may remarry (or reside with)[46] a new husband of her choice. For example, the formula in Hammurabi's code reads, "a husband of her choice [lit. of her heart] shall marry [lit. take] her" (= *mut libbiša iḫḫassi*).[47] Holtz then considers the formula of the release clause (in the event of the dissolution of the marriage) in Neo-Babylonian marriage documents. The clause in these docu-

41. For a survey of scholarship on the use of Aramaic in the Mishnah, see Christian Stadel, "Tannaitic Aramaic: Methodological Remarks and a Test Case," in *Studies in Rabbinic Hebrew*, ed. S. Heijmans (Cambridge, 2020), 97–117. Two particularly important treatments of the subject matter include David Talshir, "The Nature of the Aramaic in Tannaitic Literature," in *Sugiyot bilshon hakhamim*, ed. M. Bar-Asher (Hebrew; Jerusalem, 1991), 69–70, and Günther Stemberger, "Los Dichos Arameos de Hillel en el tratado Abot" *MEAH* 53 (2004): 387–405.

42. The text is Papyrus Murabaat 19 in *Discoveries in the Judean Desert, Volume 2: Les grottes de Murabbaat*, ed. P. Benoit et al. (Oxford, 1961), 104–9; Ada Yardeni, *Textbook of Aramaic, Hebrew and Nabatean Documentary Texts from the Judaean Desert and Related Material I* (Jerusalem, 2000), 131. On evidence for the tannaim drawing from living traditions when constructing their laws, see Milgram, *From Mesopotamia to Mishnah*, 113.

43. See the text of the *get* cited in *Sefer Hashetarot* of Rav Hai Gaon (tenth century) in Asher Gulak, *Otsar hashetarot hanehugim beyisrael* (Jerusalem, 1926), 71 (text no. 68), discussed by Holtz, "To Go and Marry," 254. See also the text of the *get* cited by Rashi at bGit 85b, *s.v. zehu tofes haget*, discussed in Shamma Friedman, "The Jewish Bill of Divorce—From Masada Onwards," in *Halakhah in Light of Epigraphy*, ed. A. I. Baumgarten, H. Eshel, R. Katzoff, and S. Tzoref (Göttingen, 2011), 175–83.

44. The phrase here is "she shall reside with a husband of her choice," (= *ana mut libbiša tuššab*); see MAL A ¶36 (in Martha Roth, *Law Collections from Mesopotamia and Asia Minor* (Atlanta, 1995), 165–66.

45. ¶13 of The Neo-Babylonian Laws states, *muti libbiša iḫḫassi* (Roth, *Law Collections*, 147–48), the same as Hammurabi's Code (see above in the body of the article).

46. See the two previous notes.

47. ¶¶137, 156, and 172 (Roth, *Law Collections*, 107, 110, 115).

ments states: "*ašar ṣebâtu tallak*," "she may go wherever she pleases."[48] That is, whereas the contracts emphasize that the wife "may go wherever she pleases," the codes highlight "remarriage."[49]

Despite the formulaic differences between the codes and the transactional records, Holtz argues that the "essential idea" that the divorced wife may do as she pleases is common to all the formulae presented. Acknowledging that in any setting the woman's freedom to move on to another husband is an intrinsic feature of a marriage's dissolution, Holtz still argues that the thematic consistency of this idea indicates a degree of possible interdependence between the ancient Near Eastern sources. Significantly, a nearly word-for-word translation into Aramaic of the Akkadian formula in the Neo-Babylonian documents appears in marriage contracts at Elephantine and is recorded as "*wthk lh 'n zy ṣbyt*."[50] As mentioned by Holtz, the proto-Semitic root **ṣby* (= 'pleasing') is present in the formulae in both the Neo-Babylonian documents (*ṣebâtu*) and the Elephantine papyri (*ṣbyt*). This important overlap establishes a historical link between the formulary traditions, affirming the shift from Akkadian to Aramaic formulae posited by Muffs.[51]

As he moves on to a discussion of the formula of a *get* discovered in the Judaean Desert and R. Judah's mishnaic release clause, Holtz correctly emphasizes the significance of the affinity between the two (despite a minor formulaic difference).[52] Furthermore, Holtz sees R. Judah's formulation, "that you may go and marry any man you please," as "bringing together what were, in the Akkadian material examined, two separate formulaic components."[53] That is, R. Judah mentions the "going" found in the documents and the "remarriage" found in the codes.

The possible fusion of themes evidenced in R. Judah's (and the Judaean Desert *get*'s) formula is certainly significant. Moreover, the persistence of the use of the proto-Semitic root **ṣby* (in mishnaic Hebrew and Aramaic, ts-b-y;[54] Akkadian, *ṣibûtu*)[55] beyond the Neo-Babylonian and Elephantine

48. See Holtz, "To Go and Marry," 248–49.

49. Holtz, "To Go and Marry," 254.

50. Holtz, "To Go and Marry," 252–53.

51. See above in the body of the article.

52. The Judaean Desert *get* states "to be a wife," as opposed to the mishnaic *get*'s, "to marry" (Holtz, "To Go and Marry," 254).

53. Holtz, "To Go and Marry," 254.

54. See Michael Sokoloff, *A Dictionary of Jewish Palestinian Aramaic* (Baltimore and Ramat Gan, 1990), 457; Michael Sokoloff, *A Dictionary of Jewish Babylonian Aramaic* (Baltimore and Ramat Gan, 2002), 950; Michael Sokoloff, *A Dictionary of Judean Aramaic* (Ramat Gan, 2003), 75.

55. Hayim Tawil, *An Akkadian Lexical Companion for Biblical Hebrew* (Jersey City, 2009), 317.

documents pointed to by Holtz—that is, even in the formula of the *get* from the Judaean Desert and in the Mishnah—better anchors any argument for historical relationships. And, while as noted by Yochanan Muffs, "[e]tymological similarity is not necessarily the best indicator of functional identity,"[56] the etymological data here actually points in the direction of Holtz's (and Muffs's) own proposition.[57] As the common denominator in all these formulations, the use of the same root provides a lexicographical basis, and not just a thematic one, for arguing that these formulaic traditions are in fact historically interconnected. The linguistic link here strengthens the argument for interdependence and the probability of the trajectory envisioned by Muffs in general, and by Holtz regarding our case: from Neo-Babylonian documents to Elephantine contracts (to Judaean Desert documents) and to the Mishnah. Indeed, we are likely witness here to a scribal tradition whose ancient Near Eastern origins—preserved both in codes and transactional documents—persisted through to the rabbinic period (and beyond), due to the diffusion of Aramaic law.

3. Parallel in Concept and Formal Literary Presentation: Damages for "Disgrace" and the Dissemination of Oral Traditions

a. Damage Payment for Disgrace in the Mishnah and in the Ancient Near East

M.BK 8.1 establishes that one who injures another is liable for five payments: injury, pain, healing, loss of time, and disgrace. In his article "The Plotting Witness and Beyond—A Continuum in Ancient Near Eastern, Biblical, and Talmudic Law,"[58] Shamma Friedman argues that early tannaitic law conceptualizes the laws of bodily injuries as punitive (and not compensatory),[59]

---

56. Muffs, *Studies*, 140 n. 1.

57. The link I point out here, between the Akkadian, Aramaic, and Hebrew, is already noted in L. Koehler and W. Baumgartner, *The Hebrew and Aramaic Lexicon of the Old Testament* (Leiden, 2000), 997.

58. See n. 4. See also Shamma Friedman, *"Hemit shorkha et shori: mamon o kenas? Perek behitpathut hahalakhah,"* in *Ketabor Beharim: Mehkarim betorah shebe'al peh mugashim li-profesor Yosef Tabory*, ed. A. Atzmon and T. Shapir (Alon Shevut, 2013), 99–123.

59. Later tannaitic law, however, does conceptualize these damages as compensatory; see Friedman, *"Hemit shorkha,"* 110–11 and 114. The legal distinction follows: "Compensatory damages are such as will compensate the injured party for the injury sustained, and nothing more; such as will simply make good or replace the loss caused by the wrong or injury" (*Black's Law Dictionary*, ed. H. C. Black (St. Paul, Minn., 1968), 467; "PUNITIVE. Relating to punishment; having the character of punishment or penalty; inflicting punishment or a penalty" (*Black's Law Dictionary*, 1399).

paralleling one approach found in ancient Near Eastern codes but absent from the Hebrew Bible's treatment of payment for bodily injury.[60] Of the five rabbinic payments, Ex 21:19 only mentions healing and loss of time, "he must pay for his idleness and his cure," corresponding to actual money loss, thereby framing both as compensatory.[61]

Regarding one of the payments, "disgrace," Friedman finds three points of overlap between the Mishnah and ancient Near Eastern law that demonstrate the laws are parallel in concept and formal literary presentation: (1) the consequences of intention, (2) the literary form in which the laws are presented, and (3) the significance of the social status of the parties involved. Combined, these provide a legal parallel of what he calls "form and understanding."[62] Let us begin with mBK 8.1:

> 'Disgrace'?—all is in accordance with [the status of] one who disgraces and the one who is disgraced. One who disgraces the naked, disgraces the blind, or the sleeping, is liable; but the sleeping [one] that disgraces is exempt. One who fell from the roof and injured and disgraced [someone], he is liable for the injury but not for the disgrace, as it is written: "And puts out her hand and seizes him by his genitals" (Deut 25:11), one is not liable for disgrace unless one has intention.

Unlike the other four payments, disgrace in tannaitic law requires intention in order for the perpetrator to be fined (see above).[63] This, suggests

---

60. Compare the following comments: "the ancient Near Eastern collections show that the amount to be paid for bodily injuries was normally regulated by a tariff, and was not based upon assessment of the actual loss" (Bernard Jackson, "The Problem of Exod. XXI:22–5 (Ius Talionis)" *VT* 23:3 (1973): 282.

61. The compensatory approach is also present in ancient Near Eastern law, see Friedman, "Plotting Witness," 819, and, for a specific law, Hammurabi ¶206 (Roth, *Law Collections*, 122). Furthermore, regarding an ox that kills another ox, the Bible preserves both conceptions, depending on the case (Ex 21:35, punitive, and 36, compensatory; see Friedman, "*Hemit Shorkha*," 107).

62. On "form" see Friedman, "Plotting Witness," 820, 822–23, and on "continuum of understanding," Friedman, "Plotting Witness," 808 and 823.

63. See also *Sifre to Deuteronomy* 292, ed. L. Finkelstein (New York and Jerusalem, 1993), 311 (cited in Friedman, "Plotting Witness," 821). On the methodological question of the origins of this ruling in the operation of a prior judicial principle (in cuneiform law), as opposed to the assignment of legal meaning to superfluous words in the verses (in line with tannaitic midrashic approaches), see Friedman, "Plotting Witness," 821 and n. 63.

Friedman, parallels the intention[64] required for liability for disgrace in the Laws of Eshnunna ¶42 (ca. 1930 BCE):

> If a man bites the nose of another man and thus cuts it off, he shall weigh and deliver 60 shekels of silver; an eye—60 shekels; a tooth—30 shekels; an ear—30 shekels; a slap to the cheek—he shall weigh and deliver 10 shekels of silver.

See also the formulation in Hammurabi ¶203:[65]

> If a member of the *awīlu*-class[66] should strike the cheek of another member of the *awīlu*-class who is equal, he shall weigh and deliver 60 shekels of silver.

Note that both the *Laws of Eshnunna* and of *Hammurabi* use the price list form to register the penalties, bringing us to Friedman's second point of comparison. Tariffs for disgrace also survived in the Mishnah:

> If a man cuffed his fellow he must pay him a *sela*. R. Judah says in the name of R. Yose the Galilean: One hundred *zuz*. If he slapped him he must pay him 200 *zuz*. If [he struck him] with the back of his hand he must pay him 400 *zuz*. If he tore his ear, plucked out his hair, spat and his spittle touched him, or pulled his cloak from off him, or loosed a woman's hair in the street, he must pay 400 *zuz*.[67]

The third area of overlap pointed to by Friedman is social stratification. mBK 8.1 (above) unambiguously states: "'Disgrace'? — all is in accordance with [the status of] one who disgraces and the one who is disgraced."[68] As Friedman puts it, "[t]his emphasis on social status as a determination of the

---

64. So, too, Yaron saw intention in the cases in the Laws of Eshnunna. See Reuven Yaron, *Laws of Eshnunna* (Jerusalem, 1969), 176 (cited in Friedman, "Plotting Witness," 820–21 n. 62).

65. Roth, *Law Collections*, 121. Cited by Friedman, "Plotting Witness," 822. On the case in question as a "pure" case of disgrace, see Friedman, "Plotting Witness," 822 n. 64.

66. The Code of Hammurabi distinguishes between a gentleman (*awīlum*) and a commoner (*muškēnum*). See G. R. Driver and J. C. Miles, *The Babylonian Laws* (Oxford, 1952–1955), 86–90.

67. mBK 8.6. On the fines as punitive see yBK 8.6 6c; bBK 27b, cited in Friedman, "Plotting Witness," 823.

68. See also tBK 9.12, cited in Friedman, "Plotting Witness," 823.

level of payment due is surprisingly similar to the Laws of Hammurapi"[69] and, as Friedman reminds us, is counter to the law observed in the Bible whereby one standard for bodily injury was held up for all (see Lev 24:22). Friedman argues, therefore, that the social stratification here may be a remnant of the ancient Near Eastern norms as expressed in the Laws of Hammurabi.[70] Only with Rabbi Akiba's restoration of the biblical view did the democratization of payments for disgrace eventually become instituted in rabbinic law: "Rabbi Akiba said: Even the poorest in Israel are looked upon as nobles who have lost their possessions, for they are the sons of Abraham, Isaac, and Jacob" (mBK 8.6).

In presenting the threefold overlap between the ancient Near Eastern legal tradition and the Mishnah, Shamma Friedman provides a new type of example of interconnection, one based in conceptualization (intention and social stratification) and literary form (price lists). He thus introduces new methodological patterns for inquiry into the search for parallels. Friedman ends his piece by suggesting that the appearance of similar laws in cuneiform legal codes and in the Mishnah is indicative of an ongoing literary tradition on a continuum.[71]

In the following section, I suggest that cases like "disgrace"—where the Bible addresses the subject in one manner and the tannaitic treatment parallels known cuneiform patterns of inquiry—may be the result of the study of biblical verses along with orally transmitted scholastic traditions somehow linked to ancient Near Eastern principles.

b. The Oral Transmission of Traditions from the Ancient Near East
to the Tannaim

Based on nine examples of ancient Near Eastern laws, absent from the Bible, that "reemerge"' in tannaitic texts, Samuel Greengus suggests, "[t]his long trail of continuity supports the post biblical Jewish claim concerning the existence of ancient 'oral laws' that had been 'handed down' alongside of the written laws of the Pentateuch."[72] It is valuable to consider the circu-

69. Friedman, "Plotting Witness," 824.
70. Friedman, "Plotting Witness," 825.
71. In his earlier work, however, Friedman was more inclined to engage in comparative work only for the sake of mutual clarification (and not in search of interdependence); see, for example, Shamma Friedman, "The Case of the Woman with Two Husbands in Talmudic and Ancient Near Eastern Law" *ILR* 15 (1980): 530–58.
72. Greengus, *Laws*, 282. On the oral tradition—*torah she-be-'al peh*—of the rabbis, see, for example, mAvot 1.1; *Sifre to Deuteronomy* par. 351 (Finkelstein ed., 408). For a similar claim by Josephus in the name of the Pharisees, see *Antiquities of the Jews*, Book 13, Chapter 10:297–98 (in *The New Complete Works of Josephus*, ed. P. L. Maier and trans. W. Whiston (Grand Rapids, Mich., 1999), 441.

lation of oral traditions in the ancient world as a possible mechanism to account for legal overlap.[73] Do Greengus's examples attest to oral traditions that necessarily accompanied the transmission of, and were studied in conjunction with, the written text of the Pentateuch?[74] As mentioned, the examples he cites are specifically of laws not addressed in the Pentateuch at all.[75] Greengus's thesis would be better buttressed by examples in which the laws are handled in one way in the Biblical canon and are embellished and elaborated upon in tannaitic literature in accordance with traditions or legal principles we know from ancient Near Eastern law (see below).[76]

In a separate category of traditions addressed in his book, Greengus gives fifteen examples of biblical laws that were subject to reinterpretation by the rabbis, "sometimes entirely changing the ancient parameters."[77] Greengus is correct that in the overwhelming number of examples, reinterpretation in the rabbinic corpus is not in accordance with ancient Near Eastern legal thinking. Yet one example among the fifteen is exceptional. Payment of monetary damages for personal injury in mBK 8.1, instead of employing the

73. Consider Yaakov Elman's discussion of possible authoritative oral traditions in neo-Assyrian scribal circles, Yaakov Elman, "Authoritative Oral Tradition in Neo-Assyrian Scribal Circles" *JANES* 7 (1975): 19–32 (not cited by Greengus), and see below in the body of the article.

74. The medieval Jewish model may be instructive. On extra-textual oral interpretations that were transmitted together with the oral text of the Babylonian Talmud, see Shraga Abramson, "*Le-toldot a nusaḥ seder tannaim ve-amoraim*," in *'Iyunim be-sifrut ḥazal ba-mikra uve-toldot yisrael mukdash li-Profesor Ezra Tziyon Melamed*, ed. Y. D. Gilat et al. (Ramat Gan, 1982), 215; republished in Shraga Abramson, *Meḥkarim besifrut hageonim* (Jerusalem, 2020), 167–99. See also Neil Danzig, *Introduction to Halakhot Pesuqot with a Supplement to Halakhot Pesuqot* (Hebrew; New York and Jerusalem, 1999), 2 n. 9; Robert Brody, *The Geonim of Babylonia and the Shaping of Medieval Jewish Culture* (New Haven and London, 1998), 180; Jonathan S. Milgram, "Between *Memra* and *Stam*: On Statements in the Babylonian Talmud that Appear as Attributed and Anonymous," in *Shapir Amar Naḥmani: Rabbinic Courts in Antiquity and the Middle Ages, Festschrift for Naḥman [Neil] Danzig*, ed. D. Danzig and N. Bickart (Leiden, forthcoming), Appendix.

75. Of the nine examples Greengus cites, only one, "payment for disgrace," has a loose connection to biblical verses and not what could be at all considered an actual legal antecedent in biblical law; see Deut 25:11–12 and the discussion above in the body of the article.

76. This may be the case, in fact, with regard to the rabbinic expansion of the biblical laws of bailment (*shomrim*), but further consideration is required. In the meantime, see Yael Landman, "The Biblical Law of Bailment in its Ancient Near Eastern Contexts," (PhD diss., Yeshiva University, 2017), 329–35, who suggests that the biblical laws of bailment (Ex 22:6–14) are expanded by the rabbis (mBM Ch. 3) to include the gratuitous (*shomer ḥinam*) and non-gratuitous bailee (*shomer sakhar*), according with ancient Near Eastern antecedents. For a list of sources, see Greengus, *Laws*, 136–39.

77. Greengus, *Laws*, 287.

talionic principle ("an eye for an eye;" see Ex 21:24), constitutes what may be called a rabbinic interpretation of a biblical verse that accords with antecedents in ancient Near Eastern law.[78] Indeed, the Laws of Urnamma[79] and the Laws of Eshnunna[80] list prices for bodily injuries, while the Code of Hammurabi offers monetary compensation or *talio*.[81]

Payment for "disgrace" (discussed above) is also worthy of further consideration in the light of the transmission of oral traditions. Indeed, it could be argued that the parallel elements regarding payments for "disgrace" in the cuneiform laws and in the Mishnah were the outcome of the study of biblical verses (Deut 25:11–12)[82] in conjunction with oral traditions that harked back to the cuneiform principles.[83]

In sum, I submit that parallels that fit this pattern—verses in the Bible that are interpreted by the rabbis in accordance with cuneiform legal principles—support the idea of a channel of transmission that included some type of oral interpretation that accompanied the study of biblical verses. If more examples like "disgrace" can be identified—where the ancient Near Eastern evidence is specifically preserved in the codes—then I propose we view the data as evidence for the persistence of orally transmitted scholastic traditions.[84] I prefer to attribute the reemergence in tan-

---

78. For a listing of all the relevant sources and discussion see Greengus, *Laws*, 130–36. To be sure, it is not at all clear that the biblical formulation "an eye for an eye" should be taken literally. It may, in fact, reflect ancient Near Eastern traditions and/or formulae for determining monetary compensation in cases of injury, a matter I hope to return to (as it relates to rabbinic interpretation) in a separate study. On the topic see, for example, Raymond Westbrook, "Lex Talionis and Exodus 21:22–25," *Revue Biblique* 93 (1986): 52–69 and Raymond Westbrook, *Studies in Biblical and Cuneiform Law* (Paris, 1988), 71–83. See also, Shamma Friedman, "Glosses and Additions in *TB BAVA QAMMA* VIII" *Tarbiz* 40.4 (1971): 431 n. 48.

79. For example, in ¶22, the payment of 2 shekels of silver for a tooth (Roth, *Law Collections*, 19).

80. ¶¶42–47 (Roth, *Law Collections*, 65–66).

81. ¶¶196–98, 200–201, 206 (Roth, *Law Collections*, 121–22).

82. See mBK 8.1, cited above.

83. Friedman alludes to as much, without making any commitment, when he offers the possibility of an earlier judicial principle operating in the midrash halakhah (see n. 63) and not typical midrashic analysis. Perhaps it could be demonstrated that the midrash itself was based on the ancient Near Eastern legal conceptions.

84. Such an approach would veer from the tendency of earlier scholarship that attempted to view the rabbinic movement in relation to Greek and Roman scholasticism. See, for example, Henry Fischel, "The Uses of Sorites (Climax, Gradatio) in the Tannaitic Period" *HUCA* 44 (1974):119–51; Anthony Saldarini, "The End of the Rabbinic Chain of Tradition" *JBL* 93 (1974):97–106; Michael D. Swartz, "Scholasticism as a Comparative Category and the Study of Judaism," in *Scholasticism: Cross-Cultural and Comparative Perspectives*, ed. J. I. Cabezon (Albany, N.Y.,1998), 91–114.

naitic texts of ancient Near Eastern laws that are absent from the Bible (in line with the former category set by Greengus and discussed above), however, to the presence of longstanding local traditions to which the rabbis may have been exposed in one way or another and which were integrated into tannaitic law (e.g., the terms for assets included in the dowry, *melug* and *tson barzel*).[85]

III. CONCLUSIONS AND FURTHER RESEARCH

1. Conclusions

The discussion above highlighted three issues. Firstly, parallels between ancient Near Eastern and tannaitic laws take different forms: terminological, formulaic, and in concept and formal literary presentation. Secondly, ancient Near Eastern antecedents to tannaitic laws can be found both in codes (pointing to their genesis in ancient Near Eastern scribal and scholastic traditions) and in transactional documents (suggesting origins in local lived practices). Thirdly, three channels of transmission have been theorized; I suggest here that some channels may have been more conducive to perpetuating certain types of analogues. For example, the parallel Akkadian terms for tannaitic assets in the dowry, *melug* and *tson barzel*, occur only in transactional documents and therefore the overlap can be attributed to the rabbis' adaptation of local traditions presumably preserved by communities of practice over millennia. The divorce formula treated above is evidenced in both codes and transactional documents from the ancient Near East, and is used in Aramaic translation in archival records from Elephantine and the Judaean desert, as well as in the Mishnah. It can be argued, therefore, that the rabbis drew from a longstanding scribal tradition, with Aramaic law serving as the agent for the formula's diffusion from its original Akkadian milieu to the sphere of rabbinic legal thinking. Payment of damages for "disgrace," on the other hand, attested to in the codes and with formal literary and thematic parallels in the Mishnah, may show that the cuneiform traditions informed the way in which the rabbis interpreted specific biblical verses (Deut 25:11–12). If so, then the tannaim potentially inherited orally transmitted scholastic traditions from the ancient Near East that were studied in conjunction with the Bible and substantively affected rabbinic legisla-

---

85. Within his conception of "oral tradition," Greengus allows for "mainly orally transmitted 'customary law'" (*Laws*, 288). I prefer, however, to make a clearer distinction between the concepts of oral tradition and local tradition (see above in the body of the article).

tion. In sum, each channel of transmission was more susceptible to preserving a specific type of parallel.

Baruch Levine contended that the overall existence of interconnections between cuneiform and mishnaic laws may be due to actual historical points of contact, as the Akkadian language continued to be in use beyond the Seleucid period (4th–1st centuries BCE) and "military confrontations between the forces of regional, Mesopotamian rulers and the Romans provided a persisting context for cultural interchange between East and West."[86] By way of suggestion alone, I would like to add to this calculus. It may be that all three channels of transmission were activated by the linguistic shift from only Akkadian to the inclusion of Aramaic as a language of diplomacy and administration in the Neo-Assyrian Empire.[87] The presence of local traditions with linguistic remnants of their original Akkadian could have been the result of the migration of practices that followed the spread of the Aramaic language and its accompanying lore.[88] So too, already existing Akkadian formulae—even if, perhaps, Old Babylonian or Neo-Babylonian in origin—would have been transmitted and translated into Aramaic, eventually finding their way into the Mishnah. As for oral traditions that were studied along with Scripture, here too we may be witness to scholastic Babylonian traditions that reached the land of Israel as part of migratory pro-

86. Levine, "*Mulūgu/Melûg,*" 271.

87. There are a number of studies on the linguistic shift from Akkadian to Aramaic in the Neo-Assyrian period. Two useful overviews include Frederick Mario Fales, "New Light on Assyro-Aramaic Interference: The Assur Ostracon," in *CAMSEMUD 2007: Proceedings of the 13th Italian Meeting of Afro-Asiatic Linguistics, Held in Udine May 21st–24th, 2007*, ed. F. M. Fales and G. F. Grassi (Padova, Italy, 2010), 189–204, and Hayim Tadmor, "The Aramaization of Assyria: Aspects of Western Impact," http://aramean-dem.org/English/History/HAYIM_TADMOR.htm. The overwhelming evidence for the linguistic phenomena suggests that these changes brought about legal transitions—including the transmission of terms, formula, local traditions—as well. Muffs, however, argued for the Neo-Babylonian origins of some formulae; see, for example, Muffs, *Studies*, 41. As Aaron Koller reminds me, there are likely multiple avenues for the diffusion of Akkadian law and lore through Aramaic and into the legal world of the tannaim. He specifically points to the Samaria papyri, which show that Neo-Babylonian law, through Aramaic intermediaries, had been integrated into Palestinian traditions by the late Persian period; see Jan Dušek, *Les manuscrits araméens du Wadi Daliyeh et la Samarie vers 450–332 av. J.-C.* (Leiden, 2007), and Aaron Koller, "Review of Jan Dušek, *Les manuscrits araméens du Wadi Daliyeh et la Samarie vers 450–332 av. J.-C.* (Leiden, 2007)," *RBL* (2009): 1–8.

88. See Milgram, *From Mesopotamia to the Mishnah*, 10, 11, 13, 35, 68, 69–70, 77, 81, 143.

cesses, accompanied even by methods of interpretation[89] that the rabbis later attributed to divine oral transmission.[90]

2. Suggestions for Further Research

In this last section, I suggest how our study may problematize some of the current thinking on the nature and scope of the Mishnah, and I propose new areas of research for further investigation. As is evident from our brief treatment, the comparative study of individual tannaitic laws and their ancient Near Eastern parallels is a fruitful endeavor. Scholars have rightly focused on comparing specific laws. In the light of the localized analyses, it is perhaps the right time for the field to begin broader discussions about the Mishnah and cuneiform law.

Further research might include considering the Mishnah as a work of legal literature—a code—on a continuum beginning with the great codes of ancient Near Eastern civilizations. Possible areas of inquiry include considering new analogies in the overall structure, genre, purpose, and audience of the Mishnah. For example, scholarship in the field of rabbinics has categorized the rabbis as members of an elite scholarly class producing theoretical laws, perhaps akin to the scribal schools that authored the cuneiform codes.[91] The Mishnah as a source of law, like the ancient Near Eastern codes, is also not cited in the transactional documents of its period.[92] Furthermore, the Mishnah is organized by tractate, generally categorized topically, as is the Code of Hammurabi, and the basic presentation of material in both is case-law based (although, perhaps significantly, cuneiform law codes do not

89. See Stephen Lieberman, "A Mesopotamian Background for the So-Called Aggadic 'Measures' of Biblical Hermeneutics?" *HUCA*, vol. 58 (1987): 157–225.

90. See note 72. Another line of inquiry suggested to me by Barry Wimpfheimer is evaluating the significance of the fact that basically the entirety of the ancient Near Eastern record has come to us in written form (already from antiquity). Further examination of this question will need to be postponed. Perhaps examining the matter in the light of Shlomo Naeh's conclusion that the midrashic compendium on Leviticus, known as *Sifra*, was committed to writing in the rabbinic period would be productive. See Shlomo Naeh, "The Structure and Division of 'Torat Kohanim' (A): Scrolls" (Hebrew), *Tarbiz* 66:4 (1997): 494–512. See also the rebuttal in Jacob Sussmann, "'Torah shebeal peh,' peshuta kemashmaah: koho shel kotso shel yod," in *Meḥkerei Talmud* 3:2, ed. J. Sussmann and D. Rosenthal (Jerusalem, 2005), 373–75, and the comments in Menahem I. Kahana, "The Halakhic Midrashim," in *The Literature of the Sages*, ed. S. Safrai et al. (Amsterdam, 2006), vol. 2, 79 n. 368. My thanks to Yitz Landes for the final bibliographic entry.

91. See Roth, *Law Collections*, 4.

92. The Judaean Desert discoveries come to mind.

seem to record disputes). Such lines of inquiry would require investigation into the substantive structural differences between the Mishnah on the one hand, and ancient Near Eastern codes and their Greek and Roman counterparts on the other, so as to better identify literary commonalities that could lead to historical conclusions.[93] Of course, as Raymond Westbrook famously and controversially argued, even Hellenistic and Roman codes may find their origins in cuneiform legal precedent and literary processes.[94] Certainly, the Mishnah could be evaluated in this light as well.[95]

A comparative approach to the rabbinic conception of "the Oral Torah" may serve to reframe and redefine aspects of tannaitic legal productivity. Indeed, that the concept of authoritative oral law is to be found in the ancient Near East has been suggested by Yaakov Elman[96] and more recently Uri Gabbay, who see in the Akkadian terms ša pi ("from the mouth of"), ša pī ummani ("according to a scholar"), and šūt pi ("those of the mouth") corollaries to the rabbinic term *torah she-be-'al peh* ("oral Torah").[97] Further fleshing out of the distinctions between the oral and written processes of interpretation found in ancient Near Eastern scribal circles and tannaitic

93. For example, a suggestive comparison between *The Institutes* of Gaius and Mishnah Kiddushin is proffered in Yaakov Elman, "Order, Sequence, and Selection: The Mishnah's Anthological Choices," in *The Anthology in Jewish Literature*, ed. D. Stern (Oxford, 2004), 66–69.

94. See, for example, Raymond Westbrook, *Ex Oriente Lex: Near Eastern Influences on Ancient Greek and Roman Law*, ed. D. Lyons and K. Raaflaub (Baltimore, 2015).

95. Towards the end of his life, Westbrook and I communicated about my work on tannaitic inheritance law in comparative perspective and he expressed interest in the possibility of linking the tannaitic tradition to the chain of his theorized trajectory. While I cannot entirely embrace Westbrook's theory of diffusion, as I state above, I certainly think it is advisable to continue research along the lines of Westbrook's methods of inquiry. For a brief attempt at identifying the ancient code as a legal genre—including ancient Mesopotamian, Greek, Roman, and Jewish (Mishnah and Tosefta)—see Barry S. Wimpfheimer, "Codes," in *A Cultural History of Law: Vol. 1—A Cultural History of Law in Antiquity*, ed. J. Etxabe (London, 2019), 59–74.

96. See Elman, "Authoritative Oral Tradition." On oral transmission in general in the region, see Victor Avigdor Hurowitz, "Spanning the Generations: Aspects of Oral and Written Transmission in the Bible and Ancient Mesopotamia," in *Freedom and Responsibility: Exploring the Dilemmas of Jewish Continuity (Graetz College Centenary Volume)*, ed. R. M. Geffen and M. B. Edelman (Hoboken, N.J., 1998), 11–30.

97. See Uri Gabbay, *The Exegetical Terminology of Akkadian Commentaries* (Leiden, 2016), 293.

scholarly circles, if at all possible, remains a scholarly desideratum.[98] Roman[99] and Greek conceptions,[100] on the other hand, seem much less relevant.

Scholarly probes of this type, grounding the Mishnah as a code on a literary and legal continuum in antiquity, and identifying the rabbis as agents for the preservation and transmission of ancient traditions and oral methods of

98. The presence of customary law in oral form among the elites in pre-literate societies was already theorized in Henry Sumner Maine, *Ancient Law* (London, 1861), 8. A full discussion of the relevant concepts in ancient law collections in comparative context is long overdue.

99. Comparison of *torah she-be-'al peh* to the Roman concept of *ius non-scriptum*, "unwritten laws" (which appears in contradistinction to *ius scriptum*, "written laws,") may be out of place. Justinian (D.1.1.61), following Ulpian, divides the law into these two categories (and points to Greek antecedents; however, see the end of the next note). *Ius non-scriptum* refers specifically to custom; all other law, derived from edicts and imperial constitutions, *responsa* of jurists, etc., is considered written. As H. F. Jolowicz tells us, "[c]ustomary law . . . is unwritten because it can be discovered, not by reading a document, but only by observing what people actually do" (*Historical Introduction to the Study of Roman Law* (Cambridge, 1932), 363. It should be noted, however, that according to some scholars the text of Justinian here is a medieval interpolation; see Jolowicz, *Historical Introduction*, 363 n. 1 and the summary of views in Paola Miceli, "La costumbre como *ius non scriptum*," in *Estudios de derecho y teología en la edad media*, ed. A. Morin (Buenos Aires, 2012), 90; on a different text of Justinian (D.1.3.32) regarding the same issue and its possible "alteration," see David Ibbetson, "Custom in Medieval Law," in *The Nature of Customary Law*, ed. A. Perreau-Saussine and J. B. Murphy (Cambridge, 2007), 151–52. Regardless, while absent from the *Institutes of Gaius*, the distinction is preserved in other Roman legal (and original texts); see the bibliography above. In two fundamental respects, *torah she-be-'al peh* is different from *ius non scriptum*. *Torah she-be-'al peh*, even when transmitted orally was treated as documentary—that is, as an oral text (see Lieberman, *Hellenism in Jewish Palestine*, 83–99), and was not merely observational. Furthermore, *torah she-be-'al peh*, like *torah she-bikhtav*, is a source of law. The title given to each is to distinguish the presumed original method of transmission. Significantly, *ius scriptum* vs. *non-scriptum* is a description of the characteristics of the ongoing and developing sources of the law. They are not, however, sources of the law in and of themselves. Furthermore, an *edict* or a *responsum*, by virtue of being written down, would be categorized as *ius scriptum*, whereas any edict or approach of a jurist in talmudic sources would be by definition part of the oral (and not written) Torah. In her recent study (above), however, Paola Miceli, resurrecting the idea presented in Carlo Manenti, *Ius ex scripto e ius ex non scripto: Osservazioni critiche sulla teoria delle fonti secondo il diritto romano* (Torino, 1905), suggests that the Roman distinction is not between law and custom, but rather between law that originates in the written vs. law that does not originate in the written, see Paola Miceli, "La costumbre," 92–93, a matter certainly worthy of further investigation. My thanks to Bernard Jackson for discussing the theoretical issues with me.

100. It is true that the texts of Homer and Hesiod, for example, first became authoritative in oral form. Whether the general statements in these texts regarding social and

inquiry, could certainly problematize the regnant view of the Mishnah as a work whose raison d'être was political and whose concept of oral law came to subvert or supplement biblical authority. Such a view considers the Mishnah a replacement for Temple worship in the aftermath of its destruction, and a rabbinic "constitution" of sorts, designed to promote rabbinic authority.[101] In the end, research may affirm that the rabbis' intellectual pursuits may be viewed as akin to those of scholars in ancient Near Eastern scribal circles. Furthermore, we might begin to view the Mishnah not as a work of reconstruction composed primarily for the pursuit of power, but also as an achievement in preservation and continuity.[102]

---

moral behavior can be called authoritative "laws," however, has been called into question; see Michael Gagarin, *Early Greek Law* (Berkeley, 1986), 10–11, 53. On the prohibition of writing laws at Sparta and, in general, the exceptionality of Spartan evidence, see 56–59; on original oral rhythmic patterns recorded in Spartan *rhētra*, see 53–54 nn. 9–10, 57 n. 19. On the concept of *agraphos nomos*, that is, unwritten law, in classical Greece, see Martin Oswald, "Was There a Concept of *Agraphos Nomos* in Classical Greece?," in *Exegesis and Argument: Studies Presented to Gregory Vlastos,* ed. E. N. Lee, A. P. D. Mourelatos, and R. M. Rorty (Assen, Netherlands, 1973), 70–104.

101. On this, see most recently Naftali S. Cohn, *The Memory of the Temple and the Making of the Rabbis* (Philadelphia, 2013). Cohn's work would have benefited from a consideration of ancient Near Eastern antecedents. For example, for an important comparison between Ugaritic and mishnaic descriptive rituals (in tractates *Yoma* and *Tamid*), see Baruch Levine, "Ugaritic Descriptive Rituals," *JCS* 17 (1963): 106 n. 10.

102. The trend among scholars has been to prefer viewing the rabbis and the Mishnah as new and innovative in their time, even independent of other ancient bodies of law. See, most recently, David C. Kraemer, *A History of the Talmud* (Oxford, 2019), 72. In contrast, I am suggesting here that ancient Near Eastern scholarly programs of study and legal productivity may have been antecedents.

3. The Mishnah and the Dead Sea Scrolls

Vered Noam

A. THE UNIQUENESS OF THE MISHNAH VIS-À-VIS EARLIER LITERATURE

The Mishnah is a groundbreaking, revolutionary project; never before had anyone in Jewish society attempted to author or edit a work so broad in its aims, scope, or content. In prior corpora, such as the Apocrypha and Pseudepigrapha, the Qumran library, the New Testament, or Josephus's and Philo's writings, the collections and traditions of Jewish law are sporadic, scanty, and laconic. None approaches the sheer volume of the Mishnah or shares its ambitious objective of setting all-encompassing regulations for every realm of Jewish religious life. Nor were any earlier attempts made to meticulously categorize and subcategorize vast halakhic material, to create an elaborate, thematically organized edifice, the consummate accomplishment of the Mishnah's editors.[1]

Unprecedented features of the Mishnah include its discursive, dialectic nature; its inclusion of overt disputes in which most of the halakhic opinions are associated with identified rabbinic figures;[2] its independence from

---

1. Ishay Rosen-Zvi, "Mishnah," in *The Oxford Encyclopedia of the Bible and Law*, ed. P. Barmash, C. E. Fonrobert, C. Rothschild, J. Stackert, and J. Witte (Oxford, 2013), https://www.oxfordreference.com/view/10.1093/acref:obso/9780199843305.001.0001/acref-9780199843305-e-95; and in greater detail, Rosen-Tzvi, *Between Mishnah and Midrash: The Birth of Rabbinic Literature* (Hebrew; Ra'ananah, 2020), 23, 84–85, 124.

2. For discussion and references, see Vered Noam, *Shifting Images of the Hasmoneans: Second Temple Legends and Their Reception in Josephus and Rabbinic Literature* (Oxford, 2018), 9 n. 32. On the transition from monolithic traditions to multiplicity and dispute within Pharisaic-rabbinic circles, see Shaye J. D. Cohen, "The Significance of Yavneh:

biblical law and subsequent scarcity of biblical justifications, references, and allusions;[3] and its use of rabbinic—rather than biblical—Hebrew, which accentuates its separation from the Bible on the one hand, and the distinct statuses of these two corpora on the other.[4]

In contrast, pre-rabbinic legal material never identifies its proponents, nor does it legitimate disagreement with the authoritative law. The regulations (when preserved in the original Hebrew or Aramaic, namely in the case of traditions appearing in the Dead Sea Scrolls (DSS) are often formulated in pseudo-biblical Hebrew, replete with biblical allusions and often formulated as rewritten Bible. The small clusters of religious rulings in these libraries represent diverse halakhic domains and possess mixed themes in no apparent order.[5] Only rarely, and with great effort, can an underlying biblical or thematic sequence be deciphered for a list of religious laws.[6]

The most striking distinction, however, between the Mishnah and previous legal literature lies in the very nature of the legal material, regarding both content and level of resolution. With respect to content, the pre-rabbinic legal material differs from its mishnaic counterpart not only in date, scope, and level of organization, but mainly because the two corpora reflect opposite practices and contradictory legal, exegetical, and theological conceptions, as demonstrated below. The other feature—resolution—exemplifies the shift from Second Temple to rabbinic legal culture, defined by Moshe Halbertal as a "transition from commandment to *halakhah*." In his opinion, the very phenomenon of "halakhah" to which the Mishnah is dedicated—"the establishment of dense, intricate fields of instruc-

Pharisees, Rabbis, and the End of Jewish Sectarianism," *Hebrew Union College Annual* 55 (1984): 27–53; Vered Noam, "Beit Shammai and Sectarian Halakha" (Hebrew), *Jewish Studies* 41 (2001–2): 45–67; Yair Furstenberg, "From Tradition to Controversy" (Hebrew), *Tarbiz* 85.4 (2018): 587–642.

3. Alexander Samely, *Rabbinic Interpretation of Scripture in the Mishnah* (Oxford, 2002); Menahem Kahana, "The Relations between Exegeses in the Mishnah and Halakhot in the Midrash" (Hebrew), *Tarbiz* 84.1–2 (2015): 17–76; Yair Furstenberg, "Mishnah Uprooting Scripture" (Hebrew), *JSIJ* 16 (2019): 1–20; Rosen-Zvi, *Between Mishnah and Midrash*, 60–71.

4. Chaim Rabin, "Hebrew and Aramaic in the First Century," in *The Jewish People in the First Century*, ed. S. Safrai and M. Stern (Assen, 1976), 1007–39; Moshe Bar-Asher, "Mishnaic Hebrew: An Introductory Survey," in *The Literature of the Sages*, vol. 2, ed. S. Safrai et al. (Assen, 2006), 567–95; Elitzur A. Bar-Asher Siegal, "Hebrew Language," in *Encyclopedia of the Bible and Its Reception*, ed. H-J. Klauck et al. (Berlin, 2015), 11:646–53, and chapter 14 in this volume.

5. For examples, see notes 9–25 below.

6. See e.g. Aharon Shemesh, "4Q251: Midrash Mishpatim," *Dead Sea Discoveries* 12.3 (2005): 280–302.

tions at high resolution . . . which far exceed the purview of the original commandment"—is a rabbinic novelty as opposed to Second Temple literature, which merely elaborates on pentateuchal law. "Thus, the Mishnah does not only mark transformations in the content of *halakhah*, it marks the very emergence of *halakhah*."[7]

These substantial disparities notwithstanding, deeper scrutiny identifies hints, traces, and forerunners of the mishnaic phenomenon in earlier Jewish literature, in terms of form, content, and terminology. Focusing on the DSS library as a primary reflection of pre-rabbinic Jewish society, I seek to demonstrate various facets of its affinities to, as well as dissimilarities from, the later Mishnah.

1. Qumran Works That Address Religious Law

The very emergence of comprehensive collections of postbiblical religious rules toward the late Second Temple period, as discovered in the Qumran caves, is a new phenomenon that foreshadows the much later appearance of the Mishnah. On the other hand, the fundamental differences between these forerunners and the Mishnah clearly mark the well-defined borders between the early sectarian and the later rabbinic cultures. The three main legal works from the Qumran library well illustrate the similarities and differences between the sectarian legal system and compositions as compared to the Mishnah.[8] I begin my review with the genre, organization, and style of these works, and then examine the legal content and religious outlook reflected by each corpus.

The *Temple Scroll*

The *Temple Scroll* (11QT) belongs to the genre of rewritten Bible.[9] Opening with the renewal of the Sinaitic covenant in Exodus 34 and following

---

7. Moshe Halbertal, "The History of *Halakhah* and the Emergence of *Halakhah*" (Hebrew), *Diné Israel: Studies in Halakha and Jewish Law* 29 (2013): 1–23, at 2 (my translation).

8. Other Qumran texts also deal with legislation and contain "ordinances," or focus on a certain halakhic issue (harvesting; *teharot*; Sabbath laws); some compositions treat a specific type of extra-biblical sectarian law (community rules and eschatological rules: *Serekh ha-Yaḥad* and the *Rule of the Congregation*; war rules: the *War Scroll* and related texts). For a comprehensive collection of these compositions and fragments, see Donald W. Parry and Emanuel Tov, eds., *Texts Concerned with Religious Law*, 2 vols. (Leiden, 2004).

9. Although some scholars maintain that the *Temple Scroll* was not authored by members of the Qumran sect, but rather originated in a related, probably earlier group

the order of the canonical Pentateuch for the remainder of Exodus, Leviticus, and Numbers, it first articulates the sanctuary-related injunctions and the sacrificial rites in these pentateuchal books before turning to Deuteronomic topics. As its name indicates, this work focuses on the laws of the Temple, its structure and furnishings, but also incorporates sacrificial, festival, and purity laws, the prohibition against idolatry, the statute of the king, and priestly and Levitical gifts, among other religious themes. The authors redact the biblical laws by rephrasing verses, inserting additional rulings (even entire sections), compiling all the relevant material at a legislative issue's first appearance, and harmonizing contradictory laws.[10]

Although the *Temple Scroll*'s aspiration to encompass all the pentateuchal commandments—including harmonization of contradictory injunctions and addition of some extrabiblical themes—may faintly echo some characteristics of the mishnaic project, major differences mirror their incompatible religious worldviews. In sharp contradistinction to the deliberate mishnaic detachment from the biblical background, and its ascription of the statements to identifiable human figures, the author of 11QT clearly wished to ground both the content and authority of his work in Sinaitic revelation. The scroll deliberately alters the third-person references to God in the Deuteronomic commandments to first-person speech, in order to create the impression that all its directives were delivered by God, unmediated.[11] Lawrence H. Schiffman even defines this work as "a divine halakhic pseudepigraphon."[12] Aharon Shemesh and Cana Werman include the *Temple Scroll* among additional compositions found at Qumran that they ascribe to the

---

(Lawrence H. Schiffman, *The Courtyards of the House of the Lord: Studies on the Temple Scroll*, ed. F. Garcia Martinez [Leiden, 2008], xviii–xx), the affinity between its halakhah and other Qumranic legal texts suggests that this work is nonetheless representative of a legal system accepted, adopted, or created by the Qumran sect.

10. Yigael Yadin, ed., *The Temple Scroll*, 3 vols. (Jerusalem, 1983). For new readings. see Elisha Qimron, *The Dead Sea Scrolls: The Hebrew Writings*, 3 vols. (Hebrew; Jerusalem, 2013), 1:137–207; and Qimron, *The Qumran Texts: Composite Edition* (Hebrew; Tel Aviv, 2020, https://zenodo.org/record/3737950#.XoXRs6gzaiM), 1:137–207. For a recent edition with a new translation and commentary, see Lawrence H. Schiffman and Andrew D. Gross, with contributions by Martin G. Abegg, Michael Rand, Leen Ritmyer, and Marlene R. Schiffman, *The Temple Scroll: (11Q19, 11Q20, 11Q21, 4Q524 with 4Q365a)* (2021). Massive scholarly literature has been dedicated to various aspects of this work. See the collected studies of Lawrence H. Schiffman and especially the introduction and the comprehensive references to previous research in Schiffman, *Courtyards*, xvii–xxvi, xvii–xviii n. 1.

11. Yadin, *Temple Scroll*, 1:71.

12. Schiffman, *Courtyards*, 174. For discussion, see 163–74.

broad genre of works whose halakhic authority is based—in diametric contradiction to the Mishnah—on divine revelation.[13]

The *Damascus Document*

Another prominent legislative work from the *Yaḥad* library is the *Damascus Document*. Two partial medieval manuscripts of this work, CDa and CDb, were discovered in the Cairo Genizah in 1896, about half a century prior to the discovery of ten fragmentary manuscripts in Qumran Caves 4 (4Q266–73 or 4QDa–h), 5 (5Q12), and 6 (6Q15). The *Damascus Document* opens with a section titled "admonition" in the scholarly literature, and consists of moral instruction, exhortation, history of the sect, and polemic against its opponents. The main part of the work—about two-thirds—consists of laws, most of which appear in the Qumran rather than in the Genizah fragments. The legislative section addresses a variety of topics, including many passages on Temple-related matters, such as ritual impurity and consecrated food; other passages discuss the laws of the Sabbath, marriage and divorce, oaths and vows, and judicial regulations. The composition concludes with a penal code and a ceremony of covenant renewal, including expulsion of sinners.[14]

As compared to their counterparts in the *Temple Scroll,* the laws in the *Damascus Document* more closely resemble mishnaic legislation; as opposed to the former, the *Damascus Document* clearly distinguishes between

13. Aharon Shemesh and Cana Werman, "Halakhah at Qumran: Genre and Authority," *Dead Sea Discoveries* 10.1 (2003): 104–29.

14. For the gradual process of publication of this scroll, see mainly Solomon Schechter, *Documents of a Jewish Sectaries, I: Fragments of a Zadokite Work* (Cambridge, 1910); Louis Ginzberg, *An Unknown Jewish Sect* (New York, 1976, first published in German in 1922); Chaim Rabin, *The Zadokite Documents,* 2nd ed. (Oxford, 1958); Elisha Qimron, "The Text of CDC," in *The Damascus Document Reconsidered,* ed. M. Broshi (Jerusalem, 1992), 9–49; Joseph M. Baumgarten and Daniel R. Schwartz, "Damascus Document," in *The Dead Sea Scrolls: Hebrew, Aramaic, and Greek Texts with English Translations,* vol. 2, ed. J. H. Charlesworth (Tübingen, 1995), 4–79; Joseph M. Baumgarten and Joseph T. Milik, *The Damascus Document (4Q266–73),* DJD18 (Oxford, 1996); Qimron, *Dead Sea Scrolls: Hebrew Writings,* 1:1–58; and Qimron, *Qumran Texts: Composite Edition,* 1:1–58. For a recent edition with a new translation and commentary, see Steven D. Fraade, *The Damascus Document,* Oxford Commentary on the Dead Sea Scrolls (Oxford). For a collection dedicated to this work, see J. M. Baumgarten, E. G. Chazon, and A. Pinnick, eds., *The Damascus Document: A Centennial of Discovery. Proceedings of the Third International Symposium of the Orion Center for the Study of the Dead Sea Scrolls and Associated Literature, 4–8 February 1998* (Leiden, 2000). For an introduction to the text and review of the scholarship, see Charlotte Hempel, *The Damascus Texts,* Companion to the Qumran Scrolls 1 (Sheffield, 2000).

the biblical text and its own regulations, presenting them in autonomous units. Although these units sometimes open or close with a biblical citation that touches on the general theme, the laws are never interwoven into the pentateuchal text, or phrased imitatively as Scripture. Aharon Shemesh and Cana Werman categorize this work as belonging to a genre that bases its authority on human exegetical processes.[15] In this respect, the *Damascus Document* is somewhat closer to the rabbinic concept of human halakhic authority. On the other hand, Steven D. Fraade contrasts the *Damascus Document*'s more "biblicized" Hebrew, which he views as suggesting that its legislation relied on "continued prophetic authority," and the Mishnah's independent style, which attests to textual authority that stems from "the community of the rabbinic sages."[16]

One significant feature of the *Damascus Document* that may be regarded as an antecedent of the Mishnah is the organization of some of its laws.[17] This sectarian composition is one of the earliest examples in Jewish literature of topically organized units of religious rules, occasionally preceded by captions, which may remind us of mishnaic tractates. These include: "Concerning (על) one who purifies himself in water" (CD 10:10); "Concerning the Sabbath to guard it according to its law" (CD 10:14); "[Con]cerning a woman's oath" (CD 16:10); "This is the rule (סרך) for the judges of the Congregation" (CD 10:4); "This is the rule for the Overseer (מבקר) of a camp" (CD 13:7); "This is the rule of the many for meeting all their needs" (CD 14:12).

Fraade enumerates additional similarities between the *Damascus Document* and the Mishnah: the inclusion of heterogeneous legal subjects, including laws inapplicable for both communities, such as temple and sacrificial laws; the transformation and adaptation of scriptural laws; the citation and interpretation—albeit infrequent—of biblical verses; their nature as compilations and adaptations of previous sources; the fact that both contain only a selection from a larger corpus; the existence of intersecting literature (the Tosefta and legal Midrash with regard to the Mishnah; the *Community Rule* and other Qumran works with regard to CD); and a fluid transmission of the text. Fraade also calls attention to what he regards as a major difference between these works in terms of the relationship between law and narrative. Whereas the laws in the *Damascus Document* are set in the his-

---

15. Shemesh and Werman, "Halakhah at Qumran." For a discussion of the allegorical pesher in CD 6:3–9 in this light, see p. 109.

16. Steven D. Fraade, *Legal Fictions: Studies of Law and Narrative in the Discursive Worlds of Ancient Jewish Sectarians and Sages* (Leiden, 2011), 227–54, at 248.

17. See e.g. Lawrence H. Schiffman, *The Halakhah at Qumran* (Leiden, 1975), 82–83.

torical and liturgical framework of the admonition and covenant renewal ceremony, the Mishnah lacks any "ritual frame or grand-narrative." Minor narrative elements are rather integrated, according to Fraade, throughout the entire legal discourse of the Mishnah.[18]

In my opinion, however, the major distinction between the *Damascus Document* and the Mishnah inheres in the laws themselves. In addition to the "astonishing dissimilarity" in content[19]—discussed below—comparison of the topical groups of laws in the *Damascus Document* to mishnaic tractates treating the same topics probably best exemplifies the giant leap "from commandment to halakhah." One of the largest topical groups of laws in CD, and in the Qumran library at large, is the one "concerning the Sabbath to guard it according to its law." It spans some twenty verses (CD 10:14–11:18 and parallels in 4QDa and 4QDe) and contains about twenty extrabiblical laws. There is, however, no comparison between this short list of laconic instructions, some of which do resemble halakhic principles in the Mishnah,[20] and the massive, thirty-four-chapter edifice of tractates *Shabat* and *'Eruvin*. The brief instruction "A man may not carry anything outside his house, nor should he carry anything in. If he is in a temporary shelter, he should not take anything out of it or bring anything in" (CD 10:7–9) is illustrative. In the Mishnah, this halakhic principle spans no fewer than fifteen chapters. The sectarian document lacks not only the volume, scope, intricacy, density, and "high resolution" of the thousands of details of the mishnaic Sabbath laws, it also lacks basic conceptions which characterize rabbinic thinking on the Sabbath: the concept of thirty-nine prohibited categories of work (mShab 7.2); the rabbinic division of private and public space into four domains in the context of the prohibitions against carrying (mShab 11 and throughout the two tractates); the substantive halakhic devices of *'eruv* and *shittuf*; the measures and quantities that stipulate a transgression through work (mShab 7.3–8.7, 9.5–10.1, 12, 13.1–2); and the principle of intention as a condition for transgression (mShab 10.4, 13.3 and elsewhere), among many others.

Miqtsat Ma'ase Ha-Torah

The third composition, *Miqtsat Ma'ase ha-Torah* (4QMMT), is a major source not just for the halakhah of the Qumran sect but also for its opponents' views. Framed as a letter aimed at convincing an unidentified political leader of the veracity of the sect's halakhic stance, it has three main

18. Fraade, *Legal Fictions*, 246–54, citation at 252.
19. Qimron, *Dead Sea Scrolls: Hebrew Writings*, 1:2.
20. Schiffman, *Halakhah at Qumran*, 84–134.

sections. The first (A), of which only a small part has survived, is a solar calendar, of the type familiar to us from other Qumran works; the second (B) is a sequence of polemically formulated legal statements framed as a group declaration and worded in the first-person plural. The formula "and concerning X: we are of the opinion" introduces some of these statements, and in certain cases a group of addressees is invoked: "and you [in the plural] know that. . ." Some of the statements note their opponents' adherence to incorrect religious praxis: "[they] leave over [sacrifices from one day to the following one]" (B 10); "[they] unite with each other (מתוככים)." The final section (C) is addressed to another group and its leader, pleading with them to do "what is righteous and good in His eyes" (C 31), while referring to the blessings and curses due in the end-time, and to parts of the biblical canon, namely "the book of Moses," "the books of the prophets," and "[the writings of] David," probably Psalms. This part of the scroll also famously relates that the speakers have separated themselves "from the multitude of the peop[le]" (C 7). The name of the scroll in scholarly literature derives from the reference to the contents of the epistle in sections B and C as מקצת דברינו [. . .] מ[מעשים] "some of our rulings [. . .]*m* [. . .] precepts" (B 1–2); and מקצת מעשי התורה, "some of the precepts of the Torah" (C 27).[21]

The legal controversies at the heart of the dispute in 4QMMT enable recovery of many of the issues fueling the sectarian controversies of the day. These revolved around such topics as the sacrificial offerings, the Red Heifer, the sanctity of Jerusalem and the Temple, purity laws, priestly gifts, and the prohibition against incest, among others. The practices criticized by the scroll's author are the ones attested in rabbinic literature as the later rabbinic consensus, and sometimes the Pharisaic view, whereas the views espoused by 4QMMT represent the stance commonly found in the DSS. The latter is, in several cases, identical to the Sadducean or Boethusian position as described in rabbinic literature.

21. For editions, see Elisha Qimron and John Strugnell (in consultation with Y. Sussmann and with contributions by Y. Sussmann and A. Yardeni), *Qumran Cave 4.V: Miqsat Ma'ase Ha-Torah*, DJD 10 (Oxford, 1994); Qimron, *Dead Sea Scrolls: Hebrew Writings*, 2:204–11; Qimron, *Qumran Texts: Composite Edition*, 2:204–11; and a recent new edition with collected articles, Reinhard G. Kratz, ed., *Interpreting and Living God's Law at Qumran: Miqṣat Ma'aśe Ha-Torah: Some of the Works of the Torah*, SAPERE 37 (Tübingen, 2020). I am currently preparing a new edition with new readings and a comprehensive commentary: Vered Noam, *"Some Precepts of the Torah"—An English Translation and Commentary of 4QMMT*, Decipherment and Reconstruction by Eshbal Ratzon, The Oxford Commentary on the Dead Sea Scrolls (forthcoming). See also John Kampen and Moshe J. Bernstein, eds., *Reading 4QMMT: New Perspectives on Qumran Law and History* (Atlanta, 1996).

The distinctive nature of 4QMMT as a short polemic treatise and as a letter, or pseudo-letter,[22] is fundamentally different from the Mishnah as a vast corpus of religious law, directed at a community which *ab initio* accepts its authority. As for 4QMMT's legislative content, it is not only opposed to the later rabbinic system reflected in the Mishnah, but even explicitly disputes its earlier expressions.

That said, some aspects of 4QMMT place this composition in closest proximity to the Mishnah. Of the DSS, its language is the least "biblicized" and more greatly resembles mishnaic Hebrew than any other Qumranic work, albeit in terms of vocabulary rather than grammar.[23] Although Menahem Kister argues that most of Qimron's examples of MH in 4QMMT are in fact Aramaic words or calques,[24] he nevertheless admits that a specific kind of rabbinic terminology is indeed conspicuously present in 4QMMT, namely halakhic expressions such as פרת החטאת (cow of purification, B 13); טהרת הקודש (sacred food, B 23); תערובת (mixture, B 48, 50); מוצקות (liquid streams, B 55); לחה (liquid, B 58); and ארץ ישראל (land of Israel, B 63).[25] Moreover, the discussion in 4QMMT of minute halakhic details, rather than general rules, probably part of its explicitly polemic nature, more resembles rabbinic discourse than any other Qumran composition.

22. As some scholars argue; see Fraade, *Legal Fictions*, 69–91. This question is not relevant to the comparison of the scroll's genre—be it a genuine or a pseudo-letter—to the mishnaic genre.

23. Qimron and Strugnell, *Miqsat Ma'ase Ha-Torah*, 65–108. Qimron attributes this similarity to "the fact that both MMT and MH reflect spoken forms of Hebrew current in the Second Temple period" (108). Shelomo Morag, on the other hand, describes the latter as a low-level, defective, fragmentary vernacular, totally different from the Mishnah's aristocratic literary style (Shelomo Morag, "'Language and Style in 'Miqsat Ma'ase Ha-Torah' — Did Moreh Ha-Ṣedeq Write This Document?" (Hebrew), *Tarbiz* 65.2 (1996): 209–23.

24. Menahem Kister, "Studies in 4Q Miqsat Ma'ase Ha-Torah and Related Texts: Law, Theology, Language and Calendar" (Hebrew), *Tarbiz* 68.3 (1999): 355–59. See more recently Noam Mizrahi, "The Language of MMT," in Kratz, *Interpreting and Living God's Law*, 67–83, who observed that the different manuscripts of this work reflect distinct morphological forms.

25. Qimron and Strugnell, *Miqsat Ma'ase Ha-Torah*, 138–43; Kister, "Studies in 4Q Miqsat Ma'ase Ha-Torah," 358.

2. *The Halakhic Dispute*

The Qumranic works reflect a system of religious law that differs from, and is often opposed to, rabbinic halakhah as known to us from the Mishnah and later rabbinic compositions.[26] The sectarian group which authored—or, in certain cases, adopted—the books mentioned above and similar legislative texts, undoubtedly adhered to legal and theological conceptions alien to the later rabbinic ones. This is apparent not only from 4QMMT, which explicitly refutes practices quite similar to the tannaitic ones, but also from non-polemical DSS texts whose contents contradict both the general principles and minutiae of the rabbinic instructions. In what follows I single out some major features that characterize the two opposing halakhic frameworks.

Stringency versus Leniency

Since the publication of the first scrolls, scholars have noted the stringent positions adopted by the sect as compared to the later rabbinic halakhah.[27]

26. For a survey of the large corpus of scholarly literature dedicated to the legislative components of the DSS library, see Alex P. Jassen, "American Scholarship on Jewish Law in the Dead Sea Scrolls," in *The Dead Sea Scrolls in Scholarly Perspective: A History of Research,* ed. D. Dimant, STDJ 99 (Leiden, 2012), 101–54; Aharon Shemesh, "Trends and Themes in Israeli Research of the Halakhah in the Dead Sea Scrolls," *The Dead Sea Scrolls in Scholarly Perspective,* 345–46.

27. Saul Lieberman, "Light on the Cave Scrolls from Rabbinic Sources," *PAAJR* 20 (1951): 398; Joseph M. Baumgarten, "The Pharisaic-Sadducean Controversies about Purity and the Qumran Texts," *JJS* 31 (1980): 157–70, esp. 165; a similar observation was repeatedly made by Yadin throughout his discussion of the Temple Scroll (*Temple Scroll,* 1:98, 115–16, 136, 162–63, 168, 275, 278–89, 291–93, 295, 306–7, 310, 312–15, 318–20, 323, 325, 326, 328–32, 336–38, 338–41, 354–57, 367, 369–70, 372, 374–87, and esp. 400–401); Hannah K. Harrington, "Holiness in the Laws of 4QMMT," in *Legal Texts and Legal Issues: Proceedings of the Second Meeting of the International Organization for Qumran Studies, Cambridge, 1995. Published in Honour of Joseph M. Baumgarten,* ed. M. J. Bernstein, F. García Martínez, and J. Kampen, STDJ 23 (Leiden, 1997), 109–28; Lawrence H. Schiffman, "The Dead Sea Scrolls and Rabbinic Halakhah," in *The Dead Sea Scrolls as Background to Postbiblical Judaism and Early Christianity: Papers from an International Conference at St. Andrews in 2001,* ed. J. R. Davila, STDJ 46 (Leiden, 2003), 3–24 (esp. 21); Eyal Regev, *The Sadducees and Their Halakhah* (Hebrew; Jerusalem, 2005), 203–46. Regev distinguishes Qumranic from Sadducean law but asserts that both developed from a single early, stringent, priestly system. I used this widespread characteristic as evidence of the similarity between the *halakhah* in the DSS and that of Beit Shammai. See Noam, "Beit Shammai and Sectarian Halakha," 45–67. Cf. Hillel Newman, *Proximity to Power and Jewish Sectarian Groups of the Ancient Period* (Leiden, 2007), 201–3; and Shemesh, *Halakhah in the Making,* 129–40. Cf. Yaakov Elman, "Some Remarks on 4QMMT and the Rabbinic Tradition, or, When Is a Parallel Not a Parallel?" in *Reading 4QMMT: New Perspectives on Qumran Law and History,* ed. M. J. Bernstein and J. Kampen (Atlanta, 1996), 99–128.

Yaakov Sussmann characterized 4QMMT's rulings as "invariably consistent in their stringent rulings: what is forbidden is always forbidden, and what is unclean is absolutely unclean."[28] The editors of this scroll also noted "the sect's pronounced tendency toward strictness."[29] This observation was in fact made by the members of the sect themselves, who accused their rivals of "choosing the path of lenience": כיא בחרו בקלות.[30]

Consideration of some of the Sabbath rules in the *Damascus Document* illustrates where the two systems diverge.[31] A famous difference concerns saving a life on the Sabbath. According to CD 11:16–17 and the parallel in 4Q265 (f6: 5–8), someone who falls into a water cistern on the Sabbath may not be pulled out using any implement, such as "a ladder, rope, or tool" (CD 11:17), but rather only by extending a garment to him (4Q265 f6:7). In contrast, the Mishnah and other tannaitic sources rule that "any matter of doubt as to danger to life overrides the prohibitions of the Sabbath" (mYom 8.5–7).[32]

Whereas CD forbids drawing water into a vessel on the Sabbath (CD 11:1–2),[33] according to the Mishnah (m'Eruv 10.6) a person can draw water as long as his head and most of his body are in the same domain as the water source. The Mishnah also permits drawing water from a well located in the public domain that is deeper than ten handbreadths, which is considered

28. Yaakov Sussmann, "Appendix 1: The History of the Halakha and the Dead Sea Scrolls," in Qimron and Strugnell, *Miqsat Ma'ase Ha-Torah*, 187. See also esp. 190 (originally published as "The History of Halakha and the Dead Sea Scrolls: A Preliminary to the Publication of 4QMMT" [Hebrew], *Tarbiz* 59.1 [1989–90]: 11–76). For a review of earlier opinions see Sussmann, "History," 27 n. 61; Sussmann, "Appendix 1," 187 n. 29.

29. Elisha Qimron, "The Halakha," in Qimron and Strugnell, *Miqsat Ma'ase Ha-Torah*, 132.

30. 4Q171 (4QpPsA) f1_2 i:19. See Maurya P. Horgan, "Psalm Pesher 1," in *The Dead Sea Scrolls: Hebrew, Aramaic, and Greek Texts with English Translations,* vol. 6B, ed. J. H. Charlesworth et al. (Tübingen, 2002), 8–9. It seems that the correct translation is the one suggested above; see David Flusser, "Pharisees, Sadducees, and Essenes in Pesher Nahum," in *Judaism of the Second Temple Period: Qumran and Apocalypticism,* trans. A. Yadin (Grand Rapids, Mich., 2007), 1:256–57.

31. For the sake of convenience, I refer only to the CD fragments, without specifying the Qumran parallels, unless pertinent. For discussion and further references to the CD laws enumerated below, see Schiffman, *Halakhah at Qumran*, 77–133; Fraade, *Damascus Document.*

32. See *Mekhilta de-Rabbi Yishmael, Shabbata* 1 (Horovitz-Rabin ed., 34–41). For a discussion of, and references to, previous literature, see Aharon Shemesh, "The History of the Halakhic Concept שבת דוחה נפש פיקוח (Hebrew), *Tarbiz* 80.4 (2012): 481–505.

33. On the precise meaning of the prohibition, see Vered Noam and Elisha Qimron, "A Qumran Composition of Sabbath Laws and Its Contribution to the Study of Early Halakah," *Dead Sea Discoveries* 16 (2009): 55–96, at 64.

a private domain, due to a unique device of partial fencing (m'Eruv 2.1). The Mishnah suggests additional symbolic constructions which enable the drawing of water from one domain to another (m'Eruv 8.6–8), a strategy of which the Qumranites are totally unaware. As opposed to CD's prohibition on opening "a sealed vessel on the Sabbath" (CD 11:9),[34] the majority opinion in the Mishnah (mShab 22.3) even permits breaking a jar on the Sabbath in order to eat from it. Similarly, there is no rabbinic equivalent to CD's ban on staying in a place in proximity to gentiles on the Sabbath (CD 11:14–15).

The same is true with regard to the *Temple Scroll*. Its stringency as compared to rabbinic halakhah is evident in almost every column; therefore, I limit myself to a few, varied examples. In excluding the impure and others from holy precincts, the *Temple Scroll* banishes the severely impure from all Israelite cities (48.14–17), whereas according to the Mishnah (mKel 1.6–9), the most extreme form of exclusion is restricted to Jerusalem.[35] The scroll also instructs that a man who lies with his wife "shall not come to any part of the city of the temple, where I settle my name, for three days" (45.11–12).[36] This means that marital relations cannot take place in Jerusalem, a concept unimaginable in the rabbinic worldview. In addition, the *Temple Scroll* enumerates lesser degrees of human purity never mentioned in tannaitic literature, such as boys under twenty and proselytes, whom it limits to the outer court of the temple (39. 4–8), and the blind who are excluded from the entire temple city (45.12).[37]

Another rule (47.7–10, 11–13) forbids bringing hides of nonsacral animals, and even vessels made from them, into the Temple City,[38] whereas

34. A parallel fragment from Qumran (4Q421 f11:2) adds the words: "to eat and to drink any of it" in accordance with the wording of the [contrary] Mishnah (mShab 22.3): "A person breaks a jar *to eat dried figs from it.*" See Noam and Qimron, "Qumran Composition," 64.

35. See n. 51 below.

36. Yadin, *Temple Scroll*, 2:193.

37. See also 4QMMT B: 49–54. Yadin thought that the *Temple Scroll* "uses the word blind as a general term" for all kinds of physical defects (*Temple Scroll*, 1:291), but see Qimron and Strugnell, *Miqsat Ma'ase Ha-Torah*, 160–61.

38. See Lv 17:1–9. A parallel law should probably be reconstructed in 4QMMT B:18–24; see Qimron and Strugnell, *Miqsat Ma'ase Ha-Torah*, 48–49, 154–56. This law has been widely discussed in the scholarly literature. See e.g. David Henshke, "The Sanctity of Jerusalem: The Sages and Sectarian Halakhah" (Hebrew), *Tarbiz* 67.1 (1998): 5–28; Kister, "Studies in 4QMiqsat Ma'aśe Ha-Torah," 335–39; Aharon Shemesh, "'Three-Days' Journey from the Temple': The Use of This Expression in the Temple Scroll," *Dead Sea Discoveries* 6.2 (1999): 126–38; Schiffman, *Courtyards*, 297–313; Reinhard G. Kratz, "'The Place Which He Has Chosen': The Identification of the Cult Place of Deut. 12 and Lev. 17 in 4QMMT," *Meghillot* 5–6 (2008): 57*–80*.

rabbinic—and probably Pharisaic—halakhah does not recognize any ban on slaughter and eating of nonsacral animals in the land of Israel, including Jerusalem,[39] and even in cases of impure flesh excludes hides, bones, sinews, horns, and hooves from impurity (mHul 9.1 [=Teh 1.4], 5; m'Eduy 6.3).[40]

As to purity issues in everyday life, the *Temple Scroll* viewed stone vessels as subject to impurity (49.14), whereas the sages exempted them (mKel 10.1; mOhal 5.5). Another extrabiblical principle which is totally absent from rabbinic halakhah is the extreme impurity ascribed to a pregnant woman carrying a dead embryo (50.10–19).[41]

In the sphere of sacrifices and holy gifts, the *Temple Scroll* commands that the Passover sacrifice be eaten "in the courts of the holy (place)" (1.8–9), namely, the Temple court, whereas according to the Mishnah (mZev 5.8) it may be eaten throughout Jerusalem. The scroll also enjoins that the tithe eaten in Jerusalem as described in Deut 14:22–27 (named by the rabbis "second tithe"), is supposed to be eaten only on festivals (53.15–17), a law unheard of in tannaitic legislation.

Throughout all the polemic issues raised in 4QMMT, the author berates his adversaries' lenience. Thus, for example, he accuses the opponents of the sect, who used to eat the edible parts of the thanksgiving offering after sunset, of leaving the sacrifice "from one day to the following one" (B 9–13), in contrast to the biblical precept that it be eaten "on the day that it is offered; none of it shall be left over until morning" (Lev 7:15). The bone of contention is that according to rabbinic and probably Pharisaic halakhah, the biblical "day" with regard to sacrifices includes the following night.[42] Therefore, a thanksgiving offering, like any other sacrifice designated to be eaten on the same day, can be eaten during the day and the following night, though the rabbis limited this permission to midnight (mZev 5.6; see mBer 1.1). In contrast, sectarian works contend that the biblical "day" ends before

39. *Sifre Deut.*, 75, *Re'eh*, 139–40; bHul 16b; *Lev. Rab.* 22:7; *Sifra, Aharei-Mot, Perek* 8, *Parashah* 6, 83b; mZevah 14.1; bZevah 106a–b. See Cana Werman, "Consumption of the Blood and Its Covering in the Priestly and Rabbinic Traditions," (Hebrew), *Tarbiz* 63.1 (1994): 179–81. Even inside the temple yard, one who slaughters nonsacral animals is not liable to punishment (*Sifra, Aharei-Mot, Perek* 8, *Parashah* 6:5, 83b).

40. See also *Sifra, Shemini* 10 [*perek* 11], 5–6, p. 55d; bHul 77b, 117b, cf. mZevah 3.4, 9.5.

41. See mHul 4.3; m'Ohal 7.4; tYeb. 9.5; *Sifre Num.* 127 (Horovitz ed., 164); *Sifre Zuta* 19:16; bHul 72a. For discussion, see Yadin, *Temple Scroll*, 1:336–38; Vered Noam, "Qumran and the Rabbis on Corpse-Impurity: Common Exegesis—Tacit Polemic," in *The Dead Sea Scrolls: Text and Context*, ed. C. Hempel, STDJ 90 (Leiden, 2010), 397–430, at 407–15.

42. TZev 6.8; *Sifra, 'Emor* 8.8 (12); yYom 1.1 [38b]; bHul 83a; bTem 14a.

sunset.[43] This treatise also forbids bringing dogs into Jerusalem (B 58–60), whereas the rabbis prohibited only rearing chickens (mBK 7.7).[44] 4QMMT bans slaughter of pregnant animals and enjoins ritual slaughter of a living fetus found within a slaughtered pregnant animal (B 36–38), as opposed to rabbinic law which considered an embryo part of its mother's body (mḤul 4.1–5).[45]

Proximity to Scripture

Despite this clear-cut distinction, I have argued elsewhere that because it subconsciously takes rabbinic halakhah as its starting point, the sweeping claim that sectarian law invariably tends to stringency is biased. Closer examination indicates that sectarian law rather often reflects simple, necessary inferences from Scripture, whereas tannaitic leniency represents a surprisingly revolutionary divergence from the plain meaning of biblical commandments.[46] This is not to say that sectarian law is identical to the pentateuchal regulations—on the contrary. The Qumran scrolls manifestly deviate from biblical law by way of filling exegetical gaps, addressing practical needs, incorporating ancient traditions,[47] and even through major, fundamental innovations like extra-biblical festivals (*Temple Scroll* 19.11–24.16) and adoption of the 364-day calendar.[48] Yet when compared to rab-

43. Joseph M. Baumgarten, "The Beginning of the Day in the Calendar of Jubilees," in *Studies in Qumran Law* (Leiden, 1977), 124–30; Yadin, *Temple Scroll*, 2:89; Lawrence H. Schiffman, "'Miqtsat Maʿaseh Ha-Torah' and the 'Temple Scroll,'" *Revue de Qumran* 14.3 (1990): 435–38; Qimron and Strugnell, *Miqtsat Maʿaseh Ha-Torah*, 150–52; Hanan Birenboym, "The Law of the Well-Being Sacrifice in the 'Miqtsat Maʿaśeh Ha-Torah' Scroll" (Hebrew), *Tarbiz* 67 (1998): 241–44. A similar dispute is evident in the *Temple Scroll* 20:12–13 regarding the independent cereal offering. See also *Jub.* 21.10.

44. Sussmann, "Appendix 1," 33–34.

45. See also 11QT 52:5–7. For discussion see the references in Sussmann, "Appendix 1," 33 n. 93, 35 n. 110; Qimron and Strugnell, *Miqsat Maʿase Ha-Torah*, 157 and n. 115, Noam, *From Qumran to the Rabbinic Revolution*, 158–59, 296–300.

46. Vered Noam, "Stringency in Qumran: A Reassessment," *JSJ* 40.3 (2009): 342–55.

47. Vered Noam, "The Emergence of Rabbinic Culture from the Perspective of Qumran," *Journal of Ancient Judaism* 6 (2016): 253–74; Jonathan Ben-Dov, "An Investigation into the Continuity between Biblical Literature and the Scrolls," in *The Religious Worldviews Reflected in the Dead Sea Scrolls: Proceedings of the Fourteenth International Symposium of the Orion Center for the Study of the Dead Sea Scrolls and Associated Literature, 28–30 May, 2013*, ed. R. A. Clements, M. Kister, and M. Segal, STDJ 127 (Leiden, 2018), 1–24.

48. Jonathan Ben-Dov, "Calendars and Festivals," in *The Oxford Encyclopedia of the Bible and Law*, ed. B. A. Strawn (New York, 2015), 87–93; Ben-Dov, "Investigation," 13–19.

binic halakhah, sectarian law is immeasurably less removed from the simple sense of Scripture than its rabbinic counterpart.[49]

Let us return to the above-mentioned Qumranic directive that banished the severely impure—lepers, people with discharge, menstruants and parturients—from *all* Israelite cities, whereas those defiled by a corpse, seminal emissions, or conjugal relations, as well as the blind, are excluded only from the Temple City;[50] note that according to the rabbis the most extreme form of exclusion goes no further than Jerusalem, and other Israelite settlements are not required to banish the impure.[51]

49. Numerous scholarly works have discussed the continuity between the Bible and the DSS from various angles. In fact, in modern scholarly treatments of Qumranic works or fragments, it is almost impossible to avoid the biblical background. For our purposes, it suffices to mention Shemaryahu Talmon, "Between the Bible and the Mishnah," in *The World of Qumran from Within* (Leiden, 1989), 11–52; Menahem Kister, "A Common Heritage: Biblical Interpretation at Qumran and Its Implications," in *Biblical Perspectives: Early Use and Interpretation of the Bible in Light of the Dead Sea Scrolls: Proceedings of the First International Symposium of the Orion Center for the Study of the Dead Sea Scrolls and Associated Literature, 12–14 May, 1996*, ed. M. Stone and E. G. Chazon, STDJ 28 (Leiden, 1998), 1–11; Adiel Schremer, "'[T]He[Y] Did Not Read in the Sealed Book': Qumran Halakhic Revolution and the Emergence of Torah Study in Second Temple Judaism," in *Historical Perspectives: From the Hasmoneans to Bar Kokhba in Light of the Dead Sea Scrolls: Proceedings of the Fourth International Symposium of the Orion Center for the Study of the Dead Sea Scrolls and Associated Literature, 27–31 January, 1999*, ed. D. M. Goodblatt, A. Pinnick, and D. R. Schwartz (Leiden, 2001), 105–26; Aharon Shemesh, *Halakhah in the Making: The Development of Jewish Law from Qumran to the Rabbis* (Berkeley, 2009), 72–106; Yitzhak D. Gilat, *R. Eliezer ben Hyrcanus: A Scholar Outcast* (Ramat Gan, 1984), 68–88; Noam, "Emergence," 261–71; Ben-Dov, "Investigation," 1–24.

50. *Temple Scroll* 45:7–10; 48:14–17.

51. See, e.g., m Kel 1.6–9; tKel.-B. Kam 1.12; *Sifre Num.* 1; *Sifre Zuta Num.* 5:2; b. Pesaḥ 67a. For a comparison of the sectarian and the rabbinic halakhah, see Yadin, *Temple Scroll*, 1:277–94; Jacob Milgrom, "Studies in the Temple Scroll," *Journal of Biblical Literature* 97 (1978): 512–18; Lawrence H. Schiffman, "Exclusion from the Sanctuary and the City of the Sanctuary in the Temple Scroll," *Hebrew Annual Review* 9 (1985): 301–20; Qimron, "The Halakha," 142–47; David Henshke, "The Sanctity of Jerusalem"; Menahem Kister, "Studies in 4QMiqtsat Ma'ase Ha-Torah and Related Texts: Law, Theology, Language and Calendar," *Tarbiz* 68 (1999): 335–39 (Hebrew); Hannan Birenboim, "The Halakhic Status of Jerusalem According to 4QMMT, *1Enoch*, and Tannaitic Literature" (Hebrew), *Meghillot: Studies in the Dead Sea Scrolls* 7 (2009): 3–17. See also Vered Noam, "Creative Interpretation and Integrative Interpretation in Qumran," *Proceedings of the Conference the Dead Sea Scrolls and Contemporary Culture: Celebrating 60 Years of Discovery* (Leiden, forthcoming). On the distancing of burials from regular cities in Qumranic and rabbinic legislation see Noam, "The Dual Strategy of Rabbinic Purity Legislation," *JSJ* 39 (2008): 493–500

Scriptural references to the sending away of the impure invariably relate exclusively to two domains: exclusion from the "Tabernacle" or the "Sanctuary," including related matters, such as sacrifices;[52] and exclusion from "the camp," which in the plain sense means the physical precincts of the Israelites in the desert.[53] Accordingly, the distinction between two domains for exclusion—the City of the Temple on the one hand, and "your cities" on the other—as depicted in the sect's literature, is quite close to the plain meaning of the verses.[54]

The radical, revolutionary innovation was actually the complex system formulated by the rabbis. The rabbinic ruling compressed all of the scriptural domains compelling exclusion, including the everyday domain, into the area of Jerusalem, and exempted all other Jewish settlements from purity regulations. The terms "camp of Divine Presence, camp of Levites, and camp of Israel," used by the sages to indicate the Temple, the Temple Mount, and Jerusalem respectively[55] as the areas requiring banishment, create an illusion of a scriptural source for the tannaitic purity/impurity system. But in reality, these terms are all based on the biblical description of the order in which the Israelites camped in the desert,[56] and have nothing to do with the biblical directive to send away the impure. There is no explicit scriptural basis for sending a person away from the Levites' camp and permitting him to stay in the Israelite one, or for an impure person being sent away from the Tabernacle and being allowed in the camp of the Levites. In fact, no mention is ever made of the camping site of the Levites in the context of sending away the impure. To sum up, the contraction of the purity-demanding domain, as well as its division into three realms, is a rabbinic invention.

Another prominent example concerns fourth-year fruit. 4QMMT as well as other Dead Sea Scrolls and *Jubilees* prescribe that fourth-year fruit (Lev 19:23–25) be given to the priests, as opposed to the Pharisaic-rabbinic insistence that it be eaten by the owner in Jerusalem in a state of purity

---

52. See, for instance, Lev 7:19–21; 12:4; 21:1–12; 22:1–9; Num 9:6–13; 19:13, 20:

53. Lev 13:46; 14:3, 8; Num 5:1–4, 12:14–15 (see also 2 Kgs 7:3, 15:5); on exclusion from the war-camp, see Num 31:19–20, 24; Deut 23:11–12.

54. Some components of this law however, such as the differentiation between the two groups of impurities, do lack clear biblical justification. See Noam, *From Qumran to the Rabbinic Revolution*, 167–70; Ben-Dov, "Investigation," 11–12.

55. See esp. tKel-BK 1.12; *Sifre Num.* 1.

56. Num 1:53; 3:23, 29, 35.

(e.g. mMS 4.3–5).[57] The plain meaning of the verse, that the fourth-year fruit is "holy for giving praise before the Lord," and that only "in the fifth year you may eat its fruit," clearly conveys that the owner is *not* allowed to enjoy it, in accord with the priestly-sectarian opinion and in contrast to rabbinic tradition.[58]

In the sphere of matrimonial law, the case of Deut 22:13–21 is instructive. According to this biblical injunction, when a bride is accused by her husband of not being a virgin following the wedding-night, the parents "spread out the cloth before the elders of the town" (17) as evidence of her virginity. If "the charge proves true" (20), the girl is stoned to death. Tannaitic law—against the gist of the biblical pericope—replaced the charge of premarital sexual relations with the charge of adultery by a betrothed woman, and substituted the material evidence of the "cloth" with statements by witnesses.[59] In contrast, Qumran law states: "if a man brings an accusation against a virgin of Israel, if he says so [at the time] he marries her, trustworthy [women] shall examine her. If he has not lied about her, she shall be put to death" (4Q159 f2_4:8–9).[60] Although the Qumranites replaced the "cloth" with physical inspection, overall they adhered to the plain meaning of the verses.

Another example in which Qumran law relies on Scripture is that of the house in which a person has died. According to the *Temple Scroll* as well as the *Damascus Document*, the house of the dead person is defiled, together with its floors and ceilings, and all that is attached thereto, in accordance

---

57. For references and discussion, see Menahem Kister, "Some Aspects of Qumranic Halakhah," in *The Madrid Qumran Congress: Proceedings of the International Congress on the Dead Sea Scrolls, March 1991*, 2 vols., ed. J. T. Barrera and L. V. Montaner (Leiden, 1992), 2:571–88, at 576–86; Shemesh, *Halakhah*, 7–15. On certain complexities within *Jubilees* on the one hand and within rabbinic sources on the other hand, see Shemesh, *Halakhah*, 11–15; for the exegetical battle between the two opinions, see Vered Noam, "Early Signs of Halakhic Midrash at Qumran" (Hebrew), *Diné Israel: Studies in Halakhah and Jewish Law* 26–27 (2009–10): 3–26, at 7–18.

58. In this particular case, the Pharisaic-rabbinic deviation from Scripture appears to stem from an ancient custom which probably preceded the law formulated in Leviticus 19. See Kister, "Some Aspects," 576–86; Itamar Kislev, "The Struggle over the Character of the Israelite Cult: The Case of the Law of *O'rla* and the Fourth-Year Produce (Leviticus 19:23–25)" (Hebrew), *Shenaton* 14 (2004): 27–50.

59. See e.g. *Sifre Deut.* 235, 236, 240. See Moshe Halbertal, *Interpretative Revolutions in the Making: Values as Interpretative Considerations in Midrashei Halakhah* (Hebrew; Jerusalem, 2004), 84–92.

60. See also 4Q271f3, and Aharon Shemesh, "4Q271.3: A Key to Sectarian Matrimonial Law," *JJS* 49 (1998): 244–63.

with the plain sense of Scripture "and sprinkle on the tent" (Num 19:18).[61] Tannaitic halakhah totally exempts them from impurity.[62]

Abstraction and Intention

Another characteristic of rabbinic halakhah absent from previous Jewish law is a proclivity to sophistication and abstraction, including the novel tannaitic concepts of "intention" and "thought" in determining the validity of performance of commandments or transgressions.[63] As shown above, the *Temple Scroll* (20.12–13), 4QMMT (B: 9–13), and *Jub.* 21.10[64] hold that those who eat a sacrifice beyond the specified time sin, in accord with the biblical text (Lev 7:18, 19:7). The rabbis, however, determined that a sacrifice is considered abomination (*pigul*) only when slaughtered with the *intention* to eat it beyond the specified time, but not when *actually* eaten beyond it (mZev 2.3).[65]

The conditions required for foods to become susceptible to impurity present a similar picture. Scripture states: "All food therein which may be eaten, upon which water comes, shall be unclean; and all drink in every such vessel that may be drunk shall be unclean" (Lev 11:34). Both sectarian (4Q284a f1:2–8, 4Q274 f3 i–ii:6–9) and tannaitic law (mTer 11.2) inferred from the words "all drink" that not only water but also other liquids cause susceptibility to impurity in foodstuffs.[66] Joseph Baumgarten described

---

61. *Temple Scroll* 49.5–7, 11–13; 50:10–12; CD 12:15–18. For further elaboration on these passages, see Vered Noam, "Qumran and the Rabbis on Corpse-Impurity: Common Exegesis—Tacit Polemic," in *The Dead Sea Scrolls. Text and Context*, ed. C. Hempel, STDJ 90 (Leiden, 2010), 397–430.

62. This fundamental rule derives from several partial statements in tannaitic literature: mShab 2.3; mKel 27.1; *Sifre Zuta* 19:13. The rule is stated more clearly in bShab 28a; yShab 2.3, 4d. See Maimonides, *Code: Book of Cleanness*, "Corpse Uncleanness," 5:12, quoted by Yadin, *Temple Scroll*, 1:326.

63. Howard Eilberg-Schwartz, *The Human Will in Judaism: The Mishna's Philosophy of Intention* (Atlanta, 1986); Jeffrey L. Rubenstein, "On Some Abstract Concepts in Rabbinic Literature," *JSQ* 4 (1997): 33–73; Joshua Levinson, "From Narrative Practice to Cultural Poetics: Literary Anthropology and the Rabbinic Sense of Self," in *Homer and the Bible in the Eyes of Ancient Interpreters: Between Literary and Religious Concerns*, ed. M. Niehoff (Leiden, 2012): 345–68; Mira Balberg, *Purity, Body and the Self in Early Rabbinic Literature* (Berkeley, 2014): 148–79; Ishay Rosen-Zvi, "The Mishnaic Mental Revolution: A Reassessment," *JJS* 65.1 (2015): 36–58.

64. See also Philo, *Spec.* 1.22.

65. See also *Sifra, Tsav* 8:12 (1)–(3); bZev 29a.

66. Whereas the Mishnah (mTer 11.2) stresses that these include only water and six other liquids, Qumran law prohibits the harvesting of figs, pomegranates, and olives by impure laborers, lest they defile the harvest, since these juices also make the fruits

how rabbinic halakhah created "an elaborate theory of 'susceptibility' to which it devoted an entire mishnaic tractate, *Makhshirin*." He stressed that according to the Mishnah (mMakh 1.1, 3.6) the owner must be aware of, and desire, the wetting of the fruits in order to cause susceptibility, a concept entirely nonexistent in the Qumran fragments.[67]

Another example of sweeping sophistication also touches on the above-mentioned "tent containing a corpse" (Num 19:14). Tannaitic halakhah broadens this biblical construct to the point of an absolute halakhic abstraction. It divorces "tent" from its definition as a dwelling place, whether movable or stationary, and transforms it from a noun to a present participle describing a state, "overshadowing," which, depending on circumstances, may apply to people, animals, vegetation, or inanimate objects that project over a corpse (mOhal 6.1 and ch. 8).[68] The implications of this conceptual expansion are far-reaching, and the extent of the innovation involved can be gauged only by comparing it with Qumranic legislation.

Priestly Law

We have seen that in certain cases Qumran laws are identical to practices described by the Mishnah as Sadducean.[69] Consequently, some scholars posit that the *Yaḥad* shared the same legal system with the Sadducees,[70] who were a priestly oligarchy, and that this common legal background was "a conservative, elitist priestly conception, advocating a severe separation between priests and people,"[71] whereas the rabbinic system was heir to a more inclusive, popular Second Temple faction. Several scholars even sug-

---

susceptible to impurity "if their juice comes out when pressed" (4Q284a f1:2–8). On this dispute see Vered Noam, "Traces of Sectarian Halakha in the Rabbinic World," in *Rabbinic Perspectives: Rabbinic Literature and the Dead Sea Scrolls, Proceedings of the Eighth International Symposium of the Orion Center*, ed. S. D. Fraade et al., STDJ 62 (Leiden, 2006), 67–85, at 70–73.

67. Joseph M. Baumgarten, "Liquids and Susceptibility to Defilement in New 4Q Texts," *JQR* 85.1–2 (1994–95): 92.

68. See also *Sifre Num.* 126; *Sifre Zuta* 19:14; Noam, "Qumran and the Rabbis," 418–28.

69. Qimron and Strugnell, *Miqsat Ma'aseh Ha-Torah*, 152, 162.

70. Baumgarten, "The Pharisaic-Sadducean Controversies"; Israel Knohl, "Post-Biblical Sectarianism and the Priestly Schools of the Pentateuch: The Issue of Popular Participation in the Temple Cult on Festivals," in *The Madrid Qumran Congress*, 601–9; Daniel R. Schwartz, "Law and Truth: On Qumran-Sadducean and Rabbinic Views of Law," in *The Dead Sea Scrolls: Forty Years of Research*, ed. D. Dimant and U. Rappaport (Jerusalem, 1992), 229–30; Sussmann, "Appendix 1," 192–96; Schiffman, *Courtyards*, xviii–xix; Shemesh, *Halakhah*, 15–19, 129–40.

71. Knohl, "Post-Biblical Sectarianism," 608.

gest that the roots of these rival traditions lie in the biblical era.[72] Although
the hypothesis regarding the generic connection between the Qumranite
and Sadducean systems of law has not received universal acceptance,[73] it
is commonly assumed that Qumran law is indeed "priestly." The DSS frequently mention the priests, "sons of Zadok," as "preservers of the Covenant" (1QS 5:9), emphasize the privileged priestly status and their role in religious rituals inside and outside the temple as well as in the communal life
of the sect, and deal mostly with the priestly realms of purity, temple, and
sacrifices.[74] The rabbinic system, on the other hand, commends non-priestly
legal authority, placing rabbis as supervisors of, and divorcing priests from,
certain rituals (e.g. mYom 1.3–5; 6.3; mSot 1.4; mPar 3.7–8). Thus, for example, where the Mishnah (mPar 12.10) teaches that "all are eligible to sprinkle
(the water containing the ashes of the Red Heifer)," Qumran law demands
that "[no] man [shall sprinkle] the water for cleansing upon those defiled
by a c[orpse.] Only a clean priest [shall sprinkle] [upo]n them" (4Q277 1 ii
7). Similarly, where the Mishnah (mNeg 3.1) states that all are eligible to in-
spect skin afflictions, though only a priest can declare the person "impure"
or "pure,"[75] CD 13.2–7 instructs that even if the priest is "a simpleton," the
decision to quarantine the affected person is still his own.[76] As shown above,
the Dead Sea Scrolls typically prescribe that the fourth-year fruit be given
to the priests, as opposed to rabbinic insistence that it be eaten by the owner
in Jerusalem. The same is true regarding the cattle tithe, which according
to 4QMMT (B: 63–64) belongs to the priests, but according to the Mishnah
(mZev 5.8) is eaten by the owner. Another manifestation of the priestly nature of the Scrolls is the inclination to follow the biblical Priestly School in

72. Knohl, "Post-Biblical Sectarianism"; Knohl, "Between Voice and Silence: The
Relationship between Prayer and Temple Cult," *JBL* 115 (1996): 17–30; Israel Knohl and
Shlomo Naeh, "*Milluim Ve-Kippurim*," *Tarbiz* 62.1 (1993): 17–44, at 35–38; for a slightly
different view see Eyal Regev, "Reconstructing Qumran and Rabbinic Worldviews: Dynamic Holiness vs. Static Holiness," in *Rabbinic Perspectives*, 87–112, at 106.

73. Kister, "Studies in 4Q Miqsat Ma'aśe Ha-Torah," 325–30; Regev, *The Sadducees
and their Halakhah*, 209–15, 416–18. Regev distinguishes Qumranic from Sadducean
law, but asserts that both developed from a single early, stringent, priestly system.

74. Schwartz, "Law and Truth"; Cana Werman, "'The Price of Mediation: The Role
of Priests in the Priestly Halakhah," in *Dead Sea Scrolls and Contemporary Culture: Proceedings of the International Conference Held at the Israel Museum, Jerusalem (July 6–8,
2008)*, ed. A. D. Roitman, L. H. Schiffman, and S. Tzoref (Leiden, 2011), 377–409.

75. See also *Sifra: Tazri'a, Parashat Nega'im, Perek* 1.8–10.

76. For a comprehensive discussion, see Fraade, *Legal Fictions*, 193–210.

cases of conflicting scriptural commands, whereas the rabbis usually follow Deuteronomy.[77]

Nominalism versus Realism, Static versus Dynamic Holiness

Some additional overarching features that distinguish between these two opposing systems of law have been suggested in the scholarship. Daniel R. Schwartz proposes that Sadducean and Qumranic law be characterized as realistic, and rabbinic halakhah in general as nominalistic. If the realistic approach anchors law in nature, in independently existing situations, and therefore ascribes legal implications to actual facts (such as CD 4:21's rationale for the prohibition on polygamy: that it violates the "principle of creation" as stated in Gen 1:27: "male and female he created them"), the nominalist approach views the law as autonomous, resulting from divine will, and not contingent on preexisting circumstances. It therefore subordinates legislation to human logic and juristic decision-making mechanisms. Accordingly, the Mishnah, as opposed to 4QMMT, regards the stream of liquid feeding a body of impure water as pure, referring to their separate legal definitions, but ignores the empirical unity of both liquids.[78] An outstanding example of rabbinic "nominalism" is the subjection of the calendar to human discretion and decision (mRH 2.8–9).[79] Aharon Shemesh refined the "realistic" characterization of the sectarian system. In his opinion, "it is not just that the law supposedly is based on reality and nature, but rather, that reality is supposed to reflect the law because God, by his will, created the world according to the law."[80] Countering Schwartz's theory, Jeffrey Rubenstein argues for the largely realistic nature of rabbinic halakhah, while not-

77. Werman, "Consumption of the Blood," 173–84; Schiffman, *Courtyards*, 297–313; Regev, "Reconstructing Qumran and Rabbinic Worldviews," 106.

78. Schwartz, "Law and Truth." These definitions follow Yochanan Silman, "Halakhic Determinations of a Nominalistic and Realistic Nature: Legal and Philosophical Considerations" (Hebrew), *Diné Israel* 12 (1984–85): 249–66. For subsequent debates regarding the case of the liquid, see Rubenstein and Hayes in the following notes.

79. On the calendar, see also Christine Hayes, "Legal Realism and the Fashioning of Sectarians in Jewish Antiquity," in *Sects and Sectarianism in Jewish History*, ed. S. Stern (Leiden. Boston, 2011), 124–28; Vered Noam, "Essentialism, Freedom of Choice, and the Calendar: Contradictory Trends in Rabbinic Halakhah," in *Nominalism and Realism in Halakha Revisited: Studies in the Philosophy of Halakha,* ed. S. L. Stone, Y. Lorberbaum, and J. Rubenstein, *Diné Israel* 30 (2015): 121*–137*.

80. Shemesh, *Halakhah*, 109.

ing that it also encompasses some marginal nominalistic phenomena.[81] In my past research of the halakhic field of impurity I arrived at a conclusion similar to Rubenstein's findings for other fields of halakhah: namely, that the tannaitic approach to impurity is grounded in a natural, immanent perception, though a secondary stratum represents a diametrically opposed perception, which subjects the concept of impurity to human sensibilities and intention.[82] Christine Hayes observes that although Rubenstein correctly pointed at certain dominant "realistic" conceptions within the rabbinic world, it is nonetheless true that "rabbinic law differs from Qumran law in that it incorporates *a strain of nominalism* according to which epistemological certainty in general and empirical considerations in particular may occasionally be devalued or overruled in the determination of law."[83]

Eyal Regev explains the controversies between the two systems as emanating from conflicting perceptions of the character of holiness. The sectarians viewed holiness as a dynamic entity which is sensitive to desecration, and therefore strove to protect the holy and avoid defilement through rigorous restrictions regarding sacred space, time, and food. The rabbis, in contrast, perceived holiness as "static," that is, as a halakhic status, unaffected by human desecration, and consequently held to much more lenient views regarding the laws of purity and sacrificial rites.[84]

B. A COMMON HERITAGE

Despite the yawning gap between the Qumran and rabbinic legal systems, both corpora have preserved a primary layer of basic praxis and exegesis which, although lacking an obvious, identifiable scriptural source, is deeply rooted in both cultures. The identical existence of these "ancestral traditions" points to an ancient legacy of shared material that predates the split

81. Jeffrey L. Rubenstein, "Nominalism and Realism in Qumranic and Rabbinic Law: A Reassessment," *DSD* 6.2 (1999): 157–83.

82. Vered Noam, "Ritual Impurity in Tannaitic Literature: Two Opposing Perspectives," *Journal of Ancient Judaism* 1 (2010): 65–103. Previously, I also utilized this distinction to indicate the similarity between the Qumranic worldview and the remnants of early halakhah within the tannaitic oeuvre; see my "Traces of Sectarian Halakha," esp. 82–84. For a collection of studies dedicated to a reassessment of this topic, see Stone, Lorberbaum, and Rubenstein, eds., *Nominalism and Realism in Halakha Revisited.*

83. Hayes, "Legal Realism," 129. Moreover, Hayes has shown that "rabbinic representations of heretics . . . share a common element—a realist resistance to rabbinic legal nominalism" (145).

84. Regev, "Reconstructing Qumran and Rabbinic Worldviews."

between the sects. These traditions frequently appear in early strata of tannaitic halakhah, either explicitly or in reworked form, vestiges that were often rejected by the Mishnah and preserved only in more marginal works of rabbinic literature, mostly in legal midrashim.[85]

Such similarity is explicit with respect to many features of the Qumran Sabbath regulations, also found in rabbinic halakhah, including the ban on labor on Friday well before sunset, the prohibition against speaking on the Sabbath about post-Sabbath tasks, the ban on walking further than the Sabbath limit, the obligation to wear clean clothes and consume already-prepared food on the Sabbath, and the essence of the Sabbath as "to bless God [. . .] eating and drinking."[86]

Similarly, an ancient tradition lacking an actual scriptural basis concerns the ability of liquids to convey and intensify impurity.[87] This ability is very dominant in tannaitic halakhah as well, from its earliest phases, albeit in a different and more developed form (e.g., mPar 8.5–7; mKel 8.4; tYom 1.6). But, as opposed to the legislation of the *Yaḥad*, which holds that any liquid can become impure and render foodstuffs susceptible to impurity, rabbinic halakhah arbitrarily and secondarily limits this capacity to seven liquids (mMakh 6.4; mTer 11.2; *Sifra, Shemini* 8:1). The same is true for corpse-blood impurity. Underscored in the *Temple Scroll* (50.6), this ability is also found in the earliest strata of tannaitic halakhah (mOhal 2.2; tNaz 5.1; bNaz 53a), despite the fact it is not expounded in Scripture as we know it.[88]

There are cases in which the rabbinic mainstream, particularly in the Mishnah, presents halakhah diametrically opposed to the sectarian one, but vestiges of a contradictory, semi-sectarian halakhah are hidden in other tannaitic sources, or in statements made by marginal or rejected sages, such as Beit Shammai,[89] Eliezer ben Hyrcanus,[90] or the school of Rabbi Ishmael. These are probably residues of the early, common heritage which were later

85. This phenomenon was frequently demonstrated by Aharon Shemesh. For a methodological discussion, see his *Punishments and Sins from Scripture to the Rabbis* (Hebrew; Jerusalem, 2003), 207–16. See also Kister, "A Common Heritage"; Noam, *From Qumran to the Rabbinic Revolution*, passim and 352, 355–56; Kister, "Emergence."

86. CD 10–11, see above. For discussion, see Schiffman, *Halakhah at Qumran*, 77–133. See also 4Q264a and 4Q421, citation from 4Q264 fi I 8. See Noam and Qimron, "A Qumran Composition."

87. E.g. 1QS 6.20–21; 4Q274 3 i 6–9, ii 4–12; 4Q284a 1 1–4; 11QT 49.7–10.

88. Vered Noam, "Corpse-Blood Impurity: A Lost Biblical Reading?" *JBL* 128.2 (2009): 243–51.

89. Vered Noam, "Beit Shammai and Sectarian Halakha" (Hebrew), *Jewish Studies* 41 (2001–2): 45–67.

90. Vered Noam, "Traces of Sectarian Halakha."

overruled by later rabbinic doctrine. For example, the tannaitic tradition in
Sifre Num. 6 presents a series of considerations in support of the rabbinic
law that fourth-year fruit should be eaten by its owners. Rabbi Ishmael presents the common rabbinic stance, "it is holy to the owner," and goes on to
refute the opposing position: "you say holy for the owner or holy for the
priests?" However, the best manuscript, MS Vatican 32, reads: "it is holy
for the priests. You say, holy for the priests or holy for the owner?" According to this version, Rabbi Ishmael was actually attempting to refute the accepted view in rabbinic literature, and to teach, in accord with the priestly-
sectarian opinion, that it is "holy for the priests." Menahem Kahana has
surmised that this wording is a relic of an exceptional halakhic position held
by Rabbi Ishmael, which was identical to the priestly position recorded, as
seen above, in many nonrabbinic sources.[91]

While prohibition of, or restrictions on, divorce appear in Qumranic
writings and also in the Gospels, the rabbinic approach is a lenient one
(mGit 9.10). However, the midrash in *Sifre Numbers* introduces a unique,
exceptional ruling, which contradicts everything found in other rabbinic
sources, namely that in order for a husband to divorce his wife, the wife
must be accused of adultery. There must be witnesses to the act who issued
a prior warning, and there must also be an organized judicial procedure—
as is customary in capital offenses. This opinion exhibits partial agreement
with the stringent, excluded opinion of Beit Shammai, probably representing an ancient layer of overruled halakhah.[92]

Two Models for Describing the Relationship
between Qumran and Rabbinic Law

As Aharon Shemesh has outlined, the chronological gap makes it difficult
to determine whether the disparities between Qumran legislation and rabbinic law should be ascribed to an early polemic, thus concluding that the
rabbinic system is a reflection of the Pharisaic forerunner ("the reflective
model"),[93] or instead mostly attributed to the centuries that had passed be-

91. Menahem I. Kahana, *Sifre on Numbers: An Annotated Edition*, vol. 2 (Hebrew;
Jerusalem, 2011), 69–70. See Vered Noam, "Embryonic Legal Midrash in the Qumran
Scrolls," in *The Hebrew Bible in Light of the Dead Sea Scrolls*, ed. N. David, K. De Troyer,
A. Lange, and S. Tzoref, FRLANT 239 (Göttingen, 2011), 247–50.

92. See Vered Noam, "Divorce in Qumran in Light of Early Halakha," *JJS* 56 (2005):
206–23.

93. The question of continuity between the Pharisees and the rabbis is a contested issue. However, even those who deny continuity must admit that some regulations identical to later rabbinic legislation are already extant in Second Temple times, be they Pharisaic or not. Representative studies regarding the Pharisees and the rabbis include Ellis

tween the two corpora ("the developmental model"). According to the latter, the sectarian material is understood to represent a shared protorabbinic system of halakhah used by the rabbis as a springboard to their own culture, while the nature of its Pharisaic counterpart remains unknown. As Shemesh rightly asserts, both models coexist within the framework of ancient Jewish law. When the DSS explicitly mentions opposing opinions which accord with rabbinic regulations, we can be sure that the debate is longstanding, and that the later rabbinic halakhah is actually a reflection of Second Temple practices. In this sense 4QMMT is especially valuable, as the practices it criticizes are among those that form part of the later rabbinic consensus. Thus, with 4QMMT and other cases of early sectarian polemic, we can be certain that each discrepancy between the sectarian legislation and the rabbinic framework as we know it represents an actual Second Temple controversy rather than a linear development. Tannaitic literature too contains ancient materials, recognizable by their literary characteristics, their contexts, and the names of the sages involved. Moreover, this literature also reflects and sometimes explicitly testifies to a polemic against opposing halakhic positions from the Second Temple era. Therefore, the rabbinic laws involved must have originated in a prerabbinic culture, like the sectarian laws against which they fought.

On the other hand, and in fact for most aspects of tannaitic culture as represented in the Mishnah, the prolific creation of five generations of sages—as compared to the previous Jewish literature and practice—is responsi-

---

Rivkin, "Defining the Pharisees: The Tannaitic Sources," *HUCA* 40–41 (1970): 205–49; Jacob Neusner, *From Politics to Piety: The Emergence of Pharisaic Judaism* (Englewood Cliffs, N.J., 1973); Yigael Yadin, *The Temple Scroll*, 1:400–401; Peter Schäfer, "Der Vorrabbinische Pharisäismus," in *Paulus und das antike Judentum: Tübingen-Durham-Symposium in Gedenken an den 50. Todestag Adolf Schlatters (Mai 1938)*, ed. M. Hengel and U. Heckel, WUNT 58 (Tübingen, 1988), 125–75; David Flusser, "4QMMT and the Benediction Against the Minim," in *Judaism of the Second Temple Period*, trans. A. Yadin, vol. 1: *Qumran and Apocalypticism* (Grand Rapids, Mich., 2007), 97–103; Schiffman, *Courtyards*, xxiii, 15–17; Hayim Lapin, *Rabbis as Romans: The Rabbinic Movement in Palestine, 100–400 CE* (New York, 2012), 46–49; Yair Furstenberg, *Purity and Community in Antiquity: Traditions of the Law from Second Temple Judaism to the Mishnah* (Hebrew; Jerusalem, 2016), 7–14; Noam, *Shifting Images*, 191–94, 213. For a viewpoint that detaches the Second Temple–period Pharisees from the later rabbinic establishment, see Morton Smith, "Palestinian Judaism in the First Century," in *Israel: Its Role in Civilization*, ed. M. Davis (New York, 1956), 67–81; Cohen, "Significance of Yavneh," 36–42. For a more extreme view, which maintains that rabbinic Judaism is a new "religion," see Seth Schwartz, *Imperialism and Jewish Society, 200 B.C.E. to 640 C.E.: Jews, Christians, and Muslims from the Ancient to the Modern World* (Princeton, 2001); Daniel Boyarin, *Border Lines: The Partition of Judaeo-Christianity* (Philadelphia, 2004).

ble for nothing less than a revolution, creating an innovative legal culture of mighty proportions.[94] By establishing dense, intricate fields of instructions at high resolution, these sages invented the very phenomenon of "halakhah." They initiated revolutionary divergence from the plain meaning of biblical commandments and introduced far-reaching processes of abstraction and conceptualization, including the novel concepts of "intention" and "thought." They supported nonpriestly legal authority and divorced the obligation of purification from the secular sphere. They drew on human rather than divine authority, subordinating their legislation to juristic decision-making mechanisms rather than to nature and reality alone. These combined, comprehensive, bold innovations produced the legal and theological earthquake that forms the foundation of the Mishnah.

---

94. Shemesh, *Halakhah in the Making*, 3–7; Halbertal, "The History of Halakhah;" Noam, "Emergence."

4. Mishnah and Tosefta

Shamma Friedman

The Tosefta has been called, and rightly so, a companion to the Mishnah.[1] The basic facts of the relationship between them have been noted by many scholars. Here we cite a recent summary:

> TOSEFTA [. . .] compilation of oral law designed to serve as a supplementary volume to the Mishnah. It generally follows the same arrangement as the Mishnah and is divided, like the Mishnah, into six orders, containing tractates, which are subdivided into chapters and *halakhot*. Most halakhic Mishnah tractates have corresponding Tosefta tractates, with the exception of three tractates from the order Qodashim (*Tamid*, *Midot*, and *Kinim*). The aggadic Mishnah tractate *Avot* has no corresponding Tosefta tractate, but *Avot de-Rabbi Natan*, one of the minor tractates, serves as a kind of supplement to tractate *Avot*.[2]

Within each tractate there are differences between the Tosefta and Mishnah regarding the number of chapters, and the order of arrangement of parallel material.

The current study is devoted to the phenomenon of parallels to Tosefta passages in the Mishnah and to the examination of the thesis that the Tosefta passage is often primary to its Mishnah parallel. In addition to my own studies, this thesis has been espoused by a number of contemporary scholars, including Judith Hauptman, Shaye J. D. Cohen, David Henshke, and Robert Brody.

---

1. Abraham Goldberg, "The Tosefta—Companion to the Mishna," *The Literature of the Sages, First Part*, ed. S. Safrai (Philadelphia, 1987), 283–302.

2. Avraham Walfish, "Tosefta," *The Oxford Dictionary of the Jewish Religion* (New York and Oxford, 1997), 699–700.

The question of the relationship between Mishnah and Tosefta is an ancient one, already posed to Sherira Gaon in the tenth century by R. Jacob b. Nissim, head of the scholars of Kairouan, Tunisia.

In his responsum[3] Sherira voices uncertainty as to whether the Tosefta was composed in the days of R. Judah the Prince or afterwards, but was certain however that it was compiled and redacted after the Mishnah, positing that the text of the Tosefta clearly indicates that it is posterior to the Mishnah and directly addresses its text.[4] Maimonides wrote in his foreword to Mishneh Torah: "R. Ḥiyya compiled the Tosefta to explain the subject matter of the Mishnah."[5]

The weighty authority of Sherira and Maimonides, and especially the latter, influenced subsequent scholars to regard the Tosefta *and each passage in it* as referring directly to the text of Mishnah.

For our purposes, one can subsume the mutual relation of Mishnah and Tosefta passages under three categories:

1. The Tosefta is pointing to a specific passage in the Mishnah, which it explains or expands.
2. The Tosefta presents an independent law or homily absent from the Mishnah, which falls within the subject matter of a given tractate.
3. The passage in the Tosefta is a literary parallel of that in the Mishnah.

3. *Iggeret Rav Sherira Gaon*, B. M. Lewin, ed., Haifa 1921, p. 34. See also p. 35, s.v. "*mihu.*"

4. "And as to the Tosefta, certainly it was R. Ḥiyya who redacted it, but we are uncertain whether he did it in the days of Rabbi [Judah the Patriarch] or after him. But without a doubt the Tosefta was redacted after the laws of our mishnah were redacted. And the words of the Tosefta are clearly posterior to those of the Mishnah, and were taught with reference to them" [trans. SJDC].

5. Cf. Maimonides's Introduction to his commentary on the Mishnah, ed. Qafiḥ, with Arabic original, p. 34 in the Hebrew numeration. There Maimonides defines the mission of the Tosefta as explaining what was unclear in the Mishnah, and "to add points which can be derived from the Mishnah, although with much effort, and he [R. Ḥiyya] deduced them in order to teach us how to learn and infer from the Mishnah." Maimonides's Mishnah-centricity is palpable. His Mishneh Torah was modeled after the Mishnah, even structurally. See Shamma Friedman, "The Organizational Pattern of the Mishneh Torah," *Jewish Law Annual* I (1978): 37–41. And conversely, just as the Mishneh Torah transmitted the complete corpus of *halakhah* perfectly, so, he holds, the Mishnah encompassed its entire extent, albeit sometimes encrypted. It was the Tosefta which spelled out these embedded allusions. Just as it was said that there is nothing in all of scripture that is not alluded to in the Torah, so, holds Maimonides, there is nothing in the Tosefta that you can't find in the Mishnah.

That is to say, the entire pericope is found in both the Mishnah and Tosefta, content and language, with the exception of phrases large or small which set apart each of the parallels.[6]

We have already alluded above to the prevailing predisposition among scholars to assume direct referencing of each and every Tosefta passage to the Mishnah, whenever at all possible. Undoubtedly the name Tosefta, which means "addition," was a major factor for this predilection, along with the influential stand taken by earlier scholars, especially Maimonides. The classification provided above, which is similar to that offered by Boaz Cohen,[7] differs slightly, but most significantly, in the third category:

As above	Boaz Cohen
The passage in the Tosefta is a literary parallel of that in the Mishnah. That is to say, the entire pericope is found in both the Mishnah and Tosefta, content and language, with the exception of phrases large or small which set apart each of the parallels.	Repetitions of the M. often with *explanatory glosses.*[8]

In Cohen's language, those phrases where the two differ are taken as "explanatory glosses." He does not entertain the converse: namely, that the Tosefta preserves older parallels of pericopae in the Mishnah.

Indeed, there is much reason to posit such a possibility, and after close investigation, to identify such cases. Just as the second category ("Tosefta presents an independent law or homily *absent* from the Mishnah") is widely

6. Shamma Friedman, *Tosefta Atiqta: Pesaḥ Rishon, Synoptic Parallels of Mishna and Tosefta Analyzed with a Methodological Introduction* (Hebrew; Ramat Gan, 2002), 10–11. Many scholars have presented lists categorizing the relationship of Mishnah/Tosefta passages. E.g. Moshe David Herr describes the relationship of passages thusly: "It contains (a) *beraitot* which are completely parallel to the *halakhot* of the Mishnah; (b) *beraitot* parallel to the *halakhot* of the Mishnah but differing somewhat in style or terminology; (c) *beraitot* which are totally dependent upon the *halakhot* of the Mishnah but add new material; (d) *beraitot* containing new material related to the material discussed in the *halakhot* of the Mishnah; (e) *beraitot* containing completely new material covering subjects and topics which are not discussed in the Mishnah at all, or are merely referred to indirectly" (Moshe David Herr, "Tosefta," *Encyclopaedia Judaica*, 1st edition [1997], Volume 15, col. 1283–85 at 1283). Regarding the classification provided by Boaz Cohen, see below.
7. Boaz Cohen, *Mishnah and Tosefta Shabbat* (New York 1935), 52.
8. Emphasis added.

taken to refer to pericopae *earlier* than the Mishnah, so in the third category ("the passage in the Tosefta is a literary parallel of that in the Mishnah") the Tosefta passage might be older than the corresponding Mishnah passage.

These pages are dedicated to the elucidation of this question. Its frame of reference is the sets of specific passages, and not the Tosefta as a whole. We shall claim that in a significant number of cases (but not necessarily always)[9] the comparison of Mishnah and Tosefta argues for the primacy of the Tosefta passage over against the Mishnah passage, often in such a way that the Tosefta pericope can well be taken as similar or identical to the material from which the Mishnah passage was carved. The approach is not dogmatic but rather philological, based upon critical investigation of every couplet. It does not aim to generalize from the findings, but argues that if a significant number of probabilities is established, there is a basis for considering such a relationship in other cases under analysis when such a conclusion is convincing.

Thus it will be claimed that the Tosefta contains many passages parallel to and earlier than similar Mishnah passages. This does not make the Tosefta as a whole earlier than the Mishnah, and it can be argued that the Tosefta is certainly later than the Mishnah, even though it contains some earlier material.

The dogmatic approach of viewing each Tosefta parallel of necessity addressing a passage in the Mishnah was the *modus operandi* of David Pardo, the outstanding traditional commentator on the Tosefta,[10] and maintained by Saul Lieberman in his monumental commentary *Tosefta Ki-feshutah*. This praxis viewed the opening words of the Tosefta pericope as a lemma from the parallel *mishnah*, and any difference in the Tosefta's wording vis-à-vis the Mishnah as the content of the Tosefta's comment on the given *mishnah*. Often the difference (= the supposed commentary) is minor or trivial, and the suggestion that the entire pericope was repeated in order to register a minor comment appears strained.[11]

We shall present the positions on this issue in a binary contrast: the historians of the Oral Law operating in the context of explaining the nature of the Tosefta (the traditional approach) versus those expressing an opinion in the context of critical analysis of specific passages (the philological approach). The dogmatic approach championed by Sherira generalizes from the first category of Mishnah/Tosefta relationships mentioned above ("The

---

9. See below n. 26.

10. In his work *Ḥasde David*.

11. Friedman, *Atiqta*, 11, 32–41; Friedman, *Parallels*, 15 [= *Studies*, 129]. This method was likewise employed by J. N. Epstein, cf. e.g. *Atiqta*, 23–28.

Tosefta is referring to a specific passage in the Mishnah, which it explains or expands"), for which there are indeed many examples in the Tosefta. Sherira acts as a historian of the Oral Law (indeed he pioneered this function) and as such undertakes sweeping categorization of the rabbinic works. This framework is divorced from scrutinizing the texts in question. Rather he generally builds upon explicit information within a corpus about itself or, as in this case, also bases himself upon information from the name (Tosefta = addition).

The dogmatic position does not consider the treatment of the tannaitic material in the Talmuds, which posits explicit (= named) tannaitic statements in the *baraitot* as the source material of anonymous teachings in the Mishnah, thus supplying their historical *Sitz im Leben*.[12] The term *stimta'ah* is used to identify an anonymous *mishnah* as being the words of a *tanna* named in the Tosefta (bMeg 26a).[13]

From Maimonides down to modern times, historians of the Oral Law repeated Sherira's position. Maimonides must have been the inspiration for commentators on the Tosefta who apply this rule throughout—David Pardo par excellence. An exception to this tendency is Jacob Naḥum Epstein, who posits an anterior position of Tosefta in a variety of types of Mishnah-Tosefta relationships. In discussing the attribution of anonymous Mishnah passages he calls upon "Tosefta and *baraitot* which cite the Mishnah passages in explicit attribution," i.e. the Tosefta and *baraitot* present named *tannaim* paralleling anonymous passages in the Mishnah.[14] When the Tosefta *does* refer to a *mishnah*, Epstein claims that the *mishnah* used by the Tosefta is an edition older than our *mishnah*.[15] In his introductory chap-

12. See below, n. 14. Cf. Jacob Naḥum Epstein, *Introduction to the Mishnaic Text* (Hebrew), 3rd edition (Jerusalem 2000), 7. For *mishnas* summarizing statements in the Tosefta see 641, 651, 671.

13. Cf. Shamma Friedman, *Studies in Tannaitic Literature: Methodology, Terminology and Content* (Hebrew; Jerusalem, 2013), 457–58. Also see below, re mPes 1.6–7 (example 6).

14. Jacob Naḥum Epstein, "Talmudic Study and its Needs" (Hebrew), *Yediᶜot Hamakhon Lemadaᶜe Hayahadut* 2 (1925), 5–22 at 21 [= *Madaᶜe Hayahadut* (Jerusalem, 1970)]: "the Tosefta and *the baraitot,* frequently adduce our Mishnah attributed to its author" (trans. SJDC).

15. Epstein. *Prolegomena*, 256–57; Friedman, *Atiqta*, 22 [= Friedman, *Studies*, 16]. See the following works by Judith Hauptman: "How Old is the Haggadah?", *Judaism* 51 (2002): 3–18; "Women in Tractate Pesaḥim" (Hebrew), *Atara L'Haim: Studies in the Talmud and Medieval Rabbinic Literature in Honor of Professor Haim Zalman Dimitrovsky*, ed. I. M. Ta-Shma et al. (Jerusalem 2000), 63–78; "Does the Tosefta Precede the Mishnah: Halakhah, Aggada, and Narrative Coherence," *Judaism* 50 (2001), 224–40; *Rereading the Mishnah* (Tübingen, 2005); "Mishnah as a Response to 'Tosefta,'" *The Synoptic*

ter to the Mishnah,[16] Epstein points out many Tosefta passages which he claims were the source material for parallel passages in the Mishnah,[17] often shortened by Rabbi.[18]

This being said, it is true, as pointed out above, that Epstein assigned many complete Tosefta parallels to the status of commentary to the Mishnah, considering the opening words as a lemma.

The other context in which opinions on our question are voiced is textual studies per se. Many a scholar, in the course of analyzing tannaitic material or commenting upon it, has argued for the primacy of the Tosefta parallel. The more the scholar's attention is focused upon the specific passage under study the less he or she feels bound by the dogmatic rules, if attention is directed to them at all.

A case in point is where the two tendencies exist within the same person. Abraham Goldberg, across a series of studies, carefully developed the thesis that every parallel passage in the Tosefta is secondary to its Mishnah parallel.[19] Yet as a commentator he correctly observed that the Tosefta contains some background material of the Mishnah, e.g. tShab 2.13 as the source upon which mShab 1.3 was based.[20] Other modern scholars in the course of their work have analyzed specific Mishnah pericopae as secondary to their

---

Problem in Rabbinic Literature, ed. S. J. D. Cohen (Providence, 2000), 13–34; "The Mishanh as a Reworking of an Earlier Tannaitc Collection" (Hebrew), *Neti'ot Ledavid: Jubilee volume for David Weiss Halivni*, ed. Y. Elman et al. (Jerusalem 2004), אס–אפ.

16. Jacob Naḥum Epstein, *Prolegomena ad Litteras Tannaiticas* (Hebrew; Jerusalem and Tel Aviv, 1957), 200–234.

17. See Friedman, *Atiqta*, 29–31 [= Friedman, *Studies*, 22–25]. Compare to Epstein's handling of mPes 3.2 (see *Atiqta*, 29 [= *Studies*, 23], number 2) my handling of these passages in *Atiqta*, chapter 11.

18. See Friedman, *Atiqta*, 30 [= Friedman, *Studies*, 24], number 5. In his *Introduction to the Text of the Mishnah*, an entry in the index of the 2000 edition (p. 1400) reads: "Mishnah passages shortened from . . . the Tosefta."

19. "One of the outstanding characteristics of the Tosefta is to quote the Mishnah with a stylistic change, in order to comment upon the Mishnah." Abraham Goldberg, "Order of the Laws and Characteristics of the Tosefta . . . Bava Qamma" (Hebrew), *Meḥqerei Talmud II: Talmudic Studies Dedicated to the Memory of Professor Eliezer Shimshon Rosenthal*, ed. Moshe Bar-Asher and David Rosenthal (Jerusalem, 1993), 151–96 at 152. See Friedman, *Atiqta*, 41–46 [= Friedman, 36–40].

20. Abraham Goldberg, *Commentary to Mishnah Shabbat* (Hebrew; Jerusalem, 1976), 57 n. 3 (see Friedman, *Atiqta*, 46 [= Friedman, *Studies*, 40]).

parallels in the Tosefta,[21] as have contemporary scholars, especially during the last several decades.

Jacob Neusner also fervently championed the total subjection of Tosefta to Mishnah as an ironclad rule. He writes: "Only seldom—for somewhat under a sixth—does the Tosefta present a statement that may be interpreted entirely independently of the Mishnah's counterpart, if any."[22] In his breakdown of types he states concerning "freestanding statements": "These statements can be fully understood only in dialogue with the Mishnah's counterpart."[23] He makes no explicit mention of the subject dealt with here.[24] Elsewhere he rejected Alberdina Houtman's thesis that Tosefta can be primary to Mishnah.[25]

THE PHILOLOGICAL APPROACH

David Henshke, although having voiced reservation regarding what he mistakenly viewed as my position,[26] has been an ardent champion of the theory

---

21. Among these we can point to J. H. Dünner, A. Guttmann, A. Spanier, Y. J. Weinberg, J. de Vries, B. Cohen, J. N. Epstein, A. Weiss, Ch. Albeck, and M. S. Feldblum (Friedman, *Atiqta*, 56–63 [= Friedman, *Studies*, 47–54]). D. Halivni noted: "it is clear that the source of the Mishnah is the Tosefta . . . the Mishnah in its usual way shortened the language of the Tosefta and removed the rhetorical question, and there is no doubt that one of the sources knew the other and took from it this expression . . . there is no reason to deny the primacy of this excerpt from the Tosefta" (trans. SJDC). See Friedman, *Atiqta*, 70 (= Friedman, *Studies*, 54); Jonah Fraenkel, "The Aggada in the Mishnah" (Hebrew), *Meḥqerei Talmud III: Talmudic Studies Dedicated to the Memory of Professor Ephraim E. Urbach*, ed. D. Rosenthal and Y. Sussmann (Jerusalem 2005), 655–83 at 670; see summary in Avraham Walfish, "Creative Redaction and the Power of Desire—A Study of the Redaction of Tractate Qiddushin: Mishnah, Tosefta, and Babylonian Talmud" (Hebrew), *JSIJ* 7 (2008): 31–79 at 41; Avraham Walfish, "Unity of Halakha and Aggada" (Hebrew), in *Higayon L'Yona: New Aspects in the Study of Midrash, Aggadah and Piyut in Honor of Professor Yona Fraenkel*, ed. J. Levinson et al. (Jerusalem, 2006), 309–31 at 327.

22. Jacob Neusner, "Describing Tosefta: A Systematic Account," in Fox and Meacham, *Introducing*, 39–71 at 40.

23. Neusner, "Describing Tosefta," 40.

24. See Friedman, *Atiqta*, 62 and n. 192 [= *Studies*, 53 and n. 201].

25. Jacob Neusner, *The Place of the Tosefta in the Halakhah of Formative Judaism: What Alberdina Houtman Didn't Notice* (Atlanta, 1998).

26. David Henshke, *'Mah Nishtannah': The Passover Night in the Sages' Discourse* (Hebrew; Jerusalem, 2016), 4. It is strange for Henshke to assume that my point of departure was an *a priori* assumption that Tosefta is always primary to Mishnah parallels. This

regarding the frequent dependency of Mishnah passages upon Tosefta parallels.[27] He writes:

> Although the redaction of the Tosefta was certainly posterior to that
> of the Mishnah, it is indeed well known that sometimes early traditions are found in the Tosefta, to which the redactor of the Mishnah
> directs his attention for the purpose of reworking or registering the
> opposing opinion which he holds.[28]

is nowhere stated in Tosefta Atiqta nor in any of my other publications. My only point
of departure was that it has been shown that Tosefta is *sometimes* primary to Mishnah,
and therefore *consideration* of such a determination is valid. It goes without saying (or it
should) that each case must be analyzed on its own merits. Thus in my foreword to the
Atiqta volume I indicated that "having arrived at this model we have seen that sometimes there are indications, which emerge from a meticulous investigation of the parallels, that may strengthen the possibility described [above] and may turn the scales to
its probability that sometimes [!] the Tosefta preserves an earlier version [. . .] having
proposed no small number of examples which appear convincing according to my humble opinion, we have determined it proper to investigate this phenomenon across consecutive parallels. Consequently this work examines the relationship between parallel
passages" (11). I opened the tenth chapter saying, "Concerning this mishnah it is possible
to apply, with no difficulty or problem, the conventional approach, that the Mishnah
is older than the laws in the Tosefta, and the Mishnah presents, in its tight and original formulation, the basic law, upon which the Tosefta adds two detailed laws" (249);
I also examined the obverse possibility there. In Shamma Friedman, "The Primacy of
Tosefta in Mishnah-Tosefta Parallels—*Shabbat* 16, 1: כל כתבי הקדש" (Hebrew), *Tarbiẓ* 62
(1993): 313–38 [= Friedman, *Studies*, 81–108], I considered the possible consequences
"if the hypothesis [רעיון] is found to be true and valid for most of the Mishnah/Tosefta
parallels, or a large number of them" (315 [= *Studies*, 83]). In "The Primacy of Tosefta in
Mishnah-Tosefta Parallels—Rabban Gamliel and the Sages" (Hebrew), *Bar-Ilan* 26–27
(1995): 277–88 [= Friedman, *Studies*, 109–21] I noted: "It is too early to say what percentage of the Mishnah/Tosefta parallels are convincingly explained in this manner, but I
am convinced that it is at least a considerable percentage, and perhaps most of them" [!]
(278 [= *Studies*, 119]). Blankovsky correctly observes about my position: "he insists that
every parallel should be examined on its own," Yuval Blankovsky, "Rabbinic Inquiry
(*Hakirah*) as the Place Rabbinic and Academic Talmudic Discourse Meet: The Case
of 'Two Hold a Cloak,'" *RRJ* 21 (2018): 82–107 at 102. This point is similarly correctly
described by others cited below.

27. This approach operates in his studies, see the many examples listed in the indices
of his books: *The Original Mishna in the Discourse of Later Tanna'im* (Hebrew; Ramat
Gan, 1997), see index there, 364, s.v. "Tosefta"; David Henshke, *Festival Joy in Tannaitic
Discourse* (Hebrew; Jerusalem, 2007), 453, s.v. "Mishnah"; *Mah Nishtannah*, 623, etc.;
Friedman, *Atiqta*, 63 and n. 197 [= Friedman, 54].

28. David Henshke, "What Should be Omitted in the Reading of the Bible? Forbidden Verses and Translations" (Hebrew), *Kenishta* 1 (2001): 13–42, at 16 in the Hebrew
numeration. There, in note 20, he refers affirmatively to two articles in my *Atiqta* series.

Henshke refers to the two-way relationship between the Mishnah and the Tosefta thusly: "Sometimes the Mishnah is earlier and the Tosefta is oriented to its text, and *sometimes conversely, early material preserved in the Tosefta is reworked in the Mishnah*";[29] "[. . .] the two opposite directions which serve alternately throughout the length of Mishnah/Tosefta parallels: primary material in the Tosefta which was reworked by the Mishnah [. . .] as against primary material in the Mishnah that was reworked in the Tosefta."[30]

Judith Hauptman has devoted numerous studies in support of the position that many Tosefta passages are earlier than their Mishnah parallels.[31] She has also addressed the overall relationship of the two works, claiming that the Tosefta was redacted earlier than the Mishnah. I feel, however, that this thesis (the earlier redaction of the Tosefta as a whole) is untenable,[32] due to the fact that the Tosefta includes teachings by tannaim of a generation after those found in the Mishnah,[33] including R. Ḥiyya and Rav,[34] who were of a status between tannaim and amoraim. Alongside Hauptman's position on the earlier redaction of the Tosefta is her assertion that the Tosefta refers not to our Mishnah (Rabbi), but to an earlier Mishnah collection.[35]

29. Henshke, *Festival Joy*, 6 n. 31; emphasis added. The specific case he refers to addresses the well-known lists of legal categories in mHag 1.8 and tEruv 8.24, determining that mHag 1.8 is a reworking of tEruv 8.24.

30. David Henshke, "Directing Prayer toward the Holy Place: The Plain Meaning of the Mishnah and Its Echoes in Talmudic Literature" (Hebrew), *Tarbiz* 80 (2011): 5–27 at 20 n. 64.

31. See above, n. 15. See also Alberdina Houtman, *Mishnah and Tosefta* (Tübingen, 1996); Reena Zeidman, "An Introduction to the Genesis and Nature of Tosefta," in Fox and Meacham, *Introducing*, 73–97; Merav Tubul-Kahana, "The Mishna-Tosefta Relationship in Light of Tetralemma and Trilemma Parallels" (Hebrew), *Sidra* 26 (2011): 61–80. Cf. Binyamin Katzoff, "A Story in Three Contexts: The Redaction of a Toseftan Pericope," *AJS Review* 38 (2014): 109–27; Blankovsky, *Inquiry*.

32. See Shamma Friedman, "Mishna-Tosefta Parallels" (Hebrew), *Proceedings of the Eleventh World Congress of Jewish Studies*, Div. C, vol. 1 (1993): 15–22 at 16 [= Friedman, *Studies*, 130].

33. Cf. Robert Brody, *Mishnah and Tosefta Studies* (Jerusalem, 2014), 116; Brody, *Mishnah and Tosefta Ketubbot: Text, Exegesis and Redaction* (Hebrew; Jerusalem 2015), 43.

34. tYom 1.7, tHul 6.3, tNeg 8.6. See Saul Lieberman, *Tosefta Ki-feshutah* (New York, 1955–88), *Yom Tov*, 923; Epstein, *Introduction*, 166; Epstein, *Prolegomena*, 243, 251; Friedman, *Primacy* 1993, 314 and n. 3 [Friedman, *Studies*, 82]; Friedman, *Primacy* 1995, 277 and n. 1 [= Friedman, *Studies*, 109]; Paul Mandel, "The Tosefta," *The Cambridge History of Judaism, Volume 4*, ed. S. T. Katz (Cambridge, 2006), 316–35 at 319 n. 10 [= Katz, *Tosefta* 2018, 111 n. 10].

35. Judith Hauptman, "The Tosefta as a Commentary on an Early Mishnah," *JSIJ* 4 (2005): 109–32.

In my opinion, these two claims do not necessarily go hand in hand; even though the redaction of Tosefta may have been posterior to the Mishnah (which seems to be the case), the Tosefta may still sometimes refer to an earlier Mishnah. This indeed was Epstein's position, based upon the divergence of sequence within the two works,[36] and so voiced by other scholars also.[37]

In his study on the relationship between Mishnah and Tosefta, Robert Brody writes: "In my opinion there is no doubt that Friedman is correct in claiming that the Tosefta sometimes preserves sources which are identical or very similar to those underlying specific passages of the Mishnah";[38] "On the whole I would agree with Shamma Friedman's characterization [. . .] My work on tractate Ketubbot led me to similar conclusions."[39] When comparing mKet 11.4 and tKet 11.3, Brody states: "I suggest that the Mishnah has reworked a source resembling the Tosefta and introduced a number of changes."[40]

The possibility that in *some* of the Mishnah-Tosefta parallels the Tosefta presents an earlier source has now reached general treatment by historians of the Oral Law. Shaye J. D. Cohen writes: "The Tosefta is immensely useful for reconstructing the sources of the Mishnah and Talmud. Material of

36. See Epstein, *Prolegomena*, 242, 257 ("in many places its order is the order of another Mishnah, earlier than our Mishnah") (trans. SJDC); Friedman, *Atiqta*, 12, 18, 20, 22 [= *Studies*, 6, 11, 13–14, 16], 98–99, 103. Goldberg rejected this thesis of Epstein's, and consistently correlated Tosefta with the sequence of our Mishnah, even at the cost of explaining the seeming disconnect as a "pedagogic" insight (See Goldberg, *Order*; *Companion*). Goldberg writes: "Many scholars claim that the Tosefta does not follow the order of the extant Mishna, but of an earlier recension of it"; "Epstein, *Tannaitic Literature*, 256–60 is one of the foremost exponents of this theory" (Goldberg, *Companion*, 285 and n. 8). Hauptman touched upon Epstein's tendency to speak of an early Mishnah, and thus "came close" to her idea that the Tosefta as a whole refers to an earlier Mishnah (Hauptman, *Commentary*, 112–13 and n. 15; 125). See also my comment in Primacy 1993, 321 [= *Studies*, p. 90].

37. See Friedman, *Atiqta*, 41–42, n. 117 [= *Studies*, 37–38 n. 128].

38. Brody, *Studies*, 113 [= Brody, *Ketubbot*, 43].

39. Brody, *Studies*, 115; Brody, *Ketubbot*, 122. Cf. further: "I agree with Friedman and Hauptman (and others) that in many cases the Tosefta preserves in a more original and rudimentary form material which appears in a revised and edited form in the Mishnah" (*Studies*, 141). Brody goes on (142–45) to deal at greater length with two cases in which he disagrees with my suggestion that the Tosefta may be more original. In each of these two cases, however, I claimed that it was quite possible that the Mishnah was primary, but still went on for exploration purposes to consider the converse, emphasizing supportive points (perhaps in an excessive manner). See *Atiqta*, 70, bottom, quoted by Brody, *Studies*, 141–42; *Atiqta*, 249, *Brody*, 144.

40. Brody, *Studies*, 132–33.

the second and third types may contain traces of the sources out of which the Mishnah was constructed."[41] The "second type" is described there as one in which "the Tosefta repeats more or less what is in the Mishnah, but in different language." Elsewhere Cohen states: "There is a growing consensus [. . .] that some Toseftan material is earlier than the Mishnah, that is, that the Tosefta in various places contains the literary stuff out of which the Mishnah was created. Hence the Tosefta is both earlier and later than the Mishnah."[42]

During recent decades I have seen dozens of studies that analyze specific Tosefta passages as being more original than their parallels in the Mishnah, and could have served as the Mishnah's literary source.[43] In the words of Joshua Kulp, his "article examines the relationship between two sets of parallel chapters in the Mishnah and Tosefta, uncovering phenomena which imply the primacy of the Tosefta over its mishnaic parallelism."[44] "The material in the Mishnah has been distilled, greatly abbreviated and stamped with a style common in the Mishnah."[45] Natan Braverman, in the course of his linguistic study of Mishnah and Tosefta, concludes specific investigations claiming, for example: "It would appear that the editor of the Mishnah had before him the source in the Tosefta, and the editor summarized the long conditional sentence in the Tosefta with a short conditional sentence

41. Shaye J. D. Cohen, "Tosefta," *Late Antiquity: A Guide to the Postclassical World*, ed. G. W. Bowersock et al. (Cambridge, Mass., 1999), 730.

42. Shaye J. D. Cohen, "Tosefta," *The Eerdmans Dictionary of Early Judaism*, ed. J. J. Collins and D. C. Harlow (Grand Rapids, 2001), 1317–18. See also Shaye J. D. Cohen, "Are There Tannaitic Parallels to the Gospels?," *JAOS* 116 (1996): 85–89, e.g. on mBer 8 and tBer 5.25–28: "defensible hypothesis is that the Tosefta is a fuller recension of the source from which the Mishnah derives" (88). Cf. Harry Fox, "Introducing," *Introducing Tosefta: Textual, Intratextual and Intertextual Studies* (New York 1999), ed. H. Fox and T. Meacham, 1–27 at 28; Chaim Milikowsky, "On the Formation and Transmission of Bereshit Rabba and the Yerushalmi: Questions of Redaction, Text-Criticism and Literary Relationships," *JQR* 92 (2002): 521–67 at 523–24; Stephen G. Wald, "Tosefta," *Encyclopaedia Judaica*, 2nd edition (2007), 70–72; and the coverage in Mandel, *Tosefta*, 2006, 327–28; Mandel, *Tosefta*, 2018, 124.

43. See Joshua Kulp, "Organisational Patterns in the Mishnah in Light of their Toseftan Parallels," *JJS* 58 (2007): 52–78. In his review of Harry Fox and Tirzah Meacham, eds., *Introducing Tosefta: Textual, Intratextual and Intertextual Studies* (New York, 1999), Eliezer Segal views Shamma Friedman, "The Primacy of Tosefta to Mishnah in Synoptic Parallels," in Fox and Meacham, 99–121, as "eminently persuasive," Eliezer Segal, Review of Fox and Meacham, Introducing, *JAOS* 121 (2001), 502–3.

44. Kulp, *Patterns*, 52.

45. Kulp, *Patterns*, 62.

in the Mishnah";[46] similarly, "It would appear that the passage in the Tosefta is the source of our *mishnah.*"[47]

It is frequently suggested that our subject is in dispute among the scholars. This is an improper use of the word "dispute," since no one has undertaken any research, let alone a comprehensive study, offering a challenging response to this thesis. Indeed, it would be difficult to claim that the Tosefta parallel is never primary to Mishnah. The thesis itself only claims that *sometimes* or *often* the Tosefta is primary to Mishnah. What remains to be done is to advance such an investigation across all Six Orders, to determine the relative frequency of this phenomenon. If a significant number of the cases so far studied appear reasonable, the possibility should be considered and weighed when studying Mishnah-Tosefta parallels.

Such an investigation is by its nature dependent upon subjective evaluation on the part of the researcher, as is largely true throughout the humanities, where reasoned probability serves in place of ironclad objective proof.[48]

EXAMPLES

I will present here selected examples to illustrate Mishnah-Tosefta parallels of the type we have been discussing, and hopefully demonstrate the reasonableness and probability of our conclusions. I shall open with one of the first cases I have dealt with, going back to a study published in 1971.[49] The context of these studies was not an investigation of the Tosefta, but rather philological examination of specific passages in the course of other studies; in other words, in an atmosphere divorced from any theories about the Tosefta, unencumbered by dogma, but rather in a natural and text-centered manner.

---

46. Natan Braverman, "Concerning the Language of the Mishnah and the Tosephta" (Hebrew), *Proceedings of the Ninth World Congress of Jewish Studies*, D, vol. 1 (Jerusalem 1985): 31–38 at 35.

47. Braverman, *Language*, 36.

48. As ably expressed by Naḥmanides (Milḥemet HaShem, Berakhot, beginning): שאין בחכמה הזאת מופת ברור כגון חשבוני התשבורת ונסיוני התכונה. We recall Metzger's admonition: "To teach another how to become a textual critic is like teaching another how to become a poet," Bruce M. Metzger and Bart D. Ehrman, *The Text of the New Testament: Its Transmission, Corruption, and Restoration*, 4th ed. (New York and Oxford, 2005), 305.

49. A second study was published in 1975, see Shamma Friedman, "Found Objects in the Public Domain" (Hebrew), *Dine Israel* 6 (1975): 169–75.

1.

Tosefta Shevi'it 2.4 (p. 169)	Mishnah Shevi'it 2.9
	הַבְּצָלִים הַסָּרִיסִים
פּוֹל המצרי שמנע ממנו מים שלשים יום לפני ראש השנה מתעשר לשעבר ומותר לקיימו בשביעית, אם לאו אסור לקיימו בשביעית ומתעשר לשנה הבאה	וּפּוֹל מִצְרִי שֶׁמָּנַע מֵהֶן מַיִם שְׁלֹשִׁים יוֹם לִפְנֵי רֹאשׁ הַשָּׁנָה מִיתְעַשְּׂרִין לְשֶׁעָבַר וּמוּתָּרִין בַּשְּׁבִיעִית, וְאִם לָאו אֲסוּרִין בַּשְּׁבִיעִית וּמִתְעַשְּׂרִין לְשָׁנָה הַבָּאָה.
במ׳ דברים אמורים בשל שקי, אבל	
בשל בעל שמנע הימנו שתי מריעות	וְשֶׁלַּבַּעַל שֶׁמָּנַע מֵהֶן שְׁתֵּי עוֹנוֹת
דברי ר׳ מאיר וחכמים או׳ שלש.	דְּבֵ׳ ר׳ מֵאִיר וַחֲכָמ׳ אוֹמ׳ שָׁלוֹשׁ.

The Tosefta is virtually identical with the Mishnah, except for two main differences: only the Mishnah has הבצלים הסריסים ("shallots"); Mishnah has עונות, Tosefta: מריעות ("spells"). There would be no reason for eliminating הבצלים הסריסים on the part of the Tosefta, whereas the Mishnah "improves" the text with a substantive addition. The word עונות in the Mishnah substitutes for the rare and difficult word מריעות in the Tosefta.[50] The context of my 1971 study[51] was the irregular word order caused by the addition at the beginning of the Mishnah.

2.

Tosefta Shabbat 13.14 (pp. 61–62)	Mishnah 'Eruvin 4.2
ספינה הבאה בים אין עולין מתוכה ליבשה אלא אם כן היו בתוך התחום עד שלא חשיכה.	
מעשה ברבן גמליאל וזקנים שהיו באין בספינה וקדש עליהן היום,	פַּעַם אַחַת לֹא נִבְנְסוּ לַלְּמֶן עַד שֶׁחֲשֵׁיכָה

50. See Lieberman, *Tosefta Ki-feshutah*, 500–501. The Mishnah also tightens the second clause, perhaps in order to avoid the unusual word שקי (see Lieberman, *Tosefta Ki-feshutah*).

51. Shamma Friedman, "The 'Law of Increasing Members' in Mishnaic Hebrew" (Hebrew), *Lěšonénu* 35 (1971): 117–29, 192–206 at 195 [= M. Bar-Asher, ed., *Studies in Mishnaic Hebrew* (Hebrew), vol. II (Jerusalem, 1980), 299–326].

אמ' לו לרבן גמליאל מה אנו לירד	אָמְרוּ לוֹ לְרַבָּן גַּמְלִיאֵ' מָה אָנוּ לֵרֵד
אמ' להם צופה הייתי והיינו בתוך התחום עד שלא חשיכה, אלא נטרפה הספינה פעמים הרבה.	וְאָמַר לָהֶם מוּתָּר שֶׁכְּבָר הָיִיתִי מִסְתַּכֵּל וְהָיִינוּ בְּתוֹךְ הַתְּחוּם עַד שֶׁלֹּא חָשֵׁיכָה.

Mishnah Shabbat 16.8

באותה שעה עשה גוי סקלא לירד בו, אמרו לו מה אנו לירד, אמ' להם הואיל ולא בפנינו עשאו מותרין אנו לירד בו	מַעֲשֶׂה בְרַבָּן גַּמְלִיאֵ' וְהַזְּקֵנִים שֶׁהָיוּ בָאִין בִּסְפִּינָה [וְ]עָשָׂה גוֹי כֶּבֶשׁ לֵירֵד [בּוֹ]
וירדו בו הזקנים.	וְיָרְדוּ בּוֹ הַזְּקֵנִים.

Tosefta Shabbat 13.14 reports of a case concerning the arrival of Rabban Gamaliel and the sages to a harbor by ship—one integrated report containing two stages: A—entering the port late Friday afternoon, leaving an uncertainty as to whether Shabbat had begun or not; B—the gangway having been put into place by a non-Jew, the question was raised, would they not be permitted to descend on it.[52] The two stages are described as coming in sequence in one event, with the same questioning phrase repeated twice: מה אנו לירד ("May we descend"). Of the two issues, the issue of Sabbath limits is the only one relevant to the context in the Tosefta, but the source is cited in its entirety, and thus the question regarding the gangway is also included, despite its non-pertinence to the context. In contrast, the Mishnah separates the two issues, the first being placed in Eruvin, with the laws of Sabbath limits, and the second in Shabbat, with the laws of work done by a non-Jew on the Sabbath. The Mishnah thus displays the handiwork of a skillful redactor of legal texts.

Thus the history of these texts flows from an early source now embedded in our Tosefta to a later reworking in the Mishnah.[53]

Besides the masterly "Maimonidean" skill of arrangement and classification on the part of the compiler of the Mishnah, he also shows his hand in stylistic editing. Greek-Latin סקלא becomes Hebrew כבש. mishnaic מסתכל takes the place of biblical צופה. A formal declaration of permissibility (מותר)

---

52. In the initial clause of mShab 16.8: נָכְרִי . . . עָשָׂה כֶּבֶשׁ לֵירֵד בּוֹ יֵרֵד אַחֲרָיו יִשְׂרָא' וְאִם בִּשְׁבִיל יִשְׂרָא' אָסוּר.

53. Abraham Goldberg registered the opposite opinion, taking the Tosefta as a combination of the two *mishnas*, one in 'Eruvin and one in *Shabbat* (Goldberg, *Shabbat*, 300).

is added to a halakhic explanation. Also, the word מותר ("it is permitted") is a linguistic usage later than מותרין ("[we are] permitted").

Halakhic editing is also evident. The grounds for the permission of the gangway הואיל ולא בפנינו עשאו ("since he did not make it in our presence") was eliminated in the Mishnah, because according to the context there the reason should be הואיל ולא בשבילנו עשאו ("since he did not make it for us").[54]

Thus the arrangement, language,[55] and editing point to the reworking and development in the Mishnah of an original version in the Tosefta.[56]

3.

Tosefta Bava Meṣiʿa 7.10 (p. 100)	Mishnah Bava Meṣiʿa 6.5
השוכר את החמור	הַשּׂוֹכֵר אֶת הַחֲמוֹר לְהָבִיא חִטִּים וְהֵבִיא שְׂעוֹרִים תְּבוּאָה וְהֵבִיא תֶּבֶן חַיָּב שֶׁהַנֶּפַח[57] קָשֶׁה כַּמַּשּׂוֹאִי.
להביא לתך חטין והביא שש עשרה שעורים[58] פטור, ואם הוסיף על משאו חייב.	לְהָבִיא לֶיתֶךְ חִטִּים וְהֵבִיא לֶיתֶךְ שְׂעוֹרִים פָּטוּר וְאִם הוֹסִיף עַל מַשּׂוֹאוֹ חַיָּב.
וכמה יוסיף על משאו ויהא חייב, סמכוס או' משם ר' מאיר קב לכתף, שלש סאין לעגלה, וספ' לפי מה שהיא.	וְכַמָּה יוֹסִיף עַל מַשּׂוֹאוֹ וִיהֵי חַיָּב, סוֹמְכֹס אוֹ' מִשֵּׁם ר' מֵאִיר סְאָה לַגָּמָל וּשְׁלוֹשֶׁת קַבִּים לַחֲמוֹר.

The Mishnah's second clause, לְהָבִיא לֶיתֶךְ חִטִּים וְהֵבִיא לֶיתֶךְ שְׂעוֹרִים ("to carry a *letekh* of wheat and it carried a *letekh* of barley"), is paralleled, almost identically, by the Tosefta: להביא לתך שש עשרה חטין והביא שעורים ("to carry a *letekh* of wheat and it carried sixteen [*seahs*] of barley"). However, the Tosefta is more clearly understood. Instead of carrying a *letekh* volume of wheat, which is 15 *seahs*, the hirer loaded the beast with 16 *seahs* of barley. Nonetheless he is exempt from liability for any damage suffered by the beast, for 16 *seahs* of barley weigh the same as 15 *seahs* of wheat, barley being lighter than wheat. The hirer added no weight, only volume, and *an addition of volume does not*

54. The reason given in the Tosefta was also eliminated in the parallel *baraita* in the Bavli.

55. Natan Braverman independently came to the same conclusion regarding this Mishnah/Tosefta relationship based on linguistic criteria (Braverman, *Language*, 36).

56. Friedman, *Parallels*, 18–19 [= *Studies*, 134]. The detailed study is at Friedman, Primacy 1995.

57. Codex Kaufmann reads: שֶׁהַנֶּפָה in error.

58. This word is missing in the Vienna codex, and added by Lieberman on the basis of other witnesses.

make him liable for damage. In the Mishnah however, he is exempted from damage for loading 15 *seahs* of barley in place of the contracted 15 *seahs* of wheat. Is this not obvious, for he has increased neither weight nor volume? As the *rishonim* argued, this clause is superfluous.

The Mishnah must be understood in light of its first clause. Loading an equal weight of barley when contracted for wheat makes the hirer liable, as the *additional volume constitutes a breach of contract*. The tanna of the Mishnah wanted to include the two sources he inherited. In order to do so he had to emend the second clause, making it superfluous, after the first clause already indicated a liability for change in either weight or volume. He could not include the second clause as it appears in the Tosefta (exempt on 16 *seahs*) because according to the first clause he would be liable. In any case he wanted to include the language of the Tosefta and therefore changed 16 to 15, with the result that the clause is superfluous in itself, even for serving as a source for a deduction, for we already know from the first clause that a change in either weight or volume makes him liable.[59]

4.

Tosefta Pisḥa 3.12 (p. 154)	Mishnah Pesaḥim 3.7
אי זה צופה[60], הרואה ואינו מפסיק. מיכן **אתה אומ׳**	
ההולך לשחוט את פסחו ולמול את בנו ולוכל סעוד׳ אירוסין בבית חמיו ונזכר שיש לו חמץ בתוך הבית, אם יש לו שהות כדי שיחזור חוזר, ואם לאו אין חוזר.	הַהוֹלֵךְ לִשְׁחוֹט אֶת פִּסְחוֹ וְלָמוֹל אֶת בְּנוֹ וְלֶאֱכֹל סְעוּדַּת אֵירוּסִים בְּבֵית חָמִיו וְנִזְכַּר שֶׁיֵּשׁ לוֹ חָמֵץ בְּתוֹךְ הַבַּיִת אִם יָכוֹל לַחְזוֹר וּלְבָעֵר וְלַחְזוֹר בְּמִצְוָתוֹ יַחֲזוֹר וְאִם לָאו יְבַטֵּל בְּלִבּוֹ.

---

59. See Friedman, *Parallels*, 135–36. A detailed analysis is found in Friedman, *Talmud Arukh: BT Bava Meẓi'a VI, Critical Edition with Comprehensive Commentary* (Hebrew), Commentary Volume (Jerusalem 1990), 223–38 (see especially 223–25, 232–36); Shamma Friedman, *Talmud Arukh: BT Bava Meẓi'a VI, Critical Edition with Comprehensive Commentary* (Hebrew), Text Volume and Introduction (Jerusalem, 1996); 224. For other examples from mBM see Friedman, *Arukh Commentaries*, 7 n. 25, 71 n. 1, 98 n. 5).

60. See mPes 3.8; Lieberman, *Tosefta Ki-feshutah*, Pisḥa, 531.

This Tosefta passage itself reveals that it preserves an earlier source, in quoting a halakhic Midrash with the formula מיכן אתה אומ׳, a midrash which itself quotes a *halakhah*.[61] That *halakhah* corresponds to our *mishnah*, the first 18 words verbatim. The *halakhah* in the Tosefta does not add to our *mishnah*; the opposite is true.

This *mishnah* and the almost verbatim Tosefta pericope portray a di-lemma resulting from conflicting obligations. If, on the fourteenth of Ni-san, one sets out on a journey to Jerusalem in order to slaughter the Paschal lamb, or on a journey in order to circumcise his son (two positive command-ments whose omission is punishable by *karet*), and then recalled that he had not removed *ḥametz* from his home, what should be done? If there is time to perform both the removal and the circumcision, he must return home. "If not, he should not return," says the Tosefta. No matter how disconcerting it may be to have violated the commandment of the removal of *ḥametz*, its observance has been outweighed in this case by a more binding (positive) commandment,[62] since the fulfillment of both is impossible.

In the *mishnah*, the conclusion of this otherwise practically verbatim law is "and if not [able to return] he should cancel (the *ḥametz*) in his mind!" The depressing result of the ancient law preserved in the Tosefta, offering no re-lief whatsoever, is here somewhat ameliorated, at least on the psychological level. If you can't get rid of it, at least declare it null and void (in your mind!). But according to the Tosefta, *ḥametz* cannot be canceled. There is no choice but to determine which obligation outweighs the other.

In the system of the Bavli's legal conceptualization, the remedy in our *mishnah* was apparently considered absolutely valid, and consequently the concept of toraitic cancellation of *ḥametz* was formulated.[63]

61. See Mekhilta de-Rashbi 13.7 (39); cf. Lieberman, *Tosefta Ki-feshutah*, 532.

62. ואם, דאמר רבי שמעון בן לקיש: כל מקום שאתה מוצא עשה ולא תעשה, אם אתה יכול לקיים לקיים שניהם - מוטב, ואם לאו - יבא עשה וידחה לא תעשה (bShab 133a).

63. Friedman, *Parallels*, 20 [= *Studies*, 136]. The detailed study is at Friedman, *Atiqta*, 333–37.

5.

Tosefta Pisḥa 1.4 (p. 141)	Mishnah Pesaḥim 1.4–5

ר' מֵאִיר אוֹ' אוֹכְלִים כָּל חָמֵשׁ וְשׂוֹרְפִים
בִּתְחִילַּת שֵׁשׁ ר' יְהוּדָה אוֹמֵ' אוֹכְלִים כָּל
אַרְבַּע וְתוֹלִים כָּל חָמֵשׁ וְשׂוֹרְפִים בִּתְחִילַּת
שֵׁשׁ.

ר' יהודה או' משם רבן גמליאל שתי חלות
של תודה פסולות ומונחות על גג האיסטבה,
כל זמן שהן מונחות כל העם אוכלין חולין,
ניטלא אחת מהן כל העם אוכלין תרומה,
ניטלו שתיהן שורפין אילו ואילו.

וְעוֹד אָמַ' ר' יְהוּדָה [שְׁתֵּי] חַלּוֹת שֶׁלתּוֹדָה
פְּסוּלוֹת וּמוּנָּחוֹת עַל גַּג הָאִיסְטְוָוה כָּל זְמַן
[שֶׁהֵן] מוּנָּחוֹת כָּל הָעָם אוֹכְלִים, נִיטְלָה אַחַת
מֵהֶן תּוֹלִים לֹא אוֹכְלִים וְלֹא שׂוֹרְפִים, נִיטְלוּ
שְׁתֵּיהֶן הִתְחִילוּ כָּל הָעָם שׂוֹרְפִים. רַבָּן גַּמְלִיאֵ'
אוֹ' חוּלִּים נֶאֱכָלִים כָּל אַרְבַּע וּתְרוּמָה כָּל
חָמֵשׁ וְשׂוֹרְפִים בִּתְחִילַּת שֵׁשׁ.

The Mishnah provides an hour-to-hour schedule breakdown for 14 Nisan. A question arises regarding R. Yehudah's opinion in the Mishnah. Why is the fifth hour empty, serving as a holding period? The same question applies to the middle period of R. Yehudah's second statement, when only one loaf is in place on the portico roof. The intermediate waiting period puzzled the *amoraim*, with various suggestions made, none however fully satisfying the *rishonim*.

In the Tosefta the entire subject of "the two loaves of Thank-offering" is more understandable, upon the historic background of Temple practices, with the Kohanim eating Terumah of *ḥametz* during the intermediate period. In mishnah 4 the entire issue is recast for the post-destruction period, with hours taking the place of loaves in R. Yehudah's statement, and R. Meir going one step further and eliminating the hiatus of a middle hour of waiting altogether. In mishnah 5 the compiler appends R. Yehudah's description of the Temple practice, so as not to lose this colorful portrayal. However, the middle hour was adjusted to R. Yehudah's statement in mishnah 4 (activity suspended), with its true content added through Rabban Gamaliel's statement.[64]

---

64. Friedman, *Parallels*, 21 [= *Studies*, 136–37]. The full study is at Friedman, *Atiqta*, 104–10.

6.

Tosefta Pisḥa 1.5–6 (p. 141–42)	Mishnah Pesaḥim 1.6–7

שורפין תרומה תלויה טמאה וטהורה כאחד
דברי ר׳ מאיר, וחכמים אומ׳ תלויה בפני
עצמה טהורה בפני עצמה וטמאה בפני
עצמה.

ר׳ חֲנַנְיָה סְגַן הַכֹּהֲנִים אוֹ׳ מִימֵיהֶם שֶׁלַכֹּהֲנִים
לֹא נִמְנְעוּ מִלִשְׂרוֹף אֶת הַבָּשָׂר שֶׁנִיטְמָא
בְּוֹלַד הַטֻמְאָה עִם הַבָּשָׂר שֶׁנִיטְמָא(ה) בְּאַב
הַטֻמְאָה אַף עַל פִּי [שֶׁ]מוֹסִיפִין לוֹ [טוּמְאָה]
עַל טוּמְאָתוֹ.

אמ׳ ר׳ שמעון לא נחלקו ר׳ ליעזר ור׳ יהושע
על הטהורה ועל הטמאה שישורפין זו בפני
עצמה וזו בעצמה. על מה נחלקו, על התלויה
ועל הטמאה. שר׳ ליעזר אר׳ תישרף זו
בעצמה וזו בעצמה, ור׳ יהושע או׳ שתיהן
כאחת.

הוֹסִיף ר׳ עֲקִיבָה מִימֵיהֶן שֶׁלַכֹּהֲנִים לֹא נִמְנְעוּ
מִלְהַדְלִיק אֶת הַשֶׁמֶן שֶׁנִיפְסַל בִּטְבוּל יוֹם בְּנֵר
שֶׁנִיטְמָא בְטָמֵא מֵת אַף עַל פִּי [שֶׁ]מוֹסִיפִין
לוֹ [טוּמְאָה] עַל טוּמְאָתוֹ.

אמ׳ ר׳ יוסה אין הנדון זה דומה לראיה,
בשר שנטמא בולד הטומאה עם בשר
שנטמא באב טומאה שניהן טמאין אלא שזה
טמא טומאה חמורה וזה טמא טומאה קלה,
וכן שמן שנפסל בטבול יום בנר שניטמא
טמא מת שניהן טמאין אלא שזה טמא
טומאה חמורה וזה טומאה קלה, ואני אומ׳
שישורפין תרומה שניטמאת בולד טומאה עם
תרומה שניטמאת באב הטומאה אף על פי
שמוסיפין לה טומאה על טומאתה, ותלויה
וטמאה אומ׳ אני שהתלויה טהורה, אם
נשרפת עם הטמאה נמצאת זו מטמאתה.

אָמַ׳ ר׳ מֵאִיר מִדִבְרֵיהֶם לָמַדְנוּ שֶׁשׂוֹרְפִּים
תְרוּמָה טְהוֹרָה עִם הַטְמֵאָה בַּפֶּסַח אָמַ׳ לוֹ
ר׳ יוֹסֵי אֵינָה הִיא הַמִידָה מוֹדֶה ר׳ אֱלִיעֶזֶר
וּר׳ יְהוֹשֻעַ שֶׁשׂוֹרְפִּין זוֹ לְעַצְמָהּ וְזוֹ לְעַצְמָהּ
וְעַל מָה נֶחְלְקוּ עַל הַתְלוּיָה וְעַל הַטְמֵאָה שֶׁר׳
אֱלִיעֶזֶר אוֹמֵ׳ תִּישָׂרֵף זוֹ לְעַצְמָהּ וְזוֹ לְעַצְמָהּ
וּר׳ יְהוֹשֻעַ אוֹ׳ שְׁתֵּיהֶן כְּאַחַת.

בית שמי אומ׳ אין שורפין בשר טהור עם
בשר טמא ובית הלל מתירין.

In mishnah 7 we find the statement אמ׳ לו ר׳ יוסי אינה היא המידה מודה ר׳ אליעזר
ור׳ יהושע ששורפין זו לעצמה וזו לעצמה etc. An examination of the Tosefta shows
that the Mishnah presents an abbreviated *combination* of the language of
two tannaim. In the Tosefta we find: אמ׳ ר׳ יוסה אין הנדון זה דומה לראיה and he
proceeds to provide his proof. The continuation in the Mishnah מודה ר׳ אליעזר
etc. is not part of R. Yose's speech as it is in the Tosefta, and does not constitute the proof he offered. It is rather what R. Shimon said in the Tosefta.

The Bavli was pressed to supply a forced explanation: R. Yose erred,
R. Meir pointed out his error to him, and then R. Yose went ahead and raised
a second difficulty. However, the Yerushalmi openly presents a higher-

critical explanation: תניין אינון . . . הדא דתנינן מודה ר׳ אליעזר . . . רבי שמעון שנייא.
I.e. the Mishnah's report of R. Yose's statement is composed of the speech
of two separate tannaim. The statement מודה ר׳ אליעזר etc. was actually not
said by him but was taught by R. Shimon. In other words, even though in
the Mishnah the entire statement is attributed to R. Yose, in actuality the
second part is the language of R. Shimon.

The Yerushalmi clearly indicates that the Tosefta contains the original
statements of the tannaim involved, and the Mishnah provides an editorial
reworking of these same statements.

7.

Tosefta Kiddushin 1.13 (pp. 280–81)	Mishnah Kiddushin 1.10
העושה מצוה אחת מטיבין לו ומאריכין לו ימיו ושנותיו ונוחל את האדמה.	כָּל הָעוֹשֶׂה מִצְוָה אַחַת מְטִיבִּים לוֹ וּמַאֲרִיכִים אֶת יָמָיו וְנוֹחֵל אֶת הָאָרֶץ
וכל העובר עבירה אחת מריעין לו ומקטפין את ימיו ואין נוחל את הארץ, ועל זה נאמ׳ וחוטא אחד יאבד טובה הרבה (קהלת ט יח), בחטא יחידי זה יאבד ממנו טובות הרבה.	וְכָל שֶׁאֵינוּ עוֹשֶׂה מִצְוָה אַחַת אֵין מְטִיבִּים לוֹ וְאֵין מַאֲרִיכִין אֶת יָמָיו וְאֵינוּ נוֹחֵל אֶת הָאָרֶץ

Lieberman wrote: "The Tosefta explains that 'whoever does not perform a single commandment' [Mishnah] means that he transgresses it
[Tosefta]."[65] But would it not seem simpler to say that the Mishnah is "im-
proving" and softening the harsh style throughout the second clause of the
Tosefta? This would explain the awkwardness of the Mishnah's language regarding "not performing a commandment." Lieberman writes further that
the first clause in the Tosefta is a lemma from the Mishnah. The Tosefta
would rather seem a parallel to the Mishnah representing an original version, which the Mishnah reworked to arrive at a more delicate style.[66]

---

65. *Tosefta ki-feshutah*, 927–28.
66. See Friedman, *Parallels*, 21 [= *Studies*, 137–38] (cited approvingly by Menachem
Katz, "How is the Land Acquired? One Who Does a *Mitzvah*—A Literary Analysis of
the End of *Masechet Hakinyanim* in the Mishnah" (Hebrew), *Derekh Aggada* 9 (2006):
143–54 at 149 n. 20); Walfish, *Unity*, 313 n. 20. Compare mMak 3.15, where fulfilling one
commandment is contrasted to violating one prohibition.

Chanoch Albeck (Mishnah commentary ad loc.) briefly, and somewhat hesitatingly, took the Mishnah's style ("not perform one commandment") as a euphemism for committing one sin. In his supplementary notes he deals with the Tosefta, but not in this context. David Halivni deems Albeck's explanation "improbable."[67] Judith Hauptman already posited that this *mishnah* is posterior to the parallel Tosefta and reacting to it,[68] although her frame of reference is different than mine, arguing for the Mishnah having a different message than the Tosefta.

8.

Tosefta Kippurim 1.12 (pp. 224–25)

מעשה בשנים כהנים שהיו שוים שוים רצים ועולין בכבש, דחף אחד מהן את חבירו לתוך ארבע אמות, נטל סכין ותקע לו בלבו.

בא ר׳ צדוק ועמד על מעלות האילים ואמ׳: שמעוני בית ישראל אחינו, הרי הוא או׳ כי ימצא חלל וגו׳ ויצאו זקיניך ושפטיך ומדדו (דברים כא א–ב), בואו ונמדוד על מי ראוי להביא עגלה, על ההיכל או על העזרות. געו כולם אחריו בבכיה, ואחר כך בא אביו של תינוק, אמ׳ להם אחינו אני כפרתכם עדיין בנו מפרפר וסכין לא ניטמ׳, ללמדך שטומאת סכין קשה להן לישראל יותר משפיכות דמים. וכן הוא אומ׳ וגם דם נקי שפך מנשה הרבה מאד עד אשר מלא את ירושלם פה לפה (מלכים ב כא טז). מיכן אמרו בעון שפיכות דמים שכינה נעלית ומקדש נטמא.

Mishnah 2.2

מַעֲשֶׂה שֶׁהָיוּ שְׁנַיִם שָׁוִים וְרָצִים וְעוֹלִין בַּכֶּבֶשׁ דָּחַף אֶחָד מֵהֶן אֶת חֲבֵירוֹ וְנִשְׁבְּרָה רַגְלוֹ.

וּכְשֶׁרָאוּ בֵית דִּין דִּין שֶׁהֵן בָּאִין לִידֵי סַכָּנָה הִתְקִינוּ שֶׁלֹּא יְהוּ תוֹרְמִים אֶת הַמִּזְבֵּחַ אֶלָּא בַּפָּיִיס.

67. David Halivni, *Sources and Traditions: A Source Critical Commentary on Seder Nashim* (Hebrew; Tel Aviv, 1969), תרסא.

68. Judith Hauptman, "Does the Tosefta Precede the Mishnah: Halakhah, Aggada, and Narrative Coherence," *Judaism* 50 (2001): 224–40 at 235 and n. 34.

The Bavli resolves the immense contradiction of details of these two accounts[69] by claiming that two separate events are being presented here (*bYoma* 23a). This is the explanation given by Goldberg.[70] This, however, is a classic case where the similarity in wording and structure leaves no room for doubt that an original text is being reworked. The horrifying account in the Tosefta is cushioned by turning a murderous stabbing into a broken leg, in accordance with the usual trend in the Mishnah to make its sources more palatable. The Second Temple sage R. Zadoq's admonishment is quoted.[71] Brody includes this among examples he found convincing.[72]

9.

Mishnah Bava Meṣiʿa 7.5	Tosefta Bava Meṣiʿa 8.8 (p. 104)	Sifre Devarim 266 (p. 286)
אוֹכֵל פּוֹעֵל קִישׁוּת אֲפִילוּ בְּדִינָר וְכוֹתֶבֶת אֲפִילוּ בְּדִינָר.	אוכל פועל עד שלא יתחיל במלאכה אשכל אפי' בדינר וקישות אפי' בדינר וכותבת אפי' בטריסית.	
ר' אֶלְעָזָר חִסְמָא אוֹ' לֹא יֹאכַל פּוֹעֵל יָתֵר עַל שְׂכָרוֹ,	משם ר' לעזר חסמא אמרו לא יאכל פועל יתר על שכרו,	רבי אלעזר חסמה אומר מנין שלא יאכל פועל יותר על שכרו, תלמוד לומר כנפשך,
וַחֲכָמִ' מַתִּירִין אֲבָל מְלַמְּדִים אֶת הָאָדָם שֶׁלֹּא יְהֵא רוֹעְבְּתָן וִיהֵא סוֹתֵם אֶת הַפֶּתַח לְפָנָיו.	וחכמים מתירין.	וחכמים אומרים שבעך מלמד שאוכל פועל יותר על שכרו.

Sifre Devarim records a dispute between R. Elazar Ḥisma and the Sages as to whether an agricultural worker, who has the right to eat from the fruit upon which he is working, may consume a value greater than his wages. The same dispute is found in the Mishnah and Tosefta, not as a *derashah* (deriv-

---

69. The halakhic background is found in the previous *mishnah*.

70. "The Tosefta supplements the story about the breaking of the leg with a more tragic case" (Goldberg, *Companion*, 287); cf. Abraham Goldberg, "Tosefta to the Tractate Tamid" (Hebrew), *Benjamin de Vries Memorial Volume*, ed. E. Z. Melamed (Jerusalem, 1968), 18–42 at 23.

71. See in detail Friedman, *Atiqta*, 44–45 [= *Studies*, 39–40].

72. Brody, *Studies*, 143 n. 2.

ing the law from a biblical verse), but in a pure apodictic form (*halakhah*). In both the Mishnah and Tosefta the dispute is preceded by an additional law allowing the laborer to eat any single expensive fruit he wishes. "[Even] before he begins working" is added by the Tosefta or removed by the Mishnah, which also reduces the list of fruit.

The opinion of the Sages, which is expressed in the Sifre in the form of a *derashah*, is reduced to one word in the Tosefta: "permit." This permission is outrageous! Thus the Mishnah adds a didactic admonition not to take advantage of this extreme privilege, lest he loses the opportunity of being rehired.

10.

Tosefta Shabbat 13.1–2 (p. 57)	**Mishnah 16.1**
	כָּל כִּתְבֵי הַקֹּדֶשׁ מַצִּילִין אוֹתָן מִפְּנֵי הַדְּלֵיקָה
אַף עַל פִּי שֶׁאָמְרוּ אֵין קוֹרִין בכתבי הקדש, אבל שונין בהן ודורשין בהן, ואם צריך לו דבר לבדוק נוטל ובודק. אמ׳ ר׳ נחמיה מפני מה אמרו אין קורין בכתבי הקדש, מפני שטרי הדיוטות, שיאמרו בכתבי הקדש אין קורין קול וחומר בשטרי הדיוטות.	בֵּין שֶׁקּוֹרִין בָּהֶן וּבֵין שֶׁאֵינָן קוֹרִים בָּהֶם.
היו כתובין תרגום ובכל לשון, מצילין אותן וגונזין אותן.	אַף עַל פִּי כְתוּבִין בְּכָל לָשׁוֹן טְעוּנִים גְּנִיזָה.
	מִפְּנֵי מָה אֵין קוֹרִים בָּהֶן מִפְּנֵי בִיטוּל בֵּית הַמִּדְרָשׁ.

This mishnah has always been considered a crux due to (1) the illogical arrangement of its clauses, dealing alternately with rescuing the Holy Scriptures from fire on the Sabbath and the prohibition of reading Hagiographa on the Sabbath; and (2) the ambiguous "In no matter what language they are written they require to be hidden away." In the Tosefta the two themes ("Hagiographa" and "rescuing") are quite separate, and when compared, the meaning of the ambiguous clause is clear. The wording of our *mishnah* resulted from an effort to integrate the tangential Hagiographa theme with the central "rescuing" theme, and at the same time to reduce the *mishnah* to a brief and concise style (a standard tendency of Mishnah). The "rescuing" theme is then the kernel of the *mishnah*, with "Hagiographa" intertwined, thus enhancing the loose juxtaposition in the Tosefta, but allowing the sequence of clauses to become difficult.[73]

CONCLUSION

The Tosefta, a tannaitic companion-corpus to the Mishnah, is usually viewed as a supplement to that work, in that many Tosefta passages address specific passages in the Mishnah, providing expansions and explication. However, the Tosefta also contains passages which relate to the Mishnah, but whose literary form is not that of addition or expansion. Many of these are true parallel passages, presenting the same law, in the same or similar form as that of the Mishnah, with minor (or major) variations, part and parcel of the known phenomenon of parallel passages in Talmudic-Midrashic literature.

The prevalent rule-of-thumb judgment in scholarship until recent times viewed these Tosefta parallels as secondary to their Mishnah counterparts. They are usually construed as addressing the Mishnah in parallel form, with the divergent segments affording intentional explication of issues in the Mishnah. Undoubtedly this position preferred to view the parallels as integral to the basic relationship between the Mishnah and the Tosefta.

We feel that a convincing counter-claim can be registered on this issue. If the Tosefta parallel was intended merely for explication of a specific point in the Mishnah, a literary form consistent with this purpose could have been used (e.g. במה דברים אמורים), rather than complete restatement. How much more so, if the Mishnah had already been recognized and established as the central text of *halakhah*. Furthermore, it is often difficult to construe the specific divergence as a commentary or expansion of the Mishnah.

In keeping with the Tosefta's general characteristic as an unpolished anthological collection of material, the Tosefta passages parallel to our Mishnah are often older and primary, while the Mishnah counterparts are advanced and editorially reworked, presumably by Rabbi (Judah the Patriarch, editor of our Mishnah). Indeed, close comparison of the parallels yields a series of indicators of this relationship, with the Mishnah showing the results of the more edited and reworked of the two parallels.

73. For a fuller presentation see Friedman, *Primacy* 1993, 316–23 [= Friedman, *Studies*, 84–91]. This paper was originally written as a reaction to Ephraim Elimelech Urbach, "Targum and Tosefta," *Saul Lieberman Memorial Volume*, ed. S. Friedman (Jerusalem and New York, 1993), 53–63.

The Mishnah often shortens the Tosefta parallel, and sometimes presents the content in a clearer form—"Mishnah comments on Tosefta."[74]

The above also yields a clarification of the very nature of rabbinic parallel passages. These have usually been taken as separate and independent statements of a given law (or homily). However, this study leads us to an alternative approach. The parallels are often identical verbatim for large segments of text, with the differences localized in short segments, these differences being the editorial changes we assume to have been introduced by the editor of the Mishnah.

Accordingly, we can assume that the Tosefta parallels are often identical with, or similar to, the literary sources of the Mishnah! This can be of major significance for the interpretation of the Mishnah, and for clarifying the history of *halakhah* and its development in the tannaitic period.[75]

A cadre of scholars has arrived at similar conclusions in recent decades, with a formidable corpus of their combined research coming to bear. This suffices to establish the said relationship of specific Mishnah/Tosefta passages as a reasonable possibility to be considered during investigation of such parallels, as long as the analysis of the particular parallels supports this direction.

74. See *Studies*, 14 in the Hebrew numeration, and references there.
75. Cf. English summary to Primacy 1993.

5. The Literary Evolution of the Mishnah

Yair Furstenberg

INTRODUCTION

"For our Mishnah was not created *ex nihilo* and was not stitched from one parchment." These words open Jacob Nahum Epstein's seminal discussion of Mishnah source criticism in his programmatic lecture on Talmudic Science.[1] Indeed, no Mishnah scholar can escape its literary complexities, disjunctions, and diverse forms and arrangements. Furthermore, from its very first appearance, the historical and critical study of the Mishnah was primarily concerned with the history of its composition, addressing questions such as: What are the earliest indications of Mishnah-like legal formulations? How and when were these woven into literary patterns and structures? What was the nature and intention of the redaction of these sources? Arguably, then, more than any other aspect in the study of Mishnah, a survey of this long-standing inquiry into the formation of the Mishnah allows us to trace the fundamental changes that took place in the scholarly understanding of the nature of this composition, and to suggest directions for future investigations.

In what follows I survey three major phases in the scholarly study of Mishnah source criticism. Each of them represents a radically different image of Mishnah formation, but at the same time all provide indispensable tools for Mishnah analysis. The first phase is deeply entrenched in the traditional view of the antiquity of the teachings that appear in the Mishnah.

---

1. Jacob N. Epstein, "The Talmudic Science and Its Needs," *Studies in Talmudic Literature and Semitic Languages*, ed. E. Z. Melamed, 3 vols. (Hebrew; Jerusalem, 1988), 2.1, 4.

It assumes that the literary roots of the Mishnah go back to a basically uniform legal tradition, transmitted in multiple channels of which the redactor chose at every point the version that fit him most. This scholarly approach culminated in the works of Epstein, whose authority shaped this particular image of Mishnah source criticism.

In the second phase, which currently dominates the field of Mishnah studies, source criticism has been significantly marginalized, due to a growing awareness of the degree of redactional revisionism, and the inability to adequately reconstruct the original sources embedded in the Mishnah. This approach does not deny that the Mishnah was composed over a long period from different sources, but these are arguably beyond our reach within the final composition. Consequently, it adopts a relatively holistic image of the redacted Mishnah, which scholars often take to represent the innovative nature of "Rabbinic Judaism," and the intellectual project it stands for. The first two sections are dedicated to these opposite images.

Although these two approaches suggest opposite stories regarding the history of the Mishnah, both in fact provide important tools for handling the complexity of the Mishnah's literary texture on the local level. Both critical approaches enhance the literary sensitivities necessary for unfolding the meaning of each mishnaic unit. At the same time, I will argue that both phases ultimately share a fundamentally static and stable image of the Mishnah, which neglects to adequately appreciate the Mishnah's dynamic nature. Thus, in the following sections (3–4) I advocate a third form of source criticism, one that takes into consideration the undeniable fact that the Mishnah is an evolving composition. This source-critical approach is highly aware of our limited ability to discern earlier material, but at the same time it is careful not to overlook literary indications of the Mishnah's evolution. The roots of this approach extend back to Louis Ginzberg and Chanoch Albeck, whose works on the proto-mishnaic tractates *'Eduyot* and *Tamid* will be discussed in section 3. Following their lead, we may examine the literary complexity of the Mishnah as a mirror into the formation process of rabbinic study culture.

Considering that the Mishnah is the product of an evolving composition within changing circumstances, it is hardly appropriate to ask "What is *the* Mishnah"; rather one should ask what were the forces (evidently diverse and changing over time) that generated such a multifaceted production. Identifying the literary relationship between discrete units in different stages of composition allows us to discern distinct stages of rabbinic study culture within the literary complexity of the Mishnah. A few examples of such developments will be presented in section 4. As I will seek to demonstrate, the Mishnah's literary complexity exposes the development of new forms of study, the expansion of rabbinic knowledge into new legal fields, and the creation of new legal discourses.

1. VARIATIONS OF A UNIFORM MISHNAH: RETHINKING EPSTEIN

Remarkably, the last comprehensive work written on the formation of the Mishnah is Epstein's *Introductions to Tannaitic Literature*, based on his courses from the 1940s and published in 1957.[2] It is a powerful display of innovative textual expertise, but at the same time it holds on to a conservative scholarly approach, which goes back to the historical image offered already by Rav Sherira Gaon.[3] The overall picture that emerges from the abundance of textual analyses across multiple tractates draws heavily from this tradition in two major respects. It assumes, first, that the Mishnah in some form existed already during the Second Temple period, and second, that it was a uniform and comprehensive composition from its inception. Taken together, these two points establish the existence of an ancient body of law that provided a common foundation for all subsequent versions of this corpus up to our Mishnah (as well as to the parallel Tosefta). This image strongly dictates Epstein's source-critical approach and his reconstruction of Mishnah formation. In consequence, although Epstein in his statement quoted above acknowledges the diverse sources of our Mishnah,[4] in fact these sources are quite similar to each other (as well as to the final Mishnah) since they build upon the uniform foundation of rabbinic activity.

The view of the Mishnah as a comprehensive composition that expanded gradually over time goes back to Rav Sherira and was subsequently shared by the two major scholars whom Epstein drew on: Nachman Krochmal and David Zvi Hoffmann. Krochmal claims that it was Hillel the Elder (who presumably flourished during the Herodian period) who turned away from earlier forms of Scripture-based study of law, and combined available literary units of laws into thematic tractates, thus creating the full structure of the six orders of the Mishnah. This composition was transmitted in multiple

---

2. Jacob N. Epstein, *Prolegomena ad Litteras Tannaiticas: Mishna, Tosephta et Interpretationes Halachicas, Mevo'ot le-Sifrut ha-Tannaim* (Hebrew; Tel Aviv, 1957).

3. Benjamin M. Levin, *Igeret Rabbi Sherira Gaon* (Haifa, 1921), 18–19.

4. See also Epstein, *Prolegomena*, 13: "Our Mishnah, that of Rabbi [Judah the Patriarch], is not the first composition of mishnayot; it was preceded by several compositions of mishnayot, which on the one hand were similar in the foundations of the laws, but on the other were distinct in their branches and details, interpretations and restrictions. They are distinct also in their organization and their order."

variations by later rabbis, through their interpretations and additions.[5] Hoffmann shares a similar approach.[6] As a direct precursor of Epstein, he introduced sophisticated textual and historical tools to establish the antiquity of specific literary units, which he termed "First Mishnah". Epstein further expanded this endeavor by identifying ancient mishnaic units, primarily associated with the Temple, but also applying other indications for antiquity, such as archaic language, early legal conceptions, and the groupings of teachings by early authorities, such as the Houses of Hillel and Shammai.[7]

This assumption further dictated the way Epstein described the redactional activity of R. Akiba and his disciples, whose teachings provide the backbone of our Mishnah. Zacharias Frankel had previously described R. Akiba as the first one to string together the ancient laws into a recognizable structure and form, so that they were not lost from memory.[8] Epstein, however, while naming R. Akiba "Father of the Mishnah,"[9] could not accept this description at face value. After all, in his view the laws were already organized within a clear framework into which new teachings could be added. Therefore, he claimed that R. Akiba's innovation was to fix the precise wording of the text towards its final and authoritative form. R. Akiba formulated each law in a coherent manner, even when documenting a dispute between the Houses of Hillel and Shammai. Since R. Akiba instructed his disciples to systematically examine these earlier traditions, each of these disciples formulated and transmitted these laws in his own distinct form, thus creating his own complete Mishnah.

Consequently, in the final stage of redactions, so this narrative goes, Rabbi Judah the Patriarch combined these multiple versions of the Mishnah into its final version.[10] By thoroughly comparing the parallels of each mishnaic unit, Epstein identified the source of each statement and provided

5. Nachman Krochmal, *Guide for the Perplexed of the Time* (Hebrew; London 1961; reprint: Jerusalem, 2010), 217–27.

6. David Z. Hoffmann, *The First Mishnah and the Disputes of the Tannaim*, translated from the German into Hebrew by S. Greenberg (Berlin, 1914).

7. Epstein, *Prolegomena*, 25–58.

8. Zacharias Frankel, *Darkhe ha-Mishnah* (Lipsiae, 1859), 209–11. Frankel derives this image from a later description of R. Akiba (in ADRN version A, 18) as separating the assortment of grains into different piles, presumably reflecting his role as putting order into the previously dispersed teachings.

9. Epstein, *Prolegomena*, 71, relies on references within tannaitic sources to "the Mishnah of R. Akiba" and his description as "arranging the laws to his disciples," as well as the multiple sources where he "recited" (חזר לשנות) a law in a particular fashion.

10. For a summary of this approach see Dov Zlotnick, *The Iron Pillar—Mishnah: Redaction, Form and Intent* (Jerusalem, 1988), 24–41.

a vivid image of the redactor's micro-editing. As Epstein himself states: "source criticism relates to all the cases indicated in the Talmud concerning the association of a specific Mishnah to a particular rabbi."[11] In other words, Epstein's source criticism seeks to determine whose Mishnah (from those available to him) the redactor chose at each point, and whose law he followed in each ruling. Thus, Epstein does not distinguish mishnaic sources through their literary and thematic features, but primarily through their halakhic markings, based on the assumption that each rabbi had his own Mishnah, which he adapted to his own views. Presumably this is a reasonable assumption. After all, even a cursory comparison of the Mishnah and Tosefta reveals that there were multiple ways to formulate each law, according to the perspective of different rabbis. Thus, for example, a ruling in the Mishnah formulated according to the position of R. Meir may appear in an alternative form in the Tosefta, from R. Judah's perspective.[12] Ultimately, however, Epstein's theory lacks sufficient textual evidence, since the discrete teachings of these rabbis do not accumulate into recognizable compositions, and therefore we cannot assume that each of these rabbis had a complete Mishnah of his own.[13] Furthermore, this legal-minded orientation of the textual analysis does not give due consideration to the actual tangible characteristics of textual complexity of the Mishnah. This results in an attempt to reconstruct from scattered fragments hypothetical compositions, without sufficient literary evidence for their prior existence.

Paradoxically, then, while arguing for multiple versions of the Mishnah, this approach in fact served to enhance an image of a uniform trajectory of mishnaic evolution, transmitted in a few variations in one major channel from the great master R. Akiba, through his disciples to Rabbi Judah the Patriarch. This theory has become the hallmark of the approach of Abraham Goldberg, Epstein's student.[14] Although Goldberg claims to be following Albeck in rejecting the view of the Mishnah as legal code, his image of

11. Epstein, "The Talmudic Science and Its Needs," 4.

12. Compare for example mBer 3:4 and tBer 2:13; mDem 2:2–3 and tDem 2:2–3; mMa'as 2:5 and tMa'as 2:11.

13. It is occasionally argued that when the Mishnah mentions a named rabbi, it does not just present his view, but actually quotes from his Mishnah. This for example is the underlying assumption of Israel Lewy, *Über einige Fragmente aus der Mischna des Abba Saul* (Berlin, 1876), translated into Hebrew by A. Z. Rabinowitz, "Mishnat Abba Sha'ul," *Mesilot le-Torat Ha-Tannaim* (Tel Aviv, 1928), 121–33. Due to the unique formulation of Abba Saul's positions in the Mishnah, Lewy argues that our Mishnah does not quote his views but compares his versions of the Mishnah to the standard transmission.

14. Abraham Goldberg, "The Mishna: A Study Book of Halakha," in *The Literature of the Sages*, ed. S. Safrai (Philadelphia, 1987), 211–52.

Mishnah redaction is in fact akin to that of Epstein. In Goldberg's view, the Mishnah represents the teachings of the school of Hillel as they were transmitted and interpreted by R. Akiba and his disciples, and therefore consists of four distinct layers of teachings corresponding to these generations. He suggests that "the chief aim of the final editor was to present that gamut of possible interpretations . . . the editor is interested in presenting the teachings of R. Akiba as they become reflected in the interpretive teachings of his prime pupils."[15]

Goldberg even goes on to claim that there was one "official Mishnah" that was initially edited by the patriarch during the Yavneh period, and continued to take shape during the following generations, until its final editing by R. Judah the Patriarch.[16] According to this centralized image, the rabbis of each generation incorporated the teachings of the rabbis of the previous generation into this official Mishnah. Rabbi Judah the Patriarch developed a sophisticated method for combining the views of R. Akiba's disciples, so as to guide the student of Mishnah through the various interpretations of R. Akiba's teachings. Like Epstein, Goldberg imagines the editor as weaving together fragments from the Mishnahs of different rabbis.

It is hard to deny that the Mishnah is associated with the school of R. Akiba and is founded primarily on the teaching of four of his disciples (Meir, Judah, Yosi, and Shimon). There are also indications that R. Judah the Patriarch was involved in its redaction, as assumed by the amoraim.[17] Thus, it is possible to follow the trajectory of legal development through these authorities. At the same time, with respect to the literary development of the Mishnah, it is hard to accept this monolithic image. In fact, the layers reconstructed by Goldberg are not compatible with the actual literary components of the mishnaic units. Seldom is it possible to peel off later teachings and uncover the earlier layers. Surely, the Mishnah is a composite text with a complex literary history, but as far as the literary evidence shows, this cannot be reduced to a gradual development of a single authoritative Mishnah.[18]

---

15. Goldberg, "The Mishna," 214.

16. Goldberg, "The Mishna," 216.

17. See for example yKid 3:12 (64c); bGit 29a.

18. This is a recurring theme in the critique of Jacob Neusner, *The Modern Study of the Mishnah* (Leiden, 1973). See e.g. XV–XVI. The multiplicity of mishnaic corpora associated with different schools is made apparent in the Halakhic Midrashim from the School of R. Yishmael. These include references to mishnaic rulings (through the formula "from this [verse] it is taught" etc.) that do not appear in our Mishnah, but must have belonged to the Yishmaelian mishnaic tradition. See Menahem Kahana, "The Relations between Exegeses in the Mishnah and Halakhot in the Midrash" (Hebrew), *Tarbiz* 84 (2016): 17–76.

No doubt, the achievements of this form of source criticism have substantially advanced our understanding of the mishnaic composition. The systematic comparison of the Mishnah to its parallels in other tannaitic sources served to reveal the subtle variation of legal positions, and to expose the ways the Mishnah combines different sources and positions. This method is extremely useful in tracing the development and reinterpretations of specific laws and traditions, as David Henshke for example displays extensively in his works.[19] However, such microanalysis cannot replace the wider outlook on the composition of the Mishnah from its literary components. This approach further creates the impression of a shared framework differing only in details. It tends to disregard the actual complexity of literary texture, and therefore is hardly suitable for tackling the fundamental question of the literary evolution of the Mishnah. Without assuming such a uniform history, what do the literary features of the Mishnah tell us about the creation of this composition and the form and scope of its constituent components?

2. A TEXT WITHOUT A HISTORY

Many elements of the source criticism described in the previous section have been challenged in more recent scholarship. Consequently, source-critical methods lost their grip on Mishnah study and were marginalized in favor of an alternative image of the Mishnah as a text without a history. As we shall see in this section, three groups of problems have served to undermine the previous dominance of the diachronic study of the Mishnah. In truth, these arguments do not entirely undercut the value and justification of Mishnah source criticism per se; nonetheless, in practice they seriously challenge the possibility to adequately discern these sources and reconstruct their history. At the very least, they required radical rethinking of the goal and methods of any such project. Such skepticism encouraged the turn towards alternative forms of literary analysis.

The most vulnerable component within the traditional approach to the antiquity of the Mishnah is its overstated reliance on Temple narratives as evidence for its pre-70 CE provenance. Initially, when Hoffmann attempted to identify the "first Mishnah" he focused mainly on what he considered to be hard historical data embedded in the Mishnah, such as mentions of king Agrippa and other historical figures.[20] Around these references he grouped

---

19. For example, David Henshke, *Festival Joy in Tannaitic Discourse* (Hebrew; Jerusalem, 2007).

20. Hoffmann, *First Mishnah*, 16–24.

compatible sources of seemingly early provenance. Hoffmann's judgment concerning what may be considered reliable historical data and their relevance to the reconstructions of early sources could be justly questioned; nonetheless, it offered a sound and careful methodology. Epstein, on the other hand, consistently expanded the scope of what he considered to be ancient Temple sources within the Mishnah to include almost any description of Temple rites. Furthermore, in his view, any indication of an authentic Temple tradition marked the antiquity of the whole textual unit.[21]

However, an impartial comparison with non-rabbinic sources concerning the Temple mainly reveals considerable incompatibility with the rabbinic materials. While earlier scholarship suggested complex historical reconstructions to fit in all the data,[22] more recent works exposed the extent of legal, exegetical, and ideological tendencies underlying the creative revision of Temple traditions in rabbinic literature in general and in the Mishnah in particular.[23] This scholarly inclination goes hand in hand with the changing image of the rabbis and their predecessors, the Pharisees, whose authority and access to Temple administration has been significantly downplayed.[24] It is worth mentioning in this context that the rulings of the Houses of Hil-

21. Epstein, *Prolegomena*, 25–52. In line with his approach, even the inclusion of later rabbis is dismissed as a mere addition to the earlier substratum. See for example his description of tractate *Yoma*', pp. 36–37. The general reliability of mishnaic Temple traditions is assumed with some modifications in the commentary of Ze'ev Safrai on the Mishnah. He takes these traditions to represent an authentic memory of the Temple. See Zeev Safrai, "The Memory of the Temple: Is It Really Memory and for What Purpose?" (Hebrew), *New Studies of Jerusalem* 16 (2011): 255–302.

22. According to Adolf Büchler, *The Priests and their Cult in the Last Decade of the Temple in Jerusalem* (Hebrew; Jerusalem, 1966), 14–15, the Mishnah represented the actual practice in the Temple during the last years before its destruction, when the Pharisaic law governed the Temple.

23. See Daniel Stökl Ben Ezra, *The Impact of Yom Kippur on Early Christianity: The Day of Atonement from Second Temple Judaism to the Fifth Century* (Tübingen, 2003), 19–28; Ishay Rosen Zvi, *The Mishnaic Sotah Ritual: Temple, Gender and Midrash* (Leiden, 2012); Mira Balberg, *Blood for Thought: The Reinvention of Sacrifice in Early Rabbinic Literature* (Oakland, 2017); Hillel Mali, "A City Surrounded by Walls: On the descriptions of the Bikkurim Ceremony in Tannaitic Teachings" (Hebrew), in *The Disciples of Aaron: In Memory of Prof. Aaron Shemesh*, ed. D. Boyarin, V. Noam, and I. Rosen-Zvi, *Te'uda* 31 (2021): 411–50.

24. Even if we assume the Pharisees exercised some degree of political power and influence, their social impact after the Hasmonean period evidently derived from their piety and knowledge of the Torah, and not from their position in Temple administration. The latest indication of significant Pharisaic control (albeit indirectly) over the Temple worship is 4QMMT. Only a few tannaim (outside the mainstream) exhibit direct knowledge of priestly practices, see Büchler, *The Priests*, 20–29.

lel and Shammai, which constitute the main source of early rabbinic tradition, hardly involve Temple laws. Presumably, these Pharisaic schools were concerned with non-priestly ritual practices, such as eating daily foods in purity or consuming tithes in Jerusalem, rather than with the details of the Temple service. Thus, even if one admits that discrete historical fragments are scattered within the Mishnah, the overall legal and literary structure is considered to be the product of later rabbinic study.[25] Ultimately, the emphasis on the revolutionary quality of rabbinic Judaism in this and other fields has overshadowed the study of more subtle literary dynamics that featured in earlier source-critical studies.[26]

A second feature of tannaitic study practices—one that has further undermined the possibility of recovering the sources of the Mishnah—has paradoxically been brought to light by Epstein himself. His works uncover the degree to which the teachings of the Houses of Hillel and Shammai were subjected to systematic revision by later rabbis.[27] A systematic comparison of tannaitic parallels reveals the tendency of each of R. Akiba's disciples to formulate the disputes between the Houses in his own distinct manner, and to adjust it to his own halakhic position. Faithful to the traditional approach, Epstein viewed this practice as a mere elaboration of the underlying Mishnah of the Houses, whose details were disputed by later rabbis. Thus, one can get a general sense of the concerns and topics in the earlier layer,

25. Notably, it is possible to trace the evolution of some Temple traditions within the Mishnah, through comparison to Second Temple and parallel rabbinic sources. Often the Mishnah modifies the tradition, as it appears in parallel tannaitic sources. For example, while the Mishnah regularly subjects the Temple administration to rabbinic authority, this feature is much more restrained in other sources. Compare for example the first chapters of Mishnah and Tosefta Yoma; mSot 1:4, tSot 1:6 (the rabbinic court is omitted by most manuscripts), and *Sifre* on Numbers piska 12 (p. 39; Kahana ed.); mMid 5:4 and *Sifre* on Numbers piska 116 (p. 339; concerning who is in charge of asserting the purity of priestly pedigree).

26. In this respect there is a marked difference between the laws of purity and the laws dealing with the Temple. With respect to purity laws it is possible to trace a continual development from the earliest roots in the teachings of the Houses of Hillel and Shammai, and these correspond to other Second Temple materials. See Yair Furstenberg, "Outsider Impurity: Trajectories of Second Temple Separation Traditions in Tannaitic Literature," in *Tradition, Transmission, and Transformation from Second Temple Literature through Judaism and Christianity in Late Antiquity*, ed. M. Kister, H. Newman, M. Segal, and R. Clements (Leiden, 2015), 40–68. On the other hand, the teachings of the Houses hardly address issues directly dealing with the Temple cult, and these appear only later in the teachings of later tannaim, who were compelled to turn to other sources of information.

27. E.g. Jacob N. Epstein, "On the Mishnah of R. Jehudah: A Study on the Sources of the Mishnah" (Hebrew), *Tarbiz* 15 (1944): 1–13.

even when the specific wordings and details are disputed. However, when approaching these sources with an eye on the history of rabbinic law, the inability to clearly separate between the teachings of the rabbis at each stage poses a substantial challenge to this historical endeavor.

Jacob Neusner's attempt to reconstruct the history of early rabbinic law resulted in just this sort of frustration. Having realized the considerable role of later rabbis in formulating the specific language of the Houses, Neusner turned to question the reliability of these attributions.[28] It was a short way to a more generalized argument that in referring to earlier authorities, the Mishnah is only providing a reconstruction of a "history of ideas" rather than quoting earlier sources. In Neusner's view, the redactors of each rabbinic text, including the Mishnah, presented their predecessors as representing the logical foundations of their own developed legal system and philosophy, rather than engaging in the interpretation of earlier texts.[29]

Despite the justified call for caution concerning the reconstruction of earlier sources and the extent of rabbinic revisionism, which Epstein himself was highly aware of, Neusner's alternative depiction of rabbinic scholarly activity is ultimately unpersuasive.[30] The mere literary complexity of the Mishnah, which Neusner generally ignores, defies his image of the Mishnah as a conceptual construct. This approach also disregards the subtle form of exegesis of earlier rabbinic traditions and replaces it with a falsified pseudepigraphic model. The fact is that the traditions attributed to earlier rabbis are limited to specific legal fields, corroborated by external sources on early law (such as Qumran literature). Furthermore, the range of interpretations by later rabbis is ultimately quite limited and bound to shared formulations of the earlier traditions. Thus, the kind of study the rabbis are engaged with retains the fundamental integrity of earlier traditions, even when reinterpreting or adding to them. Comparative analysis further al-

28. Jacob Neusner, "Why We Cannot Assume the Reliability of Attributions: The Case of the Houses in Mishna-Tosefta Makhshirin," in *The Mishnah in Contemporary Perspectives*, ed. A. J. Avery-Peck and J. Neusner (Leiden and Boston, 2006), 190–212.

29. See Jacob Neusner, "Redaction, Formulation and Form: The Case of Mishnah," *JQR* 70 (1980): 131–47; Neusner, *Judaism: The Evidence of the Mishnah* (Chicago and London, 1981). For a survey of Neusner's approach see Alan J. Avery-Peck, "The Mishnah, Tosefta, and the Talmuds—the Problem of Text and Context," in *Judaism in Late Antiquity, Part I—The Literary and Archaeological Sources*, ed. A. J. Avery-Peck and J. Neusner (Leiden and New York), 173–215.

30. See Shaye J. D. Cohen, "Jacob Neusner, Mishnah, and Counter Rabbinics," *Conservative Judaism* 37 (1983): 48–63; Hayim Lapin, *Early Rabbinic Civil Law and the Social History of Roman Galilee: A Study of Mishnah Tractate Baba Meṣia* (Atlanta, 1995), 22–25; John C. Poirier, "Jacob Neusner, the Mishnah, and Ventriloquism," *JQR* 87 (1996): 61–78.

lows us to trace these elaborations and assess their relative authenticity.[31] The question remains, then: how to discern distinct sources and phases in the literary evolution of the Mishnah while taking into account the extent of rabbinic revisionism? This brings us to the third, more subtle critique against the traditional form of source criticism.

The dominant modus operandi of current Mishnah scholarship brackets any form of source-critical analysis based on moderate skepticism, and consequently adopts a relatively holistic image of this composition and its project.[32] It does not deny that it was composed over a long period from different sources, but these sources are arguably beyond our reach within the final composition. Thus, even the Mishnah's complexity and incoherence become a major facet of its own intellectual statement.[33] Admittedly, there is a considerable distance between acknowledging the vast variety of materials that found their way into the Mishnah, each with its own literary and halakhic characteristics, and the actual pretension to delineate the building blocks and clearly distinguish earlier phases of the Mishnah's evolution, as in the Pentateuch documentary hypothesis. Even when the distinct underlying sources are visible, scholars have exposed traces of considerable intervention. In contrast to the way Albeck described the Mishnah as an uninterrupted amalgamation of sources,[34] it is possible to demonstrate that the sources of the Mishnah were gradually woven together by means of literary and linguistic techniques including substantial revisions. This process involved creating a multi-dimensional system of literary links that inevitably entailed a significant degree of reformulation of the underlying sources.[35]

The work of Avraham Walfish, among others, offers an elaborate reflection on these literary features of the Mishnah and the complex rela-

---

31. Such is the case concerning the multiple versions of the dispute between the houses at the head of tractate Makhshirin, discussed by Neusner (above n. 28). For a rebuttal of Neusner's argument against the reliability of attributions see Yair Furstenberg, *Purity and Community in Antiquity: Traditions of the Law from Second Temple Judaism to the Mishnah* (Hebrew; Jerusalem, 2016), 305–11.

32. This opinio communis is discussed by Christine E. Hayes, "What is (the) *Mishna*? Concluding Observations," *AJS Review* 32 (2008): 291–97.

33. Ishay Rosen Zvi, *Between Mishnah and Midrash: The Birth of Rabbinic Literature* (Hebrew; Ra'ananah, 2020), 123–24.

34. Chanoch Albeck, *Introduction to the Mishnah* (Hebrew; Jerusalem, 1967), 101.

35. An interesting case in this respect is the supposedly independent unit at the head of chapter 8 of tractate Shabat, which exhibits multiple links to its surrounding mishnahs. See Noam Zohar, "R. Akiva Said: The Significance of the Inclusion of an 'Unrelated' Unit—A Case Study in the Mishnah's Redaction" (Hebrew), *Tarbiz* 70 (2001): 353–66.

tionship between the traditional diachronic approach and the more recent synchronic forms of analysis.[36] He exposed the sophistication of linguistic choice in the Mishnah, which serves to link distinct units and highlight major motifs. This literary sensitivity serves to counter the previous tendency to explain away mishnaic complexity as a mere product of the mechanical juxtaposition of diverse sources, while the integration of such literary elements points to the redactor's attempt to create an overarching meaning.

Scholarship on the first chapter of *mKidushin* offers a fine example of the shift from a diachronic to a synchronic approach to the Mishnah.[37] Although the tractate deals with marriage, this issue hardly occupies the chapter. The first half of the chapter classifies the modes of acquisition, of which betrothal is the first category. The second half offers various classifications of the commandments, who is obligated, and where. Commentators and scholars debated the meaning of this combination. Presumably, source-critical methods serve to discern the independent sources underlying this chapter and allow us to circumvent the question of authorial intention. After all, one relevant detail in each of the sources may drag in a whole unrelated unit (to which it also belongs) into its own present literary position. This approach, however, is unsatisfactory, since many literary features in this chapter can be explained only as careful additions and revisions intended to merge the distinct sources into a unified whole. While these alterations significantly problematize any attempt to describe the exact form of the original units, and even to establish their provenance (due to the possible redactional role of biblical formulations and the like), they open the way for reconstructing the ultimate meaning of the redacted composition. At the same time, the attempt to identify the redactor's intention in turn raises new challenges: What elements within the complex mishnaic composition are relevant for the literary analysis, and how does one avoid reducing it to a simplified message?

Thus, in current scholarship the role of source criticism has been limited mainly to a general awareness of the existence of a variety of materi-

36. Avraham Walfish, "The Literary Method of Redaction in Mishnah Based on Tractate Rosh HaShana" (diss., Hebrew University 2001 [Hebrew]); Walfish, "The Poetics of the Mishnah," in *The Mishnah in Contemporary Perspective, Part Two*, ed. A. J. Avery-Peck and J. Neusner (Leiden, 2006), 153–89; Amram Tropper, "The State of Mishnah Studies," in *Rabbinic Texts and the History of Late Roman Palestine*, ed. M. Goodman and P. Alexander (Oxford, 2010), 91–115 (102–8).

37. See Epstein, *Prolegomena*, 52–54; Noam Zohar, "Women, Men and Religious Status: Deciphering a Chapter in the Mishnah," *Approaches to Ancient Judaism* 5 (1993): 33–54; Avraham Walfish, "The Study of the Redaction of Mishnah Qiddushin, Chapter 1: From Whence and to Where?" (Hebrew), *Netuim* 15 (2008): 43–77.

als available to the Mishnah redactor. While the issue of the history of the text is downplayed, this awareness serves to explain surprising literary arrangements as well as identify the traces of redactional activity, and better understand its purpose. Here again, such an approach is undoubtedly adequate on the micro level when analyzing specific units. However, when turning to the larger question concerning the nature of this unique work, we must account for the distinct phases through which it developed into its current state. Since the Mishnah as a literary genre evolved rapidly during the tannaitic period from embryonic forms for transmitting discrete rabbinic teachings, through crude attempts to link them together, to the final comprehensive composition of legal fields and the law as a whole, our very ability to understand this novel creation depends on discerning the changing powers involved in its formation.

Arguably, the Mishnah's composite literary texture does not merely reflect its multiple, even contradictory literary sources, as though it were an established genre from the start. Rather, it exposes the development of new forms of study, the expansion of rabbinic knowledge into new legal fields, and the creation of new legal discourses.[38] In the next two sections I survey works that apply source-critical analysis to uncover the developing forms of rabbinic study as reflected in the literary complexity of the Mishnah. These works identify broad changes of form, content and modes of discourse, although the exact scope and wording of the sources in each of these phases cannot be redeemed. Thus, we encounter fundamental changes in the very intention of the Mishnah through its stages of literary evolution and diversity of sources.

3. THE MANY BEGINNINGS OF THE MISHNAH

The first stage in unfolding the literary evolution of the Mishnah is to acknowledge its multiple roots. In this section we will see that the creation of the Mishnah can be traced back to different literary and scholarly antecedents. In contrast to most tractates of the Mishnah that are composed of multiple sources of diverse forms, two specific tractates, *'Eduyot* and *Tamid*, of-

---

38. Returning to the *Kidushin* case, the presence of the peculiar unit on acquisition reflects in my view a new phase of rabbinic legalism, strongly indebted to Roman legal taxonomy, which reshaped the Mishnah in several points. The unit in mKid 1:1–5 exhibits a striking similarity to Gaius, *Institutes* 1:108–24. In a forthcoming article I argue that the redaction of tractate *Kidushin* reflects substantial knowledge of Roman legal textbooks. This literary connection impacts our understanding of the circulation of Roman legal knowledge in the eastern provinces.

fer clear literary alternatives to the standard forms of mishnaic composition. They even give the impression of not belonging to the same rabbinic school as the rest of the Mishnah. Arguably, these tractates not only demonstrate the characteristic diversity of the Mishnah, but enable us to trace the gradual development of the mishnaic genre from its multiple proto-mishnaic roots. They point to earlier forms of teaching and transmission that were adopted at an early stage by the rabbis, and were gradually transformed into the more familiar literary and scholarly patterns of our Mishnah.

We start this discussion with Albeck's approach to the history of the Mishnah. Albeck fervently refuted Epstein's arguments for the existence of literary arrangement of rabbinic teachings prior to the destruction of the Temple.[39] In his view tractate *'Eduyot* was the first attempt to create such a collection; it took place in Yavneh after the destruction of the Temple and preceded all other tractates of the Mishnah. His thesis rests on two proofs. First, the Tosefta at the head of the tractate seems to provide the background for its creation: "When the Sages entered the Vineyard in Yavneh, they said, 'In the future, there will come an hour when a person seeks a teaching from the Torah and he will not find it, or in the teachings of the Scribes, and he will not find it . . . There shall not be one word of Torah similar to its fellow.' They said, 'Let us begin from Hillel and Shammai!'"[40] Then follows a quotation of a dispute from the beginning of *m'Eduyot*. Presumably this source testifies to the fear of losing the knowledge of Torah after the destruction of the Temple, which in turn resulted in the first attempt to gather the teaching of the first sages, Shammai and Hillel, as appears in *m'Eduyot*. Albeck thus argues that had there already existed a literary framework for transmitting rabbinic teachings, as Epstein assumed, there would be no place for this fear.

The second component of Albeck's thesis is the unique literary features of tractate *'Eduyot* itself. In contrast to other tractates, *'Eduyot* is not organized according to topic: rather, it assembles groups of disputes between early rabbis according to their literary features. These groups include disputes between Shammai and Hillel and the houses of Shammai and Hillel, groups of numbered disputes among the rabbis of Yavneh, and lists of disputes in fixed formulae. The second part of the tractate lists testimonies

---

39. Albeck, *Introduction to the Mishnah*, 63–87, 257–59.

40. tEdu 1:1. According to MS Vienna the final statement runs as follows: "They said: What is of the House of Shammai and what is of the House of Hillel." This variant has significant implications on the intention of this story, and the literary innovation it alludes to. See below n. 44.

of "Yavnean" rabbis on a range of disputed legal issues. As Albeck notes,[41] many of the disputes in *'Eduyot* resurface in other tractates according to their subject-matter, but it would seem pointless to assemble the disputes in this fashion, if a thematically organized framework for incorporating this knowledge has already existed. He therefore surmises that tractate *'Eduyot* was the first attempt to organize rabbinic knowledge before the further ac-cumulation of rabbinic teachings, resulting in the development of a more systematic and comprehensive form of thematic organization. Conse-quently, the disputes that already appear in tractate *'Eduyot* were duplicated in their appropriate tractates.[42]

In an attempt to explain the intention of this unique tractate, Epstein was compelled to argue that it reflects a Yavnean attempt to resolve these dis-putes (as part of a rabbinic project of legal unification).[43] This may explain the list of testimonies, but hardly fits collections of disputes according to their formal features. Albeck's position, on the other hand, although incon-clusive for reconstructing the historical background of this tractate, pro-vides a powerful literary tool for considering the evolution of the Mishnah through the changing arrangements of its materials.

Admittedly, in contrast to Albeck's assumption, the Tosefta quoted above most probably does not reflect the actual background for the creation of tractate *'Eduyot*; rather, it offers an explanation for another novel feature of rabbinic study culture, the systematic juxtaposition of opposite views side by side.[44] Also the claim that the assembly of disputes between the Houses of Shammai and Hillel belongs to the earliest stage of Mishnah formation is problematic, since it is particularly these sections that mention later rabbis,

---

41. Albeck, *Introduction to the Mishnah*, 82.

42. Compare the position of Lewy, "Mishnat Abba Sha'ul," 106, who claims that most of the disputes appeared originally in other tractates (according to R. Meir), and they were copied to *'Eduyot*.

43. Epstein, *Prolegomena*, 422, following yBer 1:3 (3b); bBer 28a. This created the dominant image of the gathering in Yavne as if it was intended to ensure uniformity of practice and eliminate sectarianism. This image is hardly confirmed in the tannaitic sources. For an alternative view see Shmuel Safrai, "The Ruling According to the House of Hillel in Yavne," *In the Day of the Temple and in the Days of the Mishnah* (Hebrew, Jerusalem, 1994), 382–405. Compare, Shaye J. D. Cohen, "The Significance of Yavneh: Pharisees, Rabbis and the End of Jewish Sectarianism," *HUCA* 55 (1984): 27–53. The most these sources hint at is an attempt to reject the halakhic positions of R. Eliezer. See Menahem Kahana, "On the Fashioning and Aims of the Mishnaic Controversy" (Hebrew), *Tarbiz* 73 (2004): 51–81 (65–66).

44. Yair Furstenberg, "From Tradition to Controversy: New Modes of Transmission in the Teachings of Early Rabbis" (Hebrew), *Tarbiz* 85 (2018): 587–641 (591–604).

the disciples of R. Akiba, who (as we have seen above) were active in formulating the teachings of the Houses. In contrast, the legal testimonies in the following chapters of the tractate feature only early rabbis. Furthermore, a close textual analysis of the tractate reveals that the sections including the disputes between the houses were woven onto the earlier strata of the testimonies, in an attempt to divert the intention of the tractate.[45] Nonetheless, despite the flaws of Albeck's historical reconstruction, on the literary level the structural difference between *'Eduyot* and other tractates, as well as the overlap between the tractates, demands our attention to the gradual transformation of literary frameworks into the typical mishnaic genre.

Turning to other tractates, these exhibit differing degrees of proximity to the *'Eduyot* literary model. This distinct model was integrated into larger thematic frameworks, while at the same time preserving much of its previous form. Consequently, some tractates belong to an intermediary stage: they are organized according to subject matter but are heavily dependent on the assemblies of early disputes. A case in point is tractate *Betsah*, whose arrangement is best understood as following the order of the generations of the tannaim, rather than any thematic plan. Thus, its first chapters are based on groups of disputes between the Houses that were transposed from *'Eduyot*, including issues that are not related to the laws of the holidays. These units were crudely transmitted together within their original literary context, and as such enable us to follow the gradual arrangement of available literary material according to subject matter.[46] Furthermore, a wider survey of the Mishnah reveals that the separation into topics and distinct legal matters is far less apparent when it comes to sources conveying the teachings of earlier rabbis. These are occasionally organized around other principles, conveying alternative aspects of rabbinic study culture.[47] Thus,

45. Furstenberg, "From Tradition to Controversy," 604–20.

46. The units in *Betsah* that are drawn from *'Eduyot* are 1:1–2 and 2:6–8. In between appear three other separate groups of disputes between the Houses. Chapter 3 is based on stories from the Yavnean period, to which relevant rulings were added. A similar case of an underlying group of stories that provide the backbone for the unit as a whole appears in mSuk ch. 2. The last two chapters of *Betsah* exhibit a clear literary pattern and are attributed to later rabbis. To the end of chapter 4 the Mishnah appends a double dispute between R. Eliezer and the rabbis. This phenomenon too recurs in tractate *Sukkah* ch. 1.

47. See e.g. mKet 13; mSot 5; mKer 3:7–10; mYad 3:5–4:4. Note that these examples do not include groups of short laws coined in the same formula (such as mMeg 1:4–11; m'Arakh 2:1–6, 3:1–5). These units do not necessarily reflect earlier forms of transmission.

units with stories concerning early rabbis on various matters are set along-side systematic legal discussions of later generations.[48]

The reception of tractate *Tamid*, another exceptional tractate, points to an additional channel by which early rabbinic materials were transformed and adapted to the standard literary patterns as they crystalized during the tannaitic period. As mentioned above, the mere treatment of the Temple cannot be considered as an indication of antiquity. At the same time, a textual phenomenon that is unique to this specific subject matter allows us to comprehend the adaptation of this field into standard forms of rabbinic study. Louis Ginzberg was the first to point out the unique features of tractate *Tamid*, dedicated to narrating the morning service in the Temple.[49] He even ventured to claim that it was not part of our Mishnah. While this claim cannot be substantiated, it clearly seems to reflect alternative forms of study.

In addition to peculiar phrases and some archaic wording, the tractate is unique for its purely descriptive form; it offers a continuous narrative and lacks any form of legal instruction. In this respect it stands out even among other units including descriptions of Temple ceremonies, which are never uniform and include legal discussions. This feature is related to the second predominant aspect of this tractate's uniqueness, its single voice and almost complete lack of disputes, which otherwise is the hallmark of rabbinic teachings and the mishnaic form of instruction. This is particularly notable since other sources testify to various disputes concerning matters mentioned in the tractate.[50] As Hillel Mali has recently argued, when reading tractate *Tamid*, one gets the impression that it never passed under the press of rabbinic study practices and interpretations.[51] Thus Ginzberg concluded

---

48. See the group of stories on Rabban Gamaliel in mBer 1–2, or the way the Mishnah links the two distinct stories in mShab 16:7–8.

49. Louis Ginzberg, "The Mishnah Tamid," *Journal of Jewish Lore and Philosophy* 1 (1919): 33–44, 197–209, 265–95.

50. The fact that several details in *Tamid* are disputed by the disciples of R. Akiba in other places was used by Neusner to attack Ginzberg's claim concerning the tractate's antiquity. Jacob Neusner, "Dating a Mishnah-Tractate: The Case of Tamid," in *History, Religion and Spiritual Democracy: Essays in Honor of Joseph L. Blau*, ed. M. Wohlgelernter (New York, 1980), 97–113. Among other arguments, Neusner claims that the explicit attestation of specific laws elsewhere to the disciples of R. Akiba points to this later provenance of this anonymous tractate as well (108). However, considering the discontinuity in the tannaitic study of the Temple laws, this argumentation is less conclusive than we would regularly assume.

51. Hillel Mali, "Descriptions of the Temple in the Mishnah: History, Redaction and Meaning" (diss., Bar Ilan University, 2018), 121–24 (Hebrew).

that this tractate, which he dated immediately after the destruction of the Temple, remained outside the general framework of the Mishnah, which continued to evolve and absorb later disputes and interpretation up to its final redaction.

Here again the chronological relationship between this and other tractates cannot be determined by supposedly ancient qualities of some literary features, but rather by tracing material that originated in one context and then was integrated in another text. And indeed scholars have demonstrated the ways other tractates dealing with the Temple have utilized sections from tractate *Tamid*, including tractates *Midot*, *Yoma'*, and *Shekalim*. As these works show, in any case of a parallel between *Tamid* and other tractates there are clear indications of the primacy of the version and context in *Tamid*. Beyond the assessment of the particular parallels, these comparisons reveal a wider and recurring phenomenon: the Mishnah consistently dissects the uniform narrative of *Tamid* and integrates select sections into the compound of concise sources, interpretations, and comments that characteristically constitute other tractates.

Arguably, this consistent textual relationship indicates that we are not dealing with parallel concurrent methods for organizing rabbinic knowledge, but rather with the development of mishnaic literary features from earlier attempts that preceded the establishment of the rabbinic manner of study and transmission. Thus, while tractate *Midot* consists of a small number of sources partially based on *Tamid*,[52] and is relatively uniform, *Yoma'* occasionally quotes and paraphrases select sections, that are subjected to redaction, interpretation, and additions,[53] and *Shekalim* creates a completely new literary construct on the basis of the materials from *Tamid*.[54] As in the case of *'Eduyot*, literary comparisons provide a useful tool for tracing the transformation of literary forms and the development of the mishnaic form of legal discourse.

---

52. Mali, "Descriptions of the Temple in the Mishnah," 140–44; Compare the synchronic view of Avraham Walfish, "Ideological Tendencies in the Description of the Temple and its Worship in Tractates Tamid and Middot" (Hebrew), *Judea and Samaria Studies* 7 (1997): 79–93.

53. Abraham Goldberg, "Tosefta of Tractate Tamid," in *Benjamin De-Vries Memorial Volume*, ed. E. Z. Melamed (Jerusalem, 1969), 18–42 (Hebrew); Yishai Glazner, "On the Use of 'Mishnayot' Tamid in Mishnah Yoma" (Hebrew), *Netuim* 19 (2014): 91–106.

54. Yair Furstenberg, "The History of Temple Sources in the Mishnah: On the Evolution of Tractate Sheqalim," *Meḥqerei Talmud* 4 (forthcoming). This is particularly evident with respect to the list of supervisors listed in mShekalim 5:1, based on an inventive interpretation of tractate *Tamid*.

In addition to mishnaic tractates representing earlier embryonic forms of rabbinic legal composition that were later adapted to more developed forms of rabbinic study, some scholars suggested that midrashic units embedded in the Mishnah belong to an earlier stage of rabbinic learning. This view was promoted by David Weiss Halivni and Abraham Goldberg, who both turned to the Qumran *Temple Scroll* as an early literary model.[55] On the literary level however, it is difficult to establish the primacy of the midrashic units in the Mishnah on the basis of this comparison as long as we lack internal literary evidence for the relative antiquity of these sections. At the same time, in other aspects the comparison to Qumran legal literature can indeed mark the developments of legal writing in the Mishnah from its earlier roots.

Scholars have amply demonstrated the close relation of early rabbinic law of the Second Temple period to Qumran legal literature.[56] But beyond the proximity of legal content and shared legal traditions or interpretations, the comparison of Qumran literature to early rabbinic teachings can also serve to mark out and characterize common assemblages of legal issues shared by both traditions. Their original form and contours are discernible even as they were integrated into expanding mishnaic compositions. The Shabbat laws in the Damascus Document provide an illuminating example.[57] This is one of the most detailed topics in the work, and it does not carry an overly polemical tone against Pharisaic-rabbinic law. Therefore, one can imagine that this issue was studied in a similar manner among the different groups, as indicated by the shared scholarly frameworks of the Qumranic composition and the earliest strata of the Mishnah.[58]

The teachings of the Houses of Shammai and Hillel, which constitute the earliest strata of the Mishnah, appear at the head of the tractate, where they deal with preparations for Shabbat, and towards the end they discuss

---

55. David Weiss Halivni, *Midrash, Mishnah and Gemara: The Jewish Predilection for Justified Law* (Cambridge, Mass., and London, 1986), 18–37; Abraham Goldberg, "The Early Midrash and the Late Midrash" (Hebrew), *Tarbiz* 50 (1980–81): 94–106. Goldberg points to the midrashic form of the section on the confession of the Tithes in mMS 5.10–13, and the ritual of the *ḥalitsa* in mYev 12:6 as early sources similar to the *Temple Scroll* embedded in the Mishnah.

56. For a detailed survey of this issue see the contribution of Vered Noam in this volume. I have demonstrated the shared foundation of Qumran and early rabbinic law in Furstenberg, *Purity and Community*, esp. chapter 5.

57. *Damascus Document* 10:14–11:18.

58. For general considerations in comparing the Mishnah to the Damascus Document, see S. Fraade, "Ancient Jewish Law and Narrative in Comparative Perspective," *Legal Fictions: Studies of Law and Narrative in the Discursive Worlds of Ancient Jewish Sectarians and Sages* (Leiden, 2011), 227–54 (246–54).

materials that cannot be carried around the house.[59] The location of these teachings is not insignificant, since a textual analysis of the whole tractate clearly points to a shift, from sporadic instructions concerning the conduct on Shabbat to a systematic attempt to define the prohibited labors on Shabbat in the middle chapters of the tractate.[60] The resemblance between the issues discussed in the Damascus Document and the first and last chapters of tractate *Shabat* is quite revealing, as both focus on the preparation of foods before the Sabbath, the prohibition to plan and discuss business matters, carrying of materials, and removing things in and out of the house. The early legal discourse, in both texts, is not concerned with actual labor on the Sabbath. This thematic similarity points to the shared halakhic world, but at times these texts even exhibit a similar literary arrangement. These literary parallels help make sense of the organizing principles of the last chapters of tractate *Shabat* that at first sight seem to comprise a random collection of instructions.

Thus, in the Damascus Document, the laws based on Isaiah 58:13 concerning business and planning on Shabbat are followed by a prohibition to eat food that was not prepared beforehand, and a prohibition to rely on the work of a gentile. These issues are combined also in the last two chapters of tractate *Shabat*, albeit in much greater detail.[61] The previous chapter addresses various issues concerning the use of liquids on Shabbat, including drinking, laundering, and opening jars, and a similar list of cases appears in the same literary context in the Damascus Document.[62] The shorter unit in the Qumranic composition allows us to identify the underlying literary pattern that has been embedded into the developed and complex mishnaic composition. This testifies to the depth of the scholarly traditions underlying the literary framework of the Mishnah, and allows us to trace the development of new ways formed by later tannaim to conceptualize the legal topics and arrange them accordingly.

The pre-rabbinic and proto-tannaitic sources surveyed in this section point to the diverse literary forms and study patterns that ultimately evolved into the distinct mishnaic discourse. Nonetheless, nascent elements are still recognizable under the massive process of unification and legal systemiza-

---

59. mShab 1:4–8, 3:1, 21:3.

60. For a helpful survey of explanations for the structure of tractate *Shabat* see Yoel Kretzmer Raziel, "The Structure of Tractate Shabbat: Like Mountains Suspended on Hair" (Hebrew), *Mishlav* 41 (2008): 7–35 (9–12). Kretzmer Raziel himself suggests that the tractate follows the biblical order as in the examples in the next section.

61. CD 10:17–11:2; mShab 23:1–4, 24:1–4.

62. CD 11:1–4; mShab 22:4–5.

tion of later rabbis in the form of cases, testimonies, Temple traditions, and distinctive legal collections. At some point these materials served the tannaim, in particular in the school of R. Akiba, as a foundation for developing a systematic, comprehensive, and unified legal discourse, as it appears in our Mishnah.

4. DYNAMIC TEXTUALITY

In the previous section we traced the development of some mishnaic literary features through comparison to earlier works from which they were drawn. In most cases, however, we are not fortunate to actually possess the original text in its earlier form. All we have are the extremely intricate multi-layered literary compounds. Nonetheless, even without an external anchor, Mishnah scholars have been able to identify the evolution process of these literary composites. Alongside the regular juxtaposition and weaving together of distinct even contradictory sources,[63] in many cases the two units exhibit some level of mutual dependence that extends beyond redactional modifications, as discussed above in section 2. This literary interdependence is crucial for examining the evolution of the Mishnah, since it allows us to separate distinct literary stages and follow the changing shape and intention of the Mishnah. For the sake of our current discussion, it is useful to distinguish between three forms of literary dependence, according to their degree of continuity: interpretation, insertion, and rearrangement. While the first fits a simple model of legal development, the latter two can point to significant, and at times radical, changes in the mishnaic form and discourse.

Interpretation. Occasionally it is possible to trace the accumulation of literary material through the names of the rabbis. Sometimes the Mishnah presents explicit interpretations by later rabbis of the teachings of earlier rabbis;[64] the dominance of early rabbis in some units allows us to isolate the additional comments by later rabbis. Thus, for example, the last chapters of *Teharot* present a nicely organized unit of the teachings of Yavnean rabbis,[65] to which clear comments of R. Akiba's disciples were added. A group of their teachings concerning *am ha-aretz* (mTeh 10.1–3) were inserted amongst the sequence of disputes between the Houses, and it reflects the

---

63. For an illuminating example see Amit Gvaryahu, "The Tannaitic Law of Battery: Scripture and Halakhah" (Hebrew), *Tarbiz* 86 (2019): 533–74 (556–66).

64. See for example mPes 1:6–7; mShek 2:2–3, 4:7.

65. mTeh 8:6–10:8. This unit opens with a general rule, appropriate as an opening statement, then follows a list of Yavnean disputes. Chapters 9–10 discuss purity in the

new legal challenge that concerned these later rabbis. To take another example: Hayim Lapin's analysis of the redactional process of tractate *Bava Metsi'a*,[66] reveals a consistent pattern by which specific rabbis added their comments to an earlier textual substratum. As Lapin writes, it is striking that material that on formal grounds is distinct from other parts of the tractate is consistently glossed by traditions attributed to the same two rabbis. Thus, the attributions serve as indicators of the hands through which the material has passed.[67]

Attributions are a crucial but insufficient tool for tracing the literary evolution of the Mishnah, considering the fact that much of the Mishnah is anonymous and that attributions scarcely provide substantial evidence for literary developments. Nonetheless, scholars have explored additional literary patterns which could indicate the accumulation of interpretive layers. This is characteristic of the work of Avraham Weiss on the Mishnah, who mapped out the mishnaic sources, predominantly on the basis of literary and formal features. Thus, for example, he discusses cases of short and general rules that are followed by later interpretations and elaborations. In some cases, he claims, the Mishnah even provides conflicting interpretations of the ancient rule.[68] His son, Moshe Weiss, expanded this approach and argued that some substantial units in the Mishnah function as an internal Tosefta, expanding upon and complementing another section within the tractate.[69] This phenomenon adds to Albeck's assertion that occasionally single Mishnahs were appended to the end of tractates so as to comment on laws earlier in the tractate.

---

production of oil and wine and are dominated by disputes between the Houses of Hillel and Shammai. Although it appears at the end of the tractate it belongs to its earliest layer. Compare Jacob Neusner, *History of Mishnaic Law of Purities*, 22 vols. (Leiden, 1974–77), 11.1, who (following Albeck) views this section as an appendix to the tractate, demonstrating the principles laid out in the previous chapters (as these were developed by later rabbis).

66. Lapin, *Early Rabbinic Civil Law*, 35–118 (Chapter 2: Literary and Redactional Problems).

67. Lapin, 114–15. In the previous chapters he identified the dominant organizational pattern through the regular use of a specific linguistic form (nominative absolute).

68. Avraham Weiss, "La-ḥeker ha-sifruti shel ha-mishna," *HUCA* 16 (1941): 1–32 (Hebrew Section); Weiss, "Perushim ve-he'arot le-text ve-leseder ha-mishna shel masekhet Shabbat", *Horev* 7 (1943): 2–74.

69. Moshe Weiss, "Tosefta-like Chapters in the Mishnah" (Hebrew), *Proceedings of the World Congress of Jewish Studies* 11 (1993), section 3.1, 55–62; Weiss, "The Order of the Mishnayot in Tractate Kinim: A Note on the Tosefta-like Chapters in the Mishna" (Hebrew), *Sidra* 13 (1997): 61–91.

Insertions. In addition to appendixes, texts are also inserted in a way that interrupts the flow of the surrounding unit, thereby indicating the later addition of text and possibly reflecting later concerns. A fine example appears in the first two chapters of tractate *Avot*. These chapters are based on a series of transmissions of the Torah from Moses to the disciples of Rabban Yohanan ben Zakkai, and these are marked by the recurring term "received from." This formal and historical sequence is interrupted after the teachings of Hillel and Shammai by a unit with an alternative organizing principle, following the Gamalielian dynasty down to the generations after R. Judah the Patriarch.[70] At this point the Mishnah returns to Rabban Yohanan ben Zakkai. While the surrounding framework is occupied with the chain of transmission up to the great rabbis of Yavneh,[71] the insertion of the Patriarchate unit evidently reflects a later interest of the third century Patriarchs to establish the antiquity and authority of their own dynasty.[72]

A halakhic example of a similar nature appears at the head of tractate *Bava Kama*. The tractate opens with a list of the four primary causes of injury (*avot nezikin*), following the biblical taxonomy (mBK 1:1). However, before discussing the four primary causes of injury in detail (3:9–6:6), the Mishnah turns to an alternative form of classification, according to the degree of danger (1:4–3:8), imposing novel, non-biblical conceptions of liability and only later returning to the basic biblical paradigm.[73] A final example is from tractate *Sanhedrin* regarding the forms of corporal punishment. Scholars have argued for the later addition of strangling as the fourth form of execution, which was considered by the rabbis to be the most lenient and the most basic form of execution in the Torah, although it is never mentioned there. Menahem Kahana has suggested that if the section on stran-

---

70. The inserted unit begins in mAv 1:16 (Rabban Gamaliel says). The ending point of the unit is less clear since it is not known who is the Hillel mentioned in 2.4–7. At any rate, the original sequence of transmission resumes with Rabban Yohanan ben Zakkai, who received from Hillel and Shammai in 2:8.

71. This section may have already been redacted at that stage, in an attempt to justify the emergence of the new rabbinic movement after the destruction.

72. See Amram Tropper, *Wisdom, Politics and Historiography: Tractate Avot in the Context of the Graeco-Roman Near East* (Oxford and New York, 2004), 88–116.

73. In his thorough analysis of tractate *Nezikin* (the three gates) David Daube identified the tension between the biblical arrangement and Romanizing legal tendencies. The complexity that the first chapters exhibit is in his view "a great flaw in the arrangement and clearly indicates limits of rabbinic systemization, the line beyond which the rabbis are incapable of remodeling their Biblical Material." See David Daube, "The Civil Law of the Mishnah: The Arrangement of the Three Gates," *Tulane Law Review* 18 (1944): 352–407 (374).

gling, as a rabbinic innovation, is removed from the Mishnah, we are left with a more coherent description of the three executions based in scripture. Here again literary indications point to literary insertions that reflect new trends in rabbinic law.[74]

Rearrangement. The changing forms of the Mishnah from its nascent stages are further exposed in cases of clashes between competing textual arrangements, as earlier material is reintegrated into new literary patterns. In the previous section we encountered such a phenomenon with respect to the integration of the *'Eduyot* material in new thematically oriented tractates. Here we will see that a careful analysis of the Mishnah's literary texture reveals traces of rearrangement of earlier material, even without an available text of origin, and even when the different arrangements pertain to the same topic. The process of literary rearrangement allows us to recognize, behind the imposition of new organizing principles, far-reaching developments within rabbinic study culture. Here I will address two such cases.

The issue of food purity occupies four tractates in the Mishnah: *Teharot, Makhshirin, Tevul Yom*, and *'Uktsim*.[75] Each of these tractates exhibits a different level of literary complexity in correlation with its length. Tractate *Teharot* offers an elaborate presentation of the principles regarding the spread of food impurity, as well as sub-tractates on doubts and *am ha-aretz* impurity. The six chapters of tractate *Makhshirin* cover various aspects of rendering foods susceptible to impurity through the contact of liquids. The shorter tractates, on the other hand, reveal a condensed literary pattern that recurs in all the tractates dealing with food impurity. Tractate *'Uktsim* deals primarily with purity of vegetables, focusing on two issues: defining the parts that are considered connected and impart impurity, and the stages when the produce becomes susceptible to impurity. These two issues, connectivity and susceptibility, are repeated in the first chapters of *Tevul Yom* in the same order, this time with respect to cooked dishes.[76]

Once we have identified this recurring pattern with respect to different kinds of foods, parallel units of this pattern surface in the other tractates as

74. Menahem Kahana, "Standard Execution: Stoning or Strangling?" *Moria Libson Memorial Volume: Studies in Jewish Studies* (Hebrew; Jerusalem, 2011), 17–26.

75. See Yair Furstenberg, "Early Redactions of 'Purities': A New Look into Mishnah Source-Criticism" (Hebrew), *Tarbiz* 80 (2012): 507–37.

76. These issues already appear in the teachings of the Houses, and arguably represent Pharisaic policy of purity observance. As such they were condemned by other groups. See Furstenberg, *Purity and Community*, 138–55; Yair Furstenberg, "Jesus against the Laws of the Pharisees: The Legal Woe Sayings and Second Temple Inter-Sectarian Discourse," *Journal of Biblical Literature* 139 (2020): 767–86.

well. This is the organizing principle of the last three chapters of tractate *Teharot*, which as we saw are almost entirely attributed to early tannaim, Yavnean rabbis, and the Houses. This unit addresses another well-defined group of foods: the triad of bread, wine, and oil. In a similar fashion, under the surface of the textual complex of the last chapter and a half of tractate *Makhshirin* relating to liquid susceptibility, lies another group of laws following the same pattern, this time regarding the unique challenge of purity observance in the market.

Four similar units are embedded in different tractates, each dealing with the same legal issues (connectivity and susceptibility) within different circumstances. This textual situation points to the existence of an early recension of these laws, which is fundamentally different from the current arrangement within the larger, more developed tractates. The original units are best understood as practical manuals for managing purity in various circumstances; therefore, they are organized according to practical considerations, and not general legal principles.[77] Only in a later stage, as these units were integrated into larger structures, these considerations were neglected in favor of a more scholastic, theoretical legal discourse.

Another example for a rearrangement of materials that indicates new forms of rabbinic study and legal thought appears in tractate *Bava Metsi'a*.[78] The order of topics in this tractate, the middle part of the larger order *Nezikin*, is admittedly quite perplexing.[79] The apparent duplication of the issue of bailees in the third and seventh chapters, where it is further disrupted by the topic of laborer rights, is particularly disturbing. In my view, the textual incoherence that is most apparent in the second half of the tractate is not a result of sporadic additions and revisions;[80] rather, it is the direct outcome of the imposition of an alternative organizing principle on the earlier literary arrangement. As in tractate *Bava Kama*, dominated by the biblical ordering of delicts, *Bava Metsi'a*, although it includes a wider range of topics, has also initially been organized according to the order of the two main scriptural units dealing with private law, starting with Ex 22–23 and then turning to Deut 22–25. Thus, for example, the laws of pledge are juxtaposed

77. Furstenberg, "Early Redactions," 530–31.

78. See Yair Furstenberg, "From the Literature of Early Halakhah to Roman Law: The Development of Tractate *Bava Metsi'a*" (Hebrew), *The Disciples of Aaron: In Memory of Prof. Aaron Shemesh*, ed. D. Boyarin, V. Noam, and I. Rosen-Zvi, *Te'uda* 31 (2020): 537–70.

79. See Daube, "The Civil Law of the Mishnah," 377–93.

80. As in the suggestions of Lapin, *Early Rabbinic Civil Law*, 85–86; David Henshke, *The Original Mishna in the Discourse of Later Tannaim* (Hebrew, Ramat Gan, 1997), 48–49.

with the unrelated laws concerning daily payments of laborers (mBM 9:11–13), since they appear alongside each other in Deut 25.[81]

In fact, the only topic that does not fit the biblical pattern is the issue of animal keepers, which we would expect to appear immediately after chapter 3, dealing with keepers of movables, as in Ex 22:6–14. At the same time, this disjoined unit is surrounded by a well-structured unit on rent and lease, including sections that share the same linguistic form and similar legal concerns. Analysis of this unit reveals its affinity to the Roman category of *locatio conductio*, a form of contract which includes hiring workers, rental of services and livestock, and leasing of houses and property.[82] Noticeably, a major component of this contract is the accountability for the damage of property held by the artisan, laborer, or lessee, subsequently leading to a reorganization of the mishnaic material.

In its final redaction the Mishnah transposed this unit concerning animal keepers from its original placement following the order of the Torah, and relocated this section at the heart of the structured unit on lease and rent, as part of a sequence of unwritten contracts that continue into tractate *Bava Batra*. The clash between two competing forms of arrangement in this part of the tractate reveals the fundamental transition that took place between two forms of study, and two approaches to these issues of private law. The earlier form, rooted in the practices of Second Temple legal literature, is bound to the biblical order and scope of topics.[83] The development of a broader conception of the field of private law entailed the adoption of Roman-like legal taxonomy, enabling the creation of new legal fields. The textual complexity is not a result of confusion as David Daube has argued; rather, it reveals the transformation of literary and conceptual frameworks in an attempt to adapt the Mishnah to familiar contemporary legal patterns.

CONCLUSION

In this paper we surveyed three general approaches to the formation of the Mishnah which draw on different groups of textual phenomena. These phenomena reflect the diverse facets of this complex creation. Classical source criticism has pointed to evidence for early literary formulations, which were

---

81. For a detailed account see Furstenberg, "Bava Metsiʿa," 548–56. A similar biblical framework determines the combination of topics in the first chapters of tractate *Shevuʿot*. See Halivni, *Midrash, Mishnah and Gemara*, 47–55.

82. This issue is concentrated in Justinian's Digest 19.2.

83. Therefore, Josephus apologized to his readers for rearranging the biblical laws in an alternative order (Josephus, *Ant.* 4:196–98).

transmitted, interpreted, and revised through multiple channels. The second approach stresses the inventiveness of both the tannaitic lawmakers in general and the redactor of the Mishnah in particular, who carefully chose each word of the condensed and precise text. Finally, in the last sections we underlined the changing literary and legal arrangements, which may well reflect developments in rabbinic study culture and law-making.

Any attempt to understand what the Mishnah is and to describe it as a composition requires consideration of all these different textual phenomena, and at the same time, the careful distinction of unique features of the Mishnah from general rabbinic patterns of study. In other words, we must ask, in what sense exactly is the Mishnah a distinct composition, and not only a segment of the continuous evolution of rabbinic study culture and flow of literary production? While classical source criticism has viewed our Mishnah as merely one version among the many compilations of rabbinic law, one whose uniqueness derives mainly from the Patriarch's authority rather than its specific literary features, it is currently common to consider the Mishnah as the first and revolutionary product of the rabbinic movement. However, this is clearly an illusion, since the Mishnah evidently absorbed earlier texts. What then sets the Mishnah apart from other rabbinic compositions, including those which have been incorporated into it? I would argue that the range of literary features surveyed in this paper, some of which reflect broader rabbinic tendencies and others that are unique to the texture of our Mishnah, point towards a process of literary differentiation, through which this specific compilation was transformed into *the* Mishnah.

Admittedly, our Mishnah is not merely an accumulation or repository of earlier sources, and it exhibits significant redactional revisionism. At the same time, it does not attempt to conceal its diverse source, and its redaction (or more accurately, its ongoing process of literary improvement) primarily pertains to the local literary level: the specific formulations of legal positions, adjustment of legal terminology, and the creation of a general aesthetic effect through a tighter literary style. In comparison to all other tannaitic compositions, the Mishnah exhibits an unprecedented degree of literary precision, which marks its unique literary texture. The most apparent effect of this literary differentiation of the Mishnah from other rabbinic sources is the consolidation of rabbinic study within a cohesive literary framework.

Notably, this literary nature of the Mishnah is not aimed towards uniformity and does not obscure gaps, tensions, and disjunctions. On the contrary, it is particularly this integrative tendency that allows a better view into the literary dynamics as I described them in sections 3–4. As we have seen, Mishnah source criticism can hardly serve to reveal the "first Mish-nah" as Hoffman expected, nor to reconstruct the mishnaic corpus of each of the tannaim, as Epstein did. At the same time, it exhibits clear literary composites, pertaining to distinct phases of rabbinic literary production, and as such points to the trajectories of rabbinic study culture. While the literary situation has proven to be too complex to clearly separate between sources and redaction, the literary tensions point to general tendencies and substantial scholarly shifts: from the expansion of legal concerns, through the employment of new legal discourse, to the separation or creation of new fields. Notably, although these developments are not limited to the Mish-nah, they are most visible here, while loose collections of sources such as those in the Tosefta cannot provide a clear image of legal and textual con-solidation. Evidently, then, the literary cohesiveness of the Mishnah serves not only to merge different sources into a tighter literary framework, but also to highlight changing literary patterns, thus revealing the evolution of rabbinic legal discourse.

Part II

Roman Context and History

6. The Presentation of the Past in the Mishnah

Martin Goodman

Most mishnaic discourse employs the continuous present tense in open-ended discussions about legal rulings, giving the reader an impression that the text is uninterested in the passage of time except in relation to such issues as changes in liability for legal obligations after the lapse of defined periods.[1] But occasionally the Mishnah uses specific references to past events to explain current halakhah, and this essay will examine briefly how the past is presented in such cases, investigating in particular which elements of the past receive attention in the text and which elements are apparently ignored. It will emerge that the Mishnah is highly selective in its presentation of Jewish history and that it has surprisingly little to say about the biblical past which produced the scriptural texts on which so much of the Mishnah's own worldview was predicated.

Some of the Mishnah's references to the past occur as explanations of changes in custom as the product of a change in circumstances. So, for instance, the "corrupt teachings" of *minim* are said to have brought about a change in the wording of blessings,[2] and the destruction of the Temple in 70 CE is said to have led to a series of *takanot* in Yavneh to deal with practical liturgical issues such as the rules to be applied in the blowing of the *shofar* and the waving of the *lulav* "since the Temple was destroyed."[3] In such

---

1. On the use of tenses in the Mishnah, see Yochanan Breuer, "Paal u-veinoni be-tivnei tekes bamishnah," *Tarbiz* 56 (1987): 299–326; on the rabbinic understanding of the nature of time in this period, see Sacha Stern, *Time and Process in Ancient Judaism* (Oxford and Portland, Ore., 2003).

2. For instance, mBer 9.5 on change in the wording of blessings "after the heretics had taught corruptly."

3. mRH 4.1, 3.

cases nothing about the past event beyond its occurrence is explored within the text. The reader of the Mishnah is assumed to know, for instance, that the Temple has been destroyed, but he or she is not told anything about the causes of the destruction of the Temple, or when it happened, or even about the role of Rome in bringing it about.[4] The fullest expression of the theme that the world has been changed since some specific named event or shift in society can be found in in the final chapter of tractate *Sotah*, although the last part of the final mishnah in this tractate, which looks not backwards to the past but forwards to the "footprints of the Messiah," is probably a later addition to the text.[5]

Rather more information is presented in the Mishnah about the history of the rabbinic movement itself, but the history presented is oddly incoherent. Best known, of course, is the assertion at the start of tractate *Avot* that "Moses received Torah from Sinai" and that the Torah was handed on by Moses to Joshua and then, through a continuous tradition of sages, down to the present: indeed, this depiction of the origins of the rabbinic tradition has often been treated as a manifesto for rabbinic Judaism in general and the Mishnah in particular. It seems plausible enough that the account in *Avot* was preserved with the rest of the Mishnah to provide authority for the opinions of the sages, but the notion that this depiction of a change of tradition since Moses was composed as part of the original project which produced the Mishnah is less plausible, since the anomalous genre of *Avot* as wisdom literature differs markedly from the rest of the Mishnah. It is probably no accident that *Avot* fits so poorly into the overall tractate structure of the Mishnah as to be in different places and within different orders in the medieval manuscripts which contain the Mishnah as a whole, and mentions of the chain of tradition since Moses are rare in the Mishnah outside tractate *Avot* itself.[6]

It is also striking that the continuous chain of tradition from Moses to the present delineated in *Avot* makes no mention of the teachings of the houses

---

4. On rabbinic responses to the destruction of the Temple in 70 CE, see, for instance, Jonathan Klawans, "Josephus, the Rabbis and Responses to Catastrophes Ancient and Modern," *JQR* 100 (2010): 278–309. The reference in mSot 9.14 to the "war of Vespasian," when "they forbade the crowns of the bridegrooms and the drum," fails to link the war to the destruction of the Temple despite the reference to the destruction in a closely preceding passage (mSot 9.12).

5. mSot 9.9–15.

6. Amram D. Tropper, *Wisdom, Politics and Historiography: Tractate Avot in the context of the Graeco-Roman Near East* (Oxford, 2004). The chain formula is found in mPe'ah 1.6, m'Eduy 8.7 and mYad 4.3 with reference to the transmission of specific traditions, but the use of the verb "received" with respect to the Torah as a whole seems

of Hillel and Shammai, which constitute such a major element of the discussions in the rest of the Mishnah in the depiction of rabbinic discourse in the decades before the destruction of the Temple, and it has even been argued that the claim of continuity since Moses represented a riposte to the presentation of the past in the rest of the Mishnah, rather than an encapsulation of the Mishnah's depiction of the emergence of different schools of halakhic interpretation and the role of the sages after 70 CE in the preservation of these different traditions. Thus Adiel Schremer has suggested that the presentation of the seamless chain of tradition since Moses in *Avot* constituted a polemical retort, emanating from the school of R. Eliezer b. Hyrcanus or his followers, against the mishnaic view that the teachings of the sages had to be collected by the rabbis when they gathered at Yavneh around Yoḥanan b. Zakkai after 70 CE, beginning by preserving the teachings of the houses of Shammai and of Hillel. The conflict between these two depictions of the rabbinic past has considerable implications for the nature and source of rabbinic authority, as Schremer observes.[7]

It is all the more remarkable (although this is not observed by Schremer in this study) that the historiographical statement which lays out the approach to the historiography of the rabbinic movement presupposed in the Mishnah is not to be found in the Mishnah but only in the Tosefta: "When the sages gathered in the vineyard at Yavneh they said: 'The time is coming at which a person will go looking for a word of Torah and will not find it, for a word of scribes and will not find it'. . . They said: 'Let us begin. What are of the House of Shammai and what is of the House of Hillel.'" One looks in vain in the Mishnah for any such account of a new beginning in the discussions of the sages in the years after 70 CE. Furthermore, although one might have expected stories about the virtuous behaviour of the sages themselves to provide a starting point for discussions of halakhah as in later rabbinic compilations, in practice such stories are rarely found in the Mishnah—indeed, it has been commonplace, since the work of Jacob Neusner and his students in the 1970s and the following decades, to observe that all the good stories about the rabbinic sages themselves are to be found not in the Mishnah but

to be unique to mAvot 1.1, cf. Gunter Stemberger, "'Moses received Torah . . .' (*mAvot* 1.1): Rabbinic Conceptions of Revelation," in *Jerusalem, Alexandria, Rome: Studies in Ancient Cultural Interaction in Honour of A. Hilhorst*, ed. F. G. Martinez and G. P. Luttikhuizen (Leiden, 2003), 285–99.

7. Adiel Schremer, "*Avot* Reconsidered: Rethinking Rabbinic Judaism," *JQR* 105 (2015): 287–311.

in legends from after the tannaitic period, so that no real rabbinic biographies can be written by anyone relying on the tannaitic evidence alone.[8]

The silence of the Mishnah about rabbinic biography is all the more surprising in light of the Mishnah's memorialisation of the non-rabbinic past through liturgical practice—from the Exodus commemorated in the celebration of Passover as discussed in tractate *Pesaḥim*, and the story of Purim which underlies the rules for the reading of the book of Esther regulated in tractate *Megilah*, to the destruction of the Temple "the first and the second time" which is marked by fasting on the 9th of Ab according to tractate *Ta'anit*.[9] Thus, for instance, the Mishnah attributes numerous teachings to Akiva and Shimon bar Yohai but betrays no trace of interest in their travails in the time of Bar Kokhba. It is true that the Mishnah occasionally includes details about the life of an individual sage, such as Rabban Gamaliel's treatment of his slave Tabi, to illustrate his attitude to specific halakhot, but when the Mishnah cites a story about "certain levites" who once went to Zoar and lost one of their companions to sickness in an inn, so that the mistress of the inn gave testimony to his death (and was believed), the characters in the story are anonymous.[10]

No less surprising than this lack of interest in the Mishnah in rabbinic biography is the lack of interest in the circumstantial details of the history of the Temple in Jerusalem, despite the great amount of attention paid to the details of the Temple cult. Discussions of the Temple and its rituals constitute over a third of the Mishnah, but one looks in vain in the text for any reference to the rebuilding project by Herod a century before the Temple's destruction, or for the names of any of the High Priests who served in the Temple during that century, apart from two mentions of Ishmael b. Phiabi, the High Priest from c. 58 to 61 CE. The only reference to any specific events clearly datable to this period is the account of the reading of the book of Deuteronomy by a king in the Temple in accordance with Deut 31:11, which unexpectedly dwells on the behaviour of a king named Agrippa (therefore either Agrippa I or Agrippa II) rather than a biblical king, but this reference to real events in the Temple is an exception.[11]

8. Jacob Neusner, *Development of a Legend: Studies in the Traditions Concerning Yohanan ben Zakkai* (Leiden, 1970).

9. mTa'an 4.6–7.

10. On Gamaliel and Tabi, see mBer 2.7; mPes 7.2; mSuk 2.1; on the Levites in Zoar, see mYev 16.7.

11. On Ishmael b. Phiabi, see mPar 3.5 (on his preparation of a red heifer) and mSot 9.15; on Agrippa, see mSot 7.8.

Even more remarkable than the lack of reference to Herod as the builder of the Temple in its final form is the lack of reference to Solomon, its first builder, even when the text cites a scriptural verse which refers to Solomon's Temple, as at mMid 4.4.[12] The description of the Temple and its rituals comprises instead a detailed account of an imagined Temple into which elements of the Solomonic and Herodian buildings are merged with rabbinic fantasy to present a picture of an idealized institution. This idealized picture was evidently considered to be of considerable import for the present day, and thus worthy of intense discussion between the sages, despite the destruction of the Herodian building and the end of sacrifice a century and a half before the Mishnah was compiled. Nothing hints at a new form of Judaism with novel religious practices to replace the sacrifices and offerings mandated in the Torah. Whether this implies that the extended discussions of the sages reflected an expectation that the Temple would soon be rebuilt, as it had been after its earlier destruction, or a belief that constructing a theory of sacrifice through elaborate descriptions was valuable in its own right, cannot be known. In either case, the entire discourse takes for granted the primacy of rabbinic opinions in shaping correct worship. Less clear is whether the Mishnah also presupposes rabbinic control over the Temple cult in the past: according to mMid 5.4, the Great Sanhedrin used to "sit and judge the priesthood," and in mSan 4.4 the Sanhedrin is described as a body comprising the pupils of the sages, so it would be reasonable to deduce that the disciples of the sages were thought to have judged the priesthood, but the text fails to make this explicit.[13]

The failure of the Mishnah to provide a clearer image of the Jewish past is surprising in light of the common claim that the Mishnah constituted in some way a response to the political and military disasters suffered by the

12. The verse cited is I Kgs 6.6, describing the relationship of three stories of cells, one above another.

13. On the depiction of the Temple and its rituals in the Mishnah, see Lee I. Levine, "Josephus' Description of the Jerusalem Temple: 'War,' 'Antiquities,' and Other Sources," in *Josephus and the History of the Greco-Roman Period: Essays in Memory of Morton Smith*, ed. F. Parente and J. Sievers (Leiden, 1994), 233–46; Steven D. Fraade, "The Temple as a Marker of Jewish Identity before and after 70 CE: The Role of the Holy Vessels in Rabbinic Memory and Imagination," in *Jewish Identities in Antiquity: Studies in Memory of Menahem Stern*, ed. L. I. Levine and D. R. Schwartz (Tübingen, 2009), 237–65; Ishay Rosen-Zvi, *The Mishnaic Sotah Ritual: Temple, Gender and Midrash* (Leiden, 2012); Naftali S. Cohn, *The Memory of the Temple and the Making of the Rabbis* (Philadelphia, 2013); Mira Balberg, *Blood for Thought: The Reinvention of Sacrifice in Early Rabbinic Literature* (Oakland, Calif., 2017); Nathan S. Schumer, "The Memory of the Temple in Palestinian Rabbinic Literature" (PhD diss., Columbia, 2017).

Jews at the hands of Rome in 70 and 135 CE, even though references to these disasters are almost absent from the Mishnah itself and almost nothing is said explicitly about Rome.[14] To some extent, such claims about the impact of disaster are a product of circular argument: if it is assumed that Jews and Judaism must have been deeply affected by the Roman world between 135 CE and the adoption of Christianity by Constantine in 312 CE because Jews saw Rome as a sibling rival for world domination, as has recently been argued, the Mishnah might reasonably be expected to reflect this somehow in its depiction of the Jewish polity. Some have even claimed optimistically that the Mishnah provided, in place of national political structures, a new identity through a law code to act as a beacon for the Jewish people in troubled times.[15]

The open-ended nature of mishnaic discourse, and amoraic debates about the interpretation of this discourse, may be thought to preclude the notion that the Mishnah was designed to provide a clear law code of any kind, but more plausible is the suggestion that the Mishnah constituted an expression of resistance to Roman rule in other ways, through its role in implicitly delegitimizing the right of the Roman state to alienate property and exercise jurisdiction in criminal cases,[16] and through its deliberate distancing of its intended audience from surrounding society by the adoption of Hebrew rather than Aramaic or Greek despite the widespread use of both Aramaic and Greek for other purposes in Palaestina, as in the rest of the Roman Near East, in this period.[17] Even if it is accepted that many Jews in Palaestina abandoned allegiance to their Jewish identity in the two centuries following the defeat of Bar Kokhba,[18] the rabbis must be seen as a counter-instance: whatever model is posited for rabbis and Romanization,[19] and

14. Ishay Rosen-Zvi, "Is the Mishnah a Roman Composition?" *The Faces of Torah*, ed. M. Bar Asher Siegal, T. Novick, and C. Hayes (Göttingen, 2017), 495, refers to subversive rabbinic discourse about Rome as Esau, Edom, and the Fourth Kingdom in Daniel, but this discourse, which is indeed so characteristic of much later rabbinic literature, is not actually a feature of the Mishnah.

15. Katell Berthelot, ed., *Reconsidering Roman Power: Roman, Greek, Jewish and Christian Perceptions and Reactions* (Rome, 2020); David Aberbach, *Revolutionary Hebrew, Empire and Crisis: Four Peaks in Hebrew Literature and Jewish Survival* (London, 1998).

16. Seth Schwartz, "The Mishnah and the Limits of Roman Power," in *Reconsidering Roman Power*, ed. K. Berthelot, 396.

17. Fergus G. B. Millar, *The Roman Near East, 31 BC–AD 337* (Cambridge, Mass., and London, 1993).

18. Seth Schwartz, *Imperialism and Jewish Society: 200 B.C.E. to 640 C.E.* (Princeton, 2001).

however minor their influence may have been beyond their own group,[20] there can be no denying their dedication to the Jewish tradition.

All of which raises the question of the mishnaic depiction of the biblical past. There is much evidence that other provincials in the eastern provinces of the Roman Empire expressed their cultural resistance to Rome by focusing on a more glorious past. This was most striking in the Greek world, where display orators of the so-called Second Sophistic selected themes from Athens in the fifth and fourth centuries BCE to demonstrate their rhetorical skill,[21] offsetting the indignities of current Roman domination and the collapse of Greek political independence in the Hellenistic period by harking back to a time when, as Romans would readily acknowledge, Greek civilization had far outshone the barbaric culture of Rome in the early Republic.[22] Athenians turned their city into a museum which celebrated the achievements of long ago in architecture, art, and ceremonies.[23] Spartans recreated a version of their famed austere lifestyle, presenting it as a return to the values of old.[24] Tourists in Greece and Asia Minor saw in the landscape and cities they visited the evidence of past glories.[25] Orators and moralists turned to well-known stories of the classical past for exempla to illustrate their arguments.[26]

The rabbis who produced the Mishnah did much the same as the authors of the Second Sophistic in respect to the recent past by also ignoring the political realities of contemporary provincial Roman life except when they impinged on matters of halakhic concern. Thus they made no mention of the

19. Ishay Rosen-Zvi, "Rabbis and Romanization: A Review Essay," in *Jewish Cultural Encounters in the Ancient Mediterranean and Near Eastern World*. ed. M. Popovic, M. Schoonover, and M. Vandenberghe (Leiden, 2017), 218–45.

20. Shaye J. D. Cohen, "The Rabbi in Second-Century Jewish Society," *The Cambridge History of Judaism: The Early Roman Period*, ed. W. Horbury, W. D. Davies, and J. Sturdy (Cambridge, 1999), 922–90.

21. Ewen Bowie, "The Greeks and Their Past in the Second Sophistic," *Past and Present* 46 (1970): 3–41; Graham Anderson, *The Second Sophistic: A Cultural Phenomenon in the Roman Empire* (London, 1993).

22. Simon Swain, *Hellenism and Empire: Language, Classicism and Power in the Greek World, AD 50–250* (Oxford, 1996), 65–100.

23. James H. Oliver, *The Civic Tradition and Roman Athens* (Baltimore, 1983).

24. Paul Cartledge and Antony Spawforth, *Hellenistic and Roman Sparta: A Tale of Two Cities*, 2nd ed. (London, 2002).

25. Susan E. Alcock, John F. Cherry, and Jas' Elsner, eds., *Pausanias: Travel and Memory in Roman Greece* (Oxford, 2001).

26. Christopher B. R. Pelling, *Plutarch and History: Eighteen Studies* (London, 2002); Joy Connolly, "Reclaiming the Theatrical in the Second Sophistic," *Helios* 28 (2001): 75–96.

Maccabees even in the context of Hanukkah and they had almost nothing to say about the dynasty of the Hasmoneans, or about Herod and his descendants, or about the war which had led to the destruction of the Temple in 70 CE and the defeat of Bar Kokhba.[27]

That this silence was the result of a deliberate exclusion of such historical material and not an accidental result of some sort of communal amnesia is clear both from the preservation of *Seder Olam* (see below) and from the evidence that wider Jewish society sometimes indulged in evocation of just such recent historical events: the rebels in 132–35 CE continued some of the coin types minted by their predecessors in the war of 66 to 70 CE, evoking in the later revolt the notion of a new era of "the freedom of Israel" which had been a novel characteristic of the first revolt; some inscriptions produced by Jews in Palaestina later in antiquity, long after the compilation of the Mishnah, referred to an era beginning with the destruction of the Temple.[28]

Thus the rabbis who produced the Mishnah could have done much the same as the authors of the Second Sophistic in reference to the distant past by using the biblical past to evoke the glorious history of Israel: precisely this was done in the late first century CE by Josephus in the heroic rewriting of the characters of biblical heroes in his *Antiquities*.[29] Both in the *Antiquities* and in his earlier *Jewish War*, Josephus referred quite frequently to the biblical significance of sites still to be seen in the geography of Judaea,[30] and rhetorical flights of fancy in the *Jewish War* evoked biblical figures like Jeremiah.[31]

That the rabbis cited in the Mishnah had just as good a knowledge of the biblical past as Josephus is clear from their citations of passages from every biblical book apart from Nehemiah, Daniel, and some of the minor prophets,[32] but these citations are not numerous for any biblical books apart from the Pentateuch, and the interest of the rabbis in the Mishnah lies more often in the specifics of the wording of the passage cited rather than an evoca-

27. The reference in mMid 1.6 to a room in the Temple where "the sons of the Hasmoneans had hidden away the stones of the altar which the Greek kings had defiled" is an exception.

28. Martin Goodman, *Rome and Jerusalem: The Clash of Ancient Civilizations* (London, 2007), 490–491.

29. Louis H. Feldman, *Josephus's Interpretation of the Bible* (Berkeley, 1998).

30. For example, Jos. *B.J.* 4. 483–5 (Sodom); 5. 303 (the "so-called Camp of the Assyrians," cf. 2 Kgs 18:17; 19:35).

31. Jos. *BJ* 6. 531–2.

32. Herbert Danby, *The Mishnah* (Oxford, 1933), 807–11. The book of Daniel is not cited, but reference to the book can be found in mYom 1.6 and mYad 4.5.

tion of the past.[33] Since the same rabbis discussed the biblical past more extensively in the tannaitic midrashim, which also cite the biblical texts much more extensively,[34] and later rabbinic texts also preserved stories about the Second Temple period in a form clearly related to their appearance in the writings of Josephus but through a separate tradition or traditions,[35] it is worth investigating whether the minimal evocation of the biblical past in the Mishnah was deliberate.

The Mishnah is not completely averse to citing biblical stories in support of a specific argument. When tractate *Berakhot* discusses the best sort of greeting to use, the first example quoted is Boaz, who according to the book of Ruth saluted the reapers with the phrase "The Lord be with you."[36] According to tractate *Ta'anit*, prayers by a community on a day of fasting should draw attention to the efficacy of prayer by Abraham on Mount Moriah, by the Israelites at the Red Sea, by Joshua in Gilgal, by Samuel at Mizpah, by Elijah on Carmel, by Jonah in the belly of the fish, and by "David and his son Solomon in Jerusalem."[37] As illustration of the principle of "measure for measure," which is said to underlie the punishment of a woman found guilty of adultery through the *sotah* ritual, the Mishnah notes the appropriateness of the punishments of Samson (blinded because he had gone after the desire of his eyes) and Absalom (hung by his hair because he gloried in his hair)[38] and, more positively, the readiness of the Israelites to wait seven days for Miriam, after she had been punished for speaking against Moses, as recompense for the "one hour" she had waited for Moses when he was a baby lying in a basket among the reeds by the bank of the Nile.[39] As illustration of the importance of confession by a criminal sentenced to death if he is to have a share in the world to come, the Mishnah quotes the example of Akhan son of Carmi, who took loot from Jericho contrary to the divine ban, and was sentenced by Joshua to be stoned. In this case, the moral drawn depends both on the confession which is intrinsic to the biblical story and on

33. See, for example, mShek 6.6, which quotes 2 Kgs 12:16 on Jehoiada and the Temple, using the wording of the verse in order to show how Lev 5:15 and Lev 5:18 can be conflated.

34. See, for example, Jacob Z. Lauterbach, *Mekhilta de-Rabbi Ishmael: A Critical Edition*, 2nd ed., 2 vols. (Philadelphia, 2014); Carol Bakhos, *Current Trends in the Study of Midrash* (Leiden, 2006).

35. Vered Noam, *Shifting Images of the Hasmonaeans: Second Temple Legends and Their Reception in Josephus and Rabbinic literature* (Oxford, 2018).

36. mBer 9.5.

37. mTa'an 2.4.

38. mSot 1.8.

39. mSot 1.9.

the precise wording of Joshua's condemnation: according to the Mishnah, since Joshua said that "The Lord shall trouble you this day," Akhan would be troubled "this day" but not in the world to come.[40]

Since such occasional uses of biblical exempla in the Mishnah show what could be done, the absence of biblical stories and characters from most of the text is striking. Our knowledge of the biblical past if we only had the Mishnah would be minimal, particularly if we exclude the wisdom tractate *Avot* (which starts with Moses on Sinai and refers to a series of incidents in the biblical narrative in chapter 5).[41] We would know little about Abraham apart from references to him as "our father" and an unspecified event on Mt. Moriah.[42] We would know a bit more about Moses, primarily as the originator of the law but also as victor over Amalek through keeping his hands raised, as we would know that he founded a system of courts still valid to the present, that he established the set feasts, that he was worthy to take the bones of Joseph for burial, that he himself was so worthy that he was buried by God himself, and that he prepared the first red heifer.[43] David is almost invisible, apart from an oblique reference to the undesirability of interpreting the story of him and Bathsheba[44] and references to his marriage to Saul's widow and behavior at Abner's funeral in a discussion of the rights and duties of a king in tractate *Sanhedrin*.[45] Even less is said about Solomon despite the extensive traditions in late Second Temple Judaism about his remarkable wealth and wisdom.[46] About Ezra we would know only that he expressly prohibited Samaritans from having a part in building the Temple[47] and that he was the second, after Moses, to prepare the ashes of the red heifer.[48] We would know about the blessings and curses on mount Gerizim and mount Ebal[49] and that there had been fighting against Philistines and the

---

40. mSan 6.2.

41. mAvot 5.2–4.

42. mKid 4.14 ("our father"); mTa'an 2.4 (Moriah).

43. mYom 3.8 (originator of law); mRH 3.8 (victor over Amalek); mSan 1.6 (founder of court system); mMeg 3.6 (set feasts); mSot 1.9 (bones of Joseph and burial by God); mPar 3.5 (red heifer).

44. mMeg 4.10.

45. mSan 2.2–3; the reference to eighteen women at mSan 2.4 presumably also refers to David, although it does not make this explicit.

46. On traditions about Solomon, see, for example, Erich S. Gruen, *Constructs of Identity in Hellenistic Judaism: Essays on Early Jewish Literature and History* (Berlin and Boston, 2016), 36–37, on Eupolemus.

47. mShek 1.5.

48. mPar 3.5.

49. mSot 7.5.

children of Ammon,[50] and a close reader might spot that at one time there were "priests of the high places" whose worship was considered an affront to the Temple in Jerusalem,[51] but we would have no sense of the impressiveness of Israel's history as it was paraded so effectively by Josephus just over a century earlier.

In sum, the attitude to the distant past in the Mishnah differs radically from that to be found in the Second Sophistic. While the writers of the Second Sophistic employed a pure Attic Greek as a way to distinguish their discourse from the debased versions of the Greek language in use by ordinary people in contemporary society,[52] the Mishnah, which also employs an artificial language which differed from the Aramaic used by ordinary people, eschewed classical Hebrew in favor of the distinctive form of the language which we characterize as mishnaic Hebrew.[53] Numerous opportunities to evoke the biblical past are passed over: to illustrate problems in implementing the principle of levirate marriage in tractate *Yevamot*, the Mishnah could have cited the story of Tamar in Genesis or the story of Boaz in the book of Ruth;[54] much more could have been said about Samson in tractate *Nazir*;[55] something on Jephthah and his daughter would have added weight to the discussion in tractate *Nedarim*, as can be seen from later rabbinic aggadah about his imprudent vow.[56]

It seems likely that the rabbis who compiled the Mishnah knew what they were doing when they decided to present their national tradition in so different a fashion from the classicizing of the Second Sophistic, but it is not easy to explain why they treated the past in this way. Since the Mishnah lacks any introduction or guide for users of the text or even any indication of the literary genre to which it should be assigned, any answer must be surmise, but some suggestions may be more plausible than others.

One possibility is that the rabbis said so little about the distant past because they did not find it interesting, preferring to focus instead on the present and the future, but if, as has been claimed, the same tannaitic rabbis were responsible for the preservation of *Seder Olam*,[57] it will not be possible

50. mSot 8.1.
51. mMen 13.10.
52. Swain, *Hellenism and Empire*.
53. Moshe Bar-Asher, *Studies in Mishnaic Hebrew*, 2 vols. (Hebrew; Jerusalem, 2009).
54. Gen 38:6-11 (Tamar); Ruth 4:3-8.
55. Jdg 13:4 (although note that mNaz 1.2 does discuss Samson as a type of nazirite).
56. Jdg 11:30-40; b. Ta'an 4a.
57. Chaim J. Milikowsky, *Seder 'Olam: mahadurah mada`it, perush u-mavo* (Jerusalem, 2013).

to characterize the period after 70 CE as a time in which Jews lost interest in historiography altogether,[58] and it may be preferable to seek an explanation in the specific purpose of the Mishnah itself, in which scriptural citations concentrate on the precise words used in the biblical text rather than the historical content of that text: it is remarkable, for instance, that the only reference to the story of Esther in tractate *Megilah*, which is dedicated to prescriptions for the reading of the book of Esther, is concerned with liturgical rules about the amount of the biblical book which must be read to fulfill the obligation on the festival of Purim.[59] In some ways, the rabbis may have thought about figures of the biblical past as sages like themselves, so that the text uses the characteristic rabbinic verb *darash* for the exposition of a biblical verse by Jehoiada, the high priest from the time of King Jehoash, and the characteristic rabbinic verb *hitkin* to describe the actions of "the first prophets" in ordaining the twenty-four courses into which the priesthood was divided.[60]

Perhaps the neatest explanation of the presentation of the past in the Mishnah is an assumption that the Mishnah was always designed by rabbis to be used in conjunction with more historiographically aware texts such as the halakhic midrashim, and that it may be wrong to try to understand the Mishnah as a text by itself rather than in the context of a complex rabbinic society of which the Mishnah only affords us occasional glimpses. If so, perhaps the lack of reference to any other contemporary rabbinic text anywhere in the text of the Mishnah constitutes simply an indication that the Mishnah was always intended as a hermetic text for insiders who could be expected to know how to use it well, and for whom glorying in the biblical past, which they knew intimately, was simply an unnecessary distraction from the fascinating task of discussing the halakhah for the present day.

58. Yosef H. Yerushalmi, *Zakhor: Jewish History and Jewish Memory* (New York, 1989).

59. mMeg 2.3.

60. mShek 6.6 on the interpretation of Lev 5:19 by Jehoiada (see note 33 above); mTa'an 4.2.

7. The Mishnah and Roman Law: A Rabbinic Compilation of *ius civile* for the Jewish *civitas* of the Land of Israel under Roman Rule

Catherine Hezser

The Mishnah was created by and is based on traditions that were generated and transmitted by rabbis who lived in the Land of Israel at a time when it was part of the wider Roman Empire. We can therefore assume that the Graeco-Roman political, social, economic, and cultural context affected many aspects of the Mishnah's content, structure, and purpose. Since the Mishnah is the first known compilation of rabbinic law, Roman jurists' law and legal compendia constitute the most important comparative material. Roman jurists were active in Roman Palaestina and other parts of the Roman Empire at the time when the Mishnah developed. Their roles as informal adjudicators resembled the roles of rabbis as legal advisors to their fellow Jews. Some of the legal areas and issues dealt with by mishnaic rabbis have analogies in Roman jurists' law. Rabbis transmitted, collected, and edited their teachers' and predecessors' legal traditions at approximately the same time as collections of jurists' law were created. Both the Mishnah and collections of Roman jurists' law were eventually integrated into the larger corpora of rabbinic and Roman civil law, the Talmud Yerushalmi and Justinian's Digest. Rabbis are likely to have been aware of Roman legal practices and discussions, even if they did not know Latin or study at Roman law schools.[1]

---

1. See Catherine Hezser, "Did Palestinian Rabbis Know Roman Law? Methodological Considerations and Case Studies," in *Legal Engagement: The Reception of Roman*

In this essay I shall suggest that the most simple and straightforward answer to the question "What is the Mishnah?" is that it is a compilation of rabbinic *ius civile* for the Jewish *civitas* within the boundaries of a rabbinically defined Land of Israel. In the post-Hadrianic period, the Roman *laissez-faire* attitude toward legal adjudication may have caused rabbis to confirm and intensify their role as legal advisors to members of the Jewish populace, serving as sources of legal knowledge that constituted an alternative to jurists who advised on the basis of Roman law. After Caracalla's reform of 212 CE, which granted citizenship to all inhabitants of the Roman Empire, rabbis may have feared that the political integration of the Jews of the Land of Israel into the Roman *civitas* might lead to complete legal integration. Jews could be subjected to Roman civil law while the centuries-old Jewish legal tradition, oriented around the Torah as the most important aspect of post-70 CE Jewish identity, might become lost. These circumstances may have motivated the editors, traditionally associated with the patriarch R. Yehudah ha-Nasi at the beginning of the third century, to compile earlier traditions into a corpus that matched the general topics and forms of Roman civil law (e.g., property law, family law) but also added areas of specifically Jewish concern (e.g., holiday observance and purity rules). A Jewish alternative to Roman *ius civile* was created that could be further developed, interpreted, and applied to new circumstances by later generations of rabbis.

1. RABBIS AND ROMAN JURISTS

Especially after the Bar Kokhba revolt, when the rabbinic Land of Israel became part of the Roman province of Syria-Palaestina, Roman jurists would have been active in major cities such as Caesarea, and private law schools may have been established in the land already in the second century.[2] In the mid-third century, Gregorius Thaumaturgus travelled to Caesarea to study Roman law there rather than at Berytus.[3] Experts in Roman law would have

Law and Tribunals by Jews and Other Inhabitants of the Empire, ed. K. Berthelot, N. B. Dohrmann, and C. Nemo-Pekelman (Rome, 2021). For earlier comparative approaches to rabbinic and Roman law see especially Boaz Cohen, *Jewish and Roman Law. A Comparative Study*, 2 vols. (New York, 1966); David Daube, *Collected Works of David Daube: Talmudic Law* (Berkeley, 1992), including "The Civil Law of the Mishnah: The Arrangement of Three Gates." For a review of scholarship on rabbinic and Roman law until 2003 see Catherine Hezser, "Introduction," in *Rabbinic Law in Its Roman and Near Eastern Context*, ed. Catherine Hezser (Tübingen, 2003), 1–15. For more recent approaches see note 71.

2. Fergus Millar, *The Roman Near East, 31 BC–AD 337* (Cambridge, 1996), 374–77.

3. Benjamin Isaac, *Empire and Ideology in the Graeco-Roman World. Selected Papers* (Cambridge, 2017), 274 n. 65.

advised the Roman governor and his officials. They would also have offered their services to the Jewish and non-Jewish inhabitants of the province, who were free to choose the informal adjudicators they considered advantageous to their cases.[4]

Harries has pointed to the "judicial diversity" in Roman Palaestina in the first centuries, when various types of informal adjudicators functioned side by side to deliver "arbitration as a means of dispute settlement."[5] Both parties had to agree to the adjudicator and accept his judgment (see the tannaitic case story about R. Yose b. Ḥalafta and the two litigants in ySan 2.1, 17b). The religious basis of the judgment—based on Torah law believed to have been revealed by God—would have served as a motivation to obey it (see the following story about R. Akiba, who tells the litigant: "Know before whom you stand, before Him who spoke and brought the world into being," ySan 2.1, 17b). For cases involving Jewish litigants, rabbis would have tried to claim a monopoly in serving as adjudicators and legal advisors. That they were not always successful is evident from rabbinic narratives such as the one about a woman named Tamar who allegedly complained about rabbis to the governor's office in Caesarea (yMeg. 3.2, 74a). According to the story, "R. Ḥiyya, R. Yose, and R. Ami found Tamar guilty, and she went and brought [a complaint] against them to the proconsul in Caesarea," R. Abahu is said to have intervened on behalf of his colleagues, though the legal issue itself is not specified here.

Although the story is set in the time of the amora R. Abahu, appeals by Jews to the governor are likely to have happened in the second century already.[6] It is also likely that Jews consulted with Roman jurists, not only in cases where non-Jews were involved. A basic knowledge of Roman civil law and legal practice could have been acquired by word of mouth and observation. If one of the legal parties thought that his or her case would be dealt with on better terms by a Roman adjudicator, that party may have approached a jurist rather than a rabbi. In fact, to be advised by a jurist and judged on the basis of Roman law may have been the unenforced default position in the first centuries CE already, despite the co-existence of indigenous (local) and imperial (empire-wide) legal systems and adjudication practices.[7] Under the emperors Arcadius and Honorius in 398 CE, Jews in

4. Millar, *Roman Near East*, 528.

5. Jill Harries, "Courts and the Judicial System," in *The Oxford Handbook of Jewish Daily Life in Roman Palestine*, ed. C. Hezser (Oxford, 2010), 85 and 91 (quote).

6. Rudolf Haensch, "The Roman Provincial Administration," in *The Oxford Handbook of Jewish Daily Life in Roman Palestine*, ed. C. Hezser (Oxford, 2010), 80.

7. Kimberley Czajkowski and Benedikt Eckhardt, "Introduction," in *Law in the Roman Provinces*, ed. K. Czajkowski and B. Eckhardt in collaboration with M. Stroth-

the eastern parts of the empire were expressly subject to Roman civil law: "The Jews, being Roman citizens, were subject to Roman law as administered by its courts." From that time onwards, rabbinic law was supposed to be used for religious and ritual purposes only.[8]

Unlike rabbis, almost all Roman jurists stemmed from the upper strata of society and were "of at least potential senatorial status."[9] Their views would therefore generally reflect the perspective of the wealthy. Frier and McGinn write: "Although Roman private law itself was nominally egalitarian . . . nonetheless there are solid reasons to believe that the outlook, values, and interests of the upper classes (from whose ranks the Roman jurists were overwhelmingly drawn) were crucially important in shaping both the overall texture and the specific rules of classical Roman family law."[10] This was true not only for family law but for Roman law in general. Jurists belonged to the leisured classes and were not paid for their legal services.[11] Only the scions of well-to-do families would have been able to obtain a higher legal education.

In his study of Mishnah tractate *Bava Metsiʿa*, Hayim Lapin has argued that tannaitic rabbis either came from the upper strata of society themselves or chose "to identify themselves with the wealthy Jewish landholders of Roman Galilee."[12] He goes on to argue that "[r]abbis were also choosing . . . to sanction—and to the extent that the image of 'egalitarianism' is maintained, to mask—a set of unequal relationships between rich and poor" (Lapin, *Early Rabbinic Civil Law*). Cohen has pointed to the "rural origin" of tan-

---

mann (Oxford, 2020), (1) emphasize recent scholarship's move toward "a more dynamic two-way process" between the Roman authorities and the empire's inhabitants, evident in many provinces at the time (Czajkowski and Eckhardt, "Introduction"), and (2) present an example from Egypt, where in 186 CE the gymnasiarch Chairemon appeals to the Roman prefect to have his daughter divorced "by the law," most likely the "Law of the Egyptians"; both local Egyptian legal traditions and Roman law were available to the inhabitants.

8. Shlomo Simonsohn, *The Jews of Italy: Antiquity* (Leiden and Boston, 2014), 150: the law was addressed to Eutychianus, praetorian prefect in the East.

9. Olivia F. Robinson, *The Sources of Roman Law: Problems and Methods for Ancient Historians* (London and New York, 1997), 8.

10. Bruce W. Frier and Thomas A. J. McGinn, *A Casebook of Roman Family Law* (Oxford, 2004), 6.

11. Bruce W. Frier, *The Rise of the Roman Jurists: Studies in Cicero's Pro Caecina* (Princeton, 1985), 33.

12. Hayim Lapin, *Early Rabbinic Civil Law and the Social History of Roman Palestine* (Atlanta, 1995), 240.

naitic rabbis before R. Yehudah ha-Nasi.[13] Yet combining this alleged rural origin with the assumption of a wealthy rabbinic elite is problematic, since wealthy landowners lived in cities in antiquity. As I have argued elsewhere, most rabbis are likely to have belonged to the so-called middling strata of society in the first two centuries.[14] Only very few tannaim are described as landowners and owners of slaves. Even if references to professions are less common in tannaitic than in amoraic texts, cognomens indicate that several tannaim were craftsmen.[15] Unlike Roman jurists' law, the Mishnah seems to reflect a broader socio-economic perspective that is not limited to the highest strata of society. In fact, local Jewish aristocrats may have preferred to be judged in accordance with Roman law, such as Tamar (a wealthy widow?) in the story above. Like Roman jurists, rabbis did not charge their "clients" for their occasional legal advice. Their income came from ordinary professions. We may assume that like Roman jurists, they would have considered it an honor and privilege to provide halakhic guidance, a practice that would have increased their reputation as scholars among their local fellow Jews.

The forms of the legal traditions transmitted by legal scholars were based on their social function of *respondere*: to provide informal legal advice to anyone who approached them.[16] As Leesen has pointed out, this function was closely linked to the casuistic nature of Roman jurisprudence: "Roman jurists were not primarily concerned with the development of a coherent system of private law; . . . their major legal activity being *respondere*, i.e. giving legal advice or *responsa* in court cases and legal disputes."[17] This legal

13. Shaye J. D. Cohen, "The Place of the Rabbi in the Jewish Society of the Second Century," in *The Significance of Yavneh and Other Essays in Jewish Hellenism* (Tübingen, 2010), 296.

14. Catherine Hezser, *Jewish Slavery in Antiquity* (Oxford, 2005), 294–96: very few rabbis (R. Yehudah ha-Nasi, R. Gamaliel) are presented as slaveholders in Palestinian rabbinic texts; tasks carried out by household slaves in upper-class families (e.g., cooking and serving food) are associated with rabbis themselves. Students seem to have carried out some of these tasks (*shimush ḥakhamim*), thereby replacing slaves. On the "middling groups" see Ben-Zion Rosenfeld, *Social Stratification of the Jewish Population of Roman Palestine in the Period of the Mishnah, 70–250 CE* (Leiden and Boston, 2020), 91–140, who distinguishes between the "low middle class" and the independent farmer but does not discuss the merchant as a distinct category.

15. Catherine Hezser, *The Social Structure of the Rabbinic Movement in Roman Palestine* (Tübingen, 1997), 261, for references.

16. Catherine Hezser, "The Codification of Legal Knowledge in Late Antiquity: The Talmud Yerushalmi and Roman Law Codes," in *The Talmud Yerushalmi and Graeco-Roman Culture*, vol. 1, ed. P. Schäfer (Tübingen, 1998), 581–98.

17. Tessa G. Leesen, *Gaius Meets Cicero: Law and Rhetoric in the School Controversies* (Leiden and Boston, 2010), 21.

advice was given *ad hoc*. Private citizens approached jurists with their specific legal problems and asked them for advice. Interestingly, Leesen refers to Cicero's work *De oratore* (1.239–40) as evidence for the proposition that as a jurist, Cicero gave "advice that served the cause of the citizen who consulted him." If that was the case, rabbis may well have competed with Roman jurists in attracting litigants, especially those from the upper strata of society.

Did tannaitic rabbis cater to the legal and religious needs of rural Jews while Roman jurists offered their services in the cities? After the Bar Kokhba revolt, rabbis may have been busy helping rural Jews accommodate to Roman territorial control and changed circumstances, as Avery-Peck has argued. In the Mishnah's division of agriculture, "rabbis do more than regulate how Israelites are to plant, harvest, process, and eat the crops they grow for sustenance."[18] They show them how holiness continued to pertain to the land (in the sense of the land being God's possession) and sanctification continued to apply to its products despite the Roman devastation.[19] But rabbis also discuss defunct institutions such as the Temple, as well as tithes for priests who had lost their ritual duties.[20] Lapin therefore emphasizes the "ideal" nature of the Mishnah's legal regulations, which may have been detached from actual social practice.[21]

Cohn has argued that the rabbinic imagination of the institution of the Temple served to establish rabbis as authorities in their own right after 70 CE.[22] (Imaginary) topics concerning the Temple cult would have aligned rabbis with Roman jurists, who dealt with issues related to the imperial cult. According to Witte, "Roman law also established the imperial cult . . . The Roman emperor was to be worshipped as a god and king in the rituals of the imperial court and in the festivals. . . . The Roman law itself was viewed as an embodiment of an immutable divine law, appropriated and applied through the sacred legal science of imperial pontiffs and jurists."[23] While rabbis as-

---

18. Alan J. Avery-Peck, "The Division of Agriculture and Second Century Judaism: The Holiness of the Devastated Land," in *The Mishnah in Contemporary Perspective: Part One*, ed. A. J. Avery-Peck and J. Neusner (Leiden and Boston, 2002), 41.

19. Avery-Peck, "The Division of Agriculture," 42.

20. Avery-Peck, "The Division of Agriculture," 43.

21. Lapin, *Early Rabbinic Civil Law*, 237. See also Jack N. Lightstone, *Mishnah and the Social Formation of the Early Rabbinic Guild: A Socio-Rhetorical Approach* (Waterloo, 2002), 67.

22. Naftali S. Cohn, *The Memory of the Temple and the Making of the Rabbis* (Philadelphia, 2013), 116.

23. John Witte, *God's Joust, God's Justice: Law and Religion in the Western Tradition* (Grand Rapids, 2006), 9.

serted legal control over their fellow Jews based on their Torah knowledge, jurists applied, developed, and interpreted the Roman legal tradition to guide their fellow citizens.

Rabbis and jurists seem to have been involved in similar types of legal activities. Their foremost function was to "respond" to the legal issues and cases that were brought to them.[24] Jurists "presented opinions on questions of law to private citizens" as well as to magistrates and judges (*respondere*); they interpreted laws and formulas, "occasionally arguing cases as advocates themselves (*agere*)"; and they "drafted legal documents, such as contracts and wills (*cavere*)."[25] Both rabbis and jurists taught students: "The jurists were also engaged in the systematic exposition and teaching of law. In performing this task, they composed opinions when their students raised questions for discussion based on hypothetical cases. These opinions were almost equal in terms of influence to those formulated for questions arising from actual cases and indirectly helped develop Roman law in new directions."[26]

Relations between rabbis and their students, as presented in rabbinic sources, are strikingly similar to those between jurists and their students. Schiller has pointed out that "the young man frequently took residence as a house guest in the family of a renowned jurist."[27] He would therefore be able to observe his teacher's actions and listen to and memorize the advice he gave to his clients. Furthermore, "[t]he young man accompanied the jurist to the places in Rome where jurists gathered for discussion and disputation of controversial legal problems and to respond to legal queries from private persons."[28] Similarly, disciples of rabbis are said to have lived with their masters and to have accompanied them wherever they went.[29] Rabbis must have been familiar with jurists' practices, imitated them in real life, and fulfilled partially analogous functions in Jewish society.

Similarities between Roman jurists' functions of *respondere*, *agere*, and *cavere* and the ways in which rabbis present themselves in the Mishnah (and Talmud Yerushalmi) are striking. Case stories, according to which rabbis

---

24. Catherine Hezser, "Roman Law and Rabbinic Legal Composition," in *The Cambridge Companion to the Talmud and Rabbinic Literature*, ed. C. E. Fonrobert and M. S. Jaffee (Cambridge, 2007), 149; Cohn, *Memory of the Temple*, 20.

25. George Mousourakis, *Roman Law and the Origins of the Civil Law Tradition* (Heidelberg and New York, 2015), 71.

26. Mousourakis, *Roman Law*, 71.

27. A. Arthur Schiller, *Roman Law: Mechanisms of Development* (The Hague, 1978), 398.

28. Schiller, *Roman Law*, 398.

29. Hezser, *Social Structure*, 332–52.

were approached by litigants and provided their responses to controversial issues, are a common feature of the Mishnah, as Moshe Simon-Shoshan has shown.[30] As I have argued elsewhere, very similar legal narratives appear among the responsa of second- to third-century CE Roman jurists such as Q. Cervidius Scaevola and Julius Paulus Prudentissimus, transmitted in Justinian's *Digest*, the early Byzantine compilation of Roman civil law.[31] Rabbis' and Roman jurists' decisions in legal matters were transmitted in much the same form. Babusiaux points out that "the basic narrative structure, the story or the case, is inspired, if not taken over from the rhetorical concept of *narratio*."[32]

As members of the elite, Roman jurists possessed rhetorical training "and therefore also used their fundamental rhetorical skills as a basis in their legal writing."[33] Hidary has argued that rabbis were also knowledgeable in the arts of rhetoric and used these skills in legal proceedings: "We see that both Roman and rabbinic legal professionals shared much of the same educational training and emphasis on rhetorical ability."[34] In general, rabbinic case stories tend to be shorter and more concise than Roman case stories. They lack explicit questions that constitute one part of the tripartite structure of the latter narratives.[35] Whether rabbis formulated such stories because they had gained formal rhetorical training, or whether they imitated Roman legal traditions they had observed or learned informally in conversations, remains an open question.[36]

The juridical functions of *agere* and *cavere* also have analogies in the Mishnah. Rabbis not only gave legal advice but could also function as judges who decided cases in court settings, as tractate *Sanhedrin* suggests. While the existence of a rabbinic high court (or "sanhedrin") after 70 CE has been questioned by scholars, individual rabbis may have held private courts or

30. Moshe Simon-Shoshan, *Stories of the Law: Narrative Discourse and the Construction of Authority in the Mishnah* (Oxford, 2012), 167–93. See also Arnold Goldberg, "Form und Funktion des Ma'ase in der Mischna," *Frankfurter Judaistische Beiträge* 2 (1974) 1–38; Catherine Hezser, *Form, Function, and Historical Significance of the Rabbinic Story in Yerushalmi Neziqin* (Tübingen, 1993), 283–303.

31. Hezser, "Codification of Legal Knowledge," 588–92.

32. Ulrike Babusiaux, "Legal Writing and Legal Reasoning," in *The Oxford Handbook of Roman Law and Society*, ed. P. J. du Plessis, C. Ando, and K. Tuori (Oxford, 2016), 177.

33. Babusiaux, "Legal Writing," 177.

34. Richard Hidary, *Rabbis and Classical Rhetoric: Sophistic Education and Oratory in the Talmud and Midrash* (Cambridge, 2016), 234.

35. See Hezser, "Codification of Legal Knowledge," 588–89, for examples.

36. On the use of classical legal rhetoric in literary contexts, e.g. by Shakespeare, see Quentin Skinner, *Forensic Shakespeare* (Oxford, 2014).

served as judges in local courts alongside other Jewish and non-Jewish judges.[37] Evidence of rabbinic judges is generally limited to amoraic sources.[38] Yet Büchler's categorical distinction between rabbis and local judges is not persuasive.[39] More likely is Goodman's suggestion that both rabbinic and non-rabbinic legislation and jurisdiction was based on "the law *as it was actually practiced*."[40] Even if the rabbis of the Mishnah were critical of judges who took the same position as advocates, "the Mishnah does not ban advocates altogether" and permits the granting of legal advice to litigants.[41] The granting of legal advice and assistance in procedural matters is something mishnaic rabbis identify with.

The jurists' third function of drafting legal documents (*cavere*) also has analogies in the Mishnah.[42] Documents and their proper formulations and usages are frequently mentioned in both tannaitic and amoraic texts. A rabbinic innovation was the *prosbol*, a type of document that was allegedly introduced by Hillel (mShevi 10.3). This document protected the right of the creditor and allowed him to collect debts even during the sabbatical year. The Mishnah provides legal guidance on the proper format, formulation, dating, and signature of the document (mShevi 10.4). Rabbis also discussed the "correct" formulation of wills (mBB 8.7), the writing of betrothal documents (mKid 1.1), and the validation of marriage documents by witnesses' signatures (mKet 2.3; 5.1). Their advice on drafting documents was not limited to family matters but included the purchase and manumission of slaves (mKid 1.1–2; mGit 1.4). The phenomenon that the acquisition and dismissal of wives and slaves is discussed together seems to be due to their status as non-kin dependents of the householder.[43] Bauman's comment on Roman jurists will have applied to rabbis as well: "In the specific area of *cavere*, the

37. H.P. Chajes,. "Les juges juifs en Palestine." *Revue des Études Juives* 39 (1899): 39–52; David Goodblatt, *The Monarchic Principle. Studies in Jewish Self-Government in Antiquity* (Tübingen, 1994); Hezser, *Social Structure*, 276–77.

38. Hezser, *Social Structure*, 276.

39. Adolf Büchler, *The Political and the Social Leaders of the Jewish Community of Sepphoris in the Second and Third Centuries* (London, 1909), 21.

40. Martin Goodman, *State and Society in Roman Galilee, A.D. 132–212* (Totowa, N.J., 1983), 159–60.

41. Hidary, *Rabbis and Classical Rhetoric*, 226.

42. On the meaning of *cavere* versus *agere* see Schiller, *Roman Law*, 273–74.

43. Hezser, *Jewish Slavery*, 69–82; Sandra R. Joshel and Sheila Murnaghan, "Introduction: Differential Equations," in *Women and Slaves in Graeco-Roman Culture: Differential Equations*, ed. S. R. Joshel and S. Murnaghan (London and New York, 1998), 1–21.

drafting of private documents, the jurists' services must have been in great demand."[44] While *cavere* and *agere*, "[i]n the sense of advising on the procedure of or conducting private suits" (Bauman, *Lawyers in Roman Republican Politics*), must have occupied at least some jurists' and rabbis' time, there is much more evidence in the surviving documents for their function of *respondere*, providing legal advice to private citizens.

2. THE MISHNAH AS RABBINIC CITIZENS' LAW (*IUS CIVILE*) FOR THE JEWISH *CIVITAS*

Although rabbinic civil law is vastly expanded in the late antique Talmud Yerushalmi, the Bavot tractates of the Mishnah already contain much civil law, and civil law is also part of discussions in other tractates.[45] Such discussions deal with damage done to a neighbor's property,[46] theft[47] and fraud,[48] employment law concerning laborers and tenants,[49] slave law including manumission,[50] the formulation and use of documents and witnesses,[51] and family law involving gifts and inheritances.[52] Almost all of these topics were also addressed by Roman jurists, whose decisions and discussions are recorded in Justinian's Codex as well as in earlier collections of individual jurists' traditions.

In Roman society, civil law (*ius civile*) "denotes the law of a given *civitas* or of the citizens; with reference to Rome, it is the *ius civile proprium Romanorum*."[53] According to Harries, "in the ancient Mediterranean world,

---

44. Richard A. Bauman, *Lawyers in Roman Republican Politics: A Study of the Roman Jurists in Their Political Setting, 316–82 BC* (Munich, 1983), 4.

45. See Lapin, *Early Rabbinic Civil Law*, 119–235, on civil law in mBava Metsiʿa.

46. Jacob Neusner, *A History of the Mishnaic Law of Damages*, 5 parts (Eugene, Ore., 2007; previously published Leiden, 1985).

47. Bernard S. Jackson, *Theft in Early Jewish Law* (Oxford, 1972).

48. Jacob Neusner, *The Economics of the Mishnah* (Chicago and London, 1990), 82–83.

49. David Farbstein, *Das Recht der freien und unfreien Arbeiter nach jüdisch-talmudischem Recht verglichen mit dem Antiken, speciell mit dem römischen Recht* (diss., Bern, 1896); Ben-Zion Rosenfeld and Haim Perlmutter, *Social Stratification of the Jewish Population of Roman Palestine in the Period of the Mishnah, 70–250 CE* (Leiden and Boston, 2020), 71–88.

50. See Hezser, *Jewish Slavery in Antiquity*.

51. Catherine Hezser, *Jewish Literacy in Roman Palestine* (Tübingen, 2001), 297-309.

52. Reuven Yaron, *Gifts in Contemplation of Death in Jewish and Roman Law* (Oxford, 1960); Jonathan S. Milgram, *From Mesopotamia to the Mishnah: Tannaitic Inheritance Law in Its Legal and Social Contexts* (Tübingen, 2016).

53. Adolf Berger, *Encyclopedic Dictionary of Roman Law* (Clark, N.J., 2004), 527.

law and citizenship in general went together."[54] She quotes the Roman jurist Gaius, who stated in the second century CE: "What each people establishes for itself as law (*ius*) is unique to that citizen body and is called the citizens' law, because it is the law unique to that citizen community (*civitas*)" (Gaius, *Institutes* 1.1). Rather than assuming that Roman law was forced on new citizens in the provinces, Czajkowski and Eckhardt describe the situation more distinctly: "People were not made citizens to promote a Roman legal order, but the possible recourse to that order was part and parcel of their elevated status. Quite without provident planning, they did become carriers of the Roman legal system; by exercising their privilege or recourse to it, they therefore helped propagate the idea of Rome as the ultimate guarantor of justice."[55]

The rabbinic editors of the Mishnah may well have considered their compilation as "appertaining to the *civitas*"[56] of the Jews of the rabbinically defined Land of Israel, in contrast to natural or international law, *ius gentium*, the law of all peoples. As such, the Mishnah would have stood in continuation to Torah law, which Seth Schwartz calls "the constitution of the Jews of Palestine"[57] that governed Jews before the incorporation of their land into the Roman Empire: "Before the rise of Rome, the Mediterranean was a mosaic of many cities and citizenships, all with their own laws. Even after the Roman conquest of the eastern provinces from the second century BCE, many cities were classified as 'free' and retained their previous laws and distinctive civic identities, although these were gradually eroded over time."[58]

This view of a pluralistic legal landscape with many local legal traditions associated with indigenous identities dominates scholarship on law in the Roman provinces nowadays. To some extent, this pluralism seems to have continued even after 212 CE. Czajkowski and Eckhardt reckon with "the survival and even thriving of local legal orderings" even after the extension of Roman citizenship to inhabitants of the provinces.[59]

In 212 CE, all inhabitants of the Roman Empire received Roman citizenship and at least theoretically, "the [Roman] *ius civile*, written and un-

---

54. Jill Harries, "Roman Law from City State to World Empire," in *Law and Empire: Ideas, Practices, Actors*, ed. J. Duindam, J. Harries, C. Humfress, and N. Hurvitz (Leiden, 2013), 47.

55. Czajkowski and Eckhardt, "Introduction," 9.

56. Harries, "Roman Law," 47.

57. Seth Schwartz, *Imperialism and Jewish Society: 200 B.C.E. to 640 C.E* (Princeton, 2001), 56.

58. Harries, "Roman Law," 47.

59. Czajkowski and Eckhardt, "Introduction," 4.

written, was the law of the Roman *civitas*, the Roman citizen body and that citizen community was now coextensive with the population of an empire extending from Hadrian's Wall to the Sahara and the Euphrates."[60] Interestingly, the compilation of the Mishnah, associated with rabbinic circles around the patriarch R. Yehudah ha-Nasi, broadly coincides with the Roman emperor Caracalla's extension of Roman citizenship to inhabitants of the Roman provinces (*Constitutio Antoniana* of 212 CE).[61] Imrie has emphasized the prominent role that Roman jurists obtained under the Severan emperors—a period that he calls "something of a golden age for jurists"—including "significant administrative positions, and even rising to the praetorian prefecture."[62] At that time, rabbis may have feared that Jewish integration into the Roman *civitas* might imply their subjection to Roman civil law, if not forcefully then at least voluntarily, and would bring about a loss or gradual fading of traditional Jewish law based on the Torah and rabbinic jurisdiction.[63]

The compilation of the Mishnah at the beginning of the third century CE may then be understood as a rabbinic attempt to create a specifically Jewish collection of citizens' law that could serve as a viable alternative to Roman *ius civile* within a rabbinically defined Land of Israel. It needs to be stressed that rabbinic halakhic rules always pertained to the boundaries of what rabbis called the Land of Israel, not the entire Roman province of Syria-Palaestina.[64] They thus defied Roman administrative boundaries and continued earlier local territorial traditions just as they maintained and developed their indigenous legal tradition when Roman law "infiltrated" their space. In both domains, territorial and legal, adjustments were made.[65]

Rabbinic reactions to Roman legal imperialism had certain analogies in other provinces of the Roman Empire that "had their own pre-existing local

60. Czajkowski and Eckhardt, "Introduction," 4.

61. On Caracalla's reform and its various rationales (fiscal, military, administrative) see Alex Imrie, *The Antonine Constitution: An Edict for the Caracallan Empire* (Leiden and Boston, 2018).

62. Imrie, *The Antonine Constitution*, 35.

63. On the concept of the Oral Torah and its relationship to the Written Torah see Martin S. Jaffee, *Torah in the Mouth: Writing and Oral Tradition in Palestinian Judaism 200 BCE–400 CE* (Oxford, 2001), 5 and 51, who dates it to the mid-second to early third century CE.

64. On the rabbinic perception of Eretz-Israel and the connection between rabbinic *halakhah* and these geographical boundaries see Eyal Ben-Eliyahu, *Identity and Territory: Jewish Perceptions of Space in Antiquity* (Berkeley and Los Angeles, 2019), 86–109.

65. For territorial adjustments to rabbinic boundaries in light of the Roman division of space and changing demographics see Ben-Eliyahu, *Identity and Territory*, 104.

legal orderings that were not eliminated with the coming of empire."[66] Czajkowski and Eckhardt emphasize "local agency . . . in the uptake, interpretation, integration or indeed rejected [*sic*] of Roman law in the provinces and indeed the construction of the various local legal cultures under Rome."[67] In her study of the legal situation in Judaea until Hadrian, Czajkowski compares the "tardiness" in the uptake of Roman legal institutions with Egypt.[68] Future comparisons between rabbinic and other local legal traditions may yield further analogies.[69]

To serve as a viable local alternative to Roman civil law, rabbinic civil law would have had to cover some of the same areas that Roman jurists' law dealt with and include other areas that were of particular interest to a Jewish constituency (e.g., regulations on Sabbath and holiday observance, purity rules, etc.). Being more or less familiar with the casuistic jurisprudence of Roman jurists in the East and having given Torah-based legal advice to their Jewish compatriots since the destruction of the Temple, rabbis may have "conceived of their traditional system of practice as law in imitation of Roman notions of the law" and "mimicked the style of presenting legal material in a heterogeneous manner."[70]

Only a few of the legal areas covered by both rabbis and Roman jurists can be addressed here.[71] One such area is property law. Mishnaic rabbis

66. Czajkowski and Eckhardt, "Introduction," 10.

67. Czajkowski and Eckhardt, "Introduction," 10.

68. Kimberley Czajkowski, "Law and Romanization in Judaca," in *Law in the Roman Provinces*, ed. K. Czajkowski and B. Eckhardt in collaboration with M. Strothmann (Oxford, 2020), 84–100. The study is based on Josephus and the New Testament. The later rabbinic period is not dealt with here.

69. The papers in the volumes edited by Kimberley Czajkowski and Benedikt Eckhardt in collaboration with Meret Strothmann, *Law in the Roman Provinces* (Oxford, 2020), and by Werner Eck in collaboration with Elisabeth Müller-Luckner, *Lokale Autonomie und römisch Ordnungsmacht in den kaiserzeitlichen Provinzen vom 1. bis 3. Jahrhundert* (Munich, 1999), provide a good basis for such a comparison.

70. Cohn, *Memory of the Temple*, 36. See also Beth A. Berkowitz, *Execution and Invention: Death Penalty Discourse in Early Rabbinic and Christian Cultures* (Oxford, 2006), 162; Simon-Shoshan, *Stories of the Law*, 81–82.

71. Other scholars have already conducted comparisons in specific areas and pointed to the likely impact of Roman on rabbinic law in the land of Israel, even if rabbinic rules are not identical and may lack the complexity of jurists' law. See, e.g., Orit Malka and Yakir Paz, "*Ab hostibus captus et a latronibus captus*: The Impact of the Roman Model of Citizenship on Rabbinic Law," *Jewish Quarterly Review* 109 (2019): 141–72; Orit Malka, "Disqualified Witnesses between Tannaitic Halakha and Roman Law: The Archaeology of a Legal Institution," *Law and History Review* 37 (2019): 937–59; Yair Furstenberg, "Between the Literature of Early Halakhah and the Roman Law: The History of Mish-

dealt with issues concerning theft and the receipt of stolen goods;[72] damage to another person's property;[73] the sale, lease, and safekeeping of goods;[74] and debts, loss, and negligence.[75] Property law, including damages, was also an important area of Roman civil law.[76] Obviously, property law was of great significance for the economy of the Roman Empire and its provinces. Epstein summarizes the broader questions that Roman property law tried to answer: "First, how is property acquired? Second, what is the property so acquired? Third, how is that property protected? Fourth, how is that property transferred? Fifth, how are divided interests created in property? Sixth, how are unintentional mergers of property sorted out?"[77] The property types dealt with in both Roman and rabbinic law included real estate as well as movable property such as material objects, animals, and slaves. One could be the individual or partial owner of these goods. Possession could be acquired, transferred, or lost. In the interest of stable possession rights, legal remedies were applied when property was unlawfully seized or stolen. As Epstein has pointed out, "endless complications could arise" in property law cases.[78] Jurists and rabbis would deal with the specific cases that litigants presented to them.

Some scholars have argued that rabbinic property law, especially in the Mishnah, mostly deals with minor cases of movable property of a low value.[79] This phenomenon might seem to be linked to our discussion above

---

nah Bava Metsia" (Hebrew), *Te'udah* 31 (2021): 541–74; Jonathan A. Pomeranz, "The Rabbinic and Roman Laws of Personal Injury," *AJS Review* 39 (2015) 303–31; Nathalie B. Dohrmann, "Law and Imperial Idioms: Rabbinic Legalism in a Roman World," in *Jews, Christians, and the Roman Empire. The Poetics of Power in Late Antiquity*, ed. N. B. Dohrmann and A. Y. Reed (Philadelphia, 2014), 63–78.

72. Boaz Cohen, "The So-called Jüdisches Hehlerrecht in the Light of Jewish Law." *Historia Judaica* 4 (1942): 145–53.

73. Neusner, *History of the Mishnaic Law of Damages*.

74. Lapin, *Early Rabbinic Civil Law*, 155–232.

75. Samuel Greengus, *Laws in the Bible and in Early Rabbinic Collections: The Legal Legacy of the Ancient Near East* (Eugene, Ore., 2011), 188–235.

76. See Herbert Hausmaninger and Richard Gamauf, *A Casebook on Roman Property Law* (Oxford, 2012), for examples; Bernhard Erwin Grueber (2004). *The Roman Law of Damage to Property: Being a Commentary on the Title of the Digest Ad Legem Aquiliam (IX. 2)* (Clark, N.J., 2004).

77. Richard A. Epstein, "The Economic Structure of Roman Property Law," in *The Oxford Handbook of Roman Law and Society*, ed. P. J. du Plessis, C. Ando, and K. Tuori (Oxford, 2016), 513.

78. Epstein, "Economic Structure," 515.

79. Jacob Neusner, *Judaism and Society: The Evidence of the Yerushalmi* (Chicago, 1983), 121.

concerning the relatively lower socio-economic status of (most) rabbis and their followers in comparison with Roman jurists who belonged to the upper strata of Roman society and would have been consulted by wealthy estate owners. Yet the property law issues addressed in Roman case stories are not limited to real property in land. As far as movable property is concerned, Roman jurists dealt with lost cows (Paul, Digest 41.2.3.13) and buried money (Papinian, Digest 41.2.44 pr.) just as rabbis did. Rabbis, like Roman jurists, discussed the acquisition, transfer, and loss of slaves[80] and other types of property.[81] While rabbis would have been more familiar with the lower-value movable property cases concerning most of their Jewish clientele, they also occasionally dealt with the transfer of real estate and slaves, which members of the upper strata of Jewish society would have possessed.

When discussing property law in the Mishnah, a focus on case stories may be too limited. Lapin has noted that "[i]n tannaitic corpora, property and status cases together make up just over a third of the total number of cases," whereas most case stories deal with issues of purity and ritual.[82] Besides case stories, legal discussions on property issues need to be taken into consideration. While case stories are not exact transcripts of cases brought before rabbis, but rather greatly reduced and abstracted mnemonic versions created for the purposes of transmission and later discussion, legal statements and discussions may not be merely theoretical but rather based on issues that were relevant in daily life.

In any case, Roman jurists also dealt with issues that had "little practical significance": "It was those problems that interested them, not the practical significance of the cases."[83] Cases, on the other hand, "were stated abstractly to include only those features that were relevant to a legal problem."[84] Both jurists and rabbis problematized and conceptualized issues known from daily life, such as possession, fault, damage, intention, and negligence: "The genius of the Roman jurists lay not in finding new concepts, but in seeing the legal significance of familiar ones."[85] The same can be said about the rabbis. Individuals learned in law were assumed to be able to give advice in ev-

---

80. See Hezser, *Jewish Slavery in Antiquity*.

81. Jacob Neusner, *Judaism: The Evidence of the Mishnah* (Eugene, Ore., 1981), 146, 254.

82. Hayim Lapin, *Rabbis as Romans: The Rabbinic Movement in Palestine, 100–400 CE* (Oxford and New York, 2012), 105.

83. James Gordley, *The Jurists: A Critical History* (Oxford, 2013), 10.

84. Gordley, *The Jurists*, 10.

85. Gordley, *The Jurists*, 10.

eryday life matters: "numerous everyday problems not needing court proceedings required settlement by a man on the spot, preferably one trained
in public consultation," such as the jurists—and by extension—rabbis.[86]

Only a few examples of property law topics that both Roman jurists and
mishnaic rabbis dealt with can be provided here. Roman jurists argued that
a householder could acquire possession through his slave or dependent son.
According to the jurist Paul, "through a slave or a son-in-power [*in potes-
tate*] we acquire possession," even of a purchase that was made with parts
of the slave's *peculium* his master did not know about.[87] On the one hand,
slaves are here treated as humans who can take possession; on the other
hand, they are equated to minor sons, unable to own property themselves.
Watson has argued that possession (the act of taking hold of or seizing an
ownerless object) by a third party on behalf of the householder was a Roman innovation.[88]

Mishnaic and other tannaitic texts suggest that rabbis were familiar with
the distinction between possession and ownership. The Mishnah states that
objects found by minor children, wives, and Canaanite slaves, all dependents of the householder, belong to the householder, who would be considered their rightful owner (mBM 1.5). By contrast, finds of adult children,
divorced wives, and Israelite slaves belong to their finders. In comparison
with Roman law, the distinction between Israelite and Cannanite, that is,
Jewish and non-Jewish slaves, is unusual here.[89] Only in the case of Canaanite slaves, slaves of a non-Jewish origin, would servile possession lead to the
householder's ownership of the objects.

Elsewhere, no such distinctions between different types of slaves are
made. Although rabbis do not use the term *peculium*, the Tosefta states:
"the son who does business with what belongs to his father, and likewise
the slave who does business with what belongs to his master, behold, they
[the proceeds] belong to the father, behold, they [the proceeds] belong
to the master" (tBK 11.2).[90] The Roman *peculium* was property which the

86. Bauman, *Lawyers in Roman Republican Politics*, 114.

87. Commentary on the Praetor's Edict, book 54, quoted and translated in Hausmaninger and Gamauf, *Casebook on Roman Property Law*, 53 case 25.

88. Alan Watson, "Acquisition of Possession per Extraneam Personam," *Tijdschrift
voor Rechtsgeschiedenis* 29 (1958): 22–42; Watson, "Acquisition of Possession and Usu-
caption *per servos et filios*," *Law Quarterly Review* 78 (1962): 205–27.

89. On the general lack of distinction between slaves of Jewish and non-Jewish origin
in rabbinic texts see Paul McCraken Flesher, *Oxen, Women, or Citizens? Slaves in the
System of the Mishnah* (Atlanta, 1988), 36; Hezser, *Jewish Slavery in Antiquity*, 36.

90. On the *peculium* see Boaz Cohen, "Peculium in Jewish and Roman Law." *Proceedings of the American Academy for Jewish Research* 20 (1951): 135–234; Elias J. Bicker-

pater familias gave to his slave (or dependent son) to invest in business.[91] According to Frier and McGinn, "[p]articularly slaves, but also children, actively traded with their *peculia*, in effect operating as managers of quasi-independent 'firms' although still within the ambits of the *familia*."[92] Ultimately, the proceeds belonged to the householder. Whether this Tosefta passage refers to money that the master has given to his slave for the explicit purpose of doing business with it or whether a *peculium*-like allocation of money is envisioned here remains uncertain. Since the slave is owned by the master, everything he possesses belongs to the master. According to a statement attributed to R. Meir, "the hand of a slave is like the hand of his master" (yPe'ah 4.6, 18b; yKid. 1.3, 60a): he is a means through which his master takes possession and acquires things.

The use of slaves (or other dependents) as intermediaries was legally (and probably also morally) advantageous for householders. In certain circumstances they could avoid having to pay damages if the damage occurred while the slave was in charge. If the owner of cattle commissioned a slave (or minor son or messenger) to transfer a cow to a prospective borrower and the cow died en route, the borrower was not liable to pay damages to the owner (mBM 8.3), even if the slave was his own. The borrower is liable to pay damages only if he explicitly asked the owner to use an intermediary for the transfer or agreed to it, that is, if he was responsible for the employment of the intermediary in whose custody the cow died (mBM 8.3).

Interestingly, Roman law also stipulates that a master is liable for a slave's actions or damage incurred through him, if the master authorized the action: "Such liability occurred, and gave a legal motivation to the injured party, whenever a slave acted under definite authorization . . . The liability incurred was limited . . . by the extent of authorization."[93] Similarly, the Mishnah rules that the borrower is liable to pay damages to the owner of the cow which dies in transit only if he authorized a slave (or minor son or messenger) to bring him the cow.

The slave himself—like minor children—could handle property but not own it, since he lacked the capacity of *dominium*, ownership: "The object

man, "The Maxim of Antigonos of Socho," in Bickerman, *Studies in Jewish and Christian History. A New Edition in English including The God of the Maccabees,* ed. A. Tropper (Leiden, 2007), 543–62.

91. William L. Westermann, *The Slave Systems of Greek and Roman Antiquity* (Philadelphia, 1955), 83.

92. Frier and McGinn, *Casebook of Roman Family Law,* 263.

93. Westermann, *Slave Systems,* 83.

itself was taken by the slave *domini animo sed servi corpore*."[94] In specific circumstances he could be authorized to act in his owner's name (*domini nomine*): "Under specific consent of his owner for a definite case or under a wider authorization which would include a given transaction a slave was able to deal in the master's name (*domini nomine*) with third parties, either for the purpose of acquiring or of alienating property for his master."[95] In the mishnaic case, the intermediary's function is more limited: the slave is merely in charge of the transfer of the property. If the owner of the cow authorized his own slave to accomplish the transfer and the cow died, the loss would be his own; if the borrower authorized either his own or the owner's slave, he would be liable to pay damages to the owner. These and other legal issues are discussed in more complex ways in Roman legal texts. As I have already argued elsewhere, a knowledge of Roman law is indispensable for understanding many of the Mishnah's (and Talmud Yerushalmi's) legal issues properly.[96]

3. RABBINIC AND ROMAN LEGAL COMPILATION

Not only the content of rabbinic legal discussions but also some of the literary forms used to transmit rabbinic *halakhah* have equivalents in Roman legal texts. Legal narratives, foremost amongst them case stories, have already been discussed extensively.[97] The structures of rabbinic and Roman case stories are very similar and have a similar *Sitz im Leben*, namely, rabbis' and jurists' role of *respondere*—responding to legal problems others brought before them. This is not to say, however, that the issues addressed in case stories happened in real life. The formulations are elliptical and abstract; some scenarios would have been invented for theoretical legal discussion. Roman case stories usually include a specific question and tend to be more detailed. Yet the structure of case description (*casus*)—question or, in the case of rabbinic case stories, the general statement that someone went and asked a certain rabbi (*quaestio*)—the jurist's or rabbi's case decision or legal advice (*responsum*) are very similar. Such case stories became primary forms of transmitting legal advice in societies with informal adjudicators who administered case law.

94. Westermann, *Slave Systems*, 83.

95. Westermann, *Slave Systems*, 83.

96. Hezser, "Did Palestinian Rabbis Know Roman Law?" (forthcoming).

97. Hezser, *Form, Function, and Historical Significance*, 283–303; 588–94; Simon-Shoshan, *Stories of the Law*, 114–16, 176–93.

Falcón y Tella emphasizes that Roman jurists were scholars who practiced jurisprudence (*prudentia iuris*), rather than legislators who issued laws.[98] This practice was not initiated by the government but arose out of the scholarship and practice of the jurists themselves. Falcón y Tella stresses "the principle of spontaneity, of the isolating of private law from political power and of aversion to the extension of bureaucracy."[99] The scholastic basis and independence from politics were shared by rabbinic *halakhah*, as was the multifarious nature of the rulings that emerged in this context. Roman law "is a 'case-specific' law, formed by case law, the product of disagreements and controversies."[100] General principles and declarations of rights are missing. What we find instead are "abstract, precise and clear" case decisions and formulae that take specific legal circumstances into account.[101]

Also important is Falcón y Tella's emphasis on the religious basis of Roman jurisprudence: "Both the lawful . . . and the unlawful . . . depended on the will of the Gods. The virtues of the citizen, of *paterfamilias*, and of the jurist . . . determined by the law itself, were religious in character."[102] Private law, dealt with by jurists, focused on the family and dealt with issues such as status, property, inheritance, loans, contracts etc.[103] As jurisconsults, jurists rather than legislators "played the fundamental role in the process of formation and creation of law. The jurisconsult, via *iurisprudentia*, adapted the scope of the existing law to new needs and requirements . . . Law was basically shaped by the judgments of the jurisconsults, those judgments constituted the principle and almost the only source of law."[104] The similarity to rabbinic *halakhah* is striking. Like Roman law, rabbinic law was based on earlier "existing law," the Torah, that was interpreted and adapted to new circumstances. It had a religious basis and traced its own rules and moral values to Moses at Sinai. Both jurists' law and rabbinic *halakhah* emerged in scholastic contexts which combined theoretical discussions with practical applications. This scholastic context and practice are crucial for understanding the emergence, transmission, and compilation of rabbinic and Roman law.

98. María José Falcón y Tella, *Case Law in Roman, Anglosaxon and Continental Law* (Leiden and Boston, 2011), 7–10.

99. Falcón y Tella, *Case Law*, 8.

100. Falcón y Tella, *Case Law*, 8.

101. Falcón y Tella, *Case Law*, 8.

102. Falcón y Tella, *Case Law*, 8–9.

103. See the contributions in Part IV of David Johnston, ed., *The Cambridge Companion to Roman Law* (Cambridge, 2013).

104. Falcón y Tella, *Case Law*, 10.

We lack direct information about the development and compilation of the Mishnah. By studying the Mishnah within the context of Roman legal scholarship and the compilation of jurists' law, we can extend our knowledge of these processes. At the very beginning stands the rabbi and legal scholar who develops new rules and decisions based on his interpretation of earlier legal traditions and in the context of Graeco-Roman culture. Classicists have pointed out that "Greek influence on Roman law cannot be denied" and that philosophical ideas, both popular and academic, had an impact on Roman jurisprudence.[105] Similarly, the rabbis of the Mishnah discussed and developed law (*halakhah*) in the context of Hellenism, especially Stoic philosophy, which Josephus associates with Pharisees.[106] The rabbis applied their legal scholarship when others approached them for advice and transmitted their rulings as case stories, rules, and legal hypotheses.

Ibbetsen distinguishes between the legal science practiced by jurists until 200 CE and the period of "authority" from that time onwards: "[A]fter the deaths of Papinian, Paul, and Ulpian, the three great jurists of the late second and early third centuries, imperial power came to dominate all aspects of the law."[107] The beginning of the third century CE constitutes "a major watershed": "the scientific work of jurists seems to come to a very sudden halt."[108] From that time onwards, there are no more "juristic works revealing any real originality of thought" (Ibbetsen, "Sources of Law"). The late second to early third century CE was also a major turning point as far as rabbinic literature is concerned. It marked the end of the tannaitic period, the emergence of the first patriarch R. Yehudah ha-Nasi, and the assumed time of the editing of the Mishnah. Although the later amoraim continued to develop *halakhah*, they considered the traditions of their tannaitic predecessors authoritative. Around that time, the notion of the Oral Torah was introduced.[109] Jurists and rabbis of the third and fourth centuries venerated their predecessors and were eager to compile and preserve their legal traditions for later generations.

As far as the first and second centuries CE are concerned, it seems that Roman jurisprudence was largely unregulated and did not need authoriza-

105. Laurens Winkel, "Roman Law and its Intellectual Context," in *The Cambridge Companion to Roman Law*, ed. D. Johnston (Cambridge, 2015), 14.
106. Josephus, Life 2.12; Steve Mason, *Flavius Josephus. Translation and Commentary*, vol. 9: *Life of Josephus* (Leiden, 2011), 21.
107. David Ibbetsen, "Sources of Law from the Republic to the Dominate," in *The Cambridge Companion to Roman Law*, ed. D. Johnston (Cambridge, 2015), 26.
108. David Ibbetsen, "Sources of Law," 40.
109. Jaffee, *Torah in the Mouth*, 5, 51.

tion by imperial authorities. According to Pomponius, "men who had confidence in their knowledge gave opinions to those who consulted them" (Justinian's Digest 1.2.2.49).[110] Augustus established the *ius respondendi* in principle but did not grant it to anyone in particular to avoid authorizing contradictory decisions.[111] Tiberius allegedly authorized Sabinus, who was of a lesser social status than other jurists, and Caligula and Nero conferred the right to certain *heads* of legal schools "for political reasons."[112] Hadrian, however, "abolished the *ius respondendi*" and "recommended them [i.e., jurists] to give advice on their own authority."[113] Legal expertise "was by custom not to be sought but to be self-evident, and so he would be delighted if anyone who trusted his own abilities should prepare himself for giving opinions to the people."[114] Rabbis seem to have gained significance within Jewish society of Roman Palaestina after the Bar Kokhba revolt, when Roman emperors encouraged self-declared legal experts to set themselves up and offer their services to the public without requiring special authorization to do so.

Also interesting is the phenomenon of legal disagreement amongst both jurists and rabbis. Robinson writes: "This freedom to disagree persisted until the end of the classical period and beyond, even under Diocletian."[115] Sometimes a *communis opinio* was reached by following a specific jurist's view or by imperial enactment on issues that were considered particularly important. The second century CE jurist Gaius reckons with the possibility that the *responsa prudentium*, the decisions of the jurisprudents, may disagree. In such cases "it is permitted for the judge to follow whichever decision he wishes" (Gaius 1.7). Only if all jurists consent is the judge bound to follow that ruling.[116] The rabbinic view that sages' opinions are of equal value (see tSot 7.12 concerning disputes between the schools of Hillel and Shammai: "all these words have been given by a single Shepherd") seems to echo that sentiment.

The earliest stages of compilation of "classical" Roman jurisprudence seem to have coincided with the development of the tannaitic tradition in the second century CE. Justinian's *Digest* refers to collections of the most famous second-century jurists' legal traditions such as the *Institutes* of Gaius,

---

110. Translation with Robinson, *Sources of Roman Law*, 8.
111. Leesen, *Gaius Meets Cicero*, 26.
112. Leesen, *Gaius Meets Cicero*, 27.
113. Leesen, *Gaius Meets Cicero*, 28.
114. Robinson, *Sources of Roman Law*, 12.
115. Robinson, *Sources of Roman Law*, 34.
116. Leesen, *Gaius Meets Cicero*, 29.

the *Sentences* of Paul, and the *Rules* of Ulpian. Of these, only Gaius's *Institutes* have survived in manuscript form. They were discovered in a palimpsest at Verona that has been dated to the fifth century CE.[117] According to Schiller, Gaius's "work was an elementary text for beginning law students, dating from the middle of the 2nd century."[118] The late antique versions of the fourth and fifth centuries CE have excerpted, paraphrased, supplemented, and altered a no-longer-existing earlier text.[119] This is also the case with the *Sentences* of Paul, excerpted in the Digest. They were "an anthology made from the writings of the jurist Paulus by a compiler about the turn of the 4th century, to which later editors added further materials from time to time to keep the work up to date . . . The writer drew his extracts from the writings of Paul, condensing the material, bringing it up to date."[120] Further alterations occurred in the following two centuries.

Besides such compilations of individual jurists' traditions, encyclopedic collections with materials attributed to different jurists were created in the fourth and fifth centuries CE. The *Fragmenta Vaticana* of the fourth century CE combine and juxtapose the traditions of the "classical" jurists Papinian, Paul, and Ulpian by presenting excerpts from their individual collections of private law on topics such as sales, gifts, and guardianship.[121] The individual and partly contradictory views and decisions are listed thematically, without being commented upon or harmonized. The transmission of disputes on particular legal issues (*disputationes* and *quaestiones*) suggests that the collection served educational as well as jurisdictional purposes. It is assumed that the editors of this by-now-fragmentary work aspired to create a comprehensive collection of private law covering all legal areas. Another collection of jurists' law, probably created around 300 CE, is the *Iuris Epitomae* of Hermogenianus, a post-classical jurist and *magister libellorum* of Diocletian.[122] Besides case decisions, the compilation contains disputationes and quaestiones—discussions of legal problems.

Just as the views and decisions of the "classical" Roman jurists of the second century CE are available only in later collections and compilations of the early Byzantine period, the Mishnah as a collection of tannaitic traditions of first- and second-century rabbis has been preserved as part of the

117. Schiller, *Roman Law*, 43–44.
118. Schiller, *Roman Law*, 43.
119. Schiller, *Roman Law*, 45.
120. Schiller, *Roman Law*, 46.
121. Theodor Mommsen, ed., *Fragmenta Vaticana: Mosaicarum et Romanarum Legum Collatio* (Berlin, 1890).
122. Detlef Liebs, *Hermogenians Iuris Epitomae. Zum Stand der römischen Jurisprudenz im Zeitalter Diokletians* (Göttingen, 1964).

Talmud Yerushalmi (and later Bavli). Lieberman has argued that the Mishnah was composed and "published" orally throughout late antiquity until its integration into the Talmud.[123] The Tosefta as a variant but partly overlapping collection of tannaitic traditions may be viewed in the context of variant compilations of jurists' law in Roman society of the third to fifth centuries CE.

The literary development of Roman jurists' law reveals complex processes of transmission, excerption, recombination, supplementation, and reformulation that were conducted for several centuries by compilers, editors, and scribes. At a time when the notion of an "original" version of a text was unknown, late antique scholars created variant compilations of the legal traditions of their venerated predecessors that served their own purposes.[124] This phenomenon resulted in various collections of "classical" private law that were partly overlapping and partly different. Excerpts from already circulating collections were integrated into the large "encyclopaedic" compendia of the Talmud and *Digest* in early Byzantine times.

To properly understand the processes of transmitting, collecting, selecting, excerpting, recombining, ordering, reformulating, supplementing, harmonizing, and commenting upon earlier material, the development of the Mishnah (and of the Tosefta and Talmud Yerushalmi) has to be examined in the context of the development of Roman private law, from the pre-Justinian collections and compilations of legal traditions associated with the second-century "classical" jurists to the creation of Justinian's Digest. The pre-Justinian compilations arranged the collected material in certain thematic orders which would have served the specific purposes of those who created them. Different collections with partly shared material seem to have circulated side by side. While the Roman legal editors seem to have mostly relied on written material (which, except for Gaius's *Institutes*, is lost to us), they may have supplemented this material with oral traditions and student notes. The practice of *respondere*, as well as the discussion of legal cases in school settings, were oral practices based on jurists' rhetorical training.[125]

123. Saul Lieberman, *Hellenism in Jewish Palestine* (2nd ed. New York, 1962), 83–99.

124. Catherine Hezser, "The Mishnah and Ancient Book Production," in *The Mishnah in Contemporary Perspective*, vol. 1, ed. J. Neusner and A. J. Avery-Peck (Leiden and Boston, 2002), 175.

125. Clifford Ando, "Introduction: The Discovery of the Fact," in *The Discovery of the Fact,* ed. C. Ando and W. P. Sullivan (Ann Arbor, 2020), 5, points to aspects of legal argumentation learned during rhetorical training; his distinction between Roman and "Semitic" argumentation and reference to Roman jurisprudence as a "Western triumph" seems biased, however, and is not backed by a comparative analysis.

For a comparative study of the editorial procedures of rabbinic and Roman legal compilations, König's and Woolf's definition of encyclopaedism as a set of shared practices rather than a genre seems most suitable: the editors "made use of shared rhetorical and compilatory techniques to create knowledge-ordering works of different kinds, works that often claimed some kind of comprehensive and definitive status."[126] They refer to "an encyclopaedic spectrum, with different texts drawing on shared encyclopaedic markers to different degrees and for very different purposes."[127] The Mishnah would have been at a different stage of this spectrum than the later and much more comprehensive Talmuds. Similarly, the compilers of the *Fragmenta Vaticana* were at a different stage in comparison with the editors of the *Digest*. The "common ground" of the compilers was "a spectrum of shared techniques," such as "[n]ote-taking, excerption and recombination, cross-referencing," that is, scholastic methods that emerged in late antiquity.[128]

Although the ideal was comprehensiveness, variant legal compilations existed side by side (cf. the Mishnah and Tosefta, Talmud Yerushalmi and Bavli). König and Woolf point out that "the ordering work of the encyclopaedist is always in tension with the inherent miscellaneousness of the materials he or she must deal with."[129] This is a phenomenon that scholars of the Mishnah and other rabbinic works know well. Last but not least, the compilatory efforts of rabbis and jurists must be seen within the context of Roman and early Byzantine culture and society of the third to fifth centuries CE, when rabbis and jurists distinguished themselves from their "classical" predecessors whose legal knowledge they held in high esteem. The later scholars realized that the preservation of this knowledge required the use of scholastic methods, an area that came easier to them than casuistic jurisprudence itself.

4. MUTUAL AWARENESS?

In view of the many striking similarities in rabbis' and jurists' roles as legal advisers, their engagement in legal discussions and the teaching of students, the similar private law topics they dealt with, their use of similar forms of

---

126. Jason König and Greg Woolf, "Introduction," in *Encyclopaedism from Antiquity to the Renaissance*, ed. J. König and G. Woolf (Cambridge, 2013), 1.

127. König and Woolf, "Introduction."

128. König and Woolf, "Introduction." 6.

129. König and Woolf, "Introduction." 8.

transmission, and the creation of compilations in which the traditions of (first- and) second-century rabbis and jurists are preserved and considered "classical" by their late antique successors, it is quite obvious that at least from the late second century CE onwards rabbis in Roman Palaestina were aware of the activities of Roman jurists in their vicinity. From the Roman perspective, rabbinic legal advice in "minor" civil law matters seems to have been tolerated as part of the pluralistic legal landscape of the eastern provinces where local "indigenous" legal traditions continued in Roman imperial times. Perhaps Roman jurists and provincial officials were even aware of the amalgamation of Roman law by local adjudicators, a process which they probably would have welcomed.[130]

As pointed out above, the post-Hadrianic stance of *laissez-faire* in jurisprudential matters enabled legal scholars to function as legal advisors on the sole basis of their expert knowledge. Rabbis who lived in or near cities would have been familiar with Roman jurists' practice of *respondere* and offered a similar service to their fellow Jews, based on their own legal heritage of the Torah. While the Torah constituted an alternative to Roman law, it had to be developed and adapted to solve legal problems in a changed political, socio-economic, and cultural environment. Neusner has claimed that mishnaic rabbis developed their own "system" of *halakhah* in distinction from biblical law: "There is no system of civil laws and institutions in the priestly and holiness codes."[131] While one may argue with Neusner's use of the term "system," the innovative nature of the Mishnah is obvious. Inspired by biblical values and concerns, the Mishnah is a compilation of rabbinic "citizens' law" that was probably meant as an alternative to and in many ways imitates Roman *ius civile*. If Romans were aware of Jewish provincial assimilation to Roman legal practices, their tolerance of rabbinic legal autonomy in private law matters would be understandable. R. Yehudah ha-Nasi's purported closeness to Roman officials[132] and the rabbis' greater involvement in city life from the turn of the second to third century CE onwards[133] would have facilitated such an alignment. Similarities between rabbinic and Roman law are especially evident in the Talmud Yerushalmi,

130. The tannaitic story about Roman officials checking on R. Gamaliel's legal teaching (yBK 4.3, 4b par. Sifre Deut. 344) and praising it (exceptions notwithstanding) might reflect general awareness of rabbinic jurisdiction amongst Roman provincial authorities.

131. Neusner, *Evidence of the Mishnah*, 199.

132. Lapin, *Rabbis as Romans*, 23.

133. Hezser, *Social Structure*, 158–64.

which expands on the Mishnah's discussion of civil law issues and approximates jurists' law in its complexity.

The study of the Mishnah in the context of Roman law is still in its early stages, despite the important contributions made to this issue in the past. Areas that would merit more detailed and comprehensive studies are rabbinic and Roman legal education, the role of the dispute form in rabbinic *halakhah* and Roman jurisprudence, and the development of the Mishnah and Talmud Yerushalmi in the context of Roman legal compilations and scholastic practices of the second to fourth centuries CE.

8. Mishnah and History

Hayim Lapin

Usually dated to about 200 CE, the Mishnah is thought to be the earliest rabbinic composition, and it continues to be the object of traditional memorization, recitation, and study to the present. It is difficult to overestimate the long-term significance of the Mishnah within the cultural and intellectual history of Jews and Judaism. Yet that significance should not overshadow its importance in its own place and time. The Mishnah is a vital pivot point in our understanding of the emergence of the rabbinic group, its internal conflicts, and subsequent developments. The Mishnah also provides densely detailed discussions of a variety of mundane (and therefore often under-documented) practices, artifacts, and materials. Finally, the Mishnah, together with other early rabbinic works, comprises some of the very few surviving examples of extensive contemporaneous vernacular composition from anywhere in the Roman world. The Mishnah thus presents a unique and particular view for understanding the cultural and intellectual impacts of conquest and annexation in the eastern Roman empire.

Problems of historical interpretation arise when we try to move beyond general pronouncements to actually working with the material. A brief look back at the history of scholarship helps to specify some of the longstanding problems of method and approach. In 1981, Jacob Neusner published *Judaism: The Evidence of the Mishnah*, following shortly on his twenty-two volume *History of the Mishnaic Law of Purities*.[1] Neusner's later work has been all but ignored in scholarship. In the 1970s and 1980s, however, he defined a moment at which the lines between scholars who thought that early rabbinic literature provided enough material to reconstruct a "history of Juda-

---

1. Jacob Neusner, *A History of the Mishnaic Law of Purities*, 22 vols. (Leiden, 1974); Jacob Neusner, *Judaism: The Evidence of the Mishnah* (Chicago, 1981).

ism," or a history of Jews, and those who did not, hardened around doctrinal and even institutional lines.

Neusner's work coincided, more or less, with analogous developments in proximate fields, in particular what was called in biblical studies the "minimalist/maximalist debate":[2] how much suspicion about events or their interpretation is appropriate, given what we think we know about the composition and bias of our sources. Although Neusner was no post-modernist, his influence also coincided with the period when debates for and against postmodern and poststructuralist approaches dominated debates across the humanities. "Theory" brought attention to new historiographical possibilities, but the insistence on the constructedness of knowledge—there was no "there" there—was received by many as relativistic, amoral, and frankly dangerous.[3] Rabbinics scholars trained in North America in the 1980s and 1990s felt the need to "answer Neusner" in their research and to justify their attempt (or their refusal to attempt) to make factual claims about the past based on their studies.[4]

Forty years on, how we read for history is deeply inflected by this problematization of sources and historicity. An oft-studied story from the Mishnah (mRH 2.8–9) provides an example. The story may refer to a conflict between Gamaliel and one or more rabbis. Some scholars will proceed on the assumption that the underlying event is an essential factor in our interpretation. Yet virtually all recognize that the transmitted story has been constructed or revised to address issues significant for rabbis, if only we could agree on what they are: calendrical authority, the legitimacy or primacy of the house of Gamaliel, or perhaps the philosophy of law distinguishing rabbis from priests.[5]

The varied approaches to *mRosh Ha-Shanah* 2.8 exemplify the common conundrum faced by historians in non-western and pre-modern fields of needing to reconstruct our sources first in order to interpret them histori-

2. Iain W. Provan, "Ideologies, Literary and Critical: Reflections on Recent Writing on the History of Israel," *JBL* 114 (1995): 585–606.

3. For one response see Himmelfarb's essay "Postmodernist History," in *On Looking into the Abyss: Untimely Thoughts on Culture and Society* (New York, 1994), 131–60.

4. Autobiographically, "answering Neusner" intersected with addressing theory: see Hayim Lapin, *Early Rabbinic Civil Law and the Social History of Roman Galilee: A Study of Mishnah Tractate Baba' Meṣiʿa'* (Atlanta, 1995), 19–33.

5. Examples: David M. Goodblatt, *The Monarchic Principle: Studies in Jewish Self-Government in Antiquity* (Tübingen, 1994), 204–7; Martin Jacobs, "Die Institution des judischen Patriarchen: Eine quellen- und traditionskritische Studie zur Geschichte der Juden in der Spätantike," *TSAJ* 52 (Tubingen, 1995): 199–200; Daniel R. Schwartz, "From Priests at Their Right to Christians at Their Left? On the Interpretation and De-

cally. The Mishnah (and rabbinic literature more broadly) also poses problems more narrowly particular to itself, ones stemming from our reconstructions. To the extent that we view the Mishnah not as a hodgepodge or a loosely edited anthology, but rather as a carefully constructed work with a specific agenda and controlled vocabulary and rhetoric, we encounter the problem of how much the overarching editorial or compositional work determines our ability to interpret the parts.[6] Neusner's solution in his later work was to give up on the parts and focus on "documents"—whole texts in their canonical forms—but this is to impose a classical Newtonian solution on what appears to be fundamentally a quantum problem. Readers who seek to break through the redactional shell of the Mishnah look for terminological shifts or chronological or prosopographical inconsistencies to recover materials that have not been fully assimilated and can therefore be read against the grain. Simultaneously, scholars (sometimes the same as in the prior set) have shown that it is possible, and in fact illuminating, to focus on the Mishnah as a coherent whole.[7]

For the purposes of discussion here, I approach the Mishnah not simply as a repository of raw historical data about the past but rather as a historical artifact in its own right. It is that artifact that we study historically. In what follows, "What is the Mishnah?" asks about raw materials, artisans, and technology—sources, strata, redaction. "What does the Mishnah Do?" provides a survey of the kinds of purposes the Mishnah appears to serve and the kinds of audience it presupposes. The final section, "What Can We Learn?," draws attention to some avenues of historical inquiry. Not surprisingly, the rabbis as a group feature very strongly among those inquiries. In fact, in practice the Mishnah first documents the existence of a group of rabbis. However, thinking of the Mishnah as an artifact suggests that we should also think about context, and in particular the provincial context of Roman Palaestina in which the Mishnah was produced and in which it first circulated.

---

velopment of a Mishnaic Story (m. Rosh HaShanah 2:8–9)" [Hebrew], *Tarbiz* 74 (2004): 21–41; David Henshke, "R. Joshua's Acceptance of the Authority of Rabban Gamaliel II: A Study of Two Versions of the Same Event" [Hebrew] *Tarbiz* 76 (2006): 81–104; Avraham Walfish, "Halakhic Confrontation Dramatized: A Study of Mishnah Rosh HaShanah 2:8–9," *HUCA* 79 (2008): 1–41.

6. See Christine Hayes, "What is (the) Mishnah? Concluding Observations," *AJS Review* 32 (2008): 291–97, commenting on collected papers from a 2006 symposium.

7. Yair Furstenberg, *Purity and Community in Antiquity: Traditions of the Law from Second Temple Judaism to the Mishnah* [Hebrew] (Jerusalem, 2016), and Mira Balberg, *Purity, Body, and Self in Early Rabbinic Literature* (Berkeley, 2014), are recent representative of these two tendencies.

WHAT IS THE MISHNAH?[8]

The Mishnah lacks a prologue or epilogue that states who produced it or why. On its surface it is a compendium of laws; of discussions and debates about law; anecdotes that illustrate evidence of practice or a sage's ruling; some explicit scriptural exegesis and considerably more implicit exegesis; and very occasional homilies or moral lessons. The named authorities in the Mishnah are exclusively men.[9] These names cluster in groups, and it is conventional practice to understand these groups as falling into "generations." Many of the men bear the title *rabbi* ("my master"), a usage that appears otherwise unattested in earlier sources. Composed in non-biblical Hebrew, the Mishnah makes use of a small set of repeating rhetorical forms and a developed vocabulary of technical terms. These features require an audience with significant knowledge and specialization. Mnemonic features in the text are consistent with a traditional understanding that there was a significant oral component to the text and its original transmission.[10]

Furthermore, the "maximalists" referred to in the introduction might rely on other ancient and medieval rabbinic traditions to provide scaffolding. "Minimalists," by contrast, might insist that however plausible, those traditions are likely to be the product of exegetical practice themselves rather than better historical information. Thus, the traditional association with the name of Judah the Patriarch is plausible but cannot be confirmed.[11] We cannot know and should not assume from within the Mishnah the scope of its audience or the extent of the Mishnah's practical significance.

---

8. This section provides only a sketch. See relevant contribution to this volume, and especially Shaye Cohen's "Introduction." Readers of Hebrew will find an excellent recent introduction to the Mishnah in Ishay Rosen-Zvi, "Introduction to the Mishnah" [Hebrew] in *The Classical Rabbinic Literature of Eretz Israel: Introductions and Studies*, ed. M. I. Kahana et al., vol. 1 (Jerusalem, 2018), 1–64. Herman L. Strack and Günter Stemberger, *Introduction to the Talmud and Midrash*, trans. Markus Brockmuehl, 2nd ed. (Minneapolis, 1996), still provides an essential guide to earlier scholarship.

9. *t. Kelim B. Qam.* 4.17 cites the daughter of Hanina b. Teradion.

10. Martin S. Jaffee, *Torah in the Mouth: Writing and Oral Tradition in Palestinian Judaism, 200 BCE–400 CE* (Oxford, 2001); Ya'akov Sussmann, "Torah she-be-'al peh: peshuṭṭah ke-mashma'ah," in *Meḥqere Talmud*, ed. Y. Sussmann and D. Rosenthal, vol. 5 (Jerusalem, 2005), 209–384; Elizabeth Shanks Alexander, *Transmitting Mishnah: The Shaping Influence of Oral Tradition* (Cambridge, 2006).

11. Yitz Landes, "The Role of the Patriarchate in the Creation and Dissemination of Early Rabbinic Literature" (Ancient Judaism Regional Seminar, Philadelphia, 2021), has recently attempted to support the association on prosopographic and other grounds.

Although we can posit underlying orality and examine the completed Mishnah as it has come down to us, we cannot know the precise format in which the Mishnah circulated. The Mishnah is organized into tractates (chunks organized around topics), and tractates into orders. Since in most cases the tractates are now ordered from longest to shortest, it is uncertain whether there was an original, preferred reading or recitation order, or even how the work was intended to be read and used.[12]

Continuity with the Past

Even as it reveals little about itself and its own production, the Mishnah reads easily as furthering a conversation over legal matters that began long in the past. Its vocabulary locates material within received tradition: "first *mishnah*"; "words of the Scribes"; "they said"; and *halakhah*. The expression "*halakhah* to Moses from Sinai" claims not only antecedent extra-biblical knowledge, but also a chain of authorities for its transmission (mPe'ah 2.6; m'Eduy 8.7; mYad 4.3). Perhaps more significant is the repeated practice of citing named tradents, with a sizable block of traditions ascribed to sages conventionally dated to 70 CE or earlier, seemingly comparable with a period described by Josephus and by the New Testament Gospels.

We have limited information at our disposal to test the apparent antiquity of the Mishnah and its component traditions. Scholars once considered the sections of the Mishnah that describe procedure (especially of Temple rites) to go back to the Second Temple era. Recent scholarship has been critical of this early dating.[13] Another approach considers the Mishnah's representation of the matters that earlier figures ruled on or discussed, and the things they did. In many respects, the topics that the Mishnah ascribes to earlier generations fit well within a late Second Temple context. The debate over the definition of legitimate grounds for divorce aligns with issues also attributed to Jesus in the Gospel of Matthew.[14] Even more strikingly, the two purity practices ascribed to Pharisees in the Gospels, namely washing

---

12. Similar strategies are attested for the prophets in the Hebrew Bible, the letters of Paul in the New Testament, and the suras of the Qur'an. For post-Mishnah traditions about the sequence of the orders see bShab 31a; Mid. Tehil. 19.14.

13. Daniel Stökl Ben Ezra, *The Impact of Yom Kippur on Early Christianity: The Day of Atonement from Second Temple Judaism to the Fifth Century* (Tübingen, 2003), 20–28; Ishay Rosen-Zvi, *The Mishnaic Sotah Ritual : Temple, Gender and Midrash* (Leiden, 2012), 239–54; Naftali S. Cohn, *The Memory of the Temple and the Making of the Rabbis* (Philadelphia, 2013), esp. Chapter 3.

14. Mt 19:8–9; mGit 9.10.

of hands and the distinction between the inside and outside of vessels for purity purposes, are ascribed to early rabbis as well.[15]

Some continuity with a Second Temple era context is also apparent in other ritual areas. The Qumran polemical text 4QMMT disputes with its interlocutors on the status of a *mamzer*, along with members of restricted ethnic groups or men with genital deformities, apparently prohibiting both marriage and entry into the Temple.[16] A variety of sources from the land of Israel during the Second Temple period know about a restriction on travel on the Sabbath with a limit of 2000 cubits,[17] and about a prohibition of "taking out" from one's house on the Sabbath.[18] Marginally better attested for the diaspora than for Palaestina is the practice of lighting lamps before the Sabbath.[19] As we will see, however, nothing prepares us for the extension of these matters in the Mishnah.

Innovation, Normalization, Invention

In other respects, the Mishnah appears discontinuous with what we know from the earlier period outside the Mishnah.[20] The range of legal topics addressed in the Mishnah extends well beyond anything addressed in surviving Second Temple texts or documents. Civil and property law, for instance, do not appear to have attracted significant interest as areas of discussion or debate at all during the Second Temple period, but are extensively treated

---

15. Mk 7:1–8; Mt 15:1–9, 23:25–26; cf. Lk 11:37–42. For extensive discussion see: Furstenberg, *Purity and Community*, 85–155.

16. See the composite edition in Elisha Qimron and John Strugnell, eds., *Qumran Cave 4. V. Miqṣat Maʿaśe Ha-Torah* (Oxford, 1994), 50, ll. 39–41. See also 4Q174 (Florilegium) 1–2 i 3–4, paraphrasing Deut. 23:2–4.

17. Shaye J. D. Cohen, "Sabbath Law and Mishnah Shabbat in Origen *de Principiis*," *JSQ* 17 (2010): 171–72 and notes thereto.

18. Charlotte Elisheva Fonrobert, "From Separatism to Urbanism: The Dead Sea Scrolls and the Origins of the Rabbinic 'Eruv," *DSD* 11 (2004): 50–51.

19. Seneca *Epistolae Morales* 95.47; Molly Whittaker, *Jews and Christians: Graeco-Roman Views* (Cambridge and New York, 1984), no. 72; Menahem Stern, *Greek and Latin Authors on Jews and Judaism* (Jerusalem, 1974), no. 188; cf. Persius *Satires* 5.179–84; Whittaker, *Jews and Christians*, no. 71; Stern, *Greek and Latin Authors*, no. 190. See also Tertullian *ad Nationes* 1.13. Assuming that Josephus, *Apion* 2.282 is talking about Sabbath lamps and not some other ritual practice (John M. G. Barclay, *Josephus, Against Apion* (Leiden, 2007), at 161 n. 1036, 230 n. 425, 328 n. 1138), the specific referent is again the diaspora.

20. For this section, see Shaye J. D. Cohen, "The Judaean Legal Tradition and the Halakha of the Mishnah," in *The Cambridge Companion to the Talmud and Rabbinic Literature*, ed. C. E. Fonrobert and M. S. Jaffee (Cambridge, 2007), 121–43.

in the Mishnah. In addition, the Mishnah's rules about real property (especially tractate Bava Batra) do not only exceed Scripture, they operate in a legal world that runs contrary to the system of tribal redistribution envisioned in the Torah. Again, relying on the Mishnah's ascriptions of opinions to individual sages, there is a corresponding lack of interest in these areas among earlier generations of rabbis.[21] It is not unreasonable to suppose that civil law marks a set of innovations on the part of rabbis of the middle- to late second century CE.

Innovation can mean outright invention through scriptural or legal speculation. Tractate *Midot* refers back to individual memories about the Temple (there are claims to this at 1.2; 2.5, 6; 3.8), but at times its descriptions are based on 1 Kings or Ezekiel 40–46, suggesting that something more complicated than simply reporting received tradition about the past is at work.[22] Chapter 2 of *Sanhedrin* sketches out a system of courts for which we have no prior attestation and some of whose assumptions (e.g., a king distinct from high priest) reflect the administrative situation neither of Hasmonean Judaea nor of the last two decades of Roman rule before 66 CE.[23]

What appears as innovation may also reflect the Mishnah's navigation, selection, and affirmation from among contemporary practices. The Mishnah includes *haroset* on the Passover meal menu, for which there is no biblical warrant or prior attestation, although it leaves unresolved whether *haroset* is "commanded" (*mitsvah*; mPes 10.3). The Mishnah's standardization of the betrothal document (*ketubah*) provides an example that affects both personal status and the disposition of real and movable property.[24] The documentary evidence for Jews adjacent to southern Judaea in the early second century is sufficient to show that some did write deeds that looked very much like rabbinic rules but that they also had alternatives (in two cases, explicitly "Greek" ones).[25]

21. Hayim Lapin, "Early Rabbinic Civil Law and the Literature of the Second Temple Period," *JSQ* 2 (1995): 149–83.

22. 2 Kgs 6 (mMid 4.1; 4.4); 7 (mMid 2.6); Ezek 40 (mMid 3.7; 4.7); 41 (mMid 3.6; 4.1; 4.4; 4.7; 5.1); 43 (mMid. 3.1); 44 (mMid 4.2); 46 (mMid 2.5).

23. Note the disagreement between the Palestinian and Babylonian Talmuds about whether the king referred to in 2.2 is a Davidic king or not: ySan 2.3, 20a: David; bSan 19a: a "king of Israel" illustrated through a story of Herod.

24. mKet 4.6–12. The presumed formulation is also itself deemed sufficiently fixed to be the basis of further exegesis (see 4:7). See Mordechai Akiva Friedman, *Jewish Marriage in Palestine: A Cairo Geniza Study* (Tel-Aviv and New York, 1980), 366–70, 374–77.

25. Discussion and literature in Jacobine G. Oudshoorn, *The Relationship between Roman and Local Law in the Babatha and Salome Komaise Archives: General Analysis and Three Case Studies on Law of Succession, Guardianship, and Marriage* (Leiden, 2007), 378–438.

The difficulty of separating specifically outright innovation from selection among multiple under-documented contemporaneous alternatives extends to core areas of mishnaic praxis. In laying out prayer obligations, the Mishnah appears to operate with some wider knowledge of existing and seemingly well-known formulae and rubrics that it refers to in shorthand, even if some issues are matters of dispute (e.g., mBer 1.4, 5; 4.3; 5.2–4). Arguably, then, blessing formulae, "long" and "short," as either frames for scriptural passages (esp. *shema'* and its blessings) or concatenated into prayers (esp. *tefillah*, or "eighteen benedictions") are part of a liturgical practice that was wider than the liturgical practice of the rabbis themselves.[26]

WHAT DOES THE MISHNAH DO?

In the same way that we might ask what a spindle whorl or a grindstone recovered through survey or excavation did, we must ask what the Mishnah does. In both cases there is an iterative process through which morphological features together with context, where we have it, allow us to posit immediate function, and connect function with people and with social processes. We have no alternative to this epistemological circle, but as the study of gender in particular shows, it can lead us badly astray.[27] Provisionally, we can begin with the description of the Mishnah as a collection of laws (not necessarily practiced or practicable) and a repository of scriptural exegesis and ancient tradition that also includes considerable innovation and invention. In presenting itself in this way, the Mishnah re-writes expectations of authoritative law and the boundaries of Torah. It also calls for a new intensively engaged and mindful subject to perform its reconfigured Torah. These in turn would appear to point to significant features about the circle of rabbis that produced the Mishnah, discussed further in the next section.

26. The relationship of the prayers in Book 7 of the *Apostolic Constitutions* to the rabbinic *tefillah* is presumably relevant to this question; Pieter Willem van der Horst and Judith H. Newman, *Early Jewish Prayers in Greek* (Berlin, 2008), 1–95.

27. See discussion and attempted correctives by Miriam Peskowitz, *Spinning Fantasies: Rabbis, Gender, and History* (Berkeley, 1997); Cynthia M. Baker, *Rebuilding the House of Israel: Architectures of Gender in Jewish Antiquity* (Stanford, 2002). The problem is not limited to gender, of course. See e.g. Stuart S. Miller, *At the Intersection of Texts and Material Finds: Stepped Pools, Stone Vessels, and Ritual Purity among the Jews of Roman Galilee* (Göttingen, 2015).

A Legal Compendium

As a compendium organized around law, the Mishnah is more comprehensive in scope, and is more systematically codificatory in its organization and argument, than any prior surviving Israelite (or Judaean or Jewish) work or indeed any subsequent work before Maimonides's *Code*. Given the mix of materials (laws rooted in scripture, some perhaps the result of "pure" exegesis; matters of practice and dispute during the Second Temple period; rules dependent on historical memory or invention; and others rooted in broader contemporary practice), the Mishnah is notable for making no attempt to account for itself and very little attempt to distinguish these materials. There is no statement by the deity or the great king justifying the issuance of the laws as in the legal tradition of the ancient Near East, but no less the later codes of Theodosius II or Justinian; no covenant-making whether of the asymmetrical form (again with a royal or divine suzerain) or of a collective form as in Nehemiah 10, the Damascus Document (CD A IV 4–6, pointing to an omitted list), or for that matter Greek inscriptions documenting the governance of voluntary associations. In laying out its model for the Temple and the governance of Israel, the Mishnah does not turn to new or exegetical revelation, as do the last chapters of Ezekiel or the *Temple Scroll* or, in its own way, Jubilees. The Mishnah does not cite a real or fictive occasion for the legislation as do Jubilees, again, or the *Didache* and, subsequently, the *Didascalia Apostolorum* or the *Apostolic Constitutions*.[28]

The purpose of the collection might be juxtaposed to that which Josephus gave to himself in laying out the Jewish-Judaean *politeia*. However, while the members of Josephus's audience were readers of Greek, the members of the Mishnah's *politeia* were the Judaeans themselves, and the scope was more comprehensive than anything Josephus or Philo compiled.[29]

28. On the *Didascalia* and the Mishnah, cf. Charlotte Elisheva Fonrobert, "The *Didascalia Apostolorum*: A Mishnah for the Disciples of Jesus," *Journal of Early Christian Studies* 9 (2001): 483–509. Note the special case of m'Eduy and the "on that day" traditions, setting Yabneh and the appointment of Eleazar b. Azariah as significant moments.

29. Philo, *Special Laws*; Josephus, *Antiquities* books 3, 4. Katell Berthelot, "Judaism as 'Citizenship' and the Question of the Impact of Rome," in *In the Crucible of Empire: The Impact of Roman Citizenship upon Greeks, Jews and Christians*, ed. K. Berthelot and J. J. Price (Leuven, 2019), 107–29; Daniel R. Schwartz, "Josephus on Jewish Constitutions and Community," *SCI* 7 (1983–84): 30–52; Yehoshua Amir, "Josephus on Jewish Constitutions and Community," *SCI* 8 (1985–88): 83–105; Tessa Rajak, "The Against Apion and the Continuities in Josephus' Political Thought," in *The Jewish Dialogue with Greece and Rome: Studies in Cultural and Social Interaction* (Leiden, 2001), 216–39. See also Catherine Hezser in this volume.

Again, like Josephus and Philo the Mishnah defines a hermeneutical present in which a self-sustaining Jewish polity can exist following its own laws. But for the framers of the Mishnah, much of what they lay out had been practically irrelevant for over a century at the time of their editorial work.

Nor do the Roman state and its local agents make significant impact on the Mishnah. They appear sporadically and in the context of particular events or stories. We hear of a *hegemon* (a Greek term for the governor) in the time of Gamaliel (m'Ed 7.7). In the context of the documentary practice required for divorce, we learn that a remarried divorcée who might suffer considerable personal loss and whose children would be classified as *mamzerim* because her divorce document was written "in the name of a kingdom that is not appropriate(?) (*hogenet*), in the name of the kingdom of Media or the kingdom of Greece, according to [the era of] the building of the Temple or to the destruction of the Temple" (mGit 8:5). What the proper formula *is* we are not told; perhaps the regnal year of the emperor. The Mishnah debates whether one form of Jewish execution was decapitation "like the kingdom does" (mSan 7:3). One may not participate in building a "basilica, *gradus*, or stadium," institutions for a public, and potentially violent, display of imperial justice (m'AZ 1.7). The fact that the Temple has been destroyed is acknowledged in a number of passages, as is the fact of a recent succession of wars in one passage.[30] References to "the danger" (*sakanah*) *may* refer to persecution during or after the Bar Kokhba revolt, although this is never spelled out.[31]

Redefining the boundaries of Torah

The format of the Mishnah levels the differences between kinds of law and between sources of authority and between domains of practice. If this leveling is purposeful, and not merely a side effect of the work of collection, one innovation of the Mishnah may well be the expansion and systematization of Torah itself. Laws pertaining to Temple ritual or a system of courts which could not be put into practice appear side by side with instructions for the non-sacrificial (or not exclusively sacrificial) celebration of Passover, or the adjudication of monetary cases. Laws that more or less directly apply scripture appear side by side with others that do not.[32] In practice, considerable knowledge of scripture and its interpretation is required to know that the Mishnah's four principal forms of damage derive from Exodus 22:4–5 (mBK

---

30. Destruction e.g., mRH 4.1, 3, 4; mSot 9. Wars: esp. mSot 9.14.
31. mMS 4.11; mKet 9.9 (mShab 19.1; m'Eruv 10.1).
32. See mḤag 1.8, for notice of this.

1.1); that the classification of bailees depends on a non-intuitive reading of Ex 22:6–14 (mBM 3.1, 7.8); that the specification of appurtenances that convey with the sale of real property bears no relationship to the Torah at all (mBB 4). Occasionally within the Mishnah and more regularly elsewhere, we have evidence of a counter discourse: one purpose of midrash *halakhah* as a textual genre may well be the re-grounding of unmoored rabbinic law in scriptural sources.[33]

It is tempting to identify the Mishnah, or at least rules given "to Moses at Sinai," with the "Oral Torah" and ancestral tradition (*paradosis*) associated with the Pharisees. We do not know the contours of that *paradosis* or of the "rules . . . not written in scripture" that the Gospels and Josephus ascribe to the Pharisees.[34] In fact, the link between rabbis and Pharisees that appears in later rabbinic literature and is so commonly assumed in secondary literature is not emphasized in the Mishnah.[35] References to the Oral Torah appear nowhere in it and only rarely in other tannaitic corpora.[36] For our purposes, the important point is that when we accept the identifications of Pharisaic tradition with the Mishnah, we must also notice that the Mishnah refuses to distinguish where things "written in scripture" end and non-scriptural material or tradition begins.

The Mishnaic Subject

Scholarship in recent years has given attention to the Mishnah's emphasis on a thinking or intending subject whose forgetfulness and mindfulness have consequences for liability or for the successful completion of ritual acts. Thus, in cases where intention designates substances as food susceptible to impurity, those who are deaf, deemed legally not competent, or minors "have [the ability to cause impurity through] action but not thought" (mToh 7.6; cf. mBM 7.6). In the wake of work by Foucault and Peter Brown, some scholars have raised the possibility that the rabbinic self is tied to the rise of the interior or multiple late-antique self.[37] Possibly, too, it reflects a

33. The literature on this is extensive; see the contribution of Azzan Yadin-Israel in this volume.

34. Mark 7; Matt. 15:2, 6; Josephus 13:297, 408.

35. Shaye J. D. Cohen, "The Significance of Yavneh: Pharisees, Rabbis, and the End of Jewish Sectarianism," *HUCA* 55 (1984): 36–42.

36. In tannaitic corpora: Sifre Deut 351 (ed. Finkelstein, 408); Sifra Be-Ḥukotay Perek 8.12. See also Mek. Shab. 1 (ed. Horovitz-Rabin 345), on the thirty-nine Sabbath labors.

37. Peter Brown, *The Body and Society: Men, Women, and Sexual Renunciation in Early Christianity* (New York: Columbia University Press, 1988); Michel Foucault, *The*

nominalist conception of law that characterized some rabbis but not others, or perhaps rabbis or their (Pharisaic) antecedents but not their (priestly, non-rabbinic) Others.[38]

A concern for what the legal subject holds in thought is pervasive and at times intensive in the Mishnah. Examples include the intention of the toucher in determining impurity or of the one offering a sacrifice (not the one on whose behalf it is brought) in determining its validity; the implication of forgetting and remembering in culpability for Sabbath infractions; and the concern to maintain constant attention on others we do not trust in order to prevent impurity.[39]

In part, this emphasis is of a piece with the persistence of distinctions among Israelites and a context that presupposed the inevitable interaction between the reliable and the unreliable and between Israelites and gentiles.[40] But some expansions are new and more intensive. To return to examples of continuity with Second Temple period groups and practices mentioned earlier, nothing prepares us for the expansion of the *mamzer* into an unmarriageable caste.[41] According to Furstenberg, the Mishnah includes discussions of purity that go back to the Second Temple period; however,

---

Care of the Self: The History of Sexuality, vol. 3, trans. Robert Hurley (New York, 1988). The association has been vigorously opposed in Ishay Rosen-Zvi, "The Mishnaic Mental Revolution: A Reassessment," JJS 66 (2015): 19.

38. Examples and reservations in Rosen-Zvi, 39–40. On realism/nominalism, Daniel R. Schwartz, "Law and Truth: On Qumran-Sadducean and Rabbinic Views of Law," in *The Dead Sea Scrolls: Forty Years of Research*, ed. D. Dimant and U. Rappaport (Leiden, 1992), 229–40; Daniel R. Schwartz, *Judeans and Jews: Four Faces of Dichotomy in Ancient Jewish History* (Toronto, 2014), 21–47; Schwartz's initial essay has generated extensive discussion in the literature.

39. Balberg, *Purity, Body, and Self in Early Rabbinic Literature* (Berkeley, 2014); Balberg, *Blood for Thought: The Reinvention of Sacrifice in Early Rabbinic Literature* (Berkeley, 2017); Balberg, "The Subject Supposed to Forget: Rabbinic Formations of the Legal Self," in *Self, Self-Fashioning and Individuality in Late Antiquity: New Perspectives*, ed. J. Levinson and M. Niehoff (Tübingen, 2019), 445–69; Yair Furstenberg, "Rabbinic Responses to Greco-Roman Ethics of Self-Formation in Tractate Avot," in *Self, Self-Fashioning and Individuality in Late Antiquity*, 125–48. See also Rosen-Zvi, "The Mishnaic Mental Revolution." Balberg and Rosen-Zvi both draw attention to the connection between act and thought.

40. This is one of the themes of Moshe Halbertal, *The Birth of Doubt: Confronting Uncertainty in Early Rabbinic Literature* (Providence, 2020).

41. Meir Bar-Ilan, "The Attitude toward *Mamzerim* in Jewish Society in Late Antiquity," *Jewish History* 14 (2000): 125–70; Shaye J. D. Cohen, "Some Thoughts on 'The Attitude toward *Mamzerim* in Jewish Society in Late Antiquity,'" *Jewish History* 14 (2000): 171–74.

the construction of the *'am ha-arets* (the non-compliant Israelite) as the object of scrutiny and supervision may be precisely the contribution of the later layers of the Mishnah's redaction.[42] Similarly, although Sabbath restrictions on travel and "removing" items from one domain to the other are known from Second Temple–period texts,[43] there is no evidence outside of rabbinic texts for the construction of a real or symbolic deposit of food that permits the extension of that limit or the merging of domains into a joint space of permitted carrying.[44] The practice of merging domains for the purposes of Sabbath activity is particularly significant, since it constructs the status of space around a compact of householders, and the presence of dissenters can threaten or nullify that compact.[45]

Is the ideal mishnaic subject a sectarian, then? Shaye Cohen and Daniel Boyarin have both rejected this characterization, Cohen in favor of a nondoctrinal, generally inclusive pluralism and Boyarin in favor of a new orthodoxy.[46] "Orthodoxy" as a category binds the rabbis into a Christian conceptual straitjacket that privileges doctrine; however, there is great value in Boyarin's juxtaposition of orthodoxy to sect. A sect is constituted by the virtuous few who alone preserve Israel in moral and physical purity, an orthodoxy, in his formulation by those who adhere to and defend the "always/ already there" Torah undermined by others (heretics; but in the Mishnah also those who reject or simply fail to comply with normative rules). This conception of Torah and practice certainly allows for the continued and

---

42. Furstenberg, *Purity and Community*, 313–59. Note also those suspected in regard to the sabbatical year, mShevi 5.9; 9.1 mMa'as 5.3; mGit 5.9; see also mDem 5.9.

43. Fonrobert, "From Separatism to Urbanism," 50–51, and Eyal Regev, "The Stance of the Saducees and the Essenes in Regard to Eruv in the Light of Rabbinic Literature" [Hebrew] *Ma'of u-Ma'aseh* 6 (2000): 183–202, draw attention to 4Q270 (the *Damascus Documentf*) 5 i 1–2 as a possible reference to *'erub*. Although attractive, it attributes a unique meaning within the corpus to a word on the edge of a lacuna and followed by a lacuna at the start of the next line.

44. Origen, *de Principiis* 4.3.2, with Cohen, "Sabbath Law," 162–70. Origen knows both the Sabbath limit of 2,000 cubits and the prohibition on carrying, but not the ability to extend the limit in some direction or the consensual lifting of the restriction in a shared domain. Jerome (*Epistulae*, 121; *CSEL* 56.48–49) also knows the Sabbath limit— and connects it with recognizable rabbinic tradition—but not the extension.

45. See m'Eruv 3.2; 6.1, for those who do not acknowledge (*modim be-*) *'erub*. Note also the appearance of a *ṣadduqi* (Zadokite or Sadducee) in m'Eruv 6.2.

46. Cohen, "Significance of Yavneh," 47–50; Daniel Boyarin, *Border Lines: The Partition of Judaeo-Christianity* (Philadelphia, 2004), 50–51. The use of "sect" in the scholarship is somewhat vexed; see, however, Albert I. Baumgarten, *The Flourishing of Jewish Sects in the Maccabean Era: An Interpretation* (Leiden, 1997).

even enhanced opportunities in the Mishnah for subjects to distinguish themselves from Israelite and non-Israelite others, although on new terms.[47]

MISHNAH AS ARTIFACT: WHAT CAN WE LEARN?

"Mishnah and History" even as delimited here is exceedingly broad. I specify three areas of historiographical inquiry that the Mishnah supports. With its interest in parts and wholes of things, the Mishnah gives us a dense picture of contemporary material culture. As we have seen, the Mishnah is a peculiar work that makes tacit claims about law and tradition. It also makes extensive demands of mindfulness and care of its legal and ritual subjects. Although actual practice (and certainly what subjects hold in thought) are inaccessible to us, the Mishnah does document for us the emergence of a school with traditions and disciplines of its own. Finally, we can read the Mishnah as a text produced within Roman provincial context that simultaneously ignores, rewrites, and comes to terms with that political context.

A History of Everyday Life

With its attention to detail, and its tendency to break complex objects down to component parts, the Mishnah promises to inform us about the stuff of everyday life: fields, villages, oxen, plows, cities, festivals, pots whole or broken, coins, loaves of bread and breadcrumbs, courtyards, houses, upper stories, cellars, sons, daughters, slaves, fathers- and mothers-in-law, and deeds written, forged, lost, or canceled all make their appearance throughout the Mishnah with various degrees of specificity. Surely, attention to all this should uncover the material culture of Jews or of provincials more generally.

Some caution is in order. First, we can never be sure that when the Mishnah is prescriptive, it reflects anything like common practice. In general, documents as described in the Mishnah share family resemblances with documents known from the Judaean Desert, Egypt, and elsewhere.[48] As we have seen, however, in "real life" the documentary and legal options for marriage were broader than the Mishnah assumes. These options may, for

47. Halbertal, *The Birth of Doubt*, 88–89, emphasizes "meticulous observance [of purity] without segregations."

48. Asher Gulak, *Das Urkundenwesen im Talmud im Lichte der griechisch-ägyptischen Papyri und des griechischen und römischen Rechts* (Jerusalem, 1935; reprinted 1994), is classic although now out of date.

instance, have included divorce initiated by the wife.[49] Second, even when descriptive, the discussion is driven by analytical purposes, as in the configurations of nested or adjoining courtyards (m'Eruv 6.8–9) as they affect Sabbath law, or the construction of a house that might become impure through disease (mNeg 12.1–4). m'AZ describes a kind of cultic calendar of "the gentiles" but the festivals are almost exclusively Roman or imperial; it does not appear to provide an account of historical cult in any real place. Still, the concreteness in the Mishnah, even when it is spinning out hypothetical situations, suggests that social historians may have much more to learn from it.

Marking a "School," a Corpus, and a Disciplinary Practice

If the standard chronology is correct, the Mishnah is the earliest rabbinic work to survive. At the time of its promulgation, it already presupposed all sorts of legal, ritual, or practical information that are not spelled out. As noted, it also assumed a set of scriptural and human authorities and methods for citing them. On that level, the Mishnah attests to an audience that we can identify as members of a rabbinic movement. Although the precise correlation of the Mishnah with contemporary practice is unknown, the Mishnah outlines distinctive forms of piety and practice, carried out by distinctively intentional subjects.

In retrospect, the Mishnah was also foundational for study and the production of texts. Whatever the relative date of materials incorporated in the Tosefta, the most economic account of the Tosefta's production is that the latter work as a literary collection postdates and is structured around the Mishnah.[50] Both Talmuds are structured as "commentaries" to the Mish-

---

49. Marriage documents, see mKet 4.6–12 and Friedman, *Jewish Marriage in Palestine.* For divorce, see XHev/Se ar 13 (a wife's renunciation of claims), which contains language familiar from rabbinic documents, but appears to imply that the wife initiated the divorce, with the discussion of Tal Ilan, "On a Newly Published Divorce Bill from the Judaean Desert," *HTR* 89 (1996): 195–202; Adiel Schremer, "Papyrus *Se'elim* 13 and the Question of Divorce Initiated by Women in Ancient Jewish Halakha" [Hebrew] *Zion* 63 (1997–98): 377–90; Robert Brody, "Evidence for Divorce by Jewish Women," *JJS* 50 (1999): 230–34, and the discussions that followed.

50. For the prior dating of Tosefta materials, see Judith Hauptman, *Rereading the Mishnah: A New Approach to Ancient Jewish Texts* (Tübingen, 2005); Shamma Friedman, "The Primacy of Tosefta in MishnahTosefta Parallels—Shabbat 16, 1" [Hebrew], *Tarbiz* 62 (1993): 313–38; Shamma Friedman, *Tosefta Atikta, Synoptic Parallels of Mishna and Tosefta Analyzed, with a Methodological Introduction* [Hebrew] (Ramat-Gan, 2003).

nah; perhaps more significantly, we can see, in the statements attributed to early amoraim, glosses to and disputes about the Mishnah. As an object of study in its own right, the Mishnah served as the foundation for a distinctly rabbinic scholastic practice. One of the most striking features of that practice is that it was transportable, so that a branch of the movement took root and flourished in Babylonia, perhaps early in the third century.[51]

The Roman Imperial Context

The Mishnah creates a world that straddles the historical and the imagined. It seems preoccupied with quite mundane interactions, while projecting them onto a context that is in no particular time. There are certainly issues that derive from the sectarian context of the Second Temple period. Not far below the surface are the continued concerns of practitioners of a particular stripe to mark the distance from themselves and others. At the same time, the Mishnah creates a totalizing world for all of Israel that includes not only a ritual calendar but a procedural guide for a Temple and a system of courts and jurisdictions. It governs all sorts of agricultural activities in fulfillment of the obligations to tithe, leave corners for the poor, and allow land to lie fallow in the sabbatical year. It defines marriage, divorce, sale, barter, loan, lease, and deposit.

This claim to talk to and for all of Israel, combined with its comprehensive scope, marks the Mishnah out as revolutionary. It is what stands behind what Shaye Cohen described as pluralism and what Boyarin described as the emergence of rabbis as an "orthodoxy,"[52] as well as what Rosen-Zvi more recently described as the "imperial consciousness" of the Mishnah in constructing an alternative world that rejects the existence of the Roman imperium.[53] The first of these views seeks to uncover the internal political and social dynamics that presented themselves to Jews in the wake of the destruction of the Temple and how rabbis responded and shaped those dynamics. The second asks us to think about the emergence of "Judaism" in

51. For scholastic practice in the Yerushalmi: Hayim Lapin, "Institutionalization, Amoraim, and Yerushalmi Shebi'it," in *The Talmud Yerushalmi and Graeco-Roman Culture*, ed. P. Schäfer et al., vol. 3 (Tübingen, 2002), 161–82. For Babylonia: Barak S. Cohen, *For out of Babylonia Shall Come Torah and the Word of the Lord from Nehar Peqod: The Quest for Babylonian Tannaitic Traditions* (Leiden, 2017).

52. Mark 7; Matt. 15:2, 6; Josephus 13:297, 408.

53. Ishay Rosen-Zvi, "Rabbis and Romanization: A Review Essay," in *Jewish Cultural Encounters in the Ancient Mediterranean and Near Eastern World*, ed. M. Popović, M. Schoonover, and M. Vandenberghe, *JSJ Supplements* 178 (Leiden, 2017), 230–31.

the context of an emerging Christianity.[54] The last foregrounds the Roman imperial context, which the Mishnah presents under erasure. In what follows I will expand on this last framing, which provides a potential avenue not only for a better understanding of rabbis or of Jews more generally, but also for a placement of the origins of the Mishnah squarely in a provincial setting that should be of interest to historians of Rome as well.

Is the Mishnah "Roman"? On a trivial level this is certainly the case. References to the empire, few though they are, were mentioned above. Although its authors lacked the ability to issue coins, the economy of the Mishnah is monetized to the extent that barter is analyzed as a special form of sale. Hot water bathing in purpose-built bathhouses has been fully naturalized. The conceptualization and measurement of the Sabbath limit from a town can be understood through the work of *agrimensores*.[55] As inhabitants of the Roman imperial world, rabbis could take for granted (some of) its institutions, in the dual senses of organized structures and of shared rules of behavior.

Beyond that political and material reality, however, something more is at stake in referring to the Mishnah or to rabbis as "Roman." It suggests, on the level of content, that the Mishnah is thinking with and of the Roman state and its claims to legitimacy, even as it constructs a legal counter-reality. Given the centrality of law to both the Roman imperial and rabbinic enterprises, the influence of Roman law upon these provincials or its appropriation by provincials is an area of some interest. Here, the jury is still out, although a number of seeming parallels have been suggested; Catherine Hezser (in this volume) describes the Mishnah as a kind of *ius civile* for the Jews.[56] By far the strongest specific claim in favor of the direct and intentional appropriation of Roman law has been made in connection with a passage in the Tosefta that deals with the status of a wife redeemed from captivity and the Roman law of citizenship.[57]

On a deeper, structural level, the question remains: Did Roman rule fundamentally make possible the production of the Mishnah? It seems perverse

54. For Boyarin's resistance to "Jews" and "Judaism" see *Judaism: The Genealogy of a Modern Notion* (New Brunswick, N.J., 2019).

55. Gil Klein, "Sabbath as City: Rabbinic Urbanism and Imperial Territoriality in Roman Palestine," in *Placing Ancient Texts: The Rhetorical and Ritual Use of Space*, ed. M. Ahuvia and A. Kocar (Tübingen, 2018), 53–86.

56. For skepticism about law in particular, Ishay Rosen-Zvi, "Is the Mishnah a Roman Composition?," in *The Faces of Torah: Studies in the Texts and Contexts of Ancient Judaism in Honor of Steven Fraade* (Göttingen, 2017), 489–90.

57. Orit Malka and Yakir Paz, "*Ab hostibus captus et a latronibus captus*: The Impact of the Roman Model of Citizenship on Rabbinic Law," *JQR* 109 (2019): 141–72.

to call such a resistant, "Other"-driven work "Roman."[58] And yet, the context in which the framers of the Mishnah lived was deeply shaped by more than two centuries of Roman intervention and a more recent history of revolt and (re-)annexation. Those interventions shaped the people called Jews living in Palaestina, and how the settlements (especially cities) they lived in functioned, as well as who was a *Iudaeus* and subject to the didrachma tax. To the extent that the slaves discussed in the Mishnah correspond to real people, they are likely to be the descendants of Judaeans enslaved in the suppression of revolts in the first and second century rather than imported slaves. In that case, the characterization of the slave—a gentile who as a consequence of Jewish ownership had the status of a defective Israelite— rewrites the ethnic map of Israel along lines created by Roman conquest.[59]

As interpretive categories, Romanness and non-Romanness are not mutually exclusive. Rather, they point to a dialectical tension in historical explanation, between the circumstantial, highly local and idiosyncratic on the one hand and the systemic and broader (regional, imperial) as well as broadly comparable on the other. Emphasizing the former draws attention to deep indigenous roots and the agency and autonomy of rabbis (and more broadly, Jews) in creating a text that in retrospect was epoch-making. But an important reason to emphasize the latter is that positing "Romanness" (even in scare quotes) demands comparison and asks to what extent the groups we are interested in lived lives shaped and impacted by military conquest, taxes, cities, markets, and consumption practices. To characterize rabbis as Roman in this context gives historians the opportunity to ask how this indigenous subject population in this time and place constructed local peoplehood and identity and difference.

I am grateful to the participants in the original conference that led to this publication, and especially to David Stern, who provided extensive written comments. Max Grossman read and commented extensively on a draft of the paper. Finally, my thanks to Shaye Cohen for his instruction, mentorship, and friendship.

58. Rosen-Zvi, "Is the Mishnah a Roman Composition?"; Rosen-Zvi, "Rabbis and Romanization"; Seth Schwartz, "The Mishnah and the Limits of Roman Power," in *Reconsidering Roman Power: Roman, Greek, Jewish and Christian Perceptions and Reactions*, ed. K. Berthelot (Rome, 2020). Some of the discussion was prompted by Hayim Lapin, *Rabbis as Romans: The Rabbinic Movement in Palestine 100–400 CE* (New York, 2012).

59. Catherine Hezser, *Jewish Slavery in Antiquity* (Oxford, 2005), 27–54 (on "denationalization"), 228–32 (on sources of enslaved).

Part III

Reading the Mishnah

9. The Rhetoric of the Mishnah

Beth A. Berkowitz

> Polus: So cookery and rhetoric are the same thing?
> Socrates: Not at all, only parts of the same practice.
> Polus: What practice do you mean?
> Socrates: I fear it may be too rude to tell the truth.
> —Plato, *Gorgias*, 462e, trans. Lamb

INTRODUCTION: THE POWER OF RHETORIC

When the Mishnah speaks of a person, place, thing, or idea, what words does it use and why? Which ideologies does the Mishnah's rhetoric promote, and which does it repress? In the following essay, I look at works of scholarship from the last decade that address these questions. Philology, redaction criticism, literary analysis, and legal history are adjacent to the research that I review, though not squarely the subject. My target is what Aristotle calls "lexis," or style, the way something is formulated, even if Aristotle was imagining the address of a public orator while the Mishnah is a text that has undergone many centuries of transmission. My understanding of rhetoric is at the same time broader than the art of persuasion that Socrates, in the epigraph above, derisively compares to cookery. My understanding comes close to what today is called discourse, that is to say, "language-in-use" or, in a more Foucauldian mode, "a set of meanings, metaphors, representations, images, stories, statements and so on that in some way together produce a particular version of events."[1] This expansive approach to rhetoric befits the sober style of the Mishnah, whose manipulations of language

---

1. Gillian Brown et al., *Discourse Analysis* (Cambridge, England, 1983); Vivien Burr, *Social Constructionism* (London and New York, 2003), 64.

tend to be more subtle and systematic than those adopted by public figures from Demosthenes to Donald Trump, and the collective authorship of the Mishnah, which reflects not the strategies of a single speaker but the idioms and ideologies of a social group.

The rhetoric of the Mishnah has historically been understood primarily as a product of mnemonics. The aim of this essay is to find strains within scholarship that complicate or move beyond this approach. I begin with the Mishnah's organizational strategy of numbered lists, which have been and continue to be interpreted as mnemonic devices, and I move from there to newer concerns in the scholarship—space and time, and discourses of identity. According to Aristotle, the rhetorician must convince the audience of their authority. How does the Mishnah do so? I look at scholarship on the Mishnah's rhetoric of rabbinic authority. Central to the authority-building enterprise of the Rabbis is their legal activity; I turn to work on the Mishnah's legal rhetoric, focusing on *maḥloket*. My last subject is the Mishnah's distinctive voice and its heady meta-rhetoric. To what extent does the Mishnah show awareness of its own rhetorical practices and assumptions about the self? I close with reflection on the scholarly trends of the last decade and aspirations for next steps in research.

NUMBERS

How does the Mishnah's use of numbers compare to that of the Bible and other ancient Jewish literatures? That is the interest of two studies by Ariel Ram Pasternak and Shamir Yona.[2] In the first study from 2016 of "numerical sayings," Pasternak and Yona identify in the Bible and Mishnah typological numbers (e.g., three, four, five, seven, ten); paired numbers that express uncertainty (e.g., "five or six times" in 2 Kings 13:19; "even four or five" in *mShabat* 18:1); paired numbers that express poetic parallelism (e.g., the use of twenty and then ten in Haggai 2:16; the use of five and then six in *mMeʿilah* 4:2); and paired numbers that express "graded numerical parallelism," or number pairs that show increase. Their conclusions emphasize continuity but highlight several rabbinic innovations: a greater use of numbers for mnemonic purposes, a greater adherence to typological numbers,

---

2. Ariel-Ram Pasternak and Shamir Yona, "Numerical Sayings in the Literatures of the Ancient Near East, in the Bible, in the Book of Ben-Sira and in Rabbinic Literature," *Review of Rabbinic Judaism: Ancient, Medieval and Modern* 19.2 (October 3, 2016): 202–44; Ariel Ram Pasternak and Shamir Yona, "The Use of Numbers as an Editing Device in Rabbinic Literature," *Review of Rabbinic Judaism: Ancient, Medieval and Modern* 20.2 (August 3, 2017): 193–234.

and less use of graded numerical parallelism. In the study from 2017, Pasternak and Yona look at numbers in *mKidushin* 1:1 ("a woman is acquired in three ways, and acquires herself in two ways") and other passages from the Mishnah, Tosefta, and Bavli to propose that the rabbinic use of numbers as editing devices is "deliberate," "premeditated," and "not random," that the numbers serve a mnemonic function, and that rabbinic usage is different from the Bible's "stylistic use of numbers."[3] Staying largely within the explanatory framework of mnemonics, the two studies are useful for contextualizing and taxonomizing numbers rhetoric in the Mishnah.

Meirav Tubul Kahana's work on "numbered sayings" in the Mishnah and Tosefta also starts with scripture and does some useful taxonomizing.[4] Kahana's aim is mostly descriptive as she treats numbers three through ten (three is by far the most popular number in the Mishnah, with four a runner-up). She lays out the most common syntactic structure for the Mishnah's numbered sayings: a title that numbers the items and announces shared features, followed by the list of the items themselves. With one type of list, the idea is to exclude—*these*, and not *those*—and the items on the list are distinctive regarding the feature that they share, such as the list in *mTerumot* 1:6 of people who should not give the priestly tithe, but whose tithe is valid should they give it. In another type of list, each item is distinctive not with respect to everything outside the list, but with respect to other items on the list, such as the list in *mSanhedrin* 11:2 of the three temple courts. Sometimes the Mishnah uses numbers to present either agreement or disagreement among sages, such as the account in *mBetsah* 2:6 of three areas in which Rabban Gamaliel follows Beit Shammai's stringencies, or the dispute in *mNedarim* 11:10 between the anonymous Mishnah and Rabbi Judah over how many unmarried women's vows cannot be canceled. Kahana goes from simple to complex forms as she describes multi-numbered sayings, parallel number-sayings, and the form "X that is Y," as well as the curious instances in which the Mishnah's announced number does not match the number of items that follow (e.g., Rabbi Eliezer's statement in *mAvot* 2:10). Kahana concludes that numbered sayings were used by the rabbis as a technique to avoid mistakes in transmission, to facilitate memory, and to prevent forgetting and confusion.

Mnemotechnics go back to the Greeks and were popular among Roman orators—see Gil Klein's work below—and are likely to have been on

3. Pasternak and Yona, "The Use of Numbers," 218, 232, 233, 234.

4. Meirav (Tubul) Kahana, "Numbered Sayings in the Mishnah and Tosefta," *Jewish Studies, an Internet Journal* 15 (2019), https://jewish-faculty.biu.ac.il/files/jewish-faculty/shared/JSIJ15/tubul.pdf.

the minds of the Rabbis, but the mnemonic approach to numbers does not capture their full rhetorical effect. Though it predates the period of scholarship on which I focus, Tzvi Novick's work on numbers is useful to mention since it suggests a fruitful direction for analysis.[5] Novick looks at a single number phrase—"four or five." When a number pair phrase of this type is used in the Bible, observes Novick, it tends not to be what Novick calls "upper-bounded," that is to say, it is not used to represent an upper limit. The phrase essentially means "a bunch." The Tosefta, on the other hand, regularly uses the phrase in an upper-bounded way to mean "a few"—and not more. The Mishnah returns to the rhetorical habits of the Bible in using the phrase in a non-upper-bounded way, sometimes adding the word "even" so that "four or five" comes to mean a potentially endless number of times. Observing that the Mishnah uses the phrase in a more precise way than the Tosefta, Novick speculates that the Mishnah's authors chose its words with an expectation that the texts would be closely studied and applied to concrete cases. Novick's work illustrates how numbers rhetoric might be used to better understand the authorial intention and audience of the Mishnah.

SPACE AND TIME

In 2009, Charlotte Fonrobert documented the previous decade's "new spatial turn" in Jewish studies. Studies of spatial representation in the Mishnah soon followed.[6] In his dissertation on the Mishnah's agricultural spaces, John Mandsager argues that they offer a distinctly Jewish, idealized rural landscape that competes with the realities of Roman imperial space and especially agricultural estates.[7] Mandsager takes account of the Mishnah's agricultural vocabulary—the "master of the household" (*ba'al ha-bayit*); the "field" (*sadeh*); the "vineyard" (*kerem*); the "garden" (*gan*)—and attends to agricultural "spatial metaphors" like the fence, which refers not only to a physical marker that separates neighbors and distinguishes Jewish farms from Roman ones but also to the rabbinic enterprise more generally.[8] Gil Klein also studies the Mishnah's spatial configurations in light of ambient Roman culture, but Klein's interest is the city, not the farm. Drawing on ar-

5. Tzvi Novick, "Crafting Legal Language: 'Four or Five' in the Mishnah and the Tosefta," *Jewish Quarterly Review* 98.3 (2008): 289–304.

6. Charlotte Elisheva Fonrobert, "The New Spatial Turn in Jewish Studies," *AJS Review* 33.1 (2009): 155–64.

7. John Robert Mandsager, "To Stake a Claim: The Making of Rabbinic Agricultural Spaces in the Roman Countryside" (PhD diss., Stanford University, 2014).

8. Mandsager, "To Stake a Claim," 23–26, 217–19.

chitectural theory and history, Klein considers geometry as a framework for '*Eruvin*'s standard measurement unit of four cubits, its extended boundary of 2,000 cubits, and its configuration of the city limits as a square. These might all be understood as land survey techniques adapted by the rabbis from contemporaneous Roman ones, Klein proposes.[9] In another study, Klein looks at the furniture and architectural features of the rabbis' banquet hall in light of Roman banquet halls.[10] Klein offers an intriguing twist on the mnemonic approach to the Mishnah in another study, this one of the organization of space by *Pe'ah* when it discusses forgotten produce (*shikhhah*). The strategies of *Pe'ah* echo that of ancient Roman memorization guides, which used space as a device for memorizing ideas, words, and images.[11] A chapter of Nathan Schumer's dissertation is similarly interested in the Mishnah's palaces of memory, though Schumer's interest is the palace par excellence of rabbinic culture: the Temple.[12] Schumer argues that *Midot*'s measurements of the Temple are intended as a commemorative monument to the Second Temple past. Shimon Fogel's dissertation turns to the *bet midrash* as an organizing space for the rabbis, and drafts for it a "map" out of its rituals of entry, its seating arrangements, and its means of banishment.[13]

The temporal turn in Jewish studies, documented by Sarit Kattan Gribetz and Lynn Kaye, is more recent.[14] The temporalities of the Mishnah have been studied extensively by Kattan Gribetz, whose study of the *Shema* shows that the "always-already" tone of the Mishnah's description has concealed the novelty of this recitation ritual.[15] Kattan Gribetz looks at the time markers used by the Mishnah to define the *Shema*'s parameters: natural processes such as sunrise and sunset, and human activities such as re-

9. Gil P. Klein, "Squaring the City: Between Roman and Rabbinic Urban Geometry," in *Phenomenologies of the City: Studies in the History and Philosophy of Architecture*, ed. M. Sternberg and H. Steiner (New York, 2016), 53–68.

10. Gil P. Klein, "Torah in Triclinia: The Rabbinic Banquet and the Significance of Architecture," *Jewish Quarterly Review* 102.3 (2012): 348.

11. Gil P. Klein, "Forget the Landscape: The Space of Rabbinic and Greco-Roman Mnemonics," *Images* 10.1 (December 14, 2017): 23–36.

12. Nathan S. Schumer, "The Memory of the Temple in Palestinian Rabbinic Literature" (PhD diss., Columbia University, 2017), 65–118.

13. Shimon Fogel, "The Orders of Discourse in the House of Study (Beit Midrash) in Palestinian Rabbinic Literature: Organizing Space, Ritual and Discipline (Hebrew)" (PhD diss., Ben Gurion University of the Negev, 2014).

14. Sarit Kattan Gribetz and Lynn Kaye, "The Temporal Turn in Ancient Judaism and Jewish Studies," *Currents in Biblical Research* 17.3 (2019): 332–95.

15. Sarit Kattan Gribetz, "The Shema in the Second Temple Period: A Reconsideration," *Journal of Ancient Judaism* 6.1 (2015): 58–84.

turning home from the field or temple. In another study of the *Shema*, Kattan Gribetz observes that while the Mishnah makes the *Shema* the marker of daily time for men, it makes menstrual purity observance the marker of daily time for women.[16] Parallels between the language of *Berakhot* and *Nidah* show that the Mishnah's discourse of time distinguishes between men's and women's experiences and constructs for them different worlds. In another study of time and gender—on women's bodies as metaphors for time— Kattan Gribetz considers the comparison in *mRosh Ha-Shanah* 2:8 between the moon's position and a pregnant woman's swollen stomach, and the parallels in *mNidah* 1:3 and *tNidah* 1:5 between menstrual and lunar cycles.[17] Kattan Gribetz proposes that "the rabbis use their understanding of women and their bodies to explain and define time."[18]

IDENTITIES (THE POOR, THE HUMAN, AND THE ANIMAL)

Leaving identities related to gender, ethnicity, and religion for other essays to explore, I turn to class. In his study of the alterity of the poor in the Mishnah, Gregg Gardner argues that the poor appear "as an undifferentiated mass characterized solely by their inability to reach certain thresholds."[19] Chapter 8 of *Pe'ah* portrays the poor as "mere vessels through which householders fulfill religious obligations that require the participation of the poor." The term *'ani* performs this work, conflating those who are in need but are stable with those who are destitute, and producing an "internal other" of rabbinic society.[20] Michael Satlow similarly argues that the Mishnah presents a world in which there is "the poor" and then there is everybody else.[21] The Mishnah's laws provide for the poor but at the same time reinforce the class hierarchy through its binary rhetoric. Satlow points out,

16. Sarit Kattan Gribetz, "Time, Gender, and Ritual in Rabbinic Sources," in *Religious Studies and Rabbinics: A Conversation*, ed. E. I. Alexander and B. A. Berkowitz (New York, 2017), 139–57.

17. Sarit Kattan Gribetz, "Women's Bodies as Metaphors for Time in Biblical, Second Temple, and Rabbinic Literature, in *The Construction of Time in Antiquity: Ritual, Art, and Identity*, ed. J. Ben-Dov and L. Doering (Cambridge and New York, 2017).

18. Gribetz, 195. Sarit Kattan Gribetz, *Time and Difference in Rabbinic Judaism* (Princeton, 2020) reached me only after I had completed this essay.

19. Gregg E. Gardner, "Who Is Rich? The Poor in Early Rabbinic Judaism," *Jewish Quarterly Review* 104.4 (2014): 526.

20. Gardner, "Who Is Rich?" 530, 535.

21. Michael L. Satlow, "The Poor and Their Relief in the Mishnah: An Economic Analysis," *Studies in Judaism, Humanities, and the Social Sciences* 2.2 (2019): 61–72.

however, that the rabbinic category of the situationally poor—people who move in and out of the category—disrupts that binary. Yael Wilfand argues by contrast that "poor" is not a marginalizing rhetoric for the rabbis; indeed, some rabbis counted themselves among them.[22] Alyssa Gray's question is "not 'were the rabbis wealthy?' or 'which rabbis were wealthy?' but rather, 'what role did wealth play in the rabbis' construction of their image and role as rabbis and in their portrayals of their relationships with non-rabbis?'"[23] Gray's target corpus is post-tannaitic, but her study of the "formerly wealthy poor" begins with the Mishnah to argue that the formulation itself is ideological, its aim to build empathy and identity between wealthy and poor Jews and to highlight their shared noble past. Gray speaks elsewhere though of a tannaitic tendency to "disappear" the poor.[24] Krista Dalton's dissertation on acts of giving in rabbinic literature is likewise oriented towards later rabbinic texts of the land of Israel but covers some Mishnah passages as she tracks the slippage within rabbinic texts between "the poor" and "the rabbis."[25] Dalton's interest is in how rabbinic texts conflate gifts to the poor with gifts to the rabbis. These studies reveal the rhetorical dynamics that not only reflect but also produce class differentiation and that cause people with limited resources to appear as a distinct social group—"the poor"—with particular associations and implications.

Turning to species discourse, Rafe Neis's studies of *Kila'im*, *Nidah*, and *Bekhorot* show that rabbinic reproductive biology "implicates humans among and as animals."[26] Neis looks at the Mishnah's rhetoric of *min* (e.g., "*ke-min* + creature"), as well as its language for female animals (including humans) who give birth—*ha-mapelet* and *ha-yaldah*—and the being or

22. Yael Wilfand, *Poverty, Charity and the Image of the Poor in Rabbinic Texts from the Land of Israel* (Sheffield, 2014).

23. Alyssa M. Gray, "Wealth and Rabbinic Self-Fashioning in Late Antiquity," in *Wealth and Poverty in Jewish Tradition*, ed. L. J. Greenspoon, Studies in Jewish Civilization (West Lafayette, Ind., 2015), 53–81.

24. Alyssa M. Gray, "The Formerly Wealthy Poor: From Empathy to Ambivalence in Rabbinic Literature of Late Antiquity," *AJS Review* 33.1 (2009): 101–33; Alyssa M. Gray, "Redemptive Almsgiving and the Rabbis of Late Antiquity," *Jewish Studies Quarterly* 18.2 (2011): 144–84.

25. Krista Dalton, "Rabbis and Donors: The Logics of Giving in the Ancient Mediterranean" (PhD diss., Columbia University, 2019).

26. Rachel Rafael Neis, "The Reproduction of Species: Humans, Animals and Species Nonconformity in Early Rabbinic Science," *Jewish Studies Quarterly* 24.4 (2018): 289–317; Rachel Rafael Neis, "When Species Meet in the Mishnah," *Ancient Jew Review*, 2018, https://www.ancientjewreview.com/articles/2018/5/8/when-species-meet-in-the-mishnah.

thing that is birthed, the *valad*. The fine line between a being and a thing, and between different sorts of beings and things, that inheres within the terms is an insight Neis brings to them, but perhaps more fundamental is the very attention that Neis gives to terms. "Creaturely nomenclature" and "kind language" must be taken seriously, Neis argues, or the Mishnah's classificatory project falls below the radar.[27] Terms like "fish and locusts" (*dagim va-ḥagavim*), which the Mishnah uses metonymically for small species; binaries like pure/impure and domesticated/wild, which sort across species; *min* and the adjective *domeh* as meta-terms of classification—together these constitute a zoology, embryology, and reproductive biology comparable to that found in contemporaneous scientific taxonomies. The Mishnah's science suggests unexpected similarities and cross-overs between human beings and other species, complicating the biblical myth of *imago dei* and unsettling the fixity of the species grid.

My own work on species discourse has centered on the Bavli, but my current research on four laws of the Torah that I call the "animal family" laws (do not cook a kid in his mother's milk; keep an animal infant with the mother for the first week of life; do not slaughter an animal and the animal's child on the same day; shoo away the mother bird before taking her chicks) focuses on mishnah *Ḥulin*. In a study of the prohibition against same-day slaughter treated in *Ḥulin* chapter 5, I consider the Mishnah's family rhetoric, such as in its references to animal grandmothers and granddaughters, that situates each animal within a family tree.[28] In a different study of *Ḥulin* chapter 5, I discuss the Mishnah's treatment of the animal parent's gender.[29] The chapter begins with masculine language for the animal parent, presents a series of cases in which the gender shifts back and forth between female and male, and closes with female language. I argue that the gender instability in the Mishnah is part of a broader trajectory of ancient interpretation in which paternal bonds are marginalized.

RABBINIC AUTHORITY

Another essay in this volume addresses divergence from rabbinic practice, that is to say, sectarianism or *minut*, so here I treat recent scholarship on rhetoric that promotes or consolidates rabbinic authority to govern Jewish

27. Neis, "The Reproduction of Species," 302.

28. Beth A. Berkowitz, "A Genealogy of the Jewish Family, Animals Included," *Jewish Law Annual*, under review.

29. Beth A. Berkowitz, "Interpretation in the Anthropocene: Reading the Animal Family Laws of the Pentateuch," In *Studies in the History of Exegesis*, ed. M. W. Elliott, R. C. Heth, and A. Zautcke (Tübingen, 2022), 39–52.

practice. Richard Hidary looks at the rhetorical strategies that the Mishnah uses to shift the locus of authority from priest to rabbi within ancient Judaism.[30] Hidary organizes the strategies into four categories: a rhetoric of comparison in which rabbis and Torah study are shown to be more valuable than priests and priesthood (e.g., *Horayot* 3:8 prioritizing the *mamzer* scholar over the ignoramus high priest); a rhetoric of legal fiction in which various commandments are declared equal to sacrificial offerings (e.g., *Avot* 3:3 equating household meals with sacrifice); a rhetoric of substitution in which the rabbi replaces the priest, or a rabbinic ritual replaces a Temple practice (e.g., *mMegilah* 3:3 transferring sanctity from temple to synagogue); and, finally, a rhetoric of appropriation in which priestly or Temple laws are absorbed into the rabbinic realm such that laypeople are called upon to act like priests (e.g., *mRosh Ha-Shanah* 4:3 decreeing that the four species should be taken on all days of Sukkot). This last type of rhetoric is possibly the earliest, Hidary speculates, but the other rhetorical strategies would not have been far behind. Hidary understands the Mishnah's rhetorics of rabbinic authority to resemble those described by the literary theorist Kenneth Burke: metaphor, metonymy, synecdoche, and irony. Hidary's study is one of the few in this review to focus on rabbinic rhetoric per se and to consider the broader agenda of that rhetoric.

Tzvi Novick's monograph on normative terminology in the Mishnah and Tosefta is likewise distinctive in its attentiveness to rhetoric.[31] Working within the framework of moral philosophy, Novick proposes that the Mishnah's rhetoric is primarily deontological, that is to say, it is oriented towards "the field of ought." A vocabulary of obligation and prohibition pervades the Mishnah, Novick shows, though he also points to alternative terminologies that suggest broader modes of normativity, such as the prudent, the good, and the perfect. Positioning his work as part of a "rhetorical turn" in rabbinics, Novick embraces rhetorical analysis because, in his view, tannaitic literature expresses normativity more often implicitly than explicitly, and it is only through the implicit assumptions of rhetoric that the tensions among tannaitic normativities most clearly emerge. Novick considers the contrast between *reshut* (license to act) and *mitsvah* (obligation to do so) in the first part of his book (e.g., war of *mitsvah* vs. war of *reshut* in *mSotah* 8:7), with pauses to consider also *ḥovah* (a different term of obligation), *gezerah* (yet

30. Richard Hidary, "The Rhetoric of Rabbinic Authority: Making the Transition from Priest to Sage," in *Jewish Rhetorics: History, Theory, Practice*, ed. M. Bernard-Donals and J. W. Fernheimer (Waltham, 2014), 16–45.

31. Tzvi Michael Novick, *What Is Good, and What God Demands: Normative Structures in Tannaitic Literature* (Leiden, 2010).

another term for obligation), and *kasher* ("valid"). He then proceeds to the attitudinal language of caution and eagerness, with the *ḥasid* ("pious man") and *tsanu'a* ("prudent man") making appearances. Novick's conclusions draw upon Bakhtin's notion of dialogism to capture the multiplicity of the Mishnah's rhetorics of normativity.

One rhetoric of normativity to which Novick points is ritual. Observance of rabbinic law is constructed in ritual terms, as a function of sometimes speedy, sometimes joyful, always painstaking participation in a process. Naftali Cohn's study of mishnaic ritual highlights that ritual's vision of an Israelite collective acting synchronously according to a supreme rabbinic authority.[32] "Israel"; "all of Israel"; "the nation"; "all the nation"; "all spectators"; "all the community of the congregation of Israel" act as one to perform various rites. Chapter 5 of *mPesaḥim* shows priests and Israelites working in perfect coordination to offer the Passover sacrifice, accompanied by the singing of the Levite chorus. In *mMen* 10:3, a description of the offering of the *omer* portrays the people speaking as one, responding over and over, "Yes!" "Yes!" "Yes!," as the priest confirms his actions with them. *Bikurim* 3:2–8's description of the offering of first fruits and *Tamid*'s description of the daily offering provides a similar portrait of Israel acting in unison despite class differences, linguistic diversity, and geographic dispersal. These descriptions of the past, Cohn proposes, redound to the authority of the rabbis in their own present, which the Mishnah otherwise suggests is replete with diverse Jewish subgroups whose reality in Roman Judaea would have been far more unruly than these ritual descriptions suggest.

Mira Balberg's study of sacrifice ritual in the Mishnah similarly highlights its rhetoric of unity, uniformity, and procedural flow.[33] Congregational offerings replace individual offerings as the main mode of worship, Balberg observes. The very binary of congregational/individual is a construction of the Mishnah that it awkwardly superimposes onto the biblical text. Tractate *Tamid*, in Balberg's telling, features an idealized portrait of daily Temple routine in which priestly activity is a well-oiled machine, the priests functioning ceaselessly with great eagerness and meticulousness to

---

32. Naftali S. Cohn, "Heresiology in the Third-Century Mishnah: Arguments for Rabbinic Legal Authority and the Complications of a Simple Concept," *Harvard Theological Review* 108.4 (2015): 508–29; Naftali S. Cohn, "Sectarianism in the Mishnah: Memory, Modeling Society, and Rabbinic Identity," in *History, Memory, and Jewish Identity*, ed. I. Robinson, N. S. Cohn, and L. DiTommaso, North American Jewish Studies (Brighton, Mass., 2016), 31–54.

33. Mira Balberg, *Blood for Thought: The Reinvention of Sacrifice in Early Rabbinic Literature* (Berkeley, 2017).

fulfill their extensive regimen of minute tasks. While Hidary outlines the ways that the Rabbis substitute X or Y for sacrifice, Balberg's argument is that for the Mishnah, sacrifice just is. Balberg's approach is closer to that of Novick: one performs sacrifice because one ought to. The Mishnah's rhetoric around sacrifice, Balberg concludes, is at the deepest level one of proper, careful fulfillment of obligation. Commitment, competence, and cooperation are its hallmarks.[34] Balberg does not identify rabbinic authority as an explicit concern of sacrifice, but her prior study of skin afflictions does.[35] *Nega'im* 1:1 produces a knowledge of skin afflictions as a form of medical expertise, in Balberg's reading, while *mNega'im* 2:4 dictates bodily investigations that sound remarkably similar to a modern doctor's exam. Situating the Mishnah within the Second Sophistic's preoccupation with medical authority and knowledge, Balberg proposes that the rabbis' medicalization of skin afflictions allows them to display their interpretive skills with bodies as well as with texts.

LEGAL RHETORIC AND *MAHLOKET*

Rafe Neis's "Seduction of Law" is not about the Mishnah per se but has implications for it.[36] Before one calls the Mishnah a work of law—whether it be code, digest, manual, or something else—one might historicize the presumptions that equate Judaism with *halakhah* and then *halakhah* with law. The reasons that the Mishnah has been categorized as "law," Neis observes, have evolved over time: first in order to accommodate it to the longstanding binary of law versus faith and Judaism versus Christianity; then, with the ge'onim, in order to divvy up the classical rabbinic canon into *halakhah* and *aggadah*; and, more recently, with professional law schools in the heyday of *Mishpat Ivri*, in order to import canonical Jewish traditions into modern law and life. In point of fact, the Mishnah is made up of multiple genres—ritual, medical knowledge, agricultural methods, ethics, exegesis, history, narrative—that this volume is designed to explore.

Neis's genealogy can be kept in mind in examining recent work on *mahloket* (dispute), the signature rhetorical form of the Mishnah (and, in the "two Jews, three opinions" motif, of Jewish culture as a whole). Yair

---

34. Balberg, *Blood for Thought*, 243.

35. Mira Balberg, "Rabbinic Authority, Medical Rhetoric, and Body Hermeneutics in Mishnah Nega'im," *AJS Review* 35.2 (2011): 323–46.

36. Rachel Rafael Neis, "The Seduction of Law: Rethinking Legal Studies in Jewish Studies," *Jewish Quarterly Review* 109.1 (2019): 119–38.

Furstenberg asks how *maḥloket* came to occupy this role.[37] Furstenberg detects in the earlier strata of tannaitic literature a different preference—the selection of a single authoritative *halakhah* to transmit. This mode of transmission was in fact the dominant one in ancient Jewish literature prior to that time. Due to anxieties about cultural decay reflected in Tosefta *'Eduyot* 1:1 and similar sources, a new format was introduced in which contradictory teachings were placed side by side rather than one being chosen over the other. Furstenberg's evidence is *'Eduyot* chapter 1, in which he finds early Yavnean strata sticking to the old single-tradition model. The later Akivan material, by contrast, promotes the preservation of disputes. These disputes, once in place, generated new positions, and the rest is history—*maḥloket* replaced the single tradition as the main mode of transmission.

Rivka Shemesh-Raiskin's interest is in the particulars of the Mishnah's *maḥloket* form.[38] Shemesh-Raiskin identifies two elements: the rabbinic debate itself, and the argumentation that either precedes or follows it. Shemesh-Raiskin uses *mTa'anit* 1:1 as an illustration. The Mishnah first presents Rabbis Eliezer's and Joshua's positions regarding the proper day on which to begin recitation of the prayer for rain within the *'Amidah*, and then follows up with a debate about the merits and demerits of each rabbi's position. Australian scholars William Turnbull and Peter Muntigl call this "conversational arguing" or "conflict talk," explains Shemesh-Raiskin, who draws upon their work to depict three main features of the Mishnah's "conflict talk": dialogism; illumination of the existing dispute between rabbis; and suasion, that is to say, each addresser striving to persuade the audience of his position. Shemesh-Raiskin counts 190 such conversations in the Mishnah, with 240 exchanges between addresser and addressee. Of these exchanges, most occur between a single individual and a group. Shemesh-Raiskin comes to the conclusion that these exchanges represent real-life conversations. Her evidence lies in the rhetoric itself: the introductory dialogic tag; use of direct address between the conversation partners; use of first-person for the featured speaker and second-person for the featured addressee. While the evidence in my view points precisely in the opposite direction, to the conclusion that the dialogues are crafted literary productions, Shemesh-Raiskin does an impressive job of breaking down speech

37. Yair Furstenberg, "From Tradition to Controversy: New Modes of Transmission in the Teachings of Early Rabbis (Hebrew)," *Tarbiz* 85.4 (2018): 587–641.

38. Rivka Shemesh-Raiskin, "Toward a Description of Halachic Give-and-Take Conversations in the Mishnah," in *Studies in Mishnaic Hebrew and Related Fields: Proceedings of the Yale Symposium on Mishnaic Hebrew, May 2014*, ed. E. A. Bar-Asher Siegal and A. J. Koller (New Haven, 2017), 265–91.

acts within the Mishnah into a variety of conversational modes: asserting, asking, declaring, reprimanding. Shemesh-Raiskin's taxonomy, based on John Searle's speech act theory, offers a rich sense of the rhetorical modes of mishnaic legal conversation.

META-MISHNAH

Rhetoric that shows awareness of its own employment as rhetoric and of the rabbis as rhetoric's authors, a phenomenon that I will call meta-rhetoric, is far more typical of the Bavli than it is of the Mishnah. As Shaye Cohen remarks about the Mishnah: "it says little about itself."[39] Nevertheless, a meta-register of discourse is not as absent from the Mishnah as one might think. The elaborate inventory of the Mishnah's rhetoric offered by Alexander Samely and Rocco Bernasconi with the assistance of Ruth Shasha identifies several self-referential types.[40] The Mishnah refers to itself as a verbal entity (e.g., *Tamid* 7:3), as a genre or speech act (e.g., *Tamid* more generally), or as something dealing with an overall theme (e.g., also *Tamid*). Also relevant is Samely's treatment of "the governing voice" of the Mishnah, which Samely argues is implying that its authority is unlimited and based on unexplained knowledge (Samely considers *mAvot* 1:1 an illustration).[41] At other times, though, the governing voice makes explicit the source of its knowledge and presents its perspective as limited. Use of first-person voice on some occasions implies a royal "we" of generic discourse *(mBava Kama* 1:2; *mBava Mets'ia* 1:7). In a few cases, the governing voice is presented as that of God. Samely's typologies suggest a complex authorial self-representation on the part of the Mishnah.

Tzvi Novick's treatment of the expression "for I say" (*she-'ani 'omer*) similarly foregrounds the Mishnah's reflexive rhetoric.[42] Novick describes the expression as a fictional legal presumption that artificially uses the first person as a strategy for rabbinic lawmakers to assert their agency. One example is *mMa'aser Sheni* 4:11, in which Rabbi Yose speaks in the first person to stake out the rather indefensible position that produce found marked with

39. Shaye J. D. Cohen, "The Judaean Legal Tradition and the Halakhah of the Mishnah," in *The Cambridge Companion to the Talmud and Rabbinic Literature*, ed. C. E. Fonrobert and M. S. Jaffee, Cambridge Companions to Religion (New York, 2007), 138.

40. Alexander Samely, *Profiling Jewish Literature in Antiquity: An Inventory, from Second Temple Texts to the Talmuds* (Oxford, 2013), 389–407.

41. Samely, *Profiling Jewish Literature*, 392–98.

42. Tzvi Novick, "The 'For I Say' Presumption: A Study in Early Rabbinic Legal Rhetoric," *Journal of Jewish Studies* 61.1 (2010): 48–61.

the word "terumah" should not in fact be treated as terumah but as non-sacred food. "For I say" introduces unconfirmable or improbable presumptions; the "I" is a mask that the rabbi dons to make a strong play for a weak case. "For I say" foregrounds the role that the rabbinic lawmaker's own preference plays in his legal position and draws attention to the act of lawmaking and to the authorial production of the Mishnah. Thus the phrase can be understood "to expose the law itself as a charade."[43] The lawmaker is revealed as an interested party, not one who personally benefits from the results of a particular case, but who wants the law to be a certain way.

Joshua Levinson's main interest is midrash, but his recent work on the "new inward turn" in rabbinic literature touches upon the Mishnah as well. In that line of inquiry, Levinson's interest is the subject produced by legal discourse, which he proposes is not only a "subject-to-the-law," but also a "subject-of-the-law," that is to say, a subject whose identity is produced through the law.[44] While in biblical law, Levinson says, the subject is defined primarily by what they do, in rabbinic law, the subject is defined by their internal world.[45] This "stratification of consciousness" introduced by the rabbis is exemplified in the exemption from punishment of a person who intends to kill one person but instead kills another (*mSanhedrin* 9:2).[46] For the Bible, by contrast, there is only the blunt distinction between premeditated murder and inadvertent homicide. Another example from Levinson is *mMakhshirin* 3:6. Whereas in the Bible, moisture makes produce susceptible to impurity, in *mMakhshirin*, moisture has that effect only if the owner expresses approval of the rain that has fallen upon his produce to make it moist. The Mishnah creates a reality in which not only does a subject's intention matter, but the subject must be ever aware of that intention. Continuous vigilance is required of the rabbinic self.

Levinson takes a cue from Mira Balberg's book on the Mishnah's purity laws, where she makes a similar case about the rabbinic self's need for vigilance.[47] Balberg argues that for the Mishnah, impurity pertains to objects only insofar as they belong to the human sphere and are understood to be in

43. Novick, "The 'For I Say' Presumption," 59.
44. Joshua Levinson, "From Narrative Practice to Cultural Poetics: Literary Anthropology and the Rabbinic Sense of Self," in *Homer and the Bible in the Eyes of Ancient Interpreters*, ed. M. Niehoff (Leiden, 2012), 346. See also Joshua Levinson, "Post-Classical Narratology and the Rabbinic Subject," in *Narratology, Hermeneutics, and Midrash: Jewish, Christian, and Muslim Narratives from the Late Antiquity through to Modern Times*, ed. G. Langer and C. Cordoni (Vienna, 2014), 85–89.
45. Levinson, "From Narrative Practice to Cultural Poetics," 352–53.
46. Levinson, "From Narrative Practice to Cultural Poetics," 349.
47. Mira Balberg, *Purity, Body, and Self in Early Rabbinic Literature* (Berkeley, 2014).

some sense an extension of the human being. Balberg shows that the Mishnah's purity laws give "unparalleled attention to questions of subjectivity, and more specifically, to the ways in which persons relate to themselves, to their bodies, and to their material surroundings."[48] Here's how: the world is infused by the rabbis with an impurity to which the self must constantly attend; the self is constituted by a "modular" body whose parts may or may not at any one moment be integrally connected and which may be sometimes extended by inanimate objects; that self's purity is more affected by a dead body the more it resembles a living one; that self, to be fully susceptible to impurity, must be Jewish. In making her case Balberg pauses over certain components of mishnaic rhetoric: *ḥibburim* ("appendages"), a term that when used with the body describes detachable parts such as hair, nails, and teeth (*mZavim* 5:4); *bet ha-setarim* ("a hidden place"), a term denoting areas of bodies or objects that are not visible to the eye (*mMikva'ot* 8:5); *hakpadah* ("fastidiousness"), to describe the experience of being bothered by something on one's body (*mMikva'ot* 9:3); *keli* ("article") as an item that is put to use (the tractate of that title); *gemar mel'akhah* ("completion of labor") to describe the process by which a *keli* is produced (*mKelim* 4:4); and *maḥshavah* ("thought"), the final ingredient that makes a *keli* susceptible to impurity (*mKelim* 26:7). And there are others (e.g., *hekhsher mashkin*, activation through liquids).

Levinson and Balberg do not, however, highlight the role of rhetoric *as such* in the production of the Mishnah's "sense of self" in the way that, for instance, Novick does, or as Michal Bar Asher-Siegal does in her study of the motif of "mountains hanging by a strand" found in *mḤagigah* 1:8, a piece of rhetoric that reflects on the rabbis as producers of law.[49] *Ḥagigah* presents three categories of rabbinic law in its relationship to scripture: laws that fly in the air and have nothing to lean on; laws that are like "mountains hanging by a strand, since they are little scripture and many laws"; and laws having "upon what to lean, and it is they that are the bodies of the Torah." Bar-Asher Siegal asks: "What does it mean to describe mountains hanging by a strand? What is the mental image that these words are supposed to evoke in the reader? What is the *realia* behind these words?"[50] The Mishnah uses this colorful simile not only as an "explicatory device that conjures up a mental picture," Bar-Asher Siegal proposes, but also as an argument by analogy. Noting suggestive manuscript variations regarding the unique form of

48. Balberg, *Purity, Body, and Self,* 4–5.
49. Michal Bar-Asher Siegal, "Mountains Hanging by a Strand?: Re-Reading Mishnah Ḥagigah 1:8," *Journal of Ancient Judaism* 4.2 (2013): 235–56.
50. Siegal, "Mountains Hanging by a Strand?" 244.

the Mishnah's word for mountains, *hararim*, Bar-Asher Siegel suggests that the word was originally *ḥararim* with a *ḥet*, and that it refers to dry desert bushes or thorns which, in *Ḥagigah*'s phrase, are practically rootless, barely attached to the ground.[51] Through this phrase the Mishnah is arguing, according to Bar-Asher Siegel, that such laws are unstable. Without a basis in scripture, the law can be easily dismissed, abolished, or misunderstood. Rabbinic law's authority is thus depicted as dependent on its proximity to scripture. With this, Bar-Asher Siegel takes us back to rhetoric's role in the production of rabbinic authority, as well as to other categories of rhetoric that I have reviewed—space and time, both critical to the suspense in the image of the dry desert bush barely hanging on to the ground by its spindly roots, and numbers, since three is this mishnah's organizing principle—showing the power of these rhetorics as they work in tandem to produce the discourse of the Mishnah.

CONCLUSIONS

The work on numbers rhetoric remains in the mnemonic mode; Novick's study of number language suggests one new direction. The promising new work on space and time in the Mishnah could be made even richer if it were to give more attention to rhetoric per se as it explores other spaces—the wild, for example, a terrain recently traversed by Alex Weisberg[52]—and temporalities. Scholarship on the discourse of the poor remains divided on whether the poor are marginalized or identified with the rabbis. Further work on these questions would be illuminating. The discourse of species and of ancient science more generally is a growing area of interest, if December 2020's session at the American Academy of Religion conference on critical animal studies and Jewish studies is any indication. The rhetorics of rabbinic authority, normativity, and legal dispute are the most well-developed area of research; they are a model for other areas. The work on reflexivity, selfhood, and meta-discourse in the Mishnah might follow in the footsteps of scholarship on the Bavli and midrash even if the road is more uphill with the Mishnah. The notion of a "governing voice" suggested by Samely may help to uncover more of the "meta-Mishnah."

What might we expect in the second quarter of the twenty-first century from research on the Mishnah's rhetoric? To research the Mishnah's rhetoric is to stand at the crossroads of politics, language, and, importantly, af-

---

51. Siegal, "Mountains Hanging by a Strand?" 239.
52. Alex Weisberg, "Before There Was Nature: Affect, Ontology, and Ethics in the Early Rabbinic Sabbatical Year Laws" (PhD diss., New York University, 2019).

fect. Rhetoric's aim is to arouse the right emotion, according to Aristotle.[53] When compared with the Bavli or even the Tosefta, the Mishnah comes across as the most affectless of rabbinic corpora. The Mishnah is the rabbinic work that would appear to be most resistant to reading for rhetoric. But as this review of scholarship has revealed, the Mishnah is replete with all sorts of rhetorics. The next wave of scholarship would do well to explore the affective dimensions of these rhetorics (even if that affect might sometimes be a deadening one: that too is a mobilization of affect), drawing upon affect theory and the history of emotions. Other presentations in this volume—on sectarians, on gentiles—may help us to imagine what that might look like.[54]

53. Christof Rapp, "Aristotle's Rhetoric," in *The Stanford Encyclopedia of Philosophy*, ed. E. N. Zalta, spring 2010 (Metaphysics Research Lab, Stanford University, 2010), 5 (b), https://plato.stanford.edu/archives/spr2010/entries/aristotle-rhetoric/.

54. Rabbinics scholars Sarah Wolf and Erez DeGolan are both pursuing this new line of inquiry.

10. Mishnah as Utopia

Naftali S. Cohn

The Mishnah has sometimes been called "utopian," or even "a utopia." The following narrative snippet helps illustrate why:

> The Passover offering was slaughtered in three groups . . . The first group entered and filled the Temple Courtyard . . . The priests were standing in rows and in their hands were gold and silver dishes . . . An Israelite slaughtered, and the priest received the blood. The priest would hand [the dish] to his fellow [next to him in the row], and his fellow to his fellow, receiving the full [vessel with blood] and returning the empty one. The priest standing closest to the Altar would toss it once toward the base of the Altar. (mPes 5.5–6)

Though the Temple had been long destroyed by the time the Mishnah was created, this passage brings to life a world in which the Temple exists and functions in all its grandeur. Moreover, in this scene, Temple ritual is not only carried out, but goes smoothly. Israelite and priest work efficiently in tandem, bowls get passed, and the blood gets to where it needs to go.

But to call the Mishnah fully utopian would be a misnomer: ritual and social interaction do not always function perfectly in the Mishnah's world of the Temple. *Yoma* 2.2, for instance, describes things going wrong during the competitive ritual to decide which priest got to clear the ashes from the Altar: "It once happened [מעשה] that the two of them were equal running up the ramp. One of them pushed his fellow and he broke his leg."[1] True,

---

1. The clearing of the ashes was a daily activity, as noted in mYom 1.8 and also in mTam 1.2 and 1.4, where, however, there is no mention of any pre-lottery phase, as narrated in mYom 2.1–2. This event could have taken place on any day, and mYom 2:2 does not imply that it was necessarily on the Day of Atonement.

this story in the Mishnah is far milder than the shocking parallel version in the Tosefta: "One pushed the other within four cubits [of the top]. He took a knife and stabbed him in the heart" (tKip 1.12).[2] In the Mishnah the harm is pushing and a broken leg, not murder. Nevertheless, this passage shows that Temple ritual does not always function smoothly, as in Mishnah *Pesaḥim*. According to mYom 2:2, the ritual procedure was even deemed so faulty that it had to be changed: "When the Court saw that they were coming to danger, they established that they should only clear the ashes from the Altar based on a lottery [and not a race]." If this is a utopia, it is not a perfect world; it is far more complex.[3]

In order to understand the more complicated, imagined world in the Mishnah, I suggest that the concept of utopia is nevertheless useful. This "analytic category," as Ruth Levitas calls it, helps tease out the precise nature of the mishnaically imagined world, how this world functions, and what ideals the mishnaic authors project in creating this world. Rabbinic notions of ideal behavior, of the ideal nature of ritual, and the ideal functioning of society emerge both in passages that are more blatantly idealized and also in those that are less so.[4] In the ideal mishnaic world, there is a fully

2. In the Tosefta's dark version, it seems the competitiveness was so fierce and egos so fragile that murder ensued, whether the murderer simply continued the violence that started with a push or was motivated by the slight of being shoved, the perceived unfairness of pushing in a race, or the loss of the privilege of clearing the ashes. On interpreting ritual failure in the Mishnah, see Naftali S. Cohn, "Ritual Failure, Ritual Success, and What Makes Ritual Meaningful in the Mishnah," in *Religious Studies and Rabbinics: A Conversation*, ed. E. S. Alexander and B. A. Berkowitz (Abingdon, 2017), 158–72; and see more detail in my forthcoming work.

3. On this narrative, see Naftali S. Cohn, "Rabbis as Jurists: On the Representation of Past and Present Legal Institutions in the Mishnah" *Journal of Jewish Studies* 60.2 (2009): 258, and Naftali S. Cohn, *The Memory of the Temple and the Making of the Rabbis* (Philadelphia, 2012), 47–49. Moshe Simon-Shoshan, *Stories of the Law: Narrative Discourse and the Construction of Authority in the Mishnah* (New York, 2012), 204–10 (and 211–16), takes up the same narratives, using them to make a different argument about the role of the law. Simon-Shoshan also argues that the Mishnah is a later version that "tames" the violent and messy version of the Tosefta. While this is one possible narrative to explain the order and difference of the sources, I do not find it more compelling than the alternative. Perhaps the Tosefta's version is a later version that spins out the violence in order to convey the moral lesson it implies (as Simon-Shoshan details). Further, "the scramble to clean off the altar" that Simon-Shoshan finds in the related passage in mTam 2.1–2 is simply not there (nor in mTam 1.4, the description of what the person who won the right to clear the ashes does), and there is no strong argument that mYom 2:2 is taming the supposedly earlier Mishnah *Tamid* passage.

4. Ruth Levitas, *The Concept of Utopia* (Oxford, 2010), esp. 212, 222, and 228–29.

Jewish society: the people of Israel live in and control its land, an authoritative Jewish judiciary and legal system is in place, and social harmony and inclusion prevail. The entire people perform ritual correctly, both locally and in the Temple, and the rabbis are the ones with authority to determine correct practice, ensuring robustness of the ritual system even when things go awry. While the reality may not live up to the ideals of this imagined world, the rabbis' vision for the Mishnah contains a system of practice that has the potential to realize them.

WHAT IS UTOPIA?[5]

The terms utopia and utopian refer to an interrelated set of literary, political, and philosophical works. Thomas More established the genre when he coined the phrase in the sixteenth century, although, as Manuel and Manuel demonstrate, the concept had earlier roots going back to the Roman world. While the Mishnah could potentially have indirect genre and literary relationships to the sources Manuel and Manuel see as the roots of More's Utopia, my purpose here is not to make any claims about such historical connections or development.[6] Rather, it is to draw on the analytic category set out by Levitas and developed by others, in order to gain insight into the ways in which the mishnaic rabbis imagined the world and what might be gained by thinking of the imagined world of the Mishnah as utopian.

The most basic way of defining a "utopia" in order to stretch its potential as an analytic category is simply as an imagined alternative world. This world may be a better world than the current one, as implied by the neologism itself, utopia as *eutopia*.[7] It may be imagined in the past or future, or in some other place, or even in an abstract space existing only in the imagination.[8] The imagined world may be a desirable one, and it is possible that those imagining see it as a possible world they hope to create or attain; or it may simply be what Levitas calls "compensation," imagination filling in for something lacking, or "criticism" of the current situation." In Levitas's

5. I would like to express gratitude to Jonathan Kaplan for suggesting readings to me and for a fruitful conversation on the theory of utopia.

6. Frank E. Manuel and Fritzie P. Manuel, *Utopian Thought in the Western World* (Cambridge, Mass., 1979), and see also Zsolt Czyganyík, "Introduction: Utopianism: Literary and Political," in *Utopian Horizons: Ideology, Politics, Literature*, ed. Z. Czyganyík (Budapest: Central European University Press, 2017), 1–16.

7. See Manuel and Manuel, *Utopian Thought*, 1; see also Miguel Abensour, "Persistent Utopia" *Constellations* 15.3 (2008): 406, and Czyganyík, "Utopianism," 6.

8. Czyganyík, "Utopianism," 2–5.

view, utopian worlds are very much culturally bound, and they serve different functions: criticizing, arguing for change, expressing need or desire.[9] And there may be other functions, too, such as entertainment, or a narrative crystallization of an idealized past.

To take up utopia as an analytic category does not necessitate treating the work or text as intentionally utopian. Rather, if the text is imagining an alternative world, the use of the category facilitates asking certain questions about how exactly the text imagines this world and why it does so. What is the context that explains this particular imagined world, and what may be accomplished by imagining the world in this way?

In the Mishnah, the most relevant passages for applying the utopia lens are those narratives that describe how Temple ritual was performed in the past, or "Temple ritual narratives."[10] These passages, including extended and also briefer narratives, imagine a rich world that certainly did not exist at the time the Mishnah was composed, more than a century after the destruction of the Temple. They imagine an alternative world.

These narratives are not the only ones to weave a larger imagined world of the land of Israel with a Temple. Even in the various rulings that make up the majority of the Mishnah, covering a wide span of topics from prayers and blessings, to agricultural practices and rituals, to Sabbath and holiday observance, to laws relating loosely to marriage practices, to Temple sacrifices, to purity practices, and to everyday commercial interactions to which civil law applies, the Mishnah projects an imagined world that is not identical to the lived world that the rabbis experienced. These rulings may bear a very close relationship to the realia experienced by the rabbinic authors, to the places, materials, activities, and power dynamics with which all living in Roman Palaestina interacted. But the rulings are representations conjured within an imagined world, and as specifically legal rulings, they operate, at least in part, in the realm of the "ought," what people ought to do. These passages, too, imagine a world defined by these rulings. As Moshe Simon-Shoshan has demonstrated, every type of passage has a degree of narrativ-

9. Levitas, *Concept of Utopia*, 208, 219–20.

10. Naftali S. Cohn, "The Ritual Narrative Genre in the Mishnah: The Invention of the Past in the Representation of Temple Ritual," (PhD diss., University of Pennsylvania, 2008). This is also true in the judicial ritual narratives which center on the court, which I understand to be primarily the Great Court, also called the Sanhedrin, and at times a system of lower courts. In my understanding, these are also set in the time of the Temple, and in relation to the Temple, as indicated by locating the great court in the Temple in mMid 5.4 and mSan 11.2, and perhaps in other passages, such as the reference to "the elders" in mSuk 4.4. I will touch on this below.

ity.[11] As with the Temple ritual narratives, the imagined world of the wider body of narrative in rulings is complex. In it there is contingency, but the ritual system has dynamic strength. There is an ideal society and ritual enactment goes smoothly. The rabbis themselves, in this conjured narrative world, play a crucial role in bringing about these ideals.

IMAGINING A WORLD OF TEMPLE RITUAL

One of the key features of the Mishnah's imagined world, as already mentioned, is the Temple. A very significant proportion of the Mishnah focuses on the Temple and its rituals, or on rituals associated with the Temple in some other way. This includes not only the majority of the order of *Kodashim*, but also multiple tractates in the order of *Mo'ed*, including *Pesaḥim*, *Yoma*, *Shekalim*, *Sukkah*, and *Ḥagigah*; most of the tractates in *Zera'im*, at least to a degree; some tractates in the order of *Nashim*, including *Nedarim*, *Nazir*, and *Sotah*; and a few of the tractates in the order of *Tohorot* that relate directly to Temple ritual (including *Parah* and *Nega'im*). It may be said that these latter tractates address the Temple in some way, due to their concern with purity and entering Temple grounds.[12]

The Temple ritual narratives are a crucial locus for interpreting the Mishnah's imagined world.[13] But even many of the Mishnah's more typical rulings bring out elements of this world. The mere mention of "the time when the priests enter to eat their *terumah*" as a time marker for reciting the *shema* in mBer 1.1 contributes to this imagined world of people moving about the Temple and partaking of ritual materials. Or even the brief rule about the place where certain kinds of sacrificial offerings are performed— "their slaughtering is to the north [of the Altar]"—in mZev 5.1 contributes to imagining the array of sacrifices in a functioning Temple.

11. Simon-Shoshan, *Stories of the Law*, 15–58. The conflicting voices in the text are a key element of Simon-Shoshan's analysis throughout *Stories of the Law*. Regarding the definition of what makes narrative, I have argued for a more expansive approach than the two variables set out by Simon-Shoshan. See Cohn, *Memory of the Temple*, 8–9, and in more detail, Cohn, "The Temple Ritual Narrative Genre," 47–51.

12. See Neusner's list of tractates that he frames as being "of principal concern to Priests: Temple and Cult," in Jacob Neusner, *Judaism: The Evidence of the Mishnah* (Chicago, 1981). Neusner also frames this as the "contribution" or "gift" of the priests to the Mishnah (*Judaism*, 248–50), which is a somewhat odd formulation, especially since it is not something given directly by any priests, but rather a set of materials that may stem especially from priestly interests. On Neusner's analysis, see further below.

13. See Cohn, *The Memory of the Temple*, 4–11, 57–72; and see Cohn, "The Temple Ritual Narrative Genre," 25–112. For earlier scholarship that treats these passages as a genre (without detailing what this means), see Martin S. Jaffee, *Torah in the Mouth: Writing and Oral Tradition in Palestinian Judaism 200 BCE–400 CE* (New York 2001),

In addition to setting out a world in which there is a functioning Temple in Jerusalem, the ritual narratives, and to a degree the briefer rulings too, imagine a fully Jewish society, a society consisting of Israelites (i.e. Jews or Judaeans), where Israelites are the main demographic. These Israelites come together to worship in the Temple as a group.[14] This can be seen, for instance, in the description of "the Temple Courtyard being filled with [the people of] Israel" (mYom 1.8), who are audience to the spectacle of the Day of Atonement ritual in the Temple, or "the entire people" who "bring their *lulavs* to the Temple Mount" (mSuk 4.4) for the first festival day of Sukkot that coincides with the Sabbath. The same sense of an Israelite people filling its land occurs in the narrative of bringing the first fruits to the Temple, in which the people of an entire district of towns gathers in the city square of the central city before going to the Temple (mBik 3.2), or the Israelites (non-priests and non-Levites) in a given district gather in the cities and towns to publicly read the Torah when the district's priests and Levites are serving on rotation in the Temple (mTa'an 2.1). This same element of group Israelite identity may even be present when there is no Temple. The narrative of the people praying in the city square on public fast days (mTa'an 2.1–5) seems to presume exclusive Jewish control over the public space and existence in the city or town, and is set specifically in the post-Temple era.[15] Outside of the Temple, there seems to be a similar assumption about Jews dominating and

---

103; Michael D. Swartz, "Ritual about Myth about Ritual: Towards an Understanding of the *Avodah* in the Rabbinic Period" *Journal of Jewish Thought and Philosophy* 6 (1997): 140; Michael D. Swartz and Joseph Yahalom, *Avodah: Ancient Poems for Yom Kippur* (University Park, Penn., 2004), 16; Yochanan Breuer, "The Perfect and the Participle in Descriptions of Ceremony in the Mishnah" [Hebrew] *Tarbiz* 56 (1987): 299–326 (from a purely grammatical point of view); and Ishay Rosen-Zvi, *The Mishnaic Sotah Ritual: Temple, Gender and Midrash*, trans. Orr Scharf (Leiden, 2012), 239–40. Jaffee notes that the genre includes narratives about both the Temple and the Court; for him, what joins them are that they are both important institutions. My own explanation is that they are linked in rabbinic memory (see below, based on Cohn, *Memory of the Temple*). For my list of these narratives, see Cohn, *Memory of the Temple*, 123–25.

14. In a very few cases there are hints of Jewish government as well, as in the few references to King Agrippa II, the last Jewish king, who however did not rule much of the land of Israel (mBik 3:4, mSot 7.8). The only reference to a king having any kind of ruling authority is in mSan 2.2, and perhaps mHor 3.3. There are also a few references to a Jewish king or kings in relation to ritual participation: mBer 5.1, mYom 7.5, mYom 8.1, mRh 1.1, mNed 2.5, mNed 3.4, mSot 7.2 and 7.8, mSan 2.3, mSan 2.4, mSan 2.5, and perhaps the references to princes or members of the royal class in mBer 1.2, mShab 6.9, and mShab 14.4.

15. The explicit setting in post-Temple times is in mTa'an 2.5, which also implies that the same ritual was done at the Temple in Temple times. The same observation is made by Ishay Rosen-Zvi, *The Mishnaic Sotah Ritual*, 245, who cites different evidence from David Levine, *Communal Fasts and Rabbinic Sermons: Theory and Practice in the Tal-*

performing ritual in cities, towns, and villages of Jews. This can be seen, for instance, in the rules about when the scroll of Esther is read—"walled cities from the days of Joshua son of Nun read on the fifteenth [of the month of Adar], villages and large towns/cities reading on the fourteenth, but villages reading earlier on the day of gathering [i.e., market day]" (mMeg 1.1).[16]

Part of what makes the elements outlined thus far utopian is that when the Mishnah was created, none of these elements existed in reality, as the Mishnah itself attests.[17] On multiple occasions, the Mishnah refers to changes that occurred "when the Temple was destroyed" or to rules that apply when "there is no Temple," or "not in the presence of the Temple" or refer to "when the Temple existed" or when it will be "rebuilt."[18] Further, parts

---

mudic Period [Hebrew] (Benei Berak:, 2001), itself a historical study that extends well beyond the Mishnah.

16. On the construction of peoplehood and local, city-based identity, both of which are imagined and necessarily bear a complex relationship to the actual demographic situation, see Naftali S. Cohn, "The Complex Ritual Dynamics of Individual and Group Experience in the Temple, as Imagined in the Mishnah," *AJS Review* 43.2 (2019): 293–318, esp. 310–15, and Naftali S. Cohn, "Sacred Space in the Mishnah: From Temple to Synagogue and . . . City," in *Actes du colloque La question de la «sacerdotalisation» dans le judaïsme chrétien, le judaïsme synagogal et le judaïsme rabbinique*, ed. S. C. Mimouni and L. Painchaud (Turnhout, Belgium, 2018), 85–121. On the rabbinic construction of the land, see Eyal Ben-Eliyahu, *Identity & Territory: Jewish Perceptions of Space in Antiquity* (Oakland, 2019), 86–109. There is also extensive scholarship on cities and the land, mostly from an archaeological and historical perspective. See, for instance: Ze'ev Safrai, *The Economy of Roman Palestine* (London, 1994), 17–46; Safrai, *The Jewish Community in the Talmudic Period* [Hebrew] (Jerusalem, 1995), 29–49; Safrai, "Urbanization and Industry in Mishnaic Galilee," in *Galilee in the Late Second Temple and Mishnaic Periods: Life, Culture, Society*, vol. 1, ed. D. A. Fiensy and J. R. Strange (Minneapolis: Fortress, 2014), 272–96; Ze'ev Yeivin, "Medium-Sized Cities" [Hebrew], *Eretz Israel* 19 (1987): 59–71; Joshua Schwartz, *Jewish Settlement in Judea: After the Bar-Kochba War until the Arab Conquest, 135 C.E–640 C.E.* (Jerusalem, 1986), esp. 51–68 (on Judaea); and David A. Fiensy, "The Galilean Village in the Late Second Temple and Mishnaic Periods," in *Galilee in the Late Second Temple and Mishnaic Periods: Life, Culture, Society*, vol. 1, ed. D. A. Fiensy and J. R. Strange (Minneapolis, 2014), 177–207 (on the Galilee). On the relationship between Rabbis and cities, see Hayim Lapin, "Rabbis and Cities in Later Roman Palestine: The Literary Evidence," *Journal of Jewish Studies* 50.2 (1999): 187–207; Lapin, "Rabbis and Cities: Some Aspects of the Rabbinic Movement in Its Greco-Roman Environment," in *The Talmud Yerushalmi and Greco-Roman Culture II*, ed. C. Hezser and P. Schäfer (Tübingen, 2000), 51–80; and Lapin, *Economy, Geography and Provincial History in Later Roman Palestine* (Tübingen, 2001).

17. While the Temple did exist and ritual was practiced there, as attested in multiple other sources such as the works of Philo and Josephus, the elements of Jews filling the land and local spaces and widespread uniform observance may never have been reality.

18. When the Temple was destroyed: mMS 5.2, mSuk 3.12, mRH 4.1 and 4.2–4, mMK 3.6, mSot 9.12 and 9.15, mMen 10.5, and in a slightly different way in mNaz 5.4; when

of most Temple ritual narratives, and some other mishnaic passages, refer to the Temple using the past tense (see further below).[19] In these there is no Temple, but Temple ritual narratives imagine a world of the Temple, and many rulings deal with Temple or Temple-related ritual. Similarly, the cities and towns in the land of Israel were controlled by Romans, and the population was not composed exclusively of Jews or of a uniform body of Jews. Some passages acknowledge that cities were not all Jewish and uniform: although many cities, towns, and villages in the Galilee may have been largely ethnically Judaean, there existed examples of a "city that has gentiles present," or "a city in which Israelites and gentiles both dwell" (mSot 9.2, m'AZ 4.11, and mMakh 2.5), or even "a city that is entirely gentile" (m'AZ 4:11).[20] As Charlotte Fonrobert shows in her analysis of the *'eruv* rituals, the Mishnah goes as far as imagining Jews living in a shared courtyard with a gentile (m'Eruv 6.1).[21] Even Galilean locales were hardly uniform, with the likelihood that many Jews were rather Roman. The Mishnah, further, frequently admits that quite a few Jews do not observe the traditional practices as the rabbis think they should.[22] And yet, in Temple ritual narratives, and in much

there is no Temple: mMS 1.5–6; in the presence and not in the presence of the Temple: mBik 2.3, mShek 8.8, mḤul 5.1, mḤul 61, mḤul 7.1, mḤul 10.1, mḤul 11.1, mḤul 12.1, and mBekh 9.1; when the Temple existed: mRH 1.3–4 and mBekh 4.1 (see also mPes 10.3, which differentiates "in the Temple" from the situation of the Passover meal it is describing); rebuilding: mMS 5.2, mTa'an4.8, and mTam 7.3. On these passages, see also Rosen-Zvi, *The Mishnaic Sotah Ritual*, 246.

19. An example of a passage outside of the Temple ritual narrative genre is mBer 9.5. This is also a kind of quasi-historical narrative rather than a ruling, but it need not necessarily have used the past tense to make its point. See also the rule in Men 9.1, which refers to measurements "that were in the Temple."

20. On gentile presence, particularly in religious culture, see esp. Nicole Belayche, *Iudaea-Palaestina: The Pagan Cults in Roman Palestine (Second to Fourth Century)* (Tübingen, 2001). On these cities as predominantly gentile, see m'AZ 1:4, 4:12, and 3:4. For relevant toseftan examples, and further discussion and references, see Cohn, *The Memory of the Temple*, 151–52 end of n. 58.

21. Charlotte E. Fonrobert, "From Separatism to Urbanism: The Dead Sea Scrolls and the Origin of the Rabbinic 'Eruv'" *Dead Sea Discoveries* 11.1 (2004): 66.

22. On the character of Galilean locales, see esp. Mark A. Chancey, *Myth of a Gentile Galilee* (Cambridge, 2005); Chancey, *Greco-Roman Culture and the Galilee of Jesus* (Cambridge, 2002); Chancey, "The Ethnicities of Galileans," in *Galilee in the Late Second Temple and Mishnaic Periods: Life, Culture, Society*, vol. 1, ed. D. A. Fiensy and J. R. Strange (Minneapolis, 2014), 112–28; Seth Schwartz, *Imperialism and Jewish Society, 200 B.C.E. to 640 C.E.* (Princeton, 2001); and many chapters in Zangenberg, Attridge, and Martin, *Religion, Ethnicity, and Identity*. For further on this topic see also Cohn, *The Memory of the Temple*, 150–53 nn. 57–63. The seeming prevalence of *'ammei ha'arets* suggests different kinds of observance, but there are other relevant categories and ways of imagining how Jews practiced (as well as archaeological evidence). Crucial

of the Mishnah, these facts are ignored and the Mishnah imagines a world with a Temple and a land with a largely Jewish population, enacting rituals as they should be done. A particularly striking example of ignoring such facts is the claim in mTa'an 3:6 that the city of Ashkelon observed a public fast as directed by the elders of Jerusalem, when according to the archaeological record, there was never any significant Jewish presence in that city![23] Ishay Rosen-Zvi has pointed out that some tractates are more prone to representing reality, while others imagine the system in an abstract, utopian way.[24] More generally, the texture of the Mishnah is variegated; in some parts there is an acknowledgement that there is no Temple and no Jewish nation; in others there is a more fully imagined world that does not exist in reality; in still others, there is a mixing.

---

scholarship on this "revisionist" view of the rabbis and their rulings includes Goodman, *State and Society*, and S. Schwartz, *Imperialism*. There is also extensive scholarship on this topic, some of which is referenced in Cohn, *Memory of the Temple*, 154–56 nn. 67–71. I have made attempts to map out the imagined social geography of Roman Palaestina in Cohn, *The Memory of the Temple*, 26–35, and Cohn, "Heresiology in the Third Century Mishnah: Arguments for Rabbinic Legal Authority and the Complications of a Simple Concept" *Harvard Theological Review* 108.4 (2015): 510–14. See also my forthcoming work on this topic. Note that variegated society and practice is evidenced in earlier Jewish sources from the time of the Temple as well. This reality can be seen throughout Josephus's *War* and in the later parts of *Antiquities*. And the sectarians represented in the Qumran sectarian documents, such as in the Damascus Document and 4QMMT, separated themselves at least in part due to difference of opinion over how Temple ritual ought to be run. Some discussion of this can be found in Joseph M. Baumgarten, "Red Cow Purification Rites in Qumran Texts," *Journal of Jewish Studies* 46.1–2 (1995): 112–19; Joseph M. Baumgarten, "The Pharisaic-Sadducean Controversies about Purity and the Qumran Texts," *Journal of Jewish Studies* 31.2 (1980): 157–70; Yaacov Sussmann, "The History of Halakha and the Dead Sea Scrolls—Preliminary Observations on *Miqsat Ma'aseh Ha-Torah* (4QMMT)" [Hebrew], *Tarbiz* 59.12 (1989–90): 11–76; and Sussmann, "Appendix I: The History of the Halakha and the Dead Sea Scrolls: Preliminary Talmudic Observations on *Miqsat Ma'ase Ha-Torah*," in *Discoveries in the Judaean Desert: Volume 10. Qumran Cave 4: Miqsat Ma'aseh Ha-torah*, ed. E. Qimron and J. Strugnell (Oxford, 1994), 179–200. On the mishnaic construction and memory of sectarianism, see Naftali S. Cohn, "Sectarianism in the Mishnah: Memory, Modelling Society, and Rabbinic Identity," in *History, Memory, and Jewish Identity*, ed. I. Robinson, L. DiTommaso, and N. S. Cohn (Boston, 2015), 31–54.

23. Ashkelon excavator Daniel Master confirmed this in a personal communication, June 10, 2015. The archeology of the monumental architecture from the Severan period—see Ryan Boem, Daniel M. Master, and Robyn Le Blanc, "The Basilica, Bouleuterion, and Civic Center of Ashkelon," *American Journal of Archaeology* 120.2 (2016): 271–324—confirms that this is a gentile Roman city of the type the Mishnah itself identifies.

24. Rosen-Zvi, *The Mishnaic Sotah Ritual*, 248–49.

We have seen, then, a number of utopian elements in the Mishnah's imagined world: the existence of the Temple, its rituals, and the people of Israel dominating its land and its cities, performing ritual as a unified group in the Temple and locally. A further key element is that rituals run smoothly, without a hitch. In most of the long narrative about events on the Day of Atonement in mYom 1–7, for instance, the ritual proceeds as it should: the priest makes his immersions, changes clothing, speaks confessions and other utterances, makes sacrifices, and reads the Torah; the people make their responses, as appropriate. Similarly, in the long narrative in tractate *Tamid*, every single step is done by the priests and other ritual actors, with the required ritual objects, in the required times, in the sequence as it should be done. This begins with "the priests guard the Temple in three places," continues through the sacrificial acts of "the one slaughtering slaughtered and the one receiving the blood received it," and going through to "the priest bowed down to pour the libation and the vice priest waved scarves, and Ben Arza hit the cymbal, and the priests spoke in song; when they reached the end of the chapter, they blew the *teqi'a* blast, the *teru'a* blast, and the *teqi'a* blast."[25] The same kind of typical functioning is conveyed in a long stretch in *Zevaḥim* (including the snippet quoted above) that simply lists the proper location for the slaughter and other sacrificial acts of various sacrifices, and even includes short ritual narratives about the priest circumambulating the Altar (5.1–6.5). There are similar examples, such as details about grain offerings, including a Temple ritual narrative about changing the showbread loaves, in mMen 11.1–9. Many ritual narratives and associated sets of rules describe the rituals as they ought to be done, unfolding flawlessly.[26]

Four ritual narratives add a further utopian element by imagining a Temple ritual world that seems particularly "good," a world not only of perfectly functioning ritual, but also social harmony and inclusiveness. In these examples the Mishnah places great stress on the social interactions that take place, describing people coming together as a group, acts done jointly, and greetings or other utterances made interactively.[27] All of these elements can be found in the first of these examples, the first fruits ritual narrative,

25. The quotations are from mTam1.1, mTam5.1, and mTam 7.3—the beginning, middle, and end of the narrative.

26. This is not an exhaustive list, but I've listed a range of examples highlighting this type of narration. At this point I have glossed over narration in which there are problems or other less-than-idyllic elements. I will return to these.

27. mBik 3.2–8, mPes 5.5–10, mMid 2.2, and mMen 10.3. On these, see Cohn, "Ritual Failure, Ritual Success," 166.

mBik 3.2–8. The Mishnah describes the coming together of the group, which "gathers together" and sleeps together in one place, in the capital of the district, before embarking as one toward the Temple (mBik 3.2); the greetings given to the pilgrims as they are welcomed by Temple officials and craftspeople of Jerusalem (3.3), and as they are feted with song by the Levites (3.4); and the individual Israelite acting in unison with the priest, as the two hold the basket together and wave it (3.6). Beyond the interactivity and social harmony, there is inclusiveness. The narrative repeatedly highlights the range of people included by describing different rules for people at the extremes of different categories. There are rules applying to "those who live near . . . and those who live far [from Jerusalem]" (3.3), "those who know how to recite [in Hebrew]" and those who do not (3.7), and "the rich . . . and the poor" (3.8). A similar range of inclusion is implied in the contrast between the people of "the cities/towns in the [local] district" from throughout the land who come on pilgrimage (3.2) and the people who work in Jerusalem and in the Temple who greet them (3.3).

In the second of these narratives, the Passover sacrifice narrative (mPes 5.5–10), there are no greetings or utterances of any kind, but the crowd enters the Temple courtyard together (5.5), the Israelite and priest work in tandem, slaughtering and catching the blood ("the Israelite slaughtered and the priest received [the blood]"; 5.6),[28] the group of priests work together to pass the blood toward the altar (5.6), and the Israelites work in tandem to flay the animal (5.9). In the third narrative, describing how people used to enter the Temple Mount in mMid 2.2, there is a very warm and caring ritualized exchange between those circulating on the Mount and the mourner or the one who has been excommunicated. Finally, in the barley offering narrative (mMen 10.3–5), a crowd of multiple towns "gathers together" for the cutting of the barley (10.3) and participates in a highly stylized ritual exchange with the one doing the cutting, repeatedly answering "yes" (10.3). The recurrence of these various elements demonstrates a propensity to imagine the world of Temple ritual in idyllic terms, where ritual goes smoothly and there are positive social interactions: between individuals, between groups, and between individuals and groups.[29] Further, Temple ritual includes the whole people of Israel, described in different narratives

28. The repeated element of Priest and Israelite working together suggests inclusiveness as well. And while Levites are not mentioned explicitly, Tosefta Pisha 4:11 says it was they who were singing the *hallel* paragraphs of Psalms (Pesaḥim 5:7). See also multiple instances of the Levites singing: mBik 3.4, mTam 5.6, and 7.3.

29. I take the term "idyllic" from Jonathan Klawans, *Purity, Sacrifice, and the Temple: Symbolism and Supersessionism in the Study of Ancient Judaism* (New York, 2006),

as "the entire people" or "Israel," and composed of different subgroups, as indicated in these examples.[30]

Even in instances when Temple ritual goes wrong, the imagined world has a response. Small mistakes, such as wrong sequence or spilled blood (mYom 5.7), can usually be corrected. In the case of a more serious problem, the Great Court (the "Sanhedrin") can step in and make a correction to fix the ritual. Indeed, the power and authority of the Great Court is an important part of this imagined world. It has judicial authority and ultimate authority over Temple ritual. As the imagined predecessors of the rabbinic group itself, the Great Court grounds a rabbinic claim to legal-ritual authority, by determining how the traditional, biblically based practices were to be carried out in post-biblical times.[31]

HOW TO READ THE "UTOPIAN" TEMPLE PASSAGES

Although Temple ritual narratives have traditionally been treated as preserving traditions that somehow give unmediated access to what once happened in the Temple, it is now widely accepted that this is not the case.[32] As

---

178, who uses it to refer to the entire Temple ritual narrative genre; as I argue here, however, some passages are more idyllic than others. Michael D. Swartz, "Judaism and the Idea Ancient Jewish Ritual Theory," in *Jewish Studies at the Crossroads of Anthropology and History: Authority, Diaspora, and Tradition*, ed. R. Boustan, O. Kosansky, and M. Rustow (Philadelphia, 2011), 299–300, shows that the Day of Atonement narrative (Mishnah *Yoma'*) is also about the social (but more about the political). In that tractate there are a few ritual utterances between actors, and it is also possible to understand that the people in the audience come together as a social unit, though this language is not used (see mYom 1.8).

30. Cohn, "Complex Ritual Dynamics." As pointed out by Gail Labovitz in a question during the conference version of this paper, the notion of the entire people ignores the fact that different kinds of Jews are more included and less included. There is a range of what I would call "ritual privilege." Able-bodied free adult men are taken as the norm. Women, boys, girls, people of other sex or gender configurations (*androginos, tumtum,* and even *saris* and *aylonit*), people who are deaf, blind, or with mental or intellectual disabilities, slaves, children, and the elderly are part of the whole people, but are not fully included and privileged (though to different degrees, and in different combinations). I take this up in detail, specifically in relation to ritual, in my forthcoming work.

31. For this argument in full, see Cohn, *Memory of the Temple*, and partially set out in Cohn, "Rabbis as Jurists." On the court and imagined, utopian, legal authority, see Beth A. Berkowitz, *Execution and Invention: Death Penalty Discourse in Early Rabbinic and Christian Cultures* (New York, 2006). See also elements of this point in Kathryn T. McClymond, *Ritual Gone Wrong: What We Learn from Ritual Disruption* (New York, 2016), 58.

32. Examples of the earlier view include: David Z. Hoffmann, *The First Mishna and*

Hayden White has shown, the act of narrating necessarily involves choices about what to include and how to recount events. Many early interpreters were swayed by the verisimilitude of these accounts, and yet, as I have argued, this verisimilitude has a rhetorical function within the narrative.[33] Comparison of these narratives to earlier material, and attention to their construction, further demonstrates that they have been shaped by the rabbinic authors.[34] These are wholly rabbinic narratives from the post-Temple era that imagine an alternative world in which the Temple exists.

------

the Controversies of the Tannaim: The Highest Court in the City of the Sanctuary, trans. Paul Forchheimer (New York, 1977); Louis Ginzberg, "Tamid: The Oldest Treatise of the Mishnah," Pts. 1, 2, and 3, *Journal of Jewish Lore and Philosophy* 1.1, 1.2, and 1.3–4 (1919): 33–44, 197–209, and 265–95; and Jacob N. Epstein, *Introduction to Tannaitic Literature* [Hebrew] (Jerusalem and Tel Aviv, 1957). This approach also lies at the heart of Emil Schürer, *The History of the Jewish People in the Age of Jesus Christ (175 B.C.–A.D. 135)*, revised and edited by Geza Vermes and Fergus Millar, vol. 2 (Edinburgh, 1973), 237–313, and Saul Lieberman, *Hellenism in Jewish Palestine*, printed with *Greek in Jewish Palestine* (New York: Jewish Theological Seminary, 1994), 144–46. On this approach and its deficiencies, see Ishay Rosen-Zvi, *The Rite That Was Not: Temple, Midrash, and Gender in Tractate Sotah* [Hebrew] (Jerusalem: Magnes, 2008), 243–44, and Ishay Rosen-Zvi, "Orality, Narrative, Rhetoric: New Directions in Mishnah Research" *AJS Review* 32 (2008): 243–44. See also my own approach in Cohn, *Memory of the Temple* and "Temple Ritual Narrative Genre."

33. Hayden White, *Metahistory: The Historical Imagination in Nineteenth-Century Europe* (Baltimore, 1973), and White, *The Content of the Form: Narrative Discourse and Historical Representation* (Baltimore, 1987). On the verisimilitude of these mishnaic narratives, see Cohn, *Memory of the Temple*, 57–60; Rosen-Zvi, "Orality, Rhetoric, Narrative," 243–45; cf. Jaffee, *Torah in the Mouth*, 196 n. 15. And see Baruch M. Bokser, *The Origins of the Seder: The Passover Rite and Early Rabbinic Judaism* (New York, 2002; originally published 1984), 89.

34. My own view is that the reworking of earlier material is the most compelling evidence. As shown by Jeffrey L. Rubenstein, *The History of Sukkot in the Second Temple and Rabbinic Periods* (Atlanta, 1995), 148 and 103–161, and Rubenstein, "The Sadducees and the Water Libation" *Jewish Quarterly Review* 84 (1994): 417–44, in relation to the narratives in Sukkah; by Daniel Stökl Ben-Ezra, *The Impact of Yom Kippur on Early Christianity: The Day of Atonement from Second Temple Judaism to the Fifth Century* (Tübingen, 2003), 19–28, in relation to the *Yoma'* narrative; by Rosen-Zvi, *Rite That Was Not*, 152–80, in relation to the narrative of the ordeal of the accused adulteress; and by me in the case of the figure of the Great Court in these narratives in Cohn, *Memory of the Temple*, the mishnaic narratives are consistently different from earlier accounts. The details have been shifted in demonstrable ways, and they evidence the rabbinic "memory," in the sense used in studies of collective or cultural memory (see Cohn, *Memory of the Temple*). Rosen-Zvi, "Orality, Rhetoric, Narrative," 244, adds that many narratives contain biblical exegesis and rabbinic opinion, further highlighting the rabbinic nature of these accounts. See also the recent dissertation that takes up interpretation of biblical accounts, Hillel Mali, "From Temple to Midrash: Descriptions of the Temple in the

Jacob Neusner was the first to read the Mishnah's Temple material as a kind of utopia. As he writes about the order of *Kodashim* (and with reference to the larger body of Temple material): "it describes, with remarkable precision, and concrete detail, a perfect fantasy."[35] Using the spatial metaphor of the map (drawn from J. Z. Smith), Neusner also writes: "Mishnah maps out nonsense. It speaks in ultimate seriousness about a never-never land, giving endless, concrete, and intimate detail about a utopian cosmos—things which are not and, for now, also cannot be."[36] In these quotations and others, Neusner layers together a complex (and not necessarily consistent) understanding of what it means for the Mishnah, or parts of the Mishnah, to be utopian in this sense. He suggests that the imagined world of the Temple is an alternative to the reality of post-Temple existence; it is a no-world ("ou-topia" in one of the senses attributed to More's neologism). For Neusner this should not be presumed to be specifically a desired future (more on this below). As an alternative world, in Neusner's view, the Mishnah "maps out the cosmology of the sanctuary and its sacrificial system, that is, the world of the Temple, which had been the cosmic center of Israelite life."[37] The imagined alternative world, a world that is no longer possible, is specifically about an organized system of sacredness or holiness. As he puts it in *Judaism: The Evidence of the Mishnah*, the Mishnah's worldview involves "a heightened perception of the sanctification of Israel in deed and in de-

Mishnah: History, Redaction, and Meaning" [Hebrew] (PhD diss., Bar Ilan University, 2018).

35. Jacob Neusner, "Map without Territory: The Mishnah's System of Sacrifice and Sanctuary" *History of Religions* 19 (1979): 110. Note that while Neusner recognizes that Temple ritual narratives are a distinct kind of passage in the Mishnah, as he does, for instance, in relation to the paragraphs describing the offering of the 'omer barley sacrifice in Menahot chapter 10, in Jacob Neusner, *A History of the Mishnaic Law of Holy Things: Part Two Menahot* (Leiden: Brill, 1978–80), 135, he does not give much significance to this mishnaic genre on its own. He merely sees this as laws "worked out through and extended narrative," "related . . . in a storytelling style," or "presented in narrative style" (Neusner, *Judaism: The Evidence of the Mishnah*, 249, and see 248–50). It is important to note as well that Jonah Fraenkel, *Studies in the Spiritual World of the Aggadic Story* [Hebrew] (Bnei Brak: Hakibbutz Hameuchad, 1981), 120, seems independently to note the nostalgic tendency of the Temple ritual narratives, emphasizing their non-antiquity (and perhaps their fictionality?), writing that they are "beautiful" rituals that take place in public with a large community present. He takes a thematic reading, which, unfortunately, he barely develops. See also Klawans, *Purity, Sacrifice, and the Temple*, 178, who briefly mentions the genre and the earlier scholarship on its historicity; Klawans' primary concern is the portrayal of priests.

36. Neusner, "Map Without Territory," 110.

37. Neusner, "Map Without Territory," 110.

liberation."[38] In the earlier piece, he seems to see a kind of contradiction in this utopian imagined world. On the one hand, he reads it as an argument that "nothing has changed" (122), that "scripture's message remains valid" (114). At the same time, Neusner sees this as a feint. In reality, the rabbis were segregating the Temple world into a non-existent realm. Sacredness, in his view, becomes transferred into the human realm, onto the people of Israel. The world of the Temple becomes transported into a text that can be studied (124). In *Judaism: The Evidence of the Mishnah*, he suggests that the Mishnah represents dual worlds, "the locative," the real world "touching all manner of dull details of ordinary and everyday life," and the utopian (42).[39] Perhaps in this tension Neusner sees a simultaneous claim for continuity with the biblical and Temple past and a shift toward a more people-centered understanding of what is important (*Judaism*, 235). This is a surprising and very clever take on the idea of utopia, imagining a non-existent world as a way to lay claim to the past while discarding the Temple as a kind of dross and shifting the focus of what he terms "Judaism" to other spaces and to the people.[40] Such an argument, however, minimizes the admittedly few references to hopes for rebuilding or the future rebuilding of the Temple (see below).

Looking at individual ritual narratives, Beth Berkowitz and Ishay Rosen-Zvi have each taken a different tack than Neusner. To them, the mishnaic ritual narratives that are focused on punishments, on the death penalty and the ordeal for the accused adulteress (*sotah*), are both types of Foucauldian discourse. Berkowitz focuses not on a Temple ritual narrative, but a judicial ritual narrative, about the Great Court (Sanhedrin) putting murderers to death. As she writes, "the rabbinic ritual of execution may be the ideal ritual." Nothing can go wrong in this imagined world.[41] For Berkowitz, a key

---

38. Neusner, *Judaism: The Evidence of the Mishnah*, 230.

39. See also a later slight reformulation in Jacob Neusner, "The Mishnah Viewed Whole," in *The Mishnah in Contemporary Perspective*, ed. A. J. Avery-Peck and J. Neusner (Boston, 2002), 8, 21–27.

40. See also Bokser, *Origins of the Seder*, xi, who argues that the rabbis shift "religious life" from Temple to individual home and synagogue.

41. Berkowitz, *Execution*, 18. While the ritual enactment may be utopian in this sense, I hesitate to say a world in which there are murders is ideal. At the same time, I find limited her argument that "the ritual of the Mishnah creates a reality that is almost impervious to contingencies." This is hardly true of all narratives, as I've noted. And even in this narrative, there are contingencies taken into account—the people being "stoned" can fall in different ways, and depending on how they fall and whether they die from the fall, the ritual proceeds in different ways. See further below on responding to contingency. Note Rosen-Zvi's extension of the idea of the alternative reality of the narratives in the sense that they become studied ("Orality," 246).

component of this utopia is that it imagines fully Jewish control over the legal system and the power to dole out the death penalty. But it is not merely the fantasy of an absent Rome and of a Jewish society helmed by a powerful Jewish court, which does not err in judgment; the function of the imagined world of the death penalty ritual, according to Berkowitz, is to resist Roman colonial power. These are not "*mere* discourse," but "*practical* discourse . . . a real critique" (178). And this is a distinctly rabbinic-Jewish world of execution specifically "constructed (at least partially) out of the discourse of Roman power that envelops the rabbis" (155).[42] The imagined world is thus a critique of the lived world in which Romans exerted authority over life and death. It differed in subtle ways from lived reality, in the manner of cultural mimicry, so that it could be an effective critique. In Berkowitz's analysis, it is crucial not only that this is a Jewish enactment of the death penalty, resisting the realities of this Roman power through mimicry, but that the ritual follows rabbinic rules. As such, it provides "an education in rabbinic authority."[43]

Ishay Rosen-Zvi also examines a judicial-punitive narrative, but one that focuses on the accused adulteress, the *sotah*. Rosen-Zvi reads the discourse of this narrative as male patriarchal, "a fantasy of total domination over the woman's body and the final annihilation of the constant threat it poses."[44] The dynamics of gender, Rosen-Zvi demonstrates, are an important part of the world imagined by male rabbis. Focusing on the Mishnah as a whole, Rosen-Zvi also takes up the relationship between the Mishnah's imagined world and the reality of being part of the Roman empire: "the Mishnah does not make do with the spaces the empire leaves for the provincials, but

---

42. Berkowitz, *Execution*, 155. Rosen-Zvi, "Orality," 247, reads Berkowitz's example as a fantasy about having a Jewish institution in a position of judicial authority. The same can be said for the other judicial narratives. Rosen-Zvi's mention of the king in a position of power as a utopia seems based on Sanhedrin 2:2, which is a brief ruling, such as others imagined for the biblical era, and I'm not sure I would also refer to this as a fully imagined world. Rosen-Zvi extends the argument about Jewish authority as resisting against Roman authority in Ishay Rosen-Zvi, "Rabbis and Romanization: A Review Essay," in *Jewish Cultural Encounters in the Ancient Mediterranean and Near Eastern World*, ed. M. Popović, M. Schooneover, and M. Vandenberge (Leiden, 2017), 218–45. For Berkowitz's point about the court in Mishnah Sanhedrin not erring, see *Execution and Invention*, 85. This is in fact a tension she sees in the text, upon which the overall narrative clamps down.

43. Berkowitz, *Execution and Invention*, 18. For more developed treatments of the specifics of arguing for rabbinic authority and how mishnaic passages argue for rabbinic authority, see Cohn, *The Memory of the Temple*, and, with regard to all kinds of mishnaic narrative, Simon-Shoshan, *Stories of the Law*.

44. Rosen-Zvi, *The Mishnaic Sotah Ritual*, 16.

purports to create an alternative space, which offers an entire world to inhabit. It is a profound alternative to the Roman world which encompasses metaphysics, religion, culture, and politics."[45] The fullness of this alternative world and its Jewishness is a kind of mental oasis, what Levitas calls "compensation."

In my *Memory of the Temple and the Making of the Rabbis*, I built on these earlier works, taking up all of the Temple ritual narratives. In my reading, a key recurring element in the imagined Temple world is the figure of the Great Court. The mishnaic authors have invented this group and read them back into the past, giving them a hybrid judicial-ritual authority. This collective memory—following Barry Schwartz's use of the term—or what we might call an "invented mythologized past," served as an origin myth for the rabbis. The members of the Great Court were the rabbis' Temple-era predecessors, a source for deriving their own juristic role issuing rulings on ritual matters.[46] Following Berkowitz, I read the key to the utopian

---

45. Rosen-Zvi, "Rabbis and Romanization," 228. His claim in 228 n. 52 that this goes against my own argument in Cohn, *The Memory of the Temple*, 24, is incorrect. My argument is that the *rabbis* (not the Mishnah) are claiming for themselves—in their lived reality—the authority to determine ritual practice, an actual authority that was made available by the realities of the Roman empire. I do note that the Mishnah covers a much wider range of topics, framed around the topics covered by the Bible, but the Mishnah's imagined world is not my main point there, and in fact my argument is rather complementary to the point that he makes; the imagined utopian world extends well beyond the role the rabbis claim for themselves in the actual world. Rosen-Zvi, "Rabbis and Romanization," 244, adds that part of the mishnaic utopia is an imagined separate Jewish nation with its own institutions. This is similar to the elements I highlighted above, a land populated by the Jewish people. Note that Seth Schwartz, "The Mishnah and the Limits of Roman Power," in *Reconsidering Roman Power: Roman, Greek, Jewish and Christian Perceptions and Reactions* [online] (Roma, 2020), 18, makes a similar (but in certain details substantially different) claim to what Rosen-Zvi and I are each suggesting.

46. The bulk of the book is devoted to filling out the shape of the claimed rabbinic role, that of the collective memory, and the specific nuanced ways the imagined, narrated past argues for rabbinic authority. As I note in the book, this central claim also explains why there are two seemingly distinct kinds of ritual narratives, those about Temple ritual and those about judicial ritual. On this way of defining collective memory, see Cohn, *Memory of the Temple*, 11–12 and 139 n. 42. See Barry Schwartz, "The Social Context of Commemoration: A Study in Collective Memory" *Social Forces* 61.2 (1982): 374–402; Schwartz, "Iconography and Collective Memory: Lincoln's Image in the American Mind" *Sociological Quarterly* 32.3 (1991): 908–27; Schwartz, "Memory as a Cultural System: Abraham Lincoln in World War II" *American Sociological Review* 61.5 (1996): 908–27; Schwartz, "Collective Memory and History: How Abraham Lincoln Became a Symbol for Racial Equality" *Sociological Quarterly* 38.3 (1997): 469–96; Schwartz, *Abraham Lincoln in the Forge of National Memory* (Chicago, 2000).

fantasy as an argument for authority in the Roman world, an authority the rabbis lacked not only in the areas of civil and criminal law fully controlled by the Romans, but even in the realm of ritual, which was outside the Roman purview. In my ongoing work, I stress two additional elements of utopia as a particularly good and more perfect world. First, the ritual narratives and other mishnaic passages suggest that Temple ritual typically functions smoothly. Second, in a handful of narratives, there is harmonious social interaction and social inclusiveness: people get along, interact in a friendly and solicitous manner, and work together efficiently even when they are from different subgroups in society. The whole people of Israel is included, and there is no tension but only harmony.[47]

As I have suggested in *The Memory of the Temple*, the temporality of this utopian fantasy is rather complex. For any utopia, Levitas notes, there is a range of possible orientations towards time. (1) Utopias may be oriented toward the future, toward a desired change; (2) they may be partially oriented toward the past, in a "conservative stance," even as they may also be oriented toward recreating that supposedly better past in the future; and (3) they may be detached from time, not even necessarily imagining a world that is possible, just simply what is desired and desirable. The relationship to time in the Mishnah's temple ritual narratives is not straightforward. These narratives typically mix together three tenses: the perfect, which in this context indicates a completed action in the past; the iterative past, *haya* + participle, to indicate an action done repeatedly in the past; and the participle, the force of which is slightly more ambiguous.[48] Drawing on the work of a variety of grammarians, I note that the participle can imply: action happening in the present, modality (what ought to happen), the historical present (events in the past made more vivid through use of the present tense), or even an elided iterative past. Among the possible explanations for the mixing and precise meaning of the tenses used, I suggest that the combination gives the entire narrative a blending of nuances of the different tenses. Thus by shifting between the three tenses, the entire narrative is given the nuances that the rituals occurred in the past, that they occurred repeatedly and iteratively, that they are timeless, and that they should be or must be performed in a certain way. The participle may also imbue the narrative

47. For early versions of these arguments, see Cohn, "Ritual Failure, Ritual Success," and Cohn, "Complex Ritual Dynamics."

48. Cohn, "Ritual Narrative Genre," 51–73. In this and the next few sentences I radically condense my argument and analysis in this section of my dissertation. See there for much more detail and references to the grammarians and narrative theorists, including those of rabbinic literature, on whose work I depend and build.

with the immanence of the present tense, and the perfect may imbue it with the specificity of a one-time occurrence.[49]

Given the temporal mélange, the mishnaic imagined alternative world cannot be pinpointed precisely in time. To a degree, this is very much a fantasy about the past, the way things were when there still was a Temple. But there is also an atemporal dimension. Being iterative, the rituals are as if eternal, always happening. To the degree that these iterative rituals are similar to the Mishnah's legal rulings, they are timeless and exist in the world of what ought to be.[50] At the same time, the Mishnah twice makes explicit reference to a hope for a future rebuilding of the Temple, "may it be rebuilt speedily in our days" (mTa'an 4.8; mTam 7.3), with *Tamid* linking the worship or service in the Temple "of the Lord our God" to the future hope. As Neusner says, it is unclear if the entire genre should be read as future-oriented based on this comment, tacked on at the very end of two Temple ritual narratives. Whether or not these statements are to be understood as typical, even just the two instances further blur the temporal understanding of the imagined world. As with tense usage, this seems likely to be by design. The imagined world is nostalgic, is a hoped-for future, and is also abstract, in the realm of what ought to be. It is possible but also not quite possible. And as those who have studied these narratives more recently have repeatedly shown, the mishnaic narratives are very much rabbinically inflected and shaped memories of the past. As utopian imaginings, their precise function, to use Levitas's language, is "ambiguous" and, very likely, multifaceted. Regardless of their function, however, these narratives express the rabbinic-mishnaic authors' ideals. One ideal is that society is a wholly Jewish one in which a relatively homogeneous people fills its land and participates in ritual in an existent Temple and falls under the jurisdiction of Jewish legal authorities. A second is that people do ritual as it is supposed to be done, and that ritual functions smoothly. A third is that people engage in positive social interaction. As I will suggest, a fourth is that the legal-ritual system has the power to respond to ritual, social interaction, and even bigger things going awry, thus restoring and maintaining a smoothly and positively functioning Jewish society.

49. Cohn, "Temple Ritual Narrative Genre," 72–73. The last point builds on Moshe Simon-Shoshan, "Halachah Lema'aseh: Narrative and Legal Discourse in the Mishnah" (PhD diss., University of Pennsylvania, 2005), 58, as well as my application of Gérard Genette on iterative narrative.

50. Some rabbinic interventions into the narrative (see Cohn, *Memory of the Temple*, 68–71) can be construed as rulings within the narrative (e.g., mYom 6.7), which further blurs this boundary (but note that most are interventions specifically into the narration of the past).

CONFLICT AND RITUAL FAILURE IN THE TEMPLE

As noted at the outset, if many Temple (and judicial) ritual narratives imagine a world that is idyllic, more perfect, and smoothly functioning, there are certain kinds of trouble in paradise that repeatedly threaten this "better world" (*eu-topia*). In three distinct but intersecting ways Temple ritual narratives or moments in these narratives depict matters as not at all ideal. They describe social conflict and violence; sectarian disagreement (and conflict); and ritual going awry or failing.[51] As I will suggest, things going wrong in these ways further highlight the ideals of rabbinic authority and social harmony, while at the same time fully engaging the imagined ritual world with the reality of lived contingency, and suggesting that such contingency can be managed by the ritual-legal system set out by the rabbis in the Mishnah.

In the example from Mishnah *Yoma* and Tosefta *Kippurim* quoted earlier, the less-than-ideal aspect of Temple ritual life can be described as violence. In the Mishnah there is pushing that leads to injury, in the Tosefta stabbing and murder. The Mishnah itself frames the problem here as "danger." In a rather similar way, mSuk 4.4 narrates violence that would erupt in the Temple when the holiday of Sukkot would coincide with the Sabbath: "the entire people would bring their *lulavs* to the Temple Mount" ahead of time, where they would be stored, but when the superintendents would "throw [the *lulavs*] out to the people, they would grab and hit one another." Again, violence, and again, the Mishnah frames the problem as "danger." A third example of violence, also on the festival of Sukkot, and presumably the reworking of a historical event known from Josephus, occurs in mSuk 4.9, the "one time" that the priest pouring the water libation "poured it on his feet, and the people stoned him with their *etrogs*."[52] Each of these instances of violence is also a ritual failure, as evidenced by the need to change the ritual to prevent the danger or the mistake (intentional or unintentional) of pouring the water on the feet.[53]

---

51. There are varying ways of using the term "ritual failure," and a variety of alternative terms, such as "mistakes," ritual going "wrong" or "awry," ritual "disruptions," and "infelicities." See Cohn, "Ritual Failure, Ritual Success." See also the crucial foundational work of Ronald L. Grimes, *Ritual Criticism: Case Studies in Its Practice, Essays in on Its Theory* (Columbia, S.C., 1990), 191–209. And see Ute Hüsken, ed., *When Rituals Go Wrong: Mistakes, Failure, and the Dynamics of Ritual* (Leiden, 2007), and McClymond, *Ritual Gone Wrong*.

52. Josephus, *Antiquities* 13.372; on the relationship, see Rubenstein, *History of Sukkot*, 117–22.

53. Cohn, *Memory of the Temple*, 47–50; Cohn, "Ritual Failure," 164–66. These analyses of ritual failure and violence are based on Cohn, "Rabbis as Jurists," 258, and Cohn,

The second recurring non-idyllic element is the existence of sectarians, and perhaps *minim*, who hold a divergent view on how things should be done, and who are considered a threat. Repeatedly, measures are taken not only to ensure the procedure does not follow or even appear to follow the sectarian view or that of the heretics, but even to publicly marginalize their views (mMen 10.3, mPar 3.7 and perhaps mYom 1.3–5).[54] While in the Tosefta sectarians actually have some control to perform Temple ritual incorrectly—including the parallel narrative to the spilt water libation (tSuk 3.16, and see tKip 1.8)—the Mishnah never imagines that anything ever followed sectarian practice in the Temple or that sectarians were even present there. The instances of failure bound up with violence and danger can also be read as threats that are prevented through the authority of the Great Court, the group the rabbis construe as their predecessors, from whom they have inherited legal-ritual authority. Sometimes things go wrong, but they can be fixed. Rabbinic-style legal-ritual authority, in the Mishnah's idealized picture of the past, maintains the ideal order.[55] This is not simply an argument for authority, but an understanding that correct performance of ritual—ensured by the rabbinic predecessors of ritual—leads to positive social relations, preventing violence and discord, the natural human impulses of competitiveness, and violence.[56] The imagined world of Temple ritual narratives includes the opposite of what should be, but the system in place responds to the breakdown of social relations and to ritual enactment, and restores them. This reparative dynamic seems to be very much part of the Mishna's utopia. The glimpses of what can go wrong confirm the ideals

"Temple Ritual Narrative Genre," 180–82 and 201–3. For a similar analysis, with a historical claim about the development of related passages, see Simon-Shoshan, *Stories of the Law*, 204–16. For a chart of who is attributed as making such changes (*hitkin/hitkinu*), including anonymous "they," who could perhaps imply the Court, see Cohn, *Memory of the Temple*, 54–55, and see references in Cohn, *Memory of the Temple*, 169 n. 58 and 165–66 n. 31. An additional crucial earlier analysis of these changes, including those in response to violence, is Martin S. Jaffee, "The Taqqanah in Tannaitic Literature: Jurisprudence and the Construction of Rabbinic Memory" *Journal of Jewish Studies* 41.2 (1990): 204–25.

54. See my analysis in Cohn, "Heresiology." Following Cohen, "Significance of Yavneh," I believe that the Mishnah restricts sectarians to the past Temple era; but I also argue that the Mishnah constructs sectarians in the mold of their imagined heretics. See also Cohn, "Sectarianism in the Mishnah."

55. This is one of the central arguments of Cohn, *Memory of the Temple*. The construction of the Court as the authorities in the Temple serves as a myth of origins for the rabbis and for rabbinic authority.

56. Cohn, "Ritual Failure, Ritual Success"; see also my current book, in preparation, Cohn, *Ritual: An Ancient Jewish Perspective*.

of the imagined world that predominate in these narratives. Further, the world in which there is the authority to control these threats, by manipulating the ritual system, is indeed an imagined utopia for the mishnaic rabbis.

Even if Court authority and later rabbinic authority maintain the stability of the social and ritual worlds, there are moments when the fantasy of this authority briefly fades. In the middle of the Passover sacrifice narrative (mPes 5.5–10), the narrator announces that on the Sabbath, "the priests would rinse the Temple Courtyard [floor], not in accordance with the will of the sages" (5.8). This is a crack in one of the ideals of the Mishnah's imagined world, an acknowledgement that the authority to control what happens in the Temple is only a fantasy. The priests were the ones in control. In a deconstructive vein, drawing on the terminology of Barbara Johnson, this moment "breaks open" the utopian fantasy, if only for a moment.[57] Other examples extend this rupture of authority outside of the Temple. In mMen 10.5, in relation to the barley offering in the Temple, the narrator admits that the market in Jerusalem would be filled with roasted flour already as soon as the offering was done, again "not in accordance with the will of the sages." Later in the chapter, perhaps also in Temple times, the people of Jericho pile up the grain, also "not in accordance with the will of the sages" (10.8)—though here this infraction is softened by the claim that the sages did not explicitly object. These admissions about lack of authority to control Temple and related practice mirror admissions that the rabbis similarly lacked authority in their own times.[58] The Mishnah's fabula, its imagined world, is a utopia in multiple senses, but it nevertheless contains aporias, moments that undermine the narrative of a better world and of another world that differs from the world as actually experienced.

The complex picture that emerges for Temple ritual, in which things do not always go smoothly, there is danger and violence, and control sometimes slips, but ultimately in which there is stability in the system, is part of the larger mishnaic image of ritual as a whole. The framework of what can be termed "ritual failure," or more neutrally "ritual infelicity," shows the extent to which the Mishnah's imagined Temple utopia and all of its discourse

---

57. Barbara Johnson, "Translator's Introduction," in Jacques Derrida, *Dissemination*, trans. with an introduction and additional notes by Barbara Johnson (Chicago, 1981), xiv. In this example, the text may work to smooth over this moment, having R. Judah argue that what the priests did was to gather up the blood and sprinkle it again, and then the sages disagree with him. This pulls "the sages" out of the Temple period within the narrative and into the rabbinical narrational frame. But it is difficult to whitewash this explicit admission.

58. Cohn, "Heresiology," 513–14, building on Cohn, *Memory of the Temple*, 31–32, in turn building on Simon-Shoshan, *Stories of the Law*, 114–16.

about ritual participate fully in the actuality of the world filled with contingency. A number of scholars of ritual note that in any ritual system, even when practitioners deny it, things go wrong.[59] Mistakes of various magnitude happen, with different potential consequences and responses. This is true for the Mishnah's Temple ritual and more widely for all of its ritual. One prominent example, mentioned earlier, occurs in Mishnah *Yoma'*:

> Regarding the entire procedure of the Day of Atonement said in a
> particular order, if he did one action earlier than the other, he has
> done nothing. If he made the blood of the goat earlier than the blood
> of the bull, he should go back and sprinkle the blood of the goat and
> then the blood of the bull. If before he finished all of the placements
> of the blood inside [the inner sacred spaces], [the blood] spilled, he
> should bring other blood and go back and sprinkle from the begin
> ning. (mYom 5.7)

Priests sometimes make mistakes, including doing things out of order or spilling the blood, and in this case the priest can make up for the mistake by going back. A similar kind of simple mistake is imagined for the water libation: "The priest ascended the [Altar] ramp and turned to his left. And there were two silver bowls there . . . The western [bowl] was for water; the eastern one for wine. If he poured that of the water into that of the wine or that of the wine into that of the water—he fulfilled the obligation" (mSuk 4.9)[60] Moving into shorter legal rulings about Temple ritual, there are numerous imagined cases of mistakes. *Zevahim* is full of such mistakes. It imagines a whole variety of cases in which the priest slaughtered or did other sacrificial acts with the wrong intent about the kind of sacrifice, the location for eating, or the timing (1.1–3.6), or even just did the actions in the wrong time or place (2.4; 13.1–14.1) or with the wrong hand (3.2) or in the wrong body position (2.1).[61]

These kinds of mistakes, some of them minor and others more serious, happen not only in the Temple, but in all kinds of ritual in the Mishnah. There is recurring language used to explicitly indicate failure. Most importantly: "one has not fulfilled the obligation," "one has done nothing," "one

59. This a recurring theme in Hüsken, *When Rituals Go Wrong*.

60. While the language may suggest that the priest is pouring from one to the other, it seems that the intent is simply that in the case of the water libation or wine libation, he pours what he brings up into the wrong bowl. This is the standard interpretation.

61. These are just selected examples of ways the Mishnah imagines things may typically go wrong.

has not fulfilled a *mitsvah*," "a ritual object is invalid," or in relation to specific rituals, "one's attempted act of creating *terumah* does not create *terumah*."[62] The Mishnah may even imagine mistakes without labelling them as
failures. The end of mBer 2.3 combines an explicit label with one not so labeled: "One who recites [the *shema*] out of order, one has not fulfilled the
obligation. If one recited and made a mistake, one should return to the place
where one made the mistake."

The mistakes imagined in the everyday setting of reciting the *shema* and
the special annual setting of working with the blood on the Day of Atonement in mYom 5:7 highlight the importance of the consequences of mistakes
or failures and of the rules for how to respond to them. As the contributions
to the volume *When Rituals Go Wrong* demonstrate, cross-culturally there
is typically a range of responses, and the responses say something about the
ritual system.[63] This is true of both ritual in general and Temple ritual in the
Mishnah. Sometimes the consequences are minor or there are no consequences. In the example of the water libation in mSuk 4.9, when the water

---

62. See Cohn, "Ritual Failure, Ritual Success," and Cohn, *Ritual: An Ancient Jewish
Perspective*, where I also talk about the interrelationship between ritual failure and ritual success. Examples of this language include: *lo yatsa* (and *yatsa*): mBer 2.1, 2.3, and
6.2; mPeah 3.8; mHal 1.2, mPes 10.5; mSuk 2.1 and 4.9; mRH 3.7, 4.6, and 4.8; mMeg
2.1–2; mNaz 3.1–2 and 6.7; mBK 9.12; mSan 6.4; mMen 12.2, 13.8, and 13.10; mHul 2.5;
and mNeg 14.9–10 and 14.12. *Lo ʿasah kelum*: mTer 2.2, mYom 5.7, m'Eruv 5.7, mNeg
14.4, and perhaps mNid 9.7. *Lo kiyam mitsvah*: mSuk 2.7, mSan 7.2, mShevu 3.6, mHor
1.3, mMen 10.4, and mHul 7.2. *Ein terumato/terumatan terumah* appears throughout
Terumot. *Pasul* is very common. The language of *ḥayyav*, is also relevant, but is bound
up with how to understand *mitsvot lo taʿaseh* as ritual, though even in cases of positive
mitsvot being obligated, a punishment can be a consequence of failure. On the consequences of failure, see below.

63. I draw my map of the Mishnah's range of views on what happens when ritual
goes wrong from the various insights in the volume edited by Ute Hüsken and cited
above. See especially Jan A. M. Snoek, "Dealing with Deviations in the Performance
of Masonic Ritual," in *When Rituals Go Wrong: Mistakes, Failure, and the Dynamics of
Ritual*, ed. U. Hüsken (Leiden, 2007), 99–120. Note that Kathryn McClymond (*Ritual
Gone Wrong*, 53–55) seems to take up the same idea from the *When Rituals Go Wrong*
volume and create a list of "consequences" of mistakes specifically in sacrifice and in the
handling of the blood. Her map, however, is narrower and very specific to the examples
in Mishnah *Zevaḥim*, and, further, does not tease out what we can learn from the range
of ways the ritualists must, the system suggests, respond to failure. I also highlight that
consequences and responses are not identical. *Karet* is a rare consequence of a ritual
failure, and not a way of responding. Axel Michaels, "Perfection and Mishaps in Vedic
Ritual," in *When Rituals Go Wrong: Mistakes, Failure, and the Dynamics of Ritual*, ed.
U. Hüsken (Leiden, 2007), 121–32, offers a useful comparison of responses in a very different ritual context, which highlights paths not taken in the Mishnah.

or wine is poured into the wrong pitcher, or in the beginning of mBer 2.3, when one recited the *shema* but didn't hear oneself or was not precise with the letters (both in R. Yose's opinion)—*yatsa*, one has fulfilled the obligation anyway. However, there is a line. In most cases, "getting it right" matters, and mistakes are not tolerated or accepted.[64] Even so, it is usually not so difficult to fix. In mYom 5.7, when one has mixed up the order or spilled the blood, or in mBer 2.3 when one has made a mistake, the response is easy and the mistake can be corrected. Presumably in most cases where one has not fulfilled the obligation, one can simply go back and repeat in order to "get it right."

Repeating, though, is not always possible. In mSuk 2.6, there is a set of debates between R. Eliezer and the sages about the extent of the obligation to eat in the *sukkah* on the festival. All seem to agree that on the first night there is an obligation. R. Eliezer holds that if one misses that night, one can make it up on the seventh night. But the sages disagree, "there is no compensation." This cannot be redone. The time has passed, and one has not fulfilled the obligation and has missed out. Presumably this is the case for the many other time-dependent daily or holiday rituals; if the time has passed, for instance to recite the *shema* or eighteen-blessing prayer of mBer 1.1 and 4.1, then presumably there is no repetition (but see the Talmudic interpretation in bBer 26a).[65] In one story in mSuk 2.7, Beit Shammai claim that Yohanan ben Hahoroni, who always ate with his table in the house, "never fulfilled the *mitsvah* of *sukkah* in his entire life," an ongoing failure to fulfill. In the Temple, the Mishnah leaves ambiguous whether any obligations were ever left unfulfilled: did the fighting Jews manage to get a *lulav* to wave? Was the water libation repeated and done correctly? But the toseftan parallel explicitly imagines just such a failure in that case. In tSuk 3.16, when the people threw their *etrogs* at the priest who poured the libation on his feet, "the horn of the altar was damaged and the [Temple] service was suspended that day," implying that the afternoon *tamid* sacrifice and perhaps other sacrifices were not offered. Missing out on fulfilling an obligation is significant

---

64. This language is Edward L. Schieffelin's in "Introduction," in *When Rituals Go Wrong: Mistakes, Failure, and the Dynamics of Ritual*, ed. U. Hüsken (Leiden, 2007), 1–20; I develop this in Cohn, "Ritual Failure, Ritual Success," and even more so in *Ritual: An Ancient Jewish Perspective*.

65. One would assume the same for all other holiday rituals, such as eating the Passover offering or the matzah and *marror* on Passover night, although the Bible itself allows for those who were impure or far away to redo the Passover offering (Num 9:6–13 and see mPes 9.1–3). For the mistaken blessing in mBer 6.2 mentioned above, it is unclear if one has the chance to repeat the blessing, as is the contemporary custom.

because it jeopardizes the promised benefits of maintaining the covenant with God, negatively impacts the relationship established with the divine through the performance of *mitsvot*, and is a failure of duty.[66] Sometimes, a failure is considered a real threat; violence, in the examples quoted, is a dangerous consequence of some failures.[67]

The consequences of ritual error in the Mishnah, as in many other cultures, range widely in their seriousness; some mistakes are minor and tolerable, but others require that the ritual be repeated or modified. Within the system, there is a balance between flexibility and sticking to the rules. Usually, the reality that mistakes happen does not doom the ritual, and it can be completed. Despite the language of *yatsa-lo yatsa* and *kasher-pasul* and even the implication that an act has failed to take hold or accomplish anything, implying a razor's edge between success and failure and emphasizing the importance of doing things correctly, there is so often the chance to correct these mistakes, even when they cannot be ignored. At the same time, in certain cases even going back and repeating the procedure is impossible: there must be consequences to getting it wrong. As Edward Schieffelin highlights in surveying the various articles in the volume *When Rituals go Wrong*, in order to retain "functionality, authority, and credibility," ritual must be robust.[68] This is precisely the case for imagined Temple ritual and all ritual. The ritual system can respond to the contingencies that necessarily arise within the performance of ritual. There is a modicum of flexibility, while asserting the importance of the rules. Everything that happens can be handled by the system.

In the Mishnah this is true not only in the imagined world in which the Temple and its ritual function, but even in the real world in which the ultimate failure of Jewish ritual has taken place—the destruction of the Temple. It is true, there was a long-term cessation of crucial ritual (mTa'an 4.6;

---

66. For an explanation and justification of these ideas about what ritual success accomplishes, see Cohn, "Ritual Failure, Ritual Success."

67. There are also rare instances of further grave consequences, when ritual failure also involves violating a *mitsvat lo ta'aseh*. Thus, for instance, if the priest slaughters or does another sacrificial act intending to eat the sacrifice in the wrong time or place (mZev 2.2–3), the meat becomes "*pigul* and there is the potential for *karet*" if one then intentionally eats the meat (mKer 1.1). McClymond, *Ritual Gone Wrong*, 54–55, seems to misinterpret this mishnaic passage. *Karet* is only an extension of the ritual failure. Additional kinds of ritual failure that involve *mitsvot lo ta'aseh* and punishment consequences appear among the examples of mKer 1.1–2 and mMak 3.2–3.

68. Schieffelin, "Introduction," 17. McClymond, *Ritual Gone Wrong*, 42, makes exactly the same point, adding that the widespread possibility of correction signals an "optimistic ritual worldview."

foreshadowed in the tSuk example above), as well as violence and destruction; but with changes to ritual made by R. Yohanan ben Zakkai, following the model of the Great Court before him (mRH 4.1–4, mSuk 3.12, and mMen 10.5), the ritual system, according to the Mishnah, remains robust. The changes made by one of the earliest rabbis, further, parallels past responses to ritual disruption in the imagined mishnaic utopia, thus authorizing this repair in the rabbis' present and affirming the ongoing strength of the ritual system.

THE MISHNAH'S IDEALS: UTOPIAN AND PRAGMATIC

As in life, in the Mishnah's imagined world of ritual things sometimes work out well and sometimes do not. Experience is full of contingency. This is true even outside the realm of ritual. Pebbles, for instance, may shoot out from under an animal's foot as it passes a store in the market and cause damage (mBK 2.1). In such a case, the legal system with its rulings and adjudicators ensures that society can continue to function smoothly. In a different example, marauding gentiles could approach a city from any direction at any time or a sage could approach from any direction in order to teach (m'Eruv 3.5). Here, too, the ritual system allows for a person to create an 'eruv with conditions, so that the person can travel beyond the Sabbath boundary to respond to such contingency.

Both non-ritual and ritual experiences can involve mistakes within or outside of one's control. The consequences can be non-existent, minor but significant, or drastic. Ritual engages directly with contingency in the world. Ritual procedures and the ritual system have the capacity to respond so that ritual continues, it is fulfilled, and the system remains robust.

The imagined world of the Mishnah, particularly that of the extended Temple and judicial ritual narratives, has many moments that veer toward a particularly perfect world. There are striking moments in which the ideals of a fully Jewish society, with Jews forming the polity, having full judicial authority, engaging as a whole body in local and especially in Temple ritual, and coming together in particularly harmonious and inclusive social interaction are especially prominent. Even in moments in which ritual enactment, social interaction, or even the very existence of the Temple falls apart or crumbles, there is a response that restores order, with moderate changes. Ritual continues to function smoothly and society continues to function smoothly—even without a Temple.

The stories about Rabban Yohanan ben Zakkai's emendations imply a set of critical links between past and present, and between the fully imagined world in which the Temple is still existent and the partially imagined world which incorporates the realities of the rabbis' own time. These relationships hint at the ways in which the present world imagined by the Mishnah can be utopian as well. The world in which there is a Temple and a fully Jewish polity enacting ritual smoothly is only one part of the Mishnah's utopia. The more realistic world full of contingency, even with no Temple and no widespread Jewish polity, in which most Jews may not even follow rabbinic dictates, can be a utopia as well. The system as set out by the rabbis, with purported deep roots and authority in the Temple past, can achieve at least some of these ideals: positive and harmonious social interactions, a larger group of Jews joining together in ritual at the local level, and wider recognition of Jewish legal institutions—even if Jews do not control the land or have a Temple.[69]

Crucially for the rabbis, imagined utopia can become present reality by carefully hewing to the dictates of the ritual system as set out by the rabbis, and under rabbinic control. In a world where rabbis maintain the flexibility, authority, and robustness of the system, imagined ideals—perhaps even extending to the rebuilding of the Temple and restoration of Jewish society—have the potential to be realized.[70]

69. This is a rather different reading than what Neusner suggests, but in a way comes back full circle to his fundamental idea of the rabbis getting on with things even without a Temple.

70. The imagined world of the Mishnah, taken seriously by later rabbinic Jews, even served as building blocks for attempting to realize some of these earlier rabbinic ideals. See Cohn, *Memory of the Temple*, 121–22.

11. Mishnah and *Halakhah*

Moshe Halbertal

I

A comparison of the legal traditions we have from the days of the Second Temple and the *halakhah* in the Mishnah points to the extraordinary legal innovations that were produced in the academies of the rabbis.[1] However, studying the details of these specific innovations obscures, at times, a greater, more fundamental and highly significant transformation: the very creation and emergence of *halakhah* itself. Although the Mishnah reveals a wide expanse of legal innovations, from the laws of Shabbat to the rules of capital punishment, it bears witness to something more foundational: the shift from *Mitzvah* (commandment) to *halakhah*. This transformation signifies one of the most essential characteristics of the Mishnah. If we wish to understand what the Mishnah is, it is essential to gain clarity on what *halakhah* is.

Second Temple literature—the Apocrypha, Qumran Scrolls, the writings of Philo and Josephus—is full to the brim with different legal tradi-

---

1. The legal traditions in the Qumran Scrolls and their comparison to rabbinic literature have received extended scholarly attention. Among the central works it is worth mentioning Lawrence Schifman, *Halakhah at Qumran* (Leiden, 1975); Joseph M. Baumgarten, *Studies in Qumran Law* (Leiden, 1977); Kana Varman and Aharon Shemesh, *Revealing the Concealed: Interpreting and Halakhah in Qumran Scrolls* (Hebrew; Jerusalem, 2011); Vered Noam, *From Qumran to the Tanaitic Revolution: Approaches to the Understanding of Impurity* (Hebrew; Jerusalem, 2010); Aharon Shemesh, *Halakhah in the Making: The Development of Jewish Law From Qumran to the Rabbis* (Berkeley, 2009); Jacob Zussman, "The Study of the History of Halakhah and the Judean Desert Scrolls—Talmudic Thoughts in Light of MMT Scroll" (Hebrew), *Tarbiz* 59 (1990): 11.

tions, yet lacks anything akin to *halakhah.* For example, in an echo of the biblical commandment, the obligation to fulfill a vow appears in this literature several times.[2] However, nothing even slightly resembling the complex mishnaic tractate of *Nedarim* (vows), with its eleven detailed chapters, appears in Second Temple literature. Even more so, the extensive interpretive elaboration of the rules entailing the taking of a vow, stretching on for dozens of pages in both the Bavli and Yerushalmi, would not have been possible based on the thin interpretive material of pre-rabbinic literature. The essence of the emergence of *halakhah* is the establishment of a dense field of highly specific instructions that are meticulously calibrated in great detail. The Mishnah represents, therefore, not only a shift in the content of *halakhah,* but rather the very emergence of *halakhah.*[3]

To make clearer the distinction between commandments and *halakhah,* and to gain a better grip on what is meant by *halakhah,* let us imagine the legal realm as a topographic map. In a topographic map the density and dispersal of the different elevation lines differ from one area to the next; a mountainous terrain will have a much higher density of elevation lines, which will appear from a distance as an indistinguishable blob, while a plain will be apparent through the sparseness of lines. Laying out the law in the form of a map will make apparent that the density of rules is not uniform; there are areas in which we have few rules, and areas that are saturated with rules. To define a certain normative space as *halakhah,* and not just as a commandment, a certain threshold of rule density must be reached.

The map of biblical law will show that the only spheres that may be named halakhic are those associated with the Temple, and this is not mere coincidence; it aids us in defining the nature of the sacred place. The sacred is the space that is saturated with instructions, in which accessibility, movement, and actions are not immediate. In this highly regulated space, actions are mediated through specific and precise norms. The Temple is like a minefield in which one must walk carefully; the price of any mistake is very high, and the norms of traversing such a place must be very clear and precise. It is therefore not surprising that the densest legal context in the Torah is the chapter which deals with the entry of the high priest into the inner sanctum

2. See for example, concerning keeping vows in Damascus Scroll, *The Judean Desert Scrolls,* ed. E. Kimron (Jerusalem, 2010), p. 39, lines 174–90.

3. Naming this new phenomenon of the creation of dense, thick legal domains that far exceed the commandments in the Torah using the term "*halakhah*" is not an arbitrary semantic choice. *Halakhah* is a unique term innovated in rabbinic literature, and among other things it designates, in this literature, the legal realm which is beyond the commandments that were explicitly written in the Torah. On this see E. E. Urbach, *The Halakhah: Its Sources and Development* (Hebrew; Jerusalem, 1984), 8.

of the Temple, and the rituals of atonement and purification that took place on Yom Kippur. In creating legal realms rich with rules in vastly diverse fields, the rabbis initiate a major expansion of the domain of *halakhah* beyond the initial sacred space of the Temple. For example, the chapter in the Mishnah in the tractate of *Sukkah*, which deals with the four plant species that are taken on the holiday of Sukkot and defines, in far greater detail than the Torah, what exactly these plants are and what constitutes their proper state, amounts to a sanctification of these plants.

Therefore, the world presented in the Mishnah is not just another rung in the developing history of *halakhah*; it is the very basis of *halakhah*'s emergence. A study of Second Temple literature teaches us that the rabbis' *halakhah* as we know it is not the culmination of a gradual process of legal expansion set off at the beginning of the Second Temple period. The Mishnah, with its creation of high-resolution legal fields, represents a quantum leap which occurred in the rabbinic academies. This phenomenon is not contingent on the question of how far back *halakhah* goes in the world of the rabbis; it is possible that *halakhah* existed even earlier than the second century BCE. The actual dating is not crucial to the argument that *halakhah* appeared in the circle of sages as a completely unique phenomenon, and was not constructed on top of what preceded it. *Halakhah* exists only in the literature which is associated with the rabbis and in its most refined literary product—the Mishnah.[4]

It is important to emphasize that by the term "the emergence of *halakhah*" I do not mean the addition of commandments and other new obligations on top of existing biblical commandments. Such obligations have actually been added over time, and new holidays. for example, can be found in the Book of Jubilees as well as in rabbinic literature. By "the emergence of *halakhah*" I mean the transformation of existing commandments into a dense field of instructions, or alternatively, in the case of a new obligation, the addition of a normative volume that will incorporate the obligation as part of *halakhah*. This is the case with the post-biblical holiday of Purim: not only did the rabbis accept it as a new obligation, but they built the highly detailed mishnaic tractate of *Megilah* around it.

An example from the laws governing the impurity of the dead will further clarify this point. Matters of impurity and purity concerned all the various denominations that existed in the days of the Second Temple, and

---

4. On this distinct legal innovation of the Mishnah and its relation to Second Temple literature see Shaye J. D. Cohen, "Judaean Legal Tradition and Halakhah of the Mishnah," in *The Cambridge Companion to the Talmud and Rabbinic Literature*, ed. C. E. Fonrobert and M. Jaffee (Cambridge, 2007), 135–39.

sometimes extant writings from these denominations add to what is explicitly written in the biblical text. One of these additions, and certainly not the most important one, concerns the impurity of the dead. The Torah declares that a human corpse defiles those who touch it, as well as persons or objects who happen to be in the same enclosed space in which a dead body resides. In a rewritten section of this biblical portion found in the Dead Sea Scrolls, we find the additional point that not only the body, but also the blood of the dead defiles: "And in the open, anyone who touches a person who was killed or who died naturally, or human bone, or the blood, or a grave, shall be unclean seven days."[5] This new assertion, that the blood of the dead also creates impurity, was also accepted by the rabbis.[6] As this innovation exists both within rabbinic literature and in Second Temple literature, a comparison between the two will be able to teach us much about the emergence of *halakhah*.

In the *Temple Scroll*, as we have seen, the defiling nature of the blood of the dead was mentioned as just one more item in the list. In contrast, in tractate *Ohalot* in the Mishnah, a thick normative field is created around this addition, thus transforming it into *halakhah*. In the discussion that follows, I will track this extensive legal development.

The first step appears in this mishnah: "A *revi'it* [specific unit of volume] of blood and a *revi'it* of mixed blood from one corpse. Rabbi Akiba says: [even] from two corpses. The blood of a child that has flowed out completely: Rabbi Akiba says any amount, the Sages say a *revi'it*."[7] The rabbis, in their typical fashion, set a minimum measure for the blood that defiles—a *revi'it*. A disagreement arises over regarding a *revi'it* of blood from two different dead bodies, and also regarding the blood of a child which constitutes all of its blood but does not amount to a *revi'it*. The settings of certain legal amounts and measures is typical of rabbinic *halakhah* and can rarely be found in Second Temple literature. However, these additional questions and discussions establish the halakhic normative field. Before the advent of the rabbis, no one had asked these questions in a form meant to produce a legal thickening of the rule. In the case in front of us, the controversy between the sages and Rabbi Akiba is related to the fact that *revi'it* was considered the amount of blood contained within a child and is thus defined as the

5. Yigael Yadin, *Temple Scroll* (Jerusalem, 1977), vol. 2, p. 156.

6. Vered Noam has thoroughly explored the history of *halakhah* from Second Temple to rabbinic literature, raising the possibility that we might have here a common tradition of both these trends from earlier stages of the Second Temple period. Noam has also raised illuminating suggestions of the interpretive process that enable this extension. See Noam (above note 1), 149–56.

7. mOhal 2.2.

minimum of a *nefesh* (a soul, a life). The disagreement centers on whether
the defiling *revi'it* must be exclusively from one dead body or indicates an
amount of blood which reaches the level of *nefesh* in a more general way.[8]
The setting of measures is, among other things, a characteristic of rabbinic
law, although it exists marginally in earlier strata of Second Temple literature. The next step, attempting to precisely clarify the meaning of this
measure—the status of various kinds of *revi'it*—is the feature that defines
the revolution of the sages and the nature of the Mishnah.

The rule is subsequently developed further in the tractate: "A *revi'it* of
blood that was absorbed in [the floor] of a house, the house is pure. If it was
absorbed in a garment: if the garment is washed and a *revi'it* of blood comes
out of it, it is impure; if not, it is pure, since anything absorbed that cannot come out is pure."[9] The mishnah states that in the case where a *revi'it*
amount of blood seeped into the floor of the house, the house is pure, and
in the case where a *revi'it* amount of blood is absorbed in a cloth but can be
wrung out, the house is impure. This discussion, which deals with the status
of absorbed blood, further signifies the emergence of *halakhah*.

The next mishnah continues to develop the normative field surrounding
the rules of blood of the dead. It examines the case of blood that has spilled,
in part inside a house:

> [Blood] that was poured out in the open air: If the place it fell on was
> a slope and [a person or vessel] overshadowed part of it, he is pure.
> If it was a cavity, or if it congealed, he is impure. If it was poured out
> on a threshold, and it was sloped either inwards or outwards and the
> house overshadowed it, [the contents of the house] are pure. If it was
> a cavity, or if it congealed, [the contents of the house] are impure.[10]

This mishnah also arises from the questions relating to the liquid nature of blood, and the necessity of distinguishing between the spillage sites
and the state of the blood. The mishnah distinguishes between a stream of
blood that was partially poured into a slope within the house, in which case
the house and its contents are pure, and blood pooled or congealed inside a
house, in which case they are impure.[11]

---

8. The *halakhah* concerning revi'it of blood is an early halakhah among the rabbis.
On this see tNazir 5.1 and the comments of J. N. Epstein, *Introductions to the Tannaitic
Literature* (Hebrew; Jerusalem, 1957), 507.
9. mOhal 3.2.
10. mOhal 3.3.
11. See tOhal 4.4.

Another mishnah presents a dual disagreement over the meaning of the expression "mixed blood." This was understood to refer to the blood which flowed both while a person was alive, and after the person died:

> What is mixed blood? The blood of a corpse of which a *sheminit* [a half of *revi'it*] came out during his lifetime and a *sheminit* after his death—the words of Rabbi Akiba. Rabbi Yishmael says: a *revi'it* during his lifetime and a *revi'it* after his death, he took a revi'it from this and from that. Rabbi Elazar bar Judah says: both this and that are as water. What then is mixed blood? A crucified person whose blood is pouring out and under him there is found a *revi'it* of blood—it is impure. But a corpse whose blood drips out and under him there is found a *revi'it* of blood, [the blood] is pure. Rabbi Judah says: This is not so, but that which pours out is pure and that which drips out is impure.[12]

Without elaborating the details of the discussion and the distinction between a dripped and poured blood, this Mishnah clarifies an internal link between the attempt to thicken the normative field and the expansion of legal controversies.[13]

The emergence of *halakhah* in rabbinic literature is not a product of gradually accumulating regulations which originated in Second Temple literature, but rather a dramatic turn which reflects a new religious sensibility and a foundational change in relation to the Torah. Empty legal spaces always exist; filling these spaces constitutes a matter of active decision-making and is not a result of the idea that law, wherever it exists, suffers no vacuums. There is no reason to assume that the Dead Sea sect, had it continued to exist, would have created something similar to the Mishnah. Different ritual traditions endure for centuries without creating the legal specificity and density of the Mishnah, and we do not find even the early shoots of such a dynamic in Second Temple literature. The Mishnah's extensive questions—such as the many inquiries regarding the status of *revi'it*—constitute a halakhic field of their own, exist only in the Mishnah, and have no mention in the legal literature prior to it.[14] It is possible that such questions emerged

---

12. mOhal 3.5.

13. For more on the controversy surrounding the meaning of "Dam ha-Tvusa" (mixed blood) see tOhalot 4.5; and *Sifrei Zuta Numbers*, 19:11.

14. The dense debates and discussion that so frequently appear in the Mishnah are absent from Second Temple literature. One fascinating example concerning this matter is expressed in the Miqtsat Ma'ase Ha-Torah (the 4QMMT scroll). This scroll, which

from a practical need in communities outside the world of the rabbis, and we should distinguish between the literary evidence and the historical reality. The latter is unknown to us in this case. What does seem clear, though, is that *halakhah*, as a literary phenomenon, has no parallel in Second Temple literature or in any external historical accounts of these non-rabbinic communities. It is possible that a member of the Dead Sea sect came upon the issue of absorbed blood. It is also possible that this issue was given a local solution by that individual or by a relevant authority figure. However, this issue and its ensuing solutions were not framed as a precedent and did not become the center of intensive discussions within Second Temple literature. Furthermore, it is very likely that those who wished to fulfill biblical commandments were able to fulfill them without going into such fine detail, and that these questions did not even bother many who were completely obligated to the Torah. Members of the Dead Sea sect were punctilious with regard to the biblical rule that defiled earthen vessels cannot be purified unless they are broken, without requiring a specific definition of what constitutes a broken earthen vessel (a matter the Mishnah defines with

---

states the legal positions of the Dead Sea sect in contrast with those of the Pharisees, has been viewed by scholars as a central document in the history of *halakhah* (on that see Zussman above note 1). The different topics that are raised in the scroll, though they extend to vast areas of Torah law, don't achieve the same level of highly calibrated, dense *halakhah*. Thus, for example, the author of the scroll criticizes the rabbis for accepting sacrifices from gentiles, while his position prohibits this. In contradiction to rabbinic law, the author prohibits the entry of the Moabites and Ammonites into the Temple, based on his reading of the verse "No Ammonite or Moabite shall be admitted into the congregation of the Lord" (Deuteronomy 23:3). In another section of the scroll the author argues against the rabbis who allow the slaughter of a pregnant animal while he prohibits it, following the legal position of the sect. These sets of debates relate to a realm of rather general rules. The only section that might begin to resemble the fine-tuned nature of *halakha* relates to the debate concerning the status of a pure vessel, where water or liquids have been spilled from it down to an impure vessel. The debate is about the column of the spilled liquids that links these two vessels, and therefore channels the impurity from downwards to upwards so that the pure vessel becomes impure. Though this debate begins to get close to the level of specificity in the Mishnah, it is worth remembering that spilling from one vessel to another is a very common occurrence. Even more so, examining the discussion of such cases in the Mishnah reveals the gap between the Scroll and the Mishnah. In the Mishnah this question is stated broadly as such, and answering it depends on the type of liquid and its degree of thickness; when honey is poured it is different from water, and the temperature of the liquids also makes a difference. On these distinctions see mMakh 5.9–10. It is apparent that even in a document in which members of the Dead Sea sect state their position against those that are held by the rabbis, they don't present to us any debates that resemble the highly calibrated nature of *halakhah*.

great specificity in tractate *Kelim*).[15] The very emergence of *halakhah*—the creation of dense and thick normative spaces addressing a wide variety of commandments—is the defining attribute of the Mishnah and the world of the rabbis. The rabbis first and foremost create *halakhah*.

Below, I will address the religious meaning of the emergence of *halakhah* and its canonical manifestation in the Mishnah, and the kind of religious sensibility and stance that such a development represents. However, before engaging with this question there is a need to clarify the phenomenon itself, as well as to explicate the operation of the mechanism that creates it. Is there a particular structure through which the rabbis thicken a normative system, and what is its purpose? My attempt to sketch an answer to the question of how *halakhah* is created will be grounded in a close analysis of tractate *Pe'ah* in the Mishnah. This example is just one drop in the ocean, but it is possible that such an analysis will expose productive foundational structures.

II

The commandment of *pe'ah* is mentioned twice in the Torah: "When you reap the harvest of your land, you shall not reap all the way to the edges [*pe'ah*] of your field, or gather the gleanings of your harvest" (Lev 19:9). This rule is repeated with the addition that the poor and the stranger will take the edges and gleanings: "And when you reap the harvest of your land, you shall not reap all the way to the edges of your field, or gather the gleanings of your harvest; you shall leave them for the poor and the stranger" (Lev 23:22). Around these two short verses the rabbis created an intense halakhic field, taking shape in four chapters in the Mishnah tractate *Pe'ah*, the parallel chapters of the Tosefta *Pe'ah*, and the extensive interpretation of these mishnaic chapters in the Talmud of the land of Israel. The obligation of *pe'ah* is mentioned in Second Temple literature, but nothing in this literature even resembles what can be described as the first stage of a halakhic creation.[16]

To gain a better grasp of the manner in which *halakhah* emerges, my analysis will focus on the following question: What are the domains that the Mishnah seeks to construct through *halakhah* when it approaches a commandment such as *pe'ah*? What can we learn about the nature of *halakhah*

15. See mKel 2.2.

16. On the mention of the obligation of *pe'ah* in Second Temple literature see Josephus, *Antiquities* 4, 231; Philo, *De Virtutibus*, 90–93, and in the Qumran Scrolls, Kimron edition, p. 32, lines 80–86.

and the Mishnah from identification of the particular domains that this intense and dense regulation is attempting to shape?

The first domain which the rabbis seek to construct through the creation of the halakhic field is that of the so-called basic elements of carrying out the obligation (referred to hereafter as such). These basic elements, which are the subject of the first chapter of tractate *Pe'ah*, include the questions of the measure of a *pe'ah*,[17] its location,[18] which crops require the leaving of a *pe'ah*,[19] and the duration of the obligation of *pe'ah*.[20]

17. "These are the things that have no definite quantity: The edges [of the field]. First-fruits; [The offerings brought] on appearing [at the Temple on the three pilgrimage festivals]. The performance of righteous deeds; And the study of the Torah. . . . They should not leave *pe'ah* of less than one-sixtieth [of the field]. But even though they said, "there is no measure for *pe'ah*," everything depends upon the size of the field, the number of poor people, and the extent of the yield" (mPe'ah 1.2). The relationship between the first and the second Mishnah in relation to the measure of *pe'ah* is quite complex. It seems that the second Mishnah doesn't recognize that *pe'ah* has no measure, and there are scholars who raised the suggestion that the first Mishnah stems from an earlier stratum of the Mishnah. On that see Moshe Weiss, "The Order of Mishnah Pe'ah and Its Relation to the Tosefta" (PhD diss., Bar Ilan University, 1978), 60, 85–87; and Aharon Shemesh "Things That Have No Measure" *Tarbiz* 73, no. 3 (1994): 387–88. In his essay Shemesh suggests that the rule of "They should not leave *pe'ah* of less than one sixtieth" is a later addition and that the first and second Mishnah can be read coherently without the sentence that was added to them at a later stage. A similar position is raised in the Babylonian Talmud (bḤul 137b) claiming that though *pe'ah* has no measure from the Torah, the rabbis instituted in the second Mishnah that its minimal measure is one of sixtieth of the field. The next section in the Mishnah—"And even though they said there is no measure for *pe'ah*"—relates back to the law of Torah. According to this reading, although the Torah didn't institute a measure for *pe'ah*, it is proper to give in proportion to the size of the field, the quantity of the poor, and the quality of the produce. Another possibility to interpret the Mishnah is that the first mishnah is concerned with the maximum measure (as in tPe'ah 1.1) and states that in distinction from other commandments whose fulfilment beyond the minimum grants no added merit, *pe'ah* has no measure and the more a person gives, the better. The Mishnah therefore doesn't address minimum measure, since the whole subject of the first mishnah is the importance of the commandment and the reward that is promised for fulfilling it. See Chanoch Albeck's commentary to the Mishnah.

18. "They may give *pe'ah* at either the beginning of the [reaping of the] field or at the middle of it. Rabbi Shimon says: as long as he gives at the end according to the set amount. Rabbi Judah says: if he leaves one stalk, he can rely on this as [fulfilling the law of] *pe'ah*; and if he did not, then he only gives as ownerless property" (mPe'ah 1.3).

19. "They said a general principle concerning *pe'ah*: whatever is food, and is looked after, and grows from the land, and is harvested all at the same time, and is brought in for storage, is subject to the law of *pe'ah*. Grain and beans are in this category; Among trees: the sumac, the carob, the nut, the almond, the grapevine, the pomegranate, the olive and the palm are subject to *pe'ah*" (mPe'ah 1.4–5)

20. "He may always give *pe'ah* and be exempt from giving tithes until he makes a stack. One who gives [to the poor] as ownerless [produce] and be exempt from giving tithes until he makes a stack" (mPe'ah 1.6).

The Torah does not provide a measure of what should be left for the poor and does not specify the relevant crops or time period designated to leaving the pe'ah to the poor. Outside of the measure of gifts to the poor which are specified in the Dead Sea Scrolls, in Second Temple literature we don't find any creative attempt to define the basic terms of the performance of the commandment.[21] The subject of the first chapter of tractate *Pe'ah* aims to construct these basic elements. It is hard to imagine that there were no common traditions with regard to these elements, since any performance of the obligation is impossible without answering them. The farmers observing the commandment of *pe'ah* most probably had a common understanding of the quantity, location, and origin of crops to designate as *pe'ah* to the poor. The genesis of the *halakhah* is the attempt to produce a systematic conceptualization of these basic elements. In this context of "basic elements," the emergence of *halakhah* is not a creation of norms in a place that had been in a state of normative vacuum. The concern of *halakhah* when it deals with this basic layer is the creation of a conceptual system which captures what must have been the unarticulated custom. Even with regard to these basic structures, many of which had answers in common practice, the development of the Mishnah and the way it deals with these questions have a unique and unprecedented meaning.

The following example will clarify this point. Let us assume that with all that concerns the location of *pe'ah*, the common practice was to leave it at the corner of the field and at the end of the harvest. The rabbis, looking for conceptual and systematic meaning, asked the following question: Is this practice derived from the idea that it is forbidden to harvest the entirety of one's field without leaving (any) portion for the poor, or is it necessary to leave the *pe'ah* specifically at the very corner of the field? If the command "you shall not reap all the way to the edges of your field" means "do not reap your field all the way," then it would be possible to leave *pe'ah* in the middle of the field. According to this approach, the common practice of leaving the *pe'ah* at the edge of the field is but *one* acceptable way of fulfilling the obligation of not harvesting the field completely. It is not the exclusive way of fulfilling this commandment, but just a good example of applying a wider rule that can, in principle, be acted upon differently. This is the position of the first view in the mishnah, arguing that the portion given to the poor does not necessarily need to be at the edge of the field, but just at the end of the harvest, and therefore it is possible to harvest the field from its edges in-

---

21. In a reconstructed section of the Damascus Covenant the measure of mPe'ah and the rest of the gifts to the poor from the field is mentioned. See Kimron's edition, p. 32, and see Shemesh (above note 17), 387–405. See as well Menachem Kahana's argument concerning the inner distinctions on this matter in the history of *halakhah*, Menachem Kahana, *Sifri ba-Midbar*, vol. 3, pp. 690–98 and note 96.

ward and to leave *pe'ah* at the middle of the field. We see here that the drive to reach a meaningful definition of *pe'ah* does not narrow the range of possibilities for fulfilling the commandment: on the contrary, the options are expanded. This definition thus creates new and unintuitive ways to fulfill the obligation.

The question of which crops are obligated in *pe'ah* was also most likely a matter of common practice. It is hard to imagine that there was no common policy on whether all vegetable gardens, or whether all orchards, require leaving of a *pe'ah*. The Mishnah adds to this an attempt to develop a general conceptual rule that will enable answering these questions: "They made a rule about *pe'ah*: all that is food, and which is guarded and grows from the ground and is collected in one crop and stored for preservation, is obligated in *pe'ah*. Grain and legumes are [included] in this rule."[22] According to this rule, a fig tree is exempt from *pe'ah* since its fruits are not picked at once, but rather are picked individually according to their respective ripeness. Vegetables are also exempt because they are not stored for preservation like legumes and grains. Let us assume that the common practice was not to leave a *pe'ah* from a vegetable plot. Grounding this custom in a general precondition that *pe'ah* is only left from crops that are "stored for preservation" does more than just describe in general terms a common practice. Sometimes such conceptualization can bring about the transformation of the common practice. For example, according to this principle, onions—although they are vegetables—require the leaving of a *pe'ah* since they are preserved dry.[23] Conceptualization also allows for the creation of a general system which encompasses different halakhic contexts. Regarding the obligation to tithe the field, the Mishnah developed a rule that was framed in contrast with the one on *pe'ah*: "They stated a rule with regard to tithes: Anything which is food, and is guarded, and grows from the earth, requires tithes."[24] We find

22. mPe'ah 1.4.

23. mPes 4.8 testifies concerning the inhabitants of Jericho that they left *pe'ah* from vegetables in spite of the objection of the Sage. The tosefta in tPes 3.20 claims that this custom concerned only turnip and shallot since "they are collected in one crop." According to the Babylonian Talmud, the custom was based on the fact that there are vegetables that are stored for preservation with cooking and pickling. On all these matters see Saul Lieberman, *Tosefta ke-Pshuta, Pesaḥim-Sukah* (New York, 1955), 542–43.

A similar observation can be made concerning the other component of the conceptualization relating to the crops that are obligated in *pe'ah*: "collected in one crop." The vineyard is obligated in *pe'ah*, but grapes designated for eating are not gathered in one crop, in contrast to grapes designated for producing wine. It is possible that a wine whose grapes are picked for eating will be exempt from *pe'ah*. On a possible source that states such a position, see Menachem Kahana's comment in *Sifrei Zuta to Devarim: Texts from a New Tannaitic Midrash* (Jerusalem, 2003), 212–13.

24. mMa'as 1.1.

that in the case of tithing, the categories of "collected in one crop and stored for preservation" are missing, and thus fig trees and vegetables need to be tithed (unlike obligation of *pe'ah*).[25]

The second domain to which *halakhah* expands its regulative net goes far beyond the basic elements. The second and third chapters of tractate *Pe'ah* address topics whose clarification is not necessary for the ordinary fulfill-ment of the obligation, and whose development constitutes an important step in the emergence of *halakhah*. The first six sections of the second chap-ter (and the first section of the third chapter) are devoted to the definition of a field. Since one cannot leave a *pe'ah* from one field in order to fulfill the ob-ligation for another field, the pertinent question is what makes one territory into two fields, so that each of them requires a *pe'ah* of its own. This ques-tion received no treatment in Second Temple literature, yet from the time it was raised among the rabbis, it became the source of intensive normative innovation. The distinction between fields is specified in the following way:

And these [features] divide [fields for the sake of] *pe'ah*: a river, a pond, a private road, a public road, a public path, a private path that is permanent during summer and winter days, uncultivated land, plowed land, and a different crop. One who harvests for the pur-pose of animal food creates a division - [these are] the words of Rabbi Meir; the sages say: He does not create a division unless he plowed.[26]

The following sections of the chapter distinguish between a seeded field and an orchard (field of fruit trees). The "spacious" orchard is not to be con-sidered two fields under the strict criteria of a seeded field, and is considered two fields only when it is divided by a fence.

The rest of the third chapter is devoted to the definition of a harvest and similarly in constructing norms that are beyond the basic elements. In this matter the Mishnah develops a complex conceptual framework, producing

25. See mNid 6.6. See as well another option that is raised in *Midrash Tanaim le-Dvarim* 14, 22. The condition of "collected in one crop" as a requirement for *pe'ah*, while not being required for tithes, makes sense, since if the fruits are not collected at once it is difficult to perceive a situation in which there will be an obligation of *pe'ah* relating to the whole field. But the condition that states that only fruits that can be preserved are obligated in *pe'ah* is not clear to me. Why should this rule serve as a restriction on the crop obligated in *pe'ah*? Why are vegetables exempt from *pe'ah* while they are obligated with tithes? It is possible that *pe'ah* was considered a gift to the poor that provides crops to them for long-term supply, and not only for immediate consumption alone (for more immediate consumption, the poor are fed from the communal soup kitchen). For more on this, see the words of Rabbeinu Tam in Tosafot tPes 56b "Klal Amru."

26. mPe'ah 2.1.

two innovative features: (1) The obligation of *pe'ah* sets in with the start of the harvest, and applies to the part of the field that was not yet harvested. Thus, if the owner of the field harvested half the field, and sold the other half, the buyer will be obligated to leave enough *pe'ah* for the whole field: "If he harvested half and sells [the other] half, the buyer gives *pe'ah* for all [the field]. If he harvested half and dedicated [the other] half [for Temple use], the one who redeems it from the treasurer gives *pe'ah* for all [the field]."[27] (2) Since the harvest creates the obligation of *pe'ah*, if no harvest took place, or the owner or his workers weren't the ones that harvested the field, the field is not obligated in *pe'ah*: "If a field was harvested by non-Jews, harvested by robbers, chewed up by ants, or broken by wind or animals, it is exempt [from *pe'ah*]."[28] Every separate act of harvesting creates its own obligation of *pe'ah*, even if two harvests take place in the same field: "One who uproots moist onions [to take] to the market, while leaving the dry ones for the granary, gives *pe'ah* or both separately."[29] Collecting the moist onions for immediate sale, and the dried onions for preservation, creates independent obligations of *pe'ah*.

In a completely distinct way from the first domain which *halakhah* has shaped, this second domain does not deal with questions which are likely to occur in the regular fulfillment of the commandment. It is possible to perform the obligation of *pe'ah* without possessing an exact definition of what is a field, or when does one field turn into two, or what is the rule in the case of a harvest that was done by two different owners in stages or by a convert, or the status of fruits co-owned by two individuals. This halakhic work deals with *outliers*, whose rare occurrence does not require the attention of the common practitioner.

The third and last domain to which *halakhah* casts its net is found in the fourth chapter of tractate *Pe'ah*, and establishes a systematic organization of the manner in which the poor are supposed to gather the *pe'ah*. The Torah is silent on this issue, and Second Temple literature provides no instruction for how the poor should gather up the left crops.[30] The Mishnah created a whole field of instructions on this matter. The normative structure it creates is driven by the tension between two ideas. The first idea is expressed in the opening section of the chapter: "*Pe'ah* is given while connected to the ground,"[31] which determines that the owner of the field may not har-

---

27. mPe'ah 2.8.

28. mPe'ah 2.7.

29. mPe'ah 3.3.

30. Both Philo and Josephus (see above note 16) seem to think that the poor entered the field and collected the crop before it was harvested.

31. mPe'ah, 4.1.

vest the *pe'ah* and hand it out. This determination prevents the possibility of the owner harvesting the *pe'ah* and handing it out to the poor people of his choice: it creates a definition of the *pe'ah* as the common property of the poor. This important rule comes with a price: since the owner does not distribute the crops, competition for the leftover, unharvested crops can occur, potentially creating conditions for inequality and violence among the poor who have come to collect them. The Mishnah therefore focuses on limiting this inequality and attempting to limit the potential dangers posed by the prohibition on the owner's selective distribution of crops. The Mishnah determines that this rule does not apply in the case of crops where the tall and strong have an advantage, or where access to the crops endangers the poor.[32] Similarly, it limits the manners in which the poor are allowed to gather, in order to prevent unequal dominance over the *pe'ah* and to prevent violence in the process of gathering: "If one took a part of the *pe'ah* and threw it on the rest, he gets no portion of it [thereby]. Even if he falls upon it or spreads his cloak on it, we remove it [the *pe'ah*] from him. And thus, it is for *leket* [fallen gleanings given to the poor], and thus it is for the sheaf of *shikhehah* [forgotten sheaves given to the poor]. *Pe'ah* cannot be harvested with a scythe, and cannot be uprooted with a spade, so that a man will not hit his fellow."[33] The Mishnah also sets three times for the distribution of the *pe'ah*: "[There are] three 'beggings' [i.e., field-access] times a day: at daybreak, at midday, and in the later afternoon. Rabban Gamaliel

---

32. "*Pe'ah* is given from [the crop] while it is still connected with the soil. But in the case of hanging vine-branches and the date-palm, the owner brings down [the fruit] and distributes it among the poor. Rabbi Shimon says: the same applies to smooth nut trees. Even if ninety-nine [of the poor] say [to the owner] to distribute it and one says to leave it in the field, this latter is listened to, since he spoke in accordance with the halakhah" (*mPe'ah* 4.1) There are two possible reasons for this rule in the Mishnah. The first is that the rule is designed to ensure a fair distribution of crops such as date-palm, in which the taller and stronger poor have a clear advantage in reaching them. The second reason is to avoid having the poor climb the trees and endang themselves. The Yerushalmi in his comments on the Mishnah quotes two readings of the Torah that state these two reasons: "It is said: 'you shall not reap all the way to the edges of your field,' from here we learn that *pe'ah* is given attached to the ground. Is this the case with palm-date and elevated vineyard? It is said: 'harvest,' what is unique about 'harvest,' that short and tall are equal in access to it, the palm tree and elevated vineyard are excluded since the short doesn't have equal access to it like the tall. Others learn this rule from 'leave': leave to them grains in their straw, dates in their branches. Is this the case as well with elevated vineyards and palm trees? It is said 'them' after the verse included it to exclude, I included the ones that don't pose danger (in harvesting them) and I exclude those that pose danger" (yPe'ah 4, 1).

33. mPe'ah 4.3–4.

says: They only said [i.e., specified that number] so that [the begging times] should not be reduced. Rabbi Akiba says: They only said so that that [the begging times] should not be increased."[34] According to the Jerusalem Talmud, these times fit different groups of the poor: "Daybreak due to breast-feeding mothers, midday for children, and later afternoon for the elderly."[35] These rules—meant to organize the distribution of *pe'ah*—are nowhere to be found in Second Temple literature.

The order of chapters in tractate *Pe'ah* signifies more or less these three distinct domains of halakhic construction. The first has to do with the basic elements of the performance of the commandment, that is, matters which are necessary for each person who fulfills it, and where it is most likely that there were common practices related to it, such as the location of *pe'ah*, the crops which are obligated in *pe'ah*, and perhaps the measure of *pe'ah*. The Halakhic work in this domain is not filling a normative vacuum, but rather conceptualizing and systematizing these elements. The second domain covered by *halakhah* has to do with matters which are beyond the basic elements, where it is likely that no common practice existed. In the case of *pe'ah*, this domain covers the detailed instructions of the definition of the field and harvest and rare boundary cases that the common practitioner can ignore. The third domain is the systematic organization of the manner of gathering of the *pe'ah* by the poor.[36] Here also, it seems that it is possible to execute the commandment without a common practice or implicit nor-

34. mPe'ah 4.5.

35. yPe'ah 4.2.

36. It is possible that we have before us an explanation not only of the different domains of the expansion of halakhah but to the way in which the tractate Pe'ah in the Mishnah was edited. The editor of the Mishnah placed the discussion of the basic elements of the laws of *pe'ah* at the beginning of the tractate and proceeded to address the subjects of what constitutes a field and a harvest, which are secondary topics. The third domain was placed at the end of tractate Pe'ah, since it connects *pe'ah* to other gifts to the poor, a passage which contains as well rules that regulate the way the poor gather what they deserve. For a different position on this topic see Moshe Weiss above note 17 pp. 136–37. It is possible that the introduction of the basic elements in the beginning of the tractate explains why the editor didn't include at this first stage the Mishnah that deals with the minimal size of a field obligated in *pe'ah*, an issue that was debated by four sages from the generation of Yavneh (mPe'ah 3.7). The question concerning the minimal size of a field doesn't emerge in every performance of the obligation of *pe'ah*, since the minimal sizes that were raised by the sages do not represent standard fields. The measure of *pe'ah* that has to be left to the poor is a far more common and meaningful question than the size of the field from which *pe'ah* must be taken. Our editor preferred therefore to move this debate to the end of the unit that deals with the questions of what is a field and what is a harvest.

mative assumptions. The poor gathered *pe'ah* one way or another, and there is no reason to assume that there was a common distinction between the gathering of grain and the gathering of dates from palm trees. However, the transformation of this domain into one ruled by a complex system of norms indicates a path of expansion which is different from the second domain that was devoted to defining a field and a harvest. Although it is possible to fulfill *pe'ah* without these norms, from the moment these norms are set forth, they must apply to every gathering of dates and grapes.

It is therefore worthwhile to distinguish between the two latter domains of the halakhic creation that go beyond the basic elements. The first is found beyond the basic elements because it deals with uncommon situations and problems, which will apply only rarely. It seems reasonable to think that the rarity of these occurrences does not bother the rabbis greatly, since they are concerned with theoretical thinking that results from the very discussion. The Mishnah devoted the same serious attention to rare boundary questions as it does to the principal question of what kind of crops are obligated in *pe'ah*. The other domain which lies beyond the basic elements deals with the components of executing the commandment which have not been precisely defined in the common practice, because it is possible to execute the commandment without having a clear sense of those elements. However, from the time this domain was regulated by instructions, it covered almost every performance of the commandment. Instructions with regard to how the *pe'ah* should be gathered are relevant every time. The *halakhah*, as the unique creation of the rabbis, shapes three distinct domains with the same kind of intensity.[37] Demarcating these domains will assist us in defining the

---

37. It is worth emphasizing that the quantum leap in the level of density creating rules produces a parallel turn in the way the Torah is read. The Torah, from now on, is supposed to provide answers to new questions, and the normative weight thrust upon it is much heavier. The verses of the Torah are read in much higher resolution: they become carriers of legal meaning in a much wider way than the straightforward reading of these verses. Thus, for example, the connection between the obligation of *pe'ah* and the harvest of the field is read from the verses by the Sifra in the following manner: "'When you harvest' this excludes when robbers harvest the field, or when it was chewed up by ants, or broken by wind or animals. 'When you harvest'—a non-Jew who harvested his field and then converted is exempt from [leaving] gleanings, the forgotten sheaf and *pe'ah*. Rabbi Judah makes him liable to leave the forgotten sheaf, since he becomes liable for the forgotten sheaf at the time of their binding" (Sifra Kodoshim 1.1). The term "when you harvest" in the verse becomes charged with additional meaning and it provides legal information that ties the obligation of *pe'ah* with the act of the harvest. We have here a new kind of intensive reading that doesn't exist in earlier layers of the interpretation of Torah during the Second Temple period. There is therefore an internal, far-reaching connection between the emergence of *halakhah* and the new development of Midrash.

religious sensibility that is expressed in the revolutionary and innovative project that culminates in the Mishnah.

III

Let us turn our gaze now towards a broader issue: the religious significance and meaning of the emergence of *halakhah* as it finds its ultimate expression in the Mishnah. In order for this shift to occur, there is a need for an echelon of rabbinic scholars which devotes itself to the meticulous expansion and elaboration of the law, and an institution of a *Beit Midrash* which provides an institutional setting for the efforts that consolidate a canonical compilation. The existence of such a rabbinic group is a necessary condition for the emergence of *halakhah*, which is further reliant on the rise of the new archetype—that of the *Talmid Ḥakham*. It can also be said that the thickening of the halakhic field endows this group with a great deal of power, since from the moment that a commandment is encompassed by a dense net of instructions, fulfilling it requires expertise. With the emergence of *halakhah*, the option of being satisfied with an open-ended common practice is rejected; the performer becomes increasingly reliant on the expert to help him or her navigate the complex network of rules.

However, the existence of such a social stratum of rabbinic scholars, and the fact that the emergence of *halakhah* increased their power, does not constitute a complete explanation for the shift. At most, it represents a background condition that enables it. What is it that motivates the type of question directed at, for example, not only the precise measure of the dead's blood that creates impurity, but also the rule concerning a measure of blood that comes from two separate dead bodies? Such a dramatic shift, the central characteristic of the mishnaic project, cannot be found in a single source or motivation. Like all shifts of this depth, several motivations come together to create it, and such motivations might also be in tension with one another. The attempt to map out a possible explanation needs to also fit the different domains of halakhic expansion and the realms that are the subject of such legal densification.

The first explanation of this shift is related to the drive towards organization and systematization of the basic elements for which a common practice existed. As was claimed above, it is likely that there was a common practice with regard to which crops were obligated in *pe'ah*, but the rabbis formulate a systematic principle—"all which is food and which is guarded and grows from the ground and collected in one crop and stored for preservation is obligated in *pe'ah*"[38]—which fits the way they understand the obliga-

---

38. mPe'ah 1.4.

tion and provides a framework for generalization and contrasting with all other obligations which deal with crops, such as tithing. This type of work, which relates to the first domain of the expansion of *halakhah* that defines the location, time, crops, and measure of *pe'ah*, instills the common practice with gravity after its basic elements have been subjected to the furnace of organizing systemic thought. Such legal awakening that aims at conceptualizing, defining, and delimiting all aspects of Torah, besides being a revolution as such, often creates substantive transformations in every subject it touches.

As we have seen, this component of the emergence of *halakhah*, which deals with the basic elements of performance, is but one domain of the expansion of *halakhah*. The question of when does a field turn into two fields, or what is the status of a field that was sold in midst of harvesting and the buyer was left with its second half, or the status of a field that was harvested by robbers, is far beyond the systemic organization of the basic elements of the obligation. It is possible to argue that what motivates such regulatory activity lies in an obsessive anxiety leading to an attempt to control all possible contingencies, out of an assumption that there is a wrong and right way to execute the obligation at every stage. Such a component certainly exists in the history of *halakhah*—when a ritual is transformed into a collective obsession. In such an atmosphere, the day is not far off that the discussion will not stop at how much Matzah should be eaten on Passover night and how fast it should be eaten, but will also take up whether it should be chewed on the left or the right side of the mouth. The very existence of a normative vacuum may raise anxiety, which must be assuaged with clear instructions that will cover all possible contingencies.

But it appears that what motivates this move in the rabbinic world is an independent interest in concepts, regardless of questions of implementation. Inquiries into legal boundary cases, such as the rule of a field whose gentile owner converted after its harvest, develop the definition of the obligation of *pe'ah* as one that applies only to standing grains. The pursuit of the definition of a field or a harvest, or of a measure of blood, is transformed into an investigation which stands independently. In this context the emergence of *halakhah* does not aim to direct behavior. It actually creates an alternative imagined universe. It aims at direct unmediated contact with the word of God for its own sake, a contact that has limited friction with the daily implementation of the commandments.

I am not trying to argue that such outlying cases will never occur; it is quite possible that a field will be sold in the middle of harvest, but the discussion concerning such a matter does not arise due to an attempt to control all possible contingencies with norms. Addressing outlying cases enables us to get a better conceptual sense of the status of unharvested crops. This second domain of halakhic expansion therefore transforms the legal realm into a matter that needs to be developed, regardless of the design of the practice itself. These instructions create a complex network inhabited by the halakhic scholars as a closed universe, and the ever-growing halakhic organism develops an independent existence which draws in all who touch it.

The third direction of the expansion of *halakhah* exposes a different drive. In this domain, as it came to light in constructing the legal norms surrounding the gathering of the *pe'ah*, the instructions are relevant to each instance of leaving *pe'ah*. Such halakhic creation transformed the act of gathering of *pe'ah* by the poor to an area rich with rules. The purpose of these instructions was to construct the gathering up in such a way that it reflected the expropriation of *pe'ah* from the owner of the field, while enabling an equal competition in the gathering up of *pe'ah*. This sphere of halakhic expansion aims at correcting the world of action and making its pattern more just.

The observer of the enormous project of *halakhah* will therefore identify a duality of meaning which internally divides it. At times it seems that the aim of *halakhah* is to construct a parallel normative world. The thick network of rules and sub-rules, which are themselves a matter of further interpretation, presents an alternative universe in which the rabbinic scholar resides. At the same time, *halakhah* is directed at reality, and seeks to correct and sanctify it through the creation of a network of rules which encompass every aspect of a person's life.[39]

What is common in all the domains of the emergence of *halakhah* is the rise of a new religious sensibility, one which will henceforth characterize much of Jewish life. It reflects the replacement of the world of the prophet and the priest with that of the rabbi-scholar. In the world of the prophet, the center of the religious drama is time. The prophet perceives history as the medium of divine revelation: God is revealed in the large strokes of historical upheavals and the prophets predict and interpret them. The priest views the Temple, space, and place as the center of divine presence. *halakhah*, as we have seen, transforms the levels of normative density relating to the Temple, creating that normative density for all other fields of religious activity. The traveling temple of *halakhah* ushers in a "micro-religion" in which individuals encounter God through the development and fulfillment of the detailed commandments. The world of *halakhah* has a non-epic quality to it, and it is therefore free from the manic-depressive pendulum of history. God, according to the rabbis, dwells in the four cubits of *halakhah*.[40] This

39. On this duality see Ishay Rosen-Zvi, *Between Mishnah and Midrash* (Ra'ananah, 2020), 122–23.

40. See D. Hartman, *A Living Covenant* (New York, 1985), 204–28.

expansion and transformation of the religious world began in the rabbinic circle before the destruction of the Temple. Yet without a doubt, after the Destruction, this movement gained great forward momentum since it had prepared a meaningful and comprehensive alternative to the sudden and complete loss of space and time.

Besides replacing the biblical paradigm of epic-religion, the religious sensibility of *halakhah* also stands in opposition to other common religious paradigms. The second paradigm which the *halakhah* rejects is the religion of other-worldliness. In its mode of other-worldliness, religion is an expression of the denial of the here and now, viewing the temporal and transient as an empty shell that must be overcome. The mishnaic positing of the law as the central realm of encounter with the Divine thus binds humans to the world with all its concreteness, directing them to reshape and sanctify the world. The affirmation of the this-worldliness of *halakhah* is expressed in the following mishnah: "He used to say: more precious is one hour in repentance and good deeds in this world, than all the life of the world to come" (*mAvot* 4.17). In a later source referring to eternal messianic life, the Talmud expresses the same sentiment: "'And the years arrive when you will say: I have no desire for them'; these are the days of Messiah, in which there is neither merit nor liability" (bShab 151b). The halakhic emphasis on practice also stands in opposition to a third religious paradigm of inwardness, a paradigm which seeks God within the inner citadel of the individual soul, cultivating withdrawal and introspection as the center of religious life. *Halakhah*, in contrast, is a thoroughly communal project, and its ethos is shaped by the idea that nothing is of meaning unless it is expressed through action. The gravity of human religious life is outward, in the visible and ongoing patterned practice.

One of the earliest liturgical texts—the blessing that precedes the recitation of the *Shm'a*—is devoted to the theme of God's love:

With an everlasting love You loved the House of Israel, Your people. You taught us Torah and commandments, statutes and laws. Therefore, God our Lord, when we lie down and when we rise, we will discuss Your statutes, and rejoice in the words of Your Torah and in Your commandments forever. For they are our life and they lengthen our days, and on them we will meditate day and night. [May] Your love never be removed from us. Blessed are you God who loves his people Israel.[41]

---

41. On the rabbinic origin of this liturgical blessing see bBer 11b.

In these few liturgical lines that constitute the finest expression of the rabbinic ethos of the religion of law, God's love is manifested in the giving of the law. The gift of the law is therefore met with utmost devotion in an ongoing joyous engagement with the Torah and its commandments, expanding its realm and reach.

12. Nomos and Mishnah: The Turn to Narrative in Recent Mishnah Scholarship

Moshe Simon-Shoshan

INTRODUCTION

Focus on the narrative aspects and elements of the Mishnah reflects a particular moment in the history of rabbinics scholarship. A survey of the scholarship on the Mishnah as it developed over the nineteenth and twentieth centuries and of the study of narrative in rabbinics as it emerged as a field in the final three decades of the twentieth century reveals only sporadic attention to questions relating to narrative and the Mishnah. But with the beginning of the twenty-first century came a sudden flurry of interest in the topic. The first decade of this century saw the emergence of a body of scholarship focusing on individual mishnaic narratives or the role of narrative in the Mishnah more broadly. In the intervening years since these studies were undertaken, the question of the narrative and the Mishnah has not received anywhere near the same degree of attention. This scholarly moment might best be understood as representing the high point of a "narrative turn" in Mishnah studies which came in the wake of a similar turn in the academy starting in the 1960s.[1]

---

1. For a review of this phenomenon see Matti Hyvärinen, "Revisiting the Narrative Turns," *Life Writing* 7 (2010): 69–82.

THE NARRATIVE TURN

Literary scholars have examined and interpreted stories since antiquity. Until recently, such scholars tended to focus on individual works or on established literary genres such as the epic, novel, and short story, rather than on a broader abstract category called "narrative." This began to change in the 1960s, when French structuralist theorists began to "look squarely at narrative itself, asking rigorous questions not about this narrative or story, but about exactly what a story is, where it occurs, how it works, what it does, and for whom."[2] This approach led to the development of the field of narratology, which aspires to develop tools for the study of narrative which can be applied universally to all narratives and seeks to understand narrative as a generalized cultural and semiotic phenomenon. Narratology opened the possibility of the literary study of stories that did not fit into the traditional categories of the western literary tradition. But in its initial stages, the narrative turn was still largely limited to the study of texts that could reasonably be defined as "literary." This first phase of the narrative turn reached the world of rabbinics scholarship already in the 1970s, as scholars such as Jonah Fraenkel and Jacob Neusner began to argue that aggadic stories needed to be studied as literary works, using the tools of narrative analysis, rather than as historical and philological artifacts.[3] The literary study of aggadic narratives would soon develop into a full-fledged academic sub-field. In line with the tendencies of early narratologists, the first generation of scholars of narrative in rabbinic literature focused on the lengthier, more literarily complex stories of the Talmuds and midrashim. Shorter, halakhically oriented stories, such as the vast majority of those found in the Mishnah, remained largely neglected.[4]

---

2. Martin Kreiswirth, "Narrative Turn in the Humanities," in *Routledge Encyclopedia of Narrative Theory*, ed. D. Herman, M. Jahn and M.-L. Ryan (London and New York, 2005), 378.

3. See especially Jonah Fraenkel, *The Aggadic Narrative: Harmony of Content and Form* (Hebrew; Tel Aviv, 2001); Jacob Neusner, "Story and Tradition in Judaism," in *Judaism: The Evidence of the Mishnah* (Chicago, 1981), 307–26.

4. Indeed, Fraenkel went to great lengths to argue for the literary nature of *some* narratives found in rabbinic literature, while rejecting the "literariness" of others, largely those which were halakhic in nature. Of the hundreds of stories which Fraenkel analyzed, only five came from the Mishnah. Joshua Levinson, *Rishimat sipurim she-nidonu be-kivei Yona Frankel* in *Higayon L'Yonah: New Aspects in the Study of Midrash, Aggadah and Piyyut in Honor of Yona Fraenkel*, ed. J. Levinson, J. Elbaum, and G. Hasan-Rokem (Jerusalem, 2007), no page numbers. Frankel would turn to the Mishnah only in one of his last articles, Jonah Fraenkel, "The Aggadah in the Mishnah," *Mehqerei Talmud* 3, 2 ed. Y. Sussmann and D. Rosenthal (Jerusalem, 2005), 655–83 [Hebrew],

In the 1980s the narrative turn entered a new phase as it moved beyond departments of literary studies. It was in this period that the notion of narrative as a fundamental constituent of all human discourse, whose relevance extends well beyond departments of literature, truly began to take hold. The range of texts that could be studied as narratives, or at the very least as possessing "narrativity," radically expanded as narrative became a central category of analysis throughout the humanities and social sciences. As scholars began to see narrative everywhere, the idea that the Mishnah might be studied for its narrative content became plausible.

Among the many sub-fields that emerged out of the narrative turn of the 1980s was the "law and narrative" movement. Scholars of this school argued for the centrality of narrative in the functioning of all legal systems and cultures.[5] They sought to understand the narrative elements of legal texts and proceedings, and the manner in which broader narratives told by legal practitioners and within society at large shaped the way law is understood and decided.

Among the earliest and most influential works devoted to the interrelationship between law and narrative is Robert Cover's seminal essay "Nomos and Narrative," first published in 1983. In the opening paragraph Cover declares:

> No set of legal institutions or prescriptions exists apart from the narratives that locate it and give it meaning. For every constitution there is an epic, for each decalogue a scripture. Once understood in the context of the narratives that give it meaning, law becomes not merely a system of rules to be observed, but a world in which we live. In this normative world, law and narrative are inseparably related.[6]

---

published at the same time as the dissertations under consideration were being written. Notably, Neusner's programmatic essay "Story and Tradition" did appear as an appendix to a book on the Mishnah and offered a brief analysis of the story of Honi Hame'agel (mḤag 3.8). However, this had little impact on future scholars. The next generation of scholars such as Jeffery Rubenstein and Inbar Raveh have focused almost exclusively on amoraic sources, especially the Bavli.

5. Among the milestones of this movement are: the special issue of *Michigan Law Review* 87:8 (1989), "Legal Storytelling"; Peter Brooks and Paul Gewirtz, eds., *Law's Stories: Narrative and Rhetoric in the Law* (New Haven, 1996); Jerome Bruner, *Making Stories: Law, Literature, Life* (Cambridge, 2002); Peter Brooks, "Narrative Transactions—Does the Law Need a Narratology?" *Yale Journal of Law and the Humanities* 18 (2006): 1–28; Brooks, "Narrativity of the Law," *Cardozo Studies in Law and Literature* 14 (2002): 1–10.

6. Cover, "Nomos and Narrative," 4–5.

In making his case for the centrality of narrative to legal discourse in "Nomos and Narrative" and other works, Cover drew heavily on examples from the Jewish tradition, from the Bible to R. Yosef Karo. In doing so, he implied that Jewish texts and culture are *paradigmatic* of the relationship between law and narrative that he described in at least two ways.[7] First, the Bible and many later Jewish legal texts combine legal and narrative elements in a way that illustrates the relationship between law and narrative that Cover saw as inherent to all legal cultures. Further, throughout history, Jewish law has mostly functioned without the benefit of a state that could impose its obligations on the community. Rather, the narratives that bound the Jewish community generated a sense of obligation among the members of the community, which was sufficient to maintain widespread adherence to the law.[8]

Cover was an important influence on many of the scholars who, somewhat belatedly, brought the "law and narrative" movement into the world of ancient Jewish studies. Starting at the end of the twentieth century, and continuing into the beginning of the second decade of the twenty-first century, a group of mostly early-career scholars produced a steady stream of studies focusing on the role of narrative in rabbinic and other ancient Jewish legal texts, including the Bible, the Dead Sea Scrolls, tannaitic and amoraic midrashim, and the Talmuds.[9]

7. On the centrality of Jewish sources in "Nomos and Narrative," see Suzanne Last Stone, "In Pursuit of the Counter-Text: The Turn to the Jewish Legal Model in Contemporary American Legal Theory," *Harvard Law Review* 106 (1993): 813–94.

8. See Robert Cover, "Obligation: A Jewish Jurisprudence of the Social Order," *Journal of Law and Religion* 5 (1987) 65–74.

9. These studies include: Assnat Bartor, *Reading Law as Narrative: A Study in the Casuistic Laws of the Pentateuch* (Atlanta, 2010); Simeon Chavel, "Oracular 'novellae' and Biblical Historiography: Through the Lens of Law and Narrative," Clio 39 (2009): 1–27; Steven Fraade, "Nomos and Narrative Before Nomos and Narrative," *Yale Journal of Law and the Humanities* 17 (2005): 81–96; Barry Wimpfheimer, *Narrating the Law: A Poetics of Talmudic Legal Stories* (Philadelphia, 2011); Daniel Boyarin, *Socrates and the Fat Rabbis* (Chicago, 2009); Natalie B. Dohrmann, "Law and Narrative in the Mekhilta De-Rabbi Ishmael: The Problem of Midrashic Coherence" (diss., University of Chicago, 1999); Jane L. Kanarek, *Biblical Narrative and the Formation of Rabbinic Law* (Cambridge, 2014). Catherine Heszer anticipated this development by nearly a decade. See Catherine Hezser, *Form, Function, and Historical Significance of the Rabbinic Story in Yerushalmi Neziqin* (Tübingen, 1993). This body of scholarship also reflects a process, described by Rachel Rafael Neis, in which "halakhah is assimilated as law" in the contemporary academy. Rachel Rafael Neis, "The Seduction of Law: Rethinking Legal Studies in Jewish Studies," *Jewish Quarterly Review* 109 (2019): 119–38.

Among these works are four books on narrative in the Mishnah: Beth Berkowitz's *Execution and Invention: Death Penalty Discourse in Early Rabbinic and Christian Cultures* (2006);[10] Ishay Rosen-Zvi's *Rite That Was Not* (2008);[11] my own *Stories of the Law: Narrative Discourse and the Construction of Authority in the Mishnah* (2012);[12] and Naftali Cohn's *The Memory of the Temple and the Making of the Rabbis* (2012).[13] These scholars directly influenced one another, and their work is held together by common methodological assumptions, generic and thematic concerns, and ultimate conclusions about the nature of narrative in the Mishnah. They might be seen as representing a distinct school of scholarship which stands at the center of the narrative turn in the study of the Mishnah.

THE FOCUS ON RITUAL NARRATIVE

Three of these books focus on a single genre of mishnaic narrative, "ritual narratives," in which the Mishnah describes the proper performance of procedures and rituals in sequential form. Overwhelmingly, these narratives describe procedures related to the Temple cult or to the operation of the high court in Jerusalem, neither of which was functional in the time of the Mishnah.[14] Berkowitz was perhaps the first to use the term "ritual narrative"[15] and to describe its workings. Her analysis of rabbinic death penalty discourse opens with an extended literary analysis of the sixth chapter of *mSanhedrin*, in which the Mishnah describes the process of execution by stoning in ritual terms. Rosen-Zvi focuses on the description of the Sotah ritual in the first chapter of *mSotah*. In the final chapter of his book, he considers the entire genre of mishnaic ritual narratives describing the Temple cult. Cohn's book is largely devoted to a systematic study of this same genre, though he also extensively discusses other genres of mishnaic discourse.

My own book, *Stories of the Law*, seeks to survey the wider phenomena of stories and narrative in the Mishnah. In the first part of the book, I argue for a broader concept of "narrativity" which ranks the degree to which a

10. Beth Berkowitz, *Execution and Invention: Death Penalty Discourse in Early Rabbinic and Christian Cultures* (Oxford, 2006).

11. Ishay Rosen-Zvi, *The Rite That Was Not* (Jerusalem: Magnes Press, 2008).

12. Moshe Simon-Shoshan, *Stories of the Law: Narrative Discourse and the Construction of Authority in the Mishnah* (Oxford, 2012).

13. Naftali Cohn, *The Memory of the Temple and the Making of the Rabbis* (Philadelphia: University of Pennsylvania Press, 2012).

14. For a list of these passages see Cohn, *Memory*, 123–26.

15. Berkowitz, *Execution and Invention*, 22.

given text portrays "specificity" and "dynamism." I use the term "narrative" to refer to texts that have a high level of dynamism such that they describe a sequence of two interrelated events. The term "stories" is reserved for narratives that contain a high degree of specificity such that the events described happen once, and only once, in the past.[16] I then argue that the Mishnah is distinguished by the wide range of narrativity in the forms which it utilizes and the manner in which these forms constantly interact with each other.[17] In the second half of the book I study the stories of the Mishnah which are overwhelmingly brief legal anecdotes. I break down these anecdotes into three major genres: "case stories," "exempla," and "etiological stories." I consider the role of each of these genres in Mishnah and the significance of numerous individual stories.

Nevertheless, I too treat the phenomenon of ritual narratives on several occasions. I seek to define their distinctive place within the range of narrativity in the Mishnah. Later in the book, I investigate the dynamic relationship between ritual narratives and the etiological stories which often appear in their midst.[18]

These works also share certain methodological assumptions regarding this genre of mishnaic narrative. They all reject the traditional scholarly position that mishnaic ritual narratives transmit historical traditions of the actual operations of the Temple and contemporaneous court procedures. They argue that these texts represent radically reworked, if not entirely invented, accounts of the rituals they describe. The argument that mishnaic ritual narratives are essentially fiction empowered these writers to treat them as literary texts with broader thematic concerns and ideological agendas. This literary approach to mishnaic ritual narratives and the Mishnah is indebted to Neusner's pioneering work in the 1970s and 1980s.[19] But Neusner's ideas did not gain much traction in the wider academic world at the time. The works of Berkowitz, Cohn, and Rosen-Zvi succeeded in bringing renewed prominence and much wider acceptance to this approach.[20]

---

16. Simon-Shoshan, *Stories of the Law*, 15–20.

17. Simon-Shoshan, *Stories of the Law*, 23–95.

18. Simon-Shoshan, *Stories of the Law*, 42–45, 204–18.

19. See for example Jacob Neusner, "Ritual without Myth: The Use of Legal Materials for the Study of Religions," *Religion* 5 (1975): 91–100; Neusner, "Map without Territory: Mishnah's System of Sacrifice and Sanctuary," *History of Religions* 19 (1979): 103–27. For a critical survey of Neusner's scholarship on the Mishnah see Shaye J. D. Cohen, "Jacob Neusner, Mishnah, and Counter-Rabbinics: A Review Essay," *Conservative Judaism* 37 (1983): 48–63.

20. On the manner in which these scholars, as well as their contemporary, Chaya T. Halberstam, build on Neusner's work but have also surpassed it see Steve Fraade,

The focus on the Mishnah's ritual narratives should not surprise us. The sorts of stories that are generally considered in studies of law and narrative are either absent or relatively marginal in the Mishnah. When Cover spoke of "narratives that locate [the law] and give it meaning" he spoke primarily of stories that provide an "account of the framing of the [legal] text."[21] Such framing narratives are found at the opening of most ancient Near Eastern and classical Mediterranean legal sources. These stories describe the origins of the laws contained in the text and establish their authority.[22] The Mishnah does not open with such a text. Its orders and tractates open *in medias res*, taking the history and authority of the Mishnah's laws for granted.[23] The only such framing narrative in the Mishnah, the chain of tradition at the beginning of *Avot*, appears precisely in the only non-legal tractate of the Mishnah, whose exact relationship to the rest of Mishnah remains an open question.[24] The stories that I focused on in the Mishnah are mostly brief anecdotes scattered irregularly through the text, rarely extending beyond a couple of sentences. They tend not to invite extensive study.

Ritual narratives, in contrast, might be described as the dominant narrative form in the Mishnah. They are generally extensive accounts spread across one or more chapters of the Mishnah, often dominating the numerous tractates in which they appear. In this sense, they are the most obvious candidates for playing the critical role which, Cover argues, narratives play in all legal culture and interpretation.

Ritual narratives are also a highly distinctive form from a narratological point of view. They do not qualify as full-fledged "stories" because stories conventionally tell about one-time happenings. Ritual narratives recount

"Jacob Neusner as Reader of the Mishnah, Tosefta, and Halakhic Midrashim," *Henoch* 31 (2009): 269; Barry Scott Wimpfheimer, "A Biography or a Hagiography?" *Religious Studies Review* 44 (2018): 76.

21. Cover, "Nomos and Narrative," 4, 17.

22. Simon-Shoshan, *Stories of the Law*, 73–94.

23. This is certainly true of *mBerakhot,* the first tractate in the Mishnah according to its received order. We cannot determine with any certainty the original ordering of the Mishnah, if indeed there was one. But there is no reason to believe that the Mishnah was ever meant to begin with *Avot*. See Menachem Kahana, "The Arrangement of the Orders of the Mishnah" (Hebrew), *Tarbiz* 76 (2006–7): 29–40 [Hebrew].

24. See Alexander Guttman, "Tractate Abot: Its Place in Rabbinic Literature," *Jewish Quarterly Review* 41 (1950): 181–93; Günter Stemberger, "Die innerrabbinische Überlieferung von Mischna Abot," in *Geschichte–Traditio—Reflexion, Festschrift für Martin Hengel zum 70. Geburtstag*, vol. I: *Judentum*, ed. H. Cancick, H. Lichtenberger, and P. Schafer (Tübingen, 1996), 511–27; Adiel Schremer, "*Avot* Reconsidered: Rethinking Rabbinic Judaism," *Jewish Quarterly Review* 105 (2015): 287–311.

iterative events that ostensibly occurred many times, generally annually in the Temple. While iterative accounts often play a role in literary narratives, few cultures have produced an entire literary genre defined by this sort of narration. Arguably, it was only the radical expansion of the concept of narrative and narrativity engendered by the narrative turn that enabled scholars to identify these accounts as narratives worthy of study as such.

But ritual narratives cannot be defined simply by their iterativity. Anticipating the narrative turn in Mishnah studies by almost two decades, Yochahan Breuer undertook the first systematic study of ritual narratives already in the late 1980s. He documented the use of two distinct verb forms in these narratives, the *qatal* form, which usually describes the simple past, and the *qotel*, which usually represents a participle form.[25] Breuer argued that in the context of mishnaic ritual narratives the *qatal* and *qotel* forms can be understood as representing "story time" and "halakhic time."[26] This points to the hybrid nature of the genre of ritual narrative itself. On the one hand, narratives function as "historical" texts representing events that purportedly happened repeatedly in the past. Furthermore, as I have argued, the use of the *qatal* form encourages the reader "to envision a single iteration of the ritual," giving the reader the experience of reading an actual story.[27] On the other hand, the *qotel* form gives ritual narrative a prescriptive character, informing the reader not how the ritual *was* performed, but how it *must be* performed, independent of any time frame. Ritual narratives cannot be viewed as simple iterative narratives recounting practices of the past. They represent a remarkable merging of idealized representation of repeated events with the experience of reading a historical account of one-time events and the presentation of a set of norms to be enacted in a timeless present.

Viewed in this light, mishnaic ritual narrative might be the ultimate literary form combining law and narrative. It embodies the tension between the *is* (or the was) and the *ought* that lay at the center of Cover's vision of law as functioning as part of a *nomos:* the "normative world [in which] law and narrative are inseparably related . . . History and literature cannot escape their location in a normative universe, nor can prescription, even when embodied in a legal text, escape its origin and its end in experience."[28] This

25. Yochanan Breuer, "Perfect and Participle in Description of Ritual in the Mishnah" (Hebrew), *Tarbiz* 56 (1987): 299–326.

26. Breuer, "Perfect and Participle," 325.

27. Simon-Shoshan, *Stories of the Law*, 45.

28. Cover, "Nomos and Narrative," 5.

most characteristic form of mishnaic narrative embodies the complex relationship between law and narrative in general.

MISHNAH AS MEANING

Perhaps Cover's most important innovation in "Nomos and Narrative" is his argument that law needs to be understood as a "resource in signification" which functions to generate meaning whose significance lies far beyond the courtroom. Law "enables us to submit, rejoice, struggle, pervert, mock, disgrace, humiliate, or dignify."[29] It has the potential to give meaning to individuals and communities shaping the totality of their existence. Cover goes on to declare, "[I]t is the thesis of this Foreword that the creation of legal meaning takes place always through an essentially cultural medium." The reading of legal codes and rulings as autonomous texts, in the style of traditional literary "close reading," will not usually generate the sort of broader meaning that Cover seeks. Rather, most legal texts need to be read against the wider social, cultural, and ideological contexts of the communities which produce them in order to elicit their meaning-generating potential. The contexts are frequently, but not necessarily, expressed in the form of stories. Cover, thus, often uses the term "narrative" as a sort of metonym for this socio-ideological framework, which together with the law creates the *nomos,* the community of legal meaning.[30]

But Cover also argues that some texts inscribe a complete *nomos,* containing within them both the laws and the broader socio-ideological framework which together can generate true legal meaning. Cover's archetypal example of such a text is the Hebrew Bible, particularly the Pentateuch, which he presents as "an illustration of the ways in which precepts and narratives operate together to ground meaning."[31] He goes on to explicate the complex relationship between the Deuteronomic law of primogeniture and the foundational stories in Genesis which "revolve around the overturning of the 'normal' order of succession."[32]

The scholarship on mishnaic narrative rests on the proposition that like the Bible, the Mishnah can be read as a complete *nomos,* containing the

29. Cover, "Nomos and Narrative," 8.

30. E.g., Cover writes, "The codes that relate our normative system to our social constructions of reality and to our visions of what the world might be are narrative. The very imposition of a normative force upon a state of affairs, real or imagined, is the act of creating narrative," "Nomos and Narrative," 10.

31. Cover, "Nomos and Narrative," 19.

32. Cover, "Nomos and Narrative," 21–22.

materials necessary to reconstruct an entire worldview and not just a legal system. This represents a paradigm shift in Mishnah scholarship. From the classical commentators through modern critical scholarship, the Mishnah has been treated almost exclusively as a resource of halakhic rulings and principles. Much of the academic discussion about the Mishnah in the latter half of the twentieth century was framed by the debate between Albeck and Epstein as to whether the Mishnah should be viewed as a definitive legal code or as a more academic collection of legal materials.[33] The underlying assumption of both sides was that the Mishnah is an essentially legal work.

Scholars of mishnaic narrative have argued that the Mishnah's narratives and broader narrativity transmit an entire ethos and worldview which both underlie and transcend its halakhic content. The idea that the Mishnah is more than a source of law does not necessarily imply a focus on the Mishnah's narratives as traditionally defined. Such an approach was first suggested by Neusner, who argued that Mishnah should be viewed as a "philosophical" work presenting a systematic ontology and metaphysics. But Neusner paid little attention to the narrative character of the Mishnah, focusing rather on its simpler "formulary patterns."[34]

Similarly, Avraham Walfish makes use of a "literary-conceptual" methodology, approaching the Mishnah from a poetic rather than narrative framework. He has worked to demonstrate the ubiquity of poetic devices throughout the Mishnah, such as parallelism, symmetry, word repetition, and wordplay. Attention to these features reveals the literary unity of mishnaic chapters and tractates, which often appear to lack a coherent sequence or ordering principle. He further argues that these literary structures accomplish the central cultural work of the Mishnah as the bearers of a wide range of thematic content, imbuing the Mishnah's technical halakhot with deeper "aggadic" meaning of a theological, moral, or existential nature.[35]

33. See Simon-Shoshan, *Stories of the Law*, 230.

34. See Jacob Neusner, "The Mishnah Viewed Whole," in *The Mishnah in Contemporary Perspective*, ed. A. J. Avery-Peck and J. Neusner (Leiden, 2002) esp. 10; Jacob Neusner, *Judaism without Christianity: An Introduction to the System of the Mishnah* (Hoboken, N.J., 1991), esp. 99.

35. Walfish's major works are Avraham Walfish, "Literary Additions in the Mishnah and Their Ideological and Value Meaning" (Hebrew; MA thesis, Hebrew University of Jerusalem, 1994); Walfish, "Literary Method of Redaction in the Mishnah Based on Tractate *Rosh Hashana*" (Hebrew; diss., Hebrew University, 2001); Walfish, *Mishnah Tapestries—Tractate Berakhot: A Literary Conceptual Study of Mishnah Berakhot* (Hebrew; Alon Shevut, 2018). For an English language summary of Walfish's approach see Avraham Walfish, "The Poetics of the Mishnah," in *The Mishnah in Contemporary Perspective*, ed. A. J. Avery-Peck and J. Neusner (Leiden and Boston, 2006), 2:152–89.

For Walfish, narratives and stories are just one of the many devices used by the editors of the Mishnah to communicate its ideological content.[36]

Though Walfish does not pay particular attention to narratives in the Mishnah and does not make use of narratological tools, the manner in which he defines the Mishnah as transmitting a self-contained *nomos* might thus be viewed as being a part of the narrative turn in mishnaic studies more broadly conceived. Cover's broad uses of the term "narrative" to potentially include a wide range of rhetorical devices and methods of generating and transmitting meaning within a culture is itself a feature of the wider narrative turn in the humanities.[37]

More recently, I have made a somewhat different argument for reading the Mishnah as a self-contained *nomos*. In a forthcoming article, I survey the aggadic material in the Mishnah, both narrative and non-narrative in form, and seek to demonstrate how it functions "to construct the political, moral, and theological framework of mishnaic halakhah."[38] The study emerges from and develops my early work on narrative in the Mishnah. This development in my own work is an example of how the turn to narrative in the study of the Mishnah is an integral part of a wider shift towards understanding the Mishnah as transmitting "meaning" beyond technical legal teachings.

AUTHORITY IN/OF THE MISHNAH

The assertion that beyond the Mishnah's technical halakhic concerns lies broader ideological content raises the question of the nature of this content. Berkowitz, Cohn, Rosen-Zvi, and I all came to strikingly similar conclusions on this count. All of us saw the question of rabbinic authority as central to the Mishnah's ideological agenda.

Walfish has not made an extended effort to publish his work in major academic forums. As such his work has not received the sort of extended academic scrutiny necessary to evaluate its validity.

36. For an example of Walfish's approach to mishnaic stories and their relationship to the wider literary and ideological fabric of the Mishnah see Avraham Walfish, "Halakhic Confrontation Dramatized: A Study of Mishnah Rosh Hashanah 2:8–9," *Hebrew Union College Annual* 79 (2008): 1–41.

37. See Marie-Laure Ryan, "Narrative," in *Routledge Encyclopedia of Narrative Theory*, ed. D. Herman, M. Jahn, M.-L. Ryan (London, 2008), 344–48.

38. Moshe Simon-Shoshan, "Halakhah and Aggadah in Tannaitic Sources," in *The Literature of the Sages*, ed. C. Hayes, Compendia Rerum Iudaicarum ad Novum Testamentum, Leiden, forthcoming.

Naftali Cohn presents the strongest version of this claim. He describes the Mishnah's narrative discourse, especially the way the rabbis portray themselves as having been the ultimate authorities in the Temple, as a form of subtle propaganda to advance the rabbis' ambitions "to serve as jurists of Judaean ritual law with the authority to determine how all Judaeans would observe ritual practices."[39]

In *Stories of the Law*, I accept the existence of this authoritarian voice in the Mishnah. However, I argue there that it represents only one strand in the Mishnah's ideological tapestry. In my account, the Mishnah's stories make a collective argument for the rabbis as the sole legitimate interpreters, legislators, and embodiments of the law. But the Mishnah's apodictic discourse makes an opposite claim, that the halakha is embodied in an abstract system of rules and principles which transcend any individual or group. The two approaches to the law stand in dialogic tension in the Mishnah. I further read many of the Mishnah's more complex stories as interrogating the rabbis' claims to authority in various ways, suggesting that their authority may be more limited and fragile than they often care to admit explicitly. I argue that Mishnah might be read both as an "authoritative discourse," which "speaks with a single voice meant to impose uniform halakhic jurisprudence and practice on its audience," and as a "discourse of authority," engaging "in an ongoing and opened-ended conversation about the workings of rabbinic authority." In particular, the Mishnah's stories might be interpreted as "sites for the exploration of tensions and inconsistencies within the rabbinic power structure."[40]

Beth Berkowitz describes how "the [Mishnah's description of] the rabbinic death penalty provides an education in rabbinic authority."[41] She argues that the ritual narrative of capital punishment in *mSanhedrin* asserts not only the rabbis' (presumably theoretical) authority to execute criminals but metonymically makes the case for their authority over all Israel. She goes so far as to declare that "the entire corpus of the Mishnah would fall without *Sanh.* 6."[42] In her reading of the text, rabbinic authority over life and death ultimately stems from the rabbis' claim to be able to deliver ultimate redemption for all. At the same time, though, she sees this ritual narrative as a deeply paradoxical text which both empowers and constrains the rabbis as well as the people. Berkowitz sees the rabbis as presenting a "vision of authority that is one in dialogue" with its intended subjects,[43]

39. Cohn, *Memory*, 119.
40. Simon-Shoshan, *Stories of the Law*, 230–31.
41. Berkowitz, "Execution and Invention," 18.
42. Berkowitz, "Execution and Invention," 93.

through which the rabbis engage the people in a delicately "negotiated participation and resistance."[44]

Most provocatively, Rosen-Zvi reads the Mishnah's description of the Sotah ritual as a rabbinic "fantasy of total and unbridled control over the female body, against the backdrop of Foucault's analysis of the constitutive role of the sovereign's hold on the body in the establishment of his power."[45] The patriarchal need to control women thus becomes part of the rabbis' efforts to assert their authority of the community at large. While exposing the elements of raw physical violence within the rabbinic discourse of authority, Rosen-Zvi also emphasizes the way in which these impulses conflict with the broader rabbinic worldview. He describes the Mishnah's depiction of the Sotah ritual as one of the "most uncharacteristic manifestations" of "Tannaitic sexual mores."[46] This tension illustrates the complexity of the development of rabbinic ethics. He concludes that paradoxically, "The *sotah* ritual does not present an ideal that cannot be actualized but a fantasy that *ought* not to be fulfilled."[47]

Cohn, and to a lesser degree Rosen-Zvi, portray the Mishnah as asserting the unrestricted authority of the rabbis over the law and the community. According to Berkowitz and myself, the rabbis of the Mishnah were both ambivalent about exercising their power and well aware of their own limitations. One way or another, though, all these scholars see rabbinic authority as the central theme of mishnaic narrative.

The focus on rabbinic authority as a theme in the Mishnah is hardly self-evident, and perhaps in need of revision. Authority is far from the only extra-legal concern to be found in the Mishnah. Avraham Walfish identifies a remarkable number of themes underlying the Mishnah discussions. He identifies rabbinic authority as being at the center of the Mishnah's concerns only in cases in which this is all but explicit in the text, such as the story of R. Joshua's confrontation with Rabban Gamaliel in mRH 2.8–9.[48] In my more recent work on mishnaic aggadah, I also have pointed to a wide range of ethical, social, and theological concerns in the Mishnah, among which rabbinic authority is only one example.[49] Most recently, Hillel Mali has brought renewed attention to the ritual narratives of the Mishnah that

43. Berkowitz, "Execution and Invention," 94.
44. Berkowitz, "Execution and Invention," 70.
45. Rosen-Zvi, *Sotah Ritual*, 225.
46. Rosen-Zvi, *Sotah Ritual*, 237.
47. Rosen-Zvi, *Sotah Ritual*, 235.
48. E.g. Walfish, "Halakhic Confrontation."
49. Simon-Shoshan, "Halakhah and Aggadah."

describe the Temple cult. In his readings of these texts, Mali finds little concern with the question of rabbinic authority. Rather, as we might expect from a Temple-centric literature, Mali sees theological themes, like submission to the direct authority of God when visiting His House, as well as communal concerns, such as the tension between the private and public natures of worship in the Temple.[50]

The focus on the theme of rabbinic authority in these contemporaneous works thus demands explanation. One possible explanation is the rise of the new historiography of the tannaitic period in the years before their publication. Traditional academic accounts of the rabbinic period describe the tannaitic rabbis as the dominant religious and political elite, a sort of first estate of the Jewish society in the Land of Israel. They inherited this position from their predecessors the Pharisees, who were similarly portrayed as controlling religious life in the late Second Temple period, particularly in the Temple itself. Over the course of the 1980s and 1990s, historians began to embrace a very different narrative, in which the rabbis of the late first and early second century were a relatively marginal group that rose to prominence gradually. When the Mishnah was edited, the rabbis had, at best, only recently achieved a major leadership position in the wider Jewish community.[51]

---

50. Hillel Mali, "Descriptions of the Temple in the Mishna: History, Redaction and Meaning" (Hebrew; diss., Bar-Ilan University, 2018); Mali. "Conceptual and Ideological Aspects in the Mishnaic Description of Bringing the First Fruits to Jerusalem," in *Ritual Dynamics in Jewish and Christian Contexts: Between Bible and Liturgy*, ed. C. D. Bergmann and B. Kranemann (Leiden and Boston, 2019), 128–47. Mali might be seen as a member of an emerging school of neo-philologists, who work to broaden and deepen the approach of traditional Israeli rabbinics scholarship. His work does not have the same focus on questions of narrative and cultural theory found in the work of the earlier scholars of mishnaic ritual narrative.

51. Major works of this school include: Shaye J. D. Cohen, "The Rabbi in Second Century Jewish Society," in *The Cambridge History of Judaism*, ed. W. Horbury, W. D. Davies, and J. Sturdy (Cambridge, England, 1999); 922–90; Joshua Efron, "The Great Sanhedrin in Vision and Reality," in *Studies on the Hasmonean Period* (Leiden, 1987), 287–338; Martin Goodman, *State and Society in Roman Galilee* (Totowa, N.J., 1983); David Goodblatt, *The Monarchic Principle: Studies in Jewish Self-Government in Antiquity* (Tübingen, 1994); Catherine Hezser, *The Social Structure of the Rabbinic Movement in Roman Palestine* (Tübingen, 1997); Lee I. Levine, *Rabbinic Class of Roman Palestine* (Tübingen, 1997); Seth Schwartz, *Imperialism and Jewish Society: 200 B.C.E. to 640 C.E.* (Princeton, 2001). For critiques of the more extreme formulations associated with this school see Adiel Schremer, "The Religious Orientation of Non-Rabbis in Second-Century Palestine: A Rabbinic Perspective," in *"Follow the Wise": Studies in Jewish History and Culture in Honor of Lee I. Levine*, ed. Z. Weiss et al. (University Park, Penn., 2010); Schremer, "The Sages in Palestinian Jewish Society of the Mishnah

This revisionist historiography presented a new context for reading the Mishnah. Previously, the Mishnah was viewed as a reflection and product of a well-established rabbinic hegemony over Jews and Judaism in the Land of Israel during the Roman period. Now, the Mishnah needed to be understood as emerging into a world in which the authority of the rabbis had only just been consolidated. Read in this context, it made sense to understand the Mishnah as a key tool in the rabbis' ongoing efforts to fabricate and disseminate their vision of themselves as the sole legitimate transmitters and interpreters of the Torah. Indeed, Cohn explicitly links his reading of the Mishnah to these new historical assumptions.[52] To the extent that the Mishnah can be read as containing self-reflective consideration of the ambiguities and limitations of rabbinic power, this too fits a context in which claims to authority were still emerging and quite possibly contested.

The tendency to see rabbinic authority as a central theme in the Mishnah can also be understood against the wider background of the narrative turn itself. As Ryan writes, "The increasing popularity of the term narrative also reflects the epistemological crisis of contemporary culture. 'Narrative' is what is left when belief in the possibility of knowledge is eroded."[53] The narrative turn was part and parcel of the contemporaneous trend in the academy of questioning the legitimacy and internal coherence of all forms of traditional knowledge and authority—what has come to be known as post-modernism. In the post-modern critique, the very distinction between knowledge and authority is an illusion. Narrative is the critical tool through which this illusion is generated and sustained. In this environment, the identification of the "master-narratives" underlying all systems of knowledge and authority, and the concomitant demonstration of the fictional nature of all narratives, became central elements of narrative studies. When viewed as products of post-modernity, it appears almost inevitable that these studies of narrative in the Mishnah would focus on the way these narratives construct (and perhaps also critique) the authority of the rabbis and their laws.[54]

Period: Torah Prestige and Social Standing," in *The Classic Rabbinic Literature of Eretz Israel: Introductions and Studies.* vol. 2, ed. M. Kahana et al. (Jerusalem, 2018) 553–82.1.

52. Cohn, *Memory*, 119.

53. Ryan, "Narrative," 344.

54. Indeed, the new historiography of the rabbinic period might itself be seen as a part of this post-modern challenging of received master narratives. In particular, Cohen, "The Rabbi in Second-Century Jewish Society," which relies heavily on his analysis of the corpus of case stories in the Mishnah and elsewhere in tannaitic literature.

Though the identification of rabbinic authority as a central theme of mishnaic narrative dovetails nicely with the narrative turn in general, it in fact complicates the relationship between these narrative scholars of the Mishnah and Robert Cover's work. Cover declares, "The *nomos* that I have described requires no state. And indeed . . . the creation of legal meaning—'jurisgenesis'—takes place always through an essentially cultural medium." Cover goes on to explain that *nomoi* are "normative worlds in which law is predominantly a system of meaning rather than an imposition of force."[55] Reading "Nomos and Narrative" in conjunction with Cover's later essay, "Obligation: A Jewish Jurisprudence of the Social Order,"[56] Suzanne Last Stone argues that "Nomos and Narrative describes an imaginary alternative world of legal meaning—an ideal nomos—that corresponds, in large measure, to Cover's later description of Jewish law . . . [As] a transnational system of law that is not dependent on a state . . . Jewish law provides a test case of a legal system lacking institutional hierarchy, in which law is primarily a system of legal meaning."[57]

Stone extensively critiques Cover's understanding of Jewish law as a model of his anarchistic vision, calling him to task for his "tendency to overly romanticize Jewish law."[58] She argues that he "overstated the lack of coercive forces in Jewish law," and that Cover "notes, but minimizes, the degree to which the Jewish legal system itself has the potential to support violence against its members."[59]

The conclusions of the very scholars who sought to read the Mishnah as a textual representation of a complete legal culture and worldview can be understood as an elaboration of Stone's critique of Cover. These scholars do not find a system devoid of hierarchy, social control, or institutional violence underlying the Mishnah. Rosen-Zvi highlights the Mishnah's dark fantasy of violence and sexual control. Berkowitz interprets the rabbis' portrayal of capital punishment precisely in terms of Cover's own ideas about the violence which inherently underlies conventional, state-backed judicial authority. I read the Mishnah's many legal anecdotes as literarily constructing an elite rabbinic class of rabbis who not only controlled the interpretation and development of the law, but physically embodied it. Cohn took this framework a step further, arguing that rabbis portrayed themselves as exerting total control over the Temple, the *axis mundi* itself. Notably, all

55. Cover, "Nomos and Narrative," 11, 12.
56. Cover, "Obligation."
57. c828.
58. Rosen-Zvi, *Sotah Ritual*, 870.
59. Rosen-Zvi, *Sotah Ritual*, 868, 872.

these scholars argue that the rabbis' notions of authority and social control were influenced by and created in dialogue with the legal, social, political, and ideological framework of the Roman Empire. The Roman Empire is the ultimate example of the sort of "imperial" order that Cover contrasts with the meaning-infused *nomos*. The scholars of mishnaic narrative may have portrayed the Mishnah as constructing *halakhah* as a system of meaning, but that meaning was not divorced from social hierarchy and even violence. The Mishnah's halakhic *nomos* is hardly the irenic environment Cover imagined.

The work of these scholars may even be read as challenging Cover's belief in the very concept of a law that is not enmeshed in the state. Underlying all of their readings of the Mishnah is the proposition that it is precisely in the absence of a full-fledged state and its hierarchical apparatus of social control and violence that the question of authority and enforcement became so central to the Mishnah's narratives and ideological agenda. Questions of authority preoccupied the rabbis because they lacked state-backed power. To the extent that they did have authority, it needed to be constantly reinforced through the culture that they created and disseminated.

Cover may have ultimately understood his vision—a society and system of law held together by mutual commitment to shared meaning, devoid of coercion—in aspirational terms.[60] But the evidence of the Mishnah suggests that even the construction of a literary *nomos* of the sort he imagined may not be feasible. The absence of the apparatus of the state to enforce the law in the historical world of the Mishnah's authors appears to have led to hierarchy and coercion asserting themselves in the narrative and cultural fabric meant to take the state's place. Coercive authority may be an indelible element of any legal culture or discourse worthy of the name.[61]

THE MISHNAH'S FRAMING NARRATIVES

Early twenty-first century scholarship on narrative in the Mishnah focused on the Mishnah's dominant narrative forms: ritual narratives and, to a lesser degree, legal anecdotes. In contrast, the wider body of law and narrative

60. Cover writes regarding the *nomos* that "The unification of meaning that stands at its center exists only for an instant, and that instant is itself imaginary."

61. Gillian Hadfield and Barry R. Weingast, "Law without the State: Legal Attributes and the Coordination of Decentralized Collective Punishment," *Journal of Law and Courts* 1 (2013): 3–34, make theoretical and historical cases for the viability of law without a centralized state. However, they operate with a model very different from that of Cover. Most notably they emphasize the need for enforcement through "collective punishment," and the need for a recognized central legal authority.

studies tended to focus on the "framing narratives," which account for the origins and authority of the given legal text or system. But though the Mishnah does not open with such a framing narrative, such narratives most certainly do exist. In the past five years several scholars have turned their attention to the question of mishnaic framing narratives, identifying three candidates for this group and considering their relationship with the Mishnah and its laws. These studies might be seen as representing a second, more limited phase in the narrative turn in Mishnah studies.

The most widely recognized framing narrative for the Mishnah is the chain of tradition found in the first two chapters of Mishnah *Avot,* which traces the transmission of the Torah from Moses at Sinai to the rabbis of the Yavneh generation. Scholars have traditionally taken for granted that this account represents *the* framing narrative in which the Mishnah, and rabbinic *halakhah* in general, were meant to be understood.[62] But in his 2015 article "*Avot* Reconsidered: Rethinking Rabbinic Judaism," Adiel Schremer challenged this consensus.[63] He called attention to the significant discrepancy between the hierarchy of the students of R. Yoḥanan ben Zakkai in the *Avot* narrative and in the rest of the Mishnah. *Avot* establishes R. Eliezer as the leading figure among the sages of the Yavneh generation. R. Joshua, R. Eliezer's usual disputant throughout rabbinic literature, is given no special notice. *Avot* also records an alternative position which declares R. Eleazar ben Arakh to be R. Yoḥanan ben Zakkai's leading student. The Mishnah, in contrast, consistently favors R. Joshua's rulings over those of R. Eliezer and makes no mention whatsoever of R. Eleazar ben Arakh. On this basis, Schremer argues that *Avot* reflects the work of a dissident group of rabbis who rejected the primacy attributed by the rabbinic mainstream to R. Joshua and his rulings.

Schremer goes further, arguing that the underlying values of *Avot*'s account reflect the distinctive worldview of R. Eliezer and his students. R. Eliezer is reputed to have championed the authority of received tradition from Sinai over all other sources of Torah. Schremer presents this as the central message of the chain of tradition of the first two chapters of *Avot*. In his reading, *Avot* sees the Oral Law as a homogeneous body of divinely revealed teachings revealed to Moses at Sinai. It denies the human role in the development of *halakhah* and the distinction between rulings rooted in revelation (*de-oraita*) and those rooted in rabbinic enactment (*de-rabbanan*).

Schremer contrasts the origin narrative in *Avot* with the story that opens *'Eduyot* 1.1, recounting the events that occurred "when the sages gathered at the Vineyard at Yavneh." Concerned that "the time is coming when a person

62. Schremer, "*Avot* Reconsidered," 287–88.
63. Schremer, "*Avot* Reconsidered."

will seek out a teaching from the teachings of the Torah and not find it, from the teachings of the scribes and not find it," the sages declared a new beginning for the transmission of *halakhah*, announcing, "Let us begin from Hillel and Shammai." The Tosefta then proceeds to present its version of tractate *'Eduyot*, which, like that of the Mishnah, opens with a series of disputes between Hillel and Shammai. The account presents the compilation of *'Eduyot* as the originating act of the post-Destruction sages. It parallels the scholarly consensus that *'Eduyot* was the earliest tractate to be redacted and contains the earliest strata of the Mishnah. The *'Eduyot* narrative can legitimately be read as presenting an alternative to the account of origins of the halakhic project of the Tannaim found in *Avot*.

In Schremer's reading, by choosing the gathering of the rabbis in Yavneh as its point of origin, the story emphasizes the human factor in *halakhah*. This contrasts with the *Avot* account, which sees the *halakhah* as entirely rooted in divine revelation. Schremer argues that the rabbis' primary agenda in the *'Eduyot* story is to distinguish "teachings of Torah" and form "teachings of scribes": "The sages who gathered in the vineyard at Yavneh . . . [were] emphasizing the human origin of rabbinic teachings . . . in order to pursue their grand project of adjusting both the law and the 'tradition of the fathers' to the new circumstances in which they lived."[64]

Despite the fact that this text appears only in the Tosefta and quite possibly was actively removed from the Mishnah by its editors, Schremer argues that this narrative more accurately reflects the vision of the editors of the Mishnah than the "Eliezer" account of *Avot*.

Both Rosen-Zvi and Yair Furstenberg have criticized Schremer's interpretations of these two narratives. Rosen-Zvi argues that *Avot* and its master narrative cannot be regarded as the product of a truly dissident group of rabbis. The idea of "Torah from Sinai" appears elsewhere in the Mishnah and the overall value system of *Avot* is indistinguishable from that of the rest of the Mishnah.[65] Furstenberg focuses on the *'Eduyot* narrative. He demonstrates that belief in the primacy of inherited tradition was widespread among the Tannaim and is not a specifically Eliezerian doctrine. According to Furstenberg, the revolutionary aspect of the Mishnah is not human involvement in *halakhah*, but a shift from transmitting only normative legal positions to transmitting both sides of halakhic disputes.[66] Through a

64. Schremer, "*Avot* Reconsidered," 310–11.
65. Ishay Rosen-Zvi, "The Wisdom Tradition in Rabbinic Literature and Mishnah *Avot*," in *Tracing Sapiential Traditions in Ancient Judaism*, ed. H. Najman, J-S Rey, and E. Tigchelaar (Leiden, 2016), 188–89.
66. Yair Furstenberg, "From Tradition to Controversy: New Modes of Transmission in the Teachings of Early Rabbis" (Hebrew), *Tarbiz* 85 (2018): 461–587.

careful reading of the Tosefta narrative, he shows that its primary concern is this new method of halakhic transmission and not the distinction between the divine and human aspects of the Torah.

Nevertheless, Schremer is correct in emphasizing that we have two different (though not necessarily contradictory) origin stories for the Mishnah and the entire body of tannaitic *halakhah*. The *Avot* account reflects a tradition-oriented approach to Torah study, one which sees the Torah as a monistic, revealed body of teaching. It downplays the creative role of the rabbis as shapers of the tradition and does not explicitly acknowledge that the rabbis disagreed about many aspects of the law. The Tosefta narrative emphasizes Yavneh as the beginning of the rabbinic project. By declaring that the opposing views were to be transmitted together, the rabbis embraced a certain degree of pluralism. Even if the law must ultimately be decided according to one side, within the house of study there was now room for disagreement. Each story suggests its own framework for understanding and interpreting the Mishnah. Both of these texts lie at the margins of the Mishnah. The Tosefta text does not appear in the Mishnah at all. The *Avot* narrative clearly favors R. Eliezer over R. Joshua, distinguishing it from the rest of the Mishnah.

In a recent article I present a third foundational narrative for the Mishnah, the only one which appears in the Mishnah proper: the collection of halakhic rulings attributed to "72 elders on the day on which R. Eleazar b. Azariah was seated in the yeshiva" in *mYadayim* 3.5–4.4. I argue that this passage should be read as a continuous narrative which portrays the meeting of the sages "on that day" as a rebirth of Torah, which can be compared to the original revelation at Sinai.[67]

Ideologically, the *mYadayim* narrative stands between the *Avot* and *'Eduyot* accounts. The assembly of the Yavnean sages is described as an inclusive environment in which the law is decided by the vote of the majority after rigorous dialectical debate. It thus emphasizes the importance of the human contribution to *halakhah*, particularly that of the sages who gathered in Yavneh, even more aggressively than the *'Eduyot* account. Yet, precisely as part of its effort to include conflicting voices, this story also acknowledges R. Eliezer and the more tradition-oriented approach to the law associated with him. The most extensive debate in the passage, regarding the taking of tithes in the lands of Ammon and Moab during the Sabbatical year, is ultimately resolved by R. Eliezer. Though he was not among the

---

67. Moshe Simon-Shoshan, "'On That Day': The Deeds of the Seventy-Two (m.Yadayim 3:5–4:4) as Foundational Narrative for Rabbinic Judaism," *Jewish Studies Quarterly* 29 (2022): 109–134.

sages present on that day, a student subsequently reported how the assembled rabbis ruled that the poor man's tithe is to be taken, after R. Joshua's arguments carried the day. R. Eliezer responds: "Go and tell them, do not doubt your vote, for I have received a tradition from Rabban Yoḥanan ben Zakkai, who heard it from his teacher, and his teacher from his teacher, as a ruling given to Moses from Sinai, that Ammon and Moab give the poor man's tithe in the seventh year."[68]

The text affirms R. Eliezer's superior knowledge of the tradition from Sinai and implies that tradition holds decisive authority over the deliberations of the sages. Yet it also bridges the gap between Sinai and Yavneh by declaring that at least in this case, there is no conflict between the rulings emerging from the two sources of authority.

Though this narrative appears in the Mishnah itself, its relationship to the Mishnah's dominant voice is unclear. It grants R. Eliezer a privileged position vis-à-vis R. Joshua, in contrast with the wholesale rejection of R. Eliezer's ruling in the rest of the Mishnah. The *mYadayim* passage also marginalizes two of the leading figures in the Mishnah: Rabban Gamaliel and R. Akiba. In the rest of the Mishnah, R. Gamaliel is repeatedly described as the leader of the sages of the Yavneh generation who imposes his will upon them, especially R. Joshua.[69] Here R. Gamaliel appears only at the end of the passage, and he is accorded no special status. He debates R. Joshua as an equal, and ultimately loses.[70] Similarly, R. Akiba is arguably the most dominant sage in the Mishnah.[71] Yet according to the *mYadayim* narrative, he was not present at that critical meeting of the sages and his positions were repeatedly rejected there. It would thus appear that *mYadayim* 4.1–4 and the sources on which it draws is the work of a circle which had a somewhat different ideological and halakhic perspective from those who were responsible for the Mishnah overall.

If the first phase of the narrative turn in Mishnah studies viewed the Mishnah much as Cover presents the Hebrew Bible at the beginning of "Nomos and Narrative"—as a text combining laws and narratives to reflect a complete *nomos*—this second phase suggests an understanding of the Mishnah more akin to Cover's presentation of the United States Constitution at the end of his essay. There, Cover recounts the varying historical narratives that American jurists and activists have used to frame the Constitution and

68. mYad 4.3.
69. See especially mRH 2.8–9.
70. mYad 4.4.
71. See J. N. Epstein, *Prolegomena ad litteras tannaiticas* (Hebrew; Jerusalem, 1957), 71; Abraham Goldberg, "The Mishnah: A Studybook of Halacha," in *The Literature of the Sages*, ed. S. Safrai (Assen, 1987) 217–18.

the debates over its interpretation that have resulted. For all its narrative content, the Mishnah is not introduced by an authoritative account explaining the origins and authority of the text and those who produced it, unlike the Torah and many other ancient legal texts. Rather, there were multiple narratives circulating around the Mishnah's perimeter, each reflecting a somewhat different perspective and, apparently, a different group within the rabbinic community. As in Cover's vision of constitutional interpretation, these competing narratives represent alternative frameworks for interpreting the Mishnah and understanding the ultimate nature of rabbinic law. Already at the time of the Mishnah's publication, the Mishnah was a contested work, which could only be read in the context of the pluralistic discourse and society in which it was situated.

CONCLUSION

In the early 2000s a new trend in Mishnah scholarship emerged which called significant attention to the narrative elements of the Mishnah. This development can be viewed as the product of the "narrative turn" which overtook the humanities and social sciences in the later decades of the twentieth century. They reflect the impact of Robert Cover's seminal work in founding the law and narrative movement. This body of Mishnah scholarship began to read the Mishnah not just as a technical legal work, but as a source of religious and social meaning in which law plays a central but not exclusive part. As such, they portray the Mishnah as a literary *nomos*. Yet the *nomos* these scholars see in the Mishnah is not the peaceful, egalitarian community that Cover envisioned. It is a community ruled by an elite group of rabbis whose authority is sometimes exercised through violent means. The Mishnah may at times question, limit, or complicate certain elements or expressions of this authority structure, but its overall legitimacy is never challenged. More recent scholarship has viewed the Mishnah through the lens of a set of competing framing narratives situated at the Mishnah's margins, thus challenging earlier tendencies rooted in Neusner's pioneering work which read the Mishnah as a self-contained work whose narratives and meaning are to be found from within.

13. Holiness in the Mishnah

Sarit Kattan Gribetz

The concept of holiness is prevalent in the rabbinic corpus, especially in the Mishnah. The root *k-d-s* appears a few hundred times throughout the Mishnah's tractates rather than regarding a select topic or two.[1] Concerns about the status of holiness—whether regarding the temple, sacrifices, consecrated produce, Sabbaths and holidays, sacred writings, sexual relations, and so on—underpin many of the Mishnah's halakhic discussions. One of the Mishnah's orders, devoted to sacrifices, is titled *Kodashim* ("Holy Things"), and another, about the laws of purity and impurity, *Tohorot* ("Purities"); both discuss the topic of holiness extensively, and describe the temple (*beit ha-mikdash*), its rituals, and its rules throughout. But discussions of holiness are not limited to these orders nor to the realm of the temple and its cultic practices. In the order of *Nashim* ("Women"), which deals with all aspects related to marriage and divorce, the tractate on betrothals is called *Kidushin* ("Betrothal"). The order of *Mo'ed*, devoted to the laws of Sabbaths, festivals, and fasts, discusses topics related to holiness, not least because of the notion that Sabbaths are "holy" and festivals are "holy times" (*mikraei kodesh*), both distinct from mundane time (and from each other), and because new moons (that is, new months) are "made holy" (*mekadshin oto*). The orders of *Zera'im* and *Nezikin* also draw on notions of holiness in discussions of tithes, temple rituals, and sacred writings, among other topics. This chapter does not take a stand on whether holiness was more or less important to the rabbis of the Mishnah than to their predecessors.[2]

---

1. I exclude discussion of biblical passages appearing in the Mishnah that cite biblical passages, e.g. mAvot 6:10.

2. Tzvi Novick, "Holiness in the Rabbinic Period," in *Holiness in Jewish Thought*, ed. A. L. Mittleman (Oxford, 2018), 35–53, argues that "holiness becomes less important in the rabbinic period . . . This is a claim not about what holiness *is* for the rabbis, but about its theological or cultural significance" (35–36).

Rather, it maintains that the category of holiness is central to the Mishnah's worldview, and thus seeks to determine what holiness means in the Mishnah (including in relation to earlier conceptions of holiness upon which the Mishnah draws), and how those whose traditions are included within the Mishnah as well as those who compiled the Mishnah sought to present holiness to themselves and to those who encountered or observed mishnaic laws, rituals, and narratives.

I study the Mishnah's use of the term "holy" (*kadosh*), how it conceptualizes the idea of "holiness" (*kedusha*), and how holiness informs the mishnaic project more broadly.[3] The term and the concept are central in biblical texts, especially in the Priestly source (including the Holiness Code) and Deuteronomist sources, and are likewise employed widely in second temple literature, including the Dead Sea Scrolls, and in rabbinic sources, both tannaitic and later. In all of these contexts, "holiness" does not have a single meaning or usage; different texts and strata employ the notion of holiness for a variety of interrelated ends, such that it is a dynamic category and concept. Here I do not provide a survey of the concept of holiness in all of Jewish antiquity, nor even in the rabbinic corpus writ large, as much work on this topic has already been published by previous scholars.[4] Instead, I analyze the conceptualizations of holiness specifically in the Mishnah, and contend that we come closer to understanding the mishnaic project when we recog-

3. The terms "sacred/sacredness" and "holy/holiness" are interconnected, but I generally use "holy/holiness" in this chapter as it is the term most often used to translate the Hebrew *k-d-s*.

4. One of the foundational studies on holiness is Rudolf Otto, *The Idea of the Holy: An Inquiry into the Non-rational Factor in the Idea of the Divine and Its Relation to the Rational, Revised with Additions*, trans. John W. Harvery (Oxford, 1936), first published as *Das Heilige* in 1917, on which see also Robert Orsi, "The Problem of the Holy," in *The Cambridge Companion to Religious Studies*, ed. R. A. Orsi (New York, 2012), 84–105, who discusses some of the problematic ways "holiness" is employed in religious discourse and in the field of religious studies. For brief but helpful overviews of the concept of holiness in biblical sources, see Christine Hayes, *Introduction to the Bible* (New Haven, 2012), 151–52, and Cana Werman, "The Concept of Holiness and the Requirements of Purity in Second Temple and Tannaitic Literature," ed. M. Poorthuis and J. Schwartz, *Purity and Holiness: The Heritage of Leviticus* (Leiden, 2000), 163–79. Jacob Milgrom, *Leviticus 1–16* (New York, 1998), is an especially foundational study of holiness in the Hebrew Bible; see also Baruch A. Levine, "The Language of Holiness: Perceptions of the Sacred in the Hebrew Bible," in *In Pursuit of Meaning: Collected Studies of Baruch A. Levine*, ed. A. D. Gross (University Park, 2011), 321–34. On holiness in later Jewish contexts, see Eliezer Berkovits, "The Concept of Holiness," in *Essential Essays on Judaism*, ed. D. Hazony (Jerusalem, 2002), 247–314; Jacob Neusner, *A History of the Mishnaic Law of Holy Things*, 6 vols. (Leiden, 1978–80); Max Kadushin, *Worship and Ethics: A Study in Rabbinic Judaism* (Evanston, 1964), esp. 216–37; and, more recently, an in-depth over-

nize how central the idea of holiness is to it and probe the Mishnah's specific web of conceptions, some of which draw upon biblical and second temple precedents and others of which innovate or alter how holiness is imagined in intriguing new directions.[5]

I define "holy" and "holiness" (and the associated terms "sacred" and "sacredness," more common in both modern scholarship and popular discourse and usually used synonymously) as an emic category that the Mishnah itself uses and develops, rather than as a broad etic category that scholars employ to describe religious phenomena past or present. I therefore limit my analysis to what the Mishnah associates with the notion of *kedusha* (holiness), leaving aside the many ways the Mishnah conceptualizes adjacent topics that we might subsume under our scholarly-heuristic category

---

view of the concept of holiness from antiquity to modern Jewish thought in Alan L. Mittleman, ed., *Holiness in Jewish Thought* (Oxford, 2018); especially relevant are essays by Elsie R. Stern ("Reclaiming the Priestly Theology"), Tzvi Novick ("Holiness in the Rabbinic Period"), and Martin Lockshin ("Why is Holiness Not Contagious?"). On the transformation of the idea of a "holy nation" and Israel as a "holy people" from biblical to second temple and rabbinic sources, see Martha Himmelfarb, *A Kingdom of Priests: Ancestry and Merit in Ancient Jewish Culture and Context* (Philadelphia, 2006). On rabbinic sources, see Hannah K. Harrington, *Holiness: Rabbinic Judaism and the Graeco-Roman World* (London and New York, 2001); Eliezer Diamond, *Holy Men and Hunger Artists: Fasting and Asceticism in Rabbinic Culture* (New York, 2003); Michael Rosenberg, "Kedushah (Holiness) in Rabbinic Judaism: What Holiness Meant to the Sages of the Talmud," *My Jewish Learning* (https://www.myjewishlearning.com/article /kedushah-holiness-in-rabbinic-judaism/). On sacred space see Seth Daniel Kunin, *God's Place in the World: Sacred Space and Sacred Place in Judaism* (New York, 1998); on the holiness of synagogues, see Steven Fine, *This Holy Place: On Sanctity of the Synagogue in the Greco-Roman World* (Notre Dame, 1997); on the sacredness of cities, see Naftali S. Cohn, "Sacred Space in the Mishnah: From Temple to Synagogue and . . . City," in *La question de la "sacerdotalisation" dans le judaïsme synagogal, le christianisme et le rabbinisme*, ed. S. C. Mimouni and L. Painchaud (Turnhout, 2018); on sanctification of places, see Eyal Ben Eliyahu, "The Rabbinic Polemic against Sanctification of Sites," *Journal for the Study of Judaism* 40.2 (2009): 260–80. On the holiness of scripture, see Michael L. Satlow, *How the Bible Became Holy* (New Haven, 2014); Shamma Friedman, "'The Holy Scriptures Defile the Hands': The Transformation of a Biblical Concept in Rabbinic Theology," in *Minhah le-Nahum: Biblical and Other Studies Presented to Nahum M. Sarna in Honour of his 70th Birthday*, ed. M. Brettler and M. Fishbane (Sheffield, 1993), 117–32. On holiness and sexuality, see Naomi Koltun-Fromm, *Hermeneutics of Holiness: Ancient Jewish and Christian Notions of Sexuality and Religious Community* (New York, 2010). On holiness in ancient Christianity, see Patricia Cox Miller, *Corporeal Imagination: Signifying the Holy in Late Antique Christianity* (Philadelphia, 2009).

5. Here I follow a similar methodology I employed with Mika Ahuvia in our article "'The Daughters of Israel': An Analysis of the Term in Late Ancient Jewish Sources," *Jewish Quarterly Review* 108.1 (2018): 1–27.

of "holiness" but that the Mishnah itself presents under rubrics other than *kedusha*. This approach draws on Naomi Koltun-Fromm's notion of the "hermeneutics of holiness," which studies how and why a text or set of texts presents or names certain practices, dispositions, spaces, times, and so on with the language of holiness.[6]

I begin by outlining the ways the Mishnah conceives of the category of the holy, exploring notions of the divine, the temple and other spaces, sacrifices and consecrated objects (animals, produce, vessels, etc.), times (of the week, month, and year), and certain types or groups of people (priests, Nazarites, Israel)—all of whom the Mishnah conceives of as "holy" in some way. I then turn to how the Mishnah imagines holiness to interact with other overarching categories, including (im)purity and the mundane; presents holiness itself as variegated and hierarchal; and conceptualizes "holiness" as an abstract category. I conclude by addressing how the concept of holiness fits into the broader project of the Mishnah.[7]

Following recent scholarship, I argue that in the Mishnah holiness functions simultaneously as a halakhic category, an organizing principle, an ontological state, and an aspirational goal; is deeply enmeshed with ritual and other types of actions; and is used to conceptualize and regulate human relationships with the world, other people, objects, spaces, and times, in addition to its relationship with God and the divine realm. While holiness remains firmly connected to the temple precinct and cult, as numerous mishnaic passages attest, the Mishnah's category of holiness is not confined to the temple (nor to the Sabbath, with which it is likewise connected in biblical sources). Rather, we find in the Mishnah an expanded concept of holiness that reaches beyond the temple both spatially and conceptually—to walled cities, synagogues, city squares, marriage and sexual relationships, calendrical ritual, sacred texts, and the Hebrew language. In these varied contexts, particular actions (such as prayer or betrothal) and contents (such as sacred writings in a synagogue) deem objects, people, and places holy or consecrated though they are not connected to the temple. Yet even within its discussions of the temple, sacrifices, tithes, and consecrated objects, the Mishnah develops its ideas about holiness in ways that are not confined to the space or time of the temple, adapting key concepts from the realm of the temple to its overarching worldview, and incorporating ideas from outside the temple to its interpretation of the holiness of the temple. These shifts

6. Koltun-Fromm, *Hermeneutics of Holiness*.

7. Situating the Mishnah's concept of holiness within its Greco-Roman context is another important task, but beyond the scope of this essay.

not only expand the realms of holiness but also provide the mechanisms by which to contain or neutralize holiness through human agency.

CATEGORIES OF HOLINESS

Reading through the Mishnah, it becomes clear that the discourse of holiness permeates several areas of inquiry and practice, and becomes one of the threads that weaves its way throughout the entire composition. Here, I organize the material into five categories: (1) God as the source or epitome of holiness; (2) the temple as a holy place with various areas of different levels of holiness, along with additional places considered holy; (3) consecrated items, including property, produce, animals, vessels, and other objects that have the status of holy and thus must be handled with particular care; (4) times of the week and year, including Sabbaths, festivals, and new moons, that are considered holy and thus require certain guidelines to be followed at those times, to ensure that the sanctity of those days is respected and cultivated; and (5) people, whose status of holiness sometimes depends on their inherent identity, social group, personal status, or status of purity.

"The Holy One Blessed Be He" and "The Holy Spirit"

In line with biblical and second temple sources, the Mishnah defines God as holy and characterizes God as the source of holiness. Even though the main contexts in which the Mishnah develops the idea of holiness relate to the temple and its objects and rituals, rather than direct discussions about God and the divine realm, nonetheless the Mishnah's underlying concern in its discussions of holiness is proximity or consecration to the divine, and other ways in which divine presence, including in texts and language, must be handled with care. It is perhaps no surprise, therefore, that the Mishnah marks God's holiness in a new way, through its divine nomenclature.[8] This is most apparent in the name *ha-kadosh baruh hu*, "The Holy One Blessed Be He," not attested in earlier sources.[9] One rabbinic blessing formula includes

---

8. While biblical sources often describe God as holy (e.g. Leviticus 19:2, "Be holy, for I, your Lord God am holy"), the name "The Holy One" is not attested until the Mishnah.

9. mAvot 3:1–2, 4:22, 5:4, 6:10–11, 12; mYom 8:9; mMak 3:16; mNed 3:11; mSot 5:5; mSan 4:5, 10:6; m'Ukts 3:12. On the term in rabbinic sources, see A. Spanier, "Die Gottesbezeichnungen המקום und הקדוש ברוך הוא in der frühtalmudischen Literatur," *Monatsschrift für Geschichte und Wissenschaft des Judentums* 66.10/12 (1922): 309–14. Certain prayer rituals evoke the holiness of God, such as the *kedusha* prayer (based on Isaiah 6:3 and Ezekiel 3:12), mentioned in tBer 1:11.

a description of God as the one who "made us holy through His command-ments," a phrase already in use in tannaitic sources, though it is noticeably absent in the Mishnah.[10] The rabbinic concept of *ruaḥ ha-kodesh*, "the Holy Spirit," which takes its cue from Genesis 1:2's *ruaḥ elohim* ("divine spirit or wind"), refers to a divine and even prophetic element that is present on earth in some way.[11] Because the Mishnah's halakhic discussions often veer into the technicalities of holiness, the connection to the divine can some-times be overlooked or forgotten. But the Mishnah's conception of holiness returns to the divine as the locus or source of holiness; times, places, ob-jects, people, and activities proximate, related to, or sanctified by or for God ultimately derive their holiness from a divine source.

Holy Places

In the Mishnah, certain places are considered holy.[12] First and foremost, the temple (*ha-mikdash*) represents the epitome of a holy place. As Naf-tali Cohn writes: "the extensive amount of text devoted to the Temple, to the activities done therein, and to the sacred objects associated with it, tes-tify to the Temple's singular importance as locus and source of holiness in the mishnaic understanding."[13] The Mishnah's focus on the holiness of the cult and its spatial dimensions derives from biblical sources. In Ex 25:8, for example, God announces that the Israelites should "build me a sanctuary (*mikdash*), and I will dwell among them," and Lev 24:9 instructs Aaron and his sons to eat in a "holy place" (*makom kadosh*).[14] This space—first the tab-

10. E.g. tBer 6:9–14; tPes 10:13. On the language of blessings, see Moshe Bar-Asher, "The Formula of Blessings Ordained by the Sages" (Hebrew), *Kenishta: Studies of the Synagogue World* 4 (2010): 27–49; Moshe Bar-Asher, "The Presence of Mishnaic He-brew in Blessing Formulas" (Hebrew), *Leshonenu: A Journal for the Study of the Hebrew Language and Cognate Subjects* 76.3 (2014): 247–64; on the emergence of blessings for fulfilling commandments, and the evocation of Israel's holiness in these blessings, see Tzvi Novick, "Blessings over Misvot: The Origins of a Category," *Hebrew Union College Annual* 79 (2008): 69–86. Novick suggests a possible polemical reasons for the omission in the Mishnah, given similar practices in Gentile and sectarian contexts and the Mish-nah's hesitation to use God's name in vain.

11. mSot 9:15, discussed below. On *ruaḥ ha-kodesh*, see Peter Schäfer, *Di Vorstellung vom heiligen Geist in der rabbinischen Literatur* (Munich, 1972).

12. I examine the idea of sacred space in Jewish antiquity more broadly in Sarit Kat-tan Gribetz, "Sacred Spaces," in *A Companion to Jews and Judaism, 3rd Century BCE–7th Century CE*, ed. G. Kessler and N. Koltun-Fromm (Hoboken, N.J., 2020), 455–75.

13. Cohn, "Sacred Space in the Mishnah," 89.

14. The Mishnah uses the biblical terms *mikdash* (e.g. mSuk 5.5, mSot 7.6–7, mMS 1.5–6, mBer 9:5, mShek 6:4, mBekh 4, mGit 5:4, mHor 2:4–7, mYom 2:1; mTa'an 4:6;

ernacle and then the temple—consists of different areas, each with distinct levels of holiness, including the *kodesh* and *kodesh ha-kodashim*. The closer one moves to the center of the tabernacle or temple, the holier that space becomes. The Mishnah builds on these biblical associations in its characterization of the temple, conception of the different areas of the temple and their relative holiness, and description of temple practices, many of which concern themselves with maintaining the holiness of the precinct and those who pass through it.[15] The Mishnah also addresses the disposal of consecrated items, including sacrificial leftovers, needed to maintain the integrity of the temple's holiness. Hillel Mali has noted that in contrast to earlier sources that assume the temple destroys or conceals its sacred waste, tannaitic sources imagine the unwanted remains to leave the holy precinct of the temple and to be absorbed by the surrounding landscape, a fundamental shift in notions of holiness.[16]

While the Mishnah's focus on the sanctity of the temple might appear self-evident, it requires some explanation, for despite the Mishnah's reliance on biblical conceptions of holiness, it also introduces significant changes. Cohn identifies one important shift from biblical conceptions of the temple's holiness, derived from God's presence in that space and other historical or natural associations with it, to mishnaic ideas about the temple's holiness, primarily a product of the activities performed within it and for it.[17] He writes: "the Mishnah appears to emphasize the centrality of human action in creating and maintaining sacred space. People make Temple space sacred through ritual activity and through acts of exclusion, both of which may additionally contribute to the sense of sacredness of the place by constructing boundaries."[18] In this reading, the temple is holy because of what occurs within it, rather than inherently holy because of God's sup-

---

mTam 7, mShek 1:3, 2:1, among many references) as well as *makom kadosh* (holy place, e.g., mZev 11:4–6) to refer to the temple, along with the non-biblical terms *beit ha-mikdash* (mAvot 5:5, 6:10; mMK 3:6; mMen 10:5; mMS 5:2; mNaz 5:4; mSot 9:12, 15; mSuk 3:12; mRH 1:3–4, 4:1, 3, 4; mTa'an 4:8; mMid 1:1; mTam 1:1) and *beit kodesh ha-kodashim* (mBer 4:5–6, 9:5; mMid 4:5, 7; mNeg 14:10; mPar 3:9).

15. Distinctions between different areas of the temple precinct appear prominently, for example, in tractate *Yoma*, which details the rituals in the temple, including the Holy of Holies, on the Day of Atonement. The holiness of the temple also interacts with the status of items that come into that holy space, e.g. in mZev 9:2, in which the status of disqualified items is determined by whether they were disqualified in a sacred area or not.

16. Hillel Mali, "The Removal of the Temple Leftovers and the Tannaitic Holiness Laws" (Hebrew), *Tarbiz* (forthcoming).

17. Cohn, "Sacred Space in the Mishnah," which builds on the work of Barukh M. Bokser, "Approaching Sacred Space," *Harvard Theological Review* 78 (1985): 279–99.

18. Cohn, "Sacred Space in the Mishnah," 89.

posed or prior presence.[19] This shift tracks onto similar developments in the realm of mishnaic purity and impurity. Mira Balberg writes, for example, "that the rabbis [of the Mishnah] construct the drama of contracting, conveying, and managing impurity as a manifestation of the relations between oneself and one's human and nonhuman surroundings, and . . . they create a new array of physical and mental purity-related practices that both assume and generate a particular kind of subject."[20] The Mishnah's conception of holiness seems to function in similar ways, constructed by and constructing relationships between humans and their nonhuman surroundings through particular actions and declarations, and thereby also cultivating particular selves and subjects.

Moreover, while the Mishnah regards the city of Jerusalem and the land of Israel as extensions or expansions of the temple, as holy, it provides an overall narrower scope of holy space.[21] Eyal Ben Eliyahu has observed, for example, that the Mishnah's limited view of the temple and the city and land in which it is situated as holy represents a second key difference between biblical and mishnaic attitudes.[22] Throughout its narratives of the patriarchs and matriarchs, the exodus, sojourn in the desert, revelation at Sinai, and conquest of the land, biblical passages identify many locations, including mountains, as significant and worthy of memorializing. Recall, moreover, that in biblical sources the tabernacle moved from location to location before the temple became a permanent structure, such that the "holy place" was not presented as necessarily stationary. The Mishnah, in contrast, privileges the land of Israel, its walled cities, the city of Jerusalem, and especially its temple as the locus of holiness.[23] Tractate *Kelim*, in Ben

19. Some might be inclined to view this shift as part of the Mishnah's move towards more nominalist conceptualizations, on which see e.g. Daniel R. Schwartz, "Law and Truth: On Qumran-Sadducean and Rabbinic Views of Law," *The Dead Sea Scrolls: Forty Years of Research*, ed. D. Diamant and U. Rappaport (Leiden and Jerusalem, 1992), 229–40; Jeffrey L. Rubenstein, "Nominalism and Realism in Qumranic and Rabbinic Law: A Reassessment," *Dead Sea Discoveries* 6.2 (1999): 157–83. Novick emphasizes, however, that rabbinic sources nonetheless retain the belief that holiness is still a natural property: "Rabbinic texts do take some steps toward nominalization of holiness, but there is every reason to suppose that the rabbis continue to think of holiness as a natural property, like mass" (36).

20. Mira Balberg, *Purity, Body, and Self in Early Rabbinic Literature* (Berkeley, 2014), 2–3.

21. E.g. mMeg 3:1 and mKel 1.

22. Ben Eliyahu, "The Rabbinic Polemic against Sanctification of Sites," 260–80; Werman, "The Concept of Holiness," 175–79, makes a similar observation, a trend she traces in the book of Jubilees and early Christian texts as well.

23. See especially the *locus classicus*, mKel 1:6–9, discussed at more length below.

Eliyahu's words, links "the holiness of the innermost circle—the Temple—to the sanctity of the outmost one—the entire land of Israel" through its explanation that the land of Israel is holy primarily because the barley offering (*omer*), the first fruits, and the two loaves of bread need to be brought from the land to the temple.[24] In this conception of holy place, the Mishnah centers the temple—and by extension the city and land in which the temple sits—to the exclusion of most other holy places.

The Temple, the city of Jerusalem, and the land of Israel are not the only places that the Mishnah characterizes as holy, however. The Mishnah labels other spaces, such as walled cities or villages within the Land of Israel,[25] cities more generally,[26] city squares,[27] and synagogues[28] as holy too, likely because they became sites for rituals and public gatherings. Cohn notes that the "spaces of cities were made sacred in multiple ways by human activity—by ritual activity, the construction of boundaries and spatial interiority, the parallel relationship established to the Temple, the location of Torah scrolls, and by the presence of a large crowd of the people of Israel," a specifically rabbinic outlook on the relationship between holiness and space that complements the Mishnah's notion of the temple's holiness deriving from the rituals and actions performed for and within it.[29] Cohn also observes that the Mishnah's presentation of cities as holy aligns with similar contemporaneous Roman attitudes towards urban centers in the region; for example, coins labeled cities such as Sepphoris, home to a vibrant rabbinic community, with the term *hieras*.[30]

Steven Fine, in his study of synagogues in antiquity, highlights the specific ways the Mishnah marks synagogues as holy places.[31] Synagogues were regarded as holy for a number of reasons: they house sacred writings (themselves recognized as holy—more on this below), serve as spaces for the recitation and study of scripture and prayers (including the *Amidah*, which

24. Ben Eliyahu, "The Rabbinic Polemic against Sanctification of Sites," 263; it is worth noting that the remainder of Ben Eliyahu's analysis focuses on amoraic and late midrashim, primarily from the region of Palaestine, suggesting that the rabbinic polemics against other sacred places in the region might fit most comfortably in a fourth- and fifth-century context in which Christian pilgrimage and Christianization flourished.

25. mKel 1:7.

26. mZev 14:4–8.

27. mMeg 3:1.

28. E.g. mMeg 3:1–3.

29. Cohn, "Sacred Space in the Mishnah," 85, which analyzes mKel 1:6–9.

30. Cohn, "Sacred Space in the Mishnah," 116–17.

31. Fine, *This Holy Place*, esp. 35–60, on tannaitic sources; the analysis is extended further in Cohn, "Sacred Space in the Mishnah," 100–104.

reflects on God's holiness in its blessings),[32] gather the community in worship, and were regarded as substitutes for (but not conflated with) the temple in Jerusalem, a process Fine terms "Templizaton."[33] Nonetheless, even in a single mishnaic discussion, rabbis disagree about the nature of a synagogue's holiness and whether and in what circumstances a synagogue, despite its holy status, might be sold, confirming that different rabbinic figures surely held differing notions of the relationship between holiness and space.[34] Even so, as both Cohn and Fine argue, the Mishnah uses the template of the temple's holiness to conceive of the holiness of cities and synagogues, even as these two types of places are not conflated with the temple nor do they neatly derive their holiness directly from it.

Holy Objects

The Mishnah identifies sacrifices, heave offerings and tithes (*terumot* and *ma'asrot*), and many other items as "holy" ("separated" for special use), in that they are consecrated to the temple, must remain in the temple, or are considered part of temple property unless they are redeemed or, in the case of some sacrifices, may only be consumed in the Temple Court.[35] These include dedicated produce or property, such as fields;[36] consecrated bread, water, and food;[37] firstborns;[38] consecrated animals and sacrificial meat;[39] consecrated vessels, and vessels and ovens used to hold consecrated things;[40]

---

32. And in the *kedusha*, though the Mishnah does not mention it explicitly; see instead tBer 1:19, on which Fine, *This Holy Place*, 53.

33. Fine, *This Holy Place*, 36; see e.g. mMeg 3:3, which explicitly links the temple with synagogues. mSuk 4:1–3 suggests that rituals performed in the temple were practiced in other cities after the temple's destruction, implying that they were performed in synagogues. On the relationship between the temple and synagogues in the second temple and rabbinic period, see also Shaye J. D. Cohen, "The Temple and the Synagogue," in *The Cambridge History of Judaism*, vol. 3: *The Early Roman Period*, ed. W. Horbury, W. D. Davies, and J. Sturdy (Cambridge, 1999), 298–325.

34. mMeg 3:2, discussed in Fine, *This Holy Place*, 41.

35. E.g. mBik 3:12; mBets 5:2, 5; mBekh 8:8; mHor 2:5; mTer 6:6.

36. E.g. mShab 18:1; mBM 4:7; mHal 1:3, 4:9; mYev 11:7; mKet 5:2–4; mKer 6:8; mShevu 6:4–5; mShek 8:8; mNeg 14:3; mPe'ah 7:8; mPes 2:5, 4:8. mNaz 5 discusses which things can be de-consecrated and which cannot.

37. e.g. mToh 1:9; mSan 8:2.

38. E.g. mBekh.

39. E.g. mBekh 9:1; mZev 10:2–6, 14:9–10; mBK 4:3; mBekh 5:1, 6:11; mPes 3:8; mYev 11:7; mKer 3:4, 5; mShevu 1–2; m'Orl 3:3; mMen 13:9; mMe'il 2:1.

40. E.g. mZev 3:2; mOhal 5:5, 18:4; mZev 9:7; mKel 25:9; mMen 9:5. The term כלי קדש appears in 1 Chronicles 22:19.

priestly clothing;[41] and the ashes of the Red Heifer.[42] Many of these objects were not considered intrinsically holy, but rather consecrated ("made holy") through dedication to the temple or use in the sacrificial process, and thus gain the status of holiness and must be treated accordingly.[43] The process of de-consecration occupies much mishnaic attention as well.

The language of holiness is used extensively in mNaz 5, for example, to discuss items that are "dedicated" (*hekdesh*), including livestock, coins, and liquids; the language extends towards the Nazarite himself, as someone who has dedicated himself to God and thus follows certain restrictions because of his consecrated status. In the case of consecrated ("holy") meat, the Mishnah explains that those who left the city of Jerusalem with consecrated meat in their possession must either burn it (if they have passed Mount Scopus) or, if they are still in the orbit of the city, return to the city and burn it (an interesting interplay between holiness and space). Certain rituals differ depending on whether the item that will be touched or consumed is considered holy.[44] Body parts, too, needed sometimes to be sanctified, such as when mYom 3:2 discusses the sanctification of hands and feet in the context of the sacrifices on the Day of Atonement, and when mHal 1:9 and mBik 2:1 note that *hallah*, *terumah*, and *bikurim* require hand washing.[45]

Scholars have noted that the Mishnah fundamentally reconceptualizes biblical ideas of contagious holiness, though scholars disagree about precisely what changes and how (biblical sources themselves do not contain a completely consistent perspective).[46] Various biblical sources suggest that

41. E.g. mTam 1:1.

42. In mPar 6–7 the person who mixes the ashes of the Red Heifer with water is called "he who consecrates," the ashes are called "holy," and the act of mixing is likewise described with the terminology of holiness.

43. Mira Balberg, *Blood for Thought: The Reinvention of Sacrifice in Early Rabbinic Literature* (Berkeley, 2017), 95–97, discusses the process through which blood became holy through sacrifice.

44. E.g. mHag 2:5–7, 3 explains that to consume holy things one needs not only to rinse one's hands but fully immerse them.

45. Cf. mHag 2:5, which suggests washing hands for mundane things, in contrast to these other mishnayot, and Mk 7:1–5 and Mt 15:1–2, which assume that Jews wash hands before eating anything but do not mention defilement, on which see Chaim Milikowsky, "Reflections on Hand-Washing, Hand-Purity, and Holy Scripture in Rabbinic Literature," in *Purity and Holiness: The Heritage of Leviticus*, ed. M. Poorthuis and J. Schwartz (Leiden, 2000), 149–62.

46. E.g. Jacob Milgrom, "Sancta Contagion and Altar/City Asylum," *Congress Volume Vienna 1980* (Leiden, 1981): 278–320; Friedman, "'The Holy Scriptures Defile the Hands,'" 117–32; Mali, "The Removal of the Temple Leftovers," each of which takes a

holy objects transfer holiness through touch.[47] Leviticus 6:20, for instance, notes that "anything that touches [the grain offering] shall become holy" (כל אשר יגע בבשרה יקדש) and Ex 29:37 warns that "whatever touches the altar shall become holy" (כל הנגע במזבח יקדש). Such passages suggest that things that come into contact with holy things (the grain offering and the altar, in these specific examples) themselves adopt that same status, thus imagining a transfer of holiness to objects previously not holy. Tannaitic sources, the Mishnah among them, limit such biblical ideas of contagious holiness in several ways. Most strikingly, mZev 9:1 significantly reinterprets Ex 29:37 when it states that "the altar sanctifies that which is suited for it" (המזבח מקדש את הראוי לו), implying that only objects that are valid for sacrifices (proper for sanctification) become holy when they are placed on the altar, while other things that are placed on the altar, including sacrifices that are invalid (and thus improper for sanctification) can be removed from the altar without having become consecrated through contact with the altar.[48] As Shamma Friedman summarizes, "The basic thrust of these laws is the fact that contact does *not* impart automatic holiness."[49] Similarly, tannaitic sources imagine the absorption of holiness to be limited to instances of absorption of actual liquid from something holy, rather than absorption of holiness itself, as biblical sources posit.[50] This is not to say that holiness becomes an entirely halakhic category, but that the way it is conceptualized as an ontological substance that impacts other things shifts in the Mishnah and contemporaneous rabbinic sources.[51]

The Mishnah does not only deem holy items related to the temple, Priests, Levites, and Nazarites. It also discusses holy writings and a holy language. Identifying texts as holy has a long history in the ancient world, into which the Mishnah's terminology fits.[52] Jan Bremmer has argued that the idea of sacred books or texts seems to be a product of the Hellenistic period, which then persisted in later periods: 1 Maccabees 12:9 mentions *hagia*

---

different approach to the transformation between biblical and tannaitic notions of the transfer of holiness.

47. E.g. Ex 29:37, 30:29; Lev 6:20; Deut 22:9; Isa 65:5; Ezek 46:20; discussed in Friedman, "'The Holy Scriptures Defile the Hands,'" 120–27.

48. Friedman, "'The Holy Scriptures Defile the Hands,'" 123, 127.

49. Friedman, "'The Holy Scriptures Defile the Hands,'" 129.

50. Friedman, "'The Holy Scriptures Defile the Hands,'" 122.

51. On which see also Neusner's multi-volume *A History of the Mishnaic Law of Holy Things*.

52. Jan N. Bremmer, "From Holy Books to Holy Bible: An Itinerary from Ancient Greek to Modern Islam via Second Temple Judaism and Early Christianity," in *Authoritative Scriptures in Ancient Judaism*, ed. M. Popović (Leiden, 2010), 327–60.

biblia; Alexander Polyhistor uses the term *hiera biblos*; Philo uses *hieros nomos, hieros logos, hierai graphai, hierai anagraphai,* and related terms; Paul refers to *hagiai graphai*; 2 Timothy to *hiera grammata*; and Josephus, quoting a letter of Augustus, to *hiera grammata,* while he himself uses *hierai bibloi*.[53] Still, the Mishnah's focus on the practical, ritual, and legal dimensions of these writings' holiness is unique; mShab 16:1 explains that "holy writings" (*kitvei kodesh*), presumably scrolls that contain scripture, must be saved from fire on the Sabbath, whether or not they are read, and m'Eruv 10:3 discusses whether the obligation to rest on the Sabbath includes a prohibition against moving holy books that have fallen. Both mishnaic discussions debate whether activities that violate the Sabbath are permitted if they save such holy writings from destruction or desecration. In its discussion of what defiles the hands, tractate *Yadayim* explains that handling "holy writings" (which include, in this case, phylacteries and the edges of scrolls) makes one's hands impure,[54] and insists that handling sacred texts requires special care.[55] In this context, the category of holy writings is an explicitly technical one, denoting scriptural texts with at least 85 letters, written in Assyrian script, on parchment, with ink.[56] Holy writings are also treated as special forms of property that cannot be divided, even during ownership disputes. For instance, according to mBB 1:6, "holy writings" are never divided between two parties, even if both parties agree to splitting them. This principle stands in contrast to rules that govern other types of property, which can be divided so long as dividing them does not alter their essence and if both parties agree to the split. While conceptualizing texts both as material objects and in terms of the content they contain as holy is not unique to the Mishnah, we observe in the Mishnah's rules regarding holy writings a clear set of halakhic guidelines that establish how the holiness of such writings must be treated. These writings are treated as holy not only through their study or recitation or view as authoritative or oracular, which other texts likewise address, but also through their physical handling, preservation, and possible destruction. These latter rules resemble the treat-

---

53. Bremmer, "From Holy Books to Holy Bible," 338–40.

54. mYad 3:2–5, 4:5–6.

55. E.g. as implied in mYom 7:3.

56. mYad 4:5, 3:5, on which see Friedman, "'The Holy Scriptures Defile the Hands,'" 117, who notes that "reverence for the Torah" and "the ritualization of the Torah scroll" begin already in Neh 8. Likewise, the texts must be written in their original language— by default Hebrew but the Aramaic sections of Ezra and Daniel must be written in Aramaic to be considered holy and thus defiling the hands upon usage. tYad 2:11 includes educational texts written to teach a child to read Hallel or the Shema to also render the hands impure, thus including them in the category of "holy."

ment of other holy objects, including tithes, offerings, and sacrifices. In the Mishnah, the holy status of certain writings is not a statement exclusively about their canonical importance or revelatory status, but also about the way such texts, as material objects, contain tangible holiness that must be treated with physical care.

More unusual yet is the Mishnah's use of the term "language of the holy" (*leshon ha-kodesh*) to refer to Hebrew, the language of the "holy writings." According to mSot 7:2–4 and 9:1, for example, certain biblical passages, including the Sotah pericope, the Shema, Tefillah, and Grace after Meals can be recited in any language, while others, such as the declaration of first fruits, the passage of Levirate marriage, the blessings and curses, and the Priestly Blessing, can only be recited in Hebrew.[57] Someone who has been anointed for battle must speak in Hebrew when he addresses the people.[58] While the Hebrew of the Bible is called the holy language, scripture at the time of the Mishnah was written in Assyrian script (*ketav ashuri*), which had replaced Hebrew script in Jewish texts a few centuries earlier.[59] mMeg 1:8 states, for instance, that while Torah scrolls can be written in all languages, phylacteries and *mezuzot* (in which the biblical text itself is essential to the ritual object) must be written in Assyrian script (that is, not transliterated into a different alphabet, such as Greek or Latin). This passage appears in a longer list of slight differences that distinguish between different categories of things (e.g. between the first and second month of Adar, between festivals and Sabbaths, between a *zav* with two or three emissions, and so on), the implication being that the difference between scrolls and phylacteries is seemingly slight but nonetheless categorically significant. Apparently, texts with apotropaic qualities needed an extra level of holiness, imparted by holy script.

Holy Times and the Sanctification of Time

The Mishnah's order of *Moʻed* discusses the Sabbath and festivals, enumerating many rules ensuring that the holiness of those days is respected and cultivated. The characterization of the Sabbath as holy appears consistently in biblical passages, including in one of the Genesis creation narratives and in one version of the Decalogue.[60] In Lev 19:2–3, God's command to Moses

57. See also mYev 12:6 on performing Levirite marriage only in Hebrew.

58. mSot 8:1, citing Deut 20:3.

59. With some exceptions such as the Bar Kokhba coins, which used the antiquated ancient Hebrew script deliberately because of its resonance with the past.

60. Genesis 2:3; Exodus 20:7, 20:10, 31:13, 31:15, 35:2; Leviticus 19:2–3; Deuteronomy 5:11–12; Jeremiah 17:19–27; Ezekiel 20:12, 44:24; Nehemiah 9:14, 13:22. Isaiah 58:13 calls

to tell the Children of Israel to "be holy, for I, the Lord your God, am holy" is followed by instructions to fear one's parents and keep God's Sabbaths. Biblical passages characterize festivals too as "holy" times or occasions.[61] The Mishnah focuses for the most part on the intricacies of Sabbath and festival observance rather than on theoretical discussions about what characterizes the Sabbath as a holy time, as some other rabbinic sources do, but the implication of these restrictions is that the holiness of the day must be guarded with utmost care.[62] Occasionally, though, the Mishnah discusses the Sabbath's holy status more directly, as well as distinctions between the holiness of the Sabbath and festivals, which is borne out in the Mishnah's rules for both sets of days. For example, mSuk 5:5 mentions the shofar blasts that rang out from the temple before and after the Sabbath.[63] These blasts served to separate the holy time of the Sabbath from the mundane time of the rest of the week: "on Sabbath eve, they would add another six [blasts], three to signal to the people to stop their work, and three to distinguish between holy and mundane. On Sabbath eves that were during a festival, there were 48 [blasts] . . . and three to distinguish between holy and mundane."[64] The passage, which details how the Shofar blasts were used as a sort of alarm clock, alerting people of the approaching holy time of the Sabbath or festivals, emphasizes that certain times are "holy" while other times are not, and

the Sabbath "my holy day." Lynn Kaye, "Sacred Time and Rabbinic Literature: New Directions for an Old Question," *Journal of the American Academy of Religion* 88.4 (2020) notes the limits of using the notion of "sacred time" to explore rabbinic temporality, pointing out that there are many other ways in which temporality is configured beyond notions of "sacred" and "profane" in rabbinic texts. Here, however, the focus is indeed on "sacred time"—that is, on instances in which particular days of the week or year are characterized within the Mishnah as "holy."

61. For example in Lev 23:2.

62. Other tannaitic texts, including the Mekhilta de Rabbi Ishmael on Exodus 31, discuss at some length the precise sanctity of the Sabbath in relation to festivals, and later sources such as *Genesis Rabbah* 11 explore the intricacies of how God sanctified the day.

63. See also tSuk 4:11–12; bShab 35b.

64. Josephus, *B.J.* 4:582 mentions that the shofar blasts signaled to people when to stop working before the Sabbath and when to resume working after the Sabbath, emphasizing the need to refrain from work on the Sabbath but not explicitly using the language of holiness to describe the time of the Sabbath. These two texts, along with archaeological remains of the pedestal on which the trumpet was sounded, are discussed in Shaye J. D. Cohen, "The Judean Legal Tradition and the *Halakhah* of the Mishnah," in *The Cambridge Companion to the Talmud and Rabbinic Literature*, ed. C. E. Fonrobert and M. S. Jaffee (Cambridge, 2007), 121–43, at 130–31; Lutz Doering, "The Beginning of Sabbath and Festivals in Ancient Jewish Sources," in *The Construction of Time in Antiquity: Ritual, Art, and Identity* (Cambridge, 2017), 205–26, esp. 212–15.

highlights the importance of marking transitions between holy and mundane times. A similar discussion ensues in the Mishnah's discussion of the *havdala* ritual, which distinguished between holy and mundane time at the end of the Sabbath or a festival.[65]

Still, not all holy time is considered equivalent in the Mishnah. The holiness of the Sabbath stands above the holiness of festival days (with the exception of the Day of Atonement), considered holy times (*mikraei kodesh* in biblical sources) but not quite as holy as the Sabbath (termed *kadosh* in the Bible). The status of intermediate festival days is likewise distinguished from the first and last days of the festivals, which are accorded a higher status of holiness. Thus mHul 1:7 distinguishes between both holy and mundane time as well as between different gradations of holy time: the transition between the Sabbath and a holiday (*yom tov*) is marked differently than the transition between the Sabbath and a mundane day. The transition between two different holy days, for example from a Sabbath to a festival, is marked by one of two declarations, either "who distinguishes between holy and holy" or "between major holy and minor/light holy (בין קדש חמור לקדש הקל)" (different rabbinic figures hold different opinions about which declaration ought to be recited). In this mishnaic discussion, not only is the distinction between holy and mundane time marked, but so is the distinction between different gradations of holy time. The status of each day then dictates both the types of prohibited labors and the forms of worship associated with it.

The Mishnah also describes the sanctification of the new moon with the language of holiness. mRH 2:7 recounts how, after witnesses attest to their sighting of the new moon before three judges and their testimony is verified, the head of the Beit Din announces *"mekudash"* while the nation repeats after him, *"mekudash, mekudash,"* and thus they sanctify the new month (*mekadshin oto*) on that day.[66] The moon is consecrated in the process of declaring the start of a new month and the dates of upcoming festivals. Rabbi Elazar be-Rabbi Zaddok explains further that if the moon is not seen in time, the ritual of sanctification is not performed, because the heavens have already sanctified it without human intervention. Consecrating the moon seems to work in ways similar to the consecration of other objects, though it eventually became its own ritual, imbued with theological significance.[67]

65. mHul 1:7.

66. See further in mRH 3:1, and the extensive study of Sacha Stern, *Calendar and Community: A History of the Jewish Calendar, Second Century BCE—Tenth Century CE* (Oxford, 2001), esp. 157–64.

67. bSan 42a connects the ritual of *kidush levana* to God's divine presence, but this theological dimension is not present in the Mishnah. See also Sof 19:7, which mentions a

Finally, time figures more fundamentally into mishnaic conceptions of holiness. The holiness of sacrifices, for example, lapses after the proper time for their slaughter or consumption has passed, as it does when the Sabbath ends and a new week begins.[68] So while holy times are marked in various ways—the sounding of the shofar to mark the start of the Sabbath or a festival, and the sanctification of the moon—in many instances the passage or window of time also determines the holiness of other things.

Holy People and Actions that Lead to Holiness

Certain groups of people are associated, in the Mishnah as in biblical and second temple sources, with holiness. mYom 4:2, in its description of the High Priest's declaration on the day of Atonement, refers to the priestly caste (Aaron's children) as "your sacred people." In other passages, the Mishnah regards all of Israel as holy, an idea that likewise stems from biblical sources such as Ex 19:6 that expect all of Israel to follow God's commandments (including observance of the Sabbath, bodily purity, kashrut, refraining from idolatry, and so on) as a way of separating themselves from others and thereby achieving or embodying holiness.[69] The Mishnah not only maintains biblical hierarchies of holiness between Israelites, priests, and high priests but also expands them to include different types of Israelites, some holier than others. In its discussion of levirate marriage, for example, mYev 2:4 prohibits a widow from marrying a high priest, a divorcée from marrying a priest, a *mamzeret* or *netinah* from marrying an Israelite, and an Israelite woman from marrying a *netin* or a *mamzer,* due to an "*issur kedusha*," a prohibition related to the personal status of holiness of each type of person. While some of these marital restrictions stem from biblical prohibitions, the Mishnah for the first time encompasses different types of regular Israelites within its hierarchy of holiness.[70]

---

crowd, a festive meal, wine and blessings, discussed in Stern, *Calendar and Community,* 231.

68. Mali, "The Removal of the Temple Leftovers," identifies this temporal feature of tannaitic holiness as new and radical. I discuss the effect of the lapse of time on the efficacy of sacrifices in *Time and Difference in Rabbinic Judaism* (Princeton, 2020), 152.

69. The links between conceptions of holiness and separation from others are important tropes in biblical sources, and are carried through in later traditions as well, on which see, e.g., Adi Ophir and Ishay Rosen-Zvi, *Goy: Israel's Multiple Others and the Birth of the Gentile* (Oxford, 2018); Christine E. Hayes, *Gentile Impurities and Jewish Identities: Intermarriage and Conversion from the Bible to the Talmud* (Oxford, 2002); Jonathan Klawans, *Impurity and Sin in Ancient Judaism* (Oxford, 2002).

70. This example is discussed in Diamond, *Holy Men and Hunger Artists,* 77, and

Tzvi Novick argues, in light of this and other, similar passages, that the Mishnah innovates by characterizing Jewishness itself "as a manifestation of holiness."[71] For example, the Mishnah discusses the status of a person whose mother was not Jewish when she conceived her child but who converted during the course of her pregnancy as someone whose "conception was not in holiness and [whose] birth was in holiness."[72] In this passage, a child who is conceived by a Gentile woman who then converts to Judaism before the baby is born has a different status (that of a convert) from a child of this same woman who is conceived after her conversion (such a child is not considered a convert). The way that the Mishnah discusses this situation is that the former's conception was "not in the holiness of Israel" even though his birth was "in the holiness of Israel," while the latter's conception and birth were both "in the holiness of Israel."[73] The Mishnah's conceptualization of holiness in these examples marks the technical identity of a person. Koltun-Fromm notes further that "while the Tannaitic rabbis maintain a notion of Israel as a holy community ... they allow a more porous border: a nonholy Israelite may convert and become a holy Israelite," an approach to outsiders that stands in contrast to many earlier positions, such as those held by the authors of the book of Ezra and Jubilees, and that envisions a possibility for them to join into the holiness of Israel, transforming their status of holiness.[74]

While these examples all constitute different types of ascribed holiness, the Mishnah also promotes, to a more limited degree, notions of achieved or aspirational holiness. Koltun-Fromm notes that "holiness by achievement ... takes the form of building on an already inherent Israelite holiness by creating a new level of holiness for those who are able ... Achieved holiness ... refers, then, to the idea that a higher degree of holiness can be acquired

---

Koltun-Fromm, *Hermeneutics of Holiness*, 218–19, who writes "Every Israelite (male) fits somewhere along the continuum of 'holy' to 'very holy.' Marriage partners are then influenced by one's place on that continuum ... Whatever their origin, the *Mishnah* brings these restrictions on Israelite marriage as a parallel category to the restrictions on the priests" (219).

71. Novick, "Holiness in the Rabbinic Period," 46. Some rabbinic notions of holiness do not appear explicitly in the Mishnah even though they appear in other tannaitic works; for example, the portion of the blessing formula אשר קדשנו, "who makes us holy [through the commandments]," is found in the Tosefta and the Talmudim but not in the Mishnah. Likewise, martyrs, which in later sources are called "holy ones" (קדשים), are not so called in the Mishnah.

72. mYev 11:2.

73. mKet 4:3 discusses a similar case.

74. Koltun-Fromm, *Hermeneutics of Holiness*, 212.

through prescribed practice."[75] One example of such achieved holiness is the Nazarite, which the Mishnah treats in one of its tractates, emphasizing in particular the Nazarite's abstention from wine and other grape products as an ascetic practice, as Eliezer Diamond has argued.[76] Diamond likewise notes that while many aspects of rabbinic holiness overlap with those of the Bible, "what is new in rabbinic literature, at least apparently so, is the frequent use of *qdš* in connection with forbidden sexual relations and activities" beyond the priesthood.[77] Koltun-Fromm agrees, stating that "sexual restraint—often in legitimate sexual unions—comes to the fore as the primary rabbinic way to 'be holy'"[78] and that sexual practices "are consistently couched within a hermeneutic of holiness";[79] what begins as concern about proper marriage partners designed to maintain priestly hierarchy transforms into "a new paradigm of holy achievement through restricted sexual practices with legitimate sexual partners."[80] The link between sexual practices, marriage, and holiness is thus expanded, the Mishnah reiterating its concern over proper lineage, genealogy, and communal boundaries, creating, on the one hand, new categories of Jews, including the *mamzer*, whose marriage partner options are restricted because of their tainted lineage, and promoting, on the other hand, supererogatory sexual behaviors for some who wish to be holier than regular Jews.[81] Though these ideas are

75. Koltun-Fromm, *Hermeneutics of Holiness*, 213.

76. Diamond, *Holy Men and Hunger Artists*, 81–82.

77. Diamond, *Holy Men and Hunger Artists*, 76. Though, importantly, some biblical sources do connect sexuality and holiness, e.g. Deut 23:18, which discusses the *kadesha* and *kadesh*, often (mis)translated as "cult prostitute" connected to the temple and its rituals, on which see Tikva Frymer-Kensky, *Reading the Women of the Bible: A New Interpretation of Their Stories* (New York, 2002), 271; Tikva Frymer-Kensky, "Sex and the People: The Myth of Orgy," in *In the Wake of the Goddesses: Women, Culture, and the Biblical Transformation of Pagan Myth* (New York, 1992); for a comparative example, see Frédérique Apffel Marglin, *Wives of the God-King: The Rituals of the Devadasis of Puri* (Oxford, 1985).

78. Koltun-Fromm, *Hermeneutics of Holiness*, 214.

79. Koltun-Fromm, *Hermeneutics of Holiness*, 216.

80. Koltun-Fromm, *Hermeneutics of Holiness*, 213; Koltun-Fromm argues that "the rabbinic practice of sexual restraint in particular, and the general notion of withdrawal as holy behavior, is modeled on the marriage restrictions applied to the priesthood ... the rabbinic notion of sexual practice as *kedushah* is further influenced by the Moses at Sinai tradition ... in which Israel's three days of celibacy and Moses' permanent sexual renunciation stand as exemplars of spiritual and physical purity, as well as devotion to God" (216).

81. Yedidah Koren, "The Persons Who May Not 'Enter the Congregation' in Rabbinic Literature" (Hebrew; PhD diss, Tel Aviv University, 2021).

developed more fully in later rabbinic sources, their seeds are already sown in the Mishnah.

The intersection of holiness and sexual discourse is not limited, however, to forbidden unions, anxiety over communal boundaries, or ascetic inclinations; it appears most prominently in the Mishnah in the context of standard marital laws.[82] The process of betrothal, as it is outlined in tractate *Kidushin*, posits that a woman becomes consecrated or sanctified for marriage to a particular man when he declares her *"mekudeshet."* The root *kds* for betrothal is tannaitic, rather than biblical (Gail Labovitz notes that it is "a rabbinic locution, even a rabbinic neologism" that likely dates to the early tannaitic period), and later rabbinic sources attempt to explain its meaning (and why it replaces other terms used in the Bible).[83] Diamond explains the multivalence of the term's meaning in the context of rabbinic betrothal as follows:

> [T]his usage derives in part from the general meaning of *qdš* as separation . . . Thus she [the betrothed woman] is *mequdeshet* in at least two senses: in being separated from, and forbidden to, other men to whom she was previously permitted; and in being in some sense holy by virtue of having accepted the sexual restrictions that define betrothal . . . like the priests, who are dedicated to the service of God, a betrothed woman is designated for an exclusive relationship with the man who has betrothed her. . . . The priests are forbidden to engage in sexual relations with certain women both because they are and so that they will remain set apart to serve God in His temple, while a betrothed woman is forbidden to all other men both because she is, and so that she remains, set apart to be in an exclusive relationship with her husband.[84]

82. On which see Gail Labovitz, *Marriage and Metaphor: Constructions of Gender in Rabbinic Literature* (Lanham, 2009), esp. 63–96; Michael Satlow, *Jewish Marriage in Antiquity* (Princeton, 2001); Judith Romney Wegner, *Chattel or Person? The Status of Women in the Mishnah* (New York, 1988).

83. Labovitz, *Marriage and Metaphor*, 64, though she notes that there are some references to *kedusha* in marital contexts in earlier texts, e.g. 4Q269–271 and 4Q415, which refer to marriage as *brit kodesh*. bKid 2b, which tries to understand the Mishnah's terminology for betrothal, explains that the Mishnah chose the word "consecrated" because the wife becomes "a consecrated object." The language of betrothal is found throughout the Mishnah, e.g. mBM 4:7; mMS 1:2. Labovitz notes, however, that the shift in terminology does not necessarily mean a shift in conceptions of marriage as the purchase of a wife, which remains in the Mishnah as well.

84. Diamond, *Holy Men and Hunger Artists*, 76, 79.

Just as objects consecrated for use in the temple cannot be used for other things, so too a betrothed woman cannot be wed to another man. Judith Romney Wegner notes further that "the procedure [of betrothal, literally sanctification] uses the terminology of holiness . . . the rules rest on the belief that intercourse with a forbidden women—one consecrated to another man's use—is a prime cause of pollution. That defilement destroys a man's sanctify (*q*e*dushah*) and purity (*taharah*) and disqualifies him from participating in the sacred rites of the cult. Thus the entire corpus of rules governing men's contacts and relationships with women exhibits the same concern with sanctity that pervades the Mishnah as a whole."[85] Indeed, this terminology aligns not only with priests but also with the consecration of first-born sons, Nazirites, sacrifices, and the new moon in that they have been separated, their use and affiliation determined, and, in most cases, they must undergo a formal ritual before being de-consecrated. It also jibes well with the Mishnah's tendency to expand the types of things that its hermeneutic of holiness encompasses.

CONCEPTS OF HOLINESS IN THE MISHNAH

A number of overarching themes related to the Mishnah's conception of holiness emerge from the sources. First is the connection between holiness and impurity, two states that are intricately connected with one another because a person's state of purity or impurity often determines the ability of that person to approach, inhabit, or handle holy spaces or objects. The goal of maintaining a status of purity, in many instances, is for the purpose of encountering the holy in some way. But holiness and impurity are not technically opposites. The Mishnah explicitly juxtaposes things that are "holy" with those that are called "mundane" (defined as "not holy"), while it likewise presents purity and impurity as opposite states. "Holiness" is that which is connected to the sanctity or holiness of God, while "impurity" is that which poses a danger to that holiness, by proximity or otherwise, and thus what prevents access to that which is holy. Moreover, the Mishnah's halakhot as well as several of its narrative passages conceptualizes holiness itself as tiered, such that certain days, spaces, or objects are not either holy or mundane, but rather some can be holier than others, a theme that began to emerge in the sources discussed above. These three overlapping concepts related to holiness allow us to map the Mishnah's theories of holiness in more detail, and connect the notion of holiness with other dominant themes present throughout the mishnaic corpus.

85. Wegner, *Chattel or Person?*, 180.

The Relationship between Holiness and Impurity

The relationship between holiness and impurity is complicated. Even though impurity is not itself the antithesis of holiness, in the Mishnah (as in biblical and second temple sources) impurity prevents access or proximity to holy spaces and objects; punishments are doled out to those who are impure but nonetheless enter the Temple or consume consecrated foods or use consecrated items; some holy objects paradoxically cause impurity when they are touched, and when they are taken outside the realm of holiness (e.g. when they are taken outside of Jerusalem) they need to be burned or discarded.[86] The Mishnah devotes much space to the topic of impurity, the minutiae of when access to holiness is disrupted, and the process by which one can purify oneself or particular objects in order to be able to access that which is holy.[87] To cite a few examples of many: tractate *Zevaḥim* discusses whether the meat of an animal that was originally fit for sacrifice (that is, a "holy" or "consecrated" animal) and then disqualified (no longer "holy" or "consecrated") renders the person who consumes its meat ritually impure. Tractate *Tohorot* details the relationship between different levels of impurity and how they interact with consecrated foods, and mYom 3:3 mentions the High Priest's purification and sanctification in the context of the Day of Atonement, highlighting in yet another way how purity and holiness were interrelated.

The interrelatedness of purity and holiness figures prominently in the first chapter of tractate *Kelim* ("Vessels"), which provides two lists, one dedicated to categories and degrees of impurity and the second to degrees of holiness.[88] The first list enumerates various broad categories that cause impurity to varying degrees, including creeping things, semen, someone who has come into contact with a human corpse, a leper, the water to be sprinkled in a sin-offering, a menstruant, and so on.[89] After listing the ten

---

86. E.g. mPes 3:8; mKer 1:1–2. On the intersection of purity and holiness, see the essays in Marcel Poorthuis and Joshua Schwartz, eds., *Purity and Holiness: The Heritage of Leviticus* (Leiden, 2000); Jacob Neusner and Bruce D. Chilton, "Uncleanness: A Moral or an Ontological Category in the Early Centuries A.D.," *Bulletin for Biblical Research* 1 (1991): 63–88; and Neusner's multi-volume *A History of the Mishnaic Law of Holy Things*.

87. See e.g. Balberg, *Purity, Body, and Self*.

88. With regard to the discussion of impurity, the chapter begins by listing the "fathers of impurity" (that is, the large categories of things that cause impurity) and then lists the ten gradations of impurity that emanate from a person, which parallels the following list of ten realms of holiness.

89. mKel 1:5. The Mishnah explains that impure men are prohibited from eating consecrated food even as they are permitted to eat *terumot* and *maʿasrot*.

degrees of impurity (*tum'ot*), the Mishnah lists the ten degrees of holiness (*kedushot*), highlighting how the two concepts are in many ways two sides of a single coin, even as they are not conceptually opposites.[90] The first degree of holiness listed is the Land of Israel, which the Mishnah explains is "holier" than all other lands. What is the nature of its holiness (ומה היא קדשתה), the Mishnah asks. It answers plainly that it is (only) from that land that one brings the *omer*, *bikurim*, and *shtei ha-lehem*, while these are not brought from outside the Land of Israel. The second degree of holiness entails cities enclosed by a wall (presumably within the Land of Israel), which are holier than non-walled cities, because lepers are sent out from such walled cities, and because once a corpse leaves such a city it cannot return to it (lepers and corpses both convey impurity, and thus they are not permitted in walled cities, which have elevated statuses of holiness). Next comes Jerusalem, the ultimate walled city, the only city in which *kadashim kalim* and *ma'aser sheni* can be eaten. Then come, in ascending order of holiness, the Temple Mount, upon which *zavim*, *zavot*, menstruants, and parturients are not permitted to stand; the rampart area, from which Gentiles and those with corpse impurity are prohibited from entering; the women's section, in which a *tvul yom*, who has immersed on that day, is not permitted; the Israelite section, from which those whose atonement is incomplete are excluded; and the Priestly section, which no Israelites may enter except for specific reasons related to sacrificial rituals (laying on of hands, slaughtering, and waving). The ninth area is the space between the *ulam* and the altar, in which priests with blemishes or loosened hair may not enter, and the tenth is the *heikhal*, which only those deemed permitted to enter the temple who have washed their hands and feet can enter. More sacred than all of these—and indeed beyond the ten realms enumerated until this point—is the holy of holies (*kodesh hakodashim*), which the High Priest, having fully purified himself, enters only once a year, on the Day of Atonement.[91] This level of detailed determination of levels of holiness, though it relies on basic principles about the holiness of cultic space in biblical sources, is a new development in the Mishnah's conception of holiness. Its placement alongside levels of impurity highlights the conceptual relationship between holiness and purity.

What makes a place holy, according to this chapter of *Kelim*, are the restrictions imposed upon it regarding objects or people who are impure or who convey impurity. It is not that certain people or objects are not permit-

---

90. mKel 1:6–9.

91. A similar hierarchy of spatial holiness is articulated in the Tosefta's discussion of prayer direction in tBer 3:16.

ted in these spaces because the spaces are intrinsically holy; rather, these places are holy because these people or objects are prohibited from entering them. Rabbi Yose shares an opinion that at certain times (when incense is burned), the space between the *ulam* and the altar is of equal holiness as the *heikhal*, because at that time those with blemishes, those with loose or disheveled hair, those who have consumed alcohol, and those who have not washed their hands and feet are all forbidden to enter this space. A single space may attain different levels of holiness depending on what ritual is performed at a particular time and who may exist within it.

We can now examine the logic that underpins the idea that holy things can defile. Tractate *Yadayim* expresses the principle that holy writings defile the hands and cause impurity,[92] and presents a Sadducee critique of Pharisaic purity practices in which holy writings defile the hands while the books of Homer do not.[93] Why should sacred scriptures make hands impure while Homer's epics do not, the Sadducean position wonders? Rabbi Yohanan ben Zakkai responds that the Sadduccees also deride the Pharisaic idea that the bones of a donkey are pure while the bones of Yohanan the Priest are impure. The Mishnah concludes that the level of affection determines an object's impurity or ability to transfer impurity, such that a person cannot turn his father's or mother's bones into spoons (because human bones have a higher level of affection and are thus impure, while animal bones are not). The rabbi thus explains that the same logic applies to holy writings: Homer's works are not beloved (to the rabbis) and can be repurposed, and therefore they do not defile the hands, but holy writings are indeed beloved and must be preserved intact.[94] That they defile the hands ensures that they are not repurposed or treated disrespectfully. Ironically, the ability of holy things to impart impurity preserves their holiness. Scholars offer a variety of historical explanations of this mishnaic rule.[95] Friedman argues that the idea that holy writings defile the hands stems from an original assumption that holy writings impart holiness, and that washing hands after handling holy writings was designed to prevent the spread of holiness to other objects; once holiness was no longer considered primarily contagious, holy writings were

92. mYad 3:2, 5; tYad 2:12 also notes that some items that regularly come into contact with holy texts, such as cases, wrappings, and chests, also defile the hands, on which see Fine, *This Holy Place*, 39.

93. mYad 4:6. tYad 2:13 states that gospels and heretical books do not defile the hands, and tYad 2:14 notes that Ecclesiastes does not defile the hand because it was written by Solomon rather than divinely inspired.

94. tYad 2:19 similarly explains that holy writings defile the hands specifically because they are precious or beloved.

95. Friedman, "'The Holy Scriptures Defile the Hands,'" 131.

said to impart impurity, which remained contagious, thus maintaining the ritual of hand-washing after their use. Yair Furstenberg suggests that the ritual of washing hands transformed from a practice related to ridding one's hands of impurity in order to eat the *terumah* to one that was conceived as being related to the sanctification of priests for work in the temple, and Timothy Lim connects that idea that holy writings impart impurity to the lethal power of the Ark of the Covenant.[96] Regardless of exactly why holy writings defile the hands, the principle highlights the Mishnah's presentation of impurity and holiness as related, if in counterintuitive and innovative ways.

Distinguishing between Holy and Mundane

While holiness is often conceptualized as being in tension with impurity, the Mishnah conceptualizes "mundane" (*hol*) as the opposite of "holy" (*kadosh*). Holy vessels are juxtaposed with mundane vessels, consecrated *shekalim* are juxtaposed with non-consecrated *shekalim*, consecrated animals set aside for sacrifices are juxtaposed with those that are not consecrated, holy times are contrasted with mundane times, and so on.[97] For example, mBekh 9:1 discusses the difference between consecrated animals (*mekudashin*) and unconsecrated animals (*hulin*), and mZev 3:2 mentions holy and regular vessels—though countless examples of such passages exist throughout the Mishnah. In certain cases, the transition between holy and mundane is marked. mSuk 5:5, for instance, describes how shofar blasts signal the transition from "mundane" to "holy" time at the start of the Sabbath, and then again mark the transition from "holy" to "mundane" at the conclusion of the Sabbath.

This is not to say, however, that "holy" and "mundane" cannot coexist in the same space. In some passages, the Mishnah develops a spatial theory of holiness in which holy and mundane spaces indeed co-exist. mMS 3:8 explains the specific interplay between the temple's holy and mundane spaces in architectural terms: (1) For those chambers that were built on holy

---

96. Yair Furstenberg, "Hand-Washing in Tannaitic Literature: From Purification to Sanctification" (Hebrew), in *Minchat Yizchaq: Festschrift for Y. Sapir*, ed. I. Rozenson et al. (Rehovot, 2013), 107–30; Timothy H. Lim, "The Defilement of the Hands as a Principle Determining the Holiness of Scriptures," *Journal of Theological Studies* 61.2 (2010): 501–15.

97. Tractate Temurah is devoted to whether consecrated animals can be exchanged for non-consecrated animals, but the topic is discussed elsewhere in the Mishnah too, e.g. mZev 3:2, 7:5.

ground and opened onto mundane ground, their interior is deemed mundane and their roofs holy. (2) For those chambers that were built on mundane ground and opened onto holy ground, their interior is deemed holy and their roofs mundane. (3) For those built on a combination of holy and mundane ground and open onto holy and mundane ground, the interior and roofs that were on holy ground are holy, and the interior and roofs that were on mundane ground are mundane. M.Mid 4:5 also discusses the interplay of spaces with differing states of holiness, describing a row of stones on the top of the roof of the Temple's upper chamber that marked the division in the upper chamber between the Holy and the Holy of Holies. This division was somewhat permeable, however, for trap doors helped people lower baskets into the Holy of Holies without seeing the space itself or entering into it, which was not permitted given the high level of holiness in the space. In both of these passages, the holiness of space extends inwards and upwards, and has a carefully framed relationship with spaces of lesser holiness around it.

Hierarchies of Holiness

While holiness is juxtaposed with both impurity and the mundane, the Mishnah conceives of holiness itself as tiered, such that people, places, times, and objects are not just holy or mundane but some can be holier than others. In some cases, holiness is ordered hierarchically from least to greatest, while in others holiness is conceived concentrically, such that holiness increases as one approaches the most sacred center. Sometimes these conceptions are also merged, as we observed in the lists complied in tractate *Kelim,* in which the holiness of the Land of Israel functions in concentric circles, such that holiness increases as one approaches the most sacred center (Jerusalem is portrayed as the most holy of cities, and then the area closer to the Holy of Holies gets progressively more holy). In this conception, certain spaces are holier than the spaces that surround them, all the way to the Holy of Holies, the holiest place of all. Not all hierarchies of holiness operate concentrically, however. The Day of Atonement is considered the holiest day of the year. The "holy time" of the Sabbath, characterized as very holy, is distinguished from the "holy time" of festivals, considered less holy, or "holy-light."[98] The intermediate days, couched between the first and last festival days, are called *ḥol ha-moed,* a combination of holy and mundane.[99]

---

98. mḤul 1:7.
99. Kadushin, *Worship and Ethics,* 220–22, discusses the hierarchy of holy days.

Levels of holiness are not just a feature of places and times, either. Relative holiness determines the order in which sacrifices and offerings are brought and also the order in which they are eaten.[100] Gradations of holiness apply to different types of sacrifices and offerings, sacrifices brought by or on behalf of certain people, and different parts of the sacrifices (e.g. blood). The "holiest" offerings are called קדשי קדשים. Logics of precedent based on holiness status are discussed extensively in mZev 10 and mMeʿi 1–2; in general, that which is more holy precedes that which is less holy, both in the order of its sacrifice and in its consumption. In mHor 3:6, if both the High Priest's bullock and the congregation's bullock await sacrifice, the High Priest's precedes that of the congregation. Nevertheless, sometimes sacrifices of different holiness status are treated equally. mZev 3:1 explains that sacrifices brought by people unfit to perform a slaughter are still valid, and that this rule applies even to the holiest sacrifices reserved for priests (קדשי קדשים), as long as an impure person does not touch the flesh of the animal.[101] mSot 3:7 explains that a priest is permitted to eat the most holy offerings (*kodshei kodashim*), while the daughter of a priest cannot, while mKid 2:8 notes that a priest cannot betroth a woman with the most holy nor the lesser holy offerings (because neither are technically his property). These passages, like others, take for granted that there are levels of holiness with regard to sacrifices, and yet also articulate a rule that applies to all of them seemingly equally. As we observed above, hierarchies of holiness also apply to personal status in the context of permitted and prohibited marital unions.

Objects too exist on a hierarchy or spectrum of holiness. M.Meg 3:1 offers the general guideline that when one sells something, one can use the profits earned to buy something that is holier than what was sold, and that it is forbidden to purchase something that is of lesser holiness than that which was sold.[102] The Mishnah explains this rule through the following example: one cannot sell public property to an individual because doing so lowers its status of holiness. From this generalizing principle, we understand that all of the examples enumerated in the longer passage regard items of varying degrees of holiness in relation to one another. The passage explains as follows:

---

100. Some offerings, for example, are called the "holy of holies," to distinguish them from other offerings that are just "holy," e.g. mZev 3:1, 7:4, 10:3.

101. The gradation of sacrifices stems from biblical sources, e.g. Leviticus 6–7, discussed in Balberg, *Blood for Thought*, 44.

102. See also mNed 4:2 for a similar discussion.

Residents of a city who sell the city square can take their profits and purchase a synagogue; [if they sell] a synagogue, they can purchase an ark; [if they sell] an ark, they can purchase wrapping cloths; [if they sell] wrapping cloths, they can purchase books; [if they sell] books, they can purchase a Torah. But if they sell a Torah, they cannot purchase books; [if they sell] books, they cannot purchase wrapping cloths; [if they sell] wrapping cloths, they cannot purchase an ark; [if they sell] an ark, they cannot purchase a synagogue; [if they sell] a synagogue, they cannot purchase a city square.

Here again, we see a hierarchy of holiness employed to prohibit certain types of purchases. But in an added dimension, one ought to move only in one direction in that hierarchy: from lower to higher.

The idea that one ought to move towards the more holy is articulated most clearly through an idiom in mShek 6:4, which states that "one raises in holiness but does not diminish holiness" (*ma'alin ba-kodesh ve-lo moridin*).[103] This principle applies, in the Mishnah's discussion, to the placement of the showbread. There were several marble, silver, and gold tables in the temple. Some of these tables were used to rinse the sacrificial animal's entrails, place the limbs of the offering, or rest the vessels being used in the process. The showbread was placed on one of the marble tables when it was brought in, and then placed on the gold table when it was taken out, because of the principle that you always elevate in holiness. Apparently, a gold table is holier than a marble one, fitting for showbread that may also have increased in holiness as it entered and exited different spaces. The passage concludes with a final gold table, on which the showbread always lay in the temple. A well-known discussion in bShab 21b about lighting Hanukkah candles invokes this principle of rising in holiness to argue, according to Beit Hillel's position, that one must increase the number of candles each night of the holiday, such that one begins with a single candle on the first evening of Hanukkah and builds all the way to eight candles on the final night.

Finally, we can see how conceptualizations of the hierarchies of holiness are applied to sacred texts, too. Tractate *Yadayim*, for example, characterizes scripture as "holy"[104] and the Song of Songs as the "holiest," ap-

---

103. This logic of the holy is applied in later sources (e.g. bShab 21b) to the debate between Hillel and Shammai about the proper way to light Hanukkah candles.

104. In this passage, perhaps it refers specifically to the section of scripture known as Writings as "holy."

plying the same type of tiered temporal and spatial holiness to works of scripture.[105] In this example, "holy writings" exist on a hierarchy, with certain works "holier" than others—metaphorically or rhetorically if not practically. The characterization of the Song of Songs as "holy of holies" (a formulation used to imply a superlative: holiest) also evokes the hierarchies of holiness applied to the space of the temple, in which "the Holy of Holies" represents the holiest place in the world and the place of greatest contact between God and Israel (even if the association between the Song of Songs and the Temple's Holy of Holies was not originally intended by the phrasing of the passage, as Jonathan Kaplan argues). Rabbi Akiva's explanation in the passage might further link the Song of Songs to the time of revelation at Sinai, connecting the text in yet another way to the realm of holiness—and thus to its status as a holy writing that defiles the hands.

Kedusha: The Concept of Holiness

While the concept of holiness is central in biblical texts, the term קדושה, "holiness," does not appear in the Bible. It does, however, appear a few times in the Mishnah.[106] For example, mSot 9:15 states: "Rabbi Pinhas ben Yair says: Scrupulousness begets cleanliness, cleanliness begets purity, purity begets modesty, modesty begets holiness, holiness begets humility, humility begets fear of sin, fear of sin begets righteousness, righteousness begets *ruah ha-kodesh*, *ruah ha-kodesh* begets the resurrection of the dead, which brings about Elijah, who is remembered for good, amen."[107] Here, terms related to holiness stand, on the one hand, alongside other virtues that bring people closer to God, such as swiftness to act, cleanliness, purity, modesty, humility, fear of sin, and righteousness, and on the other hand, describe divine acts that bridge the divide between the heavenly and earthly, such as *ruah ha-kodesh*, resurrection of the dead, and the prophet Elijah, who is often associated with the final redemption. This passage appears in the

105. mYad 3:5; the discussion about the Song of Songs' status unfolds in the context of debate about whether Ecclesiastes and the Song of Songs should be counted among sacred scripture and whether they convey impurity to hands. The text is clear that they do—and goes further by suggesting that in fact the Song of Songs is not only part of scripture but an important part at that. On whether the text characterizes the Song of Songs simply as "holy" or deliberately wants to associate the text with the temple's Holy of Holies, see Jonathan Kaplan, "The Holy of Holies or the Holiest? Rabbi Akiva's Characterization of Song of Songs in Mishnah Yadayim 3:5," in *"It's Better to Hear the Rebuke of the Wise Than the Song of Fools" (Qoh 7:5): Proceedings of the Midrash Section, Society of Biblical Literature*, vol. 6, ed. W. D. Nelson and R. Ulmer (Piscataway, N.J., 2015), 63–81.

106. mYev 2, 3, 11; mKet 4, mSot 1, 9; m'Eduy 8, mTem 1, 2, 5 7.

107. *Ruah ha-kodesh* also appears in mSot 9:6.

context of a longer discussion about the loss of sages and the destruction of the temple. It ends on this hopeful note: that cultivating personal virtuous behaviors, like being scrupulous (to observe commandments), modest, or righteous will ultimately lead to God's redemption of the world. There holiness is a personal attribute rather than a divine one, and it appears in the middle of the list rather than on top.

CONCLUSION

This survey of holiness in the Mishnah highlights how foundational holiness, in all of its facets, is to the project of the Mishnah as a whole. Even though many discussions about holiness revolve around the temple and its cultic rituals, no longer practiced when the Mishnah was redacted, some concepts about holiness that derive from the temple nonetheless continue to impact life beyond and after the temple in significant ways. Other concepts related to holiness are rabbinic innovations that take hold apart from a temple context. Both arenas of holiness, including conceptualizations of ritual, space, time, food, human interactions, and God, comingle in the Mishnah's discussions, blurring distinctions between past and present and ensuring that holiness remains a central concern of the mishnaic enterprise, and thus an important locus for theorization and conceptualization within the Mishnah. The Mishnah inherited and revised biblical and second temple conceptions of holiness. It no doubt was also aware of contemporaneous conceptions of holiness in the thought and writings of other Jews, and the rituals, laws, and texts of their neighbors in Roman Palestine and the Roman Empire. Ultimately, the Mishnah integrated these various traditions into its own intellectual project.

The Mishnah's conception of holiness may help us understand the views and values of those whose traditions are embedded within it and even more so those of the compilers who composed the work. But it also helps us imagine the ideas imparted to those who made use of the text, inherited it, studied it, or tried to apply it to their lives. If they took the Mishnah's rhetoric and regulations seriously, they would have been concerned about respecting and caring for the sanctity embedded in the world—its times, places, people, and objects—or that was imbued into it through various channels, not only when the effects of doing so were positive, but also when they caused potential pain or complication for individuals and communities.

Many thanks to Shaye Cohen, David Stern, Noah Feldman, and Jay Harris for the invitation to participate in the workshop that led to this volume; Susan Kahn for her organization of the conference and volume; and Shaye Cohen, Jonathan Gribetz, Lynn Kaye, and Yevgeniy Safronov for providing helpful feedback on drafts.

14. The Language of the Mishnah— Between Late Hebrew and Mishnaic Hebrew

Elitzur A. Bar-Asher Siegal

1. INTRODUCTION

Hebrew is a Canaanite dialect belonging to the Northwest Semitic family of languages. It was spoken by the population of ancient Israel in the region of Palaestina until the early centuries of the Common Era. Most of the texts canonized in the Hebrew Bible were composed in this language, and as a result it acquired the status of a sacred tongue. Later in the Roman Period (74–220 CE), the legal corpus of the Mishnah and the Tosefta was composed, featuring rulings by rabbinic sages of this period, the Tannaim. This corpus is complemented by the legal midrashim, which, broadly speaking, propose connections between the rabbinic law and the Biblical sources. It is believed that the Roman period literature was initially transmitted orally and only later recorded in writing.[1] Therefore, although the earliest manuscripts of this literature date from the Middle Ages, they mostly reflect the language of the first to third centuries.

In discussing the history of the Hebrew language, a distinction must be made between its history as a linguistic system and the history of its written forms. The former assumes an idealized periodization of the language and

---

1. Yaacov Sussmann, "Oral Torah Understood Literally: The Power of the Tittle of the [Letter] Yod," in *Mehqerei Talmud, Vol. III, Part 1—Talmudic Studies Dedicated to the Memory of Professor Ephraim E. Urbach* (Hebrew), ed. Y. Sussmann and D. Rosenthal (Jerusalem, 2005), 209–384.

distinguishes between Early Hebrew (EH) and Late Hebrew (LH).[2] The latter bases the division on corpora, resulting in the traditional classification into Biblical Hebrew, Qumranic Hebrew, and Mishnaic Hebrew, with further sub-divisions such as early vs. late Biblical Hebrew, Early vs. Late Mishnaic Hebrew, Babylonian vs. Palaestinian Talmudic Hebrew, etc. Although these two perspectives are fundamentally different, they are clearly interrelated: on the one hand, our knowledge about the history of the structure(s) of the language is based on data gathered from the Hebrew corpora and on the historical setting of these texts; on the other hand, the analysis of the linguistic information in the corpora is a de facto description of how the different linguistic systems were used in each corpus.

This chapter aims to examine the language of the Mishnah from these two perspectives and explore the conceptual distinction between the two categories with which it is associated, namely Late Hebrew and Mishnaic Hebrew. I will outline what it means to provide a description of Late Hebrew as a linguistic system, and what it means to examine Mishnaic Hebrew as the language of a written corpus. Accordingly, this paper has a twofold goal: (1) to explain the difference between the two perspectives as relevant to the language of the Mishnah; (2) to demonstrate the advantages of keeping them separate.

The structure of the chapter is as follows: in section 2 we will briefly review the question of whether the Hebrew of the Mishnah reflects an artificial language, and I will explain why we should not deal with this question at all. In section 3, I discuss linguistic heterogeneity and explain why the awareness of heterogeneous states compels us to consider the language of the Mishnah from two different perspectives. Section 4 proposes a practical methodology for dealing with the "noisy" data in the corpora and classifying the linguistic forms according to their periods: EH vs. LH. This discussion also involves a diachronic analysis of the kinds of historical relations that may hold between the two linguistic systems. Following this discussion, section 5 considers Mishnaic Hebrew (MH), i.e., the language of the Mishnah. While the default assumption in the literature is that MH

---

2. For a discussion of the periodization of Hebrew, see Ze'ev Ben-Ḥayyim. "The Historical Unity of the Hebrew Language and Its Division into Periods" (Hebrew), *Language Studies* 1 (1985): 3–25, and Moshe Bar-Asher, "The Historical Unity of Hebrew and Mishnaic Hebrew Research," *Language Studies* 1 (1985): 75–99. For a good presentation of the standard approach that divides the history of Hebrew into four stages, and does not make the distinction between the two perspectives introduced here, see Angel Sáenz-Badillos, *A History of the Hebrew Language* (Cambridge, 1993).

is largely synonymous with LH, we will examine the various ways in which EH is present in the Mishnah corpus as well.

2. WAS MISHNAIC HEBREW AN ARTIFICIAL LANGUAGE?

A major debate among the early scholars of Mishnaic Hebrew is whether this language was an "artificial" variety of Hebrew created by speakers of Aramaic, or actually a living, spoken language. At the heart of the debate was the question of whether all differences between EH and LH (to use our terms) can be explained by pointing to parallel phenomena in Aramaic (see below section 4.2.2.1). Those who answered this question in the negative argued that Mishnaic Hebrew exhibits various analogical changes (see below section 4.2.2.1), and that such changes can only occur in spoken languages.[3]

What is common to both sides in this debate is the structure of their argument, as both rely on a *modus ponens* syllogism: (If X then Y; X is given; therefore Y). Those who argue that Hebrew at the time of the Mishnah was an artificial language assume that *if the grammar of Mishnaic Hebrew is similar to Aramaic, then Mishnaic Hebrew must be artificial,* and those who argue that it was a spoken language assume that *if there were analogical changes, then Hebrew must have been a live language.* However, both assumptions are intuitive, and in fact baseless. First, it is well known that languages with bilingual speakers can become very similar, especially when their grammars were close in the first place (as is the case with Hebrew and Aramaic).[4] Second, it has been observed that even literary languages that lack a community of speakers can still go through analogical changes.[5] Thus, the assumptions at the basis of those *modus ponens* syllogisms are groundless.

---

3. See M. Hirsh Segal, "Mišnaic Hebrew and its Relation to Biblical Hebrew and Aramaic," *Jewish Quarterly Review* (Oxford,1908), 649–51, for a review of this literature. Segal himself tries to downplay as much as possible the significance of Aramaic influence on LH.

4. See, for example, Luna Filipović and John A. Hawkins, "The Complex Adaptive System Principles Model for Bilingualism: Language Interactions within and across Bilingual Minds," *International Journal of Bilingualism* 23 (2019) : 1223–48, which among other things argues for the "Maximise common ground" principle, according to which "Bilingual learners and speakers maximise common grammatical and lexical representations and their associated processing mechanisms in two languages, L1a and L1b, within the grammatical constraints and conventions imposed by each" (1229).

5. Elitzur A. Bar-Asher Siegal, "The Formation and Cognitive Knowledge of Literary Languages: the Case of Hebrew and Aramaic in the Middle Ages," *Hebrew Studies* 62 (2021): 343–63.

Generally speaking, I would like to note that such arguments, based on intuitive assumptions not anchored in empirical data, are not a good methodology for making historical claims. As for whether Hebrew was a spoken language, there seems to be no evidence, direct or even indirect, to answer this question; therefore, it is better to leave it open. Instead, this chapter attempts to characterize the language of the Mishnah, regardless of whether it was spoken or not. To this end, let us now describe the language of the rabbinic corpus from the two perspectives introduced in section 1.

3. FROM HETEROGENEITY TO IDEALIZED GRAMMARS

An examination of the inventory of independent pronouns in the Mishnah, specifically in MS Kaufmann,[6] reveals that even in tractate *Shabat* alone there are two different variants of the third-person masculine plural pronoun: הם (mShab 6.4) and הן (mShab 12.4). Heterogeneity of this sort can be found at all levels of mishnaic grammar. Some words have different spellings representing different phonology. For example, guttural consonants alternate with their non-guttural counterparts,[7] e.g., כאור and כעור "ugly."[8] Furthermore, some verbal and nominal patterns alternate between their "contextual" and "pausal" forms (נִכְתְּבָה/נִכְתָּבָה, הוּלְבְּשׁוּ/הוּלְבָּשׁוּ),[9] exhibiting another instance of heterogeneity. In some cases, the heterogeneity is evi-

---

6. Scholars such as Epstein, Lieberman, Yalon, and Kutscher emphasized that the research of Mishnaic Hebrew must rely on high-quality manuscripts, which differ significantly from the printed editions of the Mishnah. E. Y. Kutscher "Mishnaic Hebrew," in *Henoch Yalon Jubilee Volume on the Occasion of his Seventy-Fifth Birthday*, ed. S. Lieberman et al. (Hebrew; Jerusalem, 1963) 246–80, insisted that the grammatical description must be based on "reliable manuscripts" (אבות טקסטים), i.e., manuscripts which faithfully reflect the original version of the text, and identified MS Kaufmann as the best source of this kind. In fact, Kutscher seems to ascribe all deviations from MS Kaufmann to copyists influenced by the Tiberian tradition of Biblical Hebrew or by the language of the Babylonian Talmud. This approach was modulated in Moshe Bar-Asher, "The Mishnah in Ms. Parma B of Seder Teharot—Introduction" (Hebrew), in M. Bar-Asher, ed., *A Collection of Articles on the Language of the Sages*, vol. 1 (Jerusalem, 1971): 166–85. Nevertheless, unless stated otherwise, all examples in this chapter are indeed taken from MS Kaufmann.

7. Shimon Sharvit, "Gutturals in Rabbinic Hebrew," *Studies in the Hebrew Language and the Talmudic Literature: Dedicated to the Memory of Dr. Menahem Moreshet*; (Ramat-Gan, 1989), 225–43.

8. Moshe Bar Asher, *A Morphology of Mishnaic Hebrew: Introductions and Noun Morphology* (Jerusalem, 2015), 887–88. While in MS Kaufmann the spelling is always with *aleph*, in MS Parma A both spellings are found.

9. Moshe Bar Asher, *Contextual Forms and Pausal Forms in Mishnaic Hebrew According to MS Parma B* (Hebrew), *Language Studies* 4 (1990): 51–100.

dent within the very same text (i.e., the same part of a given manuscript), and in other cases it is evident in different parts of the same manuscript (e.g., in a specific tractate)[10] or between different manuscripts.[11]

The term "heterogeneity" is used here in the sense of Labov's observation that "it is common for a language to have many alternate ways of saying 'the same' thing".[12] Indeed, all languages exhibit variation at all levels of the linguistic system: certain words have alternate pronunciations, and it is not so rare for a language to have different forms of the same grammatical category. A study that highlighted heterogeneity was Weinreich et al.,[13] which contended that linguistic analysis should seek to identify structure in multiple versions.[14] From a methodological point of view, the task of detecting such multiple structures has two components: first, identifying the separate idealized grammars, and second, determining their functional distribution by identifying the circumstances in which each of them is used. These two stages correspond to the two perspectives mentioned in the introduction with respect to the language of the Mishnah.

The idea that it is possible, or necessary, to distinguish between idealized grammars rests on the assumption, well-established in both the structuralist and generative theoretical frameworks, that languages exist as independent (cognitive) systems with identifiable structure. This common theoretical approach considers languages as systems operating on various levels—phonological, morphological, and syntactic—whereby all the elements, taken together, convey a message, i.e., combine in a compositional manner to produce a meaningful expression. Each level involves an inventory of elements that relate to one another in specific ways. For example, at the morphological level, there are systematic paradigms, such as the paradigm of independent pronouns, and this is the context in which forms like הם and הן, mentioned above, are examined. In our context, it is worth noting that the paradigms of EH and LH differ in terms of whether the 2nd and 3rd person

10. An example is Tractate Abot, which is unique in its content and style, as it contains ethical teachings. See Shimon Sharvit, *Leshonah ve-Signonah shel Massekhet Avot le-Doroteha* (Hebrew; Beer-Sheba, 2004).

11. See Moshe Bar-Asher, *Studies in Classical Hebrew* (Berlin and Boston, 2014), chapter 19, for systematic differences between groups and types of manuscripts.

12. William Labov, *Sociolinguistic Patterns* (Philadelphia, 1972).

13. U. Weinreich, W. Labov, and M. I. Herzog, "Empirical Foundations for a Theory of Language Change," in *Directions for Historical Linguistics: A Symposium*, ed. W. P. Lehmann and Y. Malkiel (Austin, 1968), 95–188.

14. On the significance of this paper, see Brian D. Joseph, "Historical Linguistics in the 50 Years since Weinrich, Labov, and Herzog (1968)," in *New Directions for Historical Linguistics*, ed. H. C. Boas and M. Pierce (Leiden, 2019), 153–73.

masculine plural pronouns are identical to their feminine counterparts (this process of merging of forms that were originally distinct to be pronounced identically is termed syncretism). Having recognized certain collections of elements as forming a paradigm, we can compare alternate paradigms and characterize the synchronic relations between their respective elements, or examine them diachronically and identify historical processes that result from the membership of various elements in the same inventory (as in cases of leveling, which is a process of generalizing an inflection across a paradigm so that all members of the given paradigm become more similar).

Thus, the standard methodology employed by linguists assumes "an ideal speaker-listener, in a completely homogeneous speech-community."[15] Given this methodological assumption, intra-speaker variations must be regarded as cases of optional rules.[16] Thus, in our context, we would aim to reconstruct two "ideal systems"—one for EH and another for LH—and to identify the systematic differences between them, and at the same time we will also aim to recognize the rules that govern the choices between these systems, within specific corpora. We turn now to illustrate how the two systems can be set apart.

Table 1 in the Appendix presents the standard verbal stems (binyanim) of EH and LH and outlines, in broad strokes, their semantic-syntactic distribution in each period: in EH, each active stem had a passive counterpart, whereas LH demonstrates a systematic syncretism of the passive and middle categories, i.e., the same forms are used both to express the middle lexical function and to mark passive sentences.[17]

---

15. Noam Chomsky, *Aspects of the Theory of Syntax* (Cambridge, 1965), 3.

16. See, among others, William Labov, *The Study of Nonstandard English.* (Washington, 1969); Antony Kroch, "Reflexes of Grammar in Patterns of Language Change," *Language Variation and Change* 1 (1989): 199–244; D. Lightfoot, *The Development of Language: Acquisition, Change and Evolution.* (Oxford, 1999). It should be noted, however, that many linguists, especially proponents of usage-based approaches, think that the idea of a systematic homogeneous linguistic system is illusory. For them, attempts to portray homogeneous varieties are merely a "game" fraught with methodological problems. Sinfree Makoni and Alastair Pennycook, "Disinventing and Reconstituting Languages," in *Disinventing and Reconstituting Languages*, ed. S. Makoni and A. Pennycook (Cleveland, 2007); J. E. Schmidt, "Versuch zum Varietätenbegriff," in *Varietäten—Theorie und Empirie* (Frankfurt, 2005), 61–74. For a review of the literature on this topic see Anne-Sophie Ghyselen and Gunther De Vogelaer, "Seeking Systematicity in Variation: Theoretical and Methodological Considerations on the 'Variety' Concept," *Frontiers in Psychology* (2018).

17. For a review of all the verbal patterns in the language of the Mishnah, see Bar-Asher, *Classical Hebrew*, chapter 20.

The difference between EH and LH in this context can be described in terms of the loss of certain stems (the two פֻּעַל stems), and a formal shift of הִתְפַּעֵל <= נִתְפַּעֵל. From a wider perspective, as noted, these changes add up to a formal syncretism between the middle and passive grammatical categories.

Observations of this kind involve a theoretical abstraction and idealization of the data itself. In reality, when comparing forms from various corpora, one encounters heterogeneity everywhere. Forms characterized as belonging to EH appear next to forms associated with LH. For example, the Mishnah contains instances of the form התפללתה "you prayed" (mTaʿan 3. 8), prefixed with ה- rather than נ-.[18] But as explained above, such heterogeneity is not unique to the language of the Mishnah. All languages, spoken and written, exhibit variations of form and structure. Speakers and writers always employ more than one linguistic system. Often, the variants belong to different registers and are used in different social settings. This phenomenon is difficult to detect in ancient texts, but it is occasionally discernible even there. In our context, Nathan argued that the distinction between two forms of the root ק.ב.ל depends on genre: in Tannaitic texts, the EH form התקבל is used in legal formulae, while the expected LH form נתקבל is found elsewhere.[19]

Heterogeneity cannot and should not always be explained in sociolinguistic terms, as it can stem from other factors as well. Variation in written texts may be due to multiple authors using different grammars (from different areas or periods), or to the instability of authors' linguistic knowledge. Variation can also arise in the process of transmission, i.e., when the original texts were copied by hand or rendered in print.[20] This can be either accidental or deliberate (based on some norm or ideal, and in the case of the language of the Mishnah, the norm was often based on the grammar of EH), or due to the influence of foreign languages.

Before describing the language of the Mishnah and its place in the history of Hebrew from the two perspectives introduced here, let me note an-

---

18. Gideon Haneman, *Morphology of Mishnaic Hebrew, Based on the Tradition of MS Parma (De Rossi 138)* (Hebrew; Tel-Aviv, 1980), 208–11.

19. Hayya Nathan, "The Linguistic Tradition of MS Erfurt of the Tosefta" (Hebrew; PhD diss., Hebrew University, 1981), 148–49. Cf. Yochanan Breuer *The Hebrew in the Babylonian Talmud according to the Manuscripts of Tractate Pesahum* (Hebrew; Jerusalem, 2020), 176–78.

20. Michael Ryzhik. "From Manuscript to Print Edition: The Development of Vocalization Patterns in the Late-Fifteenth and Mid-Sixteenth-Century Printed Editions of the Italian Prayer Book," *Lěšonénu* (2012), 333–57.

other significant difference between these two approaches that indirectly affects the linguistic discussion. It is important to note that a diachronic investigation of the linguistic system is rarely based on one specific text. In periodizing a language, scholars seek to reconstruct a grammar of each era. They therefore utilize as many texts as possible in order to distill a consistent grammar that eliminates the "noise" in the texts and untangles the mixture of grammars. In contrast, when focusing on the history of the written forms, it is important to consider the nature of each individual text and keep in mind the historical context of its composition. For our purposes, when comparing the language of the Bible with the language of the Mishnah, it is not enough to think in diachronic terms. It is also crucial to keep in mind, for example, that the Mishnah is very different from the Bible in terms of its genre. Generally speaking, the Mishnah is a legal text, a collection of brief rulings on specific issues. Unlike the Bible, it contains few narrative passages, and those that do appear are very short. Poetic texts are likewise almost absent from the Mishnah, and indeed, the tractate of *Avot*, which does have poetic features, is linguistically very different from the other tractates of the Mishnah.[21]

Such stylistic differences must be kept in mind when comparing the language of the two corpora. For example, differences of genre are crucial to the analysis of the tense system. Narrative text presents events taking place in a certain temporal sequence, while legal texts are largely modal, setting out laws and rules regarding possible states of affairs.[22] Many languages use different modes of expression to convey factual statements and modal ones. Therefore, a comparison between these aspects of EH and LH grammar is not straightforward, and must take into account this gap in genre.

To conclude, in studying the language of a certain corpus—in our case the language of the Mishnah—one must first inventory all the grammatical elements found in this corpus, and then try to account for its grammatical heterogeneity. In broad strokes, the goals are: (1) to distinguish between separate grammars; (2) to examine the historical relationship between these grammars, and (3) to identify regularities in the distribution of the competing grammars.

---

21. Moshe Bar-Asher, *A Morphology of Mishnaic Hebrew*, 887–88.

22. See Elitzur A. Bar-Asher Siegal, "Towards a Reconsideration of the Tense-Aspect-Mood System of Tannaitic Hebrew," in *Studies in Mishnaic Hebrew and Related Fields: Proceeding of the Yale Symposium on Mishnaic Hebrew, May 2014*, ed. E. A. Bar-Asher Siegal and A. J. Koller (Jerusalem-New-Haven 2017): 59–66.

4. THE HISTORY OF HEBREW FROM THE PERSPECTIVE OF LINGUISTIC SYSTEMS

4.1 Principles for Distinguishing between EH and LH

Given that all texts exhibit some level of linguistic heterogeneity, it seems reasonable to begin the discussion with a few notes on how to determine which grammatical category belongs to which linguistic system. It is beyond the scope of this chapter to fully address this complicated theoretical question. Moreover, it is not even clear that linguists have a consistently reliable method of resolving it. Hence, I will only demonstrate that in practice, there are several principles that can guide us in assessing which elements belong to EH and which belong to LH:

1. Prevalence in early vs. late texts: Given any attested variation, an option that appears mostly in early texts can be assumed to belong to EH, while one that appears mostly in later texts can be assumed to be part of LH.
2. Derivation: When it is evident that one variant is derived from the other, it is reasonable to assume that the derived variant is younger.
3. Internal structure: When systematic connections between two forms can be identified, it is preferable to treat them as part of the same linguistic system.

These principles are only rules of thumb for drawing a tentative distinction between grammars; furthermore, as we shall see, they occasionally yield conflicting results. In such cases, the first principle can usually be given primacy. Let us therefore start by surveying some of the linguistic differences between the two corpora—the Mishnah and the Bible—and then proceed to characterize these differences in historical linguistic terms.

A convenient place to begin is the lexicon, because it has been recognized for centuries that the Mishnah and the Bible differ in this respect, using different words for the same concept. For example, in the Bible the standard word for "tree" is עץ, whereas in the Mishnah it is אילן. The Biblical word for "fasting" is צום, while the mishnaic word is תענית. Further pairs of this sort are איש-אדם "man" and רע-חבר "friend."[23] Similar relations hold between grammatical morphemes: the standard relative pronoun in the Bible is אשר while in the Mishnah it is -ש (although both forms appear in both corpora).

---

23. For a substantial survey of this kind of differences see Abba Bendavid, *Leshon Miqra u-Lshon Hakhamim*, 2 vols., 2nd ed. (Hebrew; Tel-Aviv, 1971).

Sometimes the variants exhibit only minor morphological differences, as with the Biblical demonstratives הזה/הזאת and their mishnaic counterparts זו/זה. Conversely, there are elements that have a different meaning in each corpus. In the Bible the root ב.ע.ל refers to ownership whereas in the Mishnah it refers to sexual intercourse;[24] in the Bible the word מזוזה denotes a doorpost while in the Mishnah it denotes the ritual object affixed to the doorpost.[25]

So far we have only stated which variants are common in which corpus. In some instances, the variant distribution can be accounted for in terms of historical development, as with מזוזה, which seems to be an example of metonymy—a semantic change based on proximity in space or time. In other cases, it is possible to rely on principle 3 and demonstrate that semantic changes in the meaning of specific words correspond to other changes in the same semantic field.[26]

Taking the approach of comparing linguistic systems, and following principle 1, it is possible to map many grammatical differences between EH and LH with a high level of certainty. For example, in terms of the inventory of phonemes, it is reasonable to assume that while EH had the consonant /ɬ/, represented by the letter שׂ, in LH this consonant merged with the consonant /s/. This assumption is supported by the alternate spellings of words like שאור (mMen 5.1) סאור (mTY 3.4). Another example from phonology is the widespread assumption that LH had no distinction between /m/ and /n/ in word-final position, as both were either pronounced as /n/ or turned into a nasalized vowel in final position, as evident from spellings like אדן "man" (mBer 1.3) instead of the standard אדם, or כרן "vineyard" (mBB 4.9) instead of the standard כרם.[27]

Similarly, it is widely accepted that EH and LH had different versions of many morphological forms. For example, the infinitive construct in LH always begins with *l-*, and with weak verbs its form mirrors the form of the prefix-conjugation (compare EH לאמר with LH לומר). In EH the masculine singular form of the independent pronoun "you" was אַתָּה, but there are reasons to believe that in LH it was אַתְּ, identical to the feminine form.[28] Yet another example is the form of the presentative particle, which is הנה in EH

24. Elitzur A. Bar-Asher Siegal and Michal Bar-Asher Siegal, "The Hebrew-Based Traditions in Galatians 4:21–31," *Ancient Christianity* 9 (2018): 404–31.

25. Bar-Asher, *Classical Hebrew*, 238.

26. Gad B. Sarfatti, *Hebrew Semantics* (Hebrew, Jerusalem 1985), 179–80.

27. See Bar-Asher, *Morphology of Mishnaic Hebrew*, 63.

28. In MS Kaufmann the form את of the masculine pronoun appears 19 times while the EH from אתה appears 140 times. Some manuscripts exhibit only the EH form. See also Michael Ryzhik, "Direct Speech in Mishnaic Hebrew," *Leshonenu* 84 (2022), 82–90.

and הרי in LH. This difference is also accompanied by a syntactic one: While in EH nominal clauses, the presentative particle is followed by a cliticized pronoun denoting the subject of the clause (הנני, הנך, הנו), in LH the presentative can also be accompanied by an independent subject pronoun (הרי אני/ הרי את/ הרי הוא).[29]

Following this method, it is possible to construct two independent grammars for each grammatical category. Next, we turn to principle 2 and consider the diachronic relationship between the two grammars by asking the following question with regard to each difference: Did the LH variant develop from the EH one? What motivated the change from one grammar to the other? I will now outline several types of changes that occurred between the early and late periods.

4.2 Types of Change from EH to LH

4.2.1 Lexical Changes

Some grammatical changes are merely the result of lexical changes. For example, the replacement of the early construction featuring the components איש-אחיו/רעהו with the late construction featuring the components אדם-חבירו is at least partly a reflection of the lexical change mentioned above:[30]

(1)

(a) וְכִי יָזִד אִישׁ עַל רֵעֵהוּ לְהָרְגוֹ בְּעָרְמָה
"If a man willfully attacks his neighbor to kill him cunningly" (Ex 21:14)

(b) התקינו שיה(ו)א אדם שואל את שלום חבירו בשם
"It was decreed that every man should greet his friend by the name of the Lord" (mBer 9.5)

Similarly, genitive constructions, used to express possession and other relations, consisting of relative-pronoun+ל+Noun Phrase were used in both periods, but EH uses its relative pronoun *šer* as in אשר לשלמה,[31] whereas LH uses the relative element *še-* as in שלשלמה. In such cases, the difference

29. Ruth Stern, "What Does Modern Hebrew Continue? The Case of the Presentatives הנני and הריני", *Hebrew Studies* 62 (2021): 403–29.

30. It is more accurate to describe the function of the expressions as indefinite pronouns, used also to express reciprocity. On this topic, and with a discussion on these forms, see Elitzur A. Bar-Asher Siegal, *The NP-Strategy for Expressing Reciprocity: Typology, History, Syntax and Semantics*, Typological Studies in Language 127 (Amsterdam, 2020), especially chapter 4.

31. It should be noted, however, that this construction is quite rare in BH and appears mostly in the later books.

between the two grammars involves nothing more than a difference in the inventory of forms or components used in the various grammatical constructions.

In other differences, chronological order is a crucial factor. This is very clear at the phonological level. For example, as mentioned above, in EH the contrast between /m/ and /n/ was consistently maintained, whereas in LH it was neutralized in word-final position.

Clear cases of chronological development also exist at the morphological level. For example, the Bible has two forms, לולי and אילו,[32] which introduce negative and positive counterfactual conditionals, respectively. The Mishnah, on the other hand, has the form אילולי, which seems to be a combination of both and marks negative counterfactual conditionals. It seems reasonable to assume that the combined form is a later development.[33] In other cases, LH features grammatical elements that cannot be related to any specific phenomenon in EH. An example is the construction consisting of כל "all"+relative pronoun+3rd-person independent pronoun (כל שהוא/שהיא/ שהן), which either appears as a free relative, quantifying universally over kinds (2a), or is embedded within a clause (2b) to universally quantify over quantity (and later as an indefinite pronoun/determiner (2c)):[34]

(2)

(a) כל שהוא מין קללה אין מברכין עליו

"No blessing should be pronounced over things which had their origin in a curse" (mBer 6.3)

(b) קרקע כל שהוא חייב בפיאה ובבכורים

"Whatever the size of the ground it is subject to *Pe'ah* and to '*first fruits*'" (mPe'ah 3.6)

(c) הבונה כמה יבנה ויהא חייב. הבונה כל שהוא המסתת והמכה בפטיש ו[ב]מעצד הקודיח כל שהוא חייב

"He who builds, how much must he build to become guilty? Whoever builds at all [be it ever so little], whoever chops a stone, strikes with a hammer, or uses a plane, or bores a hole; [whosoever] at all [does any of these] is guilty." (mShab 12.1)

This is a new development within LH. Its emergence can be explained internally as a grammaticalization of expressions that arose in a composi-

---

32. It must be noted that אילו appears only in later books of the Bible (specifically Ecclesiastes and the Book of Esther).

33. See Elitzur A. Bar-Asher Siegal, "The History of the Forms אילולי and אלמלי— Part I: linguistic diachrony," *Leshonenu* 81 (2019): 95–115.

34. For a discussion of this construction see Elitzur A. Bar-Asher Siegal, "*Kol-še-hu* in Rabbinic Hebrew and Modern Hebrew," *Leshonenu 84* (2022), 110–143.

tional manner. From a broader perspective, the emergence of these forms in LH should be considered in light of the emergence of other indefinite expressions consisting of relative pronoun+3rd independent pronoun, such as משהו.[35]

4.2.2 Typical Diachronic Changes

Alongside these considerations, it is often possible to apply standard methodologies of historical linguistics to account for the data collected from all the relevant corpora. This essentially involves applying principle 2 and tracing diachronic developments in the history of Hebrew. These developments are of various kinds:

4.2.2.1 Contact-Induced Changes

Many of the forms that appear in the later texts but not in the earlier ones have parallels in Aramaic, and consequently are often regarded as the result of Aramaic influence. For example, the standard NP-strategy for expressing reciprocity (strategies whose components are Nominal Phrases such as "one-another" and "each other") in the Bible employs the construction איש-רעהו/אחיו lit."a man-his companion/brother" (3a).The equivalent construction in LH features a repetition of the proximal demonstrative, such as זה-זה lit. "this-this" (3b), which mirrors the Aramaic construction and therefore seems to be borrowed from that language (3c).

(3)

(a) וַיַּחֲזִקוּ אִישׁ בְּרֹאשׁ רֵעֵהוּ
"Then each man grabbed his opponent by the head" (2 Sam 2:16)

(b) השוכר את האומנים והיטעו זה את זה ואין לו זה על זה אלא זה תרעומת
"If one engaged craftsmen and they deceived one another, they have only resentment against each other" (mBM 6. 1)

(c) וְאַרְכֻבָּתֵהּ דָּא לְדָא נָקְשָׁן
"and his knees were knocking against one another" (Dan 5:6)

Similarly, the LH reflexive pronoun consists of the noun עצם "bone" suffixed with a dependent pronoun that agrees with the antecedent. This is a calque of an Aramaic construction in which the noun גרם "bone" is used in a similar way.[36]

---

35. M. Hirsh Segal, *A Grammar of the Language of the Mishnah* (Hebrew and Tel-Aviv, 1936), 64, proposes that כל שהוא is related to the pronominal use of כל "all" in the Bible. However, this association does not explain the presence of the relative pronoun and independent pronoun in this construction.

36. Segal, "Mišnaic Hebrew," 679.

It must be noted, however, that it is often hard to determine whether parallels between LH and Aramaic reflect contact-induced change or should be considered as an isogloss, in which Hebrew and Aramaic have the same linguistic feature. For example, with the 2nd-person masculine singular independent pronoun את, shared by LH and the Aramaic of this period, it is almost impossible to determine whether the shift from אתה to את in Hebrew is a reflection of Aramaic influence or a shared feature involving an apocopation (loss of a sound at the end of a word) of the final vowel.

4.2.2.2 *Internal Developments*

Analogies: Some changes of form between EH and LH can be explained as cases of analogy. For example, as mentioned earlier, while in EH the middle form of פָּעֵל is הִתְפַּעֵל, in LH the form of the middle-passive is נִתְפַּעַל. The change of the prefix (from *hi-* to *ni-*) can be explained as an analogy to the middle-passive form of the *qal*-stem, נִפְעַל. Given that Aramaic has no stem with the prefix *n-*, this development cannot be the result of Aramaic influence.

Reanalysis: The word שוב, imperative of the verb שב "return," was reanalyzed as an adverb meaning "again":[37]

(4) שוב מעשה באסיא
"Once again it happened in Asya" (mYev 16.4)

This reanalysis very likely occurred via a bridging context like the one in (5):

(5) "לך שוב"
"go-return"(I Kings 19, 15, and 20, among other places)

In contexts such as this, "go return" and "go again" express the same command in reality, and therefore שוב could be interpreted as the latter instead of the former. Such situations possibly induced the semantic reanalysis of this expression.[38]

---

37. In this case there is an Aramaic equivalent, with the form תוב, so this development may be the result of Aramaic influence.

38. Consider the following context: שׁוּב קַח-לְךָ, מְגִלָּה אַחֶרֶת; וּכְתֹב עָלֶיהָ, אֵת כָּל-הַדְּבָרִים הָרִאשֹׁנִים, אֲשֶׁר הָיוּ עַל-הַמְּגִלָּה הָרִאשֹׁנָה, אֲשֶׁר שָׂרַף יְהוֹיָקִים מֶלֶךְ-יְהוּדָה

"*Return* and take another scroll and write on it all the former words that were on the first scroll, which Jehoiakim king of Judah has burned up" (Jer 36:28).

This is a context in which the reanalysis is expected to take place, where שוב can be understood from the context as "take again." I wish to thank Noah Feldman for this great example.

Structural changes: Turning now to principle 3, the Tense-Aspect-Mood (TAM) system is a good example of a context in which it is crucial to consider the morphological inventory as a system. Tense, aspect, and mood are the most common grammatical categories marked in the verbs of natural languages, and much linguistic research relates the morphosyntactic markers found in languages to their semantic values, divided according to these categories. In such morphosyntactic systems, the function of each verbal form depends to some extent on the language's TAM categories, and on the contrast between the meanings of the various forms.

Table 2 in the Appendix compares the inventories of the verbal TAM form of the two linguistic systems.

On the one hand, the shift from EH to LH can be described as a case of simplification,[39] in which a complex morphological system with a large variety of forms became a simpler system with a smaller number of forms. However, this is only part of the story, since the TAM system not only became smaller, but was also reorganized. Table 3 in the Appendix demonstrates how the grammar of LH encodes a number of TAM distinctions.[40]

According to the structure depicted in table 3, the verb forms marked for person (i.e., prefix- and suffix-conjugation verbs) are always marked for tense as well—the former for past tense and the latter for future tense—while the participle always indicates the imperfective aspect. Hence, when a suffix/prefix-conjugation verb appears on its own, it usually indicates the perfective aspect. However, it is more accurate to say that the conjugating verbs are unmarked for aspect, since they are compatible with both aspectual values, perfective and imperfective. When a participle is preceded by a verb in the suffix/prefix-conjugation form (specifically the auxiliary of the root ה.י.ה), the verb phrase as a whole indicates the imperfective aspect and the conjugated form indicates the tense. The EH system indicates other distinctions as well, mostly aspectual ones. This is an example of a context where the linguistic systems of EH and LH differ significantly. Furthermore, the changes that produced the LH TAM system are similar to changes that took place in the Aramaic dialects of the period, and which are in fact observed cross-linguistically.[41] For our purposes, the important

---

39. Cf. Shimon Sharvit, *The Tense System of Mishnaic Hebrew* (Hebrew; Sarfatti, 1980).

40. This description follows Bar-Asher Siegal "Towards a Reconsideration." See M. Mishor, "The Tense System in Tannaitic Hebrew" (Hebrew; PhD diss., Hebrew University, 1983), for a different view.

41. Kevin Grasso, "The Stative to Perfective to Perfect to Past Path in Semitic" (forthcoming).

observation is that there is a reorganization of the entire system according to some core semantics.

4.3 Conflicts between Principles 1 and 2

As noted at the beginning of this section, ideally it would be possible to demonstrate that all differences between LH and EH grammar can be explained diachronically, i.e., that LH forms are younger, and are derived from older EH forms. But in practice this is not always possible, for there are instances where principles 1 and 2 yield contradictory conclusions.

For example, the mishnaic form of the feminine singular proximal demonstrative is זו *zô*, while the Biblical form is זאת *zōt*. From a diachronic point of view, and based on comparative data from other Semitic languages, it seems easier to derive the Biblical form from the mishnaic one, rather than the other way around.

Similarly, it was noted above that the Biblical construction איש את רעהו/אחיו was replaced by the mishnaic אדם את חבירו. However, from the perspective of grammaticalization, the Biblical construction seems more "advanced," since the meaning of the word אח "sibling" is bleached and can be applied to inanimate referents, such as curtains:

(6) חֲמֵשׁ הַיְרִיעֹת, תִּהְיֶיןָ חֹבְרֹת, אִשָּׁה, אֶל-אֲחֹתָהּ
"The five curtains should be joined to one another." (Ex 26:3)

On the other hand, the equivalent element in the LH construction, namely חבר "friend," cannot be applied to inanimate referents which require a different construction involving a repetition of nouns.[42]

(7) מטבילים מגב לגב ומחבורה לחבורה ביום טוב.
"One may immerse from one purpose to another, and from one company to another" (mBets 2.3).

Finally, we saw earlier that in EH, the presentative הנה is followed by a clitic pronoun (הנני, הנך), while in LH, the presentative הרי is followed by an independent pronoun (הרי אני, הרי אתה). This syntactic change is interesting, since in most cases cliticization represents a later stage in the process of grammaticalization.

These examples illustrate a conflict between the principles proposed above for distinguishing between EH and LH elements. Such conflicts are usually resolved by giving precedence to principle 1, and also by assuming that Hebrew, like any other language, had dialects throughout its periods

---

42. Bar-Asher Siegal *The NP-Strategy*, 132–34.

of existence as a spoken tongue (an assumption that is supported by independent evidence). Accordingly, when early and late forms differ, we need not automatically assume that the latter developed from the former. Some late forms may be derived from unattested forms in a different dialect of the earlier language. In the case of the demonstratives, for example, it may be assumed that the two forms, *zōt* and *zô,* existed in different dialects of EH. The Bible has one of these variants (*zōt),* whereas the Mishnah inherited the other.[43]

5. THE HISTORY OF THE WRITTEN CORPORA

Biblical Hebrew (BH) and Mishnaic Hebrew (MH) are the languages of the Bible and the Mishnah. While the Bible is mostly written in EH and the Mishnah mostly in LH, elements associated with LH are occasionally found in the Bible, and vice versa.[44] Some scholars appear to assume that the Mishnah was originally written in "pure LH" and that any deviation from this is the result of later interference during the transmission of the texts. However, the evidence suggests that a more nuanced approach to the relationship between EH and LH is needed. While it is true that EH *per se* does not appear in the rabbinic corpus, its authors often inserted EH elements into the text. The next section presents some examples of MH texts containing EH forms, as well as examples of LH elements in the Bible. This will be followed by a reflection concerning the difference between the two approaches: the one that describes the language of the Mishnah as LH and the one that describes it as MH.

It is often the case that where BH exhibits heterogeneity, MH does not. Sometimes the BH variants are similar in their prevalence — as with the two variants of the independent pronoun "I," אנכי and אני — and sometimes one of the variants is noticeably more common than the other, as with the two variants of the independent pronoun "we," אנחנו and אנו, the first of which is the standard form in BH.[45] In both instances, LH uses only one of the variants—specifically אני and אנו—while the other is rare. The forms אני and אנו are paradigmatically related, as they follow the iconicity principle of a single difference in form (*i* vs. *u*) signaling a single difference in meaning (singular vs. plural). The pronoun אנו is thus an example of an ele-

---

43. See Bar-Asher, *Classical Hebrew,* 234–36, for a similar discussion and more examples.

44. See Bar-Asher, *Classical Hebrew,* chapters 6 and 23, for an overview of the relevant phenomena.

45. In fact, אנו appears only once in the Bible, in the *Ktiv* (Jer 42:6).

ment that is generally regarded as part of LH but that appears once in BH as well. Another example is the word אדם used as an indefinite pronoun. As mentioned above, this element is typical of LH, whereas BH usually used the word איש instead. However, the Bible does have some instances of אדם in this context.[46] Similarly, it also displays a few examples of reciprocal constructions featuring a repetition of the demonstrative, the typical LH construction:

(8)

(a) שְׂרָפִים עֹמְדִים מִמַּעַל לוֹ... וְקָרָא זֶה אֶל-זֶה וְאָמַר

"Seraphim stood above Him . . . and they called one to the other and said . . ." (Isa 6:2–3)

(b) וַיַּחֲנוּ אֵלֶּה נֹכַח אֵלֶּה שִׁבְעַת יָמִים

"For seven days they camped opposite each other" (1 Kgs 20:29)

These are all instances of a well-known phenomenon whereby early heterogeneity is the first sign of historical change, and whereby rare forms, restricted to a particular dialect or register, become standard at a later stage.[47]

From the opposite perspective, features of EH morphology and phonology are often attested in MH as well, and in some categories they are even the default. Given the differences between written and spoken languages, and the tendency of the former to preserve archaic features, it is not surprising that the rabbinic corpus often contains BH elements, despite clear evidence that the spoken language (and for our purposes, LH in general) did not adopt them. For example, as noted earlier, in LH word-final /m/ became /n/, or a nasalized vowel. Nevertheless, in the rabbinic corpora, most words that historically ended with /m/ are still written with the letter *mem*. This is an example of the phenomenon, widely attested crosslinguistically, whereby the spelling reflects an older pronunciation of the word. The same can also happen with morphological categories, and may apply to the independent pronouns mentioned above. Moreover, even when the later texts are written in LH, it is still possible that they were originally written in a more archaic style and later amended to fit new norms.

So far, I have surveyed appearances of EH features in MH, and of LH features in BH, which do not seem to be motivated by the context in any way. However, some such appearances do seem to be motivated. There are strong reasons to believe that EH and LH coexisted for a long time, and that the differences between them were used to encode socio-linguistic distinctions. Broadly speaking, the distribution of BH and LH elements can be described

46. Segal, *Grammar*, 65.
47. As claimed by Weinreich et al., "Empirical Foundations."

as a case of diglossia, a state in which two (or more) languages, or varieties of the same language, coexist within a speech community. In such situations, the functional domains of the languages tend to be in complementary distribution, with one language used in "higher" contexts—such as religious, educational, literary, and other prestigious spheres—and the other used in "lower" context, serving as the everyday spoken tongue.

Our example can be described as a form of "literary diglossia,"[48] in which literary texts utilize two linguistic varieties to produce certain effects within the text. The elements of LH occasionally encountered in BH texts were presumably meant to add a colloquial flavor; conversely, EH elements in MH texts served to elevate the style.

Thus, in the Bible, LH-like features appear in direct speech;[49] e.g. to express the meaning "hold," in direct speech the verb is א.ח.ז (LH) while in narrative it is ח.ז.ק (EH):[50]

(9) 'שְׁלַח יָדְךָ וֶאֱחֹז בִּזְנָבוֹ'

וַיִּשְׁלַח יָדוֹ וַיַּחֲזֶק בּוֹ

"'Reach out your hand and take it by the tail.' So (Moses) reached out and took hold of it" (Ex 4:4)

Similarly, it has been demonstrated that features of LH phonology (loss of distinction between word-final /m/ and /n/) are used to mark direct speech in the book of Ruth,[51] and that direct speech even exhibits a TAM system close to that of LH.[52]

Conversely, as mentioned earlier, MH employs BH elements in passages associated with the Temple (e.g., התפעל instead of נתפעל, as in the verb השתחוה), as well as in poetic expressions (and in Tractate *Avot* in general), which feature prefix-conjugation jussive forms (10a) (see table 2 in the Appendix), as well as the EH איש-רעהו reciprocal construction (10b):

48. See Elitzur Bar-Asher Siegal, *Linguistics and Philological Studies in Hebrew and in Aramaic* (Jerusalem, 2020), 17.

49. See R. S. Kawashima, *Biblical Narrative and the Death of Rhapsode* (Bloomington, 2004), 35–69, for a characterization of the language of the biblical narratives.

50. Bendavid, *Leshon Miqra u-Lshon Hakhamim*, 14–15.

51. Elitzur Bar-Asher, *Linguistic Markers in the Book of Ruth, Shnaton—An Annual for Biblical and Ancient Near Eastern Studies* 18 (2008): 25–42.

52. See *inter alia* M. S. Smith, "Grammatically Speaking: The Participle as a Main Verb of Clauses (Predicative Participle) in Direct Discourse and Narrative in Pre-Mishnaic Hebrew," *Sirach, Scrolls and Sages: Proceedings of a Second International Symposium on the Hebrew of the Dead Sea Scrolls, Ben Sira, and the Mishnah, held at Leiden University, 15–17 December 1997* (STDJ 33), ed. T. Muraoka and J. F. Elwolde (1999), 278–332, who examines the use of the participle in direct discourse and direct narratives.

(10)

(a) "אל תעש תפילתך קבע אלא תחנונים"

"When you pray, do not make your prayers routine, but [an entreaty of] mercy and a supplication" (mAvot 2.13)

(b) "אילולי מוראה איש את רעהו חיים בלענו".

"For were it not for the fear of its authority, we would swallow each other alive." (mAvot 3.2)

This leads to the conclusion that the main innovation of MH, when compared to earlier Hebrew texts, is the employment of LH as its default language. Unlike in Qumran, where most of the authors attempted to write in some variety of EH (to the extent of producing grammatical innovations resulting from hyper-correction),[53] MH generally uses the LH grammar and lexicon.[54]

According to this picture, there was a gradual shift from EH to LH in literature. Based on the textual evidence at our disposal, we can conclude that after the First Revolt, LH gained dominance in a growing number of texts, and a register that had been largely colloquial began to be used in literature. There are various theories regarding this shift; some scholars associate it with the nationalist movement of the time or with socio-economic changes among the ruling class, for example. The observations made in this chapter suggest that two additional considerations must be taken into account. Firstly, the nature of the texts: orally transmitted rabbinic texts should not be treated the same way as texts transmitted in writing. It is reasonable to assume that written texts and oral texts will transform as they enter a different register. In addition, this chapter sought to demonstrate that in examining the evolution of language as a system—such as the shift from EH to LH— we find certain shifts in perspective that are natural and expected in any language. Among them are shifts in the standards and traits associated with literary corpora. For example, it is known that over time, spoken registers and styles make their way into literary writing. Conversely, archaisms serve to elevate the language. As we saw, in the time of the Mishnah, the language of the earlier period remained available for marking certain linguistic envi-

53. Steven Fassberg, "The Preference for Lengthened Forms in Qumran Hebrew," *Meghillot: Studies in the Dead Sea Scrolls* 1 (2003) 227–40 (Hebrew).

54. Perhaps there was a gradual historical shift, for some scholars argue that certain chapters or even entire tractates of the Mishnah, among them tractates *Tamid* and *Midot* and certain chapters of *Yoma'*, should be dated to the time of the Second Temple, or to the years immediately following its destruction. These chapters refer to the Temple in the present tense, and interestingly preserve some older features of the Hebrew language. It is possible, however, that these too are cases of literary diglossia.

ronments as culturally elevated, and in those contexts EH, the language associated with the Bible, served as part of MH.

6. CONCLUSIONS

A discussion of the language of the Mishnah must consider all the linguistic data that the mishnaic corpus includes. In other words, all this data—however heterogeneous—is part of MH. Addressing it requires making a theoretical distinction between the history of the linguistic systems (EH and LH) and the history of the language of the Hebrew corpora (BH and MH). This distinction allows us to characterize the various linguistic systems that are part of MH, and to provide an accurate terminology for dealing with the attested heterogeneity. Thus, it is possible to present the many studies of MH in a more systematic way and consider them in light of the literature about linguistic heterogeneity in general.

Moreover, this type of study sheds some light on the cultural world of the composers of the Mishnah. It may tell us, among other things, in which contexts they used a higher register, and how they used this register. Paying attention to the forms used in certain contexts may also give us an indication of when the composers' language was influenced by the language of the Bible and what perspective they held on this language.

While previous studies often tended to be restricted to philological questions (such as: Which texts are earlier? What was the original language of the text?), being aware of the phenomenon of linguistic heterogeneity makes clear that it is not always possible to answer such questions, since the heterogeneity (which is often used in such studies) can reflect the original language of the composition, and as such should not be considered a deviation from a certain grammar. Instead, if one is trying to find a systematic way to explain the distribution of the various forms, a new set of inquiries emerges, and this chapter aimed to set forth some of these questions.[55]

I wish to express my gratitude to Moshe Bar-Asher, Michal Bar-Asher Siegal, Noah Feldman, and Vered Noam for reading and commenting on an earlier version of this chapter. I'm extremely grateful to the participants of the International Zoom Workshop "What is the Mishnah?" for their comments on my presentation. These comments were crucial for shaping the final version. The research leading to these results has received funding from the European Research Council under the European Union's H2020 Framework Programme (H2020/2014–2020) / ERC grant agreement n° 741360, principal investigator Edit Doron. It was also supported by the Israel Science Foundation (grant No. 2765/21), principal investigators Elitzur Bar-Asher Siegal, Nora Boneh, and Eitan Grossman.

55. See, Elitzur A. Bar-Asher Siegal, "Philological Studies with Sociolinguistic Constraints," *Carmillim* 13 (2017): 176–99.

APPENDIX

Table 1: A comparison between EH and LH standard verbal stems[56]

EH			LH	
Active	**Passive**	**Middle**	**Active**	**Middle-Passive**
פָּעַל	פֻּעַל	נִפְעַל	פָּעַל	נִפְעַל
פִּעֵל	פֻּעַל	הִתְפַּעֵל	פִּעֵל	נִתְפַּעֵל
הִפְעִיל	הֻפְעַל		הִפְעִיל	הֻפְעַל

Table 2: The inventory of verbal forms in EH and LH

	Early Hebrew		**Late Hebrew**
Suffix-conjugation	פָּעַל		פָּעַל
Prefix-conjugation	יִפְעַל	יָקוּם	יִפְעַל
Prefix-conjugation-jussive		יָקֹם	---
Prefix-conjugation-cohortative		אָקוּמָה	---
Waw-consecutive (narrative tense)	וַיִּפְעַל/וְפָעַל		---/---
Imperative	פְּעַל/פִּעֲלָה		פְּעַל
Infinitive construct:	פְּעֹל		---
Infinitive construct:	בִּפְעֹל		---
Infinitive construct:	כִּפְעֹל		---
Infinitive construct:	לִפְעֹל		לִפְעֹל
Infinitive construct:	מִפְעֹל		---
Infinitive absolute	פָּעוֹל		---
Active Participle	פּוֹעֵל		פּוֹעֵל
Active Participle	פָּעוּל		פָּעוּל

Table 3: The LH TAM system

	Past	**Present**	**Future**
Imperfective	Participle + היה	Participle	Participle + יהיה
Perfective	Suffix-conjugation		Prefix-conjugation

56. For a review of all the verbal patterns in the language of the Mishnah, see Bar-Asher, *Classical Hebrew*, chapter 20.

Part IV

The Presentation of Persons
and Groups in the Mishnah

15. Priests and Pietists in the Mishnah

Jonathan Klawans

1. INTRODUCTION

To reconsider the place of priests in the Mishnah is to evaluate controversy about controversy. It is commonplace to assume that rabbis and priests were engaged in a fierce battle for leadership of the Jewish people, and that the rabbis' eventual predominance was achieved, in part, by the force of their derogation of priests (and, particularly, high priests) as articulated in rabbinic literature.[1] While a great many rabbinic sources can be understood as articulating a rabbinic disparagement of priests, the sentiment is strikingly rare in the Mishnah itself. So one question we will have to consider is whether a later anti-priestly polemic has been concealed in the Mishnah (as Shmuel and Ze'ev Safrai would have us believe) or whether the Mishnah suggests a more irenic state of affairs (as Jacob Neusner would have us believe, at least in certain works).[2] In what follows we will review the evi-

---

1. For recent examples, see Richard Hidary, "The Rhetoric of Rabbinic Authority: Making the Transition from Priest to Sage," in *Jewish Rhetorics: History, Theory, Practice*, ed. J. W. Frenheimer and M. Bernard-Donals (Waltham, Mass., 2014), 16–45, and Peter Schäfer, "Rabbis and Priests, or: How to Do Away with the Glorious Past of the Sons of Aaron," in *Antiquity in Antiquity: Jewish and Christian Pasts in the Greco-Roman World*, ed. G. Gardner and K. Osterloh (Tübingen, 2008), 155–72. For what may be the most thorough recent statement, see Shmuel Safrai and Ze'ev Safrai, "Appendix A: Sages and Priests After the Destruction of the Second Temple," in *Mishnat Eretz Israel: Tractate Skalim (Moed E), with Historical and Sociological Commentary*, ed. S. Safrai and Z. Safrai, in cooperation with C. Safrai (Jerusalem, 2009), 289–340.

2. For "concealed polemic" see Safrai and Safrai, "Sages and Priests," 299. For a more accommodating reading, see Jacob Neusner, *Judaism: The Evidence of the Mishnah* (Chicago, 1981), esp. 248–50, and cf. "The Mishnah's Conception of the Priesthood: The

dence with an eye toward demonstrating that the non-confrontational reading of the Mishnah merits more attention. Our argument will be supported
by considering also how the Mishnah treats other potential priestly competitors, such as *ḥasidim*. The latter are mentioned much less frequently
than the former; but some infrequently discussed topics are important ones
nevertheless.

2. A PRIESTLY INHERITANCE

We do well to begin with the obvious. An enormous amount of mishnaic
material deals with priestly matters and, by extension, priests. Within this
material there is a special sub-genre: the cultic narrative, idyllically depicting the temple, its priests, and rituals (see, e.g., mBik 3:2–8; mShek 4:1–6,
6:1–6; mYom 1:1–7:5; mSot 3:1–3; mNeg 14:1–10; mPar 3:1–11, in addition to
the entire tractate *Tamid*).[3] Many scholars of earlier generations believed
these sources in general (and tractate *Tamid* in particular) to be authentic
accounts of the temple's practice, finding their origin in priestly tradition.[4]
In *Judaism: the Evidence of the Mishnah*, Neusner spoke of a priestly legacy,
though at times he downplays the impact of recent priests by highlighting
the rabbis' own direct engagement with the priestly texts of scripture.[5] Ei-

---

Aggadah versus the Halakhah," *Review of Rabbinic Judaism* 14 (2011): 92–107. Another
analysis allowing for priestly-rabbinic interaction and influence is Philip S. Alexander,
"What Happened to the Jewish Priesthood after 70?," in *A Wandering Galilean: Essays
in Honour of Seán Freyne*, ed. Z. Rodgers, with M. Daly-Denton and A. F. McKinley
(Leiden, 2009), 5–33, esp. 25–31.

    3. See discussion in Neusner, *A History of the Mishnaic Law of Holy Things*, 6 vols.
(Leiden, 1978–80), 6.202–7. For a rather full list of such ritual narratives, see Naftali
S. Cohn, *The Memory of the Temple and the Making of the Rabbis* (Philadelphia, 2012),
123–25.

    4. Jacob N. Epstein defends the antiquity of such passages; see *Introductions to
Tannaitic Literature: Mishna, Tosephta, and Halakhic Midrashim* (Hebrew), ed. E. Z.
Melamed (Jerusalem, 1957), 25–58. M. H. Segal identifies these passages as specimens of
early Mishnaic Hebrew; see *A Grammar of Mishnaic Hebrew* (Oxford, 1927), 12–13: "The
earlier *halaka* still shows a free and picturesque mode of expression." For the classic
expression of the theory that *mTamid* contains early, priestly material, see Louis Ginzberg, "The Mishnah Tamid: The Oldest Treatise of the Mishnah," *Journal of Jewish Lore
and Philosophy* 1 (1919): 33–44, 197–209, 265–95. For a critical discussion of Ginzberg's
theory, see Neusner, *History of the Mishnaic Law of Holy Things*, 6.196–207. For the view
that these narratives stem from late rabbinic creative (and tendentious) reconstruction-
imagination, see Cohn, *Memory of the Temple*.

    5. Neusner, *Judaism: The Evidence of the Mishnah*, 71, 248–50; but cf. 100–101 for
more skeptical comments; see also Neusner, *History of the Mishnaic Law of Holy Things*

ther way, no social force or biblical source compelled the sages to devote so much of the Mishnah to priestly topics, or incorporate so many narratives nostalgically depicting the priests at work. These choices reflect the sages' interests and priorities.

The priestly impact on the Mishnah can also be discerned in the sheer number of priestly figures counted among the named sages. Priests figure prominently among the earliest named sages, beginning with Simeon the Just (mAvot 1:2; mPar 3:5), commonly identified as one of two high priests named Simeon.[6] The rabbis speak of Yosi ben Yo'ezer (mAvot 1:4–5) as a "pietist of the priesthood" (*ḥasid she-ba-kehunah*; mHag 2:7).[7] Yoḥanan the High Priest (mPar 3:5; mYad 4:6) —often identified as John Hyrcanus I (served 134–104 BCE)[8]—is remembered in rabbinic tradition as an authoritative decisor of halakhah (mMS 5:15).[9] Stretching further beyond any and all limits of historical credulity, the Mishnah even attributes one piece of midrash halakhah to King Jehoash's high priest Jehoiada (see mShek 6:6; cf. 2 Kgs 12:9–16). The exegesis is forced, and the attribution even unlikelier,

---

6.26–35 on the Order of Holy Things in relation to scriptural material: the role of the priests is one of many scriptural "givens" (34; as opposed to a rabbinic creation). In comparison to the New Testament Letter to the Hebrews, Neusner observes that the Mishnah's reading of scripture is strikingly "literal": "At no point do we find a revision of Scripture's principal concerns and themes" (39). Generally, see Shaye J. D. Cohen, "Jacob Neusner, Mishnah, and Counter-Rabbinics: A Review Essay," *Conservative Judaism* 37.1 (1983): 48–63.

6. Simeon I (ca. 3rd century BCE) is labeled "the Just" by Josephus (*Ant.* 12:43–44, 12:157), and James VanderKam argues in favor of this identification; see *From Joshua to Caiaphas: High Priests after the Exile* (Minneapolis, 2004), 137–57. Ben Sira sings the praises of Simeon II (50:1–21; see VanderKam, *From Joshua to Caiaphas*, 181–88). For arguments in favor of this later figure as Simeon the Just, see George Foot Moore, "Simon the Righteous," in *Jewish Studies in Memory of Israel Abrahams*, ed. G. A. Kohut (New York, 1927), 348–64, and Ralph Marcus, "Appendix B," in *Josephus*, ed. H. St. J. Thackeray et al., 9 vols., LCL (Cambridge, Mass., 1926–65), 7.732–36.

7. This figure is also remembered as "the Permitter," for a series of mysterious, lenient rulings recorded (curiously) in Aramaic (m'Eduy 8:4); for discussions of this passage see David Weiss Halivni, *Midrash, Mishnah, and Gemara: The Jewish Predilection for Justified Law* (Cambridge, Mass., 1986), 27–30, and Neusner, *Rabbinic Traditions about the Pharisees before 70*, 3 vols. (Leiden, 1971), 1.64–66. Neusner assumes that Yosi's partner, Yosi ben Yoḥanan (mHag 2:2), was also a priest (*Rabbinic Traditions*, 1.81). Other authorities disagree; see Elia S. Hartom, "Yosi ben Yoḥanan," in *Entzyklopedyah le-ḥakhmey ha-Talmud ve-ha-Geonim*, rev. ed. M. Margaliot et al. (Tel Aviv, 1997), 2.214.

8. See Neusner, *Rabbinic Traditions*, 1.172–76, and VanderKam, *From Joshua to Caiaphas*, 285–312, esp. 309–11.

9. On these abrogations, Saul Lieberman, *Hellenism in Jewish Palestine: Studies in the Literary Transmission, Beliefs and Manners of Palestine in the I Century B.C.E.– IV Century C.E.* (New York, 1950), 139–43, and Neusner, *Rabbinic Traditions*, 160–61.

but the tradition crediting Jehoiada with legal-exegetical authority is no less remarkable for being so wildly unbelievable. While the mishnaic traditions attributed to priestly figures hardly overwhelm, the rabbis easily could have obscured the contributions of these figures, had they so wished. Their intention, rather, was to include named priests among those responsible for the transmission and development of the rabbinic tradition.[10]

A number of subsequent rabbinic figures are also remembered as priests. According to the statistics compiled by the Safrais, upwards of thirty percent of the pre- and immediately post-70 CE sages were priests; the numbers decrease significantly thereafter.[11] Among the most interesting is a pivotal, transitional sage, Ḥananiah the Prefect of the Priests, whose personal experience and memory are recorded a number of times in the Mishnah (and subsequent rabbinic sources).[12] The traditions attributed to Ḥananiah are often more descriptive than prescriptive (e.g., m'Eduy 2:2–3; mShek 4:4) and his testimony is not always accepted as accurate or authoritative (m'Eduy 2:2; mZev 9:3; mMen 10:1). Nevertheless, Ḥananiah's imprint is felt on a number of rather complicated priestly matters, and his presence in post-destruction rabbinic circles is presented as a living link to the priestly past. A similarly well-informed priestly rabbi whose traditions ostensibly reflect his own experiences is R. Eliezer ben Yaakov, frequently quoted in tractate *Midot* (1:2, 9; 2:5, 6; cf. also mTam 5:2). At times, R. Eliezer's memory fails him (mMid 2:5, 5:4). Nevertheless, subsequent tradition attributes tractate *Midot* to R. Eliezer (yYom 2:2//33d; bYom 16a).[13] While likely not historical, the attribution further confirms the perceived importance of late second temple priestly rabbis as living links. The Mishnah does not claim that the sages received written records of prior priestly laws; rather, the Mishnah records and elaborates on oral testimonies of priestly figures who affiliated with their movement. So again, we have reason to think that

10. Another early figure, Joshua ben Peraḥiah, is identified as a high priest who burnt a red heifer in *Sifre Zutta* (on Num 19:3; Horovitz ed. 302); but as Horovitz notes (*ad loc.*), the tradition may be confused, and other versions speak of (Ishmael) ben Phiabi (cf. mPar 3:5). In Elia S. Hartom's brief biography of this figure, it is suggested that ben Peraḥiah simply advised Yoḥanan the High Priest on the matter, thus preserving his non-priestly identity (*Entzyklopedyah le-ḥakhmey ha-Talmud*, 2.188).

11. Safrai and Safrai, "Sages and Priests," 334–36; according to the Safrais, the priests among the Yavneh generation include Yoḥanan ben Zakkai, R. Ishmael, R. Tarfon, R. Eleazar b. Azariah, and perhaps Eliezer b. Hyrcanus.

12. Neusner, *Rabbinic Traditions*, 1.400–413.

13. See discussion in Epstein, *Introductions*, 31–32, and Neusner, *History of the Mishnaic Law of Holy Things*, 6.207–10.

the Mishnah's treatment of priests and priestly materials reflects rabbinic priorities.

In addition to large blocks of priestly material and traditions attributed to priestly sages, there is yet another way a variety of rabbinic traditions reflect priestly priorities and concerns. Now and then, seemingly non-priestly matters are discussed by non-priestly sages in ways that presume the centrality of priestly perspectives. Examples include the opening of tractate *Berakhot*, which sets the recitation of the evening *shema* to start "when the priests enter to eat their *terumah*" (1:1). In mBekh 7:7 a categorical reference to "men" turns out to apply only to priests.[14] In mSot 1:2 women formally warned against infidelity are banned from eating *terumah*, without specifying that only women married to priests would be permitted to eat *terumah* in the first place. In addition, various passages speak of non–priests as "*zarim*" (e.g., mTer 5:4, 10:12, 11:4), even while the alternative "*yisrael*" is used elsewhere in similar contexts (mDem 6:3–4; mTer 7:2, 9:2–3). The appearance of the latter confirms that speaking of *zarim* is a choice, one that reflects a priestly point of view.

We turn, finally, to the most aggadic of mishnaic tractates, the one that mentions a great many priests and yet is at times averred to articulate an anti-priestly polemic: *mAvot*.[15] The plain text of tractate *Avot* presents the history of the Jewish tradition as one continuous consensus, from Moses to their own day.[16] Continuity over time is not interrupted by crisis (the two

14. For these two and other examples, see Safrai and Safrai, "Sages and Priests," 301–3.

15. For the view of *Avot* as articulating a polemic against priests, see (e.g.) Daniel Boyarin, *Border Lines: The Partition of Judaeo-Christianity* (Philadelphia, 2004), 76–77; Moshe David Herr, "Continuum in the Chain of Torah Transmission" (Hebrew), *Zion* 44 (1979): 43–56, esp. 48; Louis Finkelstein, *Introduction to the Treatises Abot and Abot of Rabbi Nathan* (Hebrew; New York, 1950), 9–13, and Schäfer, "Rabbis and Priests," 166–68. See also Marjorie Lehman, "And No One Gave the Torah to the Priests: Reading the Mishnah's References to the Priests and the Temple," in *Learning to Read the Talmud: What it Looks Like and How it Happens*, ed. J. Kanarek and M. Lehman (Brighton, Mass., 2016), 85–116, esp. 89–90 (this piece addresses the matter from a pedagogical perspective). For a more moderate view, see Amram Tropper, *Wisdom, Politics, and Historiography: Tractate Avot in the Context of the Graeco-Roman Near East* (Oxford, 2004), 213–14 n. 11.

16. Both Boyarin (*Border Lines*, 74–86) and Tropper (*Wisdom, Politics*, 208–40) compare *Avot* to Christian constructions of apostolic succession; Boyarin attributes to *Avot* a greater heresiological power than Tropper grants. The following analysis aligns more with Tropper's. See also Cohen, "A Virgin Defiled: Some Rabbinic and Christian Views on the Origin of Heresy," *Union Seminary Quarterly Review* 36.1 (1980): 1–11, esp. 3–4.

temple destructions go unmentioned) nor diluted by divergence (no sects or sub-groups are named).[17] And curiously, priests are not singled out among the classes of early transmitters of Torah (like prophets, elders or the members of the great assembly; mAvot 1:1).

Contrary to popular opinion, *Avot* is not anti-priestly (nor is it anti-Sadducean, but that is not our concern at the present).[18] For all that is often said about a supposedly derisive exclusion of priests from the transmission of Torah from Sinai to the sages, any such exclusion is both incomplete and potentially to the priesthood's benefit. In fact, named priests *are* included in the complete chain of succession, starting with the high priest Simeon the Righteous (mAvot 1:2). Yosi ben Yoʻezer (1:4) was, as we have already noted, one of the "pious of the priesthood" (mHag 2:7), and Joshua ben Peraḥiah (mAvot 1:6) is later remembered as having burned a red heifer (*Sifre Zutta* 19:3 [ed. Horovitz, 302]). One of Ben-Zakkai's five illustrious students is R. Yosi ha-Kohen (mAvot 2:8). Granted, these figures are sage-priests—priests who are included because they were also sages. Their inclusion nevertheless neutralizes any reading of *Avot* as a zero-sum game pitting rabbis against priests.

In addition, the exclusion of priests as a class from the earliest part of the list can be understood to the benefit of subsequent priests. To be sure, by virtue of their inclusion, prophets, elders, and the men of the great assembly are given an important historical role in the transmission of Torah. At the same time, these classes are all relegated to the past by virtue of their passing Torah to the group that follows. The prophets and great assembly members had their day and then left the scene. The exclusion of priests from the first part of the list opens the possibility for inclusion in the transmission later, and in the future. And all this is to say nothing of what may be even more important: the content of the traditions themselves. From the world resting on temple service (mAvot 1:2), to Hillel's emphatic admonition to "be disciples of Aaron" (1:12), through R. Simeon's reference to the "crown of the priesthood" (4:13; equal here to the crowns of Torah and monarchy)[19]

---

17. See Albert I. Baumgarten and Marina Rustow, "Judaism and Tradition: Continuity, Change, and Innovation," in *Jewish Studies at the Crossroads of Anthropology and History: Authority, Diaspora, Tradition*, ed. R. S. Boustan, O. Kosansky, and M. Rustow (Philadelphia, 2011), 207–37, esp. 214–15.

18. See Klawans, *Heresy, Forgery, Novelty: Condemning, Denying, and Asserting Innovation in Ancient Judaism* (New York, 2019), 72–76, upon which this and the prior paragraph are based.

19. Contrast Avot 6:5–6—universally recognized as a post-mishnaic *baraita*—which explicitly ranks Torah above both monarchy and priesthood.

to the ten miracles that occurred in the temple (5:5), *Avot* articulates concerns as priestly as Simeon the Righteous. Granted, *Avot* traces a rabbinic trajectory, not a priestly one; but the document presents no anti-priestly polemic, not even covertly. Rather, just like the Mishnah as a whole, *Avot* credits priests among early and more recent transmitters of Torah and highlights priestly themes in the content of said Torah.

3. POWERS AND PREROGATIVES

Perhaps the clearest way the Mishnah respects and preserves priestly prestige is by its emphatic reassertion of prerogatives and powers vested exclusively in the priesthood in general and the high priesthood in particular. Consider, for instance, how the opening chapter of *mKelim* delineates impurities and sanctities, reaching a crescendo with the assertion that the Holy of Holies is entered only by the high priest, only on the Day of Atonement (1:9). One must hesitate for a moment over the obvious: in the Mishnah, the temple remains a priestly domain, bounded by ritual purity; and the Holy of Holies endures, without exception, as a high priestly preserve. In the Mishnah, as in scripture, the priests (and the high priest) play determinative roles in the daily cultic liturgy (e.g., *mTamid*), the day of Atonement (*mYoma*), decisions regarding defiling afflictions (*mNegaʿim*, esp. 3:1), and the rite of the red heifer (*mParah*). Apparently when the shofar was blown at the temple, it was blown by priests (*mTaʿanit* 2:5). And of course they receive priestly dues, some directly from all (*mTerumot*), others passed through Levites, who also received a substantial portion (*mMaʿaserot*). The sages will (as we will see in the next section) assert their influence and even insert themselves in at key moments—but the general powers and prerogatives remain as they were, squarely in the hands of the priests, limited to them by scripturally ordained right.

Precisely because these rights are scripturally ordained, it could be thought that the rabbis are here only granting what they must.[20] But at times the rabbis go further in their discussion of priestly powers—and not always in ways that limit the priests. One particularly interesting example appears in mSan 2:1–2. While the king is barred from judging (and being judged), the high priest can both judge and be judged. The rabbinic ban on monarchic judging seems to divert from scriptural precedent (1 Sam 8:5, 20); the rabbinic allowance for high priestly judging seems to be mostly a judgment call on the part of the sages, one that leans decidedly in favor of high priestly power. Any thorough rabbinic effort to coopt priestly power surely could

---

20. Cf. Safrai and Safrai, "Sages and Priests," 297.

have divested the high priest of the power to judge. Priestly courts are also mentioned here and there in the Mishnah, with insufficient elaboration (mRH 1:7; mKet 1:5). Incidentally, the few seemingly non-priestly "ritual narratives" in the Mishnah concern juridical procedures, such as capital and corporal punishment (mSan 4–7; mMak 3:12–14)—are these too, in the rabbinic mind, priestly traditions?[21]

The court is not the only locus for the extension of priestly power beyond the sanctuary; for the Mishnah, the synagogue or house of prayer is another place of priestly privilege.[22] We should not be surprised that the Mishnah reserves the priestly blessing for priests (mBer 5:4; cf. mTaʿan 4:1; mTam 5:1)—but subsequent developments prove that other possibilities pertained.[23] While the rabbis record the Psalms that the Levites used to sing in the temple (mTam 7:4), in that case the past temple practice does not limit subsequent synagogal participation to Levites alone. Priests take precedence in other prayer and synagogue rites as well, including reading the first portion of the Torah ("for the sake of peace": mGit 5:8; cf. mShek 1:3, discussed below). Even when we are told that a wise *mamzer* takes precedence over an ignorant high priest (mHor 3:8), there is no indication that this pertains to priestly ritual prerogatives—in those cases, priests would surely retain their priority.

4. CHECKS AND BALANCES, EXEMPTIONS AND OBLIGATIONS

The powers and prerogatives of the priesthood are impacted in the Mishnah by the sages' system of checks and balances, which consistently presents a vision of priestly figureheads being instructed and watched by those more learned. The most dramatic illustrations appear early in *Yoma*, where the high priest is repeatedly adjured by "elders from the court" (1:3, 5, 7). These declarations presume the possibility that the high priest was unlearned or forgetful (1:3), perhaps because of old age (cf. 3:5), and in any event needing reminders to perform the ritual according to the script (cf. mPar 3:8). Some of these traditions also may reflect the rabbinic memory of prior halakhic disagreements, especially with the occasional recognition of the possibil-

21. Cf. Neusner, *Evidence of the Mishnah*, 249–50; again, for the listing of these judicial and cultic ritual narratives, see Cohn, *Memory of the Temple*, 123–25.

22. On the roles played by priests in the ancient synagogue, see Lee I. Levine, *The Ancient Synagogue the First Thousand Years*, 2nd ed (New Haven, 2005), esp. 519–29; see also Alexander, "What Happened to the Jewish Priesthood," 7–12.

23. See Ismar Elbogen, *Jewish Liturgy: A Comprehensive History*, trans. R. P. Scheindlin (Philadelphia, 1993 [1931]), 62–66.

ity that some high priests would be inclined to follow Sadducean positions (mPar 3:7).

Yet these traditions at times go further, conjuring the image of a temple controlled not by priests but by sages: preparing for the day of atonement, the priest is reminded to do exactly as he is told (mYom 1:5).[24] When priestly competition runs amok—resulting in bodily injury—the court determines that priestly roles would be assigned by lot (mYom 2:1–2).[25] When determining the purity or impurity of *negaʿim*, the priest is depicted as declaring the matter according to instructions (mNeg 3:1).[26] Just as the high priest could judge, so too he could be judged (mSan 2:1), and *mMidot* asserts that the great Sanhedrin of Israel "sat and judged the priesthood" in the Chamber of Hewn Stone (5:4). As unlikely as these depictions may be, that rabbis imagined their predecessors exercising power in priestly domains is key supporting evidence for those who believe the rabbis engaged in a long struggle, falsely subdued in the Mishnah, eventually wresting power and influence from the priesthood.[27]

24. For an analysis of these and similar traditions that emphasize how rabbinic ritual narratives serve to assert rabbinic authority, see Cohn, *Memory of the Temple*; Lehman, "And No One Gave" (106 n. 25) cites and follows Cohn (*Memory of the Temple*, 2–3), though her argument may be more pointed at priests than Cohn intended. Note also our discussion in section 6 on the problematic conception of subtle polemic. For a parallel line of argument, one that also downplays the polemical element at least as far as materials like tractates *Tamid* and *Midot* are concerned, see Mayan Orian, "Josephus's Seven Purities and the Mishnah's Ten Holinesses," *JSJ* 47 (2016): 183–211. See also Klawans, *Purity, Sacrifice, and the Temple: Symbolism and Supersessionism in the Study of Ancient Judaism* (New York, 2005), esp. 175–211, and Steven Fine, *This Holy Place: On the Sanctity of the Synagogue during the Greco-Roman Period* (Notre Dame, 1997), esp. 35–59 (on the "templization" of synagogues in tannaitic sources, not as a replacement of the temple, but as a reflection of the "temple culture" of rabbinic Judaism).

25. As we will see with regard to priestly greed, later rabbinic texts accentuate priestly shortcomings much more than the Mishnah. In the Tosefta's version of this tale (tYom 1:12), the results are deadly, and the fallout severe; see Klawans, *Purity, Sacrifice, and the Temple*, 182–83, and Shamma Friedman's essay in the present volume. Marjorie Lehman has applied a feminist analysis to these traditions, comparing the rabbis' treatment of priests to their treatment of women; see "Imagining the Priesthood in Tractate Yoma: Mishnah *Yoma* 2:1–2 and BT *Yoma* 23a," *Nashim: A Journal of Jewish Women's Studies and Gender Issues* 28 (2015): 88–105.

26. See Neusner, "Mishnah's Conception," 93–95, where Neusner speaks memorably of the aggadic portrayals of the "priest-automaton, the priest ignoramus, the priest unworthy of his charge" (93); earlier, in *History of the Mishnaic Law of Holy Things*, Neusner spoke memorably of the priest treated like a "robot" (6.222).

27. So, especially Safrai and Safrai, "Sages and Priests," 303–15, covering these and similar examples of the limitations of priestly prerogatives in rabbinic sources.

At the same time, we should not overlook the degrees of nuance in these texts. While these criticisms cluster in *mYoma'*, this tone is absent from *mTamid*. Moreover, in *mYoma'* what's criticized above all is the high priesthood in particular. And the rabbis recognize that not all priests would have invited or accepted such interventions (e.g., mKin 3:1). Importantly, there is no line-up here of wise, non-priestly, proto-rabbinic sages against ignorant, anti-rabbinic priests. The high priest is just as often advised and reminded by his own priestly subordinates, including the *memuneh* (Danby: "officer"; Neusner: "superintendent"; e.g., mYom 2:1, 3:1; mTam 1:2, 3:1, 6:3), the deputy (*segan*), and the head of the father's house (*rosh beit av*; mYom 3:9, 4:1).[28] Even the sagely "elders" are—as required by their placement—assumed to be, or explicitly stated to be, priests (mYom 1:5). Similarly, the otherwise unheard-of figure, Zechariah b. Kevutal—who claims to have read the book of Daniel to the high priest before the Day of Atonement (mYom 1:6)—was presumably a priest.[29] Reading these passages as if non-priestly (proto-) rabbis are usurping power over priestly stooges is one possibility, but not the only one. A kinder reading allows these passages to depict a priestly caste that includes knowledgeable elders among them, precisely what is suggested by the inclusion of so much priestly material in the Mishnah as a whole.[30] Had the rabbis really wished to insert themselves or their most prominent non-priestly predecessors into quasi-priestly roles they could have done so. For instance: Why not insert a Hillel or a Ben Zakkai into the *Yoma'* narrative? The rabbis settle for something much less than that, and the intimation of conflict is tempered accordingly.

The rabbis may modestly limit priestly prerogatives in another way, by allowing non-priests to participate in cultic rituals. In line with the clear implication of Leviticus 1:5, the Mishnah permits sacrificial slaughter rather widely (mZev 3:1):

> If any man slaughtered that which was ineligible, his slaughtering is nonetheless valid, since slaughtering is valid if it is done by them that are not priests, or by women or by bondservants or by them that are

28. For a classic (albeit dated) review of various priestly positions, see Adolf Büchler, *Die Priester und der Cultus im letzten Jahrzehnt des jerusalemischen Tempels* (Vienna, 1895), 90–117.

29. See Neusner, *Rabbinic Traditions*, 1.414.

30. This is not to argue, however, for seriously entertaining the possibility that these named figures are largely directly responsible for this transmission. Epstein entertains the possibility that *Yoma* was edited by Zechariah b. Kevutal (*Introductions*, 36–37); See discussion (and rejection) in Neusner, *Rabbinic Traditions*, 1.414.

impure, even the [slaughtering of the] Most Holy Things, provided that none that is impure touches the flesh.[31]

Just as slaughter is permitted for Israelites, so too is laying of hands (mMen 9:8) and waving (mMen 5:6–7). Similar permissions are scattered about the Mishnah, pertaining to the Passover sacrifice (mPes 5:5),[32] the preparation of the red heifer (mPar 5:4),[33] and the sprinkling of the waters of purification (mPar 12:10).[34] In line with this approach, mKel 1:8 explicitly allows for Israelite access to the altar, to perform permitted acts of laying hands, slaughtering, and waving. The narrative descriptions of sacrificial practice, however, seem to presume that regular priestly ritual acts were divided among priestly performers (e.g., mYom 2:3, mTam 3:1, 4:1–4). History may be on the side of the exclusive approach, as Philo attests (*Special Laws* 1:199) and Josephus implies (e.g., *War* 5:229, *Ant.* 3:228).[35] Quite possibly, an exclusive approach found justification in Ezekiel which imagines the sacrificial altar being placed within sacred precincts (40:47, 43:13–27), an area to which only priests may enter (44:15–16).[36] On the other hand, the rabbinic permission of paschal slaughter seems eminently reasonable and also finds external support (e.g., Philo, *Special Laws*, 2:145–49).[37]

31. Translations follow (with modifications for style and clarity) Herbert Danby, *The Mishnah: Translated from the Hebrew with Introduction and Brief Explanatory Notes* (Oxford, 1933).

32. See Shmuel Safrai and Ze'ev Safrai, in cooperation with Chana Safrai, *Mishnat Eretz Israel: Tractate Psachim (Moed d) Part A, with Historical and Sociological Commentary* (Jerusalem, 2009), 227–29, and Safrai and Safrai, "Sages and Priests," 326–27.

33. See Safrai and Safrai, "Sages and Priests," 327, who note the Tosefta's more restrictive approach (tPar 4(3).6 [ed. Zuckermandel, p. 633]).

34. See Safrai and Safrai, "Sages and Priests," 311.

35. Safrai and Safrai, "Sages and Priests," 327–28. So also, Chanoch Albeck, *Shishah Sidre Mishnah*, 6 vols. (Jerusalem, 1952–58), 2.139 (introduction to *Pesaḥim*). For more on Josephus and exclusions from the sanctuary in comparison with the Mishnah in particular, see Orian, "Josephus's Seven Purities."

36. Moshe Greenberg, "The Design and Themes of Ezekiel's Program of Restoration," *Interpretation* 38.3 (1984): 181–208, esp. 193–94, 206. According to some scholars the exclusion of Israelites from the altar is reflected in other late biblical sources, such as 2 Kings 12:10 (which speaks of priests collecting funds deposited within the sanctuary) and 2 Chr 4:9 (which already speaks of the inner court as the "Court of the Priests"). See Orian, "Josephus's Seven Purities," 190–91.

37. So too Safrai and Safrai, *Psachim*, 229; cf. S. Safrai, *Pilgrimage at the Time of the Second Temple* (Hebrew), 2nd ed. (Jerusalem, 1985), 235–36 (which asserts Philo's reliability on this score). See Albeck's discussion of Passover slaughter (*Mishnah* 2.139), which suggests that despite the rabbinic permission, the common practice was in fact to let priests (or Levites) slaughter the sacrifices (even on Passover) since they were more experienced in the practice.

A particularly curious passage appears in mYom 6:3, which reiterates the theoretical permission of sacrificial participation by a non-priest—in this case, leading away the scapegoat—but then steps back:

> They delivered it to him that should lead it away. All were eligible to lead it away, but the [MS Kaufmann: high] priests had established the custom not to suffer an Israelite to lead it away. R. Yosi said: It once happened that Arsela of Sepphoris led it away and he was an Israelite.

Whether some Arsela led the goat away once or not is unknowable. Still this passage may represent the Mishnah's view on the whole: as far as the rabbis are concerned, wider participation is permitted by scripture and at times mandated by practical necessity. Yet, the Mishnah indicates, the priests possessed power and displayed an inclination to arrogate many of these honors to themselves, and often did so.

The rabbis also appear to presume an Israelite presence in Jerusalem as part of the "delegation" (*ma'amad*) corresponding to the priestly and Levitical "watches" (*mishmarot*; mTa'an 4:2). While it appears that larger groups of Israelites remained in their towns scattered throughout the land, the presence of an Israelite delegation *in Jerusalem* (mTa'an 4:2) is equally presumed (cf. mTam 5:6, which recalls the presence of the "head of the delegation").[38]

Just as the Mishnah may open the door to non-priestly participation in certain sacrificial rites, the Mishnah also obligates priests to do something they may not have done before (or ever in actuality): pay the Temple tax.[39] According to the Mishnah, the Temple tax was paid annually (mShek 1:1–3, passim), though historians grant that the tax was only annualized in the second temple period.[40] The Mishnah directs these funds toward the cost of public offerings (4:1–4), though later rabbinic sources speak of Sadducean (or Boethusian) opposition (bMen 65a, scholion to *Megilat Ta'anit* 1).[41]

38. So Büchler, *Die Priester*, 92; see also Joseph Tabory, "The Liturgy of the *Ma'amad*" (Hebrew), in *From Qumran to Cairo: Studies in the History of Prayer: Proceedings of the Research Group Convened under the Auspices of the Institute for Advanced Studies of the Hebrew University of Jerusalem 1997*, ed. J. Tabory (Jerusalem, 1999), 145–69, esp. 160–65.

39. See Safrai and Safrai, "Sages and Priests," 315–17.

40. See Jacob Liver, "The Half-Shekel Offering in Biblical and Post-Biblical Literature," *HTR* 56.3 (1963): 173–98, and Albeck, *Mishnah*, 2.183–84 (introduction to *Shekalim*).

41. On the passage from the scholion to *Megilat Ta'anit*—and its relation to other rabbinic sources such as bMen 65a—see Vered Noam, *Megillat Ta'anit: Versions, In-*

The Mishnah does question whether priests should pay this tax (mShek 1:4):

> R. Judah said: Ben Bukri testified at Yavneh that if a priest paid the Shekel he committed no sin. Rabban Yoḥanan b. Zakkai answered: Not so! Rather, if a priest did not pay the Shekel he committed sin; but the priests used to expound this scripture to their advantage, "And every meal offering of the priest shall be wholly burnt: it shall not be eaten" (Lev. 6:23); since the *Omer* and the Two Loaves and the Shewbread are ours (cf. mShek 4:1), how can they be eaten?[42]

While the Mishnah decides the matter in favor of extending the half-shekel tax to the priests, the rabbis hedge their bet. The Mishnah exempts priests from the process of compulsory pledges (mShek 1:3, "for the ways of peace")[43] and spares them the surcharge (1:6), moves that may constitute concessions to priestly resistance toward paying the tax altogether. While the rabbinic retelling of the matter suggests that the priests were motivated by self-interest, Ben-Zakkai's insinuation is softened somewhat by allowing that the priests offered a plausible, if arguable, scriptural-legal justification. Importantly, the Mishnah's recollection of priestly dispute is limited to the issue of payment. In agreement with the sages, the priestly plea for exemption accepts that the funds will be used for public offerings. And this relates to the overriding concern of the Mishnah: not to disempower or disenfranchise priests in some power grab, but rather to preserve the priesthood as the highest class of the larger polity of Israelites for whom and by whom all sacrifices should be offered.[44]

terpretation, History, with a Critical Edition (Hebrew; Jerusalem, 2003), 57–59 (text of scholion), 133–35 (text of bMen 65a), and 165–73 (Noam's analysis, including a history of scholarship on the passage). Note that the Oxford MS speaks of Boethusians, while the Parma MS speaks of Sadducees.

42. Danby explains (*Mishnah, ad loc.*): "Meaning that since these three Meal-offerings are brought as public offerings at the charges of the temple fund (which is maintained by the Shekel contributions), the priests may not contribute to the temple fund: if they contributed to the cost of these Meal-offerings they would need to be burnt; and this would be contrary to Scripture."

43. Cf. mGit 4:8 for additional uses of this phrase.

44. On the half-shekel tax in relation to principles of inclusion, Klawans, *Purity, Sacrifice*, 196–98.

5. SUSPICIOUS SILENCES: PRIESTLY
GREED AND ESOTERICISM

We turn now to consider two phenomena, hardly noted in the Mishnah at all, but commonly associated with the priesthood in extra-rabbinic sources as well as post-mishnaic rabbinic traditions. And the question is, what do we make of these silences?

The first of these is priestly greed. A number of rabbinic texts speak to this notion, and a few such passages are collected together in brief "essays" on priestly greed in (among other texts) tMen 13:18–22, bPes 57a, and bKer 28a–b.[45] In some cases, the accounts of priestly greed align with similar accounts in Josephus.[46] What is both striking and curious is how little the Mishnah itself has to say on the matter. The accusation is not entirely absent: mBekh 5:4–5 expresses concerns about self-dealing priestly shepherds. But in many cases, priestly greed is wanting in the Mishnah precisely where it is present in later texts. For instance, mKer 1:7 attests merely to shortage-induced price increases, not the priestly gouging that appears in later rabbinic sources or some instance of New Testament scholarship.[47] Similarly, bYom 18a claims that Martha, the daughter of Boethus, paid a bribe to secure Joshua b. Gamala's rise to the priesthood; mYev 6:4 recalls the marriage, but not the bribe.[48] Other sources confirm that the priesthood was

---

45. See Klawans, *Purity, Sacrifice*, 177–82, 225–29.

46. See Daniel R. Schwartz, "Kata Toyton ton Kaipon: Josephus' Source on Agrippa II," *JQR* 72.4 (1982): 241–68, who argues that the rabbis and Josephus draw on common source material. On the general possibility that rabbis may have been influenced by Josephus, see Richard Kalmin, *Jewish Babylonia between Persia and Roman Palestine* (New York, 2006), 149–72.

47. See Klawans, *Purity Sacrifice*, 225–26, and the literature cited there.

48. On these traditions, see Neusner, *Rabbinic Traditions*, 1.396–97; see also Vander-Kam, *From Joshua to Caiaphas*, 484–86. There are many similar cases in which post-mishnaic literature presents an extended narrative detailing priestly corruption, expanding a mishnaic tradition that is much more oblique. Another famous example noted earlier concerns the stories of priestly murder in tYom 1:12 (and parallels), while the similar story in the Mishnah (mYom 2:2) is much more mundane; on these stories, see Klawans, *Purity, Sacrifice*, 182–84 (cf. Neusner, "Mishnah's Conception," 96–98, which takes the Tosefta as illuminating the Mishnah). Tropper uses this parallel as an example to illustrate the problem of Mishnah-Toseftan parallels in relation to the possibility of toseftan priority; see Tropper, "The State of Mishnah Studies," in *Rabbinic Texts and the history of Late-Roman Palestine*, ed. M. Goodman and P. Alexander (Oxford, 2010), 91–115, esp. 97–99, and the literature cited there; see also Shamma Friedman's essay in this volume. Our concern is with difference, not priority, and clearly the Mishnah's presentation avoids the kind of criticism of priests that appears in other sources.

at times for sale (e.g., 2 Macc 4:7–8, 23–24), and greed figures among the crimes Qumran raises against the "Wicked Priest" (1QpHab 8:8–12) and the "later priests of Jerusalem" (1QpHab 9:4–7; cf. 12:9–10). So it is all the more striking that the Mishnah praises the material generosity of ben Gamala (mYom 3:9).[49] The list of identified generous priests may be short (see also mYom 3:10), but so is the Mishnah's list of wicked kings (mSan 10:2). By contrast, the Mishnah does not name a single wicked priest.

We find a similar presumption of priestly innocence in *mShekalim*. Here the matter at hand concerns the priest tasked with collecting half-shekel offerings from the treasury (mShek 3:2):

> He that went in to take up *terumah* did not wear a sleeved cloak or shoes or sandals or phylacteries or an amulet, lest if he became poor people should say that he became poor through a sin against the Shekel-chamber, or if he became rich they should say that he became rich from the *terumah* taken up out of the Shekel-chamber.

What is pertinent here is that the passage's concern is not primarily with the possibility of priestly theft. Rather, the rulings regarding priestly attire serve to prevent priests from being falsely accused of theft, in the event they should coincidentally experience some twist of fortune subsequently to their service as shekel-collectors. Needless to say, it is easy to imagine this mishnaic passage formulated quite differently, had the Mishnah been interested in pondering the possibility of priests pilfering the sacred purse. But greedy priests are not the concern.

There is at least one explicit accusation of priestly greed in the Mishnah, but curiously it pertains to knowledge, not money (mYom 3:11):

> But [the memory of] these [was kept] in dishonor: They of the House of Garmu (cf. mShek 5:1) would not teach [any other] how to prepare the Shewbread. They of the House of Abtinas would not teach [any other] how to prepare the incense. Hygros b. Levi had a special art in singing but he would not teach it [to any other]. Ben Kamtzar would not teach [any other] in [his special] craft of writing. Of the first it is written (Prov. 10:7): "The memory of the just is blessed" and of these [others] it is written, "But the name of the wicked shall rot."

---

49. The ben Gamala of mYom 3:9 was likely a priest in any event, even if not identified with Joshua ben Gamala (who, in turn, may be equivalent to Josephus's Jesus ben Gamaliel, *Ant.* 20:223). See Neusner, *Rabbinic Traditions*, 1.396–97, and VanderKam, *From Joshua to Caiaphas*, 483–86.

As the conclusion of this passage emphasizes, these stories of priests stingy with knowledge are contrasted with aforementioned memories of priests and other aristocrats remembered for their material generosity (mYom 3:9–10).[50] It is also worth observing the obvious: priests stingy with knowledge are priests who possess, preserve, and pass on knowledge, albeit in a way other than the Mishnah might think best.

We can look at the Mishnah's approach to priestly greed in one of two ways. The first is to find here further evidence of what the Safrais have referred to as the "concealed polemic" with the priesthood: what comes out later in the Tosefta or Bavli is what the sages of the Mishnah have suppressed, perhaps "for the sake of peace" (cf. mShek 1:3).[51] But another approach may be safer, and that is to appreciate the multifarious ways in which the Mishnah respects, valorizes, and even celebrates priestly heritage and contributions. Instead of reading back the explicit polemics of post-mishnaic texts into supposedly pregnant silences of the Mishnah, we should exert more effort to appreciate what the Mishnah has chosen to say. The struggle here is not so much between priests and rabbis; the dispute is between later and earlier rabbis, with the later ones moving away from the Mishnah's nostalgic remembrance of priestly times past.

There is a second mishnaic silence worthy of suspicion, and this pertains to mysticism and its possibly priestly milieu. It is well known that the Mishnah hardly says a thing about mysticism (compare mHag 2:1 with tHag 2:1–7, e.g.). It remains uncertain whether the merkavah mystical tradition goes back to the tannaitic period (as Scholem averred),[52] or whether (as I think the majority now maintains) the Hekhalot texts reflect late rabbinic and early medieval developments.[53] Regardless of the time and place of origin of texts like *Hekhalot Rabbati*, there can be little doubt that there were more Jews engaging in mystical or ecstatic practices (of whatever kind) than the Mishnah would have us believe. What is more, scholars like Rachel

50. We noted ben Gamala's likely priestly identity already (mYom 3:9). Rabbinic traditions (and traditional commentators on the Mishnah) identify ben Katin (mYom 3:10; cf. mTam 3:8) as a high priest as well: see, e.g., Pinhas Kehati, *Mishnayot Mevo'arot* (Jerusalem, 1992), *ad loc.* to mYom 3:9–10.

51. Safrai and Safrai, "Sages and Priests," 299; note also Neusner's subtle recognition that the aggadic critiques of the priests that he relates to the Mishnah are, in fact, mostly found in the Tosefta ("Mishnah's Conception," 93–98).

52. So, e.g., Gershom G. Scholem, *Jewish Gnosticism, Merkabah Mysticism, and Talmudic Tradition* (New York, 1965).

53. See discussion in Ra'anan Boustan, "The Study of Heikhalot Literature: Between Mystical Experience and Textual Artifact," *Currents in Biblical Research* 6.1 (2007): 130–60, esp. 144–45.

Elior and Ithamar Gruenwald have argued convincingly that the late second temple mystical tradition likely flourished in priestly circles—though I reject the presumption that mystics necessarily rejected the temple.[54] What is more, Gruenwald points to post-mishnaic rabbinic sources that attest to rabbinic memories of priestly mystical experiences, including high priests encountering heavenly voices in the Holy of Holies (e.g., tSot 13:5).[55] Intriguingly, the Israelite affiliate of the priestly courses would study *ma'aseh bereshit*—a text that could be interpreted either exoterically or esoterically (cf. mḤag 2:1). Be all this as it may, the matter pertains here precisely because the Mishnah says so much about priests while saying so little about mystics or mystical things. Of course, one possibility is that Elior, Gruenwald, and those who follow them have overstated the priestly contribution to the mystical tradition. But another explanation is simpler, along the lines of the case we are building here: the Mishnah speaks of priests often, and mystics rarely, precisely because the Mishnah values the former but not the latter.

6. LESS SUSPICIOUS SILENCES: ZADOKITES, SECTARIAN POLEMICS, AND SADDUCEES

Historians of the second temple period have often pointed to the Maccabean disruption of Zadokite priestly descent as an event of prime significance.[56] A reader of the Mishnah would have no reason to think that priests or rabbis cared much about Zadokite descent. The Mishnah asserts repeatedly and emphatically that the priesthood is pan-Aaronite (mYom 4:2; mTa'an 2:5; mZev 12:1; mḤul 10:1; mMid 5:4), and the issue of Zadokite descent never comes up, whether pertaining to high priestly legitimacy or priestly service in the temple broadly speaking. Indeed, Hasmonean and subsequent

---

54. On the priestly elements in mystical sources, see Alexander, "What Happened to the Jewish Priesthood," 18–20; Rachel Elior, *The Three Temples: On the Emergence of Jewish Mysticism*, trans. D. Louvish (London, 2004); and Ithamar Gruenwald, "The Impact of the Priestly Traditions on the Creation of the Markabah Mysticism and the Shiur Komah" (Hebrew), *Jerusalem Studies in Jewish Thought* 6.1–2 (1987): 65–120. Against Elior's association between mystics and secessionist priests, see Klawans, *Purity, Sacrifice*, 128–44, and my review of Elior's volume in *AJS Review* 29.2 (2005): 376–78.

55. On tSot 13:5 and the various traditions there suggesting priestly mystical experiences, see Gruenwald, "The Impact," esp. 79–87; see also the briefer comments to this effect (drawing in part on Gruenwald) in Safrai and Safrai, "Sages and Priests," 319–20.

56. See, e.g., Geza Vermes, *The Complete Dead Sea Scrolls in English* (London, 2004), 50–53, 63 n. 1; see Klawans, *Josephus and the Theologies of Ancient Judaism* (New York, 2012), 18–19.

high priests—presumably non-Zadokites all—are mentioned without any suggestion that they were any less legitimate than Simeon the Just. For instance, mPar 3:5 relates the seven red heifers prepared since Ezra: two by Simeon the Righteous, two by Yoḥanan, and one each by Eliehoenai the son of Hakkof, Ḥanamel the Egyptian, and Ishmael the son of Phiabi.[57] The first of these was presumably a pre-Hasmonean Zadokite (Simeon I or Simeon II), the second a non-Zadokite Hasmonean (John Hyrcanus I), and the rest—well, who knows, and as far as the Mishnah is concerned, who cares?[58] The Zadokite restriction originates in Ezekiel, not Leviticus; and as we have already seen with regard to Israelite access to the altar, the Mishnah favors the Torah over Ezekiel when the two are in conflict.

It may be tempting to discern here signs of a polemic opposing sectarians who maintained an interest in Zadokite descent (esp., e.g., 1QS 5:2, 9). But the absence of concerns with Zadokites in the Mishnah matches the lack of such interest that is in evidence in Josephus and most other second temple sources (even a number of Qumranic ones).[59] Indeed, for every one of the (rather few) sources that suggest some great importance to the matter of Zadokite descent (e.g., 1QS 5:2, 9; Ben Sira 51:12i[Heb]) there is another that speaks of "all the sons of Aaron" (e.g., 1QS 5:21; Sir 46:6–25, 50:13, 16), or takes the Zadokite matter in a non-literal fashion (e.g., CD 3:20–4:6), or speaks of some Zadok other than David's last high priest (e.g., CD 5:5). There is, in fact, no single ancient Jewish source that clearly suggests that the matter of Zadokite priestly descent was a major issue of sectarian dispute. So here we have an example of one of the Mishnah's unsuspicious silences. Zadokites did not matter to the Mishnah and may have mattered much less to other ancient Jews than many scholars assume.

As we have observed, some scholars impute polemics—be they anti-priestly or anti-sectarian—into the Mishnah, even where no explicit polemic can easily or necessarily be found.[60] We can take unadorned dis-

57. On Elieohoenai—and his ostensible identification with Josephus's Elionaeus, son of Caiaphas—see VanderKam, *From Joshua to Caiaphas*, 449–53; on Ḥanamel and his ostensible identification with Josephus's Ananel (the Babylonian) see VanderKam, *From Joshua to Caiaphas*, 394–98, 405.

58. Note also mMid 1:6, which remembers the Hasmoneans' deposit of the defiled altar in the northeast sub-chamber of the Chamber of the Hearth (cf. 1 Macc 4:44–46).

59. See Klawans, *Josephus*, 18–23, 216–18; cf. A. I. Baumgarten, "The Zadokite Priests at Qumran: A Reconsideration," *DSD* 4 (1997): 137–56.

60. This generalization holds true, albeit in different ways, for Cohn, *Memory of the Temple* (e.g., 84–89); Neusner, *History of the Mishnaic Law of Holy Things* (e.g., 6.44) and "Mishnah's Conception"; and Safrai and Safrai, "Sages and Priests." For a more focused argument, see Meir Bar-Ilan, "Are Tamid and Middot Polemical Tractates?" (Hebrew), *Sidra* 5 (1989): 27–40.

agreement as a sign of polemic if we want, but then polemic will be found everywhere we want it to be. We are better off speaking of polemic when we find explicit signs of it—when, as in mPar 3:7, the practice is explicitly shaped to reject a practice deemed sectarian (cf. mMen 10:3). And perhaps we do well to find polemic in similar passages, when rituals are performed with a striking three-fold emphasis (mPar 3:10; mShek 3:3). Even scholars such as Magen Broshi who do well to distinguish between "overt" and "covert" arguments[61] leave one key question unanswered: Is a covert polemic really *polemical*? Moving back from sectarians to priests, a great deal of what is presumed to be anti-priestly polemic is more covert than overt (in Broshi's terms). We have already noted that the Safrais speak of a "concealed polemic" (*pulmus samuy*).[62] Neusner, somewhat tautologically, claims: "Silence is the most blatant of polemics."[63] Such arguments highlighting mishnaic polemic tend to overlook the contrasts between the Mishnah and other texts on these grounds, as if the later, post-mishnaic polemical texts explain the earlier, mishnaic, anodyne ones.[64] The Mishnah's approach to priestly matters, however, should not be displaced by later sources. Instead of speaking so much about "hidden struggles" and "covert polemics," maybe we would do better to speak about how the Mishnah frequently adopts an inclusive, non-confrontational stance when speaking nostalgically of priests and priestly matters such as sacrifice and purity.

There is one more mishnaic silence that may be more valuable for an evaluation of the priesthood than some scholars allow, and that is the Mishnah's reluctance to equate the priesthood with the Sadducees. To be sure, the Mishnah allows the possibility that priests were susceptible to Sadducean influence (mPar 3:7). When criticizing Sadducees, the Mishnah recalls their affection for John Hyrcanus (mYad 4:6), suggesting that rabbis may have remembered that high priest as a Sadducee. Yet the Mishnah speaks similarly of Boethusian influence on priestly practice (mMen 10:3). More importantly, the Mishnah speaks of Sadducees without speaking of priests (e.g., m'Eruv 6:2; mMak 1:6; mNid 4:2) while regularly speaking of priests without even thinking of Sadducees. Here too we may do well to attend to the Mishnah, and rethink some common presumptions equating the Saddu-

61. Magen Broshi, "Anti-Qumran Polemics in the Talmud," in Broshi, *Bread, Wine, Walls and Scrolls* (Sheffield, 2001), 211–22, esp. 217.

62. Safrai and Safrai, "Sages and Priests," 299.

63. Neusner, *History of the Mishnaic Law of Holy Things*, 6.44.

64. Indeed, this is precisely how Neusner's argument operates in "Mishnah's Conception," 93–98, where he contrasts the (Mishnah's) "halakhic empowerment of the priesthood" (98) with the "aggadic indictment of the priesthood of temple times" (93); the bulk of the aggadic evidence cited by Neusner is post-mishnaic.

cees with a priestly aristocracy.[65] This equation was always based more on inference than evidence, and the Mishnah's silence on the matter fits more with the evidence than the inference.

7. PRIESTS, PIETISTS, AND HOLY MEN

Following the seminal work of Peter Brown, it has been widely recognized that various sorts of "Holy Men" challenged institutional priesthoods in late antiquity.[66] The mishnaic sages themselves, to be clear, are no match for Brown's demon- and disease-defying, rain-making, self-mortifying charismatics. The Mishnah does however allude to such men here and there, while post-mishnaic sources reveal even more, leaving us once again to wonder about pregnant silences and possible suppressions.

The Mishnah speaks of groups of pietists: of these, the *hasidim* are mentioned most frequently:[67] mBer 5:1 clearly refers to one such group—the "first" or "early" pietists (*hasidim rishonim*) who were particularly well-intentioned in prayer.[68] In other cases, supererogatory practices are named for such folk (mKer 6:3). One passage—mSuk 5:4—juxtaposes *hasidim* with "men of deeds" (*anshe ha-ma'aseh*), speaking of both as playing prominent roles in the water celebration of Sukkot. According to mSot 9:15 (generally recognized as a post-mishnaic gloss),[69] R. Ḥanina ben Dosa was among the last of the men of deeds, and R. Yosi Katonta was among the last of the *hasidim*. We cannot be certain whether two distinct groups are meant or, as is often supposed, the two terms are roughly synonymous.[70] Other uses of the

65. For one classic view questioning the common equation of Sadducees, wealth, and priests see Joachim Jeremias, *Jerusalem in the Time of Jesus: An Investigation into the Economic and Social Conditions during the New Testament Period*, trans. F. H. and C. H. Cave (Philadelphia, 1969), 222–32 (on the "lay nobility").

66. Peter Brown, "The Rise and Function of the Holy Man in Late Antiquity," *Journal of Roman Studies* 61 (1971): 80–101; cf. Neusner, *History of the Mishnaic Law of Holy Things*, 6.288–90.

67. On *hasidim* in pre-rabbinic usages, see S. Safrai, "The Teaching of Pietists in Mishnaic Literature," *JJS* 16.1–2 (1965): 15–33, esp. 15–18. We cannot consider here the possible, but doubtful, identification of *hasidim* with Essenes or the Qumran sectarians, often a feature of the stronger forms of the Essene Hypothesis; see, e.g., Vermes, *The Complete Dead Sea Scrolls*, 62–63.

68. Safrai speculates that much of mBer chap. 5 speaks specifically of *hasidic* doctrine and practice; see "The Teaching," 28–32.

69. Epstein, *Introduction to the Text of the Mishnah* (Hebrew), 2nd ed., 2 vols. (Jerusalem, 1964), 2.976–77.

70. See S. Safrai, "The Pious ('Hassidim') and the Men of Deeds" (Hebrew), *Zion* 50 (1985): 133–54, esp. 144–54.

term *hasidim* are more general, such as the references to pious sailors (mKid 4:14, also likely a post-mishnaic gloss)[71]—probably without any suggestion that these functionaries are pietists per se. More pertinent to our concerns is Yosi ben Yo'ezer—the priest-sage whose permissive decrees were noted earlier—spoken of as a "pietist of the priesthood" (mḤag 2:7). The priest-piety connection also appears with reference to R. Yosi the Priest, a relatively unknown disciple of Yoḥanan Ben Zakkai, identified as a *hasid* in mAvot 2:8.[72]

The Mishnah also speaks in certain abstractions about piety in relation to righteousness, holiness, and learning. In line with mishnaic priorities, an *am ha-aretz* cannot be a *hasid* (mAvot 2:5). A cluster of references appears in mAvot 5, indicating that the term and concept were understood in relation to generosity (bordering on self-denial: 5:10), suppression of anger (5:11), giving while encouraging others do the same (5:13), and combining learning with action (5:14; cf. mSuk 5:4 juxtaposing *hasidim* with "men of action"). On occasion, the Mishnah speaks of acts of loving kindness as *gemilut hasadim* (mAvot 1:1, mPe'ah 1:1, mBB 9:4)—and these references too refer to acts of piety that extend beyond what is minimally required. While these aggadic abstractions focus on acts of charity, other references in the Mishnah, as we have seen, speak of the self-acceptance of ritual stringencies (mBer 5:1). The Mishnah also knows of other such categories, including the "trusted" (*ne'eman*) and the "fellow" (*haver*)—who accepted upon themselves additional stringencies regarding tithes and purity (mDem 2:2–3). While the Tosefta's elaboration of such groups' gradual admission process parallels what we find at Qumran, we should be reluctant to suppose that the rabbinic *havurah* necessarily correlates with other known groups or other rabbinic categories of self-denial.[73] Indeed, as Safrai points out, rabbinic sources rarely if ever associate *hasidim* and *hasidut* with purity-related stringencies.[74]

71. Epstein, *Introduction*, 2.977.

72. The only other mishnaic tradition to mention Yosi the Priest is m'Eduy 8:2; cf. Safrai, "The Teaching," 19.

73. Lieberman, "Discipline in the So-Called Dead Sea Manual of Discipline," *JBL* 71.4 (1952): 199–206.

74. Safrai, "The Teaching," 33; one possible exception is the final aggadic saying in the post-mishnaic gloss to mSotah (9:15) attributed to R. Pinḥas ben Yair (trans. Danby): "Heedfulness (Heb. *zerizut*) leads to cleanliness (*nekiut*), and cleanliness leads to purity, and purity leads to abstinence (*perishut*) and abstinence leads to holiness, and holiness leads to humility, and humility leads to the shunning of sin, and the shunning of sin leads to saintliness (*hasidut*), and saintliness leads to [the gift of] the holy spirit, and the holy spirit leads to the resurrection of the dead. And the resurrection of the dead shall come through Elijah of blessed memory. Amen."

It has become quite common in scholarship to speak of Ḥoni the Circle Drawer as a *ḥasid*, based in part on the well-known story told in mTaʿan 3:8. But only the Tosefta's version speaks of an (unnamed) "certain *ḥasid*."[75] And there are reasons to question this connection: as Isaiah Ben-Pazi points out, Ḥoni's defiant self-confidence—described as if he is a member of the divine household (*ben bayit*, mTaʿan 3:8)—suggests that his attributes differed from the humble self-denial commonly attributed to the *ḥasidim*.[76] In any event, the Mishnah nowhere suggests that Ḥoni was a *ḥasid*. The same holds for Ḥanina ben Dosa, whose identity as a *ḥasid* depends on the association of *ḥasidim* with the "men of deeds."[77] Pinḥas ben Yair is also commonly identified as a *ḥasid* (cf. mSot 9:15, end), based on post-mishnaic evidence.[78]

If our primary goal involved the delicate task of parsing out these categories of pietists, then we would have to proceed further along these lines. But we can safely focus here on Peter Brown's concept of the "Holy Man" in relation to priests, as depicted in the Mishnah. Deferring to Brown on his larger conceptual category allows us to take all that we have just reviewed as evidence of a single pietistic phenomenon, albeit one larger than "*ḥasidim*" per se. Taking all this mishnaic evidence together, however, requires stepping back from imagining any counter-priestly revolutions led by bands of holy men.[79] Indeed, two phenomena further underscore the broader effort of the Mishnah to downplay or disable binary disputes between priests and possible competitors. The first, once again, is suspicious silence: Safrai, Vermes, and others may well be correct that the phenomenon of charismatic holy men was more of a factor in Judea (and possibly especially in Galilee)[80] in the late second temple and early rabbinic periods than the Mishnah al-

75. See, e.g., Safrai, "The Pious," and "The Teaching"; see also Vermes, *Jesus the Jew: A Historian's Reading of the Gospels* (Philadelphia, 1981 [1973]), esp. 69–72.

76. Isaiah Ben-Pazi, "Honi the Circle Drawer: 'A Member of the Household' or 'A Son Who Implores His Father'?" *JSJ* 48 (2017): 1–13, esp. 11–13; on humility as a key feature in *ḥasidut* see, for example, Safrai, "The Pious," 138–41. Note that the identification of Ḥoni as a *ḥasid* often goes hand in hand with the identification of Jesus as one as well; see Safrai, "The Pious," 137–38, and "Jesus and the Hasidim," *Jerusalem Perspective* 42–44 (1994): 3–22. See also Vermes, *Jesus the Jew*.

77. Safrai, "The Pious," 134–38; Vermes, *Jesus the Jew*, 72–78, and Vermes, "Hanina ben Dosa: A Controversial Galilean Saint from the First Century of the Christian Era," Part I: *JJS* 23.1 (1972): 28–50; Part II: 24.1 (1973): 51–64.

78. Safrai, "The Pious," 147–49.

79. In this respect, we follow in part Brown's own self-corrections; see "The Rise and Function of the Holy Man in Late Antiquity, 1971–1997," *Journal of Early Christian Studies* 6.3 (1998): 353–76, esp. 369–76.

80. Safrai, "The Pious," 134–38; Vermes, *Jesus the Jew*, 72–78.

lows. If so, then the Mishnah can be seen as supporting the priesthood by paying so little obeisance to its pietistic challengers. At the same time, the Mishnah's breaking down of the binary opposition—by identifying priests as *ḥasidim*, by identifying cultic practices that could be part of pietistic self-identity—further downplays dispute and may well reflect a historical reality. Perhaps some pietists did actively compete with priests; but perhaps others were, just as the Mishnah suggests, priestly. Once again, it may be that the image drawn from later rabbinic texts—of charismatic pietists giving priests a run for their money, so to speak—reflects a growing post-mishnaic disconnect between the rabbis and priests, and a concomitant increasing anti-priestly bias. But we should not read into the Mishnah what is not there.

8. CONCLUSIONS

There are indeed mishnaic passages that criticize priests: for example, mYom 1:3 conjures an image of an ignorant high priest, while mYom 3:11 conjures an image of priests keeping their knowledge to themselves. The bulk of the Mishnah, however, serves a different purpose, expressing the sages' reverence for the temple, its cult, and its personnel. The rabbinic hopes for the temple's restoration are implied and reinforced throughout. In line with this—and accepting the scriptural givens that account for the priests' pride of place—the Mishnah respects and preserves the roles that the temple's priests were, are, and will again be privileged to play. Neusner correctly describes this effort as the Mishnah's "halakhic empowerment of the priesthood."[81] Going beyond what is scripturally necessary, the Mishnah also credits priests and even high priests with playing an integral role in the transmission of Torah. Of course, the transmission of Torah is not a genealogical inheritance but one of acquired learning. So it goes without saying—though it is at times said—that there will be many learned non-priests, and some ignorant priests and even high priests. For this reason, the mishnaic temple requires rabbinic review. We do well to recall how Neusner put the matter (with reference to the Yavnean stratum of the mishnaic order of Holy Things, dated 70–140 CE):

> *The Temple is holy. Its priests therefore are indispensable. But the governance of the Temple is in accord with Torah, and it is the sage who knows Torah and therefore applies it.*[82]

---

81. Neusner, "Mishnah's Conception," 98.
82. Neusner, *History of the Mishnaic Law of Holy Things*, 6.241 (italics original).

While this statement is largely accurate, these allowances do not detract fundamentally from the Mishnah's largely irenic, nostalgic presentation of priestly matters. As we grapple with the image of priests doing what the sages would want them to do, we must recall that any on-site supervision was likely understood to be carried out by sages who were also priests. And the rabbis hardly limit priestly prerogatives to the Temple, granting them power and honorifics in courts and synagogues. Moreover, while the Mishnah occasionally speaks abstractly of ignorant priests, it identifies none. Named priests—and there are a number—are remembered for their contributions: from Jehoiada (mShek 6:6), to Simeon the Righteous (mAvot 1:2), to Hananiah the Prefect of the Priests (m'Eduy 2:2–3). We must also recognize that the Mishnah stands alone among ancient Jewish literature as a text remarkably bereft of anti-priestly animus. Unlike *Pesher Habakkuk*, the Mishnah knows of no "Wicked Priest." Unlike Hebrews, the Mishnah never anticipates that the high priests of the past will be replaced by something better that comes later. Unlike in later rabbinic documents (such as the Tosefta and the Bavli), stories of priestly greed and other transgressions are hardly hinted at, let alone told, in the Mishnah. And while Simeon looms large in Ben Sira's catalogue of heroes, it is the Mishnah's consistent veneration for the work of the entire priestly cast that sets the Mishnah apart.

At times, the Mishnah's silences are suspicious. Is it really possible that priestly greed was not an issue? Probably not. Is it likely that historical priests—or at least some of them—may have been more mystically inclined than the Mishnah allows? Probably yes. Might there have been greater struggle between priests and pietists than the Mishnah cares to recall? Perhaps. Still, we ought not claim to look at the Mishnah as a whole and speak, simultaneously, of hidden struggles or silent polemics. The Mishnah's silences are not all "blatant"; nor are they all anti-priestly. In some cases, the Mishnah's silences may be in line with what a proper reevaluation of some academic presuppositions should be. The Mishnah does not pay much attention to the Zadokite issue, and that lines up with what a thorough analysis of ancient Jewish literature suggests. The Mishnah does not equate the Sadducees with the priesthood, and there is probably no good reason ever to have done so.

Some scholars will continue to read the Mishnah's various silences as if they serve to repress what appears elsewhere, so that the true meaning and message of the Mishnah are to be found in what is articulated only in the Tosefta or the Bavli. And scholars who do this may be correct (though they may need to attend better to the difference between a silent polemic and an absent one). Even so, there should be more space in contemporary scholarship for an alternative view, one that focuses on the full range of what the Mishnah does in fact say about priests and their contributions to rabbinic knowledge of priestly matters. Such an approach must recognize the stark contrast between the Mishnah on the one hand and, on the other, earlier anti-priestly screeds (like *Pesher Habakkuk* and Hebrews) as well as the overt anti-priestly polemics found in post-mishnaic rabbinic literature. The Mishnah offers us something else, something different: a work produced under non-priestly auspices—albeit with priestly contributions at various levels along the way—that approaches priests and priestly matters with reverence and respect, consistently conjuring images of sages and priests conducting their interrelated activities in an atmosphere largely devoid of the conflicts attested in later sources and read into the Mishnah by modern scholarship.[83]

83. I am grateful to the editor of this volume as well as the organizers and attendees of the January 2021 conference for the helpful suggestions that improved this chapter.

16. Mishnah, Women, Gender: What Are We Reading For, Where Are We Reading It?

Gail Labovitz

For several years, I taught a seminar for students in their penultimate year at the Ziegler School of Rabbinic Studies. The underlying goal was to introduce the students to current ideas and methodologies in the academic study of rabbinic literature. I structured the class around the organizing theme of reading for gender, but with full awareness that there is no one such thing as "reading for gender"—indeed, this was where I worked in teaching scholarly approaches and methodologies. More specifically, for each unit we read a rabbinic story or sugya (section) or passage, and then compared the works of three or four scholars analyzing and explicating those passages, each of whom was interested in questions of gender but nonetheless brought different questions to, used different analytic tools on, and hence came to different (though not necessarily contradictory or mutually exclusive) conclusions about, the materials at hand. For example, the stories and texts about Beruriah look quite different from the eyes of Tal Ilan, seeking to determine if there might have been a real woman who gave rise to them, than from those of Rachel Adler, reading a literary tragedy;[1] the Talmudic "romance" of Rabbi Akiba and his wife yields some things when placed into a discursive formation by Daniel Boyarin, and others when read by Susan Marks

---

1. Tal Ilan, "The Quest for the Historical Beruriah, Rachel, and Imma Shalom," *AJS Review* 22:1 (1997): 1–17; Rachel Adler, "The Virgin in the Brothel: The Legend of Beruriah," *Tikkun* 3:6 (1988): 28–32, 102–5.

alongside information about female patrons and Greco-Roman statuary of women wearing city crowns.[2]

So too, a desire to study women or gender (which are not identical topics, as I will discuss) in Mishnah is not sufficient to predict what sorts of questions one might ask or what methods one might pursue, or even to anticipate the scope of the texts or other evidence one might examine. Is one to delve into the "status" of women in mishnaic law or tannaitic literature, and in what ways would such a study be similar or different to one regarding rabbinic "attitudes" towards women? Does Mishnah reveal anything— by itself, with other contemporaneous rabbinic literature, or in conjunction with other evidence of the time period—about women's "actual" lives, or is this literature better understood as documenting something of rabbinic imagination and fantasy about how women ideally ought to be?[3] And in any case, when we read men writing about women, aren't those men also telling us something about their own self-image and self-construction as men? Or perhaps we need to go back to the start and ask first: How do bodies of various sexes "become" men and women (or anything else) anyway? That is, there are at least two key questions to be considered in the topic I have been asked to address. First, what difference might it make if one is studying "women" or if one is studying "gender"? Secondly, what does it mean to speak of either in "Mishnah"?

Let me begin with "women" and "gender." I want to emphasize the distinction between them precisely because they are too frequently blurred in ways that are problematic, reproducing precisely the categories that the latter in particular is meant to explicate and deconstruct. By the term "women" we have historically usually meant persons who were born with female reproductive organs and who were therefore raised and expected to fulfill certain roles and qualities within society deemed "feminine." Yet we also know that "feminine" roles, qualities, etc. vary across time and place. That is, we have come to distinguish between sex (the physical) and gender (our understandings and experiences of ourselves and others as male or female).[4] As I myself have elsewhere summarized:

---

2. Daniel Boyarin, *Carnal Israel: Reading Sex in Talmudic Culture* (Berkeley, Los Angeles, and Oxford, 1993), 134–66; Susan Marks, "Follow That Crown: Or, Rhetoric, Rabbis, and Women Patrons," *Journal of Feminist Studies in Religion* 24:2 (2008): 77–96.

3. Although it should be noted that it is by now widely accepted that the Mishnah and other tannaitic documents cannot and should not be read as straightforward sources of (social) history on their own (that is, in the absence of other literary and material potential evidence). See further discussion of this point below.

4. Though I vastly oversimplify here even still. Some have also argued that even our understandings of physical differences are influenced by or even a product of our

Gender, then, entails the constant and on-going construction(s) and contestation(s) within a particular culture, and at a particular moment, of what it means (or might mean) to be a woman or a man, masculine or feminine. Put another way, gender may be understood as the process(es) by which these dichotomous categories are culturally produced and circulated, and by which all members of the culture are assigned and socialized to one category or the other.[5]

The key point here, for the moment, is that *all* human beings participate in gender. Indeed, since "masculinity" and "femininity" are commonly defined by one's being what the other is not,[6] to construct femininity or "woman" is equally and inherently to construct its counterpart, masculinity, "man."[7] It follows that to conflate gender with women is to perpetuate an equation of maleness with neutrality, the human "standard," unmarked and in no need of explanation, and to mark femaleness as deviant from the human "norm." And yet—that is precisely how women and the female/feminine have commonly been understood and treated in many and diverse cultures, most certainly including that of tannaitic Judaism. Thus, there are valid reasons for scholarly interest in either or both approaches.[8] It behooves us to know and explore how those identified as women—by them-

socio-cultural constructions of gender rather than clear physical facts. Perhaps the best-known proponent of this view is Judith Butler; see, for example, Judith Butler, *Gender Trouble: Feminism and the Subversion of Identity* (New York and London, 1990) and *Bodies That Matter: On the Discursive Limits of Sex* (New York, 1993). See also Sarra Lev, "They Treat Him as a Man and See Him as a Woman: The Tannaitic Understanding of the Congenital Eunuch," *Jewish Studies Quarterly* 17 (2010): 213 n. 1.

5. Gail Labovitz, *Marriage and Metaphor: Constructions of Gender in Rabbinic Literature* (Lantham, Md., 2009), 8–9, and see also the sources cited thereto.

6. See, for example, particularly the first chapter of Judith Lorber, *Paradoxes of Gender* (New Haven and London, 1994). Lorber titles the chapter "'Night to His Day': The Social Construction of Gender," and suggests (in section headings of the chapter) both that "For Individuals, Gender Means Sameness" (that is, an individual is expected to be, act as, appear, etc. similar to other individuals of the same gender; see 22–26) and "For Society, Gender Means Difference" (on a societal level, members of one gender must be, act as, and appear different from those of another; see 26–27).

7. Moreover, as will be seen below, gender need not be and perhaps cannot be strictly binary, divided into only the categories and poles of male/female, masculine/feminine, man/woman.

8. See, for example, the discussion of this point in Susan Marks, "Women in Early Judaism: Twenty-Five Years of Research and Revisioning," *Currents in Biblical Research* 6:2 (2008): 290–320. Note also this comment from Charlotte Elisheva Fonrobert: "Where women had to gain visibility, a voice, a presence, Jewish feminist criticism itself needed to be committed to gender duality." Charlotte Elisheva Fonrobert, "Gender Duality and Its Subversion in Rabbinic Law," in *Gender in Judaism and Islam: Common*

selves or by society—have been marginalized, suppressed, oppressed. And at the same time, we must be aware that both masculinity and femininity, and even the division of gender into a dichotomous binary, are contingent, socially constructed, and unstable, and so the workings of the processes that both create gender and destabilize it are also proper subjects for academic exploration.[9]

In either case, we must also speak to the titular topic of this project, "What is Mishnah?" There is more than a bit of a chicken-and-egg question here. Does the study of women and gender in the mishnaic text shape our understanding of and answers to that central question? Or do various scholars' intuitions and convictions about what Mishnah is shape how they study the workings of gender therein—the questions they ask and the conclusions that are therefore drawn? Are the questions of what we are looking for (be it women or gender or both), and the question of the nature of the text(s) (Mishnah, tannaitic literature) in which we are seeking it, perhaps even mutually reinforcing, a sort of "feedback loop"? Every work I will discuss below attempts to answer the question "What does the text tell us about women and gender?" but also has to speak to the question "What is this text and how should it be read?" I will attempt to loosely and broadly superimpose these two concerns onto each other, not because I believe they should be too closely identified with each other, but because they do seem to overlap in a number of recent cases in ways that address some open questions in the field and suggest avenues for future studies. First, I will try to situate works and research directions in this area, beginning with those that keep a tight focus on Mishnah, and eventually drawing the "camera" further

Lives, Uncommon Heritage, ed. F. Kashani-Sabet and B. S. Wenger (New York and London, 2014), 110.

9. What is more, there is a trend in surveys of this sort (and not just in rabbinics or the history of Jews and Judaism in Late Antiquity)—which I do not wish to simply perpetuate—to portray the chronological developments of the field as a progression (and progress) from the (early, and usually treated as naive) study of the status of women in the text to a wider (and considered more sophisticated) consideration of the workings of gender. Rather, it seems to me that even as the study of gender has entered the study of Mishnah and tannaitic literature and added greatly to our understanding, the study of women remains both persistent and insistent, valid and intellectually productive. More particularly, one significant portion of my discussion below will be the suggestion that several recent studies of women and women's "status" in rabbinic literature have important potential implications regarding wider debates about tannaitic textual and literary practices, including the central question of the recent symposium of "What is Mishnah?" That said, see, for example, Marks, "Women in Early Judaism"; Ishay Rosen-Zvi, "Misogyny and Its Discontents," *Prooftexts* 25:1–2 (2005): 221–22; Elizabeth Shanks Alexander, "The Impact of Feminism on Rabbinic Studies: The Impossible Paradox of Reading Women into Rabbinic Literature," in *Jews and Gender: The Challenge to Hierarchy*, ed. J. Frankel (New York and Oxford, 2000), 101–18.

and further back to locate Mishnah alongside other tannaitic documents (Tosefta, halakhic midrashim), or in conversation with other roughly contemporaneous Jewish literature and other artifacts of Jewish culture in Late Antiquity in the Land of Israel, and within the wider culture of Roman Palaestina. Subsequently, I will return to the question of how Mishnah and tannaitic literature can inform, and destabilize, our understandings of what gender is and what it encompasses, as understood by the tannaim.

I begin with one of the foundational works relevant to this topic, Judith Romney Wegner's *Chattel or Person?*, published in 1988.[10] It is, as stated plainly by its subtitle, an investigation of "The Status of Women in the Mishnah." What particularly distinguished Wegner's book in its time was (and is) its focus on Mishnah in and of itself. Having written her doctoral dissertation under the supervision of Jacob Neusner, Wegner in her study reflects several important features of his methodological innovations in the study of rabbinics. First is her adherence to Neusner's "documentary hypothesis," the claim that the individual works making up the rabbinic "canon" (such as Mishnah, specific midrashic collections, the two Talmuds) are typically coherent documents each shaped by an editorial hand (or set of hands),[11] and must each be read as an autonomous document with its own unique agenda and outlook.[12] Wegner also embraces a particular conception of Mishnah as a taxonomic[13] and legal document.[14] Crucial, of course, to understanding

---

10. Judith Romney Wegner, *Chattel or Person? The Status of Women in the Mishnah* (New York and Oxford, 1988).

11. Neusner indeed often evokes the term "authorships."

12. Hence she states that her aim is "to understand the Mishnah on its own terms, as a document produced during the late second century CE by a social group (the tannaitic sages) whose worldview and idealized way of life it presumably represents." Wegner, *Chattel or Person?*, 8. Also of note here is her phrasing "idealized way of life"—a phrasing which hints at the social construction of gender despite Wegner's stated topic of "women." On Neusner's influence on early studies of women and gender in rabbinic literature, see also Tal Ilan, *Mine and Yours Are Hers: Retrieving Women's History from Rabbinic Literature* (Kinderhook, N.Y., 1997), 16–27, particularly 20–25; and 22–23 regarding Wegner's book.

13. "The sages assume that everything can be classified in principle and that every category has a polar opposite. All objects placed in class X must by definition possess the attributes of that class; if excluded from class X, they must exhibit diametrically opposed qualities . . . Rather than conceding the viability of hybrid categories and thus permitting an unacceptable blurring of lines, the sages resort to describing problematic entities as 'like X' in some respects and 'not like X' in others. Then they assign the ambiguous object to category X for some purposes and to category Y for others." Wegner, *Chattel or Person?*, 7.

14. Wegner is clear that hers is "a jurisprudential approach, which focuses on the specific question of women's personal status in the law of the mishnaic system." Wegner, *Chattel or Person?*, 10.

Wegner's methodology is the central question of her title; she establishes the poles of women's possible status in the Mishnah as those of either chattel or person, defined as follows: "*Personhood* means the complex of legal entitlements and obligations that largely define an individual's status in society. The converse of *person* in this sense is *chattel*—an entity lacking powers, rights, or duties under the law."[15] In Wegner's understanding, the key to women's status in the Mishnah lies in the "sexuality factor":

> Whenever some man has a proprietary interest in the sexual and reproductive function of a specified girl or woman, the Mishnah's framers treat the woman as that man's chattel in all matters that affect his ownership of her sexuality; in all other contexts, the dependent woman is treated as a person. When, by contrast, no man has a legal claim on a woman's sexuality, the system always treats her as a person.[16]

The bulk of Wegner's book is dedicated to demonstrating that a wide variety of mishnaic laws relating to women and their status can be explained by this core principle, with the notable exception of women's exemptions from many ritual practices regardless of age or marital status.[17]

A related development in scholarship was initiated at much the same time by Judith Hauptman, and has since evolved in both her work and that of others. These works widen the lens applied by Wegner, so as to read Mishnah alongside Tosefta and sometimes other tannaitic texts, yet also bear similarities to Wegner's approach; they tend to posit or affirm a picture of the

---

And note that tannaitic and rabbinic taxonomic thinking will resurface below in a very different context, particularly in consideration of the social gendering of persons of intersex (and sexually indeterminant) body types.

15. Wegner, *Chattel or Person?*, 6–7; see also 10. Though Wegner herself notes that this means free women: "This study does not concern itself with slave women." Wegner, *Chattel or Person?*, 220 n. 19. Similarly, I will not be able to address this topic, though it is certainly of relevance. But the interested reader may see: Gail Labovitz, "More Slave Women, More Lewdness: Freedom and Honor in Rabbinic Constructions of Female Sexuality," *Journal of Feminist Studies in Religion* 28:2 (2012): 69–87; Diane Kriger, *Sex Rewarded, Sex Punished: A Study of the Status "Female Slave" in Early Jewish Law* (Boston, 2011); Catherine Hezser, *Jewish Slavery in Antiquity* (Oxford, New York, 2005); Tal Ilan, *Jewish Women in Greco-Roman Palestine: An Inquiry Into Image and Status* (Tübingen, 1995): 205–11.

16. Wegner, *Chattel or Person?*, 19.

17. For an approach similar to Wegner's, see also Paul Virgil McCracken Flesher, "Are Women Property in the System of the Mishnah?" in *From Ancient Israel to Modern Judaism: Intellect in Quest of Understanding*, vol. 1, ed. J. Neusner, E. S. Frerichs, and N. M. Sarna (Atlanta, 1989), 219–31; but see also my critique in Labovitz, *Marriage and Metaphor*, 32–36, and see below regarding the work of Miriam Peskowitz.

Mishnah (most particularly among tannaitic works) as the work of a distinct editorial hand, or at least as manifesting a distinct and discernable approach to questions of women's status within the legal system it creates or replicates. For Hauptman in particular, her research is situated within a larger project to understand the relationship of Mishnah and its nearest related text, the Tosefta; she is one of the primary recent advocates of the idea that the Tosefta often preserves material antecedent to the Mishnah and out of which mishnaic passages may have been shaped.[18]

Similarly to Wegner, Hauptman is also deeply interested in the status and roles allotted to women in rabbinic texts, and has thus frequently brought together this line of research with the methodological one just noted. That is, if one allows for the premise that individual rabbinic works may be read with an eye towards the editorial hand(s) that shaped them, and that Mishnah in particular is likely the product of a distinct editorial hand (or hands), it would follow that a scholar may deduce information about an editorial agenda, an ideological agenda—including about matters of gender relations—via comparison of Mishnah to other, possibly antecedent, texts. In 1989, presenting her first study in this vein comparing materials in Mishnah and Tosefta *Gitin*, Hauptman introduced an idea that would motivate and be borne out in a number of her subsequent works:

> the redactor of Mishnah Gittin did not just collect and arrange the tannaitic material that was available to him but rather in a consistent manner reconceived the sources in order to set halakhah in the Mishnah stringently. That is to say, when he omitted one of the opinions from a tannaitic dispute, he always omitted the more lenient opinion and included only the more stringent opinion in the Mishnah; and when he drafted anew the halakhah in the Tosefta—nearly always . . . he drafted it in a more stringent manner.[19]

---

18. While Hauptman has written a number of articles and studies on this question, the most obvious culmination and summation of her work is Judith Hauptman, *Rereading the Mishnah: A New Approach to Ancient Jewish Texts* (Tübingen, 2005).

19. Judith Hauptman, "Mishnah Gittin as a Pietistic Document" (Hebrew), *Proceedings of the Tenth World Congress of Jewish Studies* C/1 (1989): 24. Four examples of parallel passages in the two works demonstrate this conclusion. Indeed, as she notes at the conclusion of the paper, if one presumes that the redactor of the Mishnah passages under consideration was aware of the parallel toseftan sources (or something much like them) and crafted his Mishnah accordingly, one must then conclude that it is the ideological tendency towards stringency that is consistent, while the means employed towards such an end are variable, including omitting more lenient views, rewording and restructuring material to more stringent conclusions, and creating new independent positions that vary from those of the authorities in the original source. See also the conclusion on 28.

Over a series of short studies pursuing a similar methodology, Hauptman has compared mishnaic and toseftan materials on a variety of topics relating to women and gender relations—including the obligation to procreate (and hence divorce, due to infertility within a marriage), divorce provisions, women's participation in Passover rituals and other ritual acts, inheritance laws—and found similar results.[20] As she summed up in her book-length work considering a variety of issues relating to women's status in both tannaitic and later amoraic texts,

> Careful comparison of passages in the Mishnah and Tosefta shows that many mishnaic rules are based on and constitute a reworking, often very subtle, of the parallel Tosefta passage. It is likely that the redactor of the Mishnah changed the earlier formulation of the rule in order to have it conform to his views on a particular subject. By examining the roads not taken by him, we can better understand his legislative approach and goals, as well as those of his contemporaries . . . The striking fact that the views of the Tosefta are often more lenient, and hence beneficial to women, than those of the Mishnah, suggests that the redactor of the Mishnah had a more conservative bent than some of his colleagues.[21]

Lending additional significance to Hauptman's findings are a growing body of studies by other scholars that demonstrate similar phenomena—though not always claiming a direct link to Hauptman's work—in a widening body of textual examples.[22]

20. These works are: Judith Hauptman, "Maternal Dissent: Women and Procreation in the Mishna," *Tikkun* 6:6 (1991): 81–82, 94–95; Judith Hauptman, "Women's Voluntary Fulfillment of Positive Time Bound Commandments" (Hebrew), *Proceedings of the Eleventh World Congress of Jewish Studies* C/1 (1993): 161–68; Judith Hauptman, "Women and Inheritance in Rabbinic Texts: Identifying Elements of a Critical Feminist Impulse," in *Introducing Tosefta: Textual, Intratextual and Intertextual Studies*, ed. H. Fox, T. Meacham, and D. Kriger (Hoboken, N.J., 1999), 221–40; Judith Hauptman, "Women in Tractate Eruvin: From Social Dependence to Legal Independence" (Henrew), *Mada`ei haYahadut* 40 (2000): 145–58; Judith Hauptman, "Pesaḥ: A Liberating Experience for Women," *Masoret* (2013): 8–9 (accessible on-line at http://www.jtsa.edu/pesah-a-liberating-experience-for-women; all links in this chapter were accessible as of May 28, 2021).

21. Judith Hauptman, *Rereading the Rabbis: A Woman's Voice* (Boulder, Colo., and Oxford, 1998), 8.

22. Among these are four works by myself, Tal Ilan, and Natalie Polzer: Gail Labovitz, "'These Are the Labors': Constructions of the Woman Nursing Her Child in the Mishnah and Tosefta," *Nashim* 3 (2000): 15–42; Ilan, *Mine and Yours Are Hers*, 55–60; and Tal Ilan, *Silencing the Queen: The Literary Histories of Shelamzion and Other Jewish Women* (Tübingen, 2006), 111–21; Natalie C. Polzer, "'I Thought I Could Endure

Most recently and perhaps in greatest depth, Ishay Rosen-Zvi comes to some similar conclusions in his book examining the trial by ordeal of a woman suspected by her husband of adultery, as described in mSot and other tannaitic works including tSot and midrashim to the biblical source in Num 5.[23] For example, he begins by reading the opening of the tractate and most particularly mSot 1:2, describing a procedure whereby the husband warns the wife against interaction with a specific man, which becomes a condition of subjecting her to the test. This has often been interpreted as advantageous for the wife in comparison to the apparently unchecked power of the husband in the biblical description. Rosen-Zvi, however, turns his focus to a rather obvious internal contradiction in the Mishnah: the husband is said to warn his wife not to "speak" to the man he suspects, but the mishnah then rules that she is not liable to be tested if she merely speaks (publicly) with the man, but rather only if she is witnessed going into seclusion with him. From this, and in light of related sources in Tosefta and elsewhere, Rosen-Zvi therefore suggests that the laws of the warning "are revealed in these sources as a locus for discussing basic questions about sexual supervision and freedom . . . a wide-ranging polemic concerning sexual supervision of married women, which took place in the rabbinic world and its neighboring cultures."[24]

After reading several additional mishnayot in a similarly close manner, and in light of other tannaitic texts, Rosen-Zvi states among his conclusions:

> contrarian positions and attenuated versions of the ritual, found in the parallel sources, are absent from the Mishnah, as well as the stark absence of the presumption of innocence. It is therefore clear that the redactor of the Mishnah combined approaches and opinions

Him but Now I Cannot': Gendered Landscapes in MKetubot 7.7–10 and Parallels," *Women in Judaism: A Multidisciplinary Journal* 12:1 (2015): 1–63 (see particularly 9 and n. 42 thereto; also 17–23), https://wjudaism.library.utoronto.ca/index.php/wjudaism/article/view/26330.

23. Ishay Rosen-Zvi, *The Mishnaic Sotah Ritual: Temple, Gender and Midrash* (Leiden, 2012). And see also his related study, Ishay Rosen-Zvi, "'Even if One Found a More Beautiful Woman': An Analysis of Grounds for Divorce in Rabbinic Literature" (Hebrew), *Jewish Studies: An Internet Journal* 3 (2004): 1–11, https://jewish-faculty.biu.ac.il/files/jewish-faculty/shared/JSIJ3/rosen-zvi.pdf.

24. Rosen-Zvi, *The Mishnaic Sotah Ritual*, 21. Similarly 25–26: "The Mishnah's terse language, therefore, is a record of a polemic on the limits of the freedom of married women to speak to other men as they please . . . Is fear of adultery the motivation for the warning, or are more comprehensive objectives of supervision and control over the wife's actions at play here?" And see also 44–45.

25. Rosen-Zvi, *The Mishnaic Sotah Ritual*, 165–66.

of different Tannaim in order to construct a ritual with a very specific character. If we treat the materials found in parallel Tannaitic
sources as a repository of (surviving) Tannaitic constructions of the
sotah ritual, or parts thereof, we may say that the Mishnah selected
from that repository only the materials that suit the specific nature of
the ritual described above.[25]

That is, the Mishnah, in Rosen-Zvi's reading, consistently presents its vision of the ritual via the most punitive elements, based on—or as a project
of constructing—a presumption of the woman's guilt. This leads him to suggest, regarding the mishnaic depiction: "Its construction was not the result
of a succession of influences but an intentional ideological move with an
internal logic that dictated the selection of new influences and that shaped
their appearance in their new context."[26]

Significantly, although Hauptman frames her work as being very much
about "women," while Rosen-Zvi considers "gender" and the rabbis' male
self-fashioning through their (re)imaginings of Temple ritual and priestly
law,[27] both produce results suggesting that the ideology of the Mishnah appears to be less advantageous, less "positive" towards women, compared to
ideas and options manifested in other tannaitic sources. If this is the case,
though—if the Mishnah can be repeatedly shown through multiple examples to have a demonstrable tendency towards positions that are more restrictive of women's "status," ritual participation, freedom of movement
and social interaction, etc.—then, as Hauptman and Rosen-Zvi both note,
their analyses point to a picture of the Mishnah as a coherent and edited
work with a distinctive editorial agenda and ideology. This then places these
works, more or less deliberately,[28] in dialogue with a quite live and on-going

26. Rosen-Zvi, *The Mishnaic Sotah Ritual*, 168, and see also the following paragraph.

27. The functioning of accounts of Temple (and priestly) ritual in tannaitic literature
being a concurrent focus (alongside gender) in Rosen-Zvi's larger body of work. See
also, for example, "Bodies and Temple: The List of Priestly Bodily Defects In Mishnah
Bekhorot, Chapter 7" (Hebrew), *Mada'ei haYahadut* 43 (2005): 49–87; and so too the
discussion in the latter part of Ishay Rosen-Zvi, "Orality, Narrative, Rhetoric: New Directions in Mishnah Research," *AJS Review* 32:2 (2008): 235–49, for his consideration
of other studies by other scholars that come to similar conclusions about the role and
compositional context of narratives of Temple ritual in Mishnah.

28. In Hauptman's case, at least, quite deliberately, as already noted. But see also
how Moshe Simon-Shoshan reviews some of the implications of Rosen-Zvi's work for
precisely questions such as these: "There is also something deeply appealing about the
Mishnah to scholars with the sort of conceptual and ideological orientation exhibited by Rosen-Zvi . . . There is something 'clean' about the Mishnah's discourse when
compared to other halakhic texts . . . Furthermore, as Judith Hauptman and Shamma

debate in the field at this time relating to the composition and purpose of the Mishnah.[29]

Most significant here is the work of Elizabeth Shanks Alexander, whose scholarship has contributed greatly both to topics relating to gender and to theorizing compositional issues in tannaitic literature—though it is to the latter, and most particularly her book *Transmitting Mishnah*,[30] that I turn at this moment. I lack space here to fully engage with the (admirable) complexities of this work, but I do want to highlight how her methodological turn to orality theory (influenced in turn by the work of Martin Jaffee)[31] leads her to a bold thesis about the composition of and relationship between the two tannaitic independent legal works that have come down to us, Mishnah and Tosefta.[32] Describing the view she will challenge and critique in the book, Alexander could easily be addressing the works we have just discussed here:

> It is ironic that although rabbinic tradition ascribes great importance to *orality* as the Mishnah's mode, scholars have most often used *literary* paradigms to understand the transmission of Mishnah in antiq-

---

Friedman have argued, compared to its closest relative, the Tosefta, the Mishnah is a far more polished and tightly edited text." Moshe Simon-Shoshan, "Between Philology and Foucault: New Syntheses in Contemporary Mishnah Studies," *AJS Review* 32:2 (2008): 260.

29. Note here also two articles by Natan Margalit, "Not by Her Mouth Do We Live: A Literary/Anthropological Reading of Gender in Mishnah Ketubbot, Chapter 1," *Prooftexts* 20:1–2 (2000): 61–86, and "Priestly Men and Invisible Women: Male Appropriation of the Feminine and the Exemption of Women from Positive Time-Bound Commandments," *AJS Review* 28:2 (2004): 297–316, which intersect with the work of each of the three scholars highlighted so far. Like Wegner, Margalit keeps his focus on the Mishnah—if anything, even more narrowly in the sense that each piece reads a single, specific chapter of Mishnah. Similar to Hauptman, however, his aim is both to elucidate the literary qualities of the mishnaic text, and also to thereby investigate its "anthropological understandings"—and more particularly its construction of gender. Additionally, in terms of conclusions about gender, Margalit's methods and subsequent readings are in some ways of a similar sort to those later appearing in Rosen-Zvi's work.

30. Elizabeth Shanks Alexander, *Transmitting Mishnah: The Shaping Influence of Oral Tradition* (Cambridge, 2006). But see also *Gender and Timebound Commandments in Judaism* (Cambridge, 2013).

31. Martin Jaffee, *Torah in the Mouth: Writing and Oral Tradition in Palestinian Judaism, 200 BCE–400 CE* (Oxford and New York, 2001). See Alexander, *Transmitting Mishnah*, 4 n. 5.

32. Alexander does not address halakhic midrash (tannaitic works which are intertwined with exegesis of Scripture) in this book.

uity. Most significantly, scholars have assumed that transmission of Mishnah involved verbatim reproduction of a fixed text . . . Implicit in the conventional view of oral performance of mishnaic materials is the notion that they were formulated with great precision, that they consisted of fixed verbal content, and that they were reproduced in a verbatim fashion from one performance to another.[33]

In short, Alexander advances an argument that parallel texts are not to be read as having a chronological relationship (this one serving as the basis for that one), but rather represent different, fluid (and contemporaneous) oral performances of the underlying material.[34] The fixity of the mishnaic version would then be a later phenomenon of the reception of the Mishnah in subsequent (talmudic) study. Does the consistency of Hauptman's findings, bolstered by works by others and most notably Rosen-Zvi's work on *Sotah*, then lend credence to her understanding of Mishnah over Alexander's?

In a subsequent article, reviewing work on literary approaches to the Mishnah (and particularly the dissertation of Avraham Walfish),[35] Alexander in fact suggests that scholars are faced with a "genuine methodological quandary":

Walfish's work points out how important it is to establish clear criteria for distinguishing between the agenda of the mishnaic redactor (reflected in the Mishnah as we have it, as opposed to, say, toseftan or midrashic parallels) and the ethos of the rabbis generally during the tannaitic period . . . Tannaitic parallels are positioned *both* as a foil to confirm that which is distinctive to the Mishnah and in a uni-

33. Alexander, *Transmitting Mishnah*, 5.

34. In this, she also cites the influence of Jaffee's work on her own: "When considering the question of how to account for the variants among parallel versions, Jaffee bypasses the question of priority that occupies so many scholars evaluating parallels traditions. Instead of trying to resolve the question of which version came first, Jaffee illustrates how oral performance can produce just the kind of variety exhibited by the parallels. For him, parallels are best understood as different performative versions." Alexander, *Transmitting Mishnah*, 36–37.

35. Avraham Walfish, "The Literary Method of Redaction in the Mishnah Based on Mishnah Rosh HaShana" (Hebrew; PhD diss., Hebrew University, 2001). Walfish's work, much like that of Natan Margalit referenced above—as noted by Elizabeth Shanks Alexander in "Recent Literary Approaches to the Mishnah," *AJS Review* 32:2 (2008): 227 n. 8—argues that mishnaic chapters and tractates show regular literary features that reveal them to be coherent compositions (a phrase I borrow from Alexander) and thus likely the intentional products of an editorial or redactorial hand or hands.

fied context with the Mishnah, to indicate something of the ambient culture in which the Mishnah participates.[36]

My intent here, however, is not to adjudicate this dilemma, but to follow the directions it takes amongst scholars who are attentive to women and gender in tannaitic texts. And indeed here, following Alexander, we can turn to see what emerges when we move away from viewing the Mishnah as a distinctive document. Pulling the camera lens back a short distance, one may situate Mishnah as a co-equal part of tannaitic culture (represented by the tannaitic literary corpus as a whole). Or, pulling back for a yet wider shot, all of tannaitic literature may be read alongside additional materials such as other writings (Jewish or otherwise) of the time period, archaeological evidence, and inscriptions, towards a broader picture of Judaism(s) and Jewish life of Roman Palaestina in Late Antiquity. What new views of women's status, women's lives, and the workings of gender in tannaitic culture emerge when we adjust our focus in this way?

Here again, let me turn (for the sake of space) to just one of the pioneering works that take up this question. Scholars seeking the workings of gender in rabbinic literature and culture often work around a unifying theme, a particular site of gender construction in Late Antiquity, such as dress,[37] labor,[38] acts of religious devotion (Torah study, prayer, ritual),[39] or environ-

---

36. Alexander, "Recent Literary Approaches to the Mishnah," 231, and see also the following page. Further on, she also concedes that "I do not think Walfish's emphasis on the influence of a controlling redactional hand and my emphasis on the influence of transmission need necessarily be opposed. If it can be shown that a redacting hand shaped a message that was in dialogue with but uniquely positioned in the ambient rabbinic discourse, that would be an enormous contribution" (233–34).

37. For example, Ishay Rosen-Zvi, "Masculine Adornments, Feminine Adornments: A New Look at the Religious Status of Women in the Mishnah" (Hebrew), *Reishit* 2 (2010): 55–79; David Kraemer, "Adornment and Gender in Rabbinic Judaism," in *Envisioning Judaism, Studies in Honor of Peter Schäfer I*, ed. R. S. Boustan (Tübingen, 2013), 217–34; Naftali S. Cohn, "What to Wear: Women's Adornment and Judean Identity in the Third Century Mishnah," in *Dressing Judeans and Christians in Antiquity*, ed. K. Upson-Saia, C. Daniel-Hughes, and A. J. Batten (Farnham, England, 2014), 21–36; Gail Labovitz, "'He Must Buy Her New Clothes for Winter': Women's Attire in the Rabbinic Imagination of the Tannaitic Period," in *Dress in Mediterranean Antiquity: Greeks, Romans, Jews, Christians*, ed. A. J. Batten and K. Olsen (London, New York, 2021), 325–38.

38. Such as Naftali S. Cohn, "Domestic Women: Constructing and Deconstructing a Gender Stereotype in the Mishnah," in *From Antiquity to the Postmodern World: Contemporary Jewish Studies in Canada*, ed. D. Maoz and A. Gondos (Cambridge, 2011), 38–61.

39. Alexander, *Gender and Timebound Commandments*.

ments such as dwellings and markets.[40] The questions may seem to be ones of "realia"—where were the women (or men, for that matter), what did they wear, what did they do in a typical day—but are often pursued with the understanding that answers (to the extent they can be known) cannot be read solely or clearly out of tannaitic literature, and more particularly that rabbinic texts cannot be read as mimetic representations of daily life or typical religious practice during the period of their composition.[41] Indeed, this is precisely what the word "fantasies" is meant to signify[42] in the title of a foundational work in this vein, Miriam Peskowitz's *Spinning Fantasies*,[43] which takes labor (particular textile work, hence also "Spinning" in the title) and the family economy as a starting point for a discussion that encompasses gender relations, sexuality, marriage, and household labors. However, rather than making a concerted attempt to draw a coherent picture of what that life might have looked like for women (or men), Peskowitz focuses attention on the various and multiple makings and workings of gender that may be found in descriptions and artifacts of daily, "ordinary" life.

Mishnah is certainly the most frequently cited text in Peskowitz's study, and yet its centrality is problematized in at least two directions. First, precisely to the extent that Mishnah is brought to the foreground, the "real" recedes (though this is not to say that other forms of evidence necessarily bring the "real" closer or lend more clarity): "rather than searching ancient rabbinic texts for fictions of 'real law' or 'real women' I read . . . to show the difficulties rabbis encountered as they made gender. I catch rabbis in the act, so to speak, of producing characters for men and women."[44] This can also be seen in Peskowitz's (several) definition(s) of Mishnah: "While today and for centuries the Mishnah and other rabbinic texts hold special status among some Jews, and carry respect from others, in the second century these were texts in progress."[45] And also: "The Mishnah is a formal selection of rab-

---

40. Cynthia M. Baker, *Rebuilding the House of Israel: Architectures of Gender in Jewish Antiquity* (Stanford, 2002).

41. Though note Tal Ilan's expressly stated desire to know about "real women and things they really did"; Ilan, *Mine and Yours Are Hers*, 38. See also Baker's conclusion, in which she writes: "If I were now to attempt to answer one of the central questions posed at the outset of this study—where were the women? I would have to say that, by all accounts, they were *everywhere*." Baker, *Rebuilding the House of Israel*, 147 (emphasis in the original).

42. And similarly "stereotypes" in Cohn, "Domestic Women."

43. Miriam Peskowitz, *Spinning Fantasies: Rabbis, Gender, and History* (Berkeley, Los Angeles and London, 1997).

44. Peskowitz, *Spinning Fantasies*, 32.

45. Peskowitz, *Spinning Fantasies*, 12. See similarly 29 and 46.

binic argument. It is a fictionalization, a product crafted by a third-century storyteller and narrator of *halakhah*. The Mishnah is never a transparent record of 'real discussions' among rabbis, but a text that fashioned rabbis and insaturated a rabbinic movement."[46] But for this very reason, Peskowitz takes a very wide view of her topic and relevant materials. She situates Mishnah alongside not only Tosefta,[47] but also archaeological artifacts including grave goods and recovered tools and documents, funerary epitaphs, and writings in Greek and Latin and Aramaic by Jewish and non-Jewish authors as sources for her investigations:

> The word "text" expands beyond a meaning that privileges writing. "Text" refers to the many places where social imagination and practice are articulated: law, literature, tools, clothing, media, burial sites, art, economic and legal documents, and much more . . .
>
> Both as social contest and as repetition, traces of gender become visible within individual texts or when various texts are examined together . . . In different combinations and read with different types of critical tools, these textual remnants from Roman Palestine provide clues to how early rabbis made bodies into gender, and crafted gender into "sense."[48]

Among the sites where Peskowitz thus sets out to "catch rabbis in the act" of constructing gender are property ownership, textile production, paid and domestic labor, and the family and household economy.

Peskowitz's book is quite complex (in the best sense) and spins out (pun intended) in a variety of directions, but what I want to emphasize here is how her change in focus, her understanding of what Mishnah is and how she

---

46. Peskowitz, *Spinning Fantasies*, 35. But see also Baker, *Rebuilding the House of Israel*, 30.

47. See particularly Peskowitz, *Spinning Fantasies*, 54, for a statement about the significance of Tosefta to her study.

48. Peskowitz, *Spinning Fantasies* 11, 12. A quite similar approach also characterizes Baker's research, though perhaps her work tilts a bit more towards the hope of locating (rather literally as well as figuratively) Jewish women in Roman Palaestina. As she describes two central methodological questions for her work: "The first is the question of how the texts (in this case, the earliest Palaestinian rabbinic writings) are to be *read*—that is, what are the *generic* demands associated with them that help to determine appropriate reading strategies? And second, what are some practical and useful ways of thinking about the relationship between textually constructed subjects, bodies and spaces and material places and artifacts (as interpreted through archaeology)?" Cynthia M. Baker, *Rebuilding the House of Israel*, 29 (emphasis in the original).

situates it in her analysis, stands in contrast to the approaches we have already seen, to elicit some very different views and vantage points on women and gender and Mishnah. Peskowitz is clear that she is not seeking a broad, comprehensive statement on women's "status" in the Mishnah or standing in tannaitic culture, despite acknowledging that "It is tempting—and in some ways necessary—to look for gender and notice its most visible manifestations in egregious displays of sympathy and empathy; in instances of misogyny, privileging of men, and structural oppressions of women; or in examples of women who entered domains and roles that were usually defined as belonging to men." Rather, what she seeks out in her readings is the ordinary: "gender can be most powerful in its ordinariness, in things that have become common, nearly invisible, until they seem to be natural."[49] In this way, she finds an overarching framework such as Wegner's incomplete. In considering mKet 5:5, for example, which delineates domestic labors a married woman is expected to perform for her husband, Peskowitz writes: "The husband would own his wife's work (the completed products and the wages she garnered), and he held authority over his wife's labors (the repetitive daily tasks she would do)"—and then adds as a note:

> As such, I am extending Wegner's argument . . . I am arguing throughout that early rabbinic Judaism constructs gender as a wider variety of bodily disciplines. In contrast to the tendency to focus only on sexuality, I am arguing for the ways in which gender is constituted through masculinist control and ownership of the female laboring body, and for how control of the laboring body is imbricated with the sexed/biological body.[50]

Peskowitz also offers what may be read as a critique of a reading such as Hauptman's or any other attempt to identify more and less "positive" depictions of or rulings regarding women (such as from one rabbinic figure to another or, I would extrapolate, from one text to another), questioning the extent to which rabbis and their culture and literature can be atomized in this way: "The practice of plucking out individual characters—whether heroes,

---

49. Peskowitz, *Spinning Fantasies*, 20, 21.

50. Peskowitz, *Spinning Fantasies*, 97, and 196 n. 5. See also her discussion of property ownership and control (as regards mKet 8:1) more generally as a site of gender, to this conclusion: "A nearly unassailable part of masculinity was the legal right and social potential to own property. For women, the legal capacity to own and control property was variable. Early rabbinic ideas about womanhood did not include the idea that property ownership and control was a necessary element of female being." (35)

fallen heroes, or villains—removes from view the broader rabbinic culture out of which these texts were produced (and which in turn was produced by these writings) . . . It removes from view the ordinary and unnamed rabbis who repeated, read, heard, and commented upon this text."[51] Finally, I want to note how Peskowitz's attention to the tasks and social relations of the ordinary points to an important aspect of gender, i.e., its performativity. That is, that gender is often constructed by *doing* gender. Peskowitz captures this in a felicitous turn of phrase when she writes of the "transformation of task into trait."[52] This construction of gender by doing will also figure in the next part of my discussion.

Thus far, the works I have considered here have moved somewhat between studying "women" and towards a broader attention to gender as it constructs and affects both men and women, masculinity and femininity. For all their differences, though, what these studies tend to have in common is an underlying (if unstated) presumption that gender is binary, a duality of male and female, man and woman.[53] Thus, whereas until now we shifted between, as it were, poles on the axis of "what is Mishnah" (and therefore what questions about women or gender could/should/do we bring to reading it and what interpretive tools do we use to seek answers), here we pivot in a different direction: How might Mishnah (or tannaitic literature more broadly) shift our ideas of what gender is or could be? That is, I now want to turn the focus around to a recent grouping of works (within the last ten to fifteen years) that use tannaitic literature to complicate or directly challenge the presumption of gender as binary, giving analytic attention to the fact that tannaitic texts themselves incorporate persons whose physical sex may not fit the "obvious" signs of male and female.[54]

Most prominent among these persons, in this vein of scholarship, is the *androginos*, whose (borrowed Greek) name indicates their nature: *andros/* man and *gyne/*woman, a person with physical manifestations of both male

51. Peskowitz, *Spinning Fantasies*, 45.

52. Peskowitz, *Spinning Fantasies*, 51. And similarly Cohn, "Domestic Women," 46–47, also addressing m. Ket. 5:5: "According to both rabbis, all women are legally obligated to perform domestic labour and thus to *'perform'*... the gender stereotype that a woman's place is in the home" (emphasis added).

53. "Significantly, the underlying assumption of Jewish feminist critical work until very recently, arguably, has been that the logic of gender duality is the product of what is given, the product of social reality, in the sense that the rabbinic intellectual project merely reflected what in social reality is the duality of 'women' (*nashim*) and 'men' (*anashim*), merely inflecting it with their values." Fonrobert, "Gender Duality," 110.

54. Which is not to say that the scholars contributing to this new trend see themselves as making a radical break with those who have advanced the field before them,

and female genitalia.[55] Given (or imagining)[56] a person whose physical sex cannot be neatly identified as either (and only) male or female, how do tannaitic rabbis and sources suggest such a person is or should be gendered? Or as Charlotte Elisheva Fonrobert,[57] among the first scholars to publish on this topic in 2006 and 2007, has framed one of the fundamental questions,

> What effect does foregrounding the category of the hermaphrodite have for the rabbinic legal thinking about gender as a whole? Does the *androginos* inhabit a stable "sexual identity" as a third possibility, next to men and women, or as the exception to the rule, or does the very presence of a "neither-nor" or "both this and that" category in

---

such as scholars discussed above. To the contrary, see the opening to Charlotte Elisheva Fonrobert, "Regulating the Human Body: Rabbinic Legal Discourse and the Making of Jewish Gender," in *The Cambridge Companion to the Talmud and Rabbinic Literature*, ed. C. E. Fonrobert and M. S. Jaffee (Cambridge, 2007), 270, in which she cites Peskowitz and Baker (among others) as significant influences for the turn to gender in rabbinic studies.

55. That is, the *androginos* is something like what modern medical and scientific discourse would call "intersex." See Fonrobert, "Regulating the Human Body," 280–81. The *androginos* is often paired rhetorically and legally with the *tumtum*, a person whose genitalia are in some way obscured as by a cover of flesh; such a person, however, is presumed to have genitalia of only one kind or the other, and therefore is only a man or only a woman even though it not known which at the moment. I regret that in the interest of (relative) brevity I must skip over Sarra Lev's work on the *saris hammah* (congenital eunuch) and the *aylonit*, persons who are visibly male or female respectively, but do not (fully) develop secondary sex characteristics as is typical in puberty, and the possibility that they may be constructed as gender-crossers, a woman-like man and a man-like woman: Sarra Lev, "How the *'Aylonit* Got Her Sex," *AJS Review* 31:2 (2007): 297–316, and Lev, "They Treat Him as a Man." See also Charlotte Elisheva Fonrobert, "The Semiotics of the Sexed Body in Early Halakhic Discourse," in *How Should Rabbinic Literature Be Read in the Modern World?*, ed. M. Kraus (Piscataway, N.J., 2006), 86–94.

56. This is a point of debate in the sources discussed below. Fonrobert is inclined to understand the *androginos* as a "*Denkfigur,*" a "figure of legal thought"; see Fonrobert, "The Semiotics of the Sexed Body," 100, and Fonrobert, "Gender Duality," 116; but see also Fonrobert, "Regulating the Human Body," 287–88. Gwynn Kessler, on the other hand, asserts, "I can find little reason to doubt that these texts seek to represent real people with real genders": Gwynn Kessler, "Rabbinic Gender: Beyond Male and Female," in *A Companion to Late Antique Jews and Judaism: Third Century BCE to Seventh Century CE*, ed. N. Koltun-Fromm and G. Kessler (Hoboken, N.J., 2020), 364.

57. Fonrobert has also made important contributions to scholarship on the rabbinic gaze and consideration of female (and also male) bodies. See Charlotte Elisheva Fonrobert, *Menstrual Purity: Rabbinic and Christian Reconstructions of Biblical Gender* (Stanford, 2000), and particularly (of the works discussed here) Fonrobert, "Regulating the Human Body," 274–80.

the legal system suggest a hint of instability in the legislative effort of stabilizing sexual identities?[58]

Indeed, why consider such a figure at all?

Before turning to the *androginos*, Fonrobert begins from the premise that sexual dimorphism (male and female) is foundational to the evolving legal system initiated and developed in the Mishnah and other tannaitic works:

> Rabbinic legal thinking . . . aims first and foremost at instituting a rather pronounced dual gender grid, imposed on the social organization of Jewish society as the rabbis envisioned it. Most of the individual laws of rabbinic *halakhah* apply to either men or women. Differently put, in rabbinic legal thinking it is almost always important whether the halakhic agent is a man or a woman.[59]

Moreover, this intertwining of gender and legalism suggests to Fonrobert that

> the halakhic discourse on gender in its classical rabbinic form cannot be described as an *ontological* or *teleological* essentialism. That is to say, it does not posit an *essential* masculinity or femininity, nor is there a fixed nature to men and women . . . Rather, rabbinic halakhic discourse institutes what I would call a *functional gender duality*.[60]

Thus, Fonrobert continues, "the halakhic discourse aims to enforce and normativize congruence between sexed bodies and gendered identities."[61] This can be seen, for instance, in texts such as mSot 3:8 (or similarly mKid 1:7), which attempts to list, categorize, and organize commandments and religious *performances*—who is obligated or exempted (or excluded), to whom do they apply—according to dichotomous gender assignments, man or

---

58. Fonrobert, "Regulating the Human Body," 272–73; see similarly Fonrobert, "The Semiotics of the Sexed Body," 84.

59. Fonrobert, "Regulating the Human Body," 271; and see also Fonrobert, "The Semiotics of the Sexed Body," 80. Of course, as she notes, this is not unique to rabbinic Judaism; rather what is significant is how a given culture distinctively goes about doing so, and with what sorts of efforts and investments in the process.

60. Fonrobert, "The Semiotics of the Sexed Body," 82 (emphasis in the original); see also Fonrobert, "Regulating the Human Body," 272

61. Fonrobert, "The Semiotics of the Sexed Body," 82.

woman: "a list of the distinctive legal capacities attributed to both, not with an abstract determination of biological or anthropological differences."[62]

It is at this point that Fonrobert turns (and returns) to the *androginos*, and to one text in particular: tBik 2:3–7.[63] The passage opens by laying out a structuring taxonomy:

The *androginos*, he[64] is in some ways equivalent to men, he is in some ways equivalent to women, he is in some ways equivalent to men and to women, he is in some ways not equivalent to either men or to women.

Subsequent paragraphs address each permutation by providing examples of how the *androginos* is "equivalent to men," "to women," to both or to neither, relative to a number of rabbinic laws that are (more or less) dependent on gender identity. As Fonrobert observes, this list is similar in form to rabbinic considerations already noted (e.g. mSot 3:8) regarding gender differences between men and women: "The ways in which the androginos is similar to either men or women are not conceived abstractly. Rather, they are explored by means of gender-specific laws and the way they apply to the androginos as a basic conceptual paradox."[65] Moreover, what strikes Fonrobert as most significant here is that the *androginos* must be defined in terms of man and woman, male and female.

In the earlier articles, she especially notes the legislative weight given to the *androginos's* male genitalia (the penis), such that the *androginos* is directed to dress and groom as men do, and to take the male role in marriage and sexual relations.[66] While the *androginos's* gender is not fully disambigu-

---

62. Fonrobert, "Regulating the Human Body," 274–75.

63. A variant of this text also appears as mBik 4:1–5. Saul Lieberman, however, identifies them as two manuscript traditions, of which one is preserved in the Tosefta and the other became attached to the Mishnah; both are printed synoptically in his critical edition of Tosefta. See Saul Lieberman, *Tosefta Ki-feshutah: Be'ur Arokh la-Tosefta*, 2nd ed., vol. 1 (*Zeraim*) (New York, 1992), 836–37, and also Fonrobert, "Gender Duality," 111.

64. Because Hebrew is a gender-dichotomous language, the pronoun used here is masculine. It is, then, an open question whether the term itself is already indicative in any way of the rabbinic gendering of the *androginos*. For differing views on how one might or ought to handle the complexities of translation, compare Max Strassfeld, "Translating the Human: The *Androginos* in Tosefta Bikurim," *Transgender Studies Quarterly* 3:3–4 (2016): 590–91; Sarra Lev, "The Rabbinic *Androginos* as the 'Sometimes Jew': Investigating a Model of Jewishness," *Journal of Jewish Identities* 11:1 (2018): 83 n. 9 (and also 84 n. 21); and Fonrobert, "Gender Duality," 107 and 119 n. 2.

65. Fonrobert, "Regulating the Human Body," 273.

66. Though see also mYev. 8:6 and tYev. 10:12, in which at least one rabbi allows for sexual contact between an *androginos* and a male person so long as there is no anal pen-

ated, "the combination of both primary sexual organs in one body does not allow for either hybridity or choice, as if he could choose to be either man or woman. Indeed, in the project of integrating the doubly-sexed body into the binary halakhic system, the presence of the male genitalia has greater signifying force than the female organ."[67] In Fonrobert's reading, the lone voice of the tanna, Rabbi Yosi—who claims in tBik 2:7 that the *androginos* is a distinctive being with a distinctive sex, whom the rabbis could not determine to be either certainly a man or certainly a woman—is just that, a minority and (hence) non-normative position.[68] Moreover, Fonrobert's works suggest that the list of tBik can be read in two directions. Its laws attempt to integrate the person with the doubly sexed body into the roles, appearances, activities, and responsibilities assigned by a system that is already premised on a binary duality of male or female. Yet this discourse may be equally understood to function conversely, such that the *androginos* is an instrument by which to define, think through, reinforce, and normalize the gender binary and its demands for all: "I want to suggest that we read the compiler's choice to foreground gender as an organizational category of Jewish law and normativity as the product of a need to justify the logic of gender duality . . . In the act of justifying the logic of duality, therefore, the text reveals it as a cultural project in need of persuasion and convincing, rather than merely pronouncing (or reorganizing) law."[69] Either way, the *androginos* is not allowed to undermine the foundational nature of the gender binary for tannaitic thinking—though in the latest piece, Fonrobert does shift focus somewhat to note that the very energy expended in this discussion indicates that "The binary gender order certainly did not fall into place easily with the formulation of early rabbinic law. It remained a matter of negotiation as the Mishnah was compiled."[70]

---

etration (as between two male persons). These texts are central to the analysis in Lev, "The Rabbinic *Androginos*."

67. Fonrobert, "The Semiotics of the Sexed Body," 100; see also the discussion in Fonrobert, "Regulating the Human Body," 281–83. Note that Kraemer, "Adornment," 226–27, is one of few of the studies mentioned above, if not the only one, to even briefly make mention of the *androginos*, and that his analysis is similar to that of Fonrobert.

68. Indeed, she omits it from her translation of the passage in both Fonrobert, "The Semiotics of the Sexed Body," and Fonrobert, "Gender Duality."

69. Fonrobert, "Gender Duality," 111. Similarly, see Fonrobert, "The Semiotics of the Sexed Body," 96, 100; Lev, "The Rabbinic *Androginos*," 76; and particularly Strassfeld, "Translating the Human," 598: "this list is one of the technologies the rabbis use to establish gender as essential to rabbinic law [. . .] the androginos is the technology that the rabbis use to naturalize gender as a central axis in the law."

70. Fonrobert, "Gender Duality," 118–19.

Other scholars who have addressed this and other passages invoking the *androginos*, however, have often highlighted instead the contention, contradictions, and complications raised by the *androginos* in relation to a binary concept of gender. Precisely because the *androginos* can be at once "like" either men or women, or both or neither, Max Strassfeld reads tBik to present three possible options for understanding the *androginos*: male (if somewhat compromised), hybrid, or indeterminate.[71] As well as echoing this point, Sarra Lev cogently observes that the laws that are (or are not) applied to the *androginos* (in various locations in both Mishnah and Tosefta) not only may be dictated by physical factors such as the *androginos*'s mixed genitalia, but also may be situational, guided by the circumstances in which a particular law might become applicable.[72] Furthermore, it should be noted that the seemingly neat taxonomy of tBik in fact is, as Marianne Schleicher observes, not just variable as to the classification of the *androginos*, but actually internally contradictory, and would—if applied—result in rulings that materially disadvantage the *androginos* as regards either men or women.[73]

The most sustained counter-reading to Fonrobert's, however, appears in two related and quite recent articles by Gwynn Kessler.[74] There is one point regarding which Kessler agrees quite fully with Fonrobert: that within rabbinic literature, "gender is defined by performative acts, by doing as opposed to being."[75] And yet in nearly every other way, Kessler's interpretations and conclusions contrast sharply with those of Fonrobert. Here, then, we come back around to some of the methodological questions that figured in the prior sections of this chapter. This is, once again, the question of where scholars choose to train their lenses—and how that is both a function of what they hope to see, and a factor in what they find upon looking.

First, where Fonrobert concentrates much of her attention on legal texts of Mishnah and Tosefta (and especially tBik) to consider rabbinic legal thinking as it affects and effects the construction of gender, Kessler examines a wider sample of texts, including tannaitic halakhic midrash. Here she finds that while the category of the *androginos* (and similarly the *tumtum*) has no obvious antecedents in Scripture—which presents a strict gen-

---

71. See Strassfeld, "Translating the Human," 597, and similarly 598 and 602 n. 15.

72. Lev, "The Rabbinic *Androginos*," 85 n. 29.

73. Marianne Schleicher, "Constructions of Sex and Gender: Attending to Androgynes and *Tumtumim* Through Jewish Scriptural Use," *Literature and Theology* 25:4 (2012): 422–35; see particularly 426–28.

74. Kessler, "Rabbinic Gender"; Gwynn Kessler, "Perspectives on Rabbinic Constructions of Gendered Bodies," in *The Wiley Blackwell Companion to Religion and Materiality*, ed. V. Narayanan (Hoboken, N.J., 2020), 61–89.

75. Kessler, "Perspectives," 74.

der binary—rabbis regularly read the *androginos* (and *tumtum*) into scriptural laws:

> From tannaitic midrashic sources, we see that scriptural mentions of
> the word man or male, man and woman, and male and female, frequently prompt rabbinic discussion of the tumtum and androginos
> person . . . Thus these rabbinic sources remap the instances where
> the Bible appears to present binary gender as exhaustive to represent
> an expanded, non-binary construction of gender.[76]

Why would this be? Kessler's thesis emerges as something like the direct opposite of Fonrobert's: "For the rabbis, the existence of genders beyond a rigid, binary framing is so assumed, so self-evident, that scripture must reflect this reality; so much so that scripture is 'rewritten' or interpreted to teach this."[77]

Fonrobert turns her lens particularly to tBik because she reads it as a site in which the redactor gathered and reorganized rulings from a variety of other locations so as to systematize them according to gender categories, and from which therefore the implications of the category of the *androginos* for rabbinic gender construction emerge especially clearly. When Kessler turns to Mishnah and Tosefta, on the other hand, she looks to those rulings in all their various contexts throughout these works. Here too she finds that the legal texts regularly "write in" the *androginos* (and *tumtum*) into contexts where biblical law would seem to accommodate only binary gender. From this she concludes that for the rabbis, these categories of persons thus appear to be normal, expected, known, and self-evident, and that they exist as sex/gender types *in addition* to male and female:

> The significance of even the partial inclusion of the *tumtum* and
> *androginos* person lies in the fact that it exposes two underlying assumptions found in all of these texts. First, and most obviously,
> mishnaic and toseftan sources often work with the assumption, or
> reckon with the reality, of more than two categories of physical gender . . . Second, the tumtum and androginos are not assimilable to
> man/male and woman/female, and although distinct from both, halakhic stipulations expand to accommodate them. They are not always made to fit into a halakhic dual-gender grid.[78]

76. Kessler, "Rabbinic Gender," 359.
77. Kessler, "Rabbinic Gender," 359.
78. Kessler, "Rabbinic Gender," 364.

If anything, these sources often include the *androginos* and *tumtum* along with a variety of others, frequently including women,[79] as they are compared and contrasted to men in their religious responsibilities and social roles.

Kessler states outright: "I have sought, however, to decenter tBik 2:3–7 and to reject its purported framing of the *androginos* in terms of binary gender from the start."[80] To the extent that she must and does address its content, however, her reading shares much with those of Strassfeld, Lev, and Schleicher:

> It is this text, among those that discuss the *tumtum* and *androginos*
> persons, that *may be read* as an attempt to enforce binary gender,
> to fit the *androginos* person into such a system. Conceptually, I still
> struggle to suspend enough belief that one who is simultaneously
> similar to men, to women, to men and women, and not similar to
> men and women does not itself present a long-winded way of chal-
> lenging binary gender. Beyond this foundational problem alone, the
> text is fraught with difficulties and contradictions.[81]

And so, also contra Fonrobert, Kessler finds that "the final statement attributed to R. Yosi provides the key to understanding the passage, sum-marizes what has preceded it (broadened to include tBik 2:3–7 as a whole, however: not just tBik 2:7), and leaves the reader with the image of the *androginos* as *sui generis*."[82] In sum, Kessler suggests, if we must posit a gender binary that emerges in tannaitic literature, then "Perhaps it would be better to consider how rabbinic gender quite frequently operates within a male-not male binary instead of an assumed male-female one."[83]

Finally, this review of the very different readings of Fonrobert and Kessler raises this question: can one read a particular passage or text as especially "representative" or "exemplary" of rabbinic thinking on a topic, and if so—how? Concomitantly, how would we decide a particular item is anomalous, and therefore to be decentered? This is, ultimately, one more variant

---

79. Which also suggests, contra Fonrobert, that insofar as the gender of the *androginos* is sometimes slotted into the male-female binary, the tilt can also be toward the female side. But see also below.

80. Kessler, "Rabbinic Gender," 365.

81. Kessler, "Rabbinic Gender," 365 (emphasis in the original). See similarly Kessler, "Perspectives," 66.

82. Kessler, "Perspectives," 83 n. 15.

83. Kessler, "Rabbinic Gender," 368. Similarly Kessler, "Perspectives," 71.

of the question I have been considering throughout: Can we speak to a topic such as women or gender without considering how we define our subject and from where we view it? And which further brings me to this briefest of conclusions: what emerges from everything I have discussed here is the paradox of the topic I was asked to address for this forum. We cannot seek either women or gender in Mishnah without implicitly or explicitly holding or coming to a definition of "Mishnah," be it as a document, a way of rabbinic thinking, a piece of a larger picture of Judaism in Roman Palaestina in the first centuries of the Common Era, or what have you. But how we define Mishnah—and hence which pieces of it we look to, and how we situate it relative to other sources and influences—can change our understandings of the workings of gender therein as profoundly as the differences between Hauptman and Peskowitz, or between Fonrobert and Kessler. Is there any common ground to be found? Should there be? I close only with a tentative suggestion: we need not win each other over from one vantage point to another to find questions and angles of value in each other's research, such that yet new questions and interpretations—both regarding women/gender and regarding the nature of Mishnah—might emerge.

17. *Goyim* in the Mishnah

Ishay Rosen-Zvi

My designated topic—*Goyim* in the Mishnah—seems pretty straightforward. *Goy* and parallel words appear more than a hundred times in the Mishnah, a significant yet workable number. But the question itself is far from simple, as it assumes that there is such a thing as "the Mishnah" which can be analyzed synchronically. Of course, one can bypass this assumption by treating the Mishnah as but an example of tannaitic literature in general, but that would unfairly undercut the logic of this inquiry.

So, how are we to read the Mishnah thematically in a non-Neusnerian manner, that is, without presupposing we are dealing with a composition in the modern sense? It seems we have two main options before us: Either a heuristic analysis—one that does not assume anything about the Mishnah as a composition, but merely enables a comparison with other texts—or redaction criticism, an approach which assumes integration, at least at the level of editing.

What makes our case easier is that we are looking not for a theme, but rather for a category, and in the definition of this category the Mishnah is uniform. Several differences exist between different layers of the Mishnah in their treatment of *goyim*,[1] but I did not find internal differences in the category itself, which appears as self-evident from the very beginning.

This is also the main distinction between this study and Gary Porton's 1988 study of *goyim* in Mishnah and Tosefta. Porton's book presents a detailed analysis of most Mishnah and Tosefta passages, and contains use-

---

1. See for example Yair Furstenberg, "From Competition to Integration: The Laws of the Nations in Rabbinic Literature within its Roman Context" (Hebrew), *Dine Israel* 32 (2018): 21–58. See also his article on higher criticism in the study of Mishnah in this volume.

ful lists, tables, and summaries which we will use below. However, it has many methodological problems, and should be studied with caution.[2] But the main difference between our projects lies elsewhere: Porton was occupied with the attitude toward goyim, while my interest is the definition and function of the concept itself. This explains why I will offer a fairly coherent account of the gentile's *role* in the Mishnah (and Tosefta), whereas Porton finds a "variety of pictures," "complexity and inconsistency in the *image* of the non-Israelite."[3]

The Mishah thus serves as an opportunity to examine a systematic usage of the concept of gentiles in a well-defined corpus. Obviously, any such endeavor requires a close comparison with the Tosefta. In my study, I identified many localized differences regarding specific halakhot, as well as differences in format and level of expansions that are typical to the relationship between these two compositions. Thus while the Mishnah's *goyim* laws are discrete and isolated, the Tosefta contains several extended series of laws.[4]

2. Porton's main problem is that many of his conclusions are characteristic of the Mishnah in general, and so tell us very little about the specific treatment of *goyim*. Consider for example his assertion that some of the discussions of *goyim* "are based on imagined realities while others are derived from practical needs" (287). Porton also does not define his search clearly (either conceptually or philologically) and so includes passages on "the Ways of the Amorites" or "The Greek Kings" (33) as well as "Canaanite slaves" (49). His study contains also some gross mistakes, as for example his assertion that tractate 'AZ deals with Israelite idolaters rather than gentiles (243 and passim). For Porton's Neusnerian method of studying the Mishnah in general see Shaye Cohen, "Jacob Neusner, Mishna, and Counter-Rabbinics: A Review Essay," *Conservative Judaism* 37 (1983): 48–63. For a critique of Porton's approach see further nn. 3, 4, 50, 56, and 69 below.

3. Porton, *Goyim*, 42, 287. Porton refers here to the treatment of gentiles as well as the image of *goyim*. He distinguishes between "gentiles qua gentiles," "the gentile as other," "the gentile as idolater," etc. (see e.g. 36–37). Below I will argue that this manner of approaching our topic misses the main gist of the Mishnah.

4. For a complete list of the series of laws of goyim in the Tosefta see Gary G. Porton, *Goyim: Gentiles and Israelites in Mishnah-Tosefta* (Providence, R.I., 1988), 22–35. See especially 34–35, where Porton lists places in which different issues are juxtaposed in the Tosefta, only because they all discuss gentiles. Note however that most of these cases are simple expansions of mishnaic halakhot (adding cases and subcases, disputes, stories, explanations, etc.) typical to the Tosefta. Only a few are actual independent series of gentile laws. Some of these independent series will be discussed further below. For the exceptionally long series of halakhot in *tDemai* 1.15–23 (selling and buying Demai from and to the goy, and related issues) see Richard S. Sarason, *A History of the Mishnaic Law of Agriculture: A Study of Tractate Demai* (Leiden, 1979), 51–55. Recently Hannan Mazeh argued that this is a late appendix in the Tosefta which groups together and adapts halakhot from various contexts. See Hannan Mazeh, "Ha-goy, He-ḥashud ve-'aḥerim: Tahalikhey 'arikhah, halakha ve-ḥevra ba-Tosefta," in *From the Disciples of Aaron: Studies in Tannaitic Literature and Ancient Halakha, in Memory of Prof. Aaron*

The Tosefta also discuss categories[5] and innovative halakhot[6] that are missing from the Mishnah. But I found no overarching thematic difference in the presentation of *goyim* between the two compositions, and so the comparison will remain at the fringe of our discussion (i.e. mostly in the footnotes).

The classical scholarly conception (namely, the Protestant one) of the gentile category famously emphasized rabbinic particularism, which was then contrasted with early Christian cosmopolitanism. Counter-arguments emphasized rabbinic universalism, both in aggadah (two prime examples are Ephraim Urbach article on mSan 4.5 "כל המקיים נפש אחת" and Marc Hirshman's תורה לכל באי העולם on R. Ishmael's missionary ideology) and in halakhah (e.g., David Novak on the laws of Noah, and Christine Hayes on Gentile Impurities). Below I seek to unravel this dichotomy by retreating from issues of the positive versus negative treatment of gentiles, and investigating instead the very formation of the Jew/*Goy* dichotomy.

The title of the session in which this chapter was presented, "the social world of the Mishnah,"[7] must be thus read as: the social world formed in and by the Mishnah, rather than the social world mirrored in it.[8] This chapter thus continues (and somewhat refines) the 2018 monograph written with Adi Ophir, *Goy: Israel's Multiple Others and the Birth of the Gentile*.

I begin by mapping the appearances of the mishnaic gentile according to tractates, and then I offer a more generalized overview of the category.

Shemesh, ed. I. Rosen-Zvi, D. Boyarin, and V. Noam, *Teuda* 31 (2021): 315–48. A similar conclusion was reached by David Sabato regarding the most expanded series of laws regarding goyim in the Tosefta: the rules regarding the Noahide laws at the end of *'Avodah Zarah*. David Sabato, "Mitsvot bene noaḥ be-sifrut ha-Tana`im," MA thesis (Hebrew University of Jerusalem, 2014).

5. Like *meshumadim*, who appear five times in the Tosefta but none in the Mishnah. Famously, the dangers of Jesus's believers (tḤul 2:22–24) and a curse to *minim* and separatists (tBer 3.25) are also mentioned in the Tosefta but not in the Mishnah. It is hard to know whether the reason for these additions is chronological or a result of different policies of the Mishnah and Tosefta editors.

6. Like the use of Roman baths as a *miqve* in tMik 6.3–4.

7. "What is the Mishnah?": A Workshop Co-sponsored by the Harvard Center for Jewish Studies and the Program on Jewish and Israeli Law at Harvard Law School, January 12, 2021.

8. In other words, *Goyim* and *minim*, unlike *kohanim*, are discursive formations that do not exist outside the text. See on this Adi Ophir and Ishay Rosen-Zvi, "*Goy:* Toward a Genealogy," *Dine Israel* 28 (2011), 69–112; idem, *Goy: Israel's Multiple Others and the Birth of the Gentile* (Oxford, 2018), 8–14.

A. THE OCCURRENCES OF *GOYIM* IN THE MISHNAH:
A SURVEY

By my count, גוי (*goy*) and נכרי (*nokhri*) appear in the Mishnah,[9] in various grammatical forms, singular and plural,[10] 113 times (note that multiple occurrences in one sequence are counted as one instance).[11] These two terms are used interchangeably in tannaitic literature, the differences between them being a matter of linguistic preferences and registers (and later also scribal habits). Thus, the same Mishnah can use *nokhri* in the legal part and *goy* in the narrative which follows (23), and *goyim* regularly function as the plural of *nokhri/t* (there is no pl. *nokhrim* in the Mishnah according to the MSS) even in the same sequence (15, 52, 65). Note also that

9. I cite Mishnah according to MS Kaufmann A 50, and thus will not discuss the various censorship replacements (like idolater, עכו״ם) in the printed editions. (Ironically, *nochri* itself became a preferable censored substitute for *goy*, in the printed editions of the Bavli.) Translations are adapted from "Sefaria" (made by Joshua Kulp and others).

10. In order to have a minimal, well-defined corpus, I did not include other terms, like "erets ha'amim" in our search (although "mim" can be replaced by "goyim"; compare e.g. מדורות הגוים [96] with the parallel Tosefta מדור העמים [mOhal 18:6–12]). I also did not include terms in which *goyim* are only implied, as in mBK 1:2–3, which limits the law to "sons of the covenant" (בני ברית), while the parallel (and definitely later) Tosefta (1:1–2) already excludes them explicitly ("פרט ל ... שנגח לשור של גוי", "יצאו גוים").

11. A full list of *nokhri/goy* (sg./pl.; m/f) in the Mishnah: **Zera'im** (1) Ber 7.1, (2) Ber 8.6, (3) Pe'ah 2.7, (4) Pe'ah 4.6, (5) Pe'ah 4.9, (6) Dem 3.4, (7) Dem 5.9, (8) Dem 6.1–2, (9) Dem 6.10, (10) Shev 4.3, (11) Shev 5.7, (12) Shevi 5.9, (13) Ter 1.1, (14) Ter 3.9, (15) Ter 8.11–12, (16) Ter 9.7, (17) 'Ḥal 3.5, (18) 'Ḥal 4.7, (19) Or 1.2. **Mo'ed** (20) Shab 1.7–9, (21) Shab 2.5, (22) Shab 16.6, (23) Shab 16.8, (24) Shab 23.4, (25) Shab 24.1, (26) 'Eruv 3.5, (27) 'Eruv 4.1, (28) 'Eruv 6.1, (29) 'Eruv 8.5, (30) Pes 2.1, (31) Pes 2.2, (32) Pes 2.3, (33) Pes 4.3, (34) Shek 1.5, (35) Shek 7.6, (36) Yom 8.7, (37) Ta'an 3.7, (38) Betzs 3.2. **Nashim** (39) Yev 2.5, (40) Yev 2.8, (41) Yev 3.6 [*nokhrit* = a non-relative!], (42) Yev 7.5, (43) Yev 16.5, (44) Ket 2.9, (45) Ned 3.11, (46) Ned 4.3, (47) Naz 9.1, (48) Sot 9.2, (49) Git 1.5, (50) Git 2.5–6, (51) Git 4.6, (52) Git 4.9, (53) Git 5.8, (54) Git 5.9, (55) Git 9.2, (56) Git 9.8, (57) Kid 3.12. **Nezikin** (58) BK 4.3, (59) BK 4.6, (60) BM 5.6, (61) San 9.2, (62) Ed 5.1, (63) 'AZ 1.1–3, (64) 'AZ 1.5–6, (65) 'AZ 2.1, (66) 'AZ 2.3–7, (67) 'AZ 3.5, (68) 'AZ 4.4, (69) 'AZ 4.8–12, (70) 'AZ 5.3–4, (71) 'AZ 5.7, (72) 'AZ 5.10–12. **Kodashim** (73) Zev 4.5, (74) Men 5.3, (75) Men 5.5, (76) Men 6.1, (77) Men 9.8, (78) 'Ḥul 1.1, (79) 'Ḥul 2.7, (80) 'Ḥul 7.2, (81) 'Ḥul 8.5, (82) 'Ḥul 9.1, (83) 'Ḥul 10.3, (84) 'Ḥul 11.2, (85) Bekh 1.1, (86) Bekh 2.1, (87) Bekh 2.4, (88) Bekh 3.1, (89) Bekh 3.2, (90) Bekh 5.2, (91) Bekh 5.6, (92) Bekh 8.1, (93) 'Arakh 1.2. **Tohorot** (94) Kel 1.8, (95) Ohal 17.3, (96) Ohal 18.7–10, (97) Neg 3.1, (98) Neg 7.1, (99) Neg 11.1, (100) Neg 12.1, (101) Par 2.1, (102) Toh 1.4, (103) Toh 5.8, (104) Toh 7.6, (105) Toh 8.6, (106) Mik 8.4, (107) Nid 4.3, (108) Nid 7.3, (109) Nid 9.3, (110) Nid 10.4, (111) Makhsh 2.3, (112) Makhsh 2.5–10, (113) Zav 2.3. When not citing sources, we will refer below to Mishnah units by numbers only.

nokhri is more frequently found in the Mishnah while *goy* is more common in the Tosefta. This distinction may be due to chronological differences, but other explanations are possible too.[12]

Terms of ethnic identity in the Mishnah tend to follow the biblical vocabulary (with new meanings and sub-meanings, of course), as is clear, for example, with regard to the preference of "Israel" over "Yehudi."[13] The usage of the term *nokhri* is thus understandable, while the usage of *goy/im*, which has no such meaning in the Bible, demands explanation. Ophir and I have dealt with the linguistic and conceptual development of the term in our book. Here I will discuss the ethnic category itself, which is designated by *goy* and *nokhri* interchangeably (more or less, as we shall see below). We shall thus use the word "gentiles" to translate both.

Gentiles appear frequently in laws discussing the obligations Jews have towards things owned or controlled by gentiles, especially in the context of the commandments dependent on the Land (e.g. 6–9; 16–19),[14] holy things (73–76, 86–92), purity (106–12), and ritual slaughter (78–84). Damage is another site of *goyim* laws, as Jews are exempt from compensating for damage they cause to gentiles (58–61). In what follows I will review the appearances in different mishnaic orders, concentrating not on the content of the laws, but rather on their patterns of inclusion and exclusion.

In *Zera'im* gentiles appear *mostly* in the context of exempting the Israelites from tithes and related commandments (*Pe'ah, Demai*: 3–9; *Terumot, 'Orlah, Halah*: 16–19) or helping them to cope with the sabbatical year (10–12). The Mishnah also discusses the status of the gentile's own tithes (13–14), since (according to some opinions at least) the produce of the land of Israel is obligated in tithes, regardless of its owner's status. The issue however is not the gentile owner, but rather the legal implications for the *Israelite* who wishes to consume these products. A single source (15) discusses how one copes (halakhically) with gentiles endangering the purity of tithes or fatally threatening Israelite women (both cases are similarly conceptualized as matters of "purity").

In *Mo'ed* gentiles appear as enablers of activities forbidden for Israelites on Shabbat (a notion which will develop in medieval halakhah into the *shabbat goy* institution; *Shabat*: 20–25, *Betsah*: 38).[15] Their four appearances

---

12. See Natan Braverman, 'Bein leshon ha-mishnah li-leshon ha-Tosefta', *9th World Congress of Jewish Studies*, vol. B (Jerusalem, 1985), 36.

13. See Eyal Ben-Eliyahu, *Between Borders: The Boundaries of Eretz-Israel in the Consciousness of the Jewish People in the Time of the Second Temple and in the Mishnah and Talmud Period* (Hebrew; Jerusalem, 2013), 277–79 and the bibliography there.

14. The numbers in brackets refer to the list of references in note 11 above.

15. The Tosefta elaborated on that topic in tShab 13.9–12. See Porton, *Goyim*, 28–29.

in *'Eruvin* are split between the implications of gentiles and Israelites living side by side on the status of the courtyard's eruv (28–29) and the implications of gentiles' violent acts on the range permitted for an Israelite to walk on Shabbat (26–27). An additional case of gentiles' violence appears in *Ta'anit* (37). In *Pesaḥim* gentiles appear mostly in the context of the status of their ḥametz for Israelite consumption (30–32),[16] and once in the context of the legitimacy of trading with them (33, parallel to 64). In *Shekalim* they are permitted to participate in the temple worship voluntarily, as individuals, but not as part of the collective (34–35). Lastly, saving their life is deemed unworthy cause for desecrating the Sabbath (36).

In *Nashim*, the two major tractates in which *goyim* mostly appear are *Yevamot* and *Gitin*. In *Yevamot* they appear mainly in two contexts: an Israelite man having sex with a gentile woman (*nokhrit*, note however the exceptional use of this term in 41!) and exemptions from levirate marriage (39–43). In *Gitin*, they appear in two very different contexts: the legality of a divorce in which a gentile is involved (as a scribe, witness, court member, emissary, or executor: 49–50, 56) and laws due to "ways of peace" and *tikkun ha olam* (51–54). Gentiles are also excluded from testimony regarding personal status (43) and Nazirite laws (47). One source discusses the naming of gentiles ("uncircumcised"—45)[17] and another discusses their pedigree (57). In addition, gentiles appear twice as endangering Israelites (44, 51; and maybe also 48) and twice as enablers (46, 56).

In *Nezikin*, ten out of the fifteen appearances of gentiles are in tractate *'Avodah Zarah*, the only tractate dedicated to relationship with gentiles (not only in the context of idolatry!).[18] The remaining five are devoted mostly (58, 59, 61) to their exclusion from tort laws (a one-sided exclusion: gentiles are liable when harming an Israelite, while Israelites are liable only for

16. Here appears one of the longest series of *goyim* laws in tPes 2.5–15. See Porton, *Goyim*, 30. On *nokhri's ḥamets* see Joshua Kulp and Jason Rogoff, *Reconstructing the Talmud*, vol. II (New York, 2019), 125–73.

17. On the similarity between this mishnah and Rom 2:25–29 see Yedida Koren, "The 'Foreskinned Jew' in Tannaitic Literature: Another Aspect of the Rabbinic (re)Construction of Judaism" (Hebrew), *Zion* 82 (2017): 397–437.

18. The first two chapters discuss trade relationships with gentiles in general. See Ishay Rosen-Zvi, "Rereading Herem: Destruction of Avoda Zara in Tannaitic Literature," in *The Gift of the Land and the Fate of the Canaanites in the History of Jewish Thought*, ed. K. Bartlett, Y. David, and M. Hirshman (Oxford, 2014), 50–65.

harming their "fellow"),[19] as well as the permission to charge interest from them (60).[20]

Half of the occurrences of gentiles in *Kodashim* are in rulings regarding sacrifices brought by *goyim* (*Zevaḥim-Menaḥot*: 73–77), followed by rules regarding non sacrificial slaughter either *by* or *for goyim* (*Ḥulin*: 78–82). The latter half of the occurrences deal with the exemption of a gentile's animal from various tithes, and its implication for the Israelite consumer (*Ḥulin, Bekhorot*: 83–92). The last appearance discusses the ability of gentiles to dedicate to the Temple (*'Arakhin*: 93).

Tohorot opens with the prohibition of gentiles to enter into the Temple (94) and ends with a series of doubts raised by a mixture of gentiles and Israelites (111–12). In between, most of the occurrences regard gentiles' immunity from regular impurities are mentioned, along with their own special type of impurity (96–100, 103, 106, 107, 109–11, 113; in this context, both women's (107–9) and men's (106) impurities are mentioned.[21] There are also discussions of buying a red heifer from gentiles (101), the susceptibility of impurity of food designated for gentiles (102, 105), a gentile who plowed a cemetery (95), and the reliability of gentiles to testify that they did not touch (and thus render impure) the objects of Israelites (104).

The most illuminating fact revealed in this condensed review is that with the exception of tractate *'Avodah Zarah*, gentiles are distributed almost equally throughout the Mishnah, approximately twenty occurrences in each order. Gary Porton offers a diachronic analysis of the appearances of gentile laws by named sages, and on that front too the results correspond to

19. Tannaitic midrashim interpret the biblical language of brotherhood—"your brother," "your fellow," "your peer"—as referring to Israelites only, thus excluding *goyim* from social prerogatives such as the right to claim lost property or being reimbursed for damage. On the former, see Menaḥem Kahana, *Sifre zuṭa Devarim: muva'ot mi-midrash tanna'i hadash* (Jerusalem, 2002), 330 n. 15; on the latter, see Eliezer Shimshon Rosenthal, "'Shenei Devarim,'" in *Sefer Isaac Aryeh Seeligman: maamarim be-miqra u-ba'olam he-`atik*, ed. A. Rofé and Y. Zakovitch (Jerusalem, 1983), 463–68. On the rabbinic ethnic limitation of brotherhood, see Adiel Schremer, "'Aḥim `aheirim'," *Reshit* 1 (2009): 165–86. On an apologetic explanation of these laws in amoraic literature see Furstenberg, "From Competition to Integration," 48.

20. The last source in *Nezikin* is a dispute about *teharot* (62) and is paralleled there (107).

21. On the connection between these two see Vered Noam, "Another Look at the Rabbinic Conception of Gentiles from the Perspective of Impurity Laws," in *Judaea-Palaestina, Babylon and Rome; Jews in Antiquity*, ed. B. Isaac and Y. Shahar (Tübingen, 2012), 89–110.

the normal generational divide in the Mishnah (twice as many Ushan sages as Yavnean ones, for example).[22]

But most of these laws do not actually refer to gentiles as such, but rather to the Jews ("Israel" in the mishnaic terminology) who come into contact with them. The presence of gentiles in the midst of the Israelites' life-world, or on its outskirts, poses threats of various kinds. Since *goyim* are not obligated in mitzvot, contact with them creates problems (e.g., 8, 20, 30–32, 88–89) and doubts (112), and there is danger associated with their inherent impurity (69; 107) and non-observance of purity laws (96). Various ritual objects cannot be bought from *goyim* (101, compare mMik 8.1). Other objects cannot function correctly when in the presence of *goyim* or when they have been passed through their hands (28).

Gentiles are thus sometimes portrayed as a source of danger to Jews (15, 21, 26–27; 37; 44; 51–52; 65). But more often they appear as facilitators or enablers of the lifestyle prescribed by the Mishnah, in the context of the Sabbath and holidays (22–25; 28; 38; 112), Passover (30–32), food laws (46; 66; 69–72; 80–82; 92), and exemption from priestly gifts (83–92). They are also portrayed as associates and business partners of Jews (8, 60, 111–12), neighbors (28–29), and even co-inheritors (9). Usually, the Mishnah treats this reality as a given. Far from using the halakhic complications that these contacts create in order to prohibit them, the Mishnah assumes the contact as a simple fact, and takes pains to make it possible within the limitations of the law.[23]

In many of their occurrences *goyim* appear alongside other categories. The groupings change according to local legal contexts, in order to compare or contrast them: Samaritans (1, 6–8, 14, 34, 49, 95, 103, 108),[24] slaves (39–40, 42, 55, 57, 93), "deaf, mentally incapacitated and minor" (13, 22, 50, 79, 103), resident alien [*ger toshav*] (60, 97), leper (62 parallel to 107), Sadducee (28), *Am ha'arets* (6), and an Israelite who touched a corpse (94–96). These groupings are determined by the legal issue, not by any intrinsic qual-

---

22. Porton, *Goyim*, 149–55. This normal distribution makes his explanation that after Bar Kokhba was "the presence and the activity of gentiles in Palestine" expanded (157) redundant.

23. m'AZ 2.1 (65) is a notable exception. Most of the laws, in tractate AZ as in other tractates, limit and enable the contacts rather than categorically prohibit them. See also m'Eruv 6.1 (28) in which, according to the anonymous opinion, a gentile cannot live together with a Jew in the same courtyard on Shabbat. Note however the dissent view of R. Eliezer b. Yaakov there, and the ruling of the halakhah according to him already in the Tosefta (t'Eruv 5.20; cf. b'Eruv 62b).

24. See n. 57 below.

ity of the *goy*. That the association is local and legal, rather than an attempt at general designation, can be seen from the fact that gentiles are grouped with priests (regarding the priestly gifts 74–75 [as part of a list!], 84, 86–87, 91) more often than with dogs (46, 92, 105). There is no stable label that cuts across the various contexts in which the *goy* appears.

Goyim appear as a unified category. The few occurrences of different nations in the Mishnah are either in the context of the status of converts (mYev 8.3; mYad 4.3) or of "historic" memories (e.g. Egypt, in the Passover Seder in mPes 10.5, or "the Greek kings" regarding the desecration of the Temple in mMid 1.6; 2.3). The following Mishnah unit is a clear illustration of the tendency to consider the *goy* as an undifferentiated category:

> If a man found an abandoned child in the city and most of the people were gentiles, it may be deemed a gentile child. If most of them were Israelites, it may be deemed an Israelite child; if they were [demographically] equal, it may be deemed an Israelite child. R. Judah says: It should be determined by which are more wont to abandon children (Makhsh 2.7 [112]).

While the issue is realistic and even pressing—how does one decide the origin of an abandoned child?—there is no attempt to mark this origin in any manner that is more specific than "*a goy*." The "statistic" is thus completely binary. The rabbis treat *goy* as if it were a genealogical entity, similar to "Israelite." Even R. Judah's remark, which seems to be specifically hinting at and criticizing (or mocking) the Roman habit of exposing infants, makes no distinctions among gentiles.[25]

Gentiles' specific traits are usually irrelevant. The detailed characterizations of ethnic Others in the biblical and post biblical compositions (Jubilees; Wisdom of Solomon; Damascus Document, etc.) all but disappear in the Mishnah. Since the *goy* is outside the system, there is no need for tempestuous statements of the kind we find with regard to *minim* or apostates. The binary discourse makes such statements unnecessary in the case of the *goy*. Thus while the representation of the former in rabbinic sources is generally emotional and judgmental, that of gentiles is mostly matter-of-fact and "objective." An explicit contrast can be seen in the Tosefta:

---

25. Cf. tMakh 1.8: "R. Judah says: if there was [even] one gentile woman or slave-girl there, she is [the one] suspected of abandoning the child [even if the majority of women there are Jewish]." On the question of the historicity of the stereotype of Roman infanticide, see H. Bennett, "The Exposure of Infants in Ancient Rome," *Classical Journal* 18.6 (1923): 341–51.

"meat found in the hands of a *goy*—benefit from it is permitted, but in the hands of the *min*—benefit from it is forbidden [. . .] *for they said* that the slaughter of a *min* is [considered] idolatry [. . .] and their children are *mamzerim*" (tḤul 2.20; cf. 1:1).

The mishnaic ruling in *'Avodah Zarah* that gentiles are suspect regarding bestiality, murder, or fornication (65) is a notable exception.[26] In general, negative character traits and stereotypes are rare in the Mishnah, and when found, they mostly appear in a matter-of-fact manner (15, 43; compare the matter-of-fact positive evaluation in 104) rather than as a heated polemic. Gentiles need not be suspect of any specific behavior in order for Jews to stay away from them, keep them at arm's length, and limit negotiations with them. They are simply non-Jews, a simple and abstract negative.[27]

Like other figures in the Mishnah, *goyim* appear mostly in regard to their relations to Israelite obligations, prohibitions, and commandments. But *their* obligations and prohibitions are not under discussion. *Goyim can* do things with halakhic implications, but are not, in and of themselves, *obligated* to do anything. When they appear in the context of laws it is always with respect to their relations with or impact on the Jew. This is true when things related to them are exempt from specific halakhic spheres (10–12; 17; 18; 22–23; 30–32; 39; 48; 54; 55; 57; 60; 73; 85–92; 95; 97–100; 106–110; 113) or not exempt (5; 6–9; 16; 19; 20; 29; 58; 74–76; 106); and when they are qualified (13–14; 35; 49; 93) or disqualified (43; 47; 50; 56; 77; 78; 94) to act as legal agents.[28] The same holds true when they are excluded from halakhic domains, such as benedictions (1–2), Shabbat laws (28), commandments related to the land (3–4), purity (62), etc.

Gentiles are always treated *with regard to their effect on the Israelite*, i.e. the one who is commanded. Thus mMik 8.4 (106) says: "If a gentile woman discharged seed from an Israelite it is unclean; if the daughter of an Israelite discharged seed from a gentile it is clean." The sperm of gentiles is excluded from impurity, and therefore gentile women having sex with Israelite men

---

26. Nowhere else in the Mishnah is bestiality identified with gentiles specifically. See mKid 4.14 and compare tKid 5.10. On the exceptionality of mAZ 2.1 see Noam Zohar, "Partitions around a Shared Cultural Space: The Relationship to Gentiles and Their Images according to Mishnah *Avodah Zarah*," *Reshit* 1 (2009): 145–64.

27. Pace Sacha Stern's thesis that "demonization" is one of the major tools for the exclusion of gentiles in Tannaitic literature. Sacha Stern, *Jewish Identity in Early Rabbinic Writings* (Leiden, 1994).

28. The logic of inclusion and exclusion is explicated in the Tannaitic Midrashim through the technique of ריבויים and מיעוטים. See Schremer, "Thinking about Belonging."

become impure, but not vice versa. But the implication, in both cases, affects the Jew who comes into contact with the gentile.

The actions of the *goyim* have implications, real and legal. For example mGit 9.8 [56] says: "A bill of divorce given under compulsion: if ordered . . . by *goyim*—it is invalid; but if the *goyim* beat him and say to him, 'Do what the Israelites bid thee'—it is valid."[29] Gentiles are disqualified to enforce a bill of divorce when acting as judges in a court, but are qualified to act as a policing force, executing the Jewish court decision. Qualification and disqualification vary according to local contexts and traditions; but always with relations to the effects on the Jews.

Goyim appear as agents mostly in the context of Temple laws and holiness: they can dedicate tithe from their products (14), offer sacrifices (34–35; 73–77), and make vows to the Temple (93). This may mirror the reality of the attraction of the Jerusalem Temple to non-Jews,[30] and the polemic regarding gentiles' sacrifices at the end of the Second Temple period.[31] But in the Mishnah, it functions mainly to mark the different spheres of holiness and obligations circling the Temple.

But here too, a gentile's agency is discussed in the context of its influence on its Jewish surroundings. Thus, when a *goy* appears in a sacrificial context, the matter at hand is what the Temple authorities should do: "If a *goy* sent a burnt-offering from overseas and sent along with it [funds to purchase] libations—they are offered from his own, but if [he did] not [send]—they are offered from public funds" (*Shekalim* 7:6 [35]).[32]

Agency of *goyim* is also considered in the context of contract law (49), but mainly in order to exclude them (43, 56).[33] But for the most part, it is not agency but the very presence of the gentile that counts. Sometimes *goyim*

29. See Furstenberg, "From Competition to Integration."

30. See Matan Orian, "Gentiles and the House of the One God in Jewish Sources from the First Temple to the Hasmonean State." (Hebrew; PhD diss., Tel Aviv University, 2015).

31. See Israel Knohl, "Post-Biblical Sectarianism and the Priestly Schools of the Pentateuch: The Issue of Popular Participation in the Temple Cult on Festivals," in *The Madrid Qumran Congress*, ed. J. Trebolle Barrera and L. Vegas Montaner (Leiden, 1992), 601–9.

32. Compare Sifre Zutta to Numbers 15:2 (ed. Horowitz, 280) and see ה' בייטנה, 'עיונים במשנת ספרי זוטא ובדרכי שילובה במדרש', עבודת דוקטור, האוניברסיטה העברית תשע"ח, עמ' 155.

33. Under Roman law and using Roman legal institutions, it was difficult to avoid completely the participation of non-Jews. See Martin Goodman, *State and Society in Roman Galilee, A.D. 132–212* (Totowa, N.J., 1983); Zeev Safrai, "Halakhic Observance in the Judaean Desert Documents," in *Law in the Documents of the Judaean Desert*, ed. D. Schaps and R. Katzoff (Leiden and Boston, 2005), 205–36.

jeopardize the halakhic status of the Israelites (mainly due to their inherent impurity) and sometimes function as enablers (doing things for them on Shabbat or exempting them from tithes). But both occur mostly without any special intention to harm or to assist the Israelite. A clear example is pagan wine libation. Gentiles are (mistakenly, to be sure) perceived as "compulsive libationers,"[34] but are not suspected of doing so deliberately to damage the Jew.

Hers is another example:

> One who takes his wheat to a Samaritan miller or to an *am ha'arets* miller, [the ground wheat] retains its former status in respect of tithes and the law of the sabbatical year. [But if he carried it] to a gentile miller, [the wheat is considered] *demai* (mDem 3.4 [6]; Compare tDem 4.25–27).

Gentiles, unlike Samaritans and *Amei-arets* (both obligated in mitzvot),[35] are unreliable in the realm of tithes. Thus Porton: "gentiles qua gentiles are not trusted."[36] But as the commentators *ad loc.* explain, gentiles are not suspected of replacing the containers of wheat on purpose, but out of ignorance and carelessness. They are simply not part of the game.[37]

So the danger that comes from the *goyim* is either due to their very existence (impurity), their regular behavior (libation), or their ignorance (*demai*). Only rarely is it due to a deliberate act of malintention, as in *Terumot* 8.11 [15]: "If one was passing from place to place with loaves of *terumah* in his hand and a gentile said to him: 'Give me one of these and I will make it unclean; for if not, I will defile them all.'"

In this case the threatening gentile appears in the singular "a *nokhri* said to him," but this is an exception (caused by the fact that it is part of a story

---

34. See Sacha Stern, "Compulsive Libationers: Non-Jews and Wine in Early Rabbinic Sources," *Journal of Jewish Studies* 64 (2013): 19–44.

35. On the comparison between *Kuti* and *Am Haaretz*, and the assumption behind it that Kuti is an ignoramus Israelite see Steven Wald, *Perek "Elo Ovrin": A Critical Edition*, Jerusalem 2000, 57.

36. Porton, *Goyim*, 24; cf. 47. Compare Sarason, *Demai*, 140. On goyim and suspicion in general see Ishay Rosen-Zvi, "Usual Suspects: on Trust, Doubt and Ethnicity in the Mishnah," *The Role of Trust in Conflict Situations*, ed. I. Alon and D. Bar Tal (Berlin, 2016), 117–30.

37. See e.g. Maimonides's commentary *ad loc.*: "זה לפי שהסטוחן יתקבצו אליו קופות של חיטה ואפשר שיחליפם בפירות ישראל אחר". Cf. *Mishneh Torah*, Laws of Ma'asrot 11:13, and see further Shaul Lieberman, *Tosefta Ki-feshutah: Order Zera'im, Part 1* (New York, 1955), 242.

about an Israelite who goes on the way and chances upon someone).[38] In *all* other cases where gentiles appear as a threat (21, 26–27; 37; 44; 51–52; 65) they appear in the plural form, *goyim*. This is the case also in the mishnah unit which follows the one just cited: "Similarly (וכן), if *goyim* said to women: Give us one of you that we may defile her."[39] In contrast, in the passages that deal with the halakhic status of the gentiles, they appear in the singular, usually as *"nokhri"* (this distinction is blurred in many cases in the printed editions).[40] Here is an example from two laws discussing a similar issue:

> One who extinguishes the lamp because he is afraid due to *goyim* . . . (mShab 2.5 [21])
>   A *nokhri* who came to extinguish . . . (mShab 16.6 [22])

We have already seen that the Mishnah, unlike the tosefta, prefers *nokhri* over *goy*, but that there is no word *"nokhrim"* (pl.) in the Mishnah. The key is thus the plural form which tends to appear in casuistic narrative-like descriptions. Thus, images of the gentiles as a source of danger appear with the term *goyim* because they appear in a factual, narrative-like framework, rather than as a halakhic issue in and of itself. This can be seen by the fact that when gentiles appear as a danger, they appear as one example among several. Thus: "A man may make a stipulation concerning his eruv and say: 'If *goyim* came from the east, let my eruv be that of the west . . . If a sage came from the east, let my eruv be that of the east'" (m'Eruv 3.5 [26]); "One whom *goyim* or an evil spirit have taken out (of the Shabbat limit)" (m'Eruv 4.1 [27]); and: "For these they sound a blast on Shabbat: if a city is besieged by *goyim* or a river" (mTa'an 3.7 [37]). In these cases gentiles are but one example of a state of danger. In contrast, in laws like "A *nokhri* who came to extinguish—they do not say to him 'extinguish,' or: 'do not extinguish,' because [the responsibility for] his rest is not [incumbent] upon them" (mShab 16.6 [22]); or "'Hametz of a *nokhri* over which Passover has passed is permitted for benefit" (mPes 2.2 [31]), the very status of *nokhri* is under discussion.

---

38. In the parallel Tosefta it is phrased indeed in the plural "If he was passing through the goyim," tTer 1.14.

39. On the legal issues raised in these two Mishnah units see David Sabato, "Extraditing One to Save the Many: A History of a Talmudic Dilemma," *Shenaton Ha-Mishpat Ha-Ivri* 30 (2020): 183–210.

40. See e.g. mGit 4:9 [52]: "If a man sells himself and his children to a *goy* . . . If a man sells his field to a *goy*." But in the MSS preserving the Palestinian tradition the first occurrence, discussing the violent gentile, has *goyim*, while the second occurrence, discussing the halakhic implication of give and take with the gentile, has *nokhri*.

Note also that in the orders of *Kodashim* and *Tohorot*, which contain almost half of the occurrences of gentiles in the Mishnah, there are no appearances of the dangerous *goy*, but only conceptual discussions of the effect of gentiles on the world of purity and holiness. Additionally, in two places the Tosefta has long tractates about the danger of *goyim* (t.'Eruv 3:5–8: laws of war; tAZ 3.1–7: dangers of a neighbor gentile) and both are shortened greatly in the parallel Mishnah (m'Eruv 4.1 [27]; mAZ 2.1 [66]). It seems the Mishnah was especially selective in its inclusion of material that does not help to clarify the legal status of gentiles and its implications.

'Eruvin' is an especially indicative case. m'Eruv 6.1 [28] cites a debate whether a *nokhri* who lives with a Jew in the same courtyard prohibits the "merging" of the courtyard. The parallel Tosefta (5.22) adds the cases of a Roman official (*quaestor*) and soldiers (*xenoi*) who stay in the courtyard.[41] The Yerushalmi (6.4 [23c]) cites a long discussion of Amoraim of the first and second generation on the halakhic implications of the ability of the Roman government to expropriate houses.[42] Thus, the theme of living with gentiles in the courtyard and its effects on the 'eruv was linked, by both Tannaim and Amoraim, to the issue of Roman practices of taking over houses for civic and military uses.[43] But in the Mishnah there is no sign of all this. The only issue mentioned there is whether an individual *nokhri* annuls the 'eruv, not due to any deliberated (let alone violent) action, but by his very presence in the courtyard. Politics is checked at the door.

This is noteworthy: we are accustomed to thinking of the rabbinic *goy* as the Roman, and thus, automatically, as the violent conqueror and ruler. But this picture, detectable in tannaitic aggadic Midrash and in some appendixes in the Tosefta, has little place in the Mishnah, where the halakhic implications of the individualized *nokhri* stand at the center.

41. On the reality behind this halakhah see Shaul Lieberman, *Tosefta Ki-Feshutah: Order Moed, Part 3* (New York, 1962), 406–7.

42. Saul Lieberman, *Hayerushalmi Kipsuto, Part I*, Jerusalem 1934, 313; Efraim E. Urbach, "Halakhah and History," in *Jews, Greeks and Christians: Essays in Honor of W. D. Davies*, ed. R. H. Hamerton-Kelly and R. Scroggs (Leiden 1976), 125–26. In the parallel Babylonian sugia (b'Eruv 62a, 65b) the Palestinian political discussions of the Roman housing policy are transformed into discussions of the dangers of the individual goy.

43. See also Saul Lieberman, "Palestine in the Third and Fourth Centuries," *JQR* 36 (1946): 355; Shmuel Safrai, "The Relations between the Roman Army and the Jews of Eretz Yisrael after the Destruction of the Second Temple," *Roman Frontier Studies: Proceedings of the 7th International Congress* (Tel Aviv, 1971), 224–29.

B. THE OBVIOUSNESS AND THE MARKEDNESS
OF THE GOY: CHARACTERISTICS

In the Hebrew Bible the term *goy* has no legal implication. It denotes a people in a general sense or, in some cases, a foreign and hostile people, but with no specific law connected to it. The halakhization of the *goy* is a result of a long process of individuation and de-politicization of the biblical *goyim*, a long and gradual process that Adi Ophir and I struggled to narrate in our book. But in this context, the most significant fact is that these various developments leave no traces in the Mishnah.[44] Although *goy* in the singular as a synonym to *nokhri* is documented for the first time in this composition, it appears there as an obvious, self-explanatory entity, with no definition or demarcation.

Unlike other personal status terms which are meticulously defined, like Israel (mKid 3.12; 4.1), priest (mKid 4.4–7), minor (mNid 5.6), *mamzer* (mYev 4.13), and slave (mBik 1.5), or are historicized and contextualized, like Samaritan (mRH 2.2), Sadducee ('Eruv 6.1–2; mNid 4.2),[45] and Minin (mBer 9.5), *goy* and *nokhri* are taken for granted and their meaning is revealed solely by the manner of their employment. The *goy* is the negative of the Israelite ("a non-Jew" in medieval legal language), and thus implicated by the definition of the latter (especially in the context of marriage, see mKid 3.12–4.7; mYev 8.1–3).[46]

44. Only in homilies on verses referring to "*goy*" is the biblical meaning preserved, when it suits the homilists' interest. In a few cases the two meanings, the old and the new, appear side by side. See e.g. Gen Rab 52 (p. 547): "'would you kill a people (*goy*) even if innocent (*tzadik*)'—if thus you judged the generations of the flood and the generation of the division, then they too were just (and the punishment unjust). R. Berekhya says: if you kill a *goy* (i.e. Avimelekh) you kill also a tzadik (Abraham)." While the first homily reads *goy* as people, and "tzadik" as "innocent," the second reads *goy* as gentile, and thus "tzadik" is not a characterization of the *goy* but its opposite, i.e. Abraham versus Avimelech.

45. "One who does not acknowledge '*eruv*" ("מי שאינו מודה בעירוב") in mishnah 6:1 is an addition to the original contrast between goy and Israel (See the parallel tosefta 5.19–20, ed. Lieberman, 115). It seems to be taken from the subsequent narrative on the Sadducee, and therefore this term is but a generalized designation of a Sadducee. Cf. b'Eruv 68b ("צדוקי מאן דכר שמיה?").

46. The definition of an Israelite in *mYevamot* mentions various nations by name, and does not use the generalized category *goy*. The Mishnah here is an expansion on Deut 23:2–9, which couples Ammonites, Moabites, and men with damaged genitalia. But while Deuteronomy is about foreigners, the Mishnah is about converts. This is what justifies the differences between various peoples and the lack of a generalized category: only when members of certain nations convert to Judaism do the differences between them become meaningful.

Although the gentile is a category of personal status, the Tannaim are not engaged with digging into or subdividing it, as they do with other statuses (women for example, are grouped according to age, virginity, and marital status, menstrual cycles and diligence in observing the commandments) but only in terms of the encounter. Halakhic distinctions relate to opportunities, places, times, and forms for these encounters, the medium in which the encounter occurs, the kinds of activities involved, and so on.

No attempt is made to distinguish between various aspects of gentiles (friendly or hostile; a stranger from afar or a familiar neighbor) or between gentiles on the basis of their origin or appearance. Even "religious allegiances" do not seem to matter to the Mishnah (to the great surprise of Porton),[47] besides the very fact that gentiles are assumed to be idolaters. Instead, the conceptual effort is invested in creating the binary division: stabilizing the opposition between the Jews and their Other, and shifting in-between creatures to one pole or another. Thus the Kutti is pushed to the Jewish pole, while the Ger Toshav to the side of the gentile, and so forth.[48]

By and large, the binary distinction also absorbs the gender distinction. There are but a handful of occurrences of *nokhrit* in the Mishnah (which never use the word "*goyah*," probably due to lack of biblical precedent) and they deal mostly with the same issues as those discussed where masculine *nokhri* appears: regulating social relations (65); ritual uncleanliness (62, 109); questions of genealogy (39, 57); and conversion as a case study of instantaneous change (40, 92). There are differences in details, of course (the impurity of gentile women is manifested differently), but the categorization is similar. Thus, when moving from gentile men to women the rhetoric of m'AZ 2 changes from accusations and suspicions ("they are suspect regarding illicit sexual relations" etc.) to pure hostility ("An Israelite woman shall not midwife a gentile woman" etc.). Surely, there is a difference in the mode of othering, but not in its effect: a gentile woman is neither more nor less "goyish" than a gentile man.[49]

Tractate '*Avodah Zarah* is the place where the thickening of halakhic discourse on the shared domain is most intensive. Thematically, the tractate

---

47. Porton, *Goyim*, 3.

48. On the mishnaic treatment of the various in-between figures (Samaritans, slaves, *Ame-Haarets*, *minim*, etc.) see Adi Ophir and Ishay Rosen-Zvi, *Goy: Israel's Multiple Others and the Birth of the Gentile* (Oxford, 2018), 180–97. See also Yedida Koren, "The 'Foreskinned Jew.'" As Koren shows, Tannaitic literature is the first corpus in which an uncircumcised Jew is considered a full Jew. She further shows how mYev 8.2 deliberately diminishes the importance of the concept of "forbidden from entering the congregation," ascribing to it minimal halakhic consequences.

49. There is one theme, though, that appears only in relation to the female *nokhriot* in the Mishnah: sexual intercourse. See for example mYev 2.8 (40) "If a man is suspected

could be called "gentile[s]," like the order "Women" or the tractate *Nazir*. But unlike these, *'Avodah Zarah* has little to say about gentiles themselves, but rather explicates the shared spaces in rich detail (including a mapping of geographical space itself: 1.4; 1.8; 3.4–7; 4.3; and more).

Gentiles are not unique in that their presence causes distinctions, but all the distinctions they create have nothing to do with them. Gentiles remain oblivious to the legal ruckus they bring about. There is no halakhic category which expends as much effort as the *goy* and is analyzed so little. Gentiles simply create rules of conduct. Their presence and actions are responsible for the ever-growing governmentalization of the Jewish life-world, but they teach nothing about the identity or substance of Jews.[50]

The *goy* is always marked. Laws in tannaitic literature are never simply relevant to any human being, making ethnicity negligible. Unlike gender, which is often disregarded when the difference between men and women becomes irrelevant with respect to specific laws (as in the contexts of damages and most of the negative commandments), when gentiles are included in a law or qualified as its agent (e.g. to bring a sacrifice or write a document), it is always stated explicitly.[51] Local gentile-Jewish equality is marked as an exception regarding specific laws. The law never simply ignores the Jew/gentile opposition, even when it treats the two equally.

We must stress this major difference between the *goy* and other mishnaic subjects. The Mishnah writes *about all creatures* (including animals) but its *recipients* are Jews alone. Its default subjects are adult men ("*adam*" in the Mishnah can be either man or person; only the context allows for differentiation)[52] in *Eretz Yisrael* (for example "there are three districts [ארצות] regarding *ḥazakah*; Judea, Transjordan, and Galilee" mBB 3.2), but

---

of [having had relations] with a maid who was later emancipated, or with a *nokhrit* who subsequently converted." This and similar units deal with intercourse specifically in the context of a male Jew and a female gentile. The Tosefta adds in all these cases the opposite case: "A gentile or a slave that had relations with a daughter of Israel."

50. Pace Porton, who assigned to the mishnaic *goyim* the role of "defining the People Israel" (Porton, *Goyim*, 287). Porton's study as a whole is framed in the context of constructions of "ethnic groups" and boundaries (Porton, *Goyim*, 10, 288). See the critique by Stern, *Jewish Identity in Early Rabbinic Writings*, 135–37.

51. Inclusion and exclusion of gentiles are rarely explained: "For the ways of peace" and "for the betterment of the world" (12, 51–54), as well as "because they are suspect" (65). Gentiles are sometimes excluded through scriptural homiletics as well (31, 86–87, 93). See also (38): "a story of a gentile who brought fish to Rabban Gamaliel. He said: they are permitted, but I do not wish to accept them from him."

52. See for example: "A man [אדם] shall not abstain from the performance of the duty of being fruitful and multiplying ... the man [איש] is commanded to fulfill the mitzvah of propagation, but not the woman [אשה]" (tYev 6.6).

its conceptual net is cast outside of these default contexts to encapsulate also minors, women, and the world abroad. Gender and geography can both appear and disappear as a criterion according to their relevance in specific contexts. This state of flux is not true of the *goy*. Gentiles are never recipients; the ethnic distinction is never simply "forgotten." The *goy* is the only limit of mishnaic jurisprudence.

The Mishnah is the first legal corpus in which no explicit marker of its addressees is needed. No "Speak to the sons of Israel" as in the Pentateuch, no "you" plural as in the *Temple Scroll*. The Mishnah says "a person" (אדם) and we can simply assume that it refers to an Israelite (as in the very first Mishnah unit "to draw a person far from transgression" להרחיק את האדם מן העבירה). This obviousness, a marker of the mishnaic laws, is, we argue in our book, a direct result of the establishment of the Jew/*goy* discourse. The addressee, in other words, is implied in the very binary distinction.

The *goy* appears in the Mishnah in a multitude of contexts: sometimes as the instigator of a halakhic difficulty, but more often as an enabler and promoter of leniency, and usually as a neighbor and partner, and not as an intimidating ruler. What all these appearances share is that the *goy* is not a subject of the law, neither directly nor inadvertently. Unlike *gerim*, the *goyim* do not require verses to exclude them from certain commandments; they are excluded by default.

C. THE *GOY* AS THE ONLY AGENT WHO IS NOT OBLIGATED: A THESIS

As an *object* of the law the *goy* is not different from any other object, human or animal, that creates halakhic "problems" and demands decisions.[53] A clear example is the debate between the houses of Hillel and Shamai regarding the use of gentile labor on Shabbat (20), which is a direct continuation of their debate regarding "the resting of vessels" (as the Bavli conceptualizes it) in the Mishnah (mShab 1.5–6). Gentile labor is not discussed in and of itself, but only as a vessel of the Jew, similar to an olive press or oven.[54]

The appearance of gentiles in the Mishnah is thus closer to its interest in halakhic objects like cattle (בהמה appears some 180 times in the Mishnah) than to halakhic subjects like women (appearing some 300 times). Like cattle, the *goy* created doubts and halakhic matters to be solved for the Jew,

53. This is justly noted by Porton, *Goyim*, 3.
54. See Joshua Kulp and Jason Rogoff, *Reconstructing the Talmud*, vol. II (New York, 2019), 93. And see MekY, Pasḥa 9, 30–31: לא תעשה אתה ולא יעשה חבירך ולא יעשה גוי מלאכתך, אבל עושה גוי את מלאכתו.

and like cattle, the *goy* can be liable in tort law. *But* unlike cattle, *goyim* can also be halakhic agents. Not only do their actions have halakhic implications (this is true also for cattle) but they can deliberately do things that will sometimes be viable. This is true mainly in two contexts: legal procedure (43,49,56) and consecration (14, 35,73–77). Thus:

> All documents which are deposited in the archives of gentiles, even if those who signed the documents are gentiles, are valid, except bills of divorce and writs of emancipation (mGit 1.5 [49]).
>
> A gentile or a Samaritan—their *teruma* is a [valid] *teruma* and their tithes are [valid] tithes and their dedication [to the Temple] is a [valid] dedication (mTer 3.9 [14]).

But the fact that *goyim* are not obligated by the law distinguishes them from all other humans specified in the Mishnah (such as women, Samaritans, slaves, minors, *am haaretz*, converts, etc.).[55] Whereas other "legal objects," artifacts, animals, or humans who are not adult Jewish males are incorporated entirely within the realm of the law, and are made part of its never-ending expansion, the *goy* is included and is marked as different at one and the same time: a human agent who is an object of the law but never its subject or bearer.[56]

This is exactly what makes the *goy* unique: he is the only halakhic agent who is not obligated. Many agents are exempt or excluded from certain things, but none other than the *goy* is exempt from everything. The *goy* is the only agent who *can do* things with legal consequences but is *obligated to do* nothing.

---

55. On borderline statuses in the Mishnah, both inside and outside the halakhic constitution, see Orit Malka, "On Testimony of Women and of a Single Witness in Tannaitic Literature," *Dine Israel* 33 (2020): 227–70. Note that we are referring here to personal statuses, which are not to be confused with social roles like robbers, ליסטים.

56. This distinction is missed by Porton, who repeatedly talks about the "obligations" of gentiles. See for example his summary of tKil 2.15–16: "the important issue throughout is whether or not the gentile, like the Israelite, *must* take into account the holy nature of the Land of Israel" (Porton, *Goyim*, 28, emphasis added. Cf. 37, 49). But the Tosefta considers nothing like that. It rather discusses the implications of the *goy*'s agricultural activity on his fellow Israelite ("*goy* who grafted . . . the Israelite can take from him"; "One cannot participate with the *goy* in Kila'im"; etc.). See also Porton, *Goyim*, 32, who summarizes t'Hul 5.2–3 as ruling that *goyim* "are not obligated to follow those folk customs" (i.e. the prohibition to slaughter an animal and its offspring on the same day). But the Tosefta does not deal with this issue to begin with. Rather it discusses whether or not the Israelite is permitted to slaughter for a gentile ("השוחט . . . לאכילת גוים . . . אסור") and whether an Israelite is permitted to consume slaughter by a gentile ("שחיטת נוכרי מותר").

In fact, this may be the exact missing definition of *goy* in the Mishnah: a non-obligated halakhic agent. This is also the *goy*'s function in the Mishnah. His role (and it is usually a he) is to be the one who is not obligated and that thereby marks the limits and borders of halakhic jurisprudence. This is the reason for his appearances in so many diverse halakhic contexts. Whereas Samaritans,[57] Sadducees,[58] or *minim*[59] mark the limits of halakha from the inside, the *goy* marks it from the outside.[60] Thus the famous mishnah in Nid 4.1–3 [107]:

> Samaritan girls are considered menstruating women from the time they lie in their cradle . . . Sadducee girls, when they were accustomed to follow in the ways of their Sadducee ancestors their status is like that of Samaritan women. If they moved to follow in the ways of Israel their status is like Israel . . . blood of a *nokhrit*, and the blood discharged by a female leper, Beit Shammai deem them ritually pure, and Beit Hillel say: like that of her saliva and her urine.

I cannot enter here into the intricacies of this Mishnah, discussed at length by many.[61] For our purpose it is enough to note that this unit marks

57. Samaritans especially are contrasted time and again with *goyim* (1; 7; 49; 107 [both Samaritans and Sadducees], 108 [Samaritans and *gerim*]). On Samaritans as Israelites in the Mishnah—transgressive and marginal Israelites, but Israelites nonetheless—see Ophir and Rosen-Zvi, *Goy*, 185–92, and the conclusion at 186: "Samaritans are not considered in the Mishnah as an intermediate category but rather as Jews. They are grouped with the "Israelites" and in opposition to gentiles (Ber 7.1; 8.8; Dem 3.4; Ket 3.1; Git 1.5; Nid 7.3). Unlike the latter (Nid 4.3), they are part of the purity system (Nid 4.1) and are not considered inherently impure (Nid 7.3–4). Their exclusion is always a result of specific, local reasoning." For a different perspective, see Yair Furstenberg, "The Rabbis and the Roman Citizenship Model: The Case of the Samaritan," in *In the Crucible of Empire: The Impact of Roman Citizenship upon Greeks, Jews and Christians*, ed. K. Berthelot and J. Price (Leuven and Bristol, 2019), 181–216.

58. For the (likely, to my mind) possibility that Sadducees were not just a memory of old in the second century see Shaye Cohen, "The Significance of Yavneh: Pharisees, Rabbis, and the End of Jewish Sectarianism," *HUCA* 55 (1984): 27–53, esp. 33; Martin Goodman, "Religious Variety and the Temple in the Late Second Temple Period and Its Aftermath," *JJS* 60 (2009): 202–13, esp. 212.

59. On *minim* in the Mishnah see (from two very different perspectives) Adiel Schremer, "Wayward Jews: Minim in Early Rabbinic Literature," *JJS* 64 (2013): 242–63; Naftali S. Cohn, "Heresiology in the Third-Century Mishnah: Arguments for Rabbinic Legal Authority and the Complications of a Simple Concept," *HTR* 108 (2015): 508–29. *Meshomad* does not appear in the Mishnah, but only in the Tosefta. On the relationship between these two categories see Ophir and Rosen-Zvi, *Goy*, 193 n. 57.

60. See tKid 5.11–12, which compares *goy* with other classes (names there אומות!) of a slave, former slave, mamzer, and convert.

61. See e.g. Christine E. Hayes, *Gentile Impurities and Jewish Identities: Intermar-*

a distinction between "kosher" Israelites, Samaritans, and Sadducees on the basis of their practices. But then *all three* categories are contrasted to *nokhrit*, who is not part of the menstrual impurity "language game" at all (unless it is a decree "like her saliva and urine").[62]

This role of the *goy* is also the reason why conversion appears in various halakhot as a case study to examine the transformation from exemption to obligation and its implications in different contexts (4, 40, 50, 92, 98, 113).[63]

That gentiles are more popular than all the other categories mentioned above (*Kutim* appear twenty times in the Mishnah; *minim*, eight times; Sadducees, seven times) shows that marking the border from the outside is more useful than marking it from the inside.[64]

The Mishnah knows no limits to its jurisprudence: in the land of Israel and abroad; from the most mundane things to the laws of Kingship. The *goy* is the only limit of its jurisprudence, and thus can function to examine what happens in these borders. It serves, for example, to sort out the distinction between those obligated and those who are not in the realm of impurity (106–10), or between the legal capacity (to serve as scribes, judges, witnesses, executors) of those inside versus outside the system (49–50, 56).

I thus agree with Shaye Cohen that "the Mishnah does not establish strong boundaries around its community; it is not interested in defining or-

---

riage and Conversion from the Bible to the Talmud (Oxford, 2002), 122–31; Charlotte Fonrobert, "Blood and Law: Uterine Fluids and Rabbinic maps of Identity," *Henoch* 30.2 (2008): 243–66 and the references there.

62. Pace Annette Yoshiko Reed, who writes on this Mishnah: "Sadducees can through choices about 'the ways' to follow . . . move in and out the boundaries of 'Israel' . . . Samaritans, by contrast, are placed firmly on the outer boundary within." See Annette Y. Reed, "Parting Ways over Blood and Water? Beyond 'Judaism' and 'Christianity' in the Roman Near East," in *La croisée des chemins revisitée: Quand l'*Église et la Synagogue se sont-elles distinguées?, ed. S. C. Mimouni and B. Pouderon (Paris, 2010), 227–59, esp. 243. Since the Sadducees' behavior does not affect their ability to be *niddot*, it does not affect their inclusion in Israel, but rather their halakhic status inside Israel (i.e. among those who contract menstrual impurity). See also Daniel Boyarin, *Border Lines: The Partition of Judaeo-Christianity* (Philadelphia, 2004), 60–63.

63. The reason it can function thus is that rabbinic conversion is an instantaneous transformation rather than a long process, as in earlier literatures. See Ophir and Rosen-Zvi, *Goy*, 180–85.

64. The Mishnah famously uses borderline categories and doubtful cases as conceptual tools. See Moshe Halbertal, "The History of Halakha and the Appearance of Halakha," *Dine Israel* 29 (2013): 1–23 (Hebrew). Categories of personal status (Mamzer, Arel, Kohen, Ger, Kutti, Tumtum, Androginus, etc.) are especially useful as case studies for such inquiries. See for example Charlotte Elisheva Fonrobert, "Regulating the Human Body: Rabbinic Legal Discourse and the Making of Jewish Gender," *The Cambridge Companion to the Talmud and Rabbinic Literature* (2007), 270–94.

thodoxy, suppressing deviance, or establishing the limits of dissent."[65] But from my *goy*-centered perspective I would add that it is exactly the binary Jew/*goy* distinction which delineates the "Israelite" from the outside that enables the Mishnah to be so relaxed about these matters. In other words, the boundaries are indeed not established through orthodoxy and deviance,[66] but nonetheless the mishnah does present boundaries (strong, binary, total); they just need to be looked for elsewhere.[67]

My argument is that this is precisely the role of the *goy* in the Mishnah: to mark the boundaries of mishnaic jurisprudence from the outside.[68] This explains the *goy*'s unique status as a category that generated all sorts of discussions, but involved no rabbinic effort invested in analyzing it. It also explains why the *goy* is the only halakhic agent who is not a halakhic subject. And lastly, this may be the reason for the curious fact with which we started this review: that the *goy* is more or less "evenly" spread out throughout the tractates of the Mishnah.[69]

---

65. Shaye Cohen, "The Ways that Parted: Jews, Christians, and Jewish-Christians ca. 100–150 CE," in *Jews and Christians in the First and Second Centuries: The Interbellum 70-132 CE*, ed. J. Schwartz and P. J. Tomson (Leiden, 2018), 307–39. Compare Cohen, "The Significance of Yavneh," 41.

66. See also Adiel Schremer, "Thinking about Belonging in Early Rabbinic Literature: Proselytes, Apostates, and Children of Israel; or, Does It Make Sense to Speak of Early Rabbinic Orthodoxy?" *JSJ* 43 (2012): 249–75.

67. Robert Brody, "Rabbinic" and "nonrabbinic" Jews in Mishnah and Tosefta," in *The Faces of Torah: Studies in the Texts and Contexts of Ancient Judaism in honor of Steven Fraade*, ed. M. Bar-Asher Sigal, T. Novick, and C. Hayes (Göttingen, 2017), 229–75, narrates a picture of extending concentric circles from rabbis, to non rabbis, to *minim*, Samaritans, and lastly *goyim*. My analysis of the function of *goyim* in Tannaitic literature led to a very different picture, in which a binary division overpowers and encompasses all others.

68. This explains an important finding of Porton, *Goyim*, 40–44, namely that gentiles appear many times at the beginning of topics, serving as their introduction (see e.g. mNeg 3.1; 11.1; 12.1, in which *goyim* are excluded at the very openings of the laws of leprosy of persons, closes, and houses, respectively). The reason, I claim, is that they are part of the definition of the commandment, marking its limits.

69. Porton deduced from the fact that there is no tractate dedicated to gentiles, but that they are embedded instead in the "normal" discussions on each topic and "fit well into their context," that "the gentiles *qua* gentiles were of little concern to the compilers of Mishnah-Tosefta" (39. Cf. 35, 70). I agree that the *goy* is not of interest in and of itself (for the *goy* is not an addressee of the Law, a fact that as seen above, Porton missed). But my claim is that the embeddedness of gentiles in (almost all) the different topics of halakhah is not an accident, but rather the manner in which this category functions in the Mishnah.

18. "And Your People Are All Righteous": Heretics and Heresy in the Mishnah

Adiel Schremer

INTRODUCTION

"Heretics and Heresy in the Mishnah" is a challenging topic. The Greek word αἵρεσις, from which the English word "heresy" stems, does not appear in the Mishnah (or in any other rabbinic text of late antiquity), in any form. As it is obviously difficult to speak about "heretics" in a text that does not use this word even once, it is to be assumed—in order for such a title to be meaningful—that a certain Hebrew word that does appear in the Mishnah is the equivalent of "heretic," and therefore talking about "Heretics in the Mishnah" is possible.

This assumption, though widely held by students of rabbinic Judaism, is far from simple. "Heresy has to do with creedal matters, with believing wrongly."[1] It is usually defined as a *"theological or religious opinion or doctrine maintained in opposition, or held to be contrary, to the 'catholic' or orthodox doctrine of the Christian Church, or, by extension, to that of any church, creed, or religious system, considered as orthodox."*[2] Accordingly,

---

1. See Maureen A. Tilley, "When Schism Becomes Heresy in Late Antiquity: Developing Doctrinal Deviance in the Wounded Body of Christ," *Journal of Early Christian Studies* 15 (2007): 3. Admittedly, Tilley herself writes against this conventional view and suggests that in many cases "heresy" is better understood as "schism." A similar approach can be seen in Geoffrey D. Dunn, "Heresy and Schism According to Cyprian of Carthage," *Journal of Theological Studies* 55 (2004): 551–74; Einar Thomassen, "Orthodoxy and Heresy in Second-Century Rome," *Harvard Theological Review* 97 (2004): 241–56.

2. *Oxford English Dictionary*, s.v. "heresy."

a "heretic" is "One who maintains *theological or religious opinions* at variance with the 'catholic' or orthodox doctrine of the Christian Church, or, by extension, that of any church or religious system, considered as orthodox."[3] Hence, to say that there are heretics in the Mishnah is to claim that the Mishnah has a developed notion of "correct belief" and that it fights against people whose beliefs are "incorrect" (in the Mishnah's view). It is to say that religious dogmas are significant categories in its project. Is this indeed the case?

The Mishnah's dealing with creedal matters, with correct (or incorrect) belief, is extremely meager. In fact, there is only one passage in the entire Mishnah in which the issue of incorrect belief is in focus. That is, as is well known, mSan 10:1: "And these [are those] who do not have a share in the world to come: He who maintains (lit. says) that there is no resurrection of the dead; and [he who maintains that] there is no Torah from heaven; and an *epiqoros*."[4] This mishnaic passage is understandably celebrated by modern scholars whose historical outlook is shaped by western Christian cul-

---

3. *Oxford English Dictionary*, s.v. "heretic."

4. mSan 10:1 (my translation), following the reading of MS Kaufmann, Budapest A 50 (and other witnesses), in which the famous opening sentence, "All Israel have a share in the world to come" etc., does not appear at all. I emphasize this point, because it is precisely this line that enabled some readers to conclude that according to the Mishnah the espousal of incorrect belief renders one as "not Israel." See, for example: Burton L. Visotzky, "Mortal Sins," *Union Seminary Quarterly Review* 44 (1990): 49; Christine Hayes, "Displaced Self-Perception: The Deployment of Minim and Romans in B. Sanhedrin 90b–91a," in *Religious and Ethnic Communities in Later Roman Palestine*, ed. H. Lapin (Bethesda, Md., 1998), 276; Israel J. Yuval, "All Israel Have a Portion in the World to Come," in *Re-defining First-Century Jewish and Christian Identities: Essays in Honor of Ed Parish Sanders*, ed. F. E. Udoh et al. (Notre Dame, 2008), 114–38, and see his suggestion to read mSan 10.1–2 as anti-Christian polemic in Israel J. Yuval, "Christianity in Talmud and Midrash: Parallelomania or Parallelophobia?," in *Transforming Relations: Essays on Jews and Christians throughout History in Honor of Michael A. Signer*, ed. F. T. Harkins (Notre Dame, 2010), 50–74; Gail Labovitz, "The Rabbinic Origins of K'lal Yisra'el," *Conservative Judaism* 64 (2013): 12–13; Eugene Eung-Chun Park, "Covenantal Nomism and the Gospel of Matthew," *Catholic Biblical Quarterly* 77 (2015): 67. I am struck that even scholars who acknowledge the secondary character of that opening sentence still include it in their presentation of mSan 10:1, despite their full awareness of its being a later addition to the text of the Mishnah. See, for example, David M. Grossberg, "Orthopraxy in Tannaitic Literature," *Journal for the Study of Judaism* 41 (2010): 555; Jonathan Klawans, *Heresy, Forgery, Novelty: Condemning, Denying, and Asserting Innovation in Ancient Judaism* (New York and Oxford, 2019), 67. Cf. Adiel Schremer, "Negotiating Heresy: Belief and Identity in Early Rabbinic Literature," in *Canonization and Alterity: Heresy in Jewish History, Thought, and Literature*, ed. G. Sharvit and W. Goetschel (Berlin, 2020), 39–43.

ture, in which religion is frequently understood to be related to one's beliefs, so the desire to view Judaism as a religion, like Christianity, entails
focusing on those Jewish texts in which "belief," "thought," and "theology"
are highlighted and discussed.[5] However, mSan 10.1 is the *only* passage in
the Mishnah that treats dogmas as such, so it is utterly wrong to claim that
the Mishnah was occupied with dealing with correct, or incorrect, belief in
any substantial manner. It is not that belief is entirely absent from the Mishnah, but that the Mishnah is overwhelmingly uninterested in this aspect of
human life experience, and it does not consider belief as a major focal point
of its project.[6] Because "belief" occupies no major role in the Mishnah, it is
difficult to maintain that heresy and heretics are a significant aspect of its
worldview.

This point needs to be sharpened from yet another perspective. The word
"heretic" is a label. It is a word used by some members of society to paint in

5. Jonathan Klawans's section on "Heretics in the Mishnah" in his 2019 book, *Heresy,
Forgery, Novelty*, 67–72, is the most recent example of this trend. As the reader will notice, despite its title that section is devoted solely to mSan 10:1, and no other Mishnaic
passage is cited to explore the Mishnah's dealing with heretics. The reason is quite simple: there are no other passages in the Mishnah that discuss heresy and heretics, and this
is precisely my point here.

6. Despite Milikowsky's claim that "the Sages did not consider the fulfillment of the
commandments without belief as the heart of Judaism" (see Chaim Milikowsky, "Ge-
henna and 'Sinners of Israel' in the Light of *Seder 'Olam*" [Hebrew], *Tarbiz* 55 [1986]:
337), Shaye Cohen's assertion, that "ancient Judaism in general and rabbinic Judaism in
particular did not have creeds," is still valid. See Shaye J. D. Cohen, "A Virgin Defiled:
Some Rabbinic and Christian Views on the Origins of Heresy," *Union Seminar Quarterly
Review* 36 (1980): 5, reprinted in Cohen, *The Significance of Yavneh and Other Essays in
Jewish Hellenism* (Tübingen, 2010), 541. This is true with respect not only to the Mishnah, but to rabbinic Judaism more broadly. For this reason Ed P. Sanders felt the need to
comment on mSan 10:1 and to write that it is "both striking and odd in a religion which
generally insists far more on orthopraxy than on orthodoxy." See: Ed P. Sanders, *Paul
and Palestinian Judaism: A Comparison of Patterns of Religion* (Philadelphia, 1977), 151.
Jacob Neusner, too, has noted that rabbis in the Land of Israel of the Tannaitic period
usually "express their primary cognitive statements, their judgments upon large matters, through ritual law, not through myth or theology, neither of which is articulated
at all." See Jacob Neusner, *A History of the Mishnaic Law of Purities Part Ten, Parah:
Literary and Historical Problems* (Leiden, 1976), 230. A beautiful expression of this rabbinic attitude can be found in tShevu 3:6 (ed. Zuckermandel, 449–50), where Rabbi
Reuven is asked by a certain philosopher: "Who should be considered the most hated
person in the world?" Rabbi Reuven replies that it is he who denies God. When asked
again by the philosopher concerning the precise identity of such a person, he responds:
it is one who transgresses the commandments of "honor your father and mother, do not
murder, do not thieve." For the rabbinic sage, the denial of God is expressed in deeds,
not in abstract thought.

negative colors some people and certain stances which they dislike and wish to delegitimize. There are therefore no heretics "out there" in the world; there are only human beings, of whom some are condemned and delegitimized by others by assigning them the label "heretics." In other words, *"heresy" is the name of a discourse.* To speak about "heretics in the Mishnah" is to claim that there is a discourse of heresy in the Mishnah, that is, that the Mishnah engages in a discourse of identifying and classifying certain theological opinions and fighting against them by labeling those who espouse them as "heretics." Such a claim is problematic, however, for there is no "talk of heresy" or "talk of heretics" in the Mishnah.

Even if we were to suggest that a certain word in the Mishnah should be understood as the equivalent of "heretics"—and this is indeed frequently claimed, as is well known, for the Hebrew word *minim*—the number of times the Mishnah uses that word is very small. As Shaye Cohen has recently emphasized, a collection of all references to *minim* in the Mishnah yields a very modest corpus, "barely equal in length to one typical Mishnah chapter."[7] To speak, then, of the Mishnah's "discourse of *minim*," let alone its "discourse of heretics," is to create a distorted impression of this fundamental work of rabbinic Judaism.

The reasons behind the scholarly desire to speak about heresy and heretics in the Mishnah (and in early rabbinic Judaism more broadly), and thus to construct "the rabbinic discourse of Orthodoxy and Heresy," need not bother us here. One may hypothesize that it stems from the (unconscious) need of some contemporary scholars to view everything Jewish in Christian terms, so as to be able to present (to themselves and to others) their scholarly work as belonging to the wider discourse of the hegemonic scholarly community, but I shall leave this question aside. It will suffice to emphasize that no rabbinic work "against heretics" has ever been composed, and no "Irenaeus," "Tertullian," or "Epiphanius"—some of the Church Fathers whose works "against heretics" have survived and come down to us— is known to have ever existed among the early rabbis. The Mishnah contains not even a single chapter devoted to *minim*, and nothing resembling Book 16, Title 5, of the *Theodosian Code*, "De Haereticis," in which no fewer

7. See Shaye J. D. Cohen, "The Ways That Parted: Jews, Christians, and Jewish-Christians, ca. 100–150 CE," in *Jews and Christians in the First and Second Centuries: The Interbellum 70–132 CE*, ed. J. J. Schwartz and P. J. Tomson (Leiden and Boston, 2018), 320. Cohen refers to the Mishnah and the Tosefta together, and if we omit from the list the references to *minim* in the latter, the number is much reduced. The addition of the references to *minim* and *minut* found in all other rabbinic works of roughly the same period (that is, the Tannaitic midrashic compilations) does not change the picture in any significant manner.

than sixty-five laws pertaining to heretics are included, can be found in the entire rabbinic corpus of late antiquity. As Martin Goodman has written, in contrast to their Christian counterparts, the rabbis of first, second, and early third century "do not seem to have been concerned much of the time either to analyse the precise constituents of *minuth* [*sic*], or to define their own views in contrast to heresies . . . Despite their general interest in the classification of phenomena in the world about them, the rabbis do not seem from the extant evidence to have been concerned to define *minim* or *minuth*; it was enough that the general category existed."[8]

Finally, there is the matter of the nature of the question we are attempting to address. Does the title hint at a hidden assumption, according to which "the heretics" were a specific, identifiable group of people, who were recognized as such by other members of Jewish society of the Mishnah's days? In contrast to this implied assumption, I will attempt to show that the Mishnah does not consider *minim* as part of its social world. Rather, it views the *minim* as belonging to remote times, like Sadducees and Boethusians. The question I'll be asking, therefore, is: How do heretics, *as a category*, function in the Mishnah? That is, how do they appear in the Mishnah, and what discursive job do they perform therein? My suggestion is that the Mishnah uses the category *minim* as an *explanatory tool* to rationalize current halakhic stances and to justify them.

I. *MINIM* IN THE MISHNAH: AN OVERVIEW

The noun *minim* (plural), or *min* (singular), appears no more than six times in the Mishnah. In addition, the Mishnah refers once to *minut*.[9] Because there is some ambiguity concerning the text of these passages I shall present them here in Hebrew, according to the reading of MS Kaufmann, Budapest A50 (which is considered the most reliable text-witness of the Mishnah), accompanied by an English translation.

8. See Martin Goodman, "The Function of *Minim* in Early Rabbinic Judaism," in *Geschichte–Tradition–Reflexion: Festschrift für Martin Hengel zum 70. Geburtstag*, ed. H. Cancik, H. Lichtenberger, and P. Schäfer (Tübingen, 1996), 501–10.

9. *Minut* is mentioned also in mSot 9:15 ("and the Kingdom will become *minut*"). That passage, however, is a post-tannaitic interpolation and therefore should not be included in our discussion. Cf. Jacob N. Epstein, *Introduction to the Text of the Mishnah* (Hebrew; Jerusalem and Tel-Aviv, 1964), 976; *The Babylonian Talmud with Variant Readings, Tractate Sotah (II)*, ed. A. Liss (Hebrew; Jerusalem, 1979), 352 n. 157. Compare the similar post-tannaitic tradition in Song of Songs Rabbah 2:13 (ed. Donski, 71); bSan 97a; Tosefta Derekh Eretz, Chapter "Rabbi Shimon," 1 (ed. M. Higger [New York, 1935], 245).

1. mBer 9:9:

כל חותם הברכות שהיו במקדש היו מן העולם. משיקלקלו המינים [ו]אמרו אין עולם
אלא אחד היתקינו שיהוא אומרין מן העולם ועד העולם.

All the ending formulas of benedictions in the Temple were [of the following type]: "From the world."[10] Since the *minim* disrupted [the matters],[11] they said:[12] "There is but one world."[13] They ordained that they should say, "From the world to the world."

10. "From the world" (מן העולם) is the reading of the Land of Israel branch of the Mishnah (MSS Kaufmann, Budapest A50; Parma 138; Cambridge [ed. Lowe]; two Genizah fragments, and other witnesses). Other witnesses read: "To," or "Until" the world (עד העולם). See *The Mishnah with Variant Readings*, ed. N. Sacks (Hebrew; Jerusalem, 1975), 1.90. The latter reading is attested by the Tosefta (in all its witnesses). The difference between the two readings may be significant, as noted by Saul Lieberman, *Tosefta Ki-feshutah* (New York, 1955), 1.122–23. The common translation, "From everlasting," reflects a temporal understanding of the expression מן העולם. However, the noun העולם may be understood in a spatial sense (as its regular usage in rabbinic Hebrew; cf. Shamma Friedman, *Studies in the Language and Terminology of Talmudic Literature* [Hebrew; Jerusalem, 2014], 5). Compare, for this matter, Ps. 135:21 ברוך ה' מציון ("Blessed be the Lord from Zion"). I therefore rendered the expression literally, "from the world," in order to preserve the ambiguity of meaning, which is precisely the point of the text.

11. The translation of the expression משיקלקלו המינים is admittedly difficult, as the verb *qlql* may be understood either as a stative or dynamic verb. See Eliezer Ben Yehuda, *A Complete Dictionary of Ancient and Modern Hebrew* (Hebrew; Jerusalem, 1952), 12.5973. Indeed, some render the Hebrew phrase as: since the *minim* "corrupted [the practice]," thus reflecting an understanding of the verb as transitive (see, for example: Jacob Neusner, *The Mishnah: A New Translation* [New Haven and London, 1988], 14). Others, however, render the mishnah in a manner that reflects an understanding of the verb as stative, meaning: since the *minim* "became corrupted," or "perverted their ways" (that is, in fact, since the *minim* turned to be *minim*). See, for example, Ben Yehuda, *A Complete Dictionary*. Such an understanding may be related to the meaning of *qlql* as betray, as it emerges, for example, from SifDeut. 306 (ed. Finkelstein, 330): מי קלקל במי ("who has betrayed whom" [pace Reuven Hammer's translation in his *The Classic Midrash: Tannaitic Commentaries on the Bible* (New York and Mahwah, N.J., 1995), 338–39]: "who has rebuffed whom"). See also Saul Lieberman, *Hellenism in Jewish Palestine* (New York and Jerusalem, 1994), 49–50; Menahem Kahana, "'שיקור' and 'שינוי'—A Study in the Exegesis of Exegesis" (Hebrew), *Lĕšonénu: A Journal for the Study of the Hebrew Language and Cognate Subjects* 55 (1991): 77–83. Because of the stylistic and structural similarity of our Mishnah passage to that of mRH 2:1–2, in which it seems quite clear that the verb bears a transitive meaning, I tend to understand it in our passage along the same line and to translate the phrase accordingly as "disrupted [the matters]."

12. My translation follows the reading of the first scribe of MS Kaufmann, ואמרו (the *vav* is a superscript addition by a later hand). The scribe's reading (אמרו), without *vav*, is the reading of other witnesses as well. See *The Mishnah with Variant Readings*, 1.90–91. According to the reading ואמרו, the subject of the verb is the *minim*. On this reading, the *minim* said that there is only one world. On the former reading, it may be (and even required by the syntax) that other people said so.

13. I am not entirely sure how to punctuate this sentence. It may be read with a question mark: "They said: Is there but one world?" There is no way of deciding the matter.

2. mRH 2:1:

בראשונה היו מקבלין עדות החודש מכל אדם. משקילקלו המינים התקינו שלא יהו
מקבלים אלא מן המכירים. בראשונה היו משיאים משואות. משקילקלו הכותים התקינו
שיהו שלוחים יוצאין.

At first they would accept testimony about the new moon from
any person. Since the *minim*[14] disrupted [the matters] they enacted
that testimony should not be accepted [from any person], only from
known people. At first they would light torches [to inform about the
new moon]. Since the Kuttim disrupted [the matters], they enacted
that messengers should go forth."

3. mSan 4:5:

לפיכך נברא אדם יחיד בעולם . . . שלא יהו המינים אומ' רשויות הרבה בשמים.

For this reason man was created alone in the world . . . so that the
minim would not say, "[there are] many domains in heaven."

4. mḤul 2.9:

אין שוחטין בגומא, אבל עושה הוא אדן גומא לתוך ביתו בשביל שיכנס הדם לתוכה.
ובשוק לא יעשה כן שלא יחקה את המינים.

One may not slaughter [an animal] into a hole, but one may make
a hole in his house for the blood to flow into; one may not, however,
do so in the marketplace so that he not imitate[?] the *minim*.

5. mPar 3:3

ובפתח העזרה היה מותקן קלל שלחטאת ומביאין זכר שלרחלים וקושרין חבל בין קרניו
וקושרין מקל ומסבך בראשו שלחבל וזורקו לתוך הקלל ומכה את הזכר ונרתע לאחוריו
ונוטל ומקדש כדי שיראה על פני המים. ר' יוסה אומ' אל תתנו מקום למינים לרדות, אלא
[הוא] נוטל ומקדש.

At the entrance to the Temple Court was set ready a jar of [the
ashes of the] Sin-offering. And they bring a male from among the
sheep, and they tie a rope between its horns, and they tie a stick and
wound it about with the end of the rope, and he throws it into the
jar, and he strikes the male so that it startles backward, and he takes
and sanctifies [enough] to be visible on the water. R. Yosi says: Do
not give the *minim*[15] room to pressure! Rather, he takes [the ashes directly from the jar] and sanctifies them.

14. *Minim* is the reading of virtually all text-witnesses, pace Epstein's comment:
הבייתוסין, כצ"ל, כנו' כל כי"י, וכברייתא וירוש' ("'The Boethusians'—read thus, as is the reading
of all manuscripts, and as in the Baraitha and the Yerushalmi"), which, in all likelihood, is simply a *lapsus calami*. See Jacob N. Epstein, *Introduction to Tannaitic Literature: Mishna, Tosephta and Halakhic Midrashim* (Hebrew; Jerusalem and Tel-Aviv,
1957), 369. Cf. Yaakov Sussmann, "The History of *Halakha* and the Dead Sea Scrolls—
Preliminary Observations on Miqsat Maʿase Ha-Torah (4QMMT)" (Hebrew), *Tarbiz* 59
(1990): 52 n. 71.

15. "*Minim*"—this is the correct reading, and so it appears also in MS Parma 138, MS
Parma 487, and other reliable text-witnesses. This is also the reading of the parallel in

6. mYad 4:8:

אמ' מין גלילי: קובל אני עליכן פרושין שאתם כותבין את המושל עם משה בגט.

Said a Galilean *min*: "I complain against you, Pharisees, for you write in a bill of divorce the name of the ruler together with the name of Moses."

7. To these we should add mMeg 4:8–9, which refers to *minut*:

האומר "איני עובר לפני התיבה בצבועים", אף בלבנים לא יעבור. "בסנדל איני עובר", אף יחף לא יעבור. העושה תפילתו עגולה סכנה [מפני] שאין בה מצוה. נתנה על מצחו או על פס ידו הרי ז[ו] דרך המי[נות]. ציפה זהב ונתנה על בית יד שלינוקלו(!) הרי זו דרך החיצונים.

האומר "יברכוך טובים" הרי זו דרך המינות. "על קן ציפור יגיעו רחמיך" ו"על טוב יזכר שמך", "מודים", "מודים", משתקים אותו. והמכנה בעריות משתקים אותו. האומר "ומזרעך לא תתן להעביר למולך מן זרעך לא תתן למעברא בארמיתא" משתקים אותו בנזיפה.

He who says, "I do not pass before the ark[16] while wearing colored clothes," he should not [be permitted to] pass [before the ark] even when wearing white [clothes]. [He who says] I do not pass [before the ark] when wearing sandals, he should not [be permitted] even when barefoot. He who makes round tefillin, lo, it is a danger because it is not [proper for the fulfillment of] a *mitzvah*. If he put it on his forehead or on the palm of his hand, lo, this is the manner of *minut*. If he covered it with gold and put it over his sleeve, lo, this is the manner of outsiders.

He who says,[17] "May the good bless You," lo, this is the manner of *minut*. [One who says], "Your mercy extends to the bird's nest" or "May Your Name be remembered for good," [or] "We give thanks, we give thanks" he is to be silenced. He who [interprets Leviticus 18:21 and] says "And you shall not give any of your seed to make them pass through [the fire] to Molech [this means] of your seed you shall not give to impregnate a pagan woman," he is silenced reprimandingly.

Note that we confine ourselves to the Mishnah, so passages in the Tosefta and the Tannaitic Midrashim (the Mekhilta de-Rabbi Ishmael, etc.)[18] will not be included in our discussion.

---

tPar 3:3 (ed. Zuckermandel, 631), both in MS Vienna and the *editio princeps*. The vulgar printed editions of the Mishnah read: לצדוקים (to the Sadducees), but this is a secondary, erroneous reading. Cf. Sussmann, "History of Halakha," 153 n. 176.

16. That is: I refuse to lead the public service in the congregation.

17. Presumably in the liturgy.

18. For a survey of these passages see Adiel Schremer, "Wayward Jews: *Minim* in Early Rabbinic Literature," *Journal of Jewish Studies* 64 (2013): 246–47.

II. *MINUT* AND PRAXIS

It is frequently claimed that the Hebrew word *minut* should be understood as the rabbinic equivalent of the Greek word haeresis (heresy), and that *minim* should be translated accordingly "heretics." Daniel Boyarin expressed this claim in the clearest possible manner: "the concept of minut [is] the rabbinic equivalent to heresy."[19] Similarly, Ruth Langer has written: "Rabbinic discussions of *minim* . . . suggest that what was suspicious was the *min's* theology; the term thus would mean 'heretic,' or 'sectarian.'"[20] And the same view was expressed by Shaye Cohen in his recent paper mentioned above, when presenting "all mishnaic references to *min*, 'heretic,' *minim*, 'heretics,' and *minut*, 'heresy,'"[21] This is a widely held view indeed.[22]

One problem with this view is that the etymology of *minut* (and *minim*) is not really known,[23] so its relation to "heresy" necessarily derives from an

---

19. See Daniel Boyarin, *Border Lines: The Partition of Judaeo-Christianity* (Philadelphia, 2004), 74 (and already at 45: "*minim* and *minut* [heretics and heresy]").

20. See Ruth Langer, *Cursing the Christians? A History of the Birkat Haminim* (New York and Oxford, 2012), 22.

21. See Shaye J. D. Cohen, "The Ways That Parted," 318.

22. See, for example, the oft-cited Daniel Sperber, "Min," *Encyclopaedia Judaica* (Jerusalem, 1971), 12.1–3.

23. As correctly noted by Langer, *Cursing the Christians*, 22: "The term itself tells us virtually nothing, as the word simply means 'types,' or 'kinds'" (echoing Marcel Simon, *Verus Israel: A Study of the Relations between Christians and Jews in the Roman Empire AD 135–425* [London, 1996], 181). Saul Lieberman maintained that *min* is actually an ellipsis and should be understood as "other type" (שהולך, מין אחר פירושו ,'מיני' ,'מיני' ,'מינא' ואף בדרך אחרת). See his comment in *Yerushalmi Nezikin: Edited from the Escorial Manuscript with an Introduction*, ed. E. S. Rosenthal and S. Lieberman (Hebrew; Jerusalem, 1983), 206 n. 1. Lieberman may have had in mind SifDeut 218 (ed. Finkelstein, 251): "*min* is he who rules for himself a different way (מין שמורה לעצמו דרך אחרת)," for he mentions this text in his discussion of tBer 6:6—"this is a different way"—in his *Tosefta Ki-feshutah* (New York, 1955–88), 1.111. However, such a reading in the Sifre is unattested by any text-witness. See Finkelstein's comment, *ad loc.*, and Epstein's comment in his review of Finkelstein's edition: Jacob N. Epstein, *Studies in Talmudic Literature and Semitic Languages* (Hebrew; Jerusalem, 1988), 2.897. Recently, Robert Brody suggested that: "The traditional understanding of *minim* as heretics finds support in etymological data . . . the root *m-y-n* means, in Arabic and Ethiopic, 'to lie,' or 'to falsify.'" See Robert Brody, "'Rabbinic' and 'Nonrabbinic' Jews in Mishnah and Tosefta," in *The Faces of Torah: Studies in the Texts and Contexts of Ancient Judaism in Honor of Steven Fraade*, ed. M. Bar-Asher Siegal, T. Novick, and C. Hayes (Göttingen, 2017), 283. Surprisingly, Brody did not cite, as a support for his suggested etymology, the passage in *Mekhilta de-Rabbi Ishmael, Kaspa*, 20 (ed. Horovitz-Rabin, 327; ed. Lauterbach, 168–69), in which Rabbi Nathan comments on Ex 23:7, "Keep yourself far from a false matter" (מדבר שקר תרחק), and sees this as "a warning to separate from *minut*." However, Brody's following proposal, "that *minim* are those who, in the opinion of the rabbis, *misrepresent the true*

a priori assumption concerning the meaning of *minut* as "a flaw in the doctrine of God,"[24] an assumption that in fact has never been established.

Does the evidence support this view? Let us consider the above cited passages.[25] In mRH 2:1 (#2, above) we are told of a procedural change concerning the testimony of witnesses regarding the new moon. Originally testimony regarding the new moon was accepted from any person, but that was changed because of the interference of the *minim*. Since they interfered it was ordained that testimony will not be accepted from anyone but only from people who are known to the court.[26] Along the same line the Mishnah says that originally there was no need to send out messengers to inform Jewish communities outside Jerusalem of the new moon, because the decision about the new month was communicated by means of torches. However, because the Kuttim once disrupted the communication (presumably by lighting their own torches, on a different day) the method of communication had been changed, and instead of torches, messengers were sent from Jerusalem to distant communities to inform them about the new moon.

In what way the *minim* "interfered" we cannot know, as the Mishnah says nothing on this matter. This silence is significant, however, for nothing in this passage suggests that whatever they did was related in any way to belief, creed, or doctrine. In other words, nothing in this mishnaic passage would lead one to think that *minut* is heresy and that *minim* are heretics. Rather, we would probably assume that the *minim* were Jews who had a different calendar and were in opposition to the calendar system which the Mishnah represents. This opposition had nothing to do with creed.

In mMeg 4:8–9 we are told that putting phylacteries on the forehead or on the palm of the hand is "the way of *minut*" (הרי זו דרך המינות). Similarly,

---

nature of God by denying the principle of monotheism" (Brody, "'Rabbinic' and 'Non-rabbinic' Jews," 283–84 [emphasis added]), is not truly based on the relevant sources: only one mishnaic passage (mSan 4:5) suggests that *minim* espouse a view that may be understood as "denying the principle of monotheism." In none of the other passages in the Mishnah in which *minim* are mentioned are they portrayed as if they "misrepresent the true nature of God."

24. As claimed by Boyarin, *Border Lines*, 131; Boyarin, "Two Powers in Heaven; or, The Making of a Heresy," in *The Idea of Biblical Interpretation: Essays in Honor of James L. Kugel*, ed. H. Najman and J. H. Newman (Leiden and Boston, 2004), 335.

25. For a list of references to *minim* in the Mishnah see Schremer, "Wayward Jews," 246; Cohen, "The Ways that Parted," 319–20.

26. The Mishnah's style leaves the impression that מכירים is a category of certain people. If so, the Mishnah does not say that testimony is accepted only from a known person; rather it says that only a person who is a member in the group called מכירים may give a testimony concerning the new moon. But such a group is unknown to me from any other rabbinic text.

saying (presumably in the liturgy) "May the good bless you" (יברכוך טובים)
is "the way of the *minut*" (הרי זו דרך המינות). We are not told why these practices are considered "the way of *minut*" by the Mishnah, but it is clear that
neither belief nor dogma, but rather a certain ritual *practice*, is condemned
here.[27] This understanding is strongly supported by the immediate context:
the previous passage condemns one who says, "I will not go [before the ark]
in colored clothing"; one who says, "I will not go before the ark in sandals";
one who "makes his phylactery round"; or one who says (presumably in
the liturgy) "May your mercies extend even to a bird's nest," or "May your
name be remembered for good," or "We give thanks, we give thanks." It also
passes a negative judgment and demands silencing one who reads the laws
of the forbidden degrees of sexual union (Lev 18) in a non-literal manner, for
example: "He who says that 'And you shall not give any of your seed to make
them pass through [the fire] to Molech' (Lev 18:21) means 'of your seed you
shall not give to impregnate a pagan woman.'" All these are practices, not
dogmas. *Minut*, in other words, can hardly be understood as "heresy."[28]

Eager to find doctrine and belief in early rabbinic texts (but frustrated by
their almost complete absence therein), readers of the Mishnah frequently
tend to ascribe certain beliefs to these practices and to view them as expressions of these presumed beliefs. Through such a reading, these practices are delegitimized by the Mishnah because of the illegitimate beliefs
manifested by these practices. Nothing in the Mishnah hints at this direction, however. It is perfectly possible to understand the Mishnah's denun-
ciation of these practices as rooted in their identification with some sectarian groups, against which the Mishnah fought (or considered it important

27. Compare to Yair Furstenberg's suggestion that the Mishnah refers here to Sadducees, who believed that God is responsible only for the good things in the world, not
for the evil. See Furstenberg "Is it still possible to write a history of ideas in the world
of the Sages," (Hebrew) a lecture delivered at the National Library on January 13, 2020
(https://www.academia.edu/43231034). On Furstenberg's reading, the Mishnah is troubled by the [wrong] belief expressed by the practice it mentions. The context, however,
does not support this assumption. The practice is presented as illegitimate because of its
being the practice of certain sects, not because of its theological meaning.

28. Compare Boyarin, *Border Lines*, 123–24. Boyarin correctly notes that "the performers of such prayers would have been found in the synagogues and be otherwise indistinguishable from other Jews" (Boyarin, *Border Lines*, 123). However, his assumption
that the Mishnah is concerned with the theological errors manifested by the various
formulae it mentions is unnecessary. It can be perfectly understood as fighting against
remnants of sectarian practices, which were viewed as problematic because of their sectarian nature, and not necessarily because of their theological meaning.

to fight). In other words, what was considered by the Mishnah problematic in these practices was that they were understood as the practices of certain sectarian groups. Hence, *minut* should not be understood here as "heresy," but as "sectarianism."[29]

The same may be said of mḤul 2:9 (#4, above). It appears from this passage that *minim* have a certain manner in which they slaughter animals, and the Mishnah wishes to avoid the situation that a Jew would slaughter an animal in a manner that seems to follow the same practice. No theological view is mentioned, and nothing forces us to assume that some "belief" is the focus of the Mishnah's ruling. *Minim*, in other words, are not heretics. At most they are sectarians, but from the context it seems that they are not even Jews.[30]

III. *MINIM* AND SECOND TEMPLE SECTARIANISM

As is well known, the *minim* in mBer 9:9 are frequently identified as Sadducees.[31] If this interpretation is accepted, this mishnah leads in a direction of relating the *minim* in the Mishnah to Second Temple times.

In mYad 4:8 this understanding seems quite clear. That mishnah refers to "A Galilean *min*," who said: "I cry out against you, Pharisees, for you write in a bill of divorce the name of the ruler together with the name of Moses." According to the Mishnah the Pharisees responded, saying: "We cry out against you, Galilean *min*, for you write the Name with the name of the

29. Only in one passage mentioning *minim* it seems quite clear that incorrect belief is indeed the focal point. In mSan 4:5 (#3, above), "so that the *minim* would not say, '[there are] many domains in heaven,'" it is clear that the problem with the *minim* is that they "say" something, that is, they espouse a certain theological opinion, which the Mishnah considers wrong. Note, however, the style of the Mishnah at this point: it offers several explanations for the creation of just one first man, but there is no *vav consecutive* between them (as one would expect). This leaves room for the possibility that we are dealing with secondary additions to an original text, in which only one explanation appeared. Indeed, the Yerushalmi (in which one does find a comment relating to the second explanation, as well as a comment relating to the fourth) does not comment on the Mishnah's third explanation, that is, the one mentioning *minim*. Perhaps, then, this should be taken as an indication that the Yerushalmi was unfamiliar with this clause in the Mishnah.

30. The context of mḤul 2:9 indicates that it has pagan practices in mind. Cf. Chanoch Albeck, *Shishah Sidre Mishnah* (Hebrew; Jerusalem and Tel Aviv, 1956), 5.122. Saul Lieberman translated the Mishnah accordingly: "lest it appears that he is following the laws of the Gentiles." See Saul Lieberman, *Hellenism in Jewish Palestine* (New York and Jerusalem, 1994), 134–36.

31. Thus the Mishnah was interpreted already by Rashi, *ad loc.*, and he was followed by many others.

ruler on the same page, and moreover you [plural] write the [name of] the
ruler above, and the Name below."The precise nature of the point of contention between the *min* (and the group he represented)[32] and the Pharisees
is not very important for our purposes. It will suffice to note that here too
the polemic has to do with a practical matter, not with a belief or doctrine.
More important for my current concern is the chronological placement of
the dispute. As the Pharisees were a group that existed in Second Temple
period,[33] it emerges that the Galilean *min*, to whom the Mishnah refers, also
belongs to that period.

The same applies to the *minim* mentioned in mRH 2:1. True, their precise
identity is not explicitly stated by the Mishnah, but as early as the Tosefta
they were identified as Baethesians. We read as much in tRH 2:1:

בראשונה היו מקבלין עדות החדש מכל אדם. פעם אחת שכרו ביתסין שני עדים לבוא
להטעות את חכמים, לפי שאין ביתסין מודין שתהא עצרת אלא אחר שבת. בא אחד ואמ'
עדותו והלך לו. בא השני ואמ': עולה הייתי במעלה אדומים וראיתיו רבוץ בין שני סלעים,
ראשו דומה לעגל, אזניו דומות לגדי, קרניו דומות לצבי, וזנבו מונחת לו בין יריכותיו. ראיתיו,
נבעתתי, ונפלתי לאחורי, והרי מאתים זוז צרורין לי בסדיני. אמרו לו: מאתים זוז נתונין לך
במתנה והשוכרך ימתח על העמוד. מה ראית ליזק לכך? אמ' להם: שמעתי שהביתסין
מבקשין להטעות את חכמים, אמרתי מוטב אלך אני ואודיע את חכמים.

At first they would accept testimony concerning the new moon
from anybody. One time the Baethesians hired two witnesses to
come and fool the sages, for the Baethesians do not concede that
Pentecost should be at any time but after the Sabbath. One of them
came along and gave his testimony and went his way. The second one
came and said: I was ascending Ma'aleh Adumim and I saw it crouch-
ing between two rocks, its head looking like a calf, and its ears looking like a lamb, and its horns looking like a deer, and its tail lying between its thighs. I saw it, I was astonished, and I fell backward, and
lo, I found two hundred *zuz* tied up for me in my purse. They said to
him: The two hundred *zuz* are given over to you as gift, but the one
who hired you will be laid out on the post. Why did you get involved
in the matter? He said to them: I heard that the Baethesians were
planning to confuse the sages, I said to myself that it is better that I
go and tell the sages.

32. Note the plural form (שאתם) of the address in the Pharisees' response.
33. Pharisees, at any event, are not to be confused with rabbis (even if the latter had
various common traits with the former and can be seen as their "descendants" in one
way or another). Indeed, rabbinic texts never explicitly identify the rabbis as Pharisees.
Cf. Shaye J. D. Cohen, "The Significance of Yavneh," *Hebrew Union College Annual* 55
(1984): 36–42.

The opening sentence, "At first they would accept testimony concerning the new moon from anybody," is in fact a lemma from the Mishnah, to which the Tosefta attaches the subsequent story as a sort of "commentary," in order to explain the Mishnah's reference to "the *minim*." These *minim*, says the Tosefta, were Baethesians. Regardless, then, of the question concerning the historicity of the story, it is clear that already the Tosefta understood the Mishnah as speaking of a group of Second Temple times.[34]

IV. *MINIM* AND CHRISTIANS

One of the groups with which the *minim* are frequently identified is the early Christians. Despite its popularity, this identification has no firm basis with respect to the Mishnah: not a single mishnaic passage mentioning *minim* lends itself to the assumption that *minim* are specifically Christians.

Such an identification does emerge from two consecutive stories in the Tosefta:

I. There was a case with Rabbi Elazar ben Dama, who was bitten by a snake, and Jacob of Kefar Sama came to heal him in the name of Jesus son of Pantera (ישוע בן פנטרא), and Rabbi Ishmael did not allow him. They [*sic*; read: he] said to him: "You are not permitted, Ben Dama!" He said to him: "I shall bring you proof that he may heal me," but he did not manage to bring the proof before he died. Said Rabbi Ishmael: Happy are you, Ben Dama, for you have expired in peace, and you did not break down the hedge of the Sages. For whoever breaks down the hedge of the Sages calamity befalls him, as it is said: "He who breaks down a hedge is bitten by a snake" (Eccl 10:8).

II. There was a case with Rabbi Eliezer, who was arrested [literally: caught] on account of *minut,* and they brought him up to the *bema* [tribunal] for judgment. The *hegemon* [governor] said to him: Should an elder of your standing occupy himself in these matters?! He said to him: I consider the Judge[!] as trustworthy. That *hegemon*

34. In the following passage the Mishnah relates to another enactment, that is, that the news about the new moon should be passed on to distant Jewish communities by human messengers rather than by lighting torches, as was done earlier. According to the Mishnah, the decision about this change was a result of the Kuttim's attempt to interfere with the transmission of the news about the new moon. As that change took place already in Second Temple times (see Epstein, *Introduction to Tannaitic Literature*, 369; Lieberman, *Tosefta Ki-feshutah*, 5.1029; compare, however: Epstein, *Introduction*, 365; Albeck, *Shishah Sidre Mishnah*, 2.488), it strengthens the conclusion that the first enactment too (i.e. the one mentioning the *minim*) should be dated to the Second Temple period, as the Tosefta indeed took it for granted.

supposed that he referred to him, but he referred only to his Father in heaven. He said to him: Since you have deemed me reliable for yourself, I too have said [to myself]: Is it possible that these gray hairs should err in such matters?! [Surely not!] *Dimissus*, lo you are released. And when he left the court he was distressed to have been arrested on account of matters of *minut*. His disciples came in to comfort him but he was not convinced [literally: he did not accept [their words of comfort]. Rabbi Akiba entered and said to him: Rabbi, May I say something to you so that you will not be distressed? He said to him: Speak! He said to him: Perhaps some one of the *minim* told you a teaching of *minut* that pleased you? He said to him: By Heaven! You reminded me! Once I was strolling in the street of Sepphoris. I bumped into [literally: I found] Jacob of Kefar Sikhnin, and he said a teaching of *minut* in the name of Jesus son of Pantiri (ישוע בן פנטירי), and it pleased me. And I was arrested on account of matters of *minut*, for I transgressed the teachings of Torah: "Keep your way far from her and do not go near the door of her house" (Prov 5:8–7:26). For Rabbi Eliezer did teach: "One should always flee from what is ugly and from whatever appears to be ugly."[35]

These two stories are the earliest references to Jesus in classical rabbinic literature. It is little surprise, therefore, that they have been dealt with in numerous studies devoted to Christianity in Talmudic literature.[36] I shall not

35. tḤul. 2:22–24 (ed. Zuckermandel, 503 [translation mine]).

36. See, among many others, Saul Lieberman, "Roman Legal Institutions in Early Rabbinics and in the *Acta Martyrium*," *JQR* 35 (1944): 20–24; Adolf Büchler, "The *Minim* of Sepphoris and Tiberias in the Second and Third Centuries," in *Studies in Jewish History*, ed. I. Brodie and J. Rabbinowitz (London, New York, and Toronto, 1956), 246; David Rokeach, "Ben Stara and Ben Pantira" (Hebrew), *Tarbiz* 39 (1969): 9–18; Mark J. Geller, "Joshua B. Perahia and Jesus of Nazareth: Two Rabbinic Magicians" (PhD diss., Brandeis University, 1974), 144–45; Morton Smith, *Jesus the Magician* (New York, 1978), 48–49; Johann Maier, *Jesus von Nazareth in der talmudischen Überlieferung* (Darmstadt, 1978), 130–92; Ray A. Fritz, *Nazarene Jewish Christianity: From the End of the New Testament Period Until Its Disappearance in the Fourth Century* (Jerusalem, 1988), 96–97; Daniel R. Schwartz, "Ma hava ley memar . . . v-ḥai ba-hem," in *Sanctity of Life and Martyrdom: Studies in Memory of Amir Yekutiel*, ed. I. M. Gafni and A. Ravitzky (Hebrew; Jerusalem, 1992), 69–83; Joan E. Taylor, *Christians and the Holy Places: The Myth of Jewish-Christian Origins* (Oxford and New York, 1993), 28–29; Jack T. Sanders, *Schismatics, Sectarians, Dissidents, Deviants: The First One Hundred Years of Jewish-Christian Relations* (London, 1993), 61–63; Daniel Boyarin, *Dying for God: Martyrdom and the Making of Christianity and Judaism* (Stanford, 1999), 26–41; Jonah Fraenkel, *The Aggadic Narrative: Harmony of Form and Content* (Hebrew; Tel-Aviv, 2001), 102–4; Peter Schäfer, *Jesus in the Talmud* (Princeton, 2007), 41–62; Joshua Schwartz and Peter

attempt a detailed analysis of these stories here;[37] rather, it will suffice to note that in both stories a social contact with a follower of Jesus is presented as illegitimate because contact with *minim* is claimed to be problematic. In the first story, social contact with *minim* is problematic because it violates a halakhic ruling of rabbinic origin that prohibits one from receiving medical care from *minim*; in the second story, social contact with *minim* is problematic because it violates a rabbinic teaching that applied Prov 5:8–7:26 ("Keep your way far from her and do not go near the door of her house") to *minut*.

The point that both stories are trying to make is that followers of Jesus are *minim*, and this is their novelty. It is unlikely that such an identification was known and widely accepted in rabbinic circles already prior to the formation of these stories. Had the view of the early Christians as *minim* been widely held by rabbinic Jews before the events described by these stories, it would be very difficult to account for the ease with which Ben Dama (in the first story) and Rabbi Eliezer (in the second story) are in contact with a follower of Jesus, in contrast to a widely held view that social contact with followers of Jesus is proscribed. Rather, it seems, the stories should be seen as a rabbinic attempt at introducing the early Christians into an already existing halakhic category (*minim*), which initially did not refer to them and did not include them.

At any event, in the Mishnah none of the references to *minim* appears to have specifically Christians in mind.

IV. "SINCE THE *MINIM* INTERFERED"

The expression, "since the *minim* disrupted [the matters]" (משקלקלו המינים), which mRH 2:1 uses to justify the new norm it mentions, is found also in mBer 9.9.[38] What is the precise meaning of this expression?

That passage appears to be related to a specific religious belief, the belief in more than one world. "We," the mishnah appears to say, "believe in more than one world, but the *minim* caused people to maintain that there is

J. Tomson, "When Rabbi Eliezer was Arrested for Heresy," *Jewish Studies Internet Journal* 10 (2012): 145–81.

37. For a close reading of these stories see my *Brothers Estranged: Heresy, Christianity, and Jewish identity in Late Antiquity* (New York and Oxford, 2010), 87–94.

38. The connection between the two passages goes beyond the mere use of the same expression. The entire structure of the two passages is very similar. They both begin with a mention of an early state of affairs: "In the beginning . . ." and then proceed to explain why it was changed: "since the *minim* corrupted." They then conclude with a reference to the nature of the change: "they enacted that . . ." This similarity may indicate that both passages stem from one source.

only one world." It is not entirely clear whether the *minim* themselves held that there is only one world, or whether it was something they did which caused people to draw the wrong conclusion. The first possibility is usually preferred and I will not press too hard against it in favor of the second possibility.

Conventional wisdom assumes that the mishnah wishes to convey the message that the belief in two worlds is a fundamental tenet of Judaism. Based on such an understanding, that belief was so important for the early sages that they were willing to change an "old" and well-established formula—"From the world"—and extend it, even though such a change is something that is normally not done. They changed the formula—despite the reluctance to introduce changes in the Temple's norms—because the issue of the belief in two worlds was crucial in their opinion, and the need to combat those who deny it justified such an extreme measure. According to this understanding, the belief in two worlds was a belief which the sages and the Mishnah considered of prime importance. It was so dear to them that they wished to communicate the message that due to its importance, even the Temple's norms were changed.

There is much to commend in this reading, as it enables a better understanding of the relation between the Mishnah's two parts. Our mishnah reports two enactments: in its first part it tells about the extension of the concluding formula of benedictions that were said in the Temple; in its second part it reports a second enactment, namely "that one should greet his fellow with God's name" (שיהו אדם מברך את שלום חברו בשם). The latter is justified by the mishnah itself by reference to Ps 119:126, "It is time to act for the Lord, for they have abolished Your Torah" (עת לעשות לה' הפרו תורתך),[39] that is, there are circumstances that require an extreme action, despite its inherent character as an implicit annulment of the Torah. According to the reading suggested above, the same principle operates in both parts of the mishnah: certain circumstances, or issues, are important or grave enough to justify the abolition or modification of accepted norms.

A closer look at this mishnah reveals, however, that the matter is not as simple as it may appear. The typical reading of this mishnah views it as a *report* about a change in the Temple's liturgy, which was caused by the *minim*'s "interruption." The tradition, on this reading, claims that originally

---

39. Many, if not all, modern English translations of the Hebrew Bible render the verse as a call *to* God to act: "It is time for You to act, O LORD, For they have regarded Your law as void" (NKJV), or: "It is time for the Lord to act, for your law has been broken" (NRSV). My translation follows the traditional Jewish understanding, which stems from the use of that verse in our mishnah.

the concluding formula of benedictions in the Temple was short—"from the word" (or, following the Tosefta, "to the world")—but it was extended because of the *minim*'s claim that there is only one world, and it was modified to be: "from the world to the world."[40]

But this claim is quite surprising. For the long formula, "from the world to the world," is found already in the Bible (Ps 44:11; Ps 106:48; Neh 9:5; 1 Chr 16:36),[41] while the short formula ("from the world"), as a conclusion of a blessing, is unattested at all.[42] Why on earth would anybody in the Temple choose a short formula, "from the world," if such a formula has no biblical precedent and does not actually exist in any earlier tradition? Can we really accept that when choosing a concluding formula, the Temple authorities abandoned the biblical precedent, and did not use the full formula, "from the world to the world"? Is it conceivable that despite the existence of the biblical pattern, "from the world to the world," they decided to cut the full formula and use only half of it, "from the world"?! Why would anybody do this?

Urbach, relating to the difference between the Mishnah and the Tosefta in their presentation of the tradition—according to the Mishnah, the original formula was "from the world," whereas according to the Tosefta it was "to the world"—suggested that initially the formula used in the Temple was in fact the full one: "from the world to the world."[43] This may well be *historically* correct, for it is indeed difficult to accept the tradition's claim that initially the formula included only the words "from the world." Yet this suggestion flatly contradicts the tradition as it came down to us, either in the Mishnah or in the Tosefta.

Ishay Rosen-Zvi, too, doubted the historical value of the Mishnah's account as a reliable testimony concerning the evolution of the formula. He correctly noted that the full formula is a standard biblical formula, and that the short form is unknown from any other source. He therefore suggested that the Mishnah's account should be seen as a "midrashic explanation for

40. Pace Rashi (who was followed by Rabbi Ovadia of Bertinoro, *ad loc.*), the tradition's reference is to the Second Temple. Had the tradition meant that in the First Temple the formula was "from the world," it would have needed to adduce a biblical proof for that claim. It does not adduce such a proof, however, because it cannot do so, because there is not one. Hence, it is clear that the Second Temple is meant.

41. Cf. Friedman, *Studies in the Language and Terminology*, 13–15.

42. To be sure, עד העולם does occur in the Hebrew Bible, but in different contexts. See Friedman, *Studies*, 11 n. 40.

43. See: Ephraim E. Urbach, *The Sages: Their Concepts and Beliefs*, trans. Gerson Levi (Cambridge, 1987), 128–29; 737 n. 34.

the extended formula, 'from the world to the world,' which was practiced in the Temple."[44]

This brilliant suggestion is also difficult to accept, however, for two major reasons. First, according to Rosen-Zvi's suggestion, the Mishnah should have actually said: "All the concluding formulas of benedictions that were in the Temple were 'From the world to the world.'" If it was indeed this extended formula which stood at the focus of the tradition and which the tradition attempted to explain (or justify), as Rosen-Zvi suggests, it would have been expected that the tradition would present itself accordingly. Indeed, this scenario can be easily imagined: the tradition could have presented itself, for example, in the common midrashic style: "Scripture says, 'Blessed are You, O Lord, God of Israel, from the world to the world'—why so? In order not to give the *minim* opportunity to say that there is but one world." This is a perfectly standard midrashic style, quite common in tannaitic sources,[45] so there was no reason for the tradition not to use such rhetoric and present itself this way, had it really meant to explain (or justify) the extended formula.

Secondly (but in fact more importantly), the extended formula does not really call for an explanation. Precisely because it is taken from the Bible, where it appears several times, nothing in this formula really raises any difficulty so as to generate a "midrashic explanation."[46] And because this formula was also not used after the Destruction, it is difficult to assume that it caused any practical (as opposed to homiletical, or interpretive) difficulty of some sort. It did not require any excuse.

The real "novel" point that the tradition makes is that there was in use, at some time in the past, a short formula, in which the word "world" appeared only once. That formula (of which no one really ever heard) had to be abandoned, according to the tradition, in favor of a longer one, because of the disruption of the *minim*. I therefore suggest that it is this short formula which is the focal point of the tradition. The long formula and its existence are well known, as it is found in various biblical verses, and therefore

---

44. See: Ishay Rosen-Zvi, "Birkot ha-reiyah ve-hofa'at ha-ma'arechet ha-liturgit besifrut ha-tanna'im" (Hebrew), *Jewish Studies Internet Journal* 7 (2008): 22–23.

45. See, for example, the midrashic passages discussed in my "Midrash, Theology, and History: Two Powers in Heaven Revisited," *Journal for the Study of Judaism* 39 (2007): 241.

46. This point has been recognized, in fact, by Rosen-Zvi himself: "From the language of the Tosefta in [tractate] Ta'aniyot it emerges that it does not find any need to explain the language of the blessing in the Temple, which is mere biblical language" (גם מלשון התוספתא בתעניות שם עולה היא רואה שאין כל צורך להסביר את לשון הברכה במקדש, שאינה אלא לשון מקרא). See: Rosen-Zvi, "Birkot ha-reiyah," 23 n. 89.

we do not need to be taught that it was used in past times and is, therefore, a legitimate one. In contrast, a short formula, mentioning the word "the world" only once, has no biblical precedent, and therefore it requires justification if one wishes, for whatever reason, to use it.

This is indeed the case with the formula used by the rabbis in the manifold benedictions they invented and enacted. As is well known, the standard formula of rabbinic benedictions is: "Blessed are You, O God, King of the world" (ברוך אתה ה' אלהינו מלך העולם). This formula indeed contains only one reference to the word "world." From the perspective of the tradition in mBer 9:9, this rabbinic formula is problematic, as it mentions the word "world" only once, and hence it might give the *minim* room to use it and claim that "there is only one world." What, then, may justify the use of this formula? My suggestion is that the tradition in mBer. 9:9 was aimed at responding precisely to such a question. For this purpose it invented a "historical fact" (as it were) that indicates that a blessing formula that used the word "world" only once is perfectly legitimate, for it was the one used in the Temple of ancient times. The existence of the fuller formula, in which the word "world" is mentioned twice, is of course admitted by our tradition (indeed, how could it be denied?), but it is explained as the result of a deliberate change, due to a need to combat the *minim*'s assertion that "there is but one world."

If the need to combat the *minim*'s theological stance of denying the existence of two worlds had led the Temple authorities (or the ancient rabbis) to extend the formula and say "from the world to the world" (so as to publicly declare that there are two worlds), why, then, did the rabbis of post Destruction times create such a formula in the benedictions that plays right into the hands of the *minim*? The only possible answer to this question is that the *minim* and their heretical assertion were not considered a problem anymore by post-Destruction rabbis of Palaestina. This is the historical conclusion that a close and patient reading of our Mishnah leads to.

For the Mishnah, the heretics who promulgated the theological assertion that "there is only one world" belonged to remote times, and they no longer exist. Jews, according to the Mishnah, all believe in the world to come. The denial of this idea perhaps may be found among "others," but they are entirely out of the confines of the Jewish community and therefore their theological stances are of little (if any) concern.

The Mishnah is not interested in dogmas, I submit, not necessarily because it considers belief of relatively little importance, but rather because in its view the main theological tenets of Judaism are not disputed by the vast majority of the Jews. This is precisely what we are told by the famous opening passage prefixing (in some text-witnesses) mSan 10.1: "All Israel have a share in the world to come," for those who do not have a share in the world to come are only those who deny the heavenly origin of the Torah, or the concept of the resurrection of the dead, or people who espouse Epicurean views. Yet "all Israel" do believe in the divine origin of the Torah, and "all Israel" do accept the idea of the resurrection of the dead, and no Jew is truly an Epicurean. Therefore, "all Israel have a share in the world to come."[47] Indeed, in the words of Isaiah 60:21, which mSan 10.1 (in this textual tradition) quotes as a proof-text: "Your people are *all* righteous."[48]

At the time the Mishnah was composed, no one within the Jewish community seriously rejected or disputed the basic tenets of Judaism, such that the Mishnah felt no need to spend energy to reassert these beliefs. For that same reason it also refrained from combating heretics and heresy.

47. I am well aware that the passage prefixing mSan 10:1 quoted here is absent from MS Kaufmann and MS Cambridge of the Mishnah. See above, n. 4. I do not wish to be understood, therefore, as claiming that mSan 10:1 indeed claims that all Jews believe in the heavenly origin of the Torah and in the resurrection of the dead. However, in addition to the vulgar printed editions of the Mishnah and to the Mishnah as it appears in the Babylonian Talmud (bSan 90a) in all manuscripts, the above quoted sentence does appear in MS Parma 138 of the Mishnah, in the text of the Mishnah in the Palestinian Talmud, and in other text-witnesses. See Grossberg, "Orthopraxy in Tannaitic Literature," 520 n. 7.

48. Virtually all English translations of this verse use the future tense and render it accordingly: "Your people shall all be righteous" (RSV), or "All your people will be righteous" (CSB). In contrast, the rabbinic sages who placed that verse at the beginning of mSan 10:1, understood it, in all likelihood, in the present tense: that is, they read it as a statement of descriptive nature.

Part V

Reception and Transmission
of the Mishnah

19. The Halakhic Midrashim and the Canonicity of the Mishnah

Azzan Yadin-Israel

This chapter consists of two interrelated sections. The first surveys scholarship on the relationship between the Mishnah and the halakhic midrashim. The second section expands on the findings of the first, arguing that the halakhic midrashim offer a valuable corrective to the regnant tendency to study the Mishnah as a canonical work.

THE HALAKHIC MIDRASHIM

The phrase "halakhic midrashim" (also "legal midrashim" and "tannaitic midrashim") refers to the earliest midrashic collections. The primary halakhic midrashim consist of the Mekhilta of Rabbi Ishmael (to Exodus), the Sifra (to Leviticus), and the two Sifre (Sifre to Numbers and Deuteronomy).[1] There are also a number of midrashic collections reconstructed from later sources, such as the Mekhilta of Rabbi Shimon bar Yoḥai (to Exodus) and Mekhilta (to Deuteronomy), both partially preserved in the medieval Yemenite compilation *Midrash ha-Gadol*, and *Sifre Zuta* (to Deuteronomy),

---

1. The standard scholarly editions are: *Mekhilta de-Rabbi Ishmael*, ed. H. S. Horovitz and I. Rabin (Jerusalem, 1960; repr. of Frankfurt, 1931); *Sifra: Commentar zu Leviticus*, ed. H. Weiss (Vienna, 1862); *Sifre on Numbers: An Annotated Edition*, ed. M. Kahana (Jerusalem, 2011); *Siphre ad Deuteronomium*, ed. L. Finkelstein (New York, 1993). I use Jacob Lauterbach's translation of the Mekhilta, *Mekhilta de-Rabbi Ishmael*, ed. and trans. J. Z. Lauterbach (Philadelphia, 1933–36); and Reuven Hammer's for the Sifre Deuteronomy, *Sifre: A Tannaitic Commentary on the Book of Deuteronomy*, trans. R. Hammer (New Haven, 1986).

reconstructed primarily from the *Yalkut Shimoni*.[2] The most recent contribution is Menahem Kahana's edition of a commentary to Deuteronomy on the basis of passages embedded in the eleventh-century Bible commentary of the Karaite sage Yeshua ben Yehuda—*Sifre Zuta Deuteronomy*.[3]

Since David Hoffmann's pathbreaking work in the late nineteenth century, scholars have assigned the halakhic midrashim to two groups: the Mekhilta of Rabbi Ishmael and the Sifre Numbers, both associated with Rabbi Ishmael, and the Sifra and Sifre Deuteronomy, both associated with Rabbi Akiba. Whether this division redounds to the historical figures of Rabbi Ishmael and Rabbi Akiba is a complicated question that need not detain us here, except to say that such a relationship need not be assumed. The division is based on philological considerations, such as the terminology favored by the different midrashim, the sages cited, the hermeneutic practices championed, and more.[4] Abraham Joshua Heschel's brilliant but overly expansive *Theology of Ancient Judaism* demonstrates that the midrashic schools are also divided in theological matters.[5]

Though the division between Rabbi Ishmael and Rabbi Akiba is still widely accepted, recent years have witnessed two challenges to the status of the Sifra within this schema. The first comes from Yonatan Sagiv, whose dissertation maps out every midrashic statement in the Sifra and the Leviticus verses to which it corresponds, a procedure that leads to two major conclusions.[6] First, while the Sifra interprets almost every verse of Leviticus, *derashot* attributed to tannaitic sages engage only a small fraction of the verses (13 percent), while anonymous *derashot* make up a much greater proportion (>60 percent). Second, the anonymous *derashot* are evenly distributed across Leviticus, but the named interpretations are clustered around a small set of key verses that were the focus of vigorous debate in Second Temple and post–70 CE Jewish literature.[7] Sagiv concludes that "the Tan-

---

2. *Mekhilta de-Rabbi Shimon ben Yohai*, ed. J. N. Epstein and E. Z. Melammed (Jerusalem, 1959); *Midrash Tannaim zum Deuteronomium*, ed. D. Z. Hoffmann (Berlin, 1908); *Sifre Zutta*, ed. H. S. Horovitz (Leipzig, 1917), bound with Horovitz's edition of Sifre Numbers.

3. Menahem Kahana, *Sifre Zuta Deuteronomy: Citations from a New Tannaitic Midrash* (Jerusalem, 2002).

4. For an informative summary, see M. Kahana, "The Halakhic Midrashim," in *The Literature of the Sages*, ed. S. Safrai, Z. Safrai, J. Schwartz, and P. Tomson (2 vols.; Assen, 2006), 2.3–105.

5. Abraham Joshua Heschel, *Theology of Ancient Judaism* (Hebrew; London and New York, 1962–65).

6. Yonatan Sagiv, *Studies in Early Rabbinic Hermeneutics* (Hebrew; Hebrew University, 2009).

7. See Sagiv, *Studies in Early Rabbinic Hermeneutics*, 39 n. 20 and 140–47.

naim, as best as we can ascertain, did not produce a systematic interpretation of the Book of Leviticus in its entirety, but rather focused on a narrowly delimited interpretation of select words and themes."[8] According to Sagiv, then, the Sifra is made up of a relatively small number of tannaitic interpretations concentrated around select verses, embedded in a much larger and more uniformly distributed set of anonymous *derashot* that is in all probability not tannaitic.

The second challenge comes from my study of the Sifra's hermeneutics, which tracks with Sagiv's findings in identifying a significant fissure between its named and anonymous *derashot*.[9] The argument is complex, but the core claim is that much of the anonymous Sifra is engaged in what I have called a hermeneutic of camouflage—passages whose structure and terminology mimic midrash, but in fact offer ex post facto justification for extra-scriptural traditions. Of course, neither Sagiv's nor my arguments were known to the earlier scholars whose views I survey below, so my summary of their positions includes the Sifra as a tannaitic text. My own analysis, in contrast, focuses on the midrashim associated with Rabbi Ishmael.[10]

THE MISHNAH AND THE HALAKHIC MIDRASHIM: A SURVEY OF SCHOLARSHIP

The Bavli (*bKidushin* 49a) records two answers to the question "What is *mishnah*?" Rabbi Meir says it is *halakhot*, extra-scriptural traditions,[11] while Rabbi Judah identifies *mishnah* with *midrash*, i.e., biblical interpretation. The referent of *mishnah* in the Bavli is not completely clear, though it does not appear to be the redacted collection of rulings we know as the Mishnah.[12] Still, the exchange represents a succinct introduction of two modes of legal authorization in early rabbinic literature: one centered on received traditions and associated with the Mishnah, the other centered on scriptural interpretation and associated with the halakhic midrashim. The relationship between the two occupies a central place in modern scholarship, dating back to its earliest days. The critical study of midrash halakhah may

8. Sagiv, *Studies in Early Rabbinic Hermeneutics*, 40.

9. Azzan Yadin-Israel, *Scripture and Tradition: Rabbi Akiva and the Triumph of Midrash* (Philadelphia, 2015).

10. A thorough analysis of the Sifre Deuteronomy remains a desideratum.

11. In tannaitic literature *halakhot* regularly denotes extra-scriptural teachings, perhaps an ellipsis of *halakhah le-moshe mi-sinai*, "a ruling transmitted from Moses at Sinai."

12. If we accept the attributions as historical, both sages predate the redaction of the Mishnah.

be said to begin with the 1887 publication of Rabbi David Zvi Hoffmann's *Zur Einleitung in die halachischen Midraschim*, which opens with a presentation of this very question through a juxtaposition of kindred passages:[13]

> If a man slaughtered a quadruped and found therein an embryo, he whose appetite is robust may eat it . . . if the embryo emerged only partially, it is forbidden as food (mḤul 4.7).[14]

> "Any that has hoofs, with clefts, and that chews its cud from among the quadrupeds—it may you eat" (Lev 11:3): "It may you eat," to include the embryo. Might it be that this is the case even if it emerges only partially? Scripture teaches, saying "it" (Sifra Shemini 3.1; Weiss 48b).

The two passages agree on the law: one may eat the embryo of a slaughtered animal, but an exception is made in the case of an embryo that has already partially emerged from its mother's body, in which case its consumption is forbidden. But the legal agreement only highlights the striking difference in the authority claims implicit in each passage. The Mishnah presents its legal view apodictically, without reference to Scripture, while in the Sifra the law is anchored in the Book of Leviticus. By juxtaposing the two passages, Hoffmann brings to the fore the vexing difficulty of these two tannaitic models of authority.

Most scholars have affirmed the priority of one mode of authorization at a given time, some claiming that the priority is invariable. Thus Malbim (Meir Leibush ben Yeḥiel Michel), a nineteenth-century scholar and older contemporary of Hoffmann's, championed the view that all tannaitic rulings derived from Scripture. For "everyone who examines with rectitude and passes just judgment will see that [the Oral Law] is always supported by the pillar of Scripture and is scripturally derived (*nidreshet*) from the verses."[15] A century later, David Weiss Halivni reiterated this view, arguing that the Mishnah is wholly dependent on halakhic midrash:

13. David Zvi Hoffmann, *Zur Einleitung in die halachischen Midraschim* (Berlin, 1887), Hebrew edition, *Le-ḥeqer midreshei ha-tannaim*, trans. A. Z. Rabinowitz, in *Mesilot le-torat ha-tannaim* (Tel Aviv, 1927), 1–81. The Mishnah and Sifra passages appear in Hoffmann, *Le-ḥeqer*, 1.

14. Mishnah quotations are based on MS Kaufmann, and I have consulted Herbert Danby, *The Mishnah* (Oxford, 1933) for the translation.

15. Meir Leibush ben Jehiel Michel (Malbim), *Ayelet ha-shaḥar* (Benei Berak, 2000), 3. On the Malbim as an interpreter see Jay M. Harris, *How Do We Know This? Midrash and the Fragmentation of Modern Judaism* (Albany, 1994), 220–23.

No law is really binding on the Jew unless it can be shown to have its origin in the Bible . . . For the [Mishnah], Midrash served as the ground, the justification, the life support. Indeed, one may legitimately wonder whether the Mishnah would have survived at all were it not for the parallel existence of Midreshei Halakhah.[16]

On the other extreme we find Isaac Halevy, an important scholar and the founder of Agudath Israel, who argued that extra-scriptural tradition enjoyed absolute and unquestioned dominance in Second Temple and post–70 CE Judaism, and that the rabbis had no interest in biblical law. "For as is becoming progressively clearer, they never founded a ruling on a *derashah*, not even the most simple one . . . Rather, the criterion in all such matters was received tradition (*qabbalah*) and nothing else."[17]

Malbim, Halivni, and Halevy adopt extreme formulations, but their positions resonate with other scholars who attribute general priority to one mode of authorization over the other. David Zvi Hoffmann argued that midrash is ancillary to extra-scriptural traditions,[18] as did Jacob Nahum Epstein: "While scriptural prooftexts are provided for Jewish law, one does not derive or innovate legal traditions on the basis of Scripture."[19] Chanoch Albeck, in contrast, portrayed the Oral Law as an explication of the Torah, essentially a midrashic enterprise: "From the day [the Torah] was handed down to Israel it was accompanied by an oral explanation that clarified its intent and offered a detailed interpretation of its general statements,"[20] and this interpretation is the Oral Law. Other scholars argued that midrash and extra-scriptural tradition enjoyed primacy at different historical periods. David Zvi Hoffmann held that extra-scriptural traditions replaced midrashic study in the days of Hillel and Shammai; Zechariah Frankel located the shift in the days of Rabbi Akiva; and I. H. Weiss argued that midrash,

---

16. David Weiss Halivni, *Midrash, Mishnah and Gemara: The Jewish Predilection for Justified Law* (Cambridge, 1986), 47–48.

17. Yitzhak Isaac Halevy Rabinowitz, *Dorot Ha-Rishonim* (6 vols.; Frankfurt, 1906), 1.307.

18. "Rulings are not produced by means of interpretation, rather they are received, and the sages use interpretation only as a means for *ex post facto* support (*asmakht'a*), or to provide a firmer foundation, or to preserve them lest they be forgotten," David Zvi Hoffmann, *Commentary to Leviticus*, trans. T. Har-Sheffer and A. Lieberman (Jerusalem, 1966), 5.

19. J. N. Epstein, *Prolegomena to Tannaitic Literature* (Hebrew; Tel Aviv and Jerusalem, 1957), 511.

20. Chanoch Albeck, *Introduction to the Mishnah* (Hebrew; Jerusalem, 1967), 3.

the original form, was replaced for a time by abstract *halakhot*, but reasserted its priority in the days of Hillel.[21]

Alongside this dominant approach, a small group of scholars proposed—albeit tentatively— that midrashic and oral-traditional authority coexist in tannaitic sources. Despite explicitly privileging midrash (see above), Albeck writes in another section of his *Introduction to the Mishnah* that "there are *derashot* that precede the *halakhot* and *derashot* that succeed them, and it is only possible to determine the nature of the *derashot* by comparative analysis of the sources."[22] Yekutiel Neubauer likewise affirms that "alongside midrashic study there was, already in ancient times, a collection of received *halakhot*."[23] Both Albeck and Neubauer imagine the two authorization models in a state of peaceful coexistence. Ephraim Urbach, in an influential essay on the status of rabbinic *derashot*, asserts that there were proto-rabbinic "Pharisees-sages" committed to extra-scriptural mishnaic laws, but who gradually integrated the midrashic practices of the priestly scribes "insofar as the *derashot* corroborated and sustained rulings, attestations, and exemplary deeds already accepted by the sages."[24] Urbach alone among the scholars surveyed identifies a tension between the two modes of authorization, tension he alludes to when he writes that "the acceptance of the *derashah* as a foundation for halakhic adjudication was a slow process."[25]

My own work on this question has led me to conclude that scholars have failed to properly appreciate the gap between "mishnaic" and midrashic authority within tannaitic sources. One important indication is that the Rabbi Ishmael midrashim have a trenchantly scripturalist orientation.[26] Stated briefly, the Mekhilta and Sifre Numbers view midrash as a process that takes place "within" Scripture, playing out between two hypostases of the Hebrew Bible—*torah* and *ha-katuv*. The former is the text of the Torah, the latter a personification of Scripture as an interpreter that explicates *torah* and serves as hermeneutic model for rabbinic interpretation. Such a thoroughgoing commitment to scriptural authority leaves little room for extra-scriptural tradition. If Scripture provides its own interpretation, what need is there for a complementary Oral Torah?

21. For a fuller survey see Yekutiel Neubauer, *Ha-rambam 'al divre soferim* (Jerusalem, 1957), 140.

22. Albeck, *Introduction to the Mishnah*, 53.

23. Neubauer *Ha-rambam*, 139.

24. E. E. Urbach, "The Derashah as the Basis for Halakhah and the Problem of the *Soferim*" (Hebrew), *Tarbiz* 27 (1958): 166–82, here 173.

25. Urbach, "The Derashah," 175.

26. See Azzan Yadin, *Scripture as Logos: Rabbi Ishmael and the Origins of Midrash* (Philadelphia, 2004).

An additional indication of the gap between the two authorization models is that each engenders a different ideal type.[27] A sage whose authority stems from midrash must be literate and have a superlative command of the biblical text, and his scholarly genealogy is of little importance. A sage of extra-scriptural traditions, in contrast, need not be a skilled interpreter of Scripture or, for that matter, literate. Rather, he must be the disciple of a recognized master, i.e., of an earlier recipient of extra-scriptural *halakhot*. The authority of such a sage stems from his place in the oral-traditional chain of transmission and from his ability to accurately recall the traditions passed down to him. It is no coincidence that the Mekhilta of Rabbi Ishmael never cites legal dicta received "in the name of" a sage, nor does it refer to rabbinic "testimonies" or "decrees," to the "words of the scribes," or the "words of the sages"—all standard oral-traditional terminology. The issue, it must be emphasized, cannot be reduced to the question of genre (the Mishnah is not a midrashic work, the Mekhilta is), as such terminology is common to the Mishnah *and* the named tannaitic *derashot* of the Sifra.[28] As for Rabbi Ishmael—if nothing else a prominent figure in the Mekhilta and the Sifre Numbers—he does not participate in the practices of extra-scriptural tradition: the Mishnah and the Tosefta do not record him citing a ruling "in the name of" another sage, nor do tannaitic sources portray him having a teacher.[29] To be clear, I am not trucking in naive biographical reconstruction—a misguided attempt to determine what Rabbi Ishmael "really" did. Rather, my comments speak to different representations of religious authority. Without a proper scholarly genealogy, Rabbi Ishmael cannot (and in fact does not) claim authority *qua* recipient of extra-scriptural traditions.

A further point of difference is that the Mishnah and the halakhic midrashim employ incommensurate terminology. That is, the same terms refer to extra-scriptural tradition in the Mishnah but to Scripture and its explication in the midrashim. Thus, in the Rabbi Ishmael midrashim, the phrase "we have/have not heard" (*shama'nu/lo' shama'nu*) denotes information that has or has not been communicated by Scripture, but in the Mishnah it denotes a received (or not received) extra-scriptural tradition. The mid-

27. See Max Weber, *Economy and Society: An Outline of Interpretive Sociology*, ed. G. Roth and C. Wittich, trans. E. Fischoff and others (2 vols; New York, 1968), 1.9–10. I am using the term "ideal type" heuristically, as a way of distilling key elements from each ideology.

28. See *Scripture and Tradition*, 138–40.

29. Even the post-tannaitic Babylonian tradition that identifies him as the disciple of "Rabbi Nehunia ben ha-Kana, who explicated the entire Torah in *kelal u-ferat*" (bShevu 26a), frames the discipleship in terms of scriptural explication.

rashim refer to Scripture "speaking of the case under discussion" (*dibber ha-katuv ba-hoveh*), but in the Mishnah this phrase is used for sages' legal testimony. Again, for the Rabbi Ishmael midrashim, *stam* designates a biblical assertion made "without explanation," but in the Mishnah it is an unelaborated extra-scriptural tradition. A final example, the root *q-b-l*, whose primary sense is "to take, receive," is a technical term for receiving extra-scriptural traditions in the Mishnah ("Moses *qibbel* Torah from Sinai" in *mAvot* 1.1, and many more).[30] But in the midrashim, the substantive *qabbalah* denotes the prophetic books and the hagiographa as they help to interpret ambiguities in the Torah.

Why are these incommensurable couplets significant? First and foremost because they teach us that tannaitic terminology cannot be defined without reference to a particular conceptual framework. Any attempt to determine the meaning, e.g., of "we have/have not heard" (*shama'nu/lo' shama'nu*) must address the source of the phrase—whether it occurs in the Mishnah or in the Sifre Numbers. A lexicographer cannot provide a definition of *qabbalah* that does not acknowledge the break within the sources: Is it the reception of an oral tradition, or a collective term for the prophets and the hagiographa? Furthermore, the concurrence of terminological identity and semantic difference is a marker of incommensurability, a concept I am adopting from Thomas Kuhn's seminal work, *The Structure of Scientific Revolutions*.[31] Kuhn demonstrates that different paradigms may share a vocabulary, but this surface identity masks the fundamental untranslatability of one set of terms into the other.[32] Terminological continuity, he writes, is to be expected, since new approaches "ordinarily incorporate much of the vocabulary and apparatus, both conceptual and manipulative, that the traditional paradigm had previously employed" but "they seldom employ these bor-

---

30. Adiel Schremer has offered a provocative reinterpretation of the opening of *mAvot*, arguing that it originates in rabbinic circles different from those that gave rise to the Mishnah. The article merits much fuller treatment than I can offer here, except to say that while the opening of *Avot* may be the most famous statement of extra-scriptural tradition, it is by no means unique and an account of how other such statements relate to *mAvot* is a desideratum for Schremer. See Adiel Schremer, "'Avot' Reconsidered: Rethinking Rabbinic Judaism," *JQR* 105 (2015): 287–311.

31. Thomas S. Kuhn, *The Structure of Scientific Revolutions* (2nd ed.; Chicago: University of Chicago Press, 1970).

32. Kuhn's example is the shift from Newtonian to Einsteinian physics. Historians of science often underline the relatively smooth transition from Newtonian to Einsteinian physics, framing the former as a special case of the latter: Newton's world is Einstein's world when not approaching light speed. Such an account, Kuhn contends, is led astray by nominal continuity that obscures an underlying conceptual rupture. The terms may be the same, but "the physical referents of these Einsteinian concepts are by no means

rowed elements in quite the traditional way."[33] To be clear, I am not claiming that the relationship between oral-traditional and midrashic authority models should be framed in Kuhn's diachronic terms or that one "borrowed" its terms from the other. (I suspect Urbach's thesis of a "merger" between different groups giving rise to the diversity within tannaitic sources is closest to the truth, though I do not see how it can be proven.) All the same, Kuhn elegantly warns against the assumption that terminological continuity corresponds to conceptual continuity, and emphasizes the chasm that separates incommensurable conceptual frameworks.[34]

A final consideration in assessing the gap between the two authorization models is Rabbi Ishmael's famous marginalization of extra-scriptural tradition:

> Rabbi Ishmael teaches: In three places halakhah circumvents Scripture: the Torah says, "He shall pour out its blood and cover it with earth" (Lev 17:13) while halakhah says, with anything that grows plants; the Torah says, "He writes her a document of divorce" (Deut 24:1) while halakhah says, [he may write] on anything that was separated from the ground; the Torah says "with an awl" (Ex 21:6), while the halakhah says, with anything. (Sifre Deuteronomy §122, Finkelstein, p. 180; Hammer, p. 167).

I want to stress two points. First, the circumventions in question are quite modest. The Torah states that a slave's ear should be perforated by an awl, but *halakhah* includes any other boring instrument; the Torah states that blood of a hunted animal or bird is to be drained and covered by earth, but *halakhah* includes earth-like substance capable of growing plants; the Torah states that a man must write a "document (*sefer*) of divorce," but *halakhah* includes writs written on any media made of uprooted plants.[35] These

---

identical with those of the Newtonian concepts that bear the same name. (Newtonian mass is conserved; Einsteinian is convertible with energy. Only at low relative velocities may the two be measured in the same way, and even then they must not be conceived to be the same)," Kuhn, *Structure of Scientific Revolutions*, 101–2.

33. Kuhn, *Structure of Scientific Revolutions*, 149.

34. For a fuller discussion of this issue, see my "Qabbalah, Deuterōsis, and Semantic Incommensurability: A Preliminary Study" in *Envisioning Judaism: Studies in Honor of Peter Schäfer on the Occasion of his Seventieth Birthday*, ed. R. Boustan, K. Hermann, R. Leicht, et al. (Tübingen, 2013), 917–40.

35. See Sifre Deuteronomy to Deut 24:1: "*sefer*: I conclude that this refers only to a scroll (*sefer*); what about (a document of divorce) written on the leaves of reed, of nut tree, of olive tree, of carob tree?" (Sifre Deuteronomy §269, Finkelstein, p. 289; Hammer, p. 264).

minor tweaks to biblical laws hardly resemble the massive corpora of extra-scriptural rulings found, e.g., in the Sabbath laws of the Mishnah. Second, the passage fits an established pattern in the Rabbi Ishmael midrashim of rules that have three—and only three—exceptions, suggesting that the list of three circumventions is exhaustive.[36] Rabbi Ishmael's statement delimits, then, both the force of non-scriptural authority (minor alterations of scriptural law) and its scope. *Halakhah* thrice circumvents Scripture, and its interventions are consistently tame. Since extra-scriptural *halakhot* function as independent sources of authority only inasmuch as they circumvent Scripture—otherwise they are midrash—Rabbi Ishmael's list constitutes a radical diminution of extra-scriptural authority as such.

Taken together, the above considerations call for a more emphatic division between midrash and extra-scriptural tradition. Earlier attempts to marginalize the differences between these modes of authority do so either by relegating one to an ancillary role, or by framing their periods of primacy diachronically. My position, in contrast, emphasizes the synchronic dimension, the coexistence of the two models of authority within tannaitic sources, and the incommensurability of the models. The result is a portrait of tannaitic sources that is more unsettled than scholars have generally assumed, one in which these sources do not speak in a single voice even on such cardinal matters as the role of midrash and extra-scriptural tradition. Viewed in the broader context of the present volume, it is notable that the above conclusions are the result of a sustained study of the halakhic midrashim on their own terms, with the comparative (midrash-mishnah) analysis coming at a later stage. In the next section, I build on the idea that the halakhic midrashim can serve as a corrective to the outsized influence of the Mishnah on the study of tannaitic sources. That is to say, I will argue that the halakhic midrashim can militate against the effects of the Mishnah's canonicity on rabbinic scholarship.

THE MISHNAH AS CANON

What does it mean to characterize the Mishnah as a canon? It should be stated at the outset that the Mishnah is not the central text of the rabbinic

36. "This is one of the three instances in which Rabbi Ishmael interpreted the accusative particle '*et*'" (Sifre Numbers §32; Kahana 94). See too Bavli *Nidah* 16a. "Rabbi Ishmael says: Every '*im* [if] in the Torah refers to a voluntary act with the exception of three [which refer to obligatory acts]" (Mekhilta Baḥodesh 11, p. 243; Lauterbach 2.287–88).

"Thus you must say that Aaron was not directly addressed in any of the divine communications in the Torah, with the exception of three" (Mekhilta Pisḥa 1, p. 1; Lauterbach 1.1).

"This is one of three expressions in the Torah that Rabbi Ishmael used to interpret as a *mashal* [allegory]." (Mekhilta Nezikin 6, p. 270; Lauterbach 3.53).

bet midrash—the Talmud is. For the vast majority of its existence, study of the Mishnah was mediated by its inclusion in the Talmud.[37] But even though the Mishnah lived in the shadow of the Talmud in the lived practice of rabbinic study and debate, it was understood as the foundational text of rabbinic Judaism precisely in its role as the basis for the Talmud. Of course, not all Talmudic discussions derive from the Mishnah, but in its structure and self-presentation the Talmud explicitly affixes itself to the Mishnah. Further, post-tannaitic sages apply to the Mishnah similar interpretive assumptions regarding intentionality and linguistic economy as they do to the Torah, a point Elizabeth Shanks Alexander has developed in detail.[38] For the present discussion, I want to focus on two characteristics of canonicity outlined in Dirk de Geest's investigation of this concept.[39] The first is that "canonization aims at a complete independence and even self-reliance of specific literary phenomena," such that "the canonized texts are gradually detemporalized" and the contingent, historical context of their creation effaced.[40] Phrased differently, canonical status bestows on the work an ontological self-evidence that transports it beyond the particulars of its historical genesis. In the Mishnah's case, this means that readers (including scholars) habitually blur the distinction between the redacted anthology known as the Mishnah and the traditions it preserves. Let me draw an analogy from biblical studies. Bible scholars are keenly aware the compositions they study are "biblical" only in the limited sense that they were—subsequent to their composition—included in the biblical canon (more accurately: in one of the biblical canons). Biblical canonicity postdates the composition of the canonized work, and is constituted by the commitments of a later community to regard it as canonical. There is nothing inherently "biblical" about any of the books of the Bible, only their eventual inclusion in the canon. The same holds true for the status of the legal traditions preserved in the Mishnah. Just as the Book of Jeremiah did not "know" that it would be incorporated into a biblical anthology, so too the traditions collected in the Mishnah did not "know" they would form part of that collection. Yet the self-evidently "mishnaic" status of these traditions permeates much of the scholarly discourse surrounding the Mishnah. The same is true for the sages who appear in the Mishnah. From a strictly historical perspective, Rabbi Akiva,

37. Insofar as the Mishnah is a venerated work that is not studied on its own terms but only through the mediation of the Talmud, its canonicity is similar to that of the Torah.

38. Elizabeth Shanks Alexander, *Transmitting Mishnah: The Shaping Influence of Oral Tradition* (Cambridge, 2006), 77–116.

39. Dirk de Geest, "Cultural Repertoires within a Functionalist Perspective," in *Cultural Repertoires: Structure, Function, and Dynamics*, ed. G. J. Dorleijn and H. L. J. Vanstiphout (Leuven, 2003), 201–16.

40. de Geest, "Cultural Repertoires," 203.

Rabbi Eliezer, Rabbi Meir et al. are not in any meaningful historical sense "the sages of the Mishnah," since their inclusion in the Mishnah reflects an editorial choice made decades after their deaths. The tendency to "detemporalize" the Mishnah reaches its apogee in the phrase "the mishnaic period" (*tequfat ha-mishnah*). This terminology has been rightly criticized for anachronistically attributing to the Mishnah a historical significance at the time of its redaction.[41] But there is a deeper criticism to be levelled regarding the designation of the period as "mishnaic" (conventionally, from the destruction of the Jerusalem Temple to the early-third-century redaction of the Mishnah) during which *the Mishnah does not exist*. Such conspicuous anachronism speaks to a de-contextualization of the Mishnah—a blurring of the work and the content it presents—even to the point that the Mishnah is called on to characterize the period preceding its historical formation.

The second characteristic de Geest enumerates involves "a metonymical displacement . . . which moves away from specific texts towards . . . the name of its writer as such."[42] De Geest has in mind the identification of canons with their authors, as when specific plays are said to express "Shakespeare's worldview." Mishnah scholars do not make precisely the same arguments, but they regularly put forward ahistorical claims regarding the authorship of the Mishnah. The best known of these claims is that Mishnah was redacted by Rabbi Judah the Patriarch, a view found only in post-mishnaic sources and called into question by the many anonymous Mishnah traditions that contravene Rabbi Judah's positions.[43] More interesting for our purposes is the persistent notion that Rabbi Akiba was, in J. N. Epstein's words, "the father of the Mishnah."[44] Epstein adduces several arguments in support of

41. I have heard Moshe Halbertal make this point in reference to Gedalia Alon's book, whose Hebrew title can be translated as "The History of the Jews in the Land of Israel in the Period of the Mishnah and the Talmud."

42. de Geest, "Cultural Repertoires," 213.

43. See Epstein, *Prolegomena*, 200–202, and H. L. Strack and Günter Stemberger, *Introduction to Talmud and Midrash*, trans. M. Bockmuehl (Minneapolis, 1996), 133–35, who recognize the difficulties but affirm the traditional position. Catherine Hezser takes a more critical approach in *The Social Structure of the Rabbinic Movement in Roman Palestine* (Tübingen, 1997), 414.

44. Epstein, *Prolegomena*, 71. Among more recent writers, Reuven Hammer's claims are, to my knowledge, the most outlandish: "As important as compiling Midrash was, Akiva's work in creating the form and content of the Mishnah was even more crucial [. . .] It was Akiva who championed this form [the Mishnah] and who first created a complete version. Presumably it was Akiva who selected the six major categories, or orders (sedarim, sing. seder), in the Mishnah," Reuven Hammer, *Akiva: Life, Legend, Legacy* (Philadelphia, 2015), 85–86. Other scholars claim that the prominence of Rabbi Akiba and his students is evident from the Mishnah's having been edited "according

this claim. A tannaitic reference to "the *mishnah* of Rabbi Akiba."[45] A passage in the Fathers According to Rabbi Nathan (ADRN) in which Rabbi Judah the Patriarch likens Rabbi Akiba to a laborer who put different grains and legumes in his basket and sorted them upon returning home—just as "Rabbi Akiba acted, and he arranged the whole Torah in rings."[46] And the oft-cited Talmudic tradition in the name of Rabbi Yoḥanan, that "the unattributed portions of our Mishnah—Rabbi Meir; the unattributed portions of the Tosefta—Rabbi Nehemia; the unattributed portions of the Sifre—Rabbi Shimon. And all are according to Rabbi Akiba" (b. Sanhedrin 86a).

Epstein's arguments—regularly adduced by scholars who hold this view—are wanting. The "*mishnah* of Rabbi Akiba" most likely does not refer to a collection of legal dicta (a proto-Mishnah), but rather teaches that, in Saul Lieberman's phrase, "it was Rabbi Akiba who stated [the dictum]."[47] Tannaitic sources repeatedly refer to Rabbi Akiba *shoneh*, "reciting," a legal tradition, so *mishnah* could indeed refer to a discrete statement or tradition, as it does today. Moreover, in a number of passages Rabbi Akiba proclaims a legal tradition, but when he is informed that another sage proclaims a different version, Rabbi Akiba adopts the latter position (*ḥazar lehiyot shoneh*), a dynamic that makes it unlikely he had a fixed collection of extra-scriptural traditions.[48] The Fathers According to Rabbi Nathan passage similarly fails to confirm Rabbi Akiba's role in creating the Mishnah. In part because there is a growing consensus that ADRN contains material that has been "appended to the text . . . from the Mishnah and Talmud,"[49]

---

to the school of Rabbi Akiva" (Menachem Kahana, *Sifre Zuta Deuteronomy*, 110). Such statements gloss over the fact that inclusion in the Mishnah was an editorial decision that may or may not be an accurate reflection of the historical standing of Rabbi Akiba and his disciples.

45. The phrase occurs in mSan 3.4, mNaz 6.1, tMS 2.1 and 2.12.

46. *The Fathers according to Rabbi Nathan*, Chap. 18, trans. J. Goldin (New Haven, 1967), 90.

47. Saul Lieberman, *Tosefta ki-feshutah: Zeraʾim* (Jerusalem, 2001), 731.

48. See mTaʾan 4.4, mHul 4.2, tZav 1.6, tʿUqts 3.2, and tShevi 2.13. As Epstein himself notes, the same teaching is referred to as "the *mishnah* of Rabbi Akiva" (*mishnat rabbi akiva*) in one source (Sifre Zuta, Naso 5 §10; Horovitz 232), as "Rabbi Akiva transmitted [a ruling]" (*rabbi akiva shoneh*) in a second (Sifre Numbers, Naso 4 (M. I. Kahana, ed., *Sifre on Numbers: An Annotated Edition* [Jerusalem: Magnes, 2011], 1.16), and "Rabbi Akiva interpreted" (*darash rabbi akiva*) in a third (tBQ 10.17; M. S. Zuckermandel, ed. [Jerusalem: Bamberger and Wahrman, 1963], 368). In consequence, it is difficult to know how much stock to put into the *mishnah* reference.

49. M. B. Lerner, "The External Tractates," in *The Literature of the Sages*, ed. S. Safrai (2 vols.; Assen, 1987) 1.367–403, here 377.

and that it underwent a relatively late, Babylonian redaction.[50] But even if this passage could be shown to be tannaitic, it is an unreliable witness for Rabbi Akiba's paternity of the Mishnah. Rabbi Judah the Patriarch's praise of Rabbi Akiba is embedded in a chain of the scholarly encomia—one for Rabbi Tarfon precedes it, and one for Rabbi Eleazar ben Azariah follows it. In both cases, Rabbi Judah praises theses scholars for their expertise in *mishnah*: Rabbi Tarfon is able to cite *"miqra'* and *mishnah, midrash, halakhah* and *aggadah,"* while Rabbi Eleazar ben Azariah, "if questioned on *miqra'*, he answered; on *mishnah*, he answered; on *midrash*, he answered; on *halakhah*, he answered; on *aggadah*, he answered."[51] Nestled between these two is Rabbi Akiba, whose expertise in *mishnah* is not mentioned. How, then, can Rabbi Akiba's having "arranged the whole Torah in rings" count as evidence that he is the "father of the Mishnah" when Rabbi Tarfon and Rabbi Eleazar ben Azariah are the ones associated with *mishnah* in that very passage? Finally, what precisely can be deduced from Rabbi Yoḥanan's statement? It appears only in the Bavli, so it may be late; none of the attributions have historical validity—there is no evidence that Rabbi Nehemiah edited the Tosefta, Rabbi Shimon the Sifre, and so on; and in any case the editing of the Mishnah is attributed to Rabbi Meir. If we interpret "all are according to Rabbi Akiba" as proof that Rabbi Akiba was the author of a proto-Mishnah, ought we not conclude that he was the author of a proto-Tosefta and a proto-Sifre as well?[52] There are no grounds for isolating the Mishnah from the Tosefta and the Sifre and conscripting it as proof of Rabbi Akiba's paternity.

The historical and philological weakness of these arguments suggests an ideological motivation for designating Rabbi Akiba as the "father of the Mishnah." Rabbi Akiba's prominence in the Mishnah, and the prominence of his disciples, is undoubtedly significant, but it teaches us only about the editorial choices of the Mishnah's redactor(s). Absent additional evidence, it is not justified to conclude from this prominence anything about the historical Rabbi Akiba, and certainly not that he was its true founder. Let me press this argument one step further and claim that the traditional position reverses the historical cause and effect. The prominent role the Mish-

---

50. See Menahem Kister, *Studies in Avot de-Rabbi Natan: Text, Redaction, and Interpretation* (Jerusalem, 1998) [Hebrew], 193–217, especially 206–12.

51. *The Fathers according to Rabbi Nathan*, 90–91.

52. There is also a tradition in the Tosefta that describes Rabbi Akiba assembling legal traditions and soliciting potential scriptural links (tZav 1.2), activity that might be interpreted as some manner of editorial work, though it appears pedagogical aims motivate Rabbi Akiba here, not publication.

nah's redactors granted Rabbi Akiba, and the canonic status the work attained, played a critical role in cementing his standing in Jewish history. *Rabbi Akiba is not the father of the Mishnah; the Mishnah is the father of Rabbi Akiba.*

THE HALAKHIC MIDRASHIM AS CORRECTIVE:
THE IDENTITY OF THE RABBIS

I have indulged the reader's patience with this long digression on the canonicity of the Mishnah because I want to propose that the halakhic midrashim can serve as a corrective to its effects on scholarship. My argument, *in nuce*, is that the halakhic midrashim represent the rabbinic "road not taken" relative to the Mishnah—tannaitic corpora that were not the basis for the Talmud and so never truly canonical. (NB: there are no adjectival forms of Mekhilta, Sifra, or Sifre). Juxtaposing the Mishnah to these works can, then, foreground the Mishnah's status as *a* (not *the*) source for understanding the Tannaim. The first part of this essay is, in fact, a step in this direction—an examination of the Mekhilta and the Sifre Numbers on their own terms, leading to conclusions that do not accord with the Mishnah: a nuanced and conceptually coherent scripturalist view, and diminution, even effacement, of Oral Law. Such an approach can shed light on the outsized influence the Mishnah wields in our understanding of the early rabbinic identity.

To wit, it is not easy to pin down early rabbinic identity. Most scholars approach "the rabbis" as a known quantity, with any attempt to tease out a more robust definition degenerating into circular reasoning: the rabbis are the Jewish religious authorities known from rabbinic literature, and rabbinic literature is the corpus created by the rabbis. External criteria are hard to come by. The term *rabbi* is not viable since it appears in non-rabbinic contexts, including epigraphic sources[53] and the New Testament.[54] Rabbinic practices are also a problematic criterion. The standard account teaches that after the destruction of the Temple, rabbinic Judaism established two sur-

---

53. Shaye J. D. Cohen, "Epigraphical Rabbis," *JQR* 72 (1981): 1–17. Hayim Lapin revisited Cohen's article thirty years after its publication and found that despite redating of some of the epigraphic material, "on balance, Cohen's minimalist position is safest," though Lapin places greater weight on the dedication naming Rabbi Eleazar ha-Kappar as an indication of potentially greater rabbinic prominence and visibility in the fourth century and beyond. See Hayim Lapin, "Epigraphical Rabbis: A Reconsideration," *JQR* 101 (2011): 311–46, here 331.

54. The addressee is usually Jesus (e.g., Mt 26:49, Mk 9:5 and 11:21, Jn 1:38) but John the Baptist is also addressed as Rabbi (e.g., Jn 3:26); Matthew 23 exhorts its readers to reject the title *rabbi*.

rogate institutions: the *bet midrash* (house of study) and the synagogue. But the practice of scriptural study and interpretation is shared with other Jewish groups, including the Qumran community and the early followers of Jesus. The Community Rule even portrays the community engaging in ritualized nightly Torah study: "And in the place where the ten assemble there should never be missing a man to interpret the law [*torah*] day and night . . . And the Many shall be on watch together for a third of each night of the year in order to read the book, explain the regulation, and bless together" (1QS vi, 6–8).⁵⁵ Torah study, then, does not define the rabbis to the exclusion of other groups. Nor does the synagogue, as the rabbinic class was not initially associated with this institution. As Lee Levine has demonstrated, "on the basis of [non-rabbinic evidence], it would seem that in most areas concerning [the synagogue] . . . rabbinic involvement was minimal, at best."⁵⁶ There are conflicting testimonies within the rabbinic sources, but "only when the sages gained undisputed ascendancy within the Jewish community in religious matters, a process that culminated under Muslim rule in the Middle Ages, did a distinct and normative rabbinic stamp on the synagogue's religious dimension become irrevocably recognized."⁵⁷ Even the putatively rabbinic innovation of aligning the liturgy to correspond to the Temple sacrifices ("Prayers were established in correspondence to the sacrifices," *tefilot ke-neged korbanot tiknum*, bBer 26b) is already attested in the Qumran literature, where the Songs of the Sabbath Sacrifice serve as a liturgical correlate to the sacrificial calendar. Neither Torah study nor prayer, then, can serve as a distinguishing criterion for rabbinic identity.

Perhaps due to these difficulties, the one reliable criterion of rabbinic Judaism is the concept and practice of Oral Law, which has come to be seen, in Peter Schäfer's words, as a rabbinic dogma.⁵⁸ For Martin Jaffee, the ideology of "Torah in the mouth" is the *differentia specifica* of Rabbinic Judaism. The decline of scribalism and the concomitant rise of oral-tradition ideology, he argues, "may have something to do with the characteristic ideological shift that distinguishes Second Temple scribal groups—whether the Yahad, the Pharisees, or the as yet unidentified groups behind the Enochic and related literatures—from the rabbinic communities of the third century. The difference concerns perceptions of the role of oral communication in the genesis

55. *The Dead Sea Scrolls: Study Edition*, ed. F. G. Martínez and E. J. C. Tigchelaar (2 vols.; Leiden, 1997), 1.83–84.

56. Lee I. Levine, *The Ancient Synagogue: The First Thousand Years* (New Haven, 200), 472.

57. Levine, *The Ancient Synagogue*, 498.

58. Peter Schäfer, "Das 'Dogma' von der Mündlichen Torah im rabbinischen Judentum," in *Studien zur Geschichte und Theologie des rabbinischen Judentums* (Leiden, 1978), 152–97.

and transmission of literary tradition."[59] Yet if my earlier argument is correct and the Rabbi Ishmael midrashim are a thoroughly scripturalist corpus that minimizes oral-traditional authority, an ideology of Oral Law can only characterize *certain* rabbinic circles, those that created the Mishnah first and foremost, but not the rabbis as such.[60]

Let me press this argument further. The association of the rabbis with the Pharisees—the notion that "Rabbinic Judaism, as we meet it in Tannaitic literature, is a continuation of Pharisaism"[61]—was for many decades a scholarly commonplace, at least until the decisive intervention of Shaye Cohen's 1984 article "The Significance of Yavneh."[62] In this study, Cohen conclusively demonstrates the frailty of many of the arguments adduced in support of Pharisee-rabbinic continuity. These arguments include:

i. Gamaliel and his son Simon, who are identified as Pharisees in Josephus and in Acts, may be the Rabban Shimon ben Gamaliel cited in mAvot 1.18.

ii. Stories about Pharisees in Josephus recur as stories about rabbis in rabbinic sources.

iii. There may be a shift in both Josephus and the New Testament, with post-70 C.E. writings reflecting a more pronounced role for the Pharisees.

59. Jaffee, *Torah in the Mouth*, 66.

60. I want to emphasize that I am not questioning the significance of a practice and ideology of oral-traditional transmission in the Mishnah, a qualification made necessary by Halivni's adoption of this very position. Halivni suggests that the chain of transmission in *mAvot* "does not necessarily refer to Oral Law . . . the written Torah itself could very well be the sole subject." Moreover, "the entire concept of oral law . . . was shelved and disregarded . . . [since] the idea of an Oral Torah is hardly mentioned at all in Tannaitic literature," Halivni, "Reflections on Classical Jewish Hermeneutics," *Proceedings of the American Academy for Jewish Research* 62 (1996): 21–127, at 50 and 51 respectively. Halivni's first claim ignores the fact that dozens of tannaitic passages bespeak a clear and explicit committed to extra-scriptural tradition, e.g., mPe'ah 2.6, mYev 16.7, mYad 3.5, 4.2–3, mGit 6.7, m'Eduy 1.6, 8.7, and mZev 1.3. His second claim confounds the *phrase* "Oral Torah" (*torah she-be'al-peh*), which is indeed absent from tannaitic sources, and the *concept* of extra-scriptural tradition, which is robustly attested. On the absence of the phrase *torah she-be'al-peh* in tannaitic literature, see Gerald Blidstein, "A Note on Torah Be-'Al Peh" (Hebrew), *Tarbiz* 42 (1973): 496–98.

61. Chaim Rabin, *Qumran Studies* (New York, 1975), 60.

62. Shaye J. D. Cohen, "The Significance of Yavneh: Pharisees, Rabbis, and the End of Jewish Sectarianism," *HUCA* 55 (1984): 27–53. For a more recent and fundamentally similar survey, see Daniel R. Schwartz, *Judeans and Jews: Four Faces of Dichotomy in Ancient Jewish History* (Toronto, 2014), 122.

iv. Some of the practices and theological tenets Josephus attributes to the Pharisees recur in tannaitic sources, including the authority of extra-scriptural tradition.

Cohen responds to each of these claims as follows: (i) It is an error to draw conclusions regarding group identity from a single rabbinic family that may be Pharisaic.[63] (ii) The parallel stories involving the Pharisees in Josephus and rabbis in rabbinic sources are Babylonian and late, and arguably the result of the "rabbinization" of early traditions involving Pharisees. (iii) The post-70 CE shift in the prominence of the Pharisees as recorded by Josephus and the New Testament was and is debatable. (iv) Though there is significant overlap between the legal and theological concerns of the Pharisees and the rabbis, they are not exclusive to the Pharisees, and the overlaps are in case only partial: "the tannaim believe in an oral law revealed to Moses but this doctrine is never attributed to the Pharisees."[64]

Cohen also points out that "the [church] fathers of the second, third, and fourth centuries do not identify contemporary Judaism with Pharisaism,"[65] a remarkable fact given that the anti-Pharisee polemics of the New Testament could have been easily repurposed as anti-rabbinic by later authors. This last insight has been fleshed out more fully by Annette Reed in a brilliant essay on early Christian representations of Pharisees, focusing on the reception of Matthew 23.[66] It would be impossible to summarize the breadth of sources Reed adduces, except to say that her findings fundamentally support Cohen's position: in second- and third-century patristic sources, "the anti-Pharisaic statements in Matthew 23 are redeployed in various ways—mostly having nothing to do with Jews."[67] There are almost no attempts to link the Pharisees to contemporary Jews, and in some sources—the Pseudo-Clementine *Homilies*—we find remarkable parallels between the early Christian texts and the Pharisaic oral tradition.

---

63. Consider the Pharisees among Jesus's followers in Acts 15.5. If this verse does not demonstrate that Jesus's followers were Pharisees (and it does not), how can the conjectured Pharisaic identity of one rabbinic family demonstrate that the rabbis were Pharisees?

64. Cohen, "The Significance of Yavneh," 37. It should be noted that Cohen's article still accepts the probability of a prevalent "biographical" continuity between Pharisees and rabbis, though he rejects the claim that this continuity played a significant role in rabbinic self-understanding.

65. Cohen, "The Significance of Yavneh," 51.

66. Annette Yoshiko Reed, "When Did the Pharisees Become Rabbis?" in *Envisioning Judaism: Studies in Honor of Peter Schäfer*, 859–96.

67. Reed, "When Did Rabbis Become Pharisees," 880

Old habits die hard and nearly twenty years after Cohen published his article, some scholars still write that it is "generally assumed that the tannaim inherited the traditions of the Pharisees."[68] Nota bene, the *traditions* of the Pharisees, as Pharisee-rabbinic continuity with regard to oral tradition still enjoys broad currency. But if my earlier argument is correct and the Rabbi Ishmael midrashim are scripturalist and oral-traditional minimalists, the commitment to extra-scriptural tradition is the patrimony of only some tannaim, and whatever Oral Law–centered continuity exists between Pharisees and sages pertains to a subset of the tannaim.

CONCLUSION: THE VIEW FROM THE MARGINS

Many years ago, I participated in a university program that included a trip to New Jersey's Liberty State Park. The park boasts a view of the Statue of Liberty, though not the iconic image of Lady Liberty's raised torch and cradled tablets. Instead, park visitors see only her back. I was standing next to Prof. Indrani Catterjee, a scholar of South Asia, and jokingly commented to her that the vista was emblematic of the New York–New Jersey relationship—the former enjoys an iconic image, the other makes do with the statue's backside. Indrani immediately corrected me: "No, this is the better view, as we are not subject to her imperial gaze."[69] I do not intend to press the analogy between empire and canon too far, but Indrani's comment is evocative of the dominant position the Mishnah enjoys among scholars of the early rabbis. In a sense, the halakhic midrashim stand outside the canonical gaze of the Mishnah, alerting us to the force of this gaze, even as their literary, legal, and theological distinctiveness stress the need to read the Mishnah as one historical source among many. The insights such readings produce may unsettle long standing assumptions, e.g. concerning the scope of the early rabbinic commitment to Oral Law or Pharisee-rabbinic continuity. My hope is that such critical interventions ultimately lead to a fuller and more nuanced understanding of the early rabbinic corpora and of the rabbis who produced them.

I want to thank the organizers of the Harvard conference "What is Mishnah?" and especially Shaye Cohen, David Stern, and Susan Kahn. I also want to acknowledge David Stern's thoughtful and thought-provoking comments on an earlier draft of this essay.

68. Lawrence Schiffman and Jon Bloomberg, *Understanding Second Temple and Rabbinic Judaism* (New York, 2003), 292.

69. Belated thanks to Indrani, who is now at UT Austin, for this insightful comment.

20. The Publication and Early Transmission of the Mishnah

David Stern

The question of the composition and transmission of the Mishnah is, arguably the oldest debate in the history of rabbinic literature. What were the sources out of which the Mishnah was compiled by the early third-century sage R. Judah the Patriarch, to whom the editing of the Mishnah has traditionally been attributed? What was the plan behind R. Judah's editing, how did he go about it, and with what purpose? And most importantly, when R. Judah finally completed the Mishnah, how did he "publish" it, that is, make it public? Was the Mishnah released as a fixed document in writing, or as an orally composed and memorized text to be recited aloud and transmitted orally?

In past scholarship going back to learned discussions since the early Middle Ages, these questions about the composition of the Mishnah have often, and not always helpfully, been conflated with similar questions about the other documents constituting the Oral Torah, *Torah she-be'al peh* (or *'al peh*), the Oral or Memorized Law.[1] As is well known, the foundational

---

1. This chapter will deal only with a tiny selection of the scholarship that has been written on the subject of the composition and transmission of the Mishnah and of the Oral Law; I will not touch upon the important contributions made by, among many others, Zacharias Frankel, Chanoch Albeck, Jose Faur, Shmuel Safrai, and Dov Zlotnick. For full bibliographies, see Yaakov Sussmann, *"Torah She-be'al Peh, Peshutah ke-Mashma'ah: Koḥo shel Kotzo shel Yud"* [Oral Law—Taken Literally: The Power of the Tip of a Yod], in *Meḥkerei Talmud: Talmudic Studies Dedicated to the Memory of Professor Ephraim E. Urbach*, vol. 3, ed. D. Rosenthal and Y. Sussmann (Jerusalem, 2005; rev. and enlarged 2019), 209–385; H. L. Strack and G. Stemberger, *Introduction to the Talmud and Midrash*, trans. M. Bockmuehl (Minneapolis: Fortress, 1992); and Elisa-

narrative of rabbinic Judaism rests upon the belief that the Oral Torah was revealed to Moses at Mt. Sinai along with the "Written Torah," namely the Pentateuch; but it is also worth bearing in mind that as recent scholarship has shown, as late as the amoraic period, there was still no complete agreement among the rabbis as to what exactly constituted the Oral Torah or its Sinaitic revelation.[2] This chapter will attempt to focus narrowly upon the questions surrounding the composition of the Mishnah but, as we will see, it is often difficult and sometimes impossible to completely disentangle the Mishnah from the rest of the Oral Torah; sometimes, it may even be advisable to consult other documents of the Oral Law, particularly those from the tannaitic period, in order to contextualize the questions surrounding the Mishnah's composition and publication. The separate literary documents making up what we today call the Oral Torah, however, are probably always best considered first individually.

We can begin with the unhappy fact that nowhere in any classical rabbinic text is there an explicit account of the process of composing any rabbinic document. Nor is there unequivocal material evidence from the classical rabbinic period to resolve the many questions surrounding the composition of rabbinic literature generally, let alone the Mishnah in particular.[3] With a very few exceptional cases,[4] the earliest surviving texts of

---

beth Shanks Alexander, *Transmitting Mishnah: The Shaping Influence of Oral Tradition* (Cambridge, 2006).

2. The earliest statement about the Sinaitic origins of the Oral Torah is Sifre Dev. 351. The best overview of the scholarship on the topic remains Strack and Stemberger, *Introduction to the Talmud and Midrash*, 31–44; for the lack of consensus on Oral Torah and the most sophisticated recent treatment of the subject, see Abraham Rosenthal, "Oral Torah and Torah from Sinai—Halakha and Practice" (Hebrew), *Meḥkerei Talmud* 2, ed. M. Bar-Asher and D. Rosenthal (Jerusalem, 1993), 448–87.

3. I have not included the Rehov inscription in this discussion because of its unclear relation to the Yerushalmi; on which, see Yaakov Sussmann, "A Halakhic Inscription from the Beth-Shean Valley," (Hebrew) *Tarbiz* 43 (1974): 88–158, 123–24 in particular.

4. These mainly consist of quotations from the Mishnah (mZev 5.3 and mShav 4.13) found in Aramaic bowls, usually dated to the eighth or ninth century. For details and references, see Shaul Shaked, J. N. Ford, and S. Bhayro, *Aramaic Bowl Spells, Jewish Babylonian Aramaic Bowls I* (Leiden and Boston, 2013), 22–23; Shaul Shaked, "Form and Purpose in Aramaic Spells: Some Jewish Themes," in *Officina Magica: Essays on the Practice of Magic in Antiquity*, ed. S. Shaked (Leiden and Boston, 2005), 10–30; and Dan Levene, "If You Appear as a Pig: Another Incantation Bowl (Moussaieff 164), *Journal of Semitic Studies* 52 (2007): 59–70. The other possible text, an Oxyrhynchus fragment, Bod. MS Heb. C. 57 (P) c, was first published by A. E. Cowley, "Notes on Hebrew Papyrus Fragments from Oxyrhynchus," *Journal of Egyptian Archaeology* 2 (1915): 211, who dated it to the fourth or early fifth century, which would make it the earliest written inscription of the Mishnah by far. The text appears to be parallel, though not identical,

the Mishnah are undated fragments from the Cairo Genizah that were almost certainly not written before the eighth or ninth century. The earliest manuscript codices to contain the entirety (or very large portions) of the Mishnah, the Kaufmann Codex (Hungarian Academy of Sciences, MS A50) and MS Parma (Biblioteca Palatina, De Rossi 138), both of which represent the Palaestinian type text of the Mishnah (as opposed to the Babylonian), were written in southern Italy sometime between the eleventh and thirteenth centuries—that is, some nine to eleven centuries after the Mishnah was completed.[5]

Our first full account of the composition of the Mishnah is found in the earliest history of rabbinic literature, *The Epistle of Sherira Gaon*, written by the Babylonian sage in 986/7 to the Jewish community in Qayrawan (Tunisia). Sherira's Epistle was vastly influential on all subsequent accounts.[6] Like all early and late medieval rabbis, Sherira firmly believed in an oral tradition

---

to mYom 3.8–4.1, and may have been part of an early *seder avodah* for Yom Kippur. The most recent study to deal with the fragment is Michael D. Swartz, "Yoma from Babylonia to Egypt: Ritual Function, Textual Transmission, and Sacrifice," *AJS Review* 43 (2019): 339–53, esp. 351–52, who also lists all previous bibliography. I am currently working with Professor Swartz and Dr. Ezra Chwat on a project to identify this fragment more fully.

5. For a listing of Mishnah manuscripts, see Michael Krupp, "Manuscripts of the Mishnah," in *The Literature of the Sages*, ed. S. Safrai (Assen and Philadelphia, 1987–2006), I:252–62. The terms "Palaestinian" and "Babylonian text-types" are scholarly designations for two distinct traditions in the transmission of the Mishnah. The Hebrew and Aramaic dialects of Babylonia were not identical with the Hebrew and Aramaic dialects of the land of Israel, and the differences are apparent in our texts. Students of the Babylonian Talmud over the centuries regularly modified the text of the Mishnah to make it conform to the analyses of the Babylonian sages. In contrast, in the land of Israel, the Mishnah was studied both in the context of the formation of the Talmud of the land of Israel (the Yerushalmi) and as an independent text. The result was numerous differences, major and minor, between the Mishnah text as transmitted by sources in the land of Israel on the one hand, and by Babylonian sources on the other. For further discussion, see Robert Brody, *Mishnah and Tosefta Studies* (Jerusalem, 2014), 5–14; and David Rosenthal, "The History of the Mishnaic Text" (Hebrew), in *Sifrut Ḥazal Ha-Eretz-Yisraelit* (Jerusalem: Ben-Zvi Institute, 2018), I: 65–108, esp. 88–97.

6. The standard text remains Lewin, who prints both the French and Spanish recensions (see below). An English translation of the French recension is available in David Katz, "The Iggeres of Rav Sherira Gaon," in *Introduction to the Talmud*, ed. Y. Danziger and A. Biderman (Rahway, N.J., 2019), 565–624. For the best treatment of the epistle's background and current scholarly views, see Robert Brody, *The Geonim of Babylonia and the Shaping of Medieval Jewish Culture* (New Haven, 1998), 20–25; see as well Talya Fishman, "Claims about the Mishnah in the *Epistle* of Sherira Gaon: Islamic Theology and Jewish History," in David M. Friedenreich and Miriam Goldstein, *Beyond Religious Borders: Interaction and Intellectual Exchange in the Medieval Islamic World* (Philadelphia, 2011), 65–77, 184–92.

going back to Sinai and that the Mishnah's *halakhot*, laws, reflected that tradition. In *The Epistle*, however, he was the first to offer an account of how Rabbi Judah compiled the Mishnah as a document from previously existing sources and collections. Sherira's account has effectively served as a kind of template for most scholarly treatments of the Mishnah's redaction until today. As Sherira describes R. Judah's work, the sage did not "compose" the Mishnah on his own, but "redacted" it, gathering much if not all of its material from earlier or contemporaneous sources including earlier collections of mishnayot, and often leaving those sources, sometimes even complete tractates he inherited, almost unchanged.[7]

On the topic of *how* R. Judah redacted the Mishnah, whether orally or in writing, *The Epistle* is less helpful. During the Middle Ages, the text circulated in two versions known (somewhat misleadingly) as the French and Spanish recensions. While the recensions clearly represent the same work, they differ in many small points, and most blatantly on how the Mishnah was redacted.[8] According to the Spanish recension, the Mishnah was completed in writing, a view espoused by Maimonides and other Sephardi sages.[9] In contrast, the French version, which reflects the School of Rashi, states categorically that none of the Oral Torah, with the exception of Megillat Ta'anit (a list of days on which it is forbidden to fast), was ever written down during the talmudic period, in the course of which it was always transmitted and taught orally; it was first committed to writing in the geonic period.[10]

---

7. For a summary of Sherira's account of the Mishnah's compilation, Margarete Schlüter, "Was the Mishnah Written? The Answer of Rav Sherira Gaon," *RASHI 1040–1990: Hommage à Ephraim E. Urbach*, ed. G. Sed-Rajna (Paris, 1993), 213–18; cf. Strack and Stemberger, *Introduction to the Talmud and Midrash*, 124–26. The one recent exception to this model of the Mishnah's composition is that of Jacob Neusner, *The Memorized Torah: The Mnemonic System of the Mishnah* (Chico, 1985), 109 (cited and discussed in Catherine Hezser, "The Mishnah and Ancient Book Production," in *The Mishnah in Contemporary Perspective*, ed. A. J. Avery-Peck and J. Neusner (Leiden, 2002), 173, who, in line with his documentary approach, believes that the final editors eradicated most traces of earlier sources. For contemporary views on the Mishnah's redaction, see the excellent survey in Ishay Rosen-Zvi, *Between Mishna and Midrash: The Birth of Rabbinic Literature* (Hebrew; Ra'ananah, 2020), 86–109; and in English, Strack and Stemberger, *Introduction to the Talmud and Midrash*, 133–39.

8. For comparison of the passages where the two recensions differ, see Benjamin M. Lewin, ed., *Iggeret Rav Sherira Gaon* (Haifa: Itzkovsky, 1921), xlvii–liii.

9. Introductions to the Mishnah Torah and to his Commentary on the Mishnah.

10. bShabbat 13b s.v. *megilat ta'anit*; b'Eruvin 62b s,v. *Kigon megilat ta'anit*; bBM 33b s.v. *ve-einah middah*. I have excluded Megillat Ta'anit from my discussion because, according to all modern scholars, the work is believed to have been composed in the

Most scholars today believe that the French recension is closest to what Sherira himself wrote. This is not surprising. It is clear from abundant testimony that from the amoraic period on, study of Talmud in Babylonia was conducted entirely orally, at least publicly and formally, and it remained so in the geonic Babylonian yeshivot even after the time when inscribed texts of rabbinic literature existed.[11] In the oft-cited statement of the tenth-century Gaon Aaron Sargado, "it is known that the recitation (*gursa*) [of the entire academy] is from the mouths of the masters, and most of them do not know what a book is."[12] Even if this statement is hyperbolic—because written texts of the Talmud certainly existed by the tenth century—it captures the pervasively oral atmosphere of the yeshivot.[13] It would have been only natural for Sherira to believe that this had always been the case. Through the Middle Ages, the French recension's view remained the dominant one, largely because of Rashi's popularity.

Beginning with the rise of critical talmudic studies and the *Wissenschaft des Judentums* movement in the nineteenth century, this consensus changed, and the debate was revived with scholars taking positions on both

---

late Second Temple period. During the rabbinic period, a commentary on the Megilah circulated but no longer survives. The surviving Scholion, a hybrid of two earlier commentaries, was created in the ninth or tenth century CE. On both the Megilah and the Scholion, see Vered Noam, *Megillat Taanit Ve-ha-Scholion* (Jerusalem, 2004), esp. 333–63.

11. On rabbinic Babylonia, see Shai Secunda, "The Sassanian 'Stam': Orality and the Composition of Babylonian Rabbinic and Zoroastrian Legal Literature," in *The Talmud in its Iranian Context*, ed. C. Bakhos and M. Rahim Shayegan (Berlin, 2010), 140–60; on the geonic period, see Dafna Ephrat and Yaakov Elman, "Orality and the Institutionalization of Tradition: The Growth of the Geonic Yeshiva and the Islamic Madrasa," in *Transmitting Jewish Traditions: Orality, Texuality and Cultural Diffusion*, ed. Y. Elman and I. Gershuni (New Haven, 2000), 107–37, esp. 110–15 and 124–28; and Uziel Fuchs, *Talmudam shel Geonim: Yaḥasam shel Geonei Bavel le-Nusaḥ ha-Talmud ha-Bavli [The Geonic Talmud: The Attitude of Babylonian Geonim to the Text of the Babylonian Talmud]* (Jerusalem, 2017), esp. 51–58. Cf. Brody, *Geonim*, 156–61.

12. Benjamin M. Lewin, ed., *Otzar Ha-Geonim: Teshuvot Geonei Bavel U-Peirusheihem 'al-pi Seder Ha-Talmud* [Thesaurus of Geonic Responsa and Commentaries following the Order of the Talmud Tractates], 13 vols. (Haifa, 1928; Jerusalem, 1944), vol. 7, Yevamot, no. 170. Translation cited from Brody, *Geonim*, 157.

13. Brody, *Geonim*, 157: "Although this is clearly an exaggeration, what the Gaon seems to mean is that the majority of the academicians do not know what a written Talmud looks like, or at least are not accustomed to making use of one; rather, their knowledge of the Talmudic text derives from an unbroken chain of oral tradition." See as well Elman's insightful analysis of the statement in Ephrat and Elman, "Orality," 127–28; and compare Fuchs, *Talmudam*, 76–77, on the phenomenon he calls *tofa'at ba'al ha-shemu'ah*.

sides.[14] In the twentieth century the debate continued, with the most consequential position taken by J. N. Epstein.[15] Basing himself on the observable (and remarkable) stability of the mishnaic text, Epstein argued that there must have existed a written version of the Mishnah for the text to have that stability *even though*, he acknowledged, in public settings (i.e. in an academy) the Mishnah was never taught from a written text but always through the medium of the "Tanna." This figure—a "living book," in Saul Lieberman's memorable phrase[16]—was selected for his task for his extraordinary memory; his job was to memorize the entire Mishnah and other tannaitic teachings and then to repeat these teachings orally before the master and his disciples in the course of live academic sessions.[17] Epstein also acknowledged that the traditions as memorized, transmitted, and broadcast by the Tannaim enjoyed greater authority than the written text of the Mishnah—a fact that explained, he argued, why there is not a single reference in all rabbinic literature to a sage ever consulting a written document of the Oral Torah to solve a textual problem.[18]

Epstein was not alone in his view. Lieberman essentially accepted his argument although, in his typical fashion, he finessed it by seeking to contextualize the phenomenon within contemporaneous Greco-Roman book culture.[19] Epstein and others, as support for their view that the Mishnah existed in written form, had already cited talmudic passages that referred to rabbis writing and reading *halakhot* and other texts in *pinkasim* (writing-tablets, from the Greek *pinax*, pl. *pinakes*), in book-rolls (like *sifrei d'aggadeta*), in a *megilat setarim* (a secret or private scroll), or in notes written by students in *pinkasim* or on walls.[20] Lieberman built on these passages and

---

14. On scholarship on the topic in the eighteenth and nineteenth centuries, see the chapter by Ḥanan Gafni in this book.

15. Jacob N. H. Epstein, *Mavo le-Nusaḥ Ha-Mishnah* [*Introduction to the Mishnaic Text*], 2 vols. (1948; 3rd ed. Jerusalem, 2000), 2:673–726.

16. Saul Lieberman, *Hellenism in Jewish Palestine: Studies in the Literary Transmission, Beliefs, and Manners of Palestine in the I Century B.C.E.–IV Century C.E.* (New York, 1950), 90. Moulie Vidas, "What Is a *tannay*?," *Oqimta* 7 (2021): 24, has updated Lieberman's phrase to "a living audiobook." The well-known talmudic characterization is *tsana de-malei sifrei*, "a basket full of books" (bMegilah 28b).

17. See Lieberman's entire discussion of the Tanna, *Hellenism*, 88–90. Cf. Epstein, *Mavo*, 673–78.

18. Epstein, *Mavo*, 702.

19. Lieberman, *Hellenism*, 83–99. Indeed, he finessed it to the extent that it is also possible to take his argument as endorsing the oral publication stance while admitting the existence of written copies as well.

20. For *pinkasim*, see for example yMa'as 2.4, 49d; bMen 70a; bShab 156a; yKil 1.1, 27a. For book-rolls/*sifrei d'aggadeta*, Y. Shabbat 16.1, 15c; cf. Y. Berakhot 5.1 9a. I have

went further by identifying these inscribed texts with the *hypomnemata*, private notes used by Hellenistic and Late Antique Greco-Roman masters and disciples to help them compose their literary works. As Lieberman emphasized, these private notes had no legal or other such authority of their own—which is why they too are never cited authoritatively—but they did serve as the basis for later "corrected" editions of works.[21] So too, Lieberman argued, R. Judah—and before him, R. Meir, and before R. Meir, his teacher R. Akiba, each of whom is said by talmudic tradition to have previously compiled Mishnah collections of his own (which R. Judah later built upon)—consulted the *hypomnemata* of their disciples in order to produce successive editions of which R. Judah's was simply the last.[22]

None of these editions, however, were *published*. Basing his claim on the absence of any reference to a sage ever consulting a written text in cases of doubt or controversy, Lieberman proposed that the Mishnah (including those collections going back to R. Akiba and R. Meir) was not published in writing but in the persons of the *Tannaim*, those professional memorizers, the "living books."[23] On the basis of an inspired reading of *b'Eruvin* 54b, which portrays a scenario in which Moses taught the Mishnah to Aaron, Aaron's children, the Elders, and then all of Israel, with each group repeating it to the next one in the presence of the others, Lieberman argued that the rabbis used a similar mnemonic pedagogical procedure in training the Tannaim to memorize successive new editions of the Mishnah.[24] The final edition of the Mishnah may, then, have been originally based upon earlier written private notes, but it was itself published and later transmitted exclusively orally from memory.

---

translated *sefer/sifra* here as roll (scroll) because it is unlikely though not impossible that the rabbis used codices; see Sifre Dev, 160 where *niyar*, papyrus, could conceivably refer to a bifolium of papyrus sheets (because the book of Deuteronomy could never be written on a single piece of papyrus). If *sefer/sifra* is a roll, rabbis could also have used either a horizontal scroll or a vertical one (*rotulus*). For the *megilat setarim*, the same anecdote is repeated in bShab 6b, 96b; bBM 92a; as Shamma Friedman has reminded me, contrary to the frequent usage by many scholars of the term *megillot setarim*, we have evidence for only a single *megilat setarim*. For writing on the wall, yKil 1.1, 27a.

21. Lieberman, *Hellenism*, 87. For a much fuller description of the use of hypomnemata in the Late Antique world, see Matthew D. C. Larsen, *Gospels before the Book* (New York, 2018), and my discussion drawing on Larsen below. For some cautionary words about drawing conclusions from *hypomnemata* to the Mishnah, see Hezser, "Mishnah and Ancient Book Production," 174–78.

22. Lieberman, *Hellenism*, 95–96.

23. Lieberman, 88–94.

24. Lieberman, 93 and note 77. To be sure, Lieberman writes that the direction of inspiration went the other way, and that the talmudic account was probably taken from the practice of the academies.

More recently the consensus has turned again. In 2005 Yaakov Sussmann published a book-length article with the title "Oral Law—Taken Literally: The Power of the Tip of a Yod," later reissued as a book.[25] A scholarly tour de force, Sussmann's work is extraordinary if only for its comprehensive collection of nearly every rabbinic source even remotely touching on the question of the Oral Torah (including many that are not the run-of-the-mill examples usually cited), as well as an incredible bibliography of virtually everything written on the topic since the geonic period until the last third of the twentieth century; unhappily, more recent scholarship is given less attention, especially if it runs counter to Sussman's main argument.

Sussmann's argument is a sustained polemic on behalf of the *exclusive and absolute* orality of the transmission of the Mishnah, and of the Oral Law more generally, until the late geonic period. The various *hypomnemata* that Lieberman had identified—the *pinkasim, megillot setarim,* and *sifrei de-aggadeta*—are in Sussmann's view entirely incidental, occasional inscriptions of no significance in the history of the composition or transmission of the Mishnah. The very stability of the mishnaic text, which Epstein used as virtual proof that a written text must have existed, is utilized by Sussmann to argue precisely the opposite point: to prove how exact and disciplined the memory of the Tannaim must have been, and to show their selfless dedication and devotion to the study of *Torah she-be'al peh* and to preserving the Mishnah in its pristine form. In making his case, Sussmann draws upon his encyclopaedic knowledge of the text-tradition of rabbinic literature and his supreme skills as a philologist in order to refute many of Epstein's supposed proofs for the existence of written texts of the Oral Torah, the Mishnah in particular, often with stunning success. At the same time, Sussmann's case is more slippery than it seems, because he veers between on the one hand repeatedly emphasizing that he is addressing only the question of the Mishnah's publication, and on the other generalizing about the entire Oral Torah and works far beyond the Mishnah. Further, his unconditional refusal to allow for any nuanced exceptions to his rule that the Oral Torah never was inscribed has the effect, in practice, of weakening the strength of his overall argument.

Sussmann's article is a prime example of what Elizabeth Shanks Alexander has called a "literary" or "purist" approach to the question of orality.[26] The "literary" approach, in Alexander's characterization, views an

25. Sussmann, "Oral Law" and *Oral Law*. All references are to the original article. The rather enigmatic subtitle derives from bMenaḥot 34a, but in context the phrase "the tip of the Yod" actually refers to the graphological basis of Sussman's refutation of Epstein's major proof for the early inscription of the Mishnah; see "Oral Law," 221–25.

26. Shanks, "Orality," 48–51; and more expansively, Shanks, *Transmitting Mishnah*, 1–29.

orally transmitted text in exactly the same way as it does a fixed, inscribed text, while simultaneously insisting that the two modes of transmission—oral and written—are mutually exclusive and incapable of co-existing, let alone interacting. Even scholars like Epstein or Lieberman, who admit to the existence of private or unofficial or unauthoritative written texts, still subscribe to a slightly less doctrinaire version of the literary approach in as much as they accept an inherent opposition between orality and inscription. The novelty in Epstein's and Lieberman's conceptions of the Mishnah's composition is that where in most other cases inscription replaces orality, they view it as working in the other direction. Still, they do not see the two modalities of transmission interacting in any way.

In contrast to the literary approach, Shanks proposes a second contemporary approach to orality which we might call "performative," borrowing a term that Steven Fraade has used to describe "the oral circulatory system of teaching and study of Oral Torah."[27] This approach does not see orality and inscription as operating in totally separate spheres or as being inherently exclusive, but rather as two modalities between which most rabbinic texts circulate, moving from the oral to the written and sometimes back to the oral. This approach is heavily indebted to the relatively new field of oral literature, as pioneered first by Milman Parry and Albert Lord in their studies of Homeric and Slavic oral epic poetry, and then continued by scholars like Ruth Finnegan in the study of the ballad.[28] Shanks herself is a proponent of this approach, but it is especially identified with the work of Martin Jaffee, who has shown how both writing and oral performance figure in the composition of rabbinic texts (and, as a result, must also figure in their study).[29] Like Lieberman, Jaffee also enlists comparative evidence from the Greco-Roman world to bolster his model, but in his own case he used the *progymnasmata*, the rhetorical exercises developed and used during the Second Sophistic to train students in oratory.[30] Even more

27. Fraade uses "performative" in his article, Steven Fraade, "Literary Composition and Oral Performance in Early Midrashim," *Oral Tradition* 14 (1999): 36, while the latter phrase is found in: Steven Fraade, *From Tradition to Commentary: Torah and Its Interpretation in the Midrash Sifre to Deuteronomy* (Albany N.Y., 1991), 19; both are cited by Elizabeth Shanks Alexander, *Transmitting Mishnah* (Cambridge, 2006), 22.

28. Shanks, *Transmitting*, 9–18.

29. Martin Jaffee, *Torah in the Mouth: Writing and Oral Tradition in Palestinian Judaism 200 B.C.E.–400 C.E.* (New York and Oxford, 2001), 102–24.

30. Jaffee, *Torah in the Mouth*, 126–52. Jaffee here was drawing upon a considerable amount of earlier scholarship on the *chreia* or anecdote done by scholars like Harry Fishel. On connections between Avot and the Second Sophistic, see Amnon Tropper, *Wisdom, Politics, and Historiography: Tractate Avot in the Context of the Graeco-Roman Near East* (Oxford, 2004), 136–46.

importantly, Jaffee sought to demonstrate that the orality or writtenness of the Oral Torah—rabbinic tradition—is not merely an issue relating to the text's transmission. Rather, for Jaffee the real significance of orality to rabbinic tradition lies in the social reality created by the performance of orality, namely the bond between the master sage and the disciple to whom the sage orally imparted Oral Torah through his physical presence.[31] The meaningfulness of this relationship—the phrase *shimush talmidei ḥakhamim* does not even begin to capture it—was as important as the content of any single rabbinic tradition.

For all their differences, what the two approaches I have just described share is a basic ahistoricity in regard to their conception of Oral Torah; that is, they both assume that the concept was static, not subject to historical development or pressures. By this I do not mean that these scholars fail to allow for historical changes in attitudes towards the inscription of Oral Torah; how could they when it is eventually inscribed?[32] Rather, my point is that none of these scholars seriously considers the likelihood that views on textuality itself (whether oral or inscribed), among rabbis or gentiles, may have changed radically between the early tannaitic and geonic periods, or between Greco-Roman Palaestina and Sassanian Babylonia. More seriously, for all their valuable contributions to our appreciation of the complicated question of the Mishnah's publication, their solutions to the problem are each flawed in a different way. Epstein cannot adequately explain the lack of any reference to a written text of the Mishnah or of a single explicit indication of a sage consulting a written text. While Lieberman persuasively links the various references to writing *halakhot* in *pinkasim* and *megilot setarim* to hypomnemata kept by sages or their disciples, the notion of oral publication has (so far as I know) no parallel in any ancient book culture, and certainly not in Greco-Roman late antiquity, though texts certainly circulated orally *after* they were inscribed, a point to which I will return.[33] Further-

31. Jaffee, *Torah in the Mouth*, 147–52.

32. See Sussmann, "Oral Torah," 326–27 n. 25 in particular. Jaffee as well, *Torah in the Mouth, passim*, acknowledges historical changes, particularly by emphasizing that he is dealing only with tannaitic and amoraic Palaestina, and he does try to trace some historical developments between these periods; but the history of Oral Torah is in no way his theme.

33. On the lack of parallels, see Hezser, "Mishnah and Ancient Book Production," 182–83. To be sure, as noted by Ishay Rosen-Zvi, "Orality, Narrative, Rhetoric: New Directions in Mishnah Research," *AJS Review* 32 (2008): 241–42, the absence of a comparative parallel is not necessarily a weakness or defect. The rabbis (as Sussmann passionately argues) may indeed have been different from everyone else in the world, a point to which I will return. The problem with Lieberman's notion of oral publication is that he

more, in a very recent article, Moulie Vidas, through a painstaking study of every occurrence in literature of the land of Israel, tannaitic or amoraic, of the word *tannay* (or *tanna*), has cast serious doubt as to whether the term ever refers to a professional reciter of tradition or Mishnah.[34] Sussmann's polemic against Epstein, which relies even more heavily on the figure of the Tanna, is susceptible to the same criticism if Vidas is correct.[35] There is also deductive evidence pointing to the inscription of rabbinic literature at an early date that Sussmann treats dismissively or not at all, to which I will return shortly.[36] Finally, Jaffee's and Alexander's "performative" approach must also contend with the absence of any explicit evidence to support the existence or use of written texts *before* the compilation of the Mishnah, although in their respective monographs both scholars deduce through analyses of texts some passages that appear to have existed in written form, as opposed to others which appear more oral in form and sometimes in content. On the face of it, their "circulatory" model seems more plausible, if only because it is more flexible, but in practice their models work best with only a few types of mishnaic material—narratives and lists in particular—but not so well with others, like apodictic statements, dialogical disagreements, and legal disputes. Their argument for the social impact of the bond between master and disciple created by oral transmission of the Mishnah (and the Oral Law in general) is compelling, but it seems to be more of an effect or consequence of the mode of transmission than an explanation for it.

---

explicitly invokes the notion of an oral *ekdosis* as a known phenomenon in the Greco-Roman world, but he does not cite any evidence to support his assertion, and all his references to editions based on hypomnemata primarily refer to much earlier Alexandrian scholiasts like Aristarchus (3rd–2nd c. BCE); see *Hellenism*, p. 92 and notes 72–76.

34. Vidas, "What is a *tannay*?" Vidas deals with two other purported meanings of the term in literature of the land of Israel—as referring to a sage who is mentioned in the tannaitic corpus or lived in the period preceding the completion of the Mishnah; or as a person who ordered or arranged traditions associated with the Mishnah. Vidas does not find any evidence for the usage of the term in any of these sentences in literature of the land of Israel and argues that claims to the contrary derive from Babylonian sources of a different time and place. The section of the article dealing specifically with the question of the professional reciter is on pp. 24–54.

35. This does not by any means rule out the possibility that individual sages had assistants who served them as their personal "Tannaim," for example R. Yitzhak bar Avdumi (Yitzhak Rova), who served this role for R. Judah (yMS 5:1, 55d) and taught the Mishnah to Rav before he emigrated to Babylonia; see Sussmann, "Oral Torah," 306–7 and note 38. The figure may be comparable to the amanuensis (typically, however, a slave or freedman).

36. For a very judicious evaluation of Sussmann's project, see Uziel Fuchs, "The Power of the Big Picture: Reflections on Yaakov Sussman's *"Torah She-be'al Peh, Peshutah ke-Mashma'ah*," (Hebrew), *Mada'ei Ha-Yahadut* 55 (2020): 209–30.

As this brief survey of the scholarship to date and the available evidence suggests, the question of how the Mishnah was composed—whether orally or in writing—may be unresolvable at this point. The evidence is at once too contradictory and insufficient, and the scholarship to date has too frequently relied upon conjectures that are simply not backed up by the existing evidence. In recent years, however, there have been some new developments in our understanding about the composition of other early rabbinic documents as well as advances in our knowledge about Greco-Roman book culture during the early rabbinic period which, if they cannot definitively resolve the oral-written debate, may shed light on some other related questions: What were the social conditions within which the Mishnah was composed? Why, and for what purpose? And most importantly, perhaps, when we speak about the publication of the Mishnah, what kind of "book"—I use the term in the widest possible sense to include all possible platforms (scrolls, codices, even oral transmission)—do we imagine the Mishnah to have been? Any conclusions drawn from the comparative material will necessarily be speculative, but they are all worth exploring if only to possibly open up new avenues to investigate old problems.

Before we turn to these questions, however, I want to consider the single passage in rabbinic literature that has done the most in the past to shape the debate over orality and inscription. The passage of *bTemurah* 14b is the *locus classicus* for the Bavli's statement of the prohibition on writing down Oral Torah. It does not deal with the Mishnah per se but, as we will see, an analysis of its sources will provide us with a historical frame for understanding the development of the ban on writing the Oral Torah, within which we can then place the question of the composition of the Mishnah.

The *Temurah* passage occurs as part of a controversy about the permissibility of making libation offerings in the Temple. In the course of the discussion, the Talmud relates that when R. Dimi, a fourth-century amora who carried traditions between Babylonia and Palaestina, went from Babylonia to the land of Israel, he found R. Jeremiah, a Palaestinian sage, relating a tradition about these offerings in the name of R. Joshua ben Levi, a Palaestinian amora of the first half of the third century, whereupon he said, "If I had a messenger, I would have written a letter and sent it to R. Joseph in Babylonia." At this point, the Talmud asks:

And if he had a letter, could he have sent it?
    [1] Did not R. Abba the son of R. Ḥiyya b. Abba report in the name of R. Yoḥanan: Those who write the *halakhot* (laws) are like one who burns the Torah, and he who learns from them receives no reward.

[2] R. Judah b. Naḥmani, the expositor (*meturgeman*) of Resh Lakish, expounded (*darash*): One verse says: "Write down for yourself these words" (Ex 34:37) and one verse says, "For according to (*ki 'al-pi*, lit. "by the mouth") these words" (Ex 34:37), in order to teach you that matters [transmitted] orally/from memory (*'al-peh*) you are not permitted to recite from writing (*le-omram bi-khetav*) and those matters that are in writing (*bi-khtav*) you are not permitted to recite from memory (*'al-peh*).

[3] And the Tanna of the School of R. Ishmael taught: Scripture says, "Write down for yourself these words" (Ex 34:37)—these words you may write but you may not write *halakhot* (laws).

[4] They said: Perhaps a new matter is different? For R. Yoḥanan and Resh Lakish read a book of Aggadah (*sifra de-aggadata*) on the Sabbath. For which they offered this interpretation (*ve-darshei hakhi*) [of the verse], "It is time for the Lord to act, for they have made void Your Torah" (Ps 119:126); they said, It is better that [one law] of the Torah be uprooted than that the [whole] Torah should fall into oblivion in Israel.

In its present context, this passage has traditionally been read as offering an extended statement condemning the inscription of the Oral Law, albeit with qualifications.[37] Section 1 above condemns those who write down *halakhot*[38] and those who study *halakhot* from inscribed texts. Sections 2 and 3 offer separate exegeses of the first two-thirds of Ex 34:37 that appear to extend the condemnation (and perhaps even prohibition) to the entire Oral Torah, that is, *all matters* transmitted orally. Section 4 relates testimony about two Palaestinian amoraim who read books of aggadah on the Sabbath, an apparent violation of the rule explicated in the preceding passages; the sages' behavior is then rationalized through a midrash on Ps 119:126 that justifies the abrogation of a prohibition because of a state of emergency. We might call this "the catastrophe theory of writing." The midrash is borrowed from *mBerakhot* 9.5, where it appears as a generalized justification for the abrogation of law in times of emergency in general. The Bavli alone applies it to the case of writing down Oral Torah; nowhere is the midrash used in

---

37. On whether the ban on inscription was explicit or more like an accepted fact, see Sussmann, "Oral Torah," 332–33. Peter Schäfer, "Das 'Dogma' von der mündlichen Torah im rabbinischen Judentum," in Schäfer, *Studien zur Geschichte und Theologie des rabbinischen Judentums* (Leiden, 1978), calls it a "dogma" that was reflected mainly in practice though not necessarily enforced.

38. It is unclear whether the reference here is to individual *halakhot* or to a collection like the Mishnah, which is sometimes referred as *halakhot*.

this way in any Palaestinian source. As an explanation for the Mishnah's in-scription, the catastrophe theory has a remarkable persistence, repeatedly re-surfacing in learned writing about the Mishnah's inscription, most fa-mously in Maimonides, and most recently in Sussmann.[39]

Scholars have long recognized that this section in the Bavli is a confla-tion of different sources, but Yair Furstenberg has shown through an analy-sis of the passage in light of its sources in the Yerushalmi that the original meanings of its components were far different from what the section as a whole has conventionally been taken to mean.[40] In his analysis, Fursten-berg demonstrates that the *Temurah* passage is best approached through its partial parallel in *bGitin* 60b, which contains sections 2 and 3 from above; however, those sections can be traced back to Palaestinian sources that on the basis of exegeses of Ex 34:27 originally dealt with the nature and scope of the revelation of the Oral Torah at Mt. Sinai, not the nature or mode of its transmission. While there may be an intimation in the Yerushalmi of the tradition and interpretation attributed to the School of R. Ishmael (section 3 in *Temurah*), even so, Furstenberg argues, the tradition was not a con-demnation of writing down the Oral Law but a directive addressed by God to Moses alone, intended to prove that Moses received halakhot as Oral To-rah on Sinai. So too, as others have noted, the statement attributed to R. Ju-dah b. Nahmani, Resh Lakish's *meturgeman*, originally did not prohibit in-scribing the Oral Torah but rather reading aloud the Targum, the Aramaic translation, from a written text while the Torah Scroll was being chanted in the service.[41] Finally, the first report (section 1), attributed to R. Yohanan,

39. The source of the catastrophe theory remains to be determined. It is clearly not the Platonic view in the Phaedrus (14, 274c–275b). For Maimonides, see the Introduc-tion to the Mishnah Torah; for Yaakov Sussmann, *"Torah She-be'al Peh, Peshutah ke-Mashma'ah: Koho shel Kotzo shel Yud"* [Oral Law—Taken Literally: The Power of the Tip of a Yod], in *Mehkerei Talmud: Talmudic Studies Dedicated to the Memory of Pro-fessor Ephraim E. Urbach*, vol. 3, ed. D. Rosenthal and Y. Sussmann (Jerusalem, 2005), 209–385, rev. and enlarged ed. (Jerusalem, 2019), 320.

40. Yair Furstenberg, *"The Invention of the Ban against Writing Oral Torah in the Babylonian Talmud,"* AJSReview, 46 (2022):131-159. I wish to thank Yair Furstenberg for allowing me to use his article before its publication. For previous scholarship on the passage, see Epstein, *Mavo*, 696–97; Strack and Stemberger, *Introduction to the Talmud and Midrash*, 32–33.

41. In the parallel in *yMegilah* 4.1 (74d), an anecdote precedes the saying relating how R. Samuel b. R.Yitzhak entered a synagogue and saw a teacher rendering the Tar-gum from a *sifra* ("book"). It is not clear whether *sifra* refers to a Torah scroll (in which case the teacher was not literally reading the Targum from the Torah scroll but merely looking at it while he declaimed the translation, a practice elsewhere prohibited by the rabbis (*Midrash Tanhuma Va-Yera* 5; *bMegilah* 32a), or actually reading a written text of

likening those who write *halakhot* to those who burn Torah, is actually the Bavli's re-writing of Palaestinian traditions using similar language that likens writing blessings (*berakhot*) and aggadah to burning Torah because, Furstenberg persuasively argues, in their original contexts these Palaestinian traditions were literally about running the risk of burning Torah. Since verses of Scripture were often quoted in blessings and in aggadot with midrashim, and according to rabbinic law it is forbidden to violate the Sabbath in order to save written texts of blessings and aggadah from a fire, an inscribed blessing or aggadah would end up being burned in a fire on the Sabbath, and the verses inscribed in them would not be treated with the reverence Scripture requires.[42] Nowhere in Palaestinian sources is this analogy with its condemnation extended to writing halakhot (which rarely required the citation of Biblical verses). That, according to Furstenberg, was the Bavli's innovation.

In summary, in their original contexts in the Yerushalmi, none of the first three passages in *Temurah* had anything to do with a prohibition against the inscription of Oral Torah. Only by reworking these traditions and then clumping them together to serve its own purposes was the Bavli able to turn them into a blanket condemnation of writing down the Oral Torah.

In his masterly analysis of the passage, Furstenberg only deals in passing with the final anecdote (section 4). For our concerns, however, this anecdote is key. The *stam*, the Bavli's editor, was clearly aware of traditions which testified to sages, especially Palaestinian sages like R. Yoḥanan and R. Lakish, reading (and sometimes writing down) written texts of the Oral Torah, and then felt the need to rationalize their "transgression" through the exegesis of Ps 119:126. This rationalization provides us with the backdrop to the belief of Sherira and other Babylonian geonim and later medieval sages that except in the case of emergencies, the Oral Torah was never to be written down, and never was. At the same time, the effective re-dating of the ban to the time of the *editing* of the Bavli, which Furstenberg's analysis accomplishes, also enables us to appreciate why we find these stories of

---

the Targum. Furstenberg, "Invention of the Ban," 15, leans towards the former option. Talya Fishman, "Guarding Oral Transmission: Within and Between Cultures," *Oral Tradition* 25 (2010): 48, argues that the odd locution of Judah b. Nahmani's statement (in a literal translation), "matters that are oral you may not say in writing (*le-omran bi-khetav*)," suggests that the prohibition is only against chanting or reading aloud these non-scriptural texts from a written text, not against inscribing them in, to use her felicitous term, "phantom texts" like *hypomnemata*.

42. Furstenberg does not limit the Palaestinian fear of obliterating Scripture to the specific case of fire on the Sabbath; he sees it as a danger posed by any inscribed text which will eventually decay.

sages, especially Palaestinian sages (but also Babylonians), reading texts of the Oral Torah (and sometimes writing them).[43] More importantly, it can also help us appreciate the significance of two more recent studies: one of another tannaitic *collection*—not a sporadic text—suggesting that it too was inscribed during the amoraic period; and a second study, an analysis of deductive evidence relating to the Mishnah's organization, that also points in the direction of early inscription before the establishment of the ban in Babylonia.

The first of these studies deals with Sifra, the tannaitic midrash on Leviticus, which has a famously confusing organization. As printed today, Sifra is divided without any obvious logic or rationale into *megillot* (scrolls), *dibburim* (pronouncements), *parashiyyot* (sections), and *perakim* (chapters). In a lengthy two-part article, Shlomo Naeh has accounted for these divisions by proposing that the initial primary division into *megillot* stems from the way the book was originally inscribed—into nine actual scrolls, all of similar length.[44] This accords with the usual ancient Mediterranean scribal practice to write a single work (or section of significant length of a literary work) in its own scroll. (For example, the Iliad's 24 books were originally 24 separate scrolls. *Ḥamishah Ḥomshei Torah* were once five separate *ḥomashim*, small scrolls of single Pentateuch books.) Along these lines, Naeh argues that the Sifra was divided into nine separate scrolls, and these *actual* megillot are still preserved in the megillot divisions in our printed edition. (The other divisions are secondary and have to do with the way the Sifra was copied and later printed.)[45] Next, basing himself upon a late tannaitic tradition preserved in *bKidushin* 33a, in which he sees a reference to these nine scrolls, Naeh argues that the nine-fold division of Sifra into nine scrolls already existed in the late tannaitic period. Hence, he concludes, the Sifra must have been written down at least as early as this time.[46]

---

43. At least through the 4th c. See bBer 23a (= yBer 2.4c); bBer 23b; bSan 57b; bḤul 60b; bBB 52a; bShevu 46b; all in reference to books of aggadah. Cf. as well yBer 5.1. The one example of a written halakhic text is the *megilat setarim* of the Palaestinian Tanna Issi b. Yehuda that Rav is said to have found in R. Hiyya's house (with the same anecdote repeated in bShab 6b, 96b; bBM 92a).

44. Shlomo Naeh, "The Structure and Division of Midrash Torat Kohanim, 1: Scrolls (Towards a Codicology of Early Talmudic [Literature]" (Hebrew), *Tarbiz* 66 (1997): 483–515.

45. Shlomo Naeh, "The Structure and Division of Midrash Torat Kohanim, 2: Parashot, Perakim, Halakhot" (Hebrew), *Tarbiz* 69 (2000): 55–104.

46. For a critique of Naeh's argument, see Sussmann, "Oral Torah," 373–75, although his criticisms essentially boil down to whether a single case, even if persuasive, should alter the entire picture dictated by every other source. Sussmann's strongest criticism to my mind is his observation that if indeed the Sifra did exist in writing, why did the Stam

If Naeh's argument is correct, the Sifra may offer evidence of the sort that the Mishnah does not provide—*virtual* material evidence—as noted at the beginning of the chapter. There is, in addition, a second instance of deductive evidence that points to the likelihood of inscription by the amoraic period. It has long been known that the various *masekhtaot* (tractates) in the six *sedarim* (orders) of the Mishnah are organized in descending order by the number of chapters in each tractate.[47] In a recent article, however, Menachem Kahana has shown that two passages (in *bShabat* 31a and Midrash Tehillim 19.14) record two separate sequences of ordering for the six sedarim themselves, each of which contains two sets of three orders in different sequences.[48] Each of the two sets contains 30 tractates, so that both orders in total end up containing 60 tractates. R. Tanhuma's sequence even has the sedarim ordered chiastically.

Now, while organization of masekhtaot into sedarim by themes is essentially a matter of logical grouping, and can be accomplished in an environment of oral transmission, the sequential ordering of the sedarim is essentially spatial (and much more arbitrary). As Menachem Haran has shown with respect to the ordering of biblical books, this kind of sequential ordering only makes sense with written texts that need to be ordered so as to be kept together in some kind of spatial collection, like a library or an archive.[49] Orally transmitted collections (especially of legal material) can be organized non-sequentially because each tractate is its own unit, and it doesn't matter where the tractates are placed inside the human mind (even if the mind is a memory palace). In fact, Shlomo Naeh made this argument regarding the sequence of tractates within sedarim.[50] It is arguably even more evident in the case of the order of the sedarim, especially for R. Tan-

---

have to resort to a case of two sages reading a *sifra de-aggadeta*? It is possible of course that the Sifra as a written text may not have been known in Babylonia. In contrast, Menachem Kahana, in "Halakhic Midrashim," in S. Safrai *The Literature of the Sages* (Assen, 2006), 79 n. 368, points out that Naeh's argument demonstrates only that the Sifra existed in writing in Babylonia. I thank Yitz Landes for pointing me to this reference.

47. Epstein, *Mavo*, 980–87.

48. Menachem Kahana, "The Arrangement of the Orders of the Mishnah" (Hebrew), *Tarbiz* 76 (2007): 29–40.

49. Menachem Haran, "On Archives, Libraries and the Order of the Biblical Books," *Journal of the Ancient Near Eastern Society of Columbia University* 22 (1993): 51–61 (= *Hamikra Birei Mefarshav: Sefer Zikaron LeSarah Kamin*, ed. S. Japhet [Jerusalem, 1993], 223–34).

50. Naeh, "Structure and Division," 507 n. 117. Naeh also argues there that the statement *"ein seder le-mishnah"* in reference to the order of tractates (bBK 102a = bAZ 7a) makes sense only if other sages claim that there is an order or sequence to the tractates.

huma's chiastic ordering, which only makes sense with written texts.[51] To be sure, the word *seder*, unlike *megilah* (in the case of Sifra), has no material textual connotation; on the other hand, *masekhet*, which we translate as tractate, is etymologically equivalent to the Latin *textus*; both terms originally refer to something woven together, hence a composition.

The uncertain sequence of the sedarim and the masekhtaot in the Mishnah brings us to an even more basic question: What exactly are the parameters of the text we are discussing, and what sort of work is the Mishnah? According to Ma'agarim, the *Historical Dictionary of the Hebrew Language*, the Mishnah contains 188,621 words. To put that number into some perspective, the Pentateuch contains 80,054 words. The Mishnah, in other words, is a substantial if not monumental work, though relatively small in comparison with other classical rabbinic works (like the Babylonian Talmud).[52] Its size must be included as a factor when considering the question of its transmission as an oral or written document, even if it is not a determining criterion.[53]

So must the question of the Mishnah's genre. Over the past century, scholars have discussed and debated various generic possibilities of characterizing the Mishnah, as a law-code, a study-text, or a collection of teachings, but without being able to come to any conclusive or satisfying agreement on the question.[54] Given its substantial length, however, and its all-encompassing vision of Jewish existence, ranging from the most personal and mundane matters (a husband's duties to his wife, the daily liturgy, laws of civil damages) to the least practical (like those relating to the Temple cult and matters of purity and impurity), it might be more useful to consider the Mishnah under the rubric of ancient encyclopaedism. As Jason König and Greg Woolf have defined the term, encyclopaedism represents "the idea of comprehensive and systematic knowledge-ordering"; as a rubric, it encompasses a wide range of works from antiquity to the Renaissance that cannot be easily defined generically except for their interest in organizing

---

51. Kahana argues that R. Tanhuma's chiastic ordering was the original one selected by R. Judah and that Resh Lakish's more arbitrary sequence won out eventually because of the oral transmission of the Mishnah; but this seems to miss the point that the very idea of sequence here makes sense only if there was a written text at some point.

52. According to Ma'agarim, the Tosefta contains 304,097 words; the Yerushalmi, 695,910; and the Bavli, 1,739,595.

53. Fuchs, "The Power of the Big Picture," 14.

54. For the best survey of the different types, see Elman, "Order, Sequence, and Selection: The Mishnah's Anthological Choices," in *The Anthology in Jewish Literature*, ed. D. Stern (New York, 2004), 53–80.

knowledge.[55] The Mishnah, with its self-conscious ordering of the otherwise unsystematic contents of *Torah she-be'al peh*, clearly falls under this rubric. Indeed, in the light of other examples of ancient or late antique encyclopaedism, such as Varro's *Divine Antiquities* or Pliny's *Natural History*, the Mishnah and Tosefta do not appear quite as unique or singular as they are often taken to be, even considering their mode of oral transmission.[56] Like the other ancient encyclopaedic works, both tannaitic compositions can be seen as outgrowths of what König and Woolf call "the bookworld," even if this is, admittedly, an odd locution in the case of the Mishnah. The "bookworld" is a world in which, König and Woolf write, past and more contemporary authorities "coexisted in timeless proximity . . . an imaginary place, a construct created and shared by the educated, whose possession of it made them into an imaginary community of sorts," in which "the 'timelessness' of debate was an artefact deliberately created."[57] Any student of the Mishnah will recognize in it a similar "timelessness of debate" as an "artefact deliberately created." And like these other works, the compilation of the Mishnah can be seen as a reaction to the overgrowth of its "bookworld," to the problem of having "too much to know," the proliferation of traditions and authorities and the need to organize and bring them into some kind of ordering.[58]

If we think of the Mishnah as an encyclopaedic work, we can begin to discuss its material character by distinguishing between its composition and its transmission. There is virtually no disagreement that the Mishnah was publicly transmitted and always taught orally down until the geonic period. The more problematic questions concern the Mishnah's composition, initial publication, and circulation, whether these processes were oral or written. Here recent scholarship on ancient book-history may be of help in clarifying the issues, if not fully solving the problem.

We can begin with what the idea of an "edition" would have meant in the third century C. E. This question was first raised by Lieberman when he

55. *Encyclopaedism from Antiquity to the Renaissance*, ed. J. König and G. Woolf (Cambridge, 2013), 23. It is only to be regretted that this superb volume does not include a chapter on Jewish encyclopaedism, which would have enhanced the book's other contributions enormously.

56. See Duncan Macrae, *Legible Religion: Books, Gods, and Rituals in Roman Culture* (Cambridge, 2016), 79–97, who makes an enlightening comparison between Varro's *Divine Antiquities*, Cicero's *On the Gods*, and the Mishnah as works of Roman "civil religion," on the grounds that they all display a common "drive to organize religious culture in textual terms" (87) and employ similar rhetorical strategies and literary techniques to do so.

57. König and Woolf, *Encyclopaedism*, 33–34.

58. König and Woolf, *Encyclopaedism*, 35. Cf. Lieberman, *Hellenism*, 92–93.

asked how R. Judah prepared an "edition," an *ekdosis*, of the Mishnah.[59] As Lieberman noted, there were two ways in which editions of literary works were generally published: either by mass copying or by depositing the work in a library, where it could be consulted in cases of controversy. Since, however, there is no reference in all rabbinic literature to anyone ever consulting a written copy of the Mishnah, Lieberman argued that the Mishnah could not have been published in writing; instead, he proposed it was orally published by Tannaim, the professional memorizers. As noted earlier, however, these claims are problematic. First, there is no evidence for oral publication of this sort in the Greco-Roman world, and recent scholarship has seriously called into question whether the Tannaim mentioned in Palaestinian sources even designate professional memorizers. Furthermore, works were primarily deposited in libraries not so that they could be used to check other copies for accuracy, but in order to be copied.[60] An ancient edition was typically "a single, unique copy of a text," and when copies of an edition were made, they were relatively few in number.[61] Still, once a work left its author's hands or was deposited in a library or archive, the author effectively lost control of the book (a point to which we will return).

Lieberman made a very important contribution in identifying the various written texts used by rabbis—the *pinkasim, sifrei d'aggadeta*, and the *megilat setarim*—with the *hypomnemata* employed by Greco-Roman writers, the private notes that as he wrote had no legal authority or standing of their own.[62] *Hypomnemata* were not, however, sporadic or occasional phenomena as the occurrences of the terms corresponding to them in rabbinic literature may suggest. Many texts circulated in the Greco-Roman world in unrevised or non-final states. A recent study by Matthew D. C. Larsen has vastly enlarged our understanding of the wide and pervasive use of *hypomnemata* and their Latin equivalent, *commentarii*, in the first centuries in the common era. Both terms could refer to an extremely wide range of texts, from "rough drafts, public records, commentaries, birth announcements, [and]lists" to all sorts of "more fluid, less authored, and less 'bookish' texts—things put down in writing not so much to become literature as

59. Lieberman, *Hellenism*, 85–89.

60. For this account, see Raymond J. Starr, "The Circulation of Literary Texts in the Roman World," *Classical Quarterly* 37 (1987): 215–19; and B. A. van Groningen, "ΕΚΔΟΣΙΣ," *Mnemosyne* 16 (1963): 1–17. For a very similar summary in relation to the Mishnah, see Hezser, "Mishnah and Ancient Book Production," 184–85, though some of my conclusions are slightly different.

61. William A. Johnson, *Readers and Reading Culture in the High Roman Empire: A Study of Elite Communities* (New York, 2010), 179.

62. Lieberman, *Hellenism,* 87–88.

to be memoranda."[63] As such, these types of writings stood in an ambiguous relationship between the oral and the written. They were "memorial aids in the absence of the source of teaching," and provided access "to the living voice . . . through the medium of textual objects."[64] What is clear from the large number of examples that Larsen cites and analyzes—from Plato and Plutarch to Cicero, Pliny the Younger, Josephus, Galen, and Damis, to name only a sampling—is that the categories of the *hypomnemata* and *commentarii* encompassed a far larger range of texts that were considered by ancients to be "unfinished," some of them left unfinished intentionally with the plan that they be completed by others.[65] It may be helpful to note that the main subject of Larsen's book is the Gospel of Mark, which he argues was precisely such an "unfinished" text, a type of *hypomnema*, and was recognized and used as such by authors of other gospels and by early Christian readers.

Other recent scholarship has also illuminated our knowledge about the production of editions of learned books, including classical texts, compilations of information, anthologies of various sorts, and reference works on arcane subjects that would be of interest to scholars or intelligentsia. In a study of papyrus documents and book rolls from the first two centuries found at Oxyrhynchus in Egypt, William Johnson has identified a group of texts which include correspondence and scholar's texts (nearly all of them literary), some of which have marginal annotations (including attributed textual variants), and that reflect, in Johnson's words, "a circle of readers with scholarly interests" who "pursue their interests as a group." These readers collected texts in which they were collectively interested; Johnson has letters showing how they ordered copies to be made or purchased, and while their books were privately owned, they were bought for the group's collective interests and shared among themselves. Johnson goes on to describe how he sees this group at work:

> [T]he presence of textual variants in multiple hands seems likely to be, in some sense, the result of repeated group discussion and analysis of the text. That does not mean to imply that individuals do not also interact individually with texts . . . But many indicators seem to point to a typical mode of scholarly behavior in which the reading and study and analysis of difficult texts is constructed as a collective endeavor. As we have seen, that group work would itself include a variety of activities: not only the reading of *hypomnemata* but also col-

63. Larsen, *Gospels Before the Book*, 11.
64. Larsen, 32, 91.
65. Larsen, 19.

lation against other copies of the text, especially copies of particular value; the reading of works that provided background or ancillary information, such as [he goes on to list various works which inspire] vigorous discussion of points of style, structure, convention, as well as (to infer from the papyrus annotations) discussion of the constitution of the text. This scholarly work may well have typically revolved around a central figure—think of Diodorus's circle and the references to Harpocration in that same Oxyrhynchus letter—but the scene is by no means necessarily professional or scholastic: the other men in the cubiculum and at dinner need hardly be scholars in any conventional sense. Rather, the scholarly enterprise, in the second century, seems to have been at least as closely linked to a particular type of cultural elitism and indeed exclusionism, focused on Greek letters, as to professional scholarship.[66]

It is not difficult to imagine the circle of sages around R. Judah, *their* central figure, comparing *hypomnemata*, comparing traditions, collating collections of earlier mishnayot, even receiving oral testimonies in much the same way as Johnson describes for his circle of unconventional scholars.[67] The point I want to make with this admittedly speculative comparison is that the activity surrounding the compilation of the Mishnah was not unique or unprecedented, perhaps especially among those who were not scholars in a conventional sense. To be sure, there is no account in rabbinic literature even close to the one found in the lengthy passage cited above. But we need to be reminded that the preceding paragraph itself is *Johnson's* reconstruction of this circle of scholarly readers at work. Those second-century readers never thought of describing their own work scene any more than the circle around R. Judah thought of describing themselves at work compiling the Mishnah. It is only Johnson's good fortune that the papyri these readers left behind ended up buried in the garbage dump at Oxyrhynchus so that he could imagine and re-construct this scene eighteen centuries later.

66. Johnson, *Readers and Reading Culture*, 191–92.

67. Compare Sherira's description of how Rabbi Judah edited the Mishnah in Lewin, *Iggeret*, 16–31; and Lieberman, *Hellenism*, 89–93. *tEduyot* 1.1–2, though highly truncated, also suggests the beginning of a session of group compilation. On this important passage and related ones, like Sifre Devarim and *tSotah* 7.11–12 (and *bḤagigah* 3b), see most recently Shlomo Naeh, "Omanut Ha-Zikkaron: Mivnim Shel Zikkaron Ve-Tavniyyot Shel Tekst Be-Sifrut Hazal," *Meḥkerei Talmud* 3 (2005): 563–86; and Yair Furstenberg, "Mi-Mesoret Le-Maḥloket: Shinuyei Darkhei Ha-Mesirah Be-Mishnatam shel Tannaim Rishonim," *Tarbiz* 85 (2018): 587–641.

The most noteworthy feature of the scene Johnson paints is its collaborative nature: it is as much about creating a community of readers around a text as it is about producing the text itself. The discourse between its participants is both oral—intensely dialogical in the form of constant discussions and communal reading—and literary, a matter of working with written texts like *hypomnemata* and annotations. The two modes are constantly intertwined in the processes of reading and compilation. Recall, too, that *hypomnemata* and *commentarii* were themselves seen as extensions of a human voice that was simply not present itself.

Whether or not this specific example is convincing or useful, the sheer possibility of drawing it suggests that there still exist unexplored avenues to approach the conditions of the Mishnah's production. There are other things that ancient book history can also teach us that might help clarify the composition and transmission of rabbinic literature. For example, we know that literary works were regularly performed and read aloud before audiences, especially first drafts and unfinished works, both in more and in less elite circles, and that the intersection of the oral and the literary in this sphere of performance was also significant.[68] During the Second Sophistic with its emphasis on public oratory, the oral and the written text interacted even more insistently, especially in genres like the chreia and the anecdote, which moved back and forth between the two modalities.[69] When texts were performed publicly, they were typically memorized, but it is worth remembering that in the ancient world, as in the medieval, texts were written down not in order to be *not* forgotten, but in order to be memorized.[70] Shlomo Naeh's work on memory in rabbinic culture has only begun to show us how deeply immersed the rabbis actually were in the arts of memory, and how deep a role memorial techniques played in rabbinic literature.[71]

This last point brings us to the topic of oral transmission as the primary mode of public and formal instruction. The persistence of oral transmission in classical rabbinic culture cannot be viewed as anything but remarkable. Various reasons have been proposed for the persistence of orality and its maintenance, a number of which were already mentioned directly or in passing. (1) The traditional explanation, as presented already in the *Temu-*

---

68. Starr, "Circulation," 213–15.

69. Simon Goldhill, "The Anecdote," in *Ancient Literacies: The Culture of Reading in Greece and Rome* (New York, 2011), 96–113.

70. Carruthers, *The Book of Memory: A Study in Medieval Culture* (Cambridge, 1990), 8, 16–20, and especially 30–31, for only several treatments of what is the book's overall theme.

71. Naeh,"Omanut Ha-Zikkaron."

rah passage, is to draw a hard and fast line between the Written and the Oral Torahs: those things given in writing you are permitted to write down; those matters given orally must be preserved only by oral transmission. (2) Oral transmission guarantees the personal presence of the sage whose "personhood" is the subject of transmission, as much as the traditions he passes on.[72] (3) After seeing the Hebrew Bible (and the originally Jewish Greek translation of the Hebrew Bible) appropriated by Christianity, the Oral Law was invented and its orality mandated in order to maintain Jewish identity against Christian encroachment; orality thus becomes a mark of insular uniqueness.[73]

An appreciation of ancient book culture suggests still another reason. Oral transmission made it far easier to control access to the text. As already noted, once a written text was released—"published," as it were—its author effectively lost all control over it. Not only could anyone copy it; anyone could alter it as well, and without the author's (or editor's) permission.

Larsen has numerous examples of *hypomnemata*—unfinished texts— that their authors lost control of, or that were accidentally published, or that their authors wished to retract but could not.[74] Because the authors (or editors) had lost control of the text once it left their hands, there was nothing they could do except complain. The physician and philosopher Galen (b. Pergamon 129 CE; d. Rome c. 200–216), one of our richest sources for ancient Greco-Roman book culture, complained frequently. In one of his books about his own books, Galen justified the modesty of his ambitions to become a famous author:

> I long ago realized that if the Muses themselves were to write a book it would still not win more renown than the outpourings of complete imbeciles, and so I never had any ambition that my works might be valued among men. Since, however, as you know, *they were widely disseminated against my wishes* [my italics], I was extremely anxious at the idea of giving my friends a written version of any of the remainder.[75]

---

72. Thus Jaffee, *Torah in the Mouth*, and Alexander, *Transmitting Mishnah*.

73. Israel Jacob Yuval, "The Orality of Jewish Oral Law: From Pegagogy to Ideology," in *Judaism, Christianity, and Islam in the Course of History*, ed. L. Gall and D. Willoweit (Munich, 2011), 237–60; Mark Bregman, "Mishnah Ke-Misterin," *Meḥkerei Talmud* 3 (2005), 101–9.

74. Larsen, *Gospels Before the Book*, 37–58.

75. Galen, *De ord. libr. Suor.* (1, 5–6 Boudon-Millot; 19.50–51 K.), excerpted in Ralph Rosen, "Galen, Satire and the Compulsion to Instruct," in *Hippocrates and Medical Education*, ed. M. Horstmanshoff (Leiden and Boston, 2010), 330.

Elsewhere Galen wrote that things had gotten so bad he resolved to stop publishing altogether, but the desperate need he felt to counter all the misrepresentations of his work compelled him to write and publish still another book in order to refute the misrepresentations![76]

An oral environment of transmission was far more controlled, and controllable. The sage could decide whom he could allow into his disciple-circle, whom he wished to teach or permit to pass on the tradition. As Jed Wyrick has argued, the main anxiety that ancient readers felt, especially in reading canonical or sacred texts, was not whether the texts were sacred or of divine origin or of truly ancient descent, but whether the texts had been corrupted in the course of either transcription or transmission.[77] In this respect, the famous passage in 'Eruvin 54b mentioned earlier—the same passage cited by Lieberman as the model for how the tannaim memorized the Oral Torah[78]— is especially revealing because, as Alexander notes, the process of transmission described in the passage contains built-in safeguards ensuring faithful accurate transmission: after Moses teaches Aaron, Aaron remains next to Moses when he teaches Aaron's sons; after they learn, they too remain next to Moses while he teaches the Elders, and so on.[79] And when the entire cycle is completed, then each of the parties—Aaron, his sons, the Elders, the entire nation—has to go through it on its own, teaching everybody else in the same fashion with the others in the room, with the result that everyone hears and teaches the traditions four times. Within this "very complex choreography" of oral transmission there is no room for corruption.[80]

This rationale for oral transmission may also best fit the historical context, however one views that context. As is well known, historians of ancient Judaism have debated, for the last half-century, the place of rabbinic Judaism in the ancient Greco-Roman world. Minimalists have argued that rabbinic Judaism was essentially a dot in the wider Roman Near East, the rabbinic movement a minuscule upstart in the aftermath of 70 CE consisting of a few ritual experts per generation organized in master-disciple circles of

76. Rosen, "Galen," 330.

77. Jed Wyrick, *The Ascension of Authorship: Attribution and Canon Formation in Jewish Hellenistic and Christian Tradition* (Cambridge, 2004), 80–110. This anxiety does not die out with late antiquity. Essentially, the same anxiety lies behind the phenomenon of *tofaʿat baʿal ha-shemuʿah* described by Uziel Fuchs; see *Talmudam*, 76–77, and Ephrat and Elman, "Orality," 127–28.

78. See Lieberman, Hellenism, 93 and note 77.

79. Elizabeth Shanks Alexander, "The Orality of Rabbinic Writing," in *Cambridge Companion to Rabbinic Literature*, ed. C. E. Fonrobert and M. S. Jaffee (Cambridge, 2007), 38–57.

80. Alexander, *Transmitting Mishnah*, 41.

limited numbers, with little outside influence or impact. The maximalists claim for the movement a long, continuous history going back to the Second Temple period, with a powerful leadership role and a significant following among the common Jewish populace of Roman Palaestina. For the minimalist position, orality would seem to be the most viable mode of transmission, almost the natural one within small master-disciple circles. For the maximalists, orality would seem to be the safest and most efficient in controlling access within a wide population. Once it had taken hold in the first four generations of the tannaitic period, oral transmission would naturally have continued to be practiced by the rabbis in the amoraic period, in Palaestina as well as Babylonia.

To be sure, at that point oral transmission could also easily have taken on additional meanings.[81] Indeed, its use as a modality for controlling access to *Torah She-Be'al Peh* may itself have already been a secondary stage in the evolution of the practice. *Ein kotvin halakhot ba-sefer*— to use the very succinct formulation first recorded in the admittedly late Scholion to Megilat Ta'anit[82]—could possibly mean: "One doesn't *write* halakhot on parchment, that is, *in the way one writes in a Sefer Torah*."[83] As Haran has noted, the verb *q-r-'* in rabbinic Hebrew refers specifically to chanting Scripture aloud with *ne'imah* (bMegilah 32a); so too *k-t-v* may have had a special technical sense (especially when used in conjunction with *sefer*), referring specifically to scribal practices when writing a Sefer Torah.[84] These—and these alone— would be forbidden. Writing per se, as in a hypomnema, which could never be mistaken for a Torah Scroll, was never forbidden. All public or formal teaching of Mishnah, however, *all teaching aloud in a song (zimrah)*,[85] must be done orally, without a text, just like reading Targum.

Such a purpose—to distinguish between the Written and the Oral Torah—may have been the original impetus behind a limited ban, of the sort I have discussed, on inscribing Oral Torah in such a way that it might

81. See Fishman, "Guarding Oral Tradition," 48–50.

82. 4 Tammuz, Noam, *Megillat Ta'anit*, 78; cf. 206–8.

83. Taking *sefer* as meaning "parchment," which would be a synecdoche for a scroll, i.e. a Torah scroll; see mMeg 3.2 and bMen 34a. Of course, sometimes *sefer* does mean a "book," that is, a scroll, as in the example in the next note.

84. Menachem Haran, *Ha-Asupah Ha-Mikrait* [The Biblical Collection] (Jerusalem: Magnes, 1996), 134–35, specifically in reference to *'af ha-qorei bi-sfarim ha-ḥitsonim*, "even one who reads the outside books" (M. Sanhedrin 10.1). In point of fact, Sussmann comes very close to attributing this technical meaning to *k-t-v*; see his remarks in "Oral Torah," 371–72, in reference to bMeg 7a/ bYom 29a and the question in the Talmud as to whether Megillat Esther was or was not *ne'emrah li-kateiv*.

85. bMeg 32a.

have been mistaken for the Written Torah.[86] Its use as a device of controlling access to *Torah she be'al peh* may have been a second stage in its development as a normative mode of transmission. Its guarantee of the sage's presence before his disciples as an embodiment of tradition was certainly an added benefit. Since it was already a device for social control, its exploitation as a polemic tool against Christianity was simply the next step. And once the ideology of a double revelation at Sinai of the Written Torah and the Oral Torah began to crystallize, first in Palaestina and later most intensely in Babylonia, insistence on orality could easily have been enlisted as a blanket prohibition against any type of inscription. But such a complete ban would have been only a late development.

Why are there no references to rabbis consulting written copies of the Mishnah? Because they were *hypomnemata*, and had no authority until rabbis used them and thereby "authorized" them; but the Mishnah, in parts or as a whole, certainly could have circulated in the form of *hypomnemata*, as an unfinished work. In whatever way it circulated, however, in writing or orally, it seems quite clear that the spur for its compilation was not some catastrophic crisis facing the rabbis or the Jews of Palaestina. To the contrary: this appears to have been a moment when the rabbinic class first began to emerge from its relatively isolated position within the larger Jewish society of the land of Israel and to begin to assume a more active role in its leadership.[87] It was a moment of flourishing for the rabbis—indeed, in hindsight, one of the most productive and formative moments in all Jewish history. Whether the Mishnah's purpose was to serve as a law-code, a study-text, or a collection of teachings, its project to organize and textualize rabbinic tradition represented an effort on the rabbis' part at self-definition.[88] As it turned out, it was remarkably successful.

I wish to thank Shamma Friedman, Shlomo Naeh, Jay Harris, Azzan Yadin-Israel, and Yitz Landes for reading earlier drafts of this chapter and offering me valuable corrections, references, and suggestions for revisions.

86. See David Stern, "An Apocalyptic Scroll," forthcoming in *Like One of the Holy Ones: Studies in Honor of Martha Himmelfarb on the Occasion of Her 70th Birthday*, ed. R. Boustan, D. Frankfurter, and A. Y. Reed (Tübingen, 2022).

87. Again, see Hezser, "Mishnah and Ancient Book Production," 188–90, and her consideration of the specific role that R. Judah may have played.

88. See Macrae, *Legible Religion*, 79–97.

21. The Reception of the Mishnah from the Geonic Period to the Age of Print

Uziel Fuchs

INTRODUCTION

As the "iron pillar" of the Oral Law,[1] the Mishnah forms the foundation of several preeminent rabbinic works, principally the Jerusalem and the Babylonian Talmuds. But the Mishnah's very integration into the Talmuds, in conjunction with the Bavli's dominant status as the primary subject of study since the geonic period, significantly reduced the study of Mishnah as an independent composition. Rather, the study of the Mishnah has, for generations, been mainly confined to the context of the Bavli.[2]

Diminished independent study of the Mishnah is apparent as early as the mid-ninth century. *Seder Rav Amram Gaon* enjoins daily recitation of selections from Bible, Mishnah, and Midrash, in line with the talmudic statement: "one should always divide his time into three: [devoting] a third to Mikra, a third to Mishnah, and a third to Talmud" (bKid 30a).[3] Namely, in the ninth century the talmudic injunction received a minimalistic, symbolic interpretation: not to devote substantial amounts of time to Mishnah study but rather to read a single, identical Mishnah every day, as part of the

---

1. Mordecai Margulies, ed., *Midrash Wayyikra Rabbah* (Hebrew; New York and Jerusalem, 1993), 21:5 (2:481)

2. On the predominance of talmudic study in the geonic period, see Robert Brody, "The Talmud in the Geonic Period," in *Printing the Talmud: From Bomberg to Schottenstein,* ed. S. Liberman Mintz and G. M. Goldstein (New York, 2005), 29–35; Brody, *The Geonim of Babylonia and the Shaping of Medieval Jewish Culture* (New Haven and London, 1998), 155

3. Daniel S. Goldschmidt, ed., *Seder Rav Amram Gaon* (Jerusalem, 1971), 7.

daily prayers. To the citation of this statement, the tosafists appended Rabbeinu Tam's explanation for the reduced attention to Bible and Mishnah study: "Because we study the Bavli that is sufficient, for it is a mixture of Bible, Mishnah, and Talmud."[4] At a slightly later date, we find this reality reflected in the Ashkenazic work *Sefer Ḥasidim,* which contrasts the patterns of study in talmudic times with the present: "For then there was one teacher for Mikra, Mishnah, and Talmud; and now we have one for Torah, a second for Prophets, and a third for Talmud."[5] The absence of a teacher for Mishnah in this passage is notable.

Mishnayot were incorporated into the Talmud in one of two ways. In some manuscripts they appear in a body at the beginning of each chapter, followed by the talmudic discussion; in others they take the form of short passages interspersed between the talmudic discussion in the chapter. Most printed editions of the talmudic tractates adhere to the latter structure: a mishnah followed by several lines or pages of the talmudic *sugya,* another mishnah, accompanied by the talmudic *sugya,* and so forth. Only rarely do we find an entire chapter of the Mishnah cited in the opening of a chapter in the printed editions of the Talmud.[6]

That Diaspora study of the Mishnah generally took place in the context of the Babylonian Talmud could, at times, effect a change in the text of the Mishnah as a result of the *sugya* in the Bavli. One well-known example suffices: an alteration in one of the Four Questions asked on the Seder night. The manuscripts of the Mishnah read: שבכל הלילות אנו מטבלין פעם אחת—הלילה הזה שתי פעמים (on all other nights we dip once; on this night we dip twice), whereas some manuscripts of the Mishnah in the Bavli read: שבכל הלילות אין אנו מטבלין אפילו פעם אחת—הלילה הזה שתי פעמים (on all other nights we do not dip even once; on this night we dip twice). In the wake of the discussion and conclusion in the Bavli,[7] this change penetrated the versions of the Mishnah in the Bavli (as well as the Passover Haggadah).

4. Tosafot, b'AZ 19b.

5. Jehuda Wistinetzki, ed., *Sefer Hasidim* (Hebrew; Frankfurt am Main, 1924), 208, par. 820; Yaakov Sussmann, "Manuscripts and Text Traditions of the Mishnah" (Hebrew), in *Proceedings of the Seventh World Congress of Jewish Studies: Studies in Talmud, Halacha and Midrash* (Jerusalem, 1981), 225. See also Israel Ta-Shma, "The Practice of *Talmud-Torah* as a Social and Religious Problem in *Sefer-Hassidim*" (Hebrew), *Bar-Ilan* 14–15 (1977): 110.

6. J. N. Epstein, *Introduction to the Mishnaic Text,* 3d ed., 2 vols. (Hebrew; Jerusalem, 2000), 2:921.

7. Epstein, *Introduction to the Mishnaic Text,* 1:383–84.

In all likelihood, then, during this period youngsters studied mishnayot before embarking on study of the Talmud.[8] It is, moreover, possible that some groups devoted greater time to Mishnah study. Scholars have proposed that alongside the intensive study of the Talmud in the Babylonian geonic academies, there were also "tannaim" whose job was to repeat and study the Mishnah; the evidence is, however, inconclusive.[9]

In any event, from the geonic period on, Mishnah was primarily studied as part of the Bavli. It is clear that from the closing of the Talmud until the sixteenth century, the outstanding feature of Mishnah study in Jewish society is a progressive diminution in its status as an independent work. It is against this backdrop that this chapter seeks to forefront settings and circumstances in which the Mishnah nonetheless retained some of its autonomy, and to examine these particular forms of study.

MANUSCRIPTS OF THE MISHNAH: THEIR AFFINITY TO PALAESTINE AND BYZANTIUM

All the extant full and partial manuscripts of the Mishnah as an independent work are Italian-Byzantine manuscripts belonging to the branch of the land of Israel, as Yaakov Sussmann has shown. He observes: "We therefore have no manuscripts of the Mishnah without commentary—not Ashkenazic, French, Sephardic, or from any other tradition—except for the Italian-Byzantine-Palaestinian ones."[10]

As Sussmann suggests, this is not fortuitous; evidently, the early tradition of independent study of Mishnah persisted in the Greek and Italian regions.[11] Traces of this tradition can also be found among certain Ashkenazic

8. On the sources on Mishnah as an intermediate stage of study, see Sussmann, "Manuscripts and Text Traditions of the Mishnah," 226 n. 53; for a description of Mishnah study among children and adults in fourteenth-century Spain, see Yoel Marciano, *Sages of Spain in the Eye of the Storm: Jewish Scholars of Late Medieval Spain* (Hebrew; Jerusalem, 2019), 50–58.

9. For attestation to "tannaim" who also studied the Bavli, and for sources and bibliography, see Simcha Emanuel, "New Responsa of R. Hai Ga'on" (Hebrew), *Tarbiz* 69 (1999): 105–26; Uziel Fuchs, *The Geonic Talmud: The Attitude of Babylonian Geonim to the Text of the Babylonian Talmud* (Hebrew; Jerusalem, 2017), 40–41, 112.

10. Sussmann, "Manuscripts and Text Traditions of the Mishnah," 221.

11. Sussmann, "Manuscripts and Text Traditions," 235, and the bibliography cited there. For the scholarly literature on manuscripts of the Mishnah, see Günter Stemberger, *Introduction to the Talmud and Midrash*, trans. and ed. M. Bockmuehl, 2nd ed. (Edinburgh, 1996), 141–42. On the Italian origins of the scribe and vocalizer of MS Kaufmann, see Moshe Bar-Asher, *Studies in Mishnaic Hebrew* (Hebrew; Jerusalem, 2009), 1:236. For the possibility that the different mishnaic orders in MS Kaufmann

circles,[12] but the paucity of information on how studies were pursued in either Italy or Ashkenaz obviates any clear conclusion.

COMMENTARIES ON MISHNAIC ORDERS AND TRACTATES NOT EXPLICATED IN THE BAVLI

As noted, because most Diaspora communities studied Mishnah in the talmudic context, mishnaic tractates not explicated in the Bavli were generally neglected and remained unstudied. Nonetheless, it is not entirely the case that these tractates were never studied; there were rabbis, both in Babylonia and Europe, who engaged in the study of these orders and tractates, as seen from the commentaries surveyed below.[13]

Thus, in late-tenth-century Babylonia Sherira Gaon composed a brief commentary on words and halakhic terms in *Zeraʿim* and *Teharot*, in response to a Diaspora Jewish community's request and queries on these mishnaic orders.[14] This indicates that for some scholars, the late-tenth-century horizons of study also included *Zeraʿim* and *Teharot*.

The late geonic period saw the composition of a relatively long commentary on the order of *Teharot*. Attributed in the past to Hai Gaon, this supposition has been definitively rejected by Jacob Nahum Epstein, who thought that this commentary was composed in the late ninth century by a Babylonian sage, and instead suggested several possible authors. In any event, in its current form this work has several layers; one of the editorial stages may have taken place in Italy. Its author also mentions his commentary on *Zeraʿim,* but the text has not survived.[15]

---

were based on different sources, see Michael Ryzhik, "Mishnah Kaufmann: Further Evidence for the Existence of Different Manuscript Traditions," *Revue des Études Juives* 177 (2018): 269–79.

12. See Sussmann, "Manuscripts and Text Traditions," 235 n. 88. Avraham Grossman, *The Early Sages of Ashkenaz: Their Lives, Leadership and Works (900–1096)* (Hebrew; Jerusalem, 2001), 388–89, postulates that an early Ashkenazic sage, Meshulam ben Moses, wrote a commentary on the Mishnah.

13. For a brief survey of the partial and complete commentaries on the Mishnah, see Stemberger, *Introduction to the Talmud and Midrash*, 145–48. For somewhat longer surveys, see Zacharia Frankel, *Introduction to the Mishna: Tosephta, Mechilta, Siphra and Siphri* (Hebrew; Leipzig, 1859), 316–40; Albeck, *Introduction to the Mishna* (Hebrew; Jerusalem, 1959), 238–53.

14. Simha Assaf, ed., *Responsa Geonica: Ex Fragmentis Cantabrigiensibus* (Hebrew; Jerusalem, 1942), 172–79.

15. Jacob Nachum Epstein, *The Gaonic Commentary on the Order Toharoth Attributed to Rav Hay Gaon* (Hebrew; Jerusalem, 1982); Brody, *The Geonim of Babylonia and the*

Tractates lacking talmudic commentaries became the objects of scholarship not just in Babylonia but also in Europe. In the early twelfth century, Rabbi Isaac ben Melchizedek of Siponto (southern Italy) composed a commentary on the orders of *Zeraʿim* and *Teharot*; the commentary on *Zeraʿim* was published, but of the one on *Teharot*, only citations have survived in the works of early authorities.[16]

Several decades later, Rabbi Samson of Sens (France) also composed a commentary on these two orders, making fairly extensive use of Isaac ben Melchizedek's commentary. Comparison of the two underscores the expanded scope of Samson of Sens's commentary. Samson of Sens diverges from the specific mishnah being explicated and, like the tosafists, on more than one occasion also explains the sugya in the Yerushalmi or Bavli.[17] Ephraim E. Urbach postulated a link between the composition of these commentaries and Samson of Sens's aspiration to settle in the land of Israel.[18] Although Urbach's suggestion well explains Samson of Sens's need to explicate and engage in halakhic discussion of the land-of-Israel-dependent commandments in *Zeraʿim*, this is less true for *Teharot*. Perhaps the focus on these two orders emerged from a desire to augment the study of the Bavli. Backing for this supposition comes from the fact that Samson of Sens's commentary on *Zeraʿim* does not include tractate *Berakhot,* and his commentary on *Teharot* omits *Nidah,* both of which are the subject of talmudic commentary in the Bavli.[19]

Additional commentaries on *Zeraʿim* and *Teharot,* part of a similar trend, were composed in late-thirteenth-century Ashkenaz by Rabbi Meir

---

Shaping of Medieval Jewish Culture, 269–70. Because of the many Greek and Arabic words found in the commentary, it has been suggested that it was edited and reworked in southern Italy. See Israel Ta-Shma, *Studies in Medieval Rabbinic Literature* (Hebrew: Jerusalem, 2005), 3:239–40.

16. See Nisan Zaḳs, ed., *Perush ha-Rivmats le-rabenu Yitsḥak b"r Malki Tsedek mi-simfonet le-mishnah zeraʾim* (Jerusalem, 1975).

17. Albeck, *Introduction to the Mishna*, 246; Ephraim E. Urbach, *The Tosafists: Their History, Writings and Method* (Hebrew; Jerusalem, 1986), 305.

18. Urbach, *The Tosafists*, 298.

19. On fragments found in book bindings in European archives that contained a commentary similar to that of Samson of Sens, which may be a reworking of his commentary, see Simcha Emanuel, *Fragments of the Tablets: Lost Books of the Tosaphists* (Hebrew; Jerusalem, 2006), 45–47. Attestation to the study of *Zeraʿim* and *Teharot* as a means of completing the talmudic orders is found in the responsa of Rabbi Isaac ben Samuel, one of the leading twelfth-century tosafists, Rabbi Samson's teacher. The Mishnah is not mentioned in his many responsa, with the exception of mishnayot from *Zeraʿim* and *Teharot*. See Avraham (Rami) Reiner and Pinchas Roth, eds., *Responsa of Rabbi Isaac ben Samuel of Dampierre: A Critical Edition* (Hebrew; Jerusalem, 2019), 22.

of Rothenburg. Touching testimony has survived attesting to Rabbi Meir's work on revising and making additions to his commentary on *Teharot* while imprisoned in Ensisheim.[20] Rabbi Meir's disciple Asher ben Jehiel (Ha-rosh) also wrote commentaries on these orders and apparently on additional tractates as well.[21]

Additional commentaries were written for tractates belonging to the orders of *Nezikin* and *Kodashim* that have no Talmudic commentary in the Bavli; these can be regarded as extensions to the Bavli. Tractate *'Eduyot,* which is in *Nezikin,* merited several commentaries, including one by Rabbi Abraham ben David of Provence.[22] *Midot* (in the order of *Kodashim*) was explicated by Rashi's disciple Rabbi Shemaiah and other sages;[23] several medieval rabbis composed commentaries on *Kinim,* also in the order of *Kodashim.*[24] *Avot* as well merited many commentaries; these, however, were not composed as extensions of the Talmud but rather reflect this tractate's unique character, its ethical and behavioral guidelines. It was also distinctive for being recited in the synagogue (see below).[25]

COMMENTARIES ON THE ENTIRE MISHNAH

If the above-mentioned works focused on orders or tractates omitted from the Talmud, the period in question also saw the composition of noteworthy commentaries on the entire Mishnah. Their characteristic features and the motivation of their authors shed additional light on the status of Mishnah study during this era.

20. This commentary on several tractates from *Teharot* was published in the Vilna edition of the BT. On Maharam's commentary, see Albeck, *Introduction to the Mishna,* 238–39; Urbach, *The Tosafists,* 545. On the commentary by the early-thirteenth-century German rabbi Moses ben Hasdai, of which only citations are extant, see Urbach, *The Tosafists,* 422.

21. On Rabbenu Asher's commentary, see Albeck, *Introduction to the Mishna,* 247–48; Avraham H. Freimann, *Ha-rosh: Rabenu Asher b. R. Yeḥiel ve-tse'etsa'av: Ḥayehem u-fo'alam* (Jerusalem, 1986), 92–93.

22. See the sources cited by Menahem M. Kasher and Jacob B. Mandelbaum, *Sare ha-elef* (Jerusalem, 1978), 307. For Rabad's commentaries on the Mishnah, see Yaakov Sussmann, "Rabad on Shekalim: A Bibliographical and Historical Riddle" (Hebrew), in *Me'ah She'arim: Studies in Medieval Jewish Spiritual Life in Memory of Isadore Twersky,* ed. E. Fleischer et al. (Jerusalem, 2001), 138–39.

23. See the sources cited by Kasher and Mandelbaum, *Sare ha-elef,* 331.

24. Pinchas Roth, "Commentary on Tractate Kinnim by a Tosafist (R. Samson of Sens?)" (Hebrew), *Netuim* 7 (2000): 9–43. The appendix has a survey of all the commentaries on this tractate.

25. On the commentaries on *'Avot* and their orientation, see Shimon Sharvit, *Tractate Avoth through the Ages: A Critical Edition, Prolegomena and Appendices* (Hebrew;

GLOSSARIES

The earliest commentary on the Mishnah, and in actuality the first commentary on rabbinic literature, is Saadiah Gaon's *Alfaz al-Mishnah* (Words of the Mishnah) on the six orders of the Mishnah.[26] In this, as in many spheres, Saadiah was a pioneer. His very brief commentary focuses solely on explicating difficult words in the Mishnah. These include names of plants or utensils, as well as halakhic terms or words he thought might pose difficulty. The base text underlying the commentary is the Palaestinian version of the Mishnah, namely the version found in the complete manuscripts of the Mishnah on its own.[27] Perhaps Saadiah, who spent several years studying in Palaestina, brought this tradition of independent study of the Mishnah to Babylonia and sought through this commentary to inculcate the study of the Mishnah outside Palaestina.

It appears likely that this commentary was intended to facilitate basic study of the Mishnah with a minimal level of understanding. A commentary of this type certainly does not exhaustively investigate the meaning of the Mishnah; the contents of the Mishnah, and halakhic topics treated in it, require broader explanation. Its composition may have been partly motivated by Saadiah's polemic with the Karaites, who did not accept the Oral Law. Within this polemical context, Saadiah sought to accentuate the antiquity of the Mishnah and argued that its composition began in the days of the last prophets.[28] The need to underscore the Mishnah and the Oral Law may have been one of the underlying rationales for the creation of this brief commentary.

Saadiah's commentary enjoyed fairly wide distribution and was cited in geonic literature.[29] It was studied for centuries in the East,[30] and copies

---

Jerusalem, 2004), 37–52; Nahem Ilan, "The Double Canonization of Tractate Avot: Text, Commentary and Polemic" (Hebrew), *Netuim* 17 (2011): 57–72.

26. A large fragment of this work was preserved in a Genizah document housed in the Cambridge Library, T-S F5.109. On this fragment and Saadiah's commentary on the Mishnah, see Uziel Fuchs, "'*Millot HaMishnah*' by R. Saadia Gaon: The First Commentary to the Mishnah" (Hebrew), *Sidra* 29 (2014): 61–77.

27. In other of his works Saadiah cites the Mishnah as found in the *Sidre ha-Mishnah* tradition (namely, the tradition of the Mishnah as an independent work, without the BT or JT). See Yerahmeel (Robert) Brody, ed., *Ḥiburim hilkhatiyim shel rav Sa'adya Gaon* (Jerusalem, 2015), 201 n. 126. On how Palaestinian versions of the Mishnah reached Babylonia, see Fuchs, *Geonic Talmud*, 134–36, 148–49, 289–99.

28. Moshe Zucker, *Saadya's Commentary on Genesis* (Hebrew; New York, 1984), 186.

29. Fuchs, "Millot HaMishnah," 64–65.

30. See the sources cited in Fuchs, "Millot HaMishnah," 61–62.

were preserved in Cairo Genizah documents. Comparison of these Genizah documents shows that various authors added or subtracted "difficult words" from the original work, a practice that is indicative of its significance to learners, as they undertook to update it in line with what they viewed as important.[31]

Another commentary that also evidently explicated certain words in the Mishnah was composed in the eleventh century by the head of the Palaestinian yeshivah, Rabbi Nathan, Father of the Academy.[32] The original is no longer extant; portions have survived, however, in reworked form in a later commentary of an anonymous sage who also inserted the comments of additional exegetes.[33]

MAIMONIDES'S COMMENTARY ON THE MISHNAH

Maimonides's commentary on the Mishnah, which, as opposed to his predecessors' commentaries, explicated all six orders of the Mishnah at length, marks a significant shift in the study of the Mishnah as an independent work. Written when Maimonides was in his twenties, this mid-twelfth-century commentary extracts the underlying halakhic principles of the mishnaic discussion and, where necessary, explicates various details or difficult words in the Mishnah. In all likelihood, the commentary was intended for "laypersons, so that they could study Mishnah on their own and reach a good understanding of it . . . independently," as Israel Ta-Shma observed. As a philosopher and man of science, Maimonides incorporated discussions of topics into his commentary that went beyond the specific halakhic issue being explicated: halakhic principles, scientific and philosophical topics, and moral and didactic guidelines.[34] Moreover, Maimonides penned long intro-

31. At times, the geonim interpreted mishnayot in their responsa and in their works. For a list of these commentaries, see A. Kimmelman and B. M. Lewin, "A Guide to Talmudic Commentary in the Geonic Period" (Hebrew), *Shenaton ha-mishpat ha-ivri* 11–12 (1984–86): 512–81.

32. The commentary is in Arabic. A Hebrew translation was published by Joseph Kafiḥ in the *El ha-mekorot* edition of the Mishnah (Jerusalem, 1955–58). Simha Assaf attributes it to Rabbi Nathan ben Abraham II, who was appointed as gaon in the late eleventh century; *Tekufat ha-ge'onim ve-sifrutah: Hartsa'ot ve-shi'urim* (Jerusalem, 1955), 296. On the other hand, Moshe Gil ascribes it to Rabbi Nathan ben Abraham I: see Gil, *A History of Palestine, 634–1099*, trans. E. Broido (Cambridge, 1992), 719 n. 157.

33. Various scholars have located the anonymous compiler in either Egypt, Yemen, or Spain; there are, however, no definite data. See Assaf, *Tekufat ha-ge'onim ve-sifrutah*, 296; Israel M. Ta-Shma, *Talmudic Commentary in Europe and North Africa* (Hebrew; Jerusalem, 1999), 1:185.

34. Ta-Shma, *Talmudic Commentary*, 1:188.

ductions to topics he considered significant. In the general introduction to his commentary, he establishes the basic principles of the tradition of the Oral Law; in the introduction to *Sanhedrin* chapter 10 he treats the subject of reward and the rabbinic midrashim that address this question; in his introduction to *Avot* ("Eight Chapters") he discusses the parts of the soul, its strengths, and ways to improve it, as well as free will; in his introduction to *Teharot,* he provides a long, detailed halakhic survey of the major principles of purity and impurity. As noted there, it was Maimonides's awareness that most people, even scholars, were not familiar with these principles, that motivated him to pen this introduction. As Maimonides commented: "Every halakhah that concerns purity and impurity . . . is difficult even for great rabbis."[35]

These introductions reveal that Maimonides viewed his commentary as part of a much broader edifice. He conveys this in his introduction to the history of the transmission of the Oral Law. Maimonides comments that at the end of a long process, Judah the Prince "commenced to redact the Mishnah which incorporates the explanations of all the commandments written in the Torah."[36] Maimonides goes on to explain that the Mishnah contains explanations for commandments that were transmitted through tradition, alongside newly deduced principles, regulations, and *takanot.*[37] Accordingly, the Mishnah is the distillation of the entire Oral Law.

Given that the Mishnah and the tradition of Oral Law continued to be interpreted in the two Talmuds, according to Maimonides it was impossible to understand the Mishnah divorced from the talmudic explanations. He summed up his rationale for composing his commentary as follows: "That which led me to compose this work is (the fact) that I saw that the Talmud does something for the Mishnah (i.e. interpretation) which would never have been possible for anyone to arrive at by his own reasoning."[38] Maimonides also pinpoints the main benefit of studying his commentary: it facilitates understanding of the talmudic interpretation of the Mishnah and the concomitant halakhic conclusions:

The first is that we present the true meaning of the Mishnah and the explanation of its words. If you were to ask the greatest of Gaonim

35. Joseph Kafiḥ, ed., *Mishnah im perush rabenu Moshe ben Maimon* (Jerusalem, 1968), vol. 6: *Teharot,* 24.

36. F. Rosner, trans., *Moses Maimonides' Commentary on the Mishnah: Introduction to Seder Zeraim and Commentary on Tractate Berachoth* (New York, 1975), 65–66.

37. Rosner, *Moses Maimonides' Commentary,* 74–81.

38. Rosner, *Moses Maimonides' Commentary,* 135.

for the explanation of a Halachic law from a Mishnah, he would not
be able to answer at all, unless he were to know by heart the (discussion in the) Talmud regarding that *Halakhah* [. . .]

The second value (of this Commentary) consists of the final decision which I will clearly enunciate, stating each legal decision according to the opinion of the person whose viewpoint is accepted as
final.

The third benefit (of my Commentary on the Mishnah) is to serve
as an introduction for anyone beginning the study of (Talmudic) wisdom [. . .]

The fourth benefit is to serve as a reminder for one who has
learned and is knowledgeable, so that all which he learned will remain before him, and his learning and studying will be orderly in his
mouth.[39]

Maimonides's perception of the Mishnah as the distillation of the Oral
Law, whose interpretation must be grounded in talmudic exegesis, alongside the introduction of philosophical and didactic discussions, shows that
his aim in expounding the Mishnah extended beyond narrow consideration
of its contents. As Urbach notes, it is possible that even at a young age, when
Maimonides wrote his commentary on the Mishnah, "he had in mind his
major project of a new re-editing of the *halakhah*, and this directed his steps
to an initial effort to organize the Oral Law," a program later realized in
Maimonides's *Code* (*Mishneh Torah*).[40] Even though the Oral Law as organized in *Mishneh Torah* differed in not centering on a base text, Maimonides still awarded prime importance to his commentary on the Mishnah,
and continued to correct and update it throughout his lifetime.[41]

Despite the fact that Maimonides's commentary was the first comprehensive one on the Mishnah, his aim was not to treat the Mishnah as an autonomous work, but rather the opposite. His commentary was a means of
summarizing the entire corpus of the Oral Law and the talmudic interpretation of the Mishnah in particular.

This reveals another noteworthy facet of the question of the autonomy of
the Mishnah from Maimonides's perspective. Various scholars have argued
that because Maimonides's interpretation differs on occasion from that of
the Talmud, he evidently allowed himself, from time to time, to interpret the

39. Rosner, *Moses Maimonides' Commentary*, 136–37.

40. Ephraim E. Urbach, *Studies in Judaica* (Hebrew; Jerusalem, 1988), 708.

41. See Ta-Shma, *Talmudic Commentary*, 1:188 and the scholarly literature cited
there.

Mishnah in opposition to the Talmud. On the other hand, there are those who argue to the contrary that the divergences from the talmudic interpretation are only ostensible: namely, they interpret the Talmud, if somewhat differently from the accepted path.[42] Given the Maimonidean view of the Mishnah as summarizing the traditions of the Oral Law and as interpreted correctly in the Talmuds, the second viewpoint seems preferable.

Notwithstanding Maimonides's understanding of the Mishnah as part and parcel of the talmudic tradition, his commentary exerted great influence on the study of the Mishnah as an autonomous work, outside the framework of the study of the Bavli. Preserved in many manuscripts, this use reflects the commentary's distribution among, and influence on, students of the Mishnah.[43] Because Maimonides wrote his commentary in Judeo-Arabic, it had the strongest impact in Arabic-speaking lands. Parts of the commentary were translated into Hebrew during Maimonides's lifetime, but it was not until the fourteenth century that it merited an almost complete translation.[44] Maimonides and his commentary also influenced the textual version of the Mishnah: his version, which combined the traditions of Babylonia and Palaestina, became widespread and served as the basis for the printed editions of the Mishnah.

RABBI OBADIAH OF BARTENURA

The Italian rabbi Obadiah of Bartenura (or Bertinoro) composed his well-known commentary in the late fifteenth century, apparently after his immigration to the land of Israel.[45] The relatively brief commentary combines two exegetical methods. On the one hand, it explains the Mishnah step by step. Brief lemmata cited from the Mishnah are followed by an explanation of the text. Similar to Rashi's commentary on the Talmud, Bartenura explains words and halakhic concepts found in the Mishnah. On the other hand, he expands on matters discussed in the Talmud not explicated by Rashi; sometimes he also addresses the halakhic ruling, similar to Mai-

---

42. For a survey of the scholarship, see Chanan Gafni, *The Mishnah's Plain Sense: A Study of Modern Talmudic Scholarship* (Hebrew: Tel Aviv, 2011), 39 n. 8.

43. For the distribution of Maimonides's commentary on the Mishnah, see Sussmann, "Manuscripts and Text Traditions of the Mishnah," 243–44. For a list of the complete and partial manuscripts of the commentary, see Yaakov Sussmann (with Y. Rosenthal and A. Shweka), *Thesaurus of Talmudic Manuscripts* (Hebrew; Jerusalem, 2012), 3:129–63.

44. Ta-Shma, *Talmudic Commentary*, 1:190.

45. For a biography of Rabbi Obadiah of Bartenura, see Y. D. Lerner, *Rabenu Ovadyah mi-Bartenura: Ḥayav u-terumato le-perush ha-mishnah* (Jerusalem, 1988), 16–36.

monides's commentary.[46] On occasion, Bartenura incorporates citations from Rashi or Maimonides's commentaries. The Bartenura commentary's combination of two paths, brevity and halakhic discussion, contributed to its immense popularity and wide distribution—indeed, it remains the most widely disseminated, basic, traditional commentary to the present. Because Bartenura's commentary facilitated study of the Mishnah as an autonomous work, it made a vital contribution to the independent study of the Mishnah.

COMMENTARIES ON THE MISHNAH IN OTHER WORKS

As Ezra Chwat has shown, many of the commentators on Alfasi's *Sefer ha-halakhot* expended great efforts to explicate the Mishnayot included in this work. Chwat suggests that mid-level students did not study the Talmud and its commentaries, but were rather content with studying Mishnah and *halakhah*. The incorporation of expansions on the Mishnah in this work answered their didactic needs.[47]

Another type of mishnaic interpretation emerged in the thirteenth century, in *Bet ha-behirah* by Menaḥem ha-Meiri of Perpignan (southern France). In his commentary, Meiri prefaces his explanation of each talmudic *sugya* with the mishnah in question and its talmudic discussion. Only then does he proceed to explain additional matters found only in the Talmud. This interpretive method, which views the Bavli mainly as a commentary on the Mishnah and highlights its "mishnaic" aspect, can be seen as reflecting Maimonidean influence, as Maimonides sought to distill the talmudic tradition and the halakhot accompanying the Mishnah.[48] Although Meiri did not write an independent commentary on the Mishnah, his method underscores the unique place awarded the Mishnah as the basis for the Talmud.

Moreover, Meiri also broadened the scope of the three talmudic orders studied in his day: *Mo'ed, Nashim,* and *Nezikin.* He expounded on tractate *Ḥalah* and added it to the first part of *Pesaḥim;* to the study of *Mo'ed* he added the mishnayot treating the structure of the temple and its service:

46. For a brief treatment of Bartenura's integration of these two methods, see Frankel, *Introduction to the Mishna,* 338. On his halakhic method, see also Lerner, *Ovadya mi-Bartenura,* 89–133; Eliav Schochetman, "Is the Commentary of R. Obadiah of Bertinoro on the Mishna a Source for Halakhic Ruling?" (Hebrew), *Pe'amim* 37 (1988): 3–23.

47. Ezra Chwat, "Mishna Study among the Rishonim as Found in the Alfasi Gloss-Supplements" (Hebrew), *Alei Sefer* 19 (2001): 49–67.

48. For Maimonidean influence on Meiri, and the spheres in which he displays an independent stance, see Gerald J. Blidstein, "Rabbi Menahem Ha-Me'iri: Aspects of an Intellectual Profile," *Journal of Jewish Thought and Philosophy* 5 (1995): 63–79.

Tamid and *Midot*.[49] Similarly, he added *Mikva'ot*, for which there is no talmudic commentary, to tractate *Nidah*. He also interpreted two tractates from *Nezikin* without talmudic commentary: *Avot* and *'Eduyot*. Thus, his commentary incorporated the study of several mishnaic tractates into the regular round of study of the Bavli.

The desire to complete the orders of the Mishnah is also exemplified by a late-fourteenth-century German sage's *Ha-agudah*. This book contains brief halakhic rulings organized in the order of the tractates in the BT. For tractates with no talmudic commentary in *Zera'im* and *Teharot*, or *Shekalim* in *Mo'ed*, the book provides the openings of many mishnayot, even when these mishnayot are presented without additions or innovations, and even when they concern non-halakhic matters. These notes were evidently intended as a mnemonic aid for learners. This suggests a type of learner primarily interested in the study of halakhah, but one who also sought to study the entire Mishnah as a basic text of the Oral Law. It may also indicate that some students knew the Mishnah by heart and only required mnemonic devices.[50]

LITURGICAL, MYSTICAL, AND MAGICAL USE OF THE MISHNAH

To this point I have treated the Mishnah as educational material. Due to the brevity of mishnaic language, and the need for background in *halakhah* and other foundational concepts, study of the Mishnah requires prior knowledge and explanation. Nonetheless, the Mishnah, or parts of it, had non-didactic uses. First and foremost, it penetrated prayer, and portions of the Mishnah were "read" in the synagogue. Although the recitation of a text can

---

49. *Tamid* has talmudic commentary in the BT for some of its chapters. Note that Meiri also wrote a commentary on *Shekalim*, which has no talmudic commentary in the BT but does in the JT. He explained this tractate using the same method he used for the BT: he first presents the mishnah and then turns to the talmudic discussion.

50. See Eleazar Brizel, *Sefer ha-agudah al masekhet Baba Kama: Mavo* (Jerusalem, 1970), 11. Didactic and halakhic uses can also be found in the commentary of Rabbi Elijah (thirteenth century, London). This brief commentary on *Berakhot* combines short explanations of the Mishnah with the conclusions reached by the Talmud and accompanied by additional halakhic discussions. See Mordecai Judah Leib Zaksh, ed., *Perushe rabenu Eliyahu mi-Londris u-pesakav* (Jerusalem, 1956). On the function of this commentary and its relationship to its predecessors, see Pinchas Roth and Ethan Zadoff, "The Talmudic Community of Thirteenth-Century England," in *Christians and Jews in Angevin England: The York Massacre of 1190, Narratives and Contexts*, ed. S. R. Jones and S. Watson (Woodbridge and Rochester, 2013), 189–90.

have instructional aspects, it differs innately from study in order to attain understanding of a text.

The earliest extant attestation to the incorporation of the Mishnah in the liturgical system is found in an ancient *Seder avodah* for the Day of Atonement. Essentially a liturgical reworking of the mishnayot in tractate *Yoma* that describe the high priestly ritual on the Day of Atonement, this *Seder avodah*, titled *Shivat yamim*, is considered the earliest one in our possession.[51]

Although the witnesses to incorporation of mishnaic passages in the liturgy date only from the ninth century on, they may reflect earlier practices. Natronai Gaon wrote in a responsum that following the recitation of the blessings on the Torah in the preliminary service, one recites biblical verses treating the daily (*tamid*) sacrifice, then reads the fifth chapter of *Zevaḥim*, followed by the *baraita* (tannaitic tradition) of Rabbi Ishmael on the thirteen principles for interpreting the Torah.[52] As shown above, *Seder Rav Amram* explains that these readings represent the three parts of Jewish learning that must be studied daily: Bible, Mishnah, and Talmud.[53] The choice of this chapter in *Zevaḥim* apparently inheres in its concise presentation of the main laws of the sacrificial rites, which made it a fitting liturgical substitute for the sacrificial temple service.[54]

The attestation to the recitation of *Avot* on the Sabbath afternoon also dates to the mid-ninth century.[55] Accepted by many communities, this custom took a variety of forms. Some communities recited the tractate's chapters throughout the year; others, only in the spring—before or after Shavuot. In some places, a sixth chapter, titled *Kinyan Torah*, was added to the tractate's five chapters to make it possible to read a chapter on each of the six Sabbaths between Passover and Shavuot. Some Yemenite communities recited only the first chapter of the tractate every Sabbath.[56] Various

51. Michael D. Swartz and Joseph Yahalom, trans. and eds., *Avodah: An Anthology of Ancient Poetry for Yom Kippur* (University Park, Pa., 2005), 53. For additional reworkings of the Mishnah in *sidre avodah*, see David Stern's article in this volume, 445–46 and n. 47.

52. Robert Brody, ed., *Teshuvot Rav Natronai Bar Hilai Gaon* (Hebrew; Jerusalem, 1994), 110–11. The reading of this chapter is not found in *Siddur Rav Sa'adya Gaon* (early tenth century) but a Genizah fragment that reworked the siddur for everyday purposes included the recitation of this chapter from tractate *Zebaḥim*. See Naphtali Wieder, *The Formation of Jewish Liturgy in the East and the West* (Hebrew; Jerusalem, 1998), 596.

53. Goldschmidt, ed., *Seder Rav Amram*, 7.

54. For the varied explanations for the choice of this chapter, see Yaakov Gartner, *Studies in Prayer: Custom and Development* (Hebrew; Alon Shevut, 2015), 55–66.

55. B. M. Lewin, *Otzar ha-gaonim: Thesaurus of the Gaonic Responsa and Commentaries*, vol. 2, *Tractate Shabbath* (Hebrew; Jerusalem, 1931), 102–3; Brody, *Teshuvot Rav Natronai Bar Hilai Gaon*, 200–202.

explanations have been offered for what motivated the recitation of *Avot* on Sabbath. One suggests that because Moses died on Sabbath afternoon, "Moses received the Torah at Sinai" was recited in his honor. Others view the chain of transmission with which the tractate opens as anti-Karaite polemic. Perhaps the most straightforward explanation is that *Avot*'s ethical sayings, concepts, and setting out of guidelines for proper conduct made its contents accessible to laypersons, not just scholars.[56]

Another mishnah that entered the public liturgy was the second chapter of tractate *Shabat,* which treats the lighting of lamps for the Sabbath. In some communities it is recited before the Friday afternoon service; in others, it is recited before or after the evening service.[58] Naftali Wieder linked the mandating of its recitation to an anti-Karaite polemic, as the Karaites objected to the lighting of Sabbath lamps.[59]

Over the generations there were communities in which some worshipers remained in synagogue to read chapters of the Mishnah after the Sabbath morning service. Rabbi Judah of Barcelona describes an ongoing practice of reading chapters from tractates *Shabat* and *'Eruvin* on Sabbath mornings. He also notes a practice of reading several chapters from beginning to end every Sabbath, with the aim of completing the Mishnah every few years. Later authorities describe the custom of reading a chapter from tractate *Shabat* every Sabbath.[60] A list from the Cairo Genizah appends the appropriate chapters from the Mishnah to be read on festival evenings.[61] These are but a few of the ways that mishnayot were integrated into or in proximity

---

56. Sharvit, *Tractate Avoth*, 255–66.

57. Yaakov Gartner, "Why Did the Geonim Institute the Custom of Saying 'Avoth' on the Sabbath" (Hebrew), *Sidra* 4 (1988): 17–32; Sharvit, *Tractate Avoth*; Wieder, *Jewish Liturgy*, 350–51. For an opinion that dissents from the anti-Karaite rationale for the custom, see Brody, *Teshuvot Rav Natronai Bar Hilai Gaon*, 202 n. 6.

58. Its recitation is mentioned in *Seder Rav Amram Gaon* (Goldschmidt ed., 65). It is also noted in some sources that cite a responsum by Natronai Gaon; both Amram Gaon and Natronai lived in the ninth century. These sources are, however, later; see Brody, *Teshuvot Rav Natronai Bar Hilai Gaon*, 181 n. 1. This chapter's recitation is not mentioned in *Siddur Rav Sa'adya Gaon.* If this custom dates to the ninth century, it appears less likely that it is linked to the anti-Karaite polemic, because ninth-century rabbis were less aware of the Karaites and their customs. See Brody, *Teshuvot Rav Natronai Bar Hilai Gaon*, 259 n. 10; Brody, *Geonim of Babylonia*, 96.

59. Wieder, *Jewish Liturgy*, 323–47. Based on the inclusion of a benediction praising the rabbis and their tradition before this chapter in a Genizah document, Wieder concluded that its context was the anti-Karaite polemic.

60. For the sources, see Ephraim E. Urbach, *The World of the Sages* (Hebrew; Jerusalem, 1988), 274–76.

61. Genizah fragment, Oxford, Bodleian Library, Heb. f. 18, pp. 37–50. For a precis of the fragment and an initial analysis, see P. Roth, "Doing Things with Mishna: A Chapter

to prayer. As Yaakov Sussmann notes: "Dozens of fragments of mishnayot were found in the Genizah ... with headings and marking of chapters which indicate that they served a liturgical purpose: for weekdays, Sabbaths, the four special Sabbaths, holidays, etc. The headings note the days of the week or the weekly Torah portion for the Sabbath, and the like."[62] Here the border between ritual recitation and study is blurred.[63]

In the mystical context, the Mishnah is frequently mentioned or cited in zoharic literature, especially *Ra'aya mehemna* and *Tikune ha-Zohar*. The importance ascribed to the Mishnah in this literature is manifested by the many tannaim mentioned in it, and the many *derashot* cited in the name of Simeon bar Yoḥai and his circle. However, zoharic literature nowhere treats the Mishnah as an autonomous halakhic work. The opposite is the case. In many instances the mishnayot cited diverge from their halakhic meaning and are endowed with mystical meaning. Even the names of the six orders receive mystical interpretation.[64] Moreover, the terms *matnitin* or *mari matnitin* can also be used for citations from the Talmud, which are treated as if originating from the Mishnah. In many instances, these or similar terms are used to cite mystical sources or mystical novellae as if they are part of the early rabbinic tradition.[65] At times, even citations from the Mishnah itself are cited from the talmudic, not the mishnaic, context. For example, the mystical interpretation of the "four generative causes of damages" (mBK 1.1) is probably based on its talmudic interpretation,[66] and the opening mishnah of *Shabat* is cited with its talmudic interpretation.[67]

in the Cultural History of Rabbinic Literature" (Hebrew; unpublished seminar paper, Hebrew University, 2004), 7–8.

62. Sussmann, "Manuscripts and Text Traditions," 226 n. 55.

63. For an analysis of some of these lists, see Arye Olman, "Weekly Learning of the Mishnah: Evidences from the Cairo Genizah" (Hebrew), *Netuim* 19 (2014): 171–96.

64. See *Tikune ha-Zohar,* introduction, 5a.

65. Gershom Scholem, *Kabbalah* (Jerusalem, 1974), 216; Ephraim Gottlieb, *Studies in the Kabbala Literature*, ed. J. Hacker (Hebrew; Tel Aviv, 1976), 163–214; Daniel C. Matt, "Matnita Dilan: A Technique of Innovation in the Zohar" (Hebrew), *Jerusalem Studies in Jewish Thought* 8 (1989): 123–45.

66. See *Tikune ha-Zohar, tikkun yod mi-tikunim aharonim,* 146a. The list of the four generative causes of damage there includes horn, tooth, body, and foot and is not consistent with the list found in the Mishnah in the opening of *Baba Kama*. It is possible that the Mishnah here is cited according to one of its talmudic interpretations in the BT as Moses Cordovero proposed. See Moses Cordovero, *Sefer ha-Zohar im perush or yakar* (Jerusalem, 1987), 15:165.

67. See *Zohar: Ra'aya mehemna,* vol. 3 (*Be-midbar*), *parashat pinḥas* (243b–244a). The citation there includes part of the sugya from bShab 2b.

Another surprising context in which we find selections from the Mishnah is that of magic, though the findings in this realm are sparse. Two mishnayot were copied onto two incantation bowls: one from mZev 5.3, the other from mShevu 4.13.[68] Incantation bowls are thought to date to the late Sasanian period; if that is correct, these are the earliest attestations to the text of the Mishnah. Their use in magical contexts indicates the widespread distribution and knowledge of the Mishnah. Partial quotations of mishnayot are also found in magical texts from the Genizah, but their function there is obscure.[69]

CONCLUSIONS

From the geonic period until modernity the Mishnah did not have a major place as an autonomous work; rather, it was primarily studied as part of the Bavli. Attestation to its abandonment as an independent work comes from the scant testimony to its study and the limited number of commentaries devoted solely to the Mishnah. This appears to be attributable to the fact that halakhic rulings are not made on the basis of the Mishnah, but generally rely on the Bavli. Moreover, because of its size and complexity, the Bavli captured the lion's share of the learners' time, and they barely studied other rabbinic works, including the Mishnah.

That the Mishnah was barely studied as an autonomous work also explains the lack of development of commentaries on its plain meaning, without the talmudic interpretation. Study of a text on its own invites independent understanding; this explains the emergence of commentaries on the Bible, which was read in synagogue and studied independently. Such a development took place with respect to the Mishnah in the modern period, when it began to be studied autonomously, and commentaries on its plain meaning emerged.[70] This, however, did not occur in the medieval period, during which the Mishnah was not seen as an independent work.

---

68. See Shaul Shaked, "Form and Purpose in Aramaic Spells: Some Jewish Themes (The Poetics of Magic Texts)," in *Officina magica: Essays on the Practice of Magic in Antiquity* (Leiden, 2005), 3–7. The incantation bowl that interpolated the mishnah from Shevu 4.13 was published by Dan Levene, "'If You Appear as a Pig: Another Incantation Bowl (Moussaieff 164)," *Journal of Semitic Studies* 52 (2007): 59–70. For a discussion of the version of the Mishnah and the import of its citation in a magic context, see Avigail Manekin-Bamberger, "Intersections between Law and Magic in Ancient Jewish Texts" (Hebrew; PhD diss., Tel Aviv University, 2018), 14–16.

69. Joseph Naveh and Shaul Shaked, *Magic Spells and Formulae: Aramaic Incantations of Late Antiquity* (Jerusalem, 1993), 206, 219.

70. Gafni, *The Mishnah's Plain Sense.*

Nonetheless, despite its general neglect until modernity, there were places where orders and tractates not found in the Talmud were studied, and attempts were made to interpret the Mishnah or parts of it. The commentaries surveyed here evidence several stages. In the early period we find explanations of difficult words; such works assist with a basic understanding of the Mishnah. At a later stage, we find Maimonides's more comprehensive commentary that not only explicates words and expressions but addresses the halakhic principles found in the Mishnah. Obadiah of Bartenura's commentary interprets the Mishnah sequentially, sentence by sentence. Although grounded in the talmudic tradition, Bartenura's commentary facilitated independent study of the Mishnah and was a harbinger of the changes that took place in the study of the Mishnah from the sixteenth century on.

I thank the Research Authority of Herzog College for its assistance in funding the translation, which was prepared by Dena Ordan.

22. The Reception of the Mishnah in the Modern Era

Chanan Gafni

The reception of the Mishnah in the modern era can be framed as the story of its restoration to the forefront of Jewish learning and scholarship after being treated for centuries primarily as part of the Talmud and, to a certain extent, as a mere introduction to amoraic discourse. Starting with the age of printing, the Mishnah regained its status as an autonomous composition and as an independent subject of study. This dramatic shift was, however, the result of a two-stage process: the emergence of study of the Mishnah as an independent corpus in the sixteenth to eighteenth centuries, and the rise of independent interpretations of the Mishnah—that is, not through the talmudic prism—especially in the nineteenth century. In the following I discuss these two stages and conclude with some observations on the current study of the Mishnah, in the twentieth and twenty-first centuries.[1]

STUDY OF THE MISHNAH AS AN INDEPENDENT CORPUS (16TH–18TH CENTURIES)

The first phase of this long process marks a shift from treating the Mishnah almost exclusively in its talmudic context, to a willingness to allow independent study of the Mishnah without advancing to its later talmudic interpretation. In earlier periods, so it seems, Jews rarely addressed the Mish-

---

1. For some general surveys on the study of the Mishnah, including treatments of its reception in the early modern period, see Yechiel Y. Weinberg, "Le-ḥeker ha-mishnah," in *Shut seride esh* (Jerusalem, 1977), 4:222–35; Zvi M. Rabinovitz, "Le-korot limud ha-mishnah," in *Ha-mishnah la-no'ar: Darkhe hora'ata ve-'erkha ha-ḥinukhi* (Jerusalem, 1951), 45–69; Chanan Gafni, *The Mishnah's Plain Sense: A Study of Modern Talmudic Scholarship* (Hebrew; Tel Aviv, 2011).

nah in such a fashion.² The small number of manuscripts of the Mishnah alone (without the corresponding talmudic text), as well as the few commentaries (with the exception of Maimonides, of course) devoted solely to the Mishnah (especially to tractates interpreted by the Talmud) indicates the rarity of independent study of the Mishnah. Selected chapters from the Mishnah, such as the second chapter of *Shabat,* or tractate *Avot,* were recited liturgically (on Friday evening and on the Sabbath after *Minchah* respectively).³ Other mishnayot were recited liturgically after the death of a family member.⁴ Otherwise, the Mishnah was only studied as part of the Talmud.⁵ Needless to say, before approaching the Talmud, young students were first introduced to the Mishnah as an independent text; however, having reached the intellectual maturity to study the Talmud (and often even before . . .), they abandoned their mishnaic studies.

The sole exceptions to this prevailing approach can be traced in Italy and Byzantium,⁶ where, possibly under the influence of more ancient practices of study in Palaestina, the Mishnah was still discussed on its own terms and preserved independently in manuscripts. Elsewhere, in both Christian and Muslim lands, scholars focused on the Talmud as soon as they reached the appropriate intellectual level.

Numerous sociocultural factors, rooted in different realms of Jewish life, and a variety of Jewish communities, contributed to the dramatic turn in the role of the Mishnah in the Jewish curriculum.⁷ Although traces of these

2. See especially Yaakov Sussmann, "Manuscripts and Text Traditions of the Mishnah" (Hebrew), in *Proceedings of the World Congress of Jewish Studies* (Jerusalem, 1977), 3:215–50, and Uzy Fuchs's article in the present volume.

3. On the practice of reciting the second chapter of *mShabat* during the Friday evening prayers, see Naftali Wieder, *The Formation of Jewish Liturgy in the East and West* (Hebrew; Jerusalem, 1998), 1:323–47. On the origin of reciting *mAvot,* see Yaakov Gartner, "Why Did the Geonim Institute the Custom of Saying 'Avoth' on the Sabbath?" (Hebrew), *Sidra* 4 (1988): 17–32.

4. I am not sure exactly when this practice emerged. See Mordecai Mayer, "'Mishnah 'otiyot neshamah': Hashpa'at ra'ayon zeh al limud mishnah," *Ha-ma'ayan* 52.2 (2011): 39–44.

5. On the study of the Mishnah in medieval yeshivot, see Mordechai Breuer, *Oholei Torah: The Yeshivah, Its Structure and History* (Hebrew; Jerusalem, 2003), 129–33. Many sources on the study of the Mishnah, in the educational system especially, are found in Simha Assaf, *Mekorot le-toledot ha-ḥinukh bi-yisrael* (new ed. by Shmuel Glick), 5 vols. (New York and Jerusalem, 2002).

6. See, especially, Sussmann, "Manuscripts and Text Traditions," 230–31, 234–36.

7. For a detailed study of this shift, see Aaron Ahrend, "Mishnah Study and Study Groups in Modern Times" (Hebrew), *JSIJ* 3 (2004): 19–53. The following references are among the many found in his informative article.

factors can be identified in earlier periods, they did not emerge strongly until the late medieval and early modern periods.

Mysticism

One important impetus for the revival of Mishnah study was grounded in mysticism. Numerous passages in *Sefer ha-Zohar* and *Tikune ha-Zohar* strongly advocate the study of the Mishnah. Thus, for example, in relation to the biblical, six-winged seraphs (see Isa 6:2), the *Zohar* preaches: "Whoever studies Scripture and the six orders of the Mishnah, this is the one who knows how to order and bind the unification of the Lord, in a fitting manner."[8]

Inspired by such passages, but also by interesting connections formed between the word *mishnah* and the word *neshama* (soul), we find a small group of prominent scholars, concentrated mainly in sixteenth-century Safed, instituting various praxes involving the recitation of mishnaic texts.[9] Thus, as mentioned above, although the roots of the independent study of the Mishnah may have stemmed from Palaestina, it took on greater momentum in the kabbalistic context. This circle of scholars included such figures as Joseph Karo (1488–1575),[10] Moses Cordovero (1522–70),[11] Isaac Luria (1534–72),[12] Samuel Ozida (1545–1604),[13] Ḥayyim Vital (1542–1620),[14] and

---

8. See *Zohar*, Introduction, 42a: "מאן דקארי ותני שית סדרי משנה, דא הוא מאן דידע לסדרא ולק שרא קשורא ויחודא דמאריה כדקא יאות."

9. See Ben-Zion Dinaburg, "The Beginnings of Hasidism and Its Social and Messianic Elements" (Hebrew), *Zion* 9 (1944): 192–93; Ronit Meroz, "The Circle of R. Moshe ben Makhir and Its Regulations" (Hebrew), *Pe'amim* 31 (1987): 45–47; Ahrend, "Mishnah Study," 22–25.

10. On Rabbi Joseph Karo and the Mishnah, see R. J. Zwi Werblowsky, *Joseph Karo: Lawyer and Mystic* (Philadelphia, 1977), 266–77; Mor Altshuler, *The Life of Rabbi Yoseph Karo* (Hebrew; Tel Aviv 2016), 45–46, 108–11. Both scholars claim that such practices were rooted in the earlier Byzantine context. Rabbi Joseph Karo's special connection to the Mishnah is reflected in his mystical diary *Magid mesharim*, where he receives certain revelations through the Mishnah itself.

11. See, e.g., Bracha Sack, *The Kabbalah of Rabbi Moshe Cordovero* (Hebrew; Jerusalem, 1995), 117.

12. See Meir Benayahu, *Toledoth Ha-Ari* (Hebrew; Jerusalem, 1967), 228, 330.

13. Samuel Ozida was one of Isaac Luria's first students in Safed. He is especially known for his *Midrash Shemuel,* a commentary on *mAvot*. On the importance of reciting mishnayot, see his comment on *mAvot* 5.23.

14. On Ḥayyim Vital and the Mishnah, see Lawrence Fine, "Recitation of Mishnah as a Vehicle for Mystical Inspiration: A Contemplative Technique Taught by Hayyim Vital," *REJ* 141 (1982): 183–99.

Joseph Ashkenazi (16th century), also known as "the tanna from Safed" (התנא מצפת).[15] These scholars believed that they could merit divine guidance through intensive recitation of the Mishnah; they prescribed recitation of a set number of mishnayot per day, which they often chanted repeatedly to a special melody. Furthermore, some of these scholars approached the Mishnah as a mystical text and interpreted it in that light.

Pedagogic Motivations

The mystical occupation, nay obsession, with the Mishnah was essentially restricted to individuals belonging to kabbalistic circles in the Ottoman Empire, mainly Safed, and had little impact on the curriculum in the Jewish educational system worldwide. A more dramatic, widely influential pedagogical revolution, spearheaded by Judah Loew ben Bezalel (1520–1609), otherwise known as the Maharal of Prague, took place in the central European arena, namely, in Poland, Moravia, and Bohemia.[16]

In his writings, Maharal frequently expressed dissatisfaction with the prevailing educational system of his time. Strongly influenced by famous contemporary pedagogues,[17] Maharal felt that the usual curriculum in the Jewish educational system failed to take into account the students' intellectual development and capabilities (or lack thereof), nor was it attuned to the different levels of Jewish society; rather, it was directed solely at the brightest students, who intended to embark on rabbinic careers. His revolutionary vision, which called for young students not to delve into the Talmud before acquiring thorough knowledge of the Mishnah, bestowed a major role on the study of the Mishnah.[18]

Maharal furthermore encouraged the laity to pursue the study of the Mishnah rather than the Talmud, and to form *havurot* (study groups) for that purpose. Indeed, contemporary rabbis testify to the avid response to Maharal's call, describing the formation of such *havurot* in their own com-

---

15. On Joseph Ashkenazi and his interest in the Mishnah, see Gershom Scholem, "New Contributions to the Biography of Rabbi Joseph Ashkenazi of Safed" (Hebrew), *Tarbiz* 28 (1958): 59–60; Benayahu, *Toledoth Ha-Ari*, 156, 187; Zvi ha-Levi Ish Horowitz, "Toledot R. Yosef Ashkenazi, ha-tanna mi-tsefat," *Sinai* 7 (1940–41): 328–30.

16. See Breuer, *Oholei Torah*, 131–33; Ahrend, "Mishnah Study," 21–22.

17. See O. D. Kulka, "The Historical Background of the National and Educational Teaching of Rabbi Judah Loeb Ben Bezalel of Prague: A Suggested New Approach to the Study of MaHaRaL" (Hebrew), *Zion* 50 (1985): 277–320.

18. See Aharon Fritz Kleinberger, *The Educational Theory of the Maharal of Prague* (Hebrew; Jerusalem, 1962).

munities. The rabbis Yom Tov Lipmann Heller (1579–1654),[19] Ephraim Luntshitz (1550–1619),[20] and Isaiah (Yeshayahu) ben Avraham Horowitz (1588–1630)[21] are but a few of the Jewish leaders who, inspired by Maharal, actively embraced Mishnah study by young students and older laypeople alike.

In this context I also note that from the sixteenth century we find many Jewish communities establishing various *hevrot*, namely communal organizations or societies devoted to meeting the needs of their members, such as *tsedaka* (charity), *hakhnasat kalah* (charity to dower a bride), *bikur holim* (visiting the sick), but also a *hevrat mishnah* (Mishnah society). Modern scholars have described and documented these societies, whose formation was fueled by social and religious considerations (as other cultural activities hardly existed), alongside the need to assume a religious commitment to Torah study. The societies assured their participants that this would contribute to their *'ilui/tikun neshamah* (the ascent of the soul, from this to the next world, or up a level in the next world). Whether they met social or religious needs, these societies constituted another setting in which the Mishnah was studied independently from the Talmud.[22]

Printed Editions

When considering the revival of the study of the Mishnah, the impact of the invention of print cannot be overlooked. As in other fields of Jewish studies, the very existence of printed editions of various works contributed greatly to their wider circulation. Due to the low cost of printed books, their greater legibility, and the ability to combine the text with commentaries, various hitherto neglected compositions gained surprising popularity in a short time. This was to a large extent true of the Mishnah. The large number of printed editions of the Mishnah, starting from the late fifteenth century and mainly in the sixteenth to eighteenth centuries, reflected popular inter-

---

19. See especially the introduction to his commentary on the Mishnah, where he relates: "שנתחברו חבורות כתות מלכי מאן מלכי רבנן, ומתעסקין יום יום פרק מפרקי משניות וחחרין חלילה. ומאת ה' היתה זאת, חוק ולא יעבור" ("For they formed havurot and groups, on my advice and on the rabbis' advice, and they study a chapter of Mishnah every day, and then again. This is the Lord's doing; an unbreakable law"). On Heller's commentary on the Mishnah, see Joseph M. Davis, *Yom-Tov Lipmann Heller: Portrait of a Seventeenth Century Rabbi* (Oxford, 2004), 66–69.

20. See Shlomo Ephraim Luntshitz, *Amude shesh* (Warsaw, 1875), 18a, 61b.

21. See Isaiah Horowitz ha-Levi, *Shene luhot ha-berit* (Jerusalem, 1993), 3:10–11.

22. Such societies were discussed at length by Ahrend, "Mishnah Study," 31–53.

est in the study of the Mishnah and, at the same time, promoted the circulation of the Mishnah among growing numbers of Torah scholars.

Examining all the printed editions of the Mishnah and commentaries on it in this time frame provides a better sense of its considerable popularity in various Jewish communities.[23] Obviously, presentation and discussion of the entire list is beyond the scope of this chapter, but even a short survey sheds light on this matter.

To the best of our knowledge, the earliest complete edition of the Mishnah was printed in the late fifteenth century in Naples (even before the Talmud was printed in its entirety!). From the time of its appearance, and throughout the sixteenth, seventeenth, and eighteenth centuries, nearly one hundred editions of the Mishnah (that is, editions that do not include the Talmud) were produced, a clear indication of this text's popularity. These editions appeared in almost all the major Jewish centers with publishing houses, such as Amsterdam, Krakow, Istanbul, and Venice. Their diverse features—size, type of commentary, text division into daily recitation or for special occasions—reveal both their original purpose and the historical settings in which they were produced. Thus, for example, pocket-sized editions of the Mishnah were probably intended for use by traveling merchants, who primarily sought to recite and review the text, perhaps on a basic level.[24] On the other hand, folio editions were probably intended for serious analysis of the text, whether in a synagogue or a yeshivah.

Commentaries

The sixteenth to eighteenth centuries saw the composition and printing of some two dozen commentaries on the Mishnah.[25] The different types of interpretations found therein also reflect the varied intellectual and social con-

23. On the circulation of the Mishnah in sixteenth-century Italy, see Shifra Baruchson, *Books and Readers* (Hebrew; Jerusalem, 1993), 142. Baruchson lists 386 copies of Mishnayot in 171 Jewish libraries in Mantua alone.

24. In some of these editions, the tractates are divided not only into chapters, but also into daily portions for study, or for those who completed the study of the entire mishnaic corpus every month. Worth mentioning here is an edition of the mishnah published by Menasseh Ben Israel (1604–57), which appeared in Amsterdam (1632), in three (!) different formats; however, all were targeted for intensive study of the Mishnah. Perhaps it was he who introduced and popularized the study of the Mishnah in his local Dutch community. See David Sclar, "Three Mishnah Editions Published by Menasseh ben Israel," in *Report of the Oxford Centre for Hebrew and Jewish Studies 2018–2019*, ed. J. Schonfield (Oxford, 2019), 36–38.

25. See Hermann L. Strack and Günter Stemberger, *Introduction to the Talmud and Midrash* (Edinburgh, 1991), 145–48. For a detailed list of commentaries on the Mishnah,

texts for which they were intended and the purposes fueling Mishnah study. The most popular commentary on the Mishnah was undoubtedly that of Obadiah of Bartenura (c. 1450–1515). Although this sixteenth-century commentary was composed only after Bartenura settled in Jerusalem (1488), its foundations belong to the Italian milieu where he spent most of his life, and its culture of learning.[26]

Several important commentaries on the Mishnah can be viewed as an outgrowth of Maharal's pedagogic revolution. Once it had been separated from the talmudic context, scholars needed assistance in pursuing study of the Mishnah. The most popular commentary, composed by Yom Tov Lipmann Heller (1579–1654), was titled *Tosafot Yom Tov* (1614).[27] Although this monumental project was essentially based on the talmudic interpretation of the Mishnah, Heller on occasion suggested his own innovative readings. Quite famous, although atypical, is Heller's comment on mNaz 4.4: אף על פי שבגמרא לא פירשו כן, הואיל לענין דינא לא נפקא ולא מידי הרשות נתונה לפרש ("Even though that is not how the Talmud explains it, because it makes no difference as far as the law is concerned, it is permissible to interpret it [differently]"). Also extremely popular were Isaac Gabbai's *Kaf naḥat* (Venice, 1614) and Elisha b. Abraham's *Kav ve-naki* (1697), both more devoted to explicating difficult words than to serious textual analysis. Much more sophisticated, and as a result less popular, were the commentaries of Moses b. Noah Isaac Lipschuetz, *Leḥem mishneh* (Cracow, 1636), and of Moses b. Mordecai Zacut, titled *Kol remez* (Amsterdam, 1719), which appeared in single printings only.

Turning to kabbalistic circles, although many of them associated the study of the Mishnah with their mystical aspirations, it is not easy to trace the impact of this connection in earlier commentaries on the Mishnah. On the contrary, surviving remarks on the Mishnah by these scholars, such as those attributed to Joseph Ashkenazi (16th century), or Solomon Adani (1567–1624), reveal critical, not mystical tendencies. It is only later that we find some commentators providing a mystical type of interpretation. They

---

including from the sixteenth to eighteenth centuries, see P. J. Kohn, *Osar Ha-Beurim We-Ha-Perushim: Thesaurus of Hebrew Halachic Literature* (mostly Hebrew; London, 1952), 1–12.

26. On Obadiah of Bartenura and his Mishnah commentary, see Yisrael Dov Lerner, *Rabenu Ovadiah mi-Bartenura: Ḥayav u-terumato le-perush ha-mishnah* (Jerusalem, 1988).

27. On Yom Tov Lipmann Heller, see Mayer Herskovics, *Two Guardians of Faith: The History and Distinguished Lineage of Rabbi Yom Tov Lipmann Heller and Rabbi Aryeh Leib Heller* (English and Hebrew; Jerusalem, 2000), and preceding note.

include Eliezer b. Samuel Shmalka Rokeach (1685–1741), who emigrated to Safed from Amsterdam after having composed his *Ma'aseh Rokeaḥ* on the Mishnah (1740). As he declared in his introduction: ובכל מסכת שיש כמה משניות שהמה תמוהים מאד... פירשתי בס"ד בדרך פשט ובדרך רמז סוד ("In every tractate where there are several puzzling mishnayot . . . with God's help I interpreted them according to their plain and their mystical meanings"). Immanuel Ḥai Ricchi (1687-1743) made a similar comment in the introduction to his *Hon 'ashir* on the Mishnah (Amsterdam, 1730): ואל תבהל ברוחך בראותך שלפעמים נתקשה עלי איזה לשון במשנה לעניין דינא, שיישבתי אותו בדרש או רמז, כי כך היא דרכה של תורה להיות לה פשט רמז דרש סוד ("And do not be angered when you see that I had difficulty with a phrase in the Mishnah and was unable to precisely determine the law and I explained it by *derash* or *remez*, for that is the way of the Oral Law to have *peshat, derash, remez,* and *sod*"). Finally, another important commentary, titled *'Ets ḥayim* (1653), was composed by Israel Ḥaggiz (1620–74). This long list of editions and commentaries on the Mishnah mirrors the shift to its study as an independent text.[28]

The Christian Context: Censorship and Christian Hebraism

Thus far we have looked at internal Jewish catalysts for the revival of the study of Mishnah as an independent text. However, the role of external factors in this process cannot be overlooked. Two such possibly interrelated factors are considered here, both of them closely related to the invention of print that was discussed above.

The first factor is connected to the impact of Christian censorship of Jewish books in Europe, in the sixteenth century especially. As some contemporary scholars have argued, Christian censorship policy dramatically influenced the culture of Jewish learning, and at times shaped its future course. Surprisingly, whereas Christian authorities imposed various restrictions on the publication of the Talmud, at times entirely prohibiting it, the Mishnah itself was not banned. Although the precise effect of this Christian policy is difficult to evaluate, it may certainly have contributed to augmenting the status of the Mishnah.[29]

28. On the printing of the Mishnah and commentaries on it in the early modern period, see Ahrend, "Mishnah Study," 25–29. Ahrend claims that the wide circulation of the Mishnah should be viewed not just as a reflection of the growing interest in this work, but also as a factor in its elevated status.

29. See, e.g., Amnon Raz-Krakotzkin, "Burning and Printing: The Hebrew Book during the Counter-Reformation" (Hebrew), *Zmanim: A Historical Quarterly* 112 (2010): 38–39.

Perhaps even more speculative is the influence of the interest of Christian Hebraists in the Mishnah.[30] In their attempt to illumine the Jewish context in which Christianity emerged and to achieve a better understanding of the gospels, Christian Hebraists displayed great interest in early rabbinic compositions, including the Mishnah, and a significant number of translations of the Mishnah appeared in the sixteenth and seventeenth centuries. Whether the Christian preoccupation with the Mishnah indirectly influenced Jews and inspired them to devote special attention to the early tannaitic text as a separate work remains, however, conjectural.

Several editions of the Mishnah in translation appeared during this period among non-Jews. Earlier translations were evidently limited to individual tractates, including *Shabat, 'Eruvin, Yoma', Rosh Ha-Shanah, Mo'ed Katan, Ketubot, Bava Kama, Makot, Midot*, and *Yadayim*. These editions, which appeared in Latin or English, were obviously intended for Christian scholars. The leading version of the Mishnah among non-Jews, a complete Latin translation of the Mishnah, was later published by Willem Surenhuis in Amsterdam in 1698–1703.[31]

INDEPENDENT INTERPRETATIONS OF THE MISHNAH
(19TH CENTURY)

The dissociation of the study of the Mishnah from the Talmud continued and even intensified from the nineteenth century onwards. Indeed, a growing number of scholars began to interpret the Mishnah as an autonomous work, that is, not through the lens or prism of the Talmud. This dramatic shift, the result of Jewish integration into contemporary scholarly discourse, reflects the extent to which Jewish rabbis and scholars internalized the critical modes of thinking of that day, ones to which they were exposed directly or indirectly.

---

30. An Oxford seminar in advanced Jewish studies was devoted to "The Mishnah between Christians and Jews in Early Modern Europe." Brief summaries of various papers presented at the seminar appeared in *Report of the Oxford Centre for Hebrew and Jewish Studies 2018–2019*, 28–42.

31. On Christian Hebraists and their Judaic publications, see David B. Ruderman, *Early Modern Jewry: A New Cultural History* (Princeton, 2010), 115–16; for Surenhius, see 178–80. See also Eric Nelson, *The Hebrew Republic: Jewish Sources and Transformation of European Political Thought* (Cambridge and London, 2010), 9–16 (but without particular reference to the Mishnah). For a list of tractates translated into Latin or other European languages, see Stephen G. Burnett, *Christian Hebraism in the Reformation Era (1500–1660): Authors, Books, and the Transmission of Jewish Learning* (Leiden, 2012), 132–33.

New Perspectives on the Mishnah

Needless to say, the approach to the Mishnah as an independent work, particularly the willingness to offer interpretations other than the ones suggested in the Talmud, required explanation and justification. After all, the talmudic interpretations had for centuries dominated the yeshivot and constituted the foundations of Jewish law (*halakhah*). Indeed, scholars provided various explanations, from their perspective, of what led the Talmud to deviate from the plain sense of the Mishnah; this consequently justified their innovative interpretations of the tannaitic texts. Their treatment of the Mishnah shapes the scholarship in this field to the present.

Part of the Talmud's misunderstanding of the Mishnah inheres in its problematic transmission, whether orally or as a written text. Scholars pointed to various mishnayot whose language was probably already corrupted by the talmudic period, which prevented the amoraim from arriving at its plain meaning (at the same time, the amoraim did not hesitate to revise or edit the mishnaic text).[32]

Another factor in the Talmud's recurrent deviation from the Mishnah's primary meaning involved lack of understanding of its original purpose and editorial guidelines. In contrast to the consensual traditional approach, which viewed the Mishnah as a legal codex meant to serve as a binding source, later scholars of the Mishnah explored other possible underlying motivations. Whereas some emphasized the role of the Mishnah in documenting ancient traditions, others focused on its pedagogical value as a textbook of Jewish law. Such innovative ways of looking at the Mishnah had a crucial impact on its interpretation and raised various questions: Should one necessarily seek consistency in the Mishnah? How should disputes and controversies attested in the Mishnah be approached? What caused the repetition of certain laws or frequent deviations from the main theme of the tractate? These questions, which had obviously been addressed before, were now cast in a new light.

Yet another aspect of the rejection of the talmudic view of the Mishnah was an outcome of a new assessment of the Mishnah in light of, and as compared to, other tannaitic texts. Although the Talmud often (but not always) strives to harmonize the laws found in the Mishnah with those found in other tannaitic compositions, such as the Tosefta or Midrash Halakhah, seeing them as complementary, modern scholars considered other types of relationships between these texts, at times viewing them as competing

32. See Gafni, *The Mishnah's Plain Sense*, 210–14.

sources. This revolutionary approach had significant ramifications for the way the Mishnah was being decoded.[33]

Lack of familiarity with mishnaic language was yet another reason underlying its misinterpretation in the Talmud. As some scholars have claimed, the amoraim, especially those who dwelt in Babylonia, were not conversant with the Greek or Latin elements found in the Mishnah, essentially a product of a Hellenistic environment. Furthermore, the Hellenistic culture in which the tannaim of the Mishnah operated was alien to the Babylonian amoraim, whose surrounding culture differed entirely. That being the case, the amoraim were not always able to access the meaning of various terms, concepts, or objects appearing in the Mishnah.[34]

However, objections to the Talmud's interpretation of the Mishnah did not just lie in the textual-historical-cultural gaps that separated the amoraim from the tannaim. Modern scholars often criticized the basic talmudic mindset and its agenda in treating the Mishnah. One common accusation was an amoraic inclination toward *pilpul*, a term used loosely to convey their discomfort with the Talmud's noncritical modes of interpretation.[35] No less problematic in their eyes was the Talmud's attempt to interpret the Mishnah in accordance with later halakhic views. Modern scholars suspected the amoraim of manipulating the words or meaning of the Mishnah to make it meet their own legal agendas. Needless to say, this harsh criticism of the Talmud's interpretation of the Mishnah raised serious questions as to its authoritative role in shaping modern Jewish law. In any event, the Mishnah was from here on freed from the talmudic setting; it was discussed and treated on its own terms, at least in academic circles or in more liberal contexts.

33. On the Mishnah-Tosefta relationship before and after the rise of modern scholarship, see Gafni, *The Mishnah's Plain Sense*, 148–56. On the Mishnah and Midrash Halakhah, see 300–306.

34. To be sure, similar comments about the amoraim's lack of fluency in classical languages are occasionally found in medieval Jewish literature. However, with greater Jewish exposure to Greek or Latin in the nineteenth century, this critique appears much more frequently, and assumes a much harsher tone. See Gafni, *The Mishnah's Plain Sense*, 162–75.

35. The criticism of *pilpul* obviously predates the nineteenth century, but initially targeted the analytic modes of thinking employed in talmudic study in the yeshivot; see especially Elchanan Reiner, "The *Yeshivas* of Poland and Ashkenaz in the Sixteenth and Seventeenth Centuries: Historical Developments" (Hebrew), in *Studies in Jewish Culture in Honour of Chone Shmeruk*, ed. Y. Bartal, E. Mendelsohn, and C. Turniansky (Jerusalem, 1993), 9–80. It is not until the late eighteenth and early nineteenth centuries that we find such accusations being leveled against the amoraim in the Talmud itself. See Gafni, *The Mishnah's Plain Sense*, 135–40.

Translations, Interpretations, Scholarly Contributions

The study of the Mishnah in the nineteenth century was obviously not re-stricted to any particular European region, or cultural or social group. Over the course of the nineteenth century, new translations, modern interpreta-tions, and scholarly essays devoted to the Mishnah emerged throughout Eu-rope; all indicate the pivotal role ascribed to the Mishnah as a central Jewish text. Although constraints of space make it impossible to describe each one of those contributions, I will refer to at least some landmarks in the modern study of the Mishnah.

Translations

If translation of a text into the vernacular is indicative of its importance at that time, this also applies to the Mishnah. Although a full German trans-lation of the Mishnah was produced in the eighteenth century (1760–63) by Johann Jacob Rabe (1710–98), two other translations appeared in the nineteenth century, this time of Jewish origin. The first full edition of the Mishnah in German appeared in Berlin (1832–34), under the supervision of I.M. Jost, who was a central figure in Wissenschaft des Judentums circles. A completely new German translation was again published in Berlin, start-ing from 1887, this time by Orthodox scholars under the supervision of Da-vid Zvi Hoffmann. Numerous tractates of the Mishnah were also translated into English in London on two occasions, in 1813 and 1878.[36]

Commentaries

Although many commentaries on the Mishnah appeared throughout the nineteenth century, the majority took a traditional-pilpulistic, not critical, approach; therefore, they are not discussed here. At the same time, several noteworthy exceptions, written by eminent rabbis, appeared in both central and Eastern Europe.

Starting in Germany, linguistic sensitivity and critical tendencies can be traced in the commentary on the Mishnah, *Leḥem shamayim* (1728), by Ja-cob Israel b. Zevi Emden (Yaavetz, 1698–1776). In this eighteenth-century literary product, we even find occasional departures from the Talmud's in-terpretation of the Mishnah, but Emden does not elaborate a systematic

---

36. See Strack and Stemberger, *Introduction to the Talmud and Midrash*, 144–45.

theory on the nature of the Mishnah and its talmudic interpretation to justify these departures.[37]

The commentary on the Mishnah by Israel Lipschuetz's (1782-1860), *Tiferet Yisrael*, which appeared about a century later in Germany, also contains scattered comments that deviate from traditional interpretative boundaries. Although Lipschuetz's work remained entirely bound to the talmudic interpretation, it on occasion included some scientific data or even semiliberal insights, which indeed led to a harsh critique by his fellow rabbis.[38]

Turning to Eastern Europe, we must mention the commentary on the Mishnah of Elijah b. Solomon of Vilna (the Vilna Gaon, 1720–97), *Shenot Eliyahu*. This composition, like many other of the Gaon's writings, appeared posthumously (starting in 1799), and questions as to its precise origins remain unanswered. In any event, this commentary too reveals a degree of independence from the talmudic interpretations of the Mishnah. Various traditions record a rather dramatic statement by the Gaon, namely that like the Bible, the Mishnah contains layers of meaning: *peshat, derash, remez,* and *sod.* Since the Talmud only offered *derash,* it is permissible to suggest alternative explanations in line with the Mishnah's plain sense, its *peshat.* This remark certainly reflects a stance that the Mishnah should be discussed on its own terms.[39]

Scholarly Essays

The new critical trends in the reception of the Mishnah were most prominent in various publications that appeared throughout the nineteenth century by a variety of scholars, mainly in German and Hebrew. As in other fields of Jewish studies, German-Jewish scholars made an outstanding contribution. The first major work devoted to the Mishnah was produced by Abraham Geiger (1810–74), who was associated with liberal trends in modern Judaism. The study of the Mishnah occupied Geiger from early childhood. In 1836 he published his first essay on this theme, titled "The Plan and

37. On Emden's Mishnah commentary, see Jacob J. Schacter, "Rabbi Jacob Emden" (PhD diss., Harvard University, 1988), 160.

38. On Lipschuetz and his *Tiferet yisrael,* see Mordecai Mayer, "R. Yisrael Lipschuetz: His Biography, Writings and a Preliminary Examination of the Methodology in his Commentary to the Mishnah: Tiferet Yisrael" (Hebrew; PhD diss., Bar-Ilan University, 2004).

39. See Chanan Gafni, "'Peshat' and 'Derash' in the Mishna: On the Metamorphosis of a Tradition from the School of R. Elijah of Vilna" (Hebrew), *Sidra* 22 (2007): 5–20.

Order of the Mishnah."[40] The article is especially well known due to Geiger's insight on the ordering of the tractates in the Mishnah, although that was not the sole theme of this groundbreaking piece. In 1844 Geiger produced his *Lehrbuch zur Sprache der Mischnah*, followed shortly by his *Lesebuch zur Sprache der Mischnah*.[41] While the first volume was restricted to the study of mishnaic Hebrew in comparison to biblical Hebrew, the second volume presented Geiger's discomfort with its interpretation in the Talmud, as reflected in a selection of mishnayot examined in this second volume. Both volumes drew the attention of the famous historian Heinrich Graetz, then a young student, leading to a lengthy, fascinating correspondence with Geiger on the Mishnah.[42]

In 1857 Zacharias Frankel (1801–75), the head of the Breslau Rabbinical Seminary, produced a far more systematic, multifaceted treatment of the Mishnah, titled *Darkhe ha-mishnah*.[43] Unlike Geiger, Frankel extended his discussion to the general question of the origins of rabbinic law, provided a detailed list of tannaim along with their biographies and legal approaches, and formulated the guiding principles of the Mishnah. In his final chapter Frankel listed the main commentaries on the Mishnah that had appeared throughout the generations. Regarding the Talmud, Frankel expressed his opinion that it not be viewed as a commentary on the Mishnah, but rather as a further stage in the history of Jewish law, as the Talmud was not genuinely interested in deciphering the original text of the Mishnah, but rather in determining the precise way to apply its norms to constantly changing conditions.

40. Abraham Geiger, "Einiges über Plan und Anordung der Mischnah," *WZJT* 2 (Stuttgart, 1835–36): 474–92.

41. Abraham Geiger, *Lehr und Lesebuch zur Sprache der Mischnah*, 2 vols. (Breslau, 1845).

42. See mainly Heinrich Graetz, "Kurze anzeigen" (I), *Orient* 5 (1844): 822–27; 6 (1845): 13–16, 30–32, 54–59, 76–78, 86–90; Graetz, "Kurze anzeigen" (II), *Orient* 6 (1845): 631–35, 643–49, 660–64, 725–30, 754–59, 771–75, 792–96; and Abraham Geiger, "Über selbstständige Mischnaherklärung," *INJ* 6 (1845): 25–31; Geiger, "Wie Man gelehrte Recensionen schreibt," *INJ* 6 (1845): 21–24; Geiger, "Weitere Proben aus einer conservativen Recension," *INJ* 7 (1846): 17–24, 26–28, 38–41; Geiger, "Letzte Proben einer conservativen Recension," *INJ* 7 (1846): 45–49. On Geiger's and Graetz's debate, see Chanan Gafni, "Abraham Geiger's Independent Commentary to the Mishnah" (Hebrew), *HUCA* 77 (2006): 51–70.

43. See Zacharias Frankel, *Darkhe ha-mishnah* (Leipzig, 1859). On Frankel and his book, see especially Andreas Brämer, *Rabbiner Zacharias Frankel: Wissenschaft des Judentums und konservative Reform im 19. Jahrhundert* (Hildesheim, 2000); Gafni, *The Mishnah's Plain Sense*, 248–60.

Finally, David Zvi Hoffmann (1843–1921), a leading Orthodox rabbi and a dominant figure in the Berlin Rabbinical Seminary, also engaged in critical study of the Mishnah. Alongside his translation and interpretation of the Mishnah, Hoffmann devoted several essays to the long editorial process of the Mishnah, trying to detect and separate early Second Temple passages from later, post–Second Temple components in this tannaitic text.[44] Perhaps Hoffmann paved the way for many future twentieth-century scholars, who approach the Mishnah as an archeological artifact containing layers of ancient laws and later interpretations. This discovery too had important consequences for the understanding of the talmudic treatment of the Mishnah.

Turning to the Italian arena, two scholars must be singled out. The younger of the two was Samuel David Luzzatto (Shadal, 1800–65). Although Luzzatto's fame rests mainly on his biblical research, in his youth he prepared a detailed commentary or lexicon of the Mishnah, which ended up as several articles devoted to mishnayot from *Berakhot*.[45] Like Geiger, Luzzatto was mainly concerned with linguistic matters, but also addressed the difficulties that the amoraim faced when they tried to interpret the Mishnah, and justified departing from their conclusions in numerous instances.

During the same timeframe his older colleague, Isaac Samuel Reggio (Yashar, 1785–1854), also published a pioneering, two-part piece on the Mishnah and its talmudic interpretation. In the first, Reggio discussed a common misconception of the Mishnah as a binding legal codex; Reggio argued that it was initially Rabbi Judah's private collection of laws and was never intended to become a public, binding legal corpus.[46] In the second, Reggio challenged the prevailing view of the Talmud as the authorized interpretation of the Mishnah. Reggio suggested that the Talmud was merely an intellectual exercise, meant to develop the student's analytic skills or to fulfill the religious commandment of learning Torah, not an authoritative

---

44. See David Z. Hoffmann, *Die erste Mischna und die Controversen der Tannaim* (Berlin, 1882).

45. See Samuel David Luzzatto, "Be'ur ketsat leshonot mi-leshon ḥakhamim," *Bikure ha-'itim* 9 (Vienna, 1828): 123–32; Luzzatto, "Be'ur ketsat leshonot mi-leshon ḥakhamim," in *Otsar ḥokmah* 1 (Lwow, 1859), 30–36; Luzzatto, Ḥakirot shonot, mikhtav heh," *Kerem Ḥemed* 3 (Prague, 1838): 61–76; Luzzatto, "Yalkut he'arot al 'inyanim shonim," *Yeshurun* 1 (Lwow, 1856), 60–61. On Luzzatto and his scholarly work on the Mishnah, see Gafni, *The Mishnah's Plain Sense*, 121–29.

46. See Isaac Samuel Reggio, "Mikhtav he," *Kerem Ḥemed* 1 (Vienna, 1833): 11–13.

formulation of the Mishnah's meaning.[47] These two Italian scholars, each in his own way, paved the way for new perspectives on the Mishnah.

Another region where we can chart the continued process of the liberation of the Mishnah from the talmudic treatment was the Austrian Empire, particularly Galicia, among the students of Nachman Krochmal (Ranak).[48] A key figure in Galician Jewish studies was Solomon Judah Rapaport (Shir, 1790–1867).[49] Although Rapaport did not dedicate his attention to the Mishnah alone, many entries in his *Erekh milin* (1852), a rabbinic lexicon, are devoted to mishnaic terms.[50] Rapaport, like his fellow scholars, emphasized the Mishnah's Hellenistic cultural context, which allowed him to unlock many terms that seemed to be unknown to Babylonian amoraim, and consequently to later generations.[51]

The most radical of the Galician Maskilim, Joshua Heschel Schorr (1814–85), dedicated several articles to the Mishnah in his periodical *He-ḥaluts*. As part of his *tendenz* to expose flaws in rabbinic literature, and thus justify abandoning the legal system that was based on it, Schorr was determined to illustrate various defects in Rabbi Judah's work. After listing inconsistencies and repetitions in the Mishnah, or demonstrating the lack of order from which it suffered, Schorr believed it would become self-evident that the Mishnah should not have become the Jewish canonical legal codex. In a later series of articles, titled *Shigegat Talmud*,[52] Schorr went even further and accused the Talmud of quite frequently misinterpreting the Mishnah. Despite the ideological bias of this work, it contains some important insights on the Mishnah.

---

47. See Reggio, "Blick auf den Thalmud," *Israelitische Annalen*, 2 (1840):106–8, 114–15, 121–22, 130–31; 3 (1841): 12–124, 130–31, but mainly Isaac Samuel Reggio, "Mikhtav heh," *Kerem Ḥemed* 7 (Prague, 1843): 101–18. On Reggio's treatment of the Mishnah and Talmud, see Gafni, *The Mishnah's Plain Sense*, 109–18.

48. As far I know, Nachman Krochmal himself does not discuss the value of the talmudic interpretation of the Mishnah in his writings, although he contributed to the study of the Mishnah in other ways, especially by attempting to date various tractates, rather than assuming they were all produced by Judah the Prince.

49. On Rapaport (Shir), see Nathan Shifriss, "Shelomo Yehudah Rapoport (Shir), 1790–1867: Torah, Haskalah, Wissenschaft des Judenthums, and the Beginning of Modern Jewish Nationalism" (Hebrew; PhD diss., Hebrew University, 2011).

50. See Solomon Judah Rapaport, *ʿErekh milin* (Prague, 1852).

51. See Gafni, *The Mishnah's Plain Sense*, 175–88.

52. See Joshua Heschel Schorr, "Shigegat talmud," *He-ḥaluts*, 1 (Lwow, 1852): 56–65; 2 (1853): 58–60; 5 (1860): 54–66. On Schorr, see Ezra Spicehandler, "Joshua Heschel Schorr," *HUCA* 40–41 (1969–1970): 503–28. On his treatment of the Mishnah, see Gafni, *The Mishnah's Plain Sense*, 140–46.

Hirsh Mendel Pineles, a relatively unknown Galician merchant, contributed greatly to the study of the Mishnah. His *Darkah shel Torah* (1861), a composition that was entirely devoted to interpreting mishnayot differently than the Talmud, led to numerous debates over the authority of the Talmud when interpreting the Mishnah.[53]

Abraham Krochmal (1817–88), the rebellious son of Nachman Krochmal (Ranak),[54] enriched the critical study of the Mishnah by penning a lengthy biography of Judah the Prince. In this biography,[55] but also in his later volumes on the Babylonian and Jerusalem Talmuds,[56] Krochmal explored the political reality in which the Mishnah emerged, and revealed the opposition to this legal codex that led, from his perspective, to the appearance of competing enterprises such as the Tosefta. Although Krochmal too had a clear ideological bias, his works did contribute to better evaluation of the Mishnah.

Finally, Isaac Hirsch Weiss (1815–1905), a Moravian scholar who eventually settled in Vienna, had a substantial role in the modern study of the Mishnah, especially in his magnum opus *Dor ve-dorshav*.[57] Far less known is his article "Ein mishnah yotset mi-yede peshutah,"[58] in which he reinforced the governing principle of the time that the Mishnah needed to be liberated from the Talmud, and should be discussed as a separate literary work.

Although establishing the autonomous status of the Mishnah was certainly an important theme that occupied Mishnah scholars in the nineteenth century, it was not the only one. Just to note an example, special attention was devoted to determining when the Mishnah became a written, rather than an oral, tradition. Often associated with inquiries about the nature of Jewish law as a whole, whether it was a dynamic or static system, this question led to heated debate among scholars from differing religious camps.[59]

---

53. On Pineles's work, see Gafni, *The Mishnah's Plain Sense*, 189–219.

54. On Abraham Krochmal's treatment of the Mishnah, see Gafni, *The Mishnah's Plain Sense: A Study of Modern Talmudic Scholarship*, 154–62.

55. See Abraham Krochmal, "Toledot rabbi Yehudah ha-nasi," *He-ḥaluts* 2 (Lwow, 1853): 63–93; Krochmal, "Be nesi'ah," *He-ḥaluts* 3 (Lwow, 1854): 118–40.

56. See Abraham Krochmal, *Yerushalayim ha-benuyah* (Lwow, 1867); Krochmal, *Perushim ve-he'arot le-talmud ha-bavli* (Lwov, 1881).

57. See Isaac Hirsch Weiss, *Dor ve-dorshav*, 5 vols. (Vilna, 1904).

58. See Weiss, "Ein mishnah yotset mi-yede peshutah," *Bet midrash* (Vienna, 1865), 1:121–28. See also Gafni, *The Mishnah's Plain Sense*, 304–13.

59. See Chanan Gafni, *Conceptions of the Oral Law in Modern Jewish Scholarship* (Hebrew; Jerusalem, 2019).

CONTEMPORARY INSIGHTS ON THE MISHNAH (20TH–21ST CENTURIES)

The twentieth to the twenty-first centuries have seen the Mishnah retain its appeal and its central role in scholarly and popular settings. This is evidenced by the publication of numerous commentaries on the Mishnah, some on individual tractates, others on the entire corpus. These publications responded to popular interest in the study of the Mishnah and also contributed to its extensive circulation. Among the scholars who composed such commentaries we may include those of Yaacov Herzog,[60] Eliezer Levi (*Mishnah meforeshet*),[61] and above all Pinḥas Kehati,[62] which has been translated into other languages as well. It is interesting that even in nonobservant Jewish circles we find attempts, alongside the Bible, to focus on study of the Mishnah, framed as a cultural document, and as a substitute for talmudic study. It was in this context that Ḥayyim Naḥman Bialik started writing his commentary on the Mishnah, which unfortunately covered only the first order.[63] In recent years efforts have been devoted to making the Mishnah even more accessible to, and stimulating for, younger students. Illustrated versions of the Mishnah appeared starting from the 1990s, and lately some endeavors to perform or film themes from mishnayot have been made, in order to encourage the study of Mishnah at an early age.

Needless to say, the Mishnah has remained a central field of interest in the academic world as well. A new edition of the Mishnah, produced by Chanoch Albeck, was meant to provide scholars with some critical insights

60. See Michael Bar-Zohar, *The Life and Times of a Jewish Prince: A Biography of Yaacov Herzog* (Hebrew; Tel Aviv, 2003), 54–56.

61. Rabbi Eliezer Levi (1883–1964) was born in Berlin and studied in the Rabbinical Seminary with Rabbi David Zevi Hoffman. He immigrated to Israel in 1932. On his Mishnah commentary, see Mordecai Mayer, "Perush 'Mishnah meforeshet' le-rabbi Eliezer Levi," *Ha-ma'ayan* 46 (2004): 73–84.

62. On Rabbi Pinḥas Kehati (1910–77), see Zeraḥ Warhaftig, "Perush ha-mishnayot shel Pinḥas Kehati: 'Ofyo, toldotav," in *Ha-rav Pinḥas Kehati: Masekeht ḥayav u-fo'alo,* ed. Z. Kaplan (Jerusalem, 1989), 69–74; Yitshak Gilat, "Al shnato shel R. Pinḥas," in *Ha-rav Pinḥas Kehati: Masekeht ḥayav u-fo'alo,* ed. Z. Kaplan, 75–80.

63. See Mordecai Mayer, "'The Mishnah Pointed and Annotated by Haim Nahman Bialik': On Bialik's Forgotten Project" (Hebrew), *Netuim* 16 (2010): 191–208; Gafni, *The Mishnah's Plain Sense,* 95–96.

and references.[64] At the same time, several new translations of the Mishnah appeared in the twentieth century, targeting both Jewish and non-Jewish readers, including English translations by Herbert Danby,[65] Philip Blackman,[66] and Jacob Neusner.[67]

A number of important twentieth-century scholarly contributions address more specific Mishnah-related areas. Although some of these scholarly essays may be seen as building on discussions from earlier centuries, they add significant data or employ revolutionary methodologies. As mentioned above, one of the major dilemmas in the study of the Mishnah involves the shift from oral to textual transmission. Perhaps one of the greatest achievements of the twentieth century in this field, J. N. Epstein's *Introduction to the Mishnaic Text* addresses this matter.[68] In this Hebrew work Epstein traces the Mishnah's textual history, not only as reflected in printed editions, but from its very inception, i.e., in Judah the Prince's own time, through the talmudic period, and in medieval literature. In contrast to previous, especially nineteenth-century scholars, Epstein employed newly discovered medieval manuscripts (above all the Kaufmann and Parma manuscripts of the Mishnah) and some Genizah fragments in trying to resolve the Mishnah's complex transmission history.[69] Unfortunately, even he did not manage to produce a critical edition of the Mishnah (which would consult all of the existing manuscripts and Genizah fragments), and only a small number of mishnaic tractates have appeared in critical editions edited by scholars.[70] A significant contribution was also made by Saul Lieberman,

64. See Chanoch Albeck, *Shishah sidre mishnah meforashim bi-yede Ḥanokh Albeck u-menukadim bi-yede Ḥanokh Yalon* (Jerusalem and Tel Aviv, 1952–59). Note that Albeck's edition was not meant to meet the needs of scholars alone, but also targeted more popular learning circles. For E. E. Urbach's harsh critique of Albeck's work, see E. E. Urbach, "Perush ha-mishnah le-Ḥanokh Albeck (Bikoret)," *Beḥinot* 3 (1953): 74–80.

65. See Herbert Danby, *The Mishnah: Translated from the Hebrew with Introduction and Brief Explanatory Notes* (London, 1944).

66. See Philip Blackman, *Mishnayoth*, 6 vols. (London, 1951–56).

67. See Jacob Neusner, *The Mishnah: A New Translation* (New Haven, 1988).

68. See J. N. Epstein, *Introduction to the Mishnaic Text*, 2 vols. (Hebrew; Jerusalem, 2000).

69. On this work, see the numerous references in Yaakov Sussmann, "Oral Law Taken Literally: The Power of the Tip of a Yod" (Hebrew; Jerusalem, 2019); and mainly Uziel Fuchs, "On 'Introduction to the Text of the Mishna': Reflections 50 Years Later and Towards a New Edition" (Hebrew), *Jewish Studies* 38 (1998): 365–78.

70. See, e.g., Abraham Goldberg, *Commentary to the Mishna: Shabbat* (Hebrew; Jerusalem, 1976).

who examined the publication and circulation history of the Mishnah in the Hellenistic context,[71] and later by Yaakov Sussmann, who devoted a lengthy study to the early transmission history of the Mishnah.[72]

Other scholars focused on the editorial mysteries of the Mishnah, and discussed the original intent and editorial considerations surrounding this composition,[73] and even the foundations of mishnaic law itself: Should it be viewed as an elaboration of the biblical text or as a rabbinic legislative endeavor?[74] Finally, several scholars have been trying to identify the historical layers in the Mishnah, and the legal developments that can be traced within the work of Judah the Prince.[75]

But whereas these and other scholars were essentially reformulating or refining earlier theories, we can also trace some new trends in contemporary scholarship. In this context I refer to two important (and somewhat contradictory) ways in which the study of the Mishnah has been enriched in the last few decades. On the one hand, a significant number of scholars have attempted to contextualize the Mishnah in its historical setting, and thus to shed light on terms or concepts which appear in the text. Such tendencies were at times rooted in Zionistic ideology, in the assumption that familiarity with the geographical region and exposure to the archeological sites in which the Mishnah emerged enables scholars to resolve some of the Mishnah's mysteries.[76] Other scholars have made more specific contributions to the study of the realia in the Mishnah.[77]

On the other hand, a growing number of scholars have been striving to explore the Mishnah in literary rather than historical terms. Such scholars

71. Saul Lieberman, *Hellenism in Jewish Palestine* (New York, 1962); Lieberman, *Greek in Jewish Palestine* (New York, 1965).

72. See Sussmann, "Oral Law Taken Literally."

73. See Dov Zlotnick, *The Iron Pillar—Mishnah: Redaction, Form, and Intent* (Jerusalem, 1998).

74. See David Weiss Halivni, *Peshat and Derash: Plain and Applied Meaning in Rabbinic Exegesis* (New York, 1991).

75. Among these scholars, I single out David Henshke's thematic articles on tractates Bava Metsi'a, Ḥagigah, and Pesaḥim. See David Henshke, *The Original Mishna in the Discourse of Later Tanna'im* (Hebrew; Ramat Gan, 1997).

76. Thus, for example, Zeev Safrai's *Mishnat erets yisrael* commentary was intended to contextualize the Mishnah in various ways, including botanical, historical, archeological, geographical, social, and political. See Ze'ev Safrai, *Mishnat erets yisra'el: Masekhet berakhot, Seder zera'im (1)* (Jerusalem, 2011).

77. See e.g. Yehoshua Brand, *Ceramics in Talmudic Literature* (Hebrew; Jerusalem, 1953); Keren Kirshenbaum, *Furniture of the Home in the Mishnah* (Hebrew; Ramat-Gan, 2013).

prefer not to focus on its legal function, but rather to analyze the Mishnah in aesthetic terms, or attempt to uncover its underlying philosophy or ethical values. One noteworthy contribution is Avraham Walfish's groundbreaking work on tractate Rosh Hashanah,[78] but other scholars have added insights as well.[79] I will not elaborate further on twenty-first-century trends in the study of the Mishnah. After all, even a glimpse of the current volume reveals the rich, fruitful nature of the current studies in this realm.

78. See also his recent work on tractate Berakhot: Avraham Walfish, *Mishnaic Tapestries—Tractate Berakhot: A Literary-Conceptual Study of Mishnah Tractate Berakhot* (Hebrew; Alon Shevut, 2018).

79. Yaakov Nagen (Genack), *Soul of Mishnah* (Hebrew; Othniel, 2016).

Contributors

Elitzur A. Bar-Asher Siegal is Associate Professor at the Hebrew University of Jerusalem. His research focuses on philology and linguistics and he seeks to develop new methodologies for finding points of contact between these two distinct but interrelated fields. He is the author of *Introduction to the Grammar of Jewish Babylonian Aramaic*, (Ugarit-Verlag 1st edition 2013, 2nd edition 2016); *Linguistic and Philological Studies in Hebrew and Aramaic*, (The Academy of Hebrew Language Press, 2020); *The NP-strategy for Expressing Reciprocity: Typology, History, Syntax and Semantics*, (John Benjamins Publishing House, 2020) and many other articles in these fields.

Beth A. Berkowitz is Ingeborg Rennert Chair of Jewish Studies and Professor in the Department of Religion at Barnard College. She is the author of *Execution and Invention: Death Penalty Discourse in Early Rabbinic and Christian Cultures* (Oxford University Press, 2006); *Defining Jewish Difference: From Antiquity to the Present* (Cambridge University Press, 2012); and *Animals and Animality in the Babylonian Talmud* (Cambridge University Press, 2018). She is co-editor with Elizabeth Shanks Alexander of *Religious Studies and Rabbinics: A Conversation* (Routledge, 2017). Her area of specialization is classical rabbinic literature, and her interests include animal studies, Jewish difference, and Bible reception history. She is currently working on a project called *What Animals Teach Us about Families: A Study of Four Biblical Laws and Their Afterlives* that offers an interpretive history of the four "animal family" laws of the Pentateuch.

Shaye J.D. Cohen is the Nathan Littauer Professor of Hebrew Literature and Philosophy in the Department of Near Eastern Languages and Civilizations of Harvard University. He has long been interested in the history of rabbinic law.

Naftali S. Cohn is Professor in and Chair of the Department of Religions and Cultures at Concordia University in Montreal. He is author of *The Memory of the Temple and the Making of the Rabbis* (University of Pennsylvania Press, 2012), and is completing a book on ritual in the Mishnah. Currently, he is beginning a new project on the representation of Jewish ritual in recent film and television.

Shamma Friedman, laureate of the Israel Prize in Talmudic research, is Professor Emeritus at The Jewish Theological Seminary of America, where he held the Benjamin and Minna Reeves chair in Talmud and Rabbinics. Friedman's primary areas of research surround the Babylonian Talmud, including literary and conceptual development, stratification of the Talmudic sugya, linguistic studies in Hebrew and Aramaic, and the nature of variant readings of the Talmudic texts. Among his publications (in Hebrew) are *Talmud Arukh, Bava Metzi'a VI: Critical Edition with Comprehensive Commentary*, and *Tosefta Atiqta: Synoptic Parallels of Mishna and Tosefta Analyzed, with a Methodological Introduction*. Some of his over 120 articles are collected in the volumes *Talmudic Studies: Investigating the Sugya, Variant Readings, and Aggada* and *Studies in Tannaitic Literature: Methodology, Terminology, and Content.*

Uziel Fuchs is the chair of the Talmudic department at the Herzog College and teaches at Bar Ilan University. His main field of research are textual criticism of Babylonian Talmud, Geonic Studies and Rabbinics. He published *The Geonic Talmud – The Attitude of Babylonian Geonim to the Text of the Babylonian Talmud* (Jerusalem, 2017; in Hebrew)

Yair Furstenberg is assistant professor in the Talmud Department at the Hebrew University of Jerusalem. His research focuses on the emergence of early rabbinic literature from its Second Temple roots, as well as the history of Jewish law within its Greco-Roman context. His current project aims to integrate rabbinic legal activity into its Roman provincial environment.

Chanan Gafni teaches at Rothberg International School, Hebrew University of Jerusalem. His publications include of *The Mishnah's Plain Sense* (2011), and most recently: *Conceptions of the Oral Law in Modern Jewish Scholarship* (2019). His research focuses on *Wissenschaft des Judentums.*

Martin Goodman is Emeritus Professor of Jewish Studies and Emeritus Fellow of Wolfson College in the University of Oxford. His publications include *Rome and Jerusalem: the Clash of Ancient Civilizations* (Knopf, 2007) and *A History of Judaism* (Princeton, 2017). His research has focussed particularly on the history of the Jews in the Roman world.

Sarit Kattan Gribetz is Associate Professor in the Theology Department at Fordham University. Her first book, *Time and Difference in Rabbinic Judaism* (Princeton, 2020), received the National Jewish Book Award in Scholarship.

Moshe Halbertal is the John and Golda Cohen professor of Jewish Thought at the Hebrew University and the Gruss Professor at NYU Law School. His latest books are *The Birth of Doubt: Confronting Uncertainty in Early Rabinnic Literature* (Brown Judaic Studies) and *Nahmanides: Law and Mysticism* (Yale University Press).

Catherine Hezser is Professor of Jewish Studies at SOAS, University of London (UK). Her research focuses on rabbinic literature and the social history of Jews in Roman and early Byzantine Palestine. Amongst her most recent publications are *Rabbinic Body Language: Non-Verbal Communication in Palestinian Rabbinic Literature of Late Antiquity* (2017); *Bild und Kontext: Jüdische und christliche Ikonographie der Spätantike* (2018); *The Oxford Handbook of Jewish Daily Life in Roman Palestine* (pb ed. 2020).

Jonathan Klawans is Professor of Religion at Boston University. Klawans's research on ancient Judaism ranges from the Hebrew Bible through rabbinic literature, including Dead Sea Scrolls and the New Testament. Klawans is the author of four books, the most recent entitled, *Heresy, Forgery, Novelty: Condemning, Denying, and Asserting Innovation in Ancient Judaism* (Oxford University Press, 2019). Klawans is also co-editor of the *Jewish Annotated Apocrypha* (Oxford University Press, 2020).

Gail Labovitz is Professor of Rabbinic Literature at the American Jewish University, where she teaches primarily for the Ziegler School of Rabbinic Studies. She is the author of *Marriage and Metaphor: Constructions of Gender in Rabbinic Literature* (Lexington, 2009) and the volume on Mo'ed Qatan for the Feminist Commentary on the Babylonian Talmud (Mohr Siebeck, 2021). Her additional research and work addresses rabbinics, gender and sexuality, and Jewish law, particularly in the realm of marriage and divorce.

Hayim Lapin is Professor of History and Robert H. Smith Professor of Jewish Studies at the University of Maryland. He has published extensively on the intersection of rabbinic literature and social and economic history, including *Rabbis as Romans* (Oxford 2011). In recent years Lapin has been one of the editors and contributors to the *Oxford Annotated Mishnah* (forthcoming 2022) and several digital projects.

Jonathan S. Milgram (PhD, Bar Ilan) is Associate Professor of Talmud and Rabbinics at The Jewish Theological Seminary (New York). He is the author of *From Mesopotamia and the Mishnah: Tannaitic Inheritance Law in its Legal and Social Contexts* (Academic Studies Press, 2016; paperback, 2019) and articles and reviews in scholarly journals. His fields include mishnaic law in comparative context, Talmud criticism and medieval Jewish law.

Vered Noam is professor of Talmud in the Department of Jewish Philosophy and Talmud at Tel Aviv University. She has published widely in Hebrew and English on the connections between Rabbinic literature and the literature of the Second Temple period, in particular the connections between the halakhah of the Qumran scrolls and the halakhah of the tannaim. In 2020 she won the Israel Prize for Talmud.

Tzvi Novick is the Abrams Jewish Thought and Culture Professor of Theology at the University of Notre Dame. He is the author of *What is Good, and What God Demands: Normative Structures in Tannaitic Literature* (2010), and *Piyyut and Midrash: Form, Genre, and History* (2018), and of many articles on Jewish literature from the Bible to late antiquity. His research focuses on tannaitic law and on the liturgical poetry of Byzantine Palestine.

Ishay Rosen-Zvi is the Chair of the Department of Jewish Philosophy and Talmud at Tel-Aviv University. He has written on Midrash and Mishnah, as well as on self-formation and collective identity in Second-Temple Judaism and rabbinic literature. Among his publications are: *Demonic Desires: Yetzer Hara and the Problem of Evil in Late Antiquity* (University of Pennsylvania Press: Philadelphia 2011); *The Mishnaic Sotah Ritual: Temple Gender and Midrash* (Brill: Leiden 2012); *Goy: Israel's Others and the Birth of the Gentile* (with Adi Ophir) (OUP: Oxford 2018); *Between Mishnah and Midrash: The Birth of Rabbinic Literature* (Open University 2019).

Adiel Schremer is professor of ancient Jewish history at the Israel & Golda Koschitzky Department of Jewish History and Contemporary Jewry at Bar-Ilan University, and a Research Fellow of the Kogod Research Center at the Shalom Hartman Institute. He is the author of *Male and Female He Created Them: Jewish Marriage in Late Second Temple, Mishnah and Talmud Peri-*

ods (2003); *Brothers Estranged: Christianity, Heresy, and Jewish Identity in Late Antiquity* (2010); and *Ma'ase Rav: Halakhic Decision-Making and the Shaping of Jewish Identity* (2019).

Moshe Simon-Shoshan is a Senior Lecturer in the Department of the Literature of the Jewish People at Bar-Ilan University specializing in rabbinic literature. His research focuses on Rabbinic Narrative and the relationship between Halakha and Aggadah in rabbinic texts. He is the author of *Stories of the Law: Narrative Discourse and the Construction of Authority in the Mishnah* (Oxford, 2012) and numerous articles including, most recently, "These and Those are the Words Of The Living God, But . . . ": Meaning, Background, And Reception Of An Early Rabbinic Teaching," *AJS Review* 45:2 (2021) and "You Can't Go Home Again: The Bavli's Story of Honi's Big Sleep as Inversion of the Yerushalmi's Account," *Journal of Jewish Studies*, 72:2 (2012).

David Stern is Harry Starr Professor of Classical and Modern Hebrew and Jewish Literature and Professor of Comparative Literature at Harvard University. His fields of specialization are classical Hebrew literature and the history of the Jewish book. He is the author and co-editor of many books including *The Jewish Bible: A Material History*; *Parables in Midrash: Exegesis and Narrative in Rabbinic Literature*; *Jewish Literary Cultures I: The Ancient Period*; *Jewish Literary Cultures II: The Medieval and Early Modern Periods*; and the forthcoming *Jewish Literary Cultures: The Modern and Contemporary Periods*.

Azzan Yadin-Israel is a professor in the Departments of Jewish Studies and Classics at Rutgers University. He has published two books on early rabbinic midrash: *Scripture as Logos: Rabbi Ishmael and the Origins of Midrash* (University of Pennsylvania Press, 2004) and *Scripture and Tradition: Rabbi Akiva and the Triumph of Midrash* (University of Pennsylvania Press, 2015). His latest book, *Temptation Transformed: The Story of How the Forbidden Fruit Became an Apple* is forthcoming from the University of Chicago Press.

Index

Aaron, 450, 468
Abba, Rabbi, 455
Abahu, Rabbi, 143
Abner, 138
Abraham, 137, 138
Abraham ben David of Provence, Rabbi, 476
Absalom, 137
Adani, Solomon, 495
Adler, Rachel, 354
adultery, 63, 70, 137, 218–19, 362
agere, 147, 148, 150
Agrippa I, king of Judea, 104, 132, 133, 136
Agrippa II, king of Batanaea, 132, 209n14
Aicher, Georg, 7
Akhan, 137–38
Akiba, Rabbi, 8, 10–12, 143, 246, 354, 415, 426, 439, 450
   disciples of, 102–3, 106, 113, 118
   disgrace payments viewed by, 39
   Epstein's view of, 101, 436–38
   impurity of the dead viewed by, 235, 237
   positive vs. negative commandments viewed by, 6
Akkadian language, 26, 27, 29, 42
Albeck, Chanoch, 93, 99, 108, 111, 112–13, 119, 262, 429–30, 506–7
Alexander, Elizabeth Shanks, 364–66, 435, 451–52, 454, 468

Alexander Polyhistor, 287
Alfasi, 482
Alfaz al-Mishnah (Saadiah Gaon), 477
Amalek, 138
'Amidah, 198, 283–84
Ammon, 272–73
'Arakhin, 10
Aramaic language, 22, 42, 134, 139, 307, 317–18, 319
Arcadius, emperor of Rome, 144
Aristotle, 187, 188, 203
Asher ben Jehiel (Ha-rosh), 476
Ashkenazi, Joseph, 491, 495
Augustus, emperor of Rome, 161, 287
Avery-Peck, Alan J., 146
'Avodah Zarah, 384, 385, 386n23, 388, 394–95
Avot, 199, 432, 441, 479, 483
   as aggadic text, 73, 333, 349
   authorship of, 270–71
   chain of tradition in, 130–31, 138, 259, 270, 272, 333–35
   insertions in, 120
   poetic features of, 312, 323–24
   recitation of, 476, 484–85, 490
   sacrifice in, 195
   this-worldliness of, 251
Avot de-Rabbi Natan, 73

Babusiaux, Ulrike, 148
Baitner, Hallel, 18n45
Baker, Cynthia M., 368n48

Bakhtin, Mikhail, 196
Balberg, Mira, 196–97, 200–201, 282
Bar Asher-Siegal, Michal, 201–2
Bar Kokhba revolt, 132, 134, 136, 143, 146, 161, 176
barter, 183
Bathsheba, 138
Bauman, Richard A., 149–50
Baumgarten, Joseph, 64–65
Bava Batra, 123, 349
Bava Kama, 9, 14, 35–36, 39–40, 122
Bava Metsi'a, 119, 122, 144, 317
Bavli, 89, 202, 344, 427, 438, 481
    discrepancies reconciled in, 91, 94
    as dominant subject of study, 471–73, 482–83
    interpretive gaps in, 474–76
    Mishnah contrasted with, 203, 352
    numbering in, 189
    species discourse in, 194, 199
    transcribing Oral Torah prohibited in, 455–58
    vow taking in, 233
    Yerushalmi's discrepancies with, 164
Bekhorot, 193, 299
Ben Eliyahu, Eyal, 282–83
Ben-Pazi, Isaiah, 350
Ben Sira, 352
Berakhot, 137, 259n23, 412, 503
    belief in one world opposed in, 416–17, 420
    language of, 315, 316, 406
    Mishnah-Bible links in, 3
    Nidah linked to, 192
    priestly references in, 336, 348
    ritual in, 208, 227, 228, 333, 349
Berkowitz, Beth, 218–19, 257, 258, 263, 264–65, 268
Bernasconi, Rocco, 199
Betsah, 113, 189, 320
Biblical Antiquities (Josephus), 16, 136
Bialik, Ḥayyim Naḥman, 506
Bikurim, 214, 285, 374–77
Blackman, Philip, 506

Boaz, 137, 139
The Book of the Commandments (Maimonides), 5
Boyarin, Daniel, 189, 354, 409, 411n28
Braverman, Natan, 83–84
Bremmer, Jan, 286
Breuer, Yochanan, 260
Brody, Robert, 73, 82, 94, 448n13
Broshi, Magen, 337
Brown, Peter, 177, 348, 350
Büchler, Adolf, 149
Burke, Kenneth, 195

Caligula, emperor of Rome, 161
canonicity, 239, 425–43
Caracalla, emperor of Rome, 142, 152
Catterjee, Indrani, 443
cavere, 147–50
censorship, 496–97
Chwat, Ezra, 482
Cicero, Marcus Tullius, 146, 464
Cohen, Boaz, 75
Cohen, Shaye, J. D., 199, 404
    mishnaic boundaries viewed by, 399–400
    mishnaic heresy viewed by, 409
    Mishna-Tosefta links viewed by, 73, 82–83
    pluralism and, 179, 182
    rabbinic-Pharisaic link rebutted by, 441–43
    tannaitic rabbis' origins viewed by, 144–45
Cohn, Naftali S., 257, 258
    holiness viewed by, 280, 281, 283, 284
    mishnaic ritual viewed by, 196
    rabbinical authority viewed by, 146, 263–64, 265, 267
Constantine, emperor of Rome, 134
Cordovero, Moses, 491
Cover, Robert, 255–56, 259–61, 263, 268, 269, 273–74
Czajkowski, Kimberley, 151, 153

Dalton, Krista, 193
Damascus Document, 17–19, 51–53, 116–17, 175
Danby, Herbert, 507
Daniel, 317
Daube, David, 123
David, king of Israel, 137, 138
Day of Atonement, 285, 291, 484
   holiness of, 290, 296, 297, 300, 335
   ritual failure on, 226, 227
   rituals for, 209, 213, 234
Dead Sea Scrolls, 47–72, 235, 241, 276
Demai, 390
De oratore (Cicero), 146
Deuteronomy, 3, 8, 9, 13, 16, 50, 122, 425–26
   holiness and, 276
   matrimonial law in, 63
   primogeniture in, 261
   scriptural conflicts resolved by, 67
Diamond, Eliezer, 293, 294
Dimi, Rabbi, 455
Diocletian, emperor of Rome, 161, 162
disgrace, 26, 27, 35–41
Divine Antiquities (Varro), 462
divorce, 26–27, 30–35, 70, 171, 176, 181
   gentiles and, 384
   for infertility, 361
dowry, 26, 27–30

Ecclesiastes, 13
Eckhardt, Benedikt, 151, 153
'Eduyot, 110–13, 121, 198, 270–72, 476, 483
Elazar bar Judah, Rabbi, 237
Elazar ben Dama, Rabbi, 414, 416
Elazar be-Rabbi Zaddok, 290
Elazar Ḥisma, Rabbi, 94
Eleazar ben Arakh, Rabbi, 270
Eleazar ben Azariah, 272, 438
Elephantine, 30, 34–35
Eliehoenai, 346
Eliezer, Rabbi, 12, 189, 198, 228, 270, 272–73, 332, 414–16, 436

Eliezer ben Hyrcanus, Rabbi, 69, 131
Elijah, 137, 303
Elijah ben Solomon of Vilna (Vilna Gaon), 501
Elior, Rachel, 344–45
Elisha ben Abraham, 495
Elman, Yaakov, 44
Emden, Jacob Israel ben Zevi, 500–501
The Epistle of Sherira Gaon, 446–47
Epstein, Jacob Nahum, 125, 507
   Akiba viewed by, 101, 436–38
   Albeck's disagreements with, 102–3, 111–12, 262, 429
   'Eduyot viewed by, 111, 112
   mishnaic stability noted by, 449, 451–54
   Mishnah-Tosefta links viewed by, 77–78, 82
   mishnaic stability noted by, 449, 451–54
   property law viewed by, 154
   pericopes viewed by, 16, 21
   source criticism of, 98–107
   Teharot authorship viewed by, 474
'Eruvin, 53, 85, 287, 384, 391–92, 450, 468, 485
Eshnunna, Laws of, 37, 40
Esther, queen of Persia, 132, 140
Exodus, 280, 425, 456–57
   holiness in, 286, 291
   language of, 315, 320, 323
   private law in, 35–36, 122, 176
   in Temple Scroll, 49–50
Ezekiel, 173, 175, 339, 346
Ezra, 138, 292, 346

Falcón y Tella, María José, 159
Fine, Steven, 283–84
Finnegan, Ruth, 452
Fogel, Shimon, 191
Fonrobert, Charlotte Elisheva, 190, 211, 371–74, 375, 377
Foucault, Michel, 177, 187, 265
Fraade, Steven D., 52–53, 452

Fraenkel, Jonah, 254

Fragmenta Vaticana, 162, 164

Frankel, Zacharias, 101, 429, 502

Friedman, Shamma, 11, 35, 37–38, 82, 286

Frier, Bruce W., 144, 157

Furstenburg, Yair, 16–17, 178, 197–98, 271–72, 299, 457–58

Gabbai, Isaac, 495

Gabbay, Uri, 44

Gaius, 151, 161–62, 163

Galen, 464, 467–68

Gamaliel, Rabban, 86, 90, 132, 168, 176, 189, 245–46, 265, 273, 441

Gardner, Gregg, 192

Geest, Dirk de, 435–36

Geiger, Abraham, 501–2

Geller, M. J., 29

Genesis, 261, 280, 288

gentiles

  halakhah and, 380–83, 386, 388, 391, 393–96, 396–400, 416

  purity and, 383, 385, 386, 388–89, 390, 392, 394

  sacrifice and, 385, 389, 395

  in Tosefta, 379–81, 383, 388, 391, 392

Ginzberg, Louis, 99, 114–15

Gitin, 336, 360, 384, 389, 457

Goldberg, Abraham, 11–12, 21, 78, 94, 102–3, 116

Goodman, Martin, 149, 405

Gospels, 70, 171

Goy (Ophir and Rosen-Zvi), 381, 383, 393

Graetz, Heinrich, 502

Gray, Alissa, 193

Greek antiquity, 135

Greek language, 134, 139

Greengus, Samuel, 38–39

Gregorius Thaumaturgus, 142

Gruenwald, Ithamar, 345

Hadrian, emperor of Rome, 161

Ḥaggiz, Israel, 496

Ḥagigah, 4, 13, 14, 201–2, 208, 344, 349

Hai Gon, 474

Ḥalah, 18n45, 482

halakhah, 232–52

  abstraction in, 64, 72, 264

  centrality of, xii

  from commandment to, 48, 232, 233

  Damascus Document and, 52, 53

  emergence and expansion of, 234–43, 248–50

  gender in, 372, 374, 376, 396

  gentiles and, 380–83, 386, 388, 391, 393–96, 396–400, 416

  holiness in, 278, 280, 286, 287, 295

  impurity in, 69, 479

  law and Scripture linked by, xiii

  midrashic, 425–34, 498

  mishnaic study and, 482, 483

  nominalism of, 67

  other-worldliness rejected by, 251

  pe'ah and, 244–47, 249

  Qumranic works and, 53, 56–68

  Roman law linked to, 158–59, 166

  Temple Scroll and, 49–50

Halbertal, Moshe, 48

Halevi, Isaac, 429

Halivni, David Weiss, 93, 116, 428–29, 441n60

ḥametz, 89, 90

Hammurabi, Code of, 33, 37–38, 40, 43

Ḥanamel the Egyptian, 336

Ḥananiah the Prefect of the Priests, 332, 352

Ḥanina ben Dosa, 348, 350

Haran, Menachem, 460, 469

Harries, Jill, 143, 150–51

ḥasidim, 330, 348–50, 472

Hasmonean, 345–46

Hauptman, Judith, 73, 81, 93, 359–61, 363, 365, 369

Hayes, Christine, 68

Hebrew language, late vs. mishnaic, 305–26

Hebrews, 352, 353

Heller, Yom Tov Lipmann, 493

Henshke, David, 73, 79–81, 104

heresy, 401–21

Hermogenianus, 162

Herod Agrippa I, king of Judea, 104, 132, 133, 136

Herod Agrippa II, king of Batanaea, 132, 209n14

Herr, Moshe David, 75n6

Herzog, Yaacov, 506

Heschel, Abraha Joshua, 426

Hezser, Catherine, 183

Hidary, Richard, 148, 195, 197

Hillel the Elder, House of, 100, 105–6, 111, 112, 131, 271
  prosbol attributed to, 149
  Shabbat observance viewed by, 116, 396

Hirschman, Marc, 381

Ḥiyya, Rabbi, 81, 455

Hoffmann, David Zvi, 100–101, 104–5, 125, 426, 428–29, 503

holiness
  categories of, 279–95
  centrality of, 275–76, 304
  through consecration, 285
  contagious, 285–86
  defined, 277–78
  of God, 279–84
  of Hebrew language, 288
  hierarchies of, 291, 292–93, 300–303
  of the land, 146
  marriage linked to, 275, 293, 294, 301
  mishnaic conceptions of, 295–304
  mundanity vs., 299–300
  of objects, 284–88
  of people, 291–95
  purity linked to, 275, 278, 282, 295–300, 303, 349n74
  static vs. dynamic, 68
  of times, 288–91

Holtz, Shalom E., 32, 34, 35

Hon'ashir (Ricchi), 496

Ḥoni the Circle Drawer, 350

Horayot, 301, 336

Horowitz, Isaiah (Yeshayahu) ben Avraham, 493

Houtman, Alberdina, 79

Ḥulin, 194, 290, 345, 407, 428

hypomnemata, 450, 451, 453, 463–67, 470

Ibbetsen, David, 160

idolatry, 50, 291, 384, 388, 394

Ilan, Tal, 354, 367n41

Imrie, Alex, 152

inheritance, 25n13, 30, 149, 150, 261, 361

insertions, in texts, 120–21

Institutes (Gaius), 162, 163

intention, 64–65, 177–78
  to disgrace or shame, 9, 36–37
  Sabbath law and, 53

Isaac ben Melchizedek, Rabbi, 475

Isaiah, 117, 322, 491

Ishmael, Rabbi, 6, 8, 10, 31, 69–70, 237, 425–26, 430–34, 443, 456, 457, 484

Ishmael ben Phiabi, 132, 346

Jacob ben Nissim, Rabbi, 74

Jacob of Kefer Sama, 414

Jaffee, Martin, 264, 440, 452–53, 454

Jehoiada, 140, 331–32, 352

Jephthah, 139

Jeremiah, 435

Jeremiah, Rabbi, 455

Jesus Christ, 171, 414–16

Jewish War (Josephus), 136

Johnson, Barbara, 225

Johnson, William, 464–66

Jonah, 137

Josephus, 139, 171, 175–76, 289n64, 339, 442, 464
  biblical references by, 16, 136, 287
  legal summaries by, 16, 47, 232
  priestly greed noted by, 342
  Stoic philosophy and, 160
  Zadokite descent ignored by, 346

Joshua, 137–38, 198

Joshua, Rabbi, 265, 270, 272
Joshua ben Gamala, 342–43
Joshua ben Levi, Rabbi, 455
Joshua ben Peraḥiah, 332n10, 334
Jost, I. M., 500
Jubilees, 175, 234, 292
Judah ben Naḥmani, Rabbi, 456, 457
Judah of Barcelona, Rabbi, 485
Judah the Patriarch, Rabbi, 9, 11, 74, 96,
    170, 341, 387, 427, 437–38, 444, 465,
    505, 507–8
  disgrace payments viewed by, 37
  as editor, 101–3, 436, 447, 450, 463, 479
  marriage and divorce viewed by,
    32–33, 34, 189
  purity laws viewed by, 237
Justinian, 45n99, 141, 148, 150, 161–62,
    163, 175

Kaf naḥat (Gabbai), 495
Kahana, Menahem, 7–8, 21, 70, 426,
    460
Kahana, Merav Tubal, 189
Kalman, Jason, 7
Kaplan, Jonathan, 303
Karo, Joseph, 491
Kattan Gribetz, Sarit, 191–92
Katzoff, Ranon, 29
Kaufmann Codex, 21, 308, 405, 446, 507
Kav ve-naki (Elisha ben Abraham), 495
Kaye, Lynn, 191
Kehati, Pinḥas, 506
Kelim, 201, 239, 282–83, 296–97, 300,
    335, 339
Keritot, 6, 342, 348
Kessler, Gwynn, 375–77
Ketubot, 5, 82, 336, 369
Kidushin, 6, 109, 189, 275, 294, 349, 427,
    459
Kila'im, 193
Kings, 173, 318, 322
Kinim, 73, 338, 476
Kister, Menahem, 55
Klein, Gil, 189, 190–91

Kodashim, 217, 275, 385, 392, 476
Kol remez (Zacut), 495
Koltun-Fromm, Naomi, 278, 292–93
König, Jason, 164, 461–62
Krochmal, Abraham, 505
Krochmal, Nachman, 100, 504
Kuhn, Thomas, 421
Kulp, Joshua, 83

Labov, William, 309
Labovitz, Gail, 294
Langer, Ruth, 409
Lapin, Hayim, 119, 144, 146, 155
Larsen, Matthew D. C., 463, 467
law and narrative, 255–56, 259, 260, 274
Leesen, Tessa G., 145
legal language, 17–21, 22, 32
Leḥem mishneh (Lipschuetz), 495
Leḥem shamayim (Emden), 500–501
leniency, 56–60
Lev, Sarra, 375, 376
Levi, Eliezer, 505
Levine, Baruch, 27–28, 42
Levine, Lee, 440
Levinson, Joshua, 200
Levitas, Ruth, 205, 206–7, 220, 221, 222
Levites, 62, 132, 209, 214
Leviticus, 9–10, 50, 64, 239, 280, 286,
    288–89, 338, 408
  Sifra to, 425–28, 459
Lieberman, Saul, 75, 92, 163, 437,
    449–53, 462–63, 468, 507–8
Lim, Timothy, 299
Lipschuetz, Israel, 501
Lipschuetz, Moses ben Noah Isaac, 495
Loew ben Bezalel, Judah, 492–93
Lord, Albert, 452
Love and Joy (Muffs), 31
Luntshitz, Ephraim, 493
Luria, Isaac, 491
Luzzatto, Samuel David, 503

Ma'aseh Rokeaḥ (Rokeach), 496
Ma'aser Sheni, 199–200, 299–300

Maccabees, 286–87, 343

Maharal of Prague (Judah Loew ben Bezalel), 492–93

Maimonides, Moses, 5, 74, 75, 77, 457, 478–81, 482, 490

Makhshirin, 65, 121, 122, 200, 336

Malbim (Meir Leibush ben Yeḥiel Michel), 428

Mali, Hillel, 114, 265–66, 281

Mandsager, John, 190

Manuel, Frank E., 206

Manuel, Fritzie P., 206

Margalit, Natan, 364n29

Mark, Gospel of, 464

Marks, Susan, 354

marriage, 51, 109, 180–81, 294–95
  biblical laws of, 5, 291
  dissolution of, 26–27, 30–35, 70, 171, 176, 181, 361, 384
  dowry and, 27–29
  holiness linked to, 275, 293, 294, 301
  ineligibility for, 172, 178
  levirate, 139, 288, 291, 384
  in Temple Scroll, 58
  witnesses to, 149

Matthew, Gospel of, 442

McGinn, Thomas A. J., 144, 157

Megilah, 132, 140, 195, 235, 288, 301–2, 408, 410

Me'ilah, 301

Meir, Rabbi, 90, 91, 102, 157, 427, 436, 438, 450

Meir of Rothenburg, Rabbi, 475–76

Mekhilta, 425–26, 430, 431, 439

Menaḥem ha-Meiri of Perpignan, 482

Menaḥot, 196, 213, 214, 225, 339, 340, 342

Middle Assyrian Laws, 33

Midot, 5, 73, 115, 163, 191, 214, 300, 337, 345, 476, 483

Midrash, 425–43

Mikva'ot, 201, 388, 483

minim, 404–21

minimalist/maximalist debate, 168, 170, 458–69

Miqtsat Ma'ase Ha-Torah (4QMMT), xi, 53–62, 64, 66–67, 71, 172, 237–38n14

Miriam, 137

mnemonics, 188–91

Moab, 272–73

Mo'ed, 208, 275, 288, 383, 482, 483

More, Thomas, 206, 217

Moses, 16, 131, 137, 138, 270, 289, 445, 450, 468

Muffs, Yochanan, 30–32, 34, 35

'*Mulūgu/Melûg*' (Levine), 27–28

Muntigl, Peter, 198

mysticism, 344–45, 491–92

Naeh, Shlomo, 459–60, 466

narrative, 253–74

Nashim, 208, 275, 384, 482

Nathan, Father of the Academy, Rabbi, 478

Nathan, Hayya, 311

Natroni Gaon, 484

Natural History (Pliny the Elder), 462

Nazir, 139, 208, 285, 395, 495

Nedarim, 4, 20, 139, 189, 208, 233

Nega'im, 197, 297, 337

Nehemiah, 175

Nehemiah, Rabbi, 438

Neis, Rafe, 193–94, 197

Neo-Babylonian Laws, 33, 34, 35

Nero, emperor of Rome, 161

Neusner, Jacob, 114n50, 165, 222, 274, 330, 347, 351, 403n6, 506
  documentary hypothesis of, 358, 447n7
  literary approach of, 254, 258
  mishnaic utopianism viewed by, 217–18
  philosophical approach of, 262
  reconstruction of sources viewed by, 107, 131–32, 167–68, 169
  Tosefta diminished by, 79

Neubauer, Yekutiel, 430

Nezikin, 16, 122, 275, 384, 476, 483

Nidah, 192, 193, 398–99, 475, 483

nominalism, 67–68

"Nomos and Narrative" (Cover), 255, 261

Novick, Tzvi, 190, 195–96, 197, 199, 201, 202, 282n19, 292

Numbers, 4, 20, 50, 362

Obadiah of Bartenura, Rabbi, 481–82, 488, 495

Ohalot, 5n9, 235–36

Ophir, Adi, 381, 383, 393

Oppenheim, A. L., 29

Oral Law (Sussmann), 451

Ozida, Samuel, 491

Papinian, 160, 162

Parah, 208, 337, 339, 346, 347, 407

Pardo, David, 76, 77

Parma MS, 446, 507

Parry, Milman, 452

Pasternak, Ariel Lam, 188–89

Paul (apostle), 287

Paul (jurist), 160, 162

Paulus Prudentissimus, Julius, 148

Pe'ah, 191, 192, 239–48, 316, 349

peculium, 156–57

petiḥta, 12

Pettit, Peter A., 6

Pesaḥim, 17n45, 88, 90–91, 132, 196, 205, 208, 342, 391, 482
   gentiles in, 384
   leaven rules in, 11
   Passover sacrifice in, 59, 176, 196, 204, 214, 225, 339

Pesher Habakkuk, 352, 353

Peskowitz, Miriam, 367–70

Pharisees, 11, 412–13, 430, 440–43
   purity practices of, 171–72
   rabbis linked to, 70–71n93, 105–6, 177–78, 266, 441–43
   Stoic philosophy linked to, 160

Philo, 175–76, 287, 339

Pineles, Hirsh Mendel, 505

Pinhas ben Yair, Rabbi, 303, 350

Plato, 187, 464

Pliny the Elder, 462

Pliny the Younger, 464

polygamy, 67

Pomponius, Sextus, 161

Porton, Gary, 379–80, 385, 397n56, 400n69

postmodernism, 168

pregnancy, 59, 60, 192, 292

priesthood, 329–53

printing, 493–94

progymnasmata, 452

property law, 153–56, 172–73

prosbol, 149

Proverbs, 416

Psalms, 54, 417, 456, 458

Purim, 132, 140, 234

"Purities," 5

purity, impurity
   biblical, 4–5, 50
   bodily afflictions and, 61, 66, 181, 296–97, 337
   conflicting views of, 68
   of the dead, 69, 234–35, 237, 248
   degrees of, 58, 62, 287
   exemptions from, 62, 64
   of food and drink, 4, 59, 64, 67, 69, 106, 121–22, 177, 200, 237–38n14
   gentiles and, 383, 385, 386, 388–89, 390, 392, 394
   holiness linked to, 275, 278, 282, 295–300, 303, 349n74
   Maimonides on, 479
   Menstrual 61, 192, 296, 297, 398–99
   of objects vs. human beings, 200–201
   Pharisaic, 171–72
   of sacrifices, 178, 301, 338–39
   Temple system linked to, xii, 51, 208, 335
   of vessels, 58–59, 64, 172, 201, 238–39, 296, 299

Qumran community, 16, 22, 47, 51, 49–56, 65–72, 232, 440
   matrimony in, 63

Second Temple, rabbinic law linked to, 116

Temple Scroll, 49–51, 58, 63, 64, 116, 175, 235

Rebbenu Tam, 472
Rabe, Johann Jacob, 500
Rapaport, Judah, 504
Rashi, 418n40, 447, 448, 481–82
rearrangement, of texts, 121
Reed, Annette, 442
Regev, Eyal, 68
Reggio, Isaac Samuel, 503–4
Resh Lakish, 456–58
respondere, 145, 147, 150, 158, 163
Ricchi, Immanuel Ḥai, 496
ritual narrative, 257–61
Robinson, Olivia F., 161
Rokeach, Eliezer ben Samuel Shmalla, 496
Roman law, 123, 141–66, 183
Rosenblatt, Samuel, 6
Rosen-Zvi, Ishay, 365, 418–19
    judicial punishment viewed by, 218–20
    Mishnah-Bible links viewed by, 13–14, 16
    mishnaic utopianism viewed by, 182, 212
    rabbinic authority viewed by, 263, 265, 268, 271
    ritual narrative viewed by, 257, 258
    women's presumed guilt viewed by, 362–63
Rosh Ha-Shanah, 192, 195, 336, 407, 410, 413–14, 416, 509
Rubenstein, Jeffrey, 67–68
Ryan, Marie-Laure, 267

Saadiah Gaon, 477
Sabbath observance, 17, 69, 116, 153, 230, 384
Sabinus, Masurius, 161
sacral animals, 58–59

sacrifice, 50, 59, 60, 62, 196–97, 213, 440
    commandments linked to, 195
    in Damascus Document, 52
    gentiles and, 385, 389, 395
    holiness of, 68, 275, 278, 281, 284–86, 288, 291, 296, 299, 301
    by non-priests, 338–39, 340
    at Passover, 59, 176, 196, 204, 214, 225, 339
    in pilgrimage festivals, 13
    ritual failure and, 226, 228–29
    in Temple Scroll, 59
    time limits for, 54, 59, 64, 291
Sadducees, 67, 337, 393, 398–99, 405, 412
    aristocraticism ascribed to, 65–66, 347–48, 352
    Dead Sea Scrolls and, 54
    gentiles and, 386
    Pharisaic practices opposed by, 298
Safrai, Shmuel, 329, 332, 344, 347, 350
Safrai, Ze'ev, 329, 332, 344, 347
Sagiv, Yonatan, 426–27
Samaritans, 138, 386, 398
Samely, Alexander, 6–7, 13, 21, 199, 202
Samson, 137, 139
Samson of Sens, Rabbi, 475
Samuel, 137, 317, 335
Sanhedrin, 133, 337, 343, 420–21, 479
    court system described in, 148, 173, 189
    crime and punishment in, 200, 257, 264, 336
    incorrect belief noted in, 402–3
    minim in, 407
    royal rights and duties in, 138, 335
    scriptural citation in, 8
Sargado, Aaron, 448
Satlow, Michael, 192–93
Saul, king of Israel, 138
Scaevola, Quintus Cervidius, 148
Schäfer, Peter, 440
Schieffelin, Edward, 229
Schiffman, Lawrence H., 50
Schiller, A. Arthur, 147, 162
Schleicher, Marianne, 375, 377

Schorr, Joshua Heschel, 504

Schremer, Adiel, 131, 270–72, 432n30

Schumer, Nathan, 191

Schwartz, Barry, 220

Schwartz, Daniel R., 67

Schwartz, Seth, 151

Searle, John, 199

Second Sophistic, 135, 136, 139, 197, 452, 466

sexual practices, 63, 275, 278, 293–94, 411

Shabat, 53, 117, 287, 308, 316, 391, 485, 486, 490

shaming, 9

Shammai, House of, 69, 70, 101, 106, 111, 112, 131, 189, 228, 271

   Shabbat observance viewed by, 116, 396

Shasha, Ruth, 199

Shekalim, 115, 208, 302, 336, 340–41, 343, 344, 384, 483

Shemesh, Aharon, 6, 50–51, 52, 67, 71

Shemesh-Raiskin, Rivka, 198–99

Shemaiah, Rabbi, 476

Shenot Eliyahu (Elijah ben Solomon of Vilna), 501

Sherira Gaon, 74, 77, 100, 446–48, 458, 474

Shevi`it, 85, 487

Shevu`ot, 403n6

Shigegat Talmud (Schorr), 504

Shimon, Rabbi, 91–92, 438

Shimon bar Yohai, 132

Sifre, 425–27, 430–31, 439, 459

Simeon bar Yoḥai, 487

Simeon the Just, 331, 334, 335, 346, 352

Simon-Shoshan, Moshe, 148, 205n3, 207–8, 257–58, 264, 268, 363–64n28

slaves, 145, 149, 150, 155, 156–58, 184, 386

Smith, J. Z., 217

Socrates, 187

Solomon, king of Israel, 133, 137, 138

Song of Songs, 303

Sotah, 348, 365

   adultery in, 362

dichotomous gender in, 372–73

exegetical reasoning in, 10

historical change noted in, 130

holiness in, 303–4

mysticism in, 345

ritual in, 208, 257, 265, 333

source criticism, 98–100, 102, 104, 109–10, 123–25

Sparta, 135

Stoicism, 160

Stone, Suzanne Last, 268

Strassfeld, Max, 375, 376

stringency, 56–60, 189

Sukkah, 11, 12, 208, 223, 228, 234, 289, 299, 348, 349

Surenhuis, Willem, 497

Sussmann, Yaakov, 57, 451, 457, 473, 486, 508

Ta`anit, 209, 212, 335, 336, 340, 345

   fasting in, 132, 137

   gentiles in, 384, 391

   rabbinic debate in, 198

Talmud

   mishnaic basis of, xiv

Tamar, 139, 143, 145

Tamid, 199, 338, 340, 483

   atypicality of, 110–11, 114–15

   Temple ritual in, 196, 213, 222, 330, 335, 336, 339

   Tosefta counterpart lacking to, 73

Tanhuma, Rabbi, 460–61

Tarfon, Rabbi, 438

Ta-Shma, Israel, 478

Teharot, 118, 121, 122, 474–75, 479, 483; see also *Tohorot*

Temple: building of, 132–33

   destruction of (70 CE), 46, 111, 115, 129–30, 133, 136, 229

   in Mishnah's imagined world, 204–5, 208–31

Temple Scroll, 49–51, 58, 63, 64, 116, 175, 235

Temurah, 455–56, 457, 466–67

tenses, 129, 211, 221–22, 260, 312, 319, 326

Terumot, 18n45, 189, 390

Tevul Yom, 121

Theodosius II, emperor of Rome, 175

Tiberius, emperor of Rome, 161

Tiferet Yisrael (Lipschuetz), 501

Timothy, 287

tithing, 31, 59, 66, 106, 182, 239–48,
    272–73, 284
  by gentiles, 383, 389

Tohorot, 208, 275, 296, 385, 392; see also
    Teharot

Tosafot Yom Tov (Heller), 495

Tosefta, 52, 73–97, 111, 163, 413–14, 418
  dating of, 181
  differing legal views in, 102, 112
  numbers in, 189–90
  gentiles in, 379–81, 383, 388, 391, 392
  rabbinic past in, 131
  Roman law and, 183
  slavery in, 156–57
  violent competition ritual in, 205, 223
  women in, 361

Turnbull, William, 198

'Uktsin, 121

Ulpianus, Domitius, 160, 162

Urbach, Ephraim, 381, 418, 430, 433,
    475, 480

Urnamma, Laws of, 40

Varro, Marcus Terentius, 462

Vermes, Geza, 350

Vidas, Moulie, 454

Vilna Gaon (Elijah ben Solomon of
    Vilna), 501

Vital, Ḥayyim, 491

Walfish, Avraham, 108–9, 262–63, 265,
    365, 509

Watson, Alan, 156

Wegner, Judith Romney, 295, 358–59,
    369

Weinreich, Uriel, 309

Weisberg, Alex, 202

Weiss, Avraham, 119

Weiss, Isaac Hirsh, 429–30, 505

Weiss, Moshe, 119

Werman, Cana, 50–51, 52

Westbrook, Raymond, 44

White, Hayden, 216

Wieder, Naftali, 485

Wilfand, Yael, 193

Wissenschaft des Judentums, 448, 500

Witte, John, 146

women and gender, 354–78

Woolf, Greg, 164, 461, 462

Wyrick, Jed, 468

Yadayim, 5, 272–73, 283, 298, 302, 408,
    412–13

Yaḥad, 51, 65, 69

Yalkut Shimoni, 426

Yehudah, Rabbi, 90

Yehudah ha-Nasi, Rabbi, 142, 145, 152,
    160, 165

Yerushalmi, 91–92, 150, 163, 457, 458,
    475
  Roman law linked to, 141, 147, 158,
    165–66, 392
  vow taking in, 233

Yeshua ben Yehuda, 426

Yevamot, 139, 318, 342, 384

Yohanan ben Hahoroni, 228

Yoḥanan ben Zakkai, 131, 230, 270, 273,
    298, 334, 341, 349

Yoḥanan the High Priest (John
    Hyrcanus I), 331, 346, 347

Yoma', 93, 94, 115, 224, 339–40, 343–45,
    351
  Day of Atonement in, 285, 291, 296,
    335, 484
  priestly checks and balances in, 336–38
  ritual failure in, 204–5, 215, 226, 227,
    228
  Sabbath rules in, 57
  Temple ritual in, 208–9, 213, 223, 281

Yom Tom ben Avraham, Rabbi, 21

Yona, Shamir, 188–89

Yose, Rabbi, 91–92, 200, 228, 298

Yose ben Ḥalafta, Rabbi, 142

Yosef Karo, Rabbi, 256
Yosi ben Yo'ezer, 331, 334, 349
Yosi ha-Kohen, Rabbi, 334, 349
Yosi Katonta, Rabbi, 348

Zacut, Moses ben Mordecai, 495
Zadoq, Rabbi, 94
Zavim, 201
Zechariah ben Kevutal, 338

Zera'im, 208, 275, 474–75, 483
Zevaḥim, 345, 484, 487
    exegetical reasoning in, 9–12
    holiness in, 296, 299, 301
    ritual failure in, 226
    sacrifice in, 59, 64, 208, 213, 226, 286,
        338–39
    tithing in, 66